Strategic Management Communication *for* Leaders

FOURTH EDITION

Strategic Management Communication *for* Leaders

FOURTH EDITION

Robyn Walker

Department of Business Communication
Marshall School of Business
University of Southern California

Wessex Press, Inc.
www.wessexlearning.com

Noel Capon, R.C. Kopf Professor of International Marketing, Columbia Business School, founded Wessex Press, Inc. in 2007. Wessex is a small publisher with global reach focusing predominantly on marketing, management, and other higher-education textbooks. Wessex's goal is to provide top-quality learning materials at affordable prices. Publishing under the Wessex Press and AxcessCapon brands, Wessex Press, Inc. offers titles in multiple print and digital formats. Wessex also offers video books.

Library of Congress Cataloging-in-Publication Data

Walker, Robyn

    Strategic Management Communication for Leaders, 4th edition / Robyn Walker

      p. cm.

    ISBN 978-0-9994861-1-5 (hardcover)
          978-0-9994861-2-2 (softcover)

    1. Management. I. Title: Strategic management communication for leaders. II. Robyn Walker

Design/Production: Anna Botelho
Editor: Lyn Maize
Indexer: Judi Gibbs

Cover image: © Rawpixel.com / bigstockphoto.com

Brief Contents

Preface   xiv

Part 1 Strategic Elements of Business Communication

Chapter 1   What Is Strategic Communication?   2

Chapter 2   Foundations of Communication   17

Chapter 3   Step One: Identify the Purposes of Communication   44

Chapter 4   Step Two: Analyze the Audience   70

Chapter 5   Steps Three and Four: Consider the Context
             and Select a Channel of Communication   93

Part 2 Tactics of Business Communication

Chapter 6   Communicating in Writing   123

Chapter 7   Communicating in Oral Presentations   160

Chapter 8   Preparing Employment Messages   201

Chapter 9   Communicating with Employees   226

Chapter 10   Communicating in and Leading Groups and Teams   257

Chapter 11   Strategic Organizational Communication   302

Appendices

Appendix A   Model Documents   344

Appendix B   Punctuation, Sentence Structure, and Usage   369

Glossary   379
Index   384

Table of Contents

Preface   xiv

Part 1 Strategic Elements of Business Communication

Chapter 1   **What Is Strategic Communication?   2**

What Is Strategic Communication?   3

Why Is a Strategic Approach to Communication Important?   5

Changes in the Workplace   5

Evolution of Our Understanding of the Communication Process   8

*The Social Construction of Reality and Its Effects on
Conceptualizing Communication   9*

How to Analyze Case Studies   10

Initial Analysis   11

Identification of Solutions and Recommendations   12

How This Book Is Organized   12

Part 1: The Strategic Process   12

Part 2: Communication Tactics for Differing Channels and Contexts   13

Chapter Summary   15

Chapter 2   **Foundations of Communication   17**

The Case of California Design, Inc.   17

Strategic Communicators   18

Models of Communication   18

Communication as Information Transfer   19

Communication as Transactional Process   19

Communication as Strategic Control   20

Communication as Dialogic Process   21

Perception   23

Self-Awareness and Communication   26

Self-Concept   26

Self-Awareness and Emotional Intelligence   27

Cultural Intelligence   28

Needed Skills for Strategic and Ethical Communication   30

    Perceptual Mindsets   31

    Thinking Styles   34

Chapter Summary   36

Case Study — A Philosophy of Dress:
Rebuilding Trust in the Brooks Brothers Brand (A)   39

Chapter 3   **Step One: Identify the Purposes of Communication   44**

The Case of Barnaby Consulting Corp.   44

Four Purposes of Communication   45

Communicating to Inform   46

Communicating to Convey Goodwill   46

    Trust   47

    Interpersonal Communication Styles   48

Communicating to Establish Credibility   48

    Expertise and Competence   49

    Personal Ethics and Integrity   50

    Emotional Control   54

    Developing a Professional Image   54

Communicating to Persuade and to Influence   56

    Conger's Multistep Model of Persuasion   57

    Interpersonal Communication and the Role of Influence   58

Chapter Summary   61

Case Study — Cable News Network: CNN Apologizes to the Chinese People   64

Chapter 4   **Step Two: Analyze the Audience   70**

The Case of Speedy Travel Inc.   70

Analyze the Audience   71

Audience Demographics   72

    Generational Differences   73

    Culture   74

Gender   77

Professional Jargon and Plain Language Use   80

Audience Knowledge, Interests, Attitudes, and Concerns   81

    Knowledge   81

    Interests and Attitudes   81

    Concerns and Questions   82

Types of Business Audiences   82

    Managerial Audiences   82

    Nonexpert Audiences   83

Expert Audiences   83

International or Multicultural Audiences   83

Mixed Audiences   84

Audience-Centered Messages   84

Application of Audience-Centered Communication   85

Chapter Summary   88

Case Study — Apple: A Case Study in External Communication   90

Chapter 5   **Steps Three and Four: Consider the Context
and Select a Channel of Communication   93**

The Case of the Virtual Team   93

Organizational Context   94

Context Defined   94

Context as a Strategic Issue   94

Dimensions of Context   95

Organizational Culture   96

Formal Communication Networks   102

Informal Communication Networks   103

Choosing a Communication Channel and Medium   103

Richness versus Leanness   104

Need for Interpretation   104

Speed of Establishing Contact   105

Time Required for Feedback   105

Cost   106

Amount of Information Conveyed   106

Need for a Permanent Record   107

Control over the Message   107

New Media and the Organization   108

E-mail   109

Social Media   111

Chapter Summary   114

Case Study — Johnson & Johnson: A Dispute with the American Red Cross   117

Part 2 Tactics of Business Communication

Chapter 6   **Communicating in Writing   123**

The Case of the Consultants   123

A Word about the Genre of Business Writing   124

Planning and Developing Informative Messages   126

Parts of a Message   127

Planning and Developing Persuasive Messages   130

Basic Components of a Persuasive Message   133

Types of Persuasive Appeals   133

Quality of Evidence   135

Organizing Persuasive Messages   135

Using the AIDA Approach   136

Using the Indirect Approach for Resistant Audiences   137

Planning and Developing Reports and Proposals   137

Preparing to Write the Report   138

Selecting the Report Type and Organizational Pattern   138

Report Format   139

Proposal Format   140

Visual Impression in Written Messages   140

White Space   141

Use of Headings   141

Use of Lists   143

Use of Graphics   143

Revising for Organization, Coherence, and Flow   147

Check Topic Sentences   147

Ensure Paragraph Coherence   148

Provide Transitions and Forecasting   148

Revising for Style and Tone   148

Proofreading for Mechanical Correctness   150

Submitting the Message   151

Chapter Summary   153

Case Study — Cerner Corporation: A Stinging Office Memo Boomerangs   156

Chapter 7   **Communicating in Oral Presentations   160**

The Case of the Novice Presenter   160

Channel Considerations   161

Planning and Developing the Presentation   162

Planning the Presentation   162

Selecting the Appropriate Structure   164

Developing the Presentation   165

Designing Visual Aids   169

Designing PowerPoint Presentations   170

Organizing PowerPoint Presentations   171

Using PowerPoint Slides   174

Delivery in Oral Presentations   174

Vocal Delivery   174

Body Movement   175

Dress and Appearance   177

Preparing for Your Presentation   177

Reducing Presentation Anxiety   179

Handling Question-and-Answer Sessions   179

Adapting to Alternate Delivery Situations   181

Culturally Diverse Audiences   181

Group Presentations   183

Distance Presentations   184

Crisis Communication   187

Chapter Summary   189

Case Study — Airbnb: Scaling Safety with Rapid Growth   191

Chapter 8   Preparing Employment Messages   201

The Case of the Gen-Y Workforce   201

Steps in the Application Process   202

Performing the Self-Inventory   203

Analyze Your Audience, the Industry, and the Overall Job Climate   203

Drafting and Developing a Résumé   204

Drafting and Developing the Application Letter   207

Reviewing Your Social Media Content   209

Job Interviews   209

Preparing for an Employment Interview from the Applicant's Perspective   210

Performing the Employment Interview   212

Writing the Thank-You or Follow-Up Message   215

Conducting Employment Interviews   215

Performance Appraisals   217

Providing Performance Feedback   218

Dealing with Conflict   219

Receiving Performance Feedback   220

Chapter Summary   221

Case Study — RadioShack: You've Got Mail!   223

Chapter 9   Communicating with Employees   226

The Case of Resisted Change Efforts   226

Interpersonal Communication in the Workplace   227

Interpersonal Style   228

Nonverbal Communication   229

Paralanguage   230

Bodily Movement and Facial Expression   230

Bodily Appearance   231

Space   231

Time   232

Touching   233

Clothing and Other Artifacts   233

Effective Listening   234

Listening Styles   234

Listening Types   235

Verbal Tactics for Effective Listening   236

Nonverbal Tactics for Effective Listening   237

Meeting Management   238

Types of Meetings   239

Steps in Meeting Management   239

Additional Considerations for Electronic Meetings   243

Motivating Employees   243

Motivation Defined   243

Developing Communication Networks   244

Communicating Change   246

Leadership Qualities   247

Delivery Tactics   248

Cultural Adaptations   249

Chapter Summary   250

*Case Study — FedEx Corporation: A Case Study on
Employee Training and the Impact of Social Media   254*

Chapter 10 **Communicating in and Leading Groups and Teams   257**

The Case of the Virtual Marketing Team   257

Forming Groups   259

Collective Endeavors   259

Interpersonal Attraction   259

Group Roles   261

Group Member Relations   263

Status Hierarchies   263

Attraction Relations   263

Communication Networks   263

Power and Group Process   264

Stages of Group Development   265

The Effects of Group Cohesion and Conformity   266

Sources of Influence within a Group   268

Group Performance   269

Group Decision Making   271
   Stages of Group Decision Making   271
   Methods of Group Decision Making   272
   The Challenges of Group Decision Making   273
Sources of Group Conflict   274
   Personal Conflict   274
   Substantive Conflict   275
   Procedural Conflict   276
   Conflict and Competition   276
   Social Dilemmas   277
Conflict Resolution   277
Techniques for Enhancing Group and Team Creativity   280
   Brainstorming   281
   The Nominal-Group Technique   282
   The Delphi Technique   283
   Electronic Brainstorming   283
Team Leadership   284
   Leadership Decisions   284
   Leadership Actions   286
   Team Effectiveness   286
Communicating in Virtual Teams   287
   Developing Trust in Virtual Teams   288
   Cultural Differences in Virtual Teams   288
   Managing Conflict in Virtual Teams   289
   Brainstorming in Virtual Teams   290
   Proper Training for Virtual Team Success   291
Chapter Summary   292
Case Study — Nokia, OYJ: A Case Study about the
                Impact of Communication on Innovation   298

Chapter 11   Strategic Organizational Communication   302
The Case of the Exploding Muffler   302
Models of Strategic Organizational Communication   304
   Strategic Internal Communication   305
Creating an Internal Communication Plan   307
   Conducting a Communication Audit   309
   Developing the Internal Communication Plan   310
Strategic External Communication   314
   External Communication Issues   315
   Investor Relations   320

Issues Management   321

Risk Communication and Crisis Communication   323

Handling the News Media   324

Chapter Summary   328

Case Study — Amazon.com, Inc.: Big Ideas in a Bruising Workplace   331

Appendices

Appendix A   **Model Documents   344**

Appendix B   **Punctuation, Sentence Structure, and Usage   369**

Glossary   379

Index   384

Preface

Strategic Management Communication for Leaders is based upon an alternative theoretical foundation grounded in theory but with connections to communication in the world of business. The text is unique in the business communication discipline in that it shows students how various business courses are related and highlights strategic communication as a practice that is applicable to all business situations regardless of the discipline, department, or organizational level at which it takes place. Unlike many other business communication texts, it also looks at communication not only as the practice of individuals but also has an organizational concern.

Other unique aspects of *Strategic Management Communication for Leaders* include its spotlight on strategy formulation while making a clear distinction between strategic and tactical elements of communication. Because strategic issues are more difficult to understand and internalize as such, they are treated in an indepth manner before providing the discussion of tactics as they apply to differing contexts and channels of communication. Internalizing the strategic considerations will enable readers to logically make appropriate tactical choices without having to set them all to memory.

Another novel aspect of *Strategic Business Communication for Leaders* is its focus on leadership, both at the theoretical and practical level. That is, the text integrates discussions of leadership theory and practice aimed at meeting the needs and the abilities of its key audiences—advanced undergraduate and graduate students and the organizations that will employ them. Opportunities for leadership communication practice is provided through the inclusion of two types of case studies in each chapter. The opening case study is intended to look at communication practices at the individual level, while closing cases look at communication from the organizational level. This ability to work at both the micro and macro level of communication within an organization is a necessity for effective leaders and managers.

With all of these unique elements combined, the result is this textbook, which provides comprehensive coverage of the critical elements of business, management, and corporate communications in a compact, highly readable format.

Help students succeed in the business world with the features found in *Strategic Management Communication for Leaders*!

Comprehensive, yet compact. The text covers all the communication topics that are relevant and critical for successful business, management, and corporate communications—written, oral presentation, interpersonal, and small group communication as well as planning and implementing communication plans for internal and external organizational audiences—in a compact, readable format.

Integrated, comprehensive approach to strategic message formulation. The text provides a comprehensive discussion of the steps of strategy formulation that can be used for any communication context: written, oral presentations, interpersonal, small group, or organizational communications.

These four steps of strategic message formulation are covered in Part 1 of the text:

- Chapter 1: What Is Strategic Communication?
- Chapter 2: Foundations of Communication
- Chapter 3: Step One: Identify the Purposes of Communication
- Chapter 4: Step Two: Analyze the Audience
- Chapter 5: Steps Three and Four: Consider the Context and Select a Channel of Communication

Comprehensive discussion of tactical elements applied to all communication contexts. Part 2 of the text provides explanation of the tactics that can be applied to achieve strategic goals in all communication contexts—written, oral presentation, interpersonal, group, and internal and external organizational communication situations. These tactical applications are covered in the following chapters of the text:

- Chapter 6: Communicating in Writing
- Chapter 7: Communicating in Oral Presentations
- Chapter 8: Preparing Employment Messages
- Chapter 9: Communicating with Employees
- Chapter 10: Communicating in and Leading Groups and Teams
- Chapter 11: Strategic Organizational Communication

Boxed features. Each chapter includes boxed features, **Responsible Communication** as well as **Critical Thinking** questions. The Responsible Communication boxed features present an ethical situation or issue that is related to the main focus of each chapter and includes questions to encourage discussion and analysis of each of those issues. Critical Thinking questions can be found throughout each chapter and are intended to encourage more in-depth thought, analysis, and application of the materials presented in each chapter.

End-of-chapter exercises. To further support understanding and information transfer through the application of relevant concepts and principles, the following exercises are included at the end of each chapter: key terms with page number references, discussion questions, applications (or assignments), as well as two case analyses, the first which appears at the beginning of each chapter. One case analysis focuses on "micro" communication skills, developing communication understanding at a personal level, while the second case study found at the end of the chapter focuses on "macro" communication skills or those applied at the organizational level. Each case analysis provides a concise synopsis of real-life business situations as well as discussion questions and assignments, as applicable, intended to aid students in applying strategic and tactical skills.

About the Author

Robyn Walker, Ph.D.
Associate Professor of Clinical Management Communication
USC Marshall School of Business

Dr. Robyn Walker is a professor of management communication at the Department of Business Communication at the University of Southern California's Marshall School of Business, where she teaches business writing and business communication to undergraduate and graduate students. She earned a master's and a doctoral degree in Communication from the University of Utah, and a master's degree in Professional Writing from the University of Southern California, and holds an MBA. Dr. Walker has held faculty appointments at the University of Arizona and California State University, Fullerton. Before entering academia, Dr. Walker worked as a professional writer and editor with such organizations as United Press International, McGraw-Hill, and Novell. She also has worked as a writing consultant for companies such as Hoffman LaRoche Pharmaceuticals and Franklin-Covey, Inc.

She continues to write and conduct research and has delivered dozens of conference papers on intercultural communication, rhetoric, cultural studies, and business communication pedagogy and published articles on intercultural communication in groups, leadership, and place-based identity. She has been the editor of the *International Journal of Business Communication*, a contributing editor of *BCOM* (Cengage Learning), and co-editor of a volume of research entitled *Discourse Perspectives on Organizational Communication* (Fairleigh Dickinson University Press, 2011), and co-author of *Leadership Talk: A Discourse Approach to Leader Emergence* (Business Expert Press, 2014). She is a member of the Association of Business Communication, Management Communication Association, National Communication Association, Academy of Management, and the Academy of International Business.

Strategic Elements of Business Communication

Part 1 provides an in-depth discussion of the steps in the strategic formulation of business communication applicable to all communication contexts. The steps in the process are drawn from rhetorical theory but include discussions of other communication contexts, as appropriate. These contexts include interpersonal, organizational, and group communication.

(Part 2 of the text discusses the tactics to be implemented in differing communication contexts: writing, presentations, group and teamwork, employment, and organizational communication.)

In many business communication texts, the focus of discussion is primarily on tactics, presenting them as the "rules" of message formulation. This approach, though, requires memorization of the rules and thus can be difficult to internalize if the rules are not consistently practiced. For this reason, this text initially focuses on developing an in-depth understanding of the strategic elements of message formation as this understanding makes it easier to then logically deduce the appropriate tactical moves.

This text thus assumes that communication is more of an art that depends upon analysis of the contextual elements of any communication situation. It is an art that requires foundational knowledge, observational skills, critical thinking and assessment, and a willingness to "work without a net." This latter idea simply means that no one right answer generally exists in many communication situations (unlike other business disciplines) and thus one must build the needed skill base and subsequent level of confidence to master a strategic approach to messaging.

Without developing the meta-skill of strategic thinking and analysis, communication becomes more rule-bound and focused on the details, much like a copy editor approaches his or her work. This approach thus risks losing sight of the strategic, "big picture" perspective needed to be an inspirational and visionary leader.

Chapter 1

What Is Strategic Communication?

A strategic approach to communication has become of greater importance in recent years for a variety of reasons. Globalization has brought numerous opportunities to organizations while simultaneously increasing the potential for greater instability and heightened competition. Globalization and this intensified competition have increased the need for excellent communication skills as management and employees deal with diversity, greater responsibility, and rapid change. In addition, communication is beginning to receive greater recognition for its central role in the creation of our social realities, including those within organizations. Thus, management and employees have a need for a more sophisticated understanding of communication to create organizational cultures that enhance morale and productivity and lead to better organizational results.

After reading this chapter, you will be able to

- *Define strategic communication and differentiate between strategy and tactics.*

- *Understand why strategic communication is critically important in today's rapidly changing world and organizational environment.*

- *Use a case study approach to apply textbook concepts and principles, a method that will enhance your learning and hone the critical and analytical skills necessary to become a practiced strategic communicator.*

What Is Strategic Communication?

Strategy as an element of communication has been around for some time. In fact, one of the earliest attempts at formulating communication strategy dates back to at least the fourth century B.C.E. and Aristotle's *Rhetoric*, a Greek treatise on the art of persuasion. Aristotle's writing on the subject of persuasion is still seen as a foundational text for the discipline; his principles are still used today. Although the concept of strategy as an element of communication has been around for centuries, it is not a coherent system of theory or practice across the widely differentiated discipline of communication. Various definitions and aspects of strategy are practiced in rhetoric, composition, and, to some extent, organizational communication. Because of this diversity of perspectives, few are prepared to truly grasp strategy as an overarching approach to the varied situations in which communication plays a role. This text is an attempt to help bridge those disciplinary differences and provide a coherent discussion of the many ways communication research applies to business and organizational settings. Strategy not only is a developing concept and practice in communication, but also has a fairly recent history in the field of business. Strategic management, for example, originated as a discipline in the 1950s and 1960s. Although there were numerous early contributors to the literature, the most influential pioneers were Alfred D. Chandler, Philip Selznick, Igor Ansoff, and Peter Drucker. Management strategy is a future-oriented conception in which the relationship between the industry and the environment is described, and this forms the guiding principles for decision making for people in the industry. The field of strategic management is characterized by numerous definitions. Jemison (1981) defines strategic management as "the process by which general managers of complex organizations develop and use strategy to co-align their organization's competences and the opportunities and constraints in the environment." In a different vein, Smircich and Stubbart (1985) define strategic management as "organization making—to create and maintain systems of shared meanings that facilitate organized action." This text more closely subscribes to the latter definition and thus a discussion of that process follows later in this chapter.

strategy

Plan for obtaining a specific goal or result that involves big-picture analysis.

In terms of its hierarchical ordering, strategic management is a level of managerial activity below setting goals and above tactics and this ordering also applies to communication strategy. **Strategy** is thus a "big picture" look at a problem that focuses on the entire forest and not individual trees. It involves analysis and evaluation and then the subsequent synthesis of a coherent plan of action based on that analysis. Strategic communication is thus an attempt to better manage the reception of the message by the audience or stakeholders to ensure that the message is received as intended. This is more challenging that it may appear on the surface due to the uniqueness of each individual in terms of his or her intelligence, knowledge, personality, values, and experiences. To make this goal more challenging, organizational, cultural, and environmental factors can also affect the reception of a message.

tactics

Concrete actions taken to implement a strategy.

Tactics can be viewed as the concrete actions that are taken to implement a strategy. Another way of understanding the distinction between strategy and tactics is by considering each's time orientation. Strategy is focused on the long term while tactics typically have a shorter timeframe. This can be better understood if we look at strategy from a military perspective, what some consider the origins of strategic thinking and planning. From this perspective, strategy is a more global plan for dealing with a problem, while a tactical approach often is concerned with a more immediate response to our adversary's activities. Broadly speaking, a strategic approach is generally considered appropriate because of the competitive nature of the business environment.

One major way this textbook differs from others in the field of business communication is that it clearly distinguishes strategic issues from tactical ones. Many business communication textbooks focus on tactics—or skills—and emphasize the use of checklists to address communication situations.

This approach can be useful in developing skills but may overlook the importance of giving due consideration to the unique, broader context within each communication situation, including differences in the audience or, considering an organizational perspective, the stakeholders, for the message. In fact, a hallmark of a strategic communication perspective is the central role that stakeholders play in shaping strategy. Research has shown that stakeholders both internal and external to the organization play a key role in shaping communication strategy, and thus it is often an iterative—rather than a "straight-line"—process. It thus involves a continual learning process, a notion in line with the goals of a learning organization.

Another way to think about a tactical approach is to consider what Shari Veil (2011) calls "trained mindlessness" as it operates in an organizational setting. "This insensitivity occurs when individuals follow the same routine simply because 'that is the way things have always been done around here.' The goal is to 'get the job done,' even though there are warning signals that require attention and better ways available to complete the task."[1] One of the reasons that trained mindlessness or a tactical approach to problems exists at the organizational level is time pressures, which also negatively affect decision-making.

Strategic communication thus aligns to some degree with the new focus on "mindfulness" in leadership. **Mindfulness** is the basic human ability to be fully present, aware of where we are and what we're doing, and not overly reactive or overwhelmed by what's going on around us.[2] It is the psychological process of bringing one's attention to the internal and external experiences occurring in the present moment. This ability enables us to be more aware of the different contexts in which we find ourselves and to thus communicate accordingly.

Mindfulness training is becoming more popular in the business world, and many large corporations have been incorporating practicing mindfulness into their culture to reap a variety of benefits.[3] For example, companies such as Google, Apple, Procter & Gamble, General Mills, Mayo Clinic, and the U.S. Army offer mindfulness coaching, meditation breaks, and other resources to their employees to improve workplace functioning.[4] Mindfulness has been found to result in better employee well-being, lower levels of frustration, lower absenteeism and burnout, as well as improving the overall work environment.[5] Since high levels of mindfulness correlate with ethical decision-making and increase personal awareness and emotional regulation, mindfulness training has been suggested as way to promote ethical intentions and behavior for business students as well.[6] High levels of personal awareness and emotional regulation also are needed to be an effective communicator.

A strategic approach to communication and other management tasks is often what differentiates a manager from a true leader (this distinction will be discussed more fully later). One of the key purposes of this book is to show you how to differentiate yourself as a leader through your understanding and use of strategic communication. Strategy is primarily a critical thinking activity, one that is based on analysis and evaluation of a particular situation or context, and then the synthesis of that information into a fact-based plan of action.

Communication strategy is part of an effective management strategy or plan, yet most management texts give short shrift to the subject. This is because management as a discipline generally focuses more on logistical issues at the organizational level—products offered, production capability, market needs, method of distribution, size and growth, and so on—rather than on human subjects creating productive organizational cultures through thoughtful and specific communication practices. When the discipline does deal with human subjects, it is often done from a psychological perspective. This textbook takes a different approach and is based on a different paradigm or perspective—a social constructionist view of reality that places communication in a central role in the creation and reproduction of organizations. (The social constructionist view of reality will be explained later in this chapter.) This is a second distinction of this text.

Strategic communication can be applied at multiple levels. Just as strategic management is designed to be applied at the organizational level, so can strategic communication management. But strategic communication as a practice can also be applied at the individual or personal level as well as the team and department levels. This is a third distinction of this text from many others that are available in that it includes discussions that go beyond personal communication practices.

mindfulness

The psychological process of bringing one's attention to the internal and external experiences occurring in the present moment.

The first part of the book provides individual communication strategies that can also be implemented at the team and organizational levels. The second part provides a discussion of the tactics that can be used to implement those strategies in different communication contexts, connecting these practices to strategic-communication management at the organizational level. This is one of the hallmarks of a strategic approach to communication: it operates at various levels of an organization, thus bridging the traditional boundaries of communication research. In fact, some researchers have proposed that a more strategic approach to communication must be practiced throughout the organization, from the leadership down to the frontline managers. I would go further in stating that employees can reap the benefits as well.[7] By bridging multiple levels, we can begin to conceptualize strategic communication as an ongoing process that links individual cognitions, words, and actions to organization-level actions and outcomes. A final hallmark of strategic communication is thus the need for *alignment* of the message across various stakeholders to achieve communicative success.

Why Is a Strategic Approach to Communication Important?

A strategic approach to communication has become more important in recent years for several reasons. The first reason involves trends in the workplace, the second is the evolution of our understanding of the communication process, and the third is greater appreciation for the centrality of communication in terms of the creation of our social and organizational realities.

Changes in the Workplace

Globalization has had a dramatic effect on the business environment in which we now operate. Although it has presented numerous opportunities to business organizations, it has also increased the potential for greater instability, rapid change, and greater competition. These forces have had varied effects, including greater merger activity, the flattening of hierarchies within organizations, and greater entrepreneurial pressures. To remain competitive in the current business environment, organizations must be flexible; generally speaking, strict rules and procedures are a hindrance in organizations that must be able to move quickly to adapt to the changes in their environment.

These changes in the business world affect both management and employees, the primary effect being the increasing importance of communication for the success of individuals and the companies in which they work. The flattening of hierarchies and pressure for companies to improve productivity to remain competitive have made interpersonal relationships and the ability to maintain them more crucial than ever. This change began as early as the 1980s when the work of a manager was particularly affected by these changes in the business environment.[8] Instead of an emphasis on planning, organizing, and coordinating, the focus of the manager moved to communication. This move is an important one to recognize because it also helps to clarify the distinctions between **leadership** and **management**. Although some researchers disagree, this text takes the position that managers coordinate and organize activities, while leaders influence people. These differing mind-sets and courses of action often complement each other in the workplace, but it is important to note that anyone can be a leader with the proper way of thinking and skill set. As organizations recognize the need for more fluid action to address change, a greater opportunity presents itself for employees to exert greater influence within the organization.

That is, changes such as the flattening of organizational hierarchies mean that "influence must replace the use of formal authority in relationships with subordinates, peers, outside contacts, and others on whom the job makes one dependent."[9] Because positional authority is no longer sufficient to get the job done, a web of influence or a balanced web of relationships must be developed.

leadership

Influence of people within an organizational setting through the orchestration of relationships.

management

The coordination and organization of activities within an organization.

"Recently managers have begun to view leadership as the orchestration of *relationships* between several different interest groups—superiors, peers, and outsiders, as well as subordinates."[10] The successful development of relationships generally lies in our skills in interpersonal communication, as does our ability to influence others; the result is the increased emphasis on communication, particularly for those in leadership positions or those who are aspiring leaders.

The importance of communication becomes clearer when we consider that leaders potentially differ from managers in regard to the type of power they may yield. Managers are appointed; they have legitimate power that enables them to reward and punish employees. The formal authority given to them by their position gives managers the ability to influence employees. Leaders, on the other hand, may be appointed or may emerge from a group of employees. In the latter case, they have the opportunity to influence others beyond their formal authority in an organization and this influence comes in large part from the ability to communicate well. This can be more clearly seen in the following table that illustrates the six key **power bases** that arise in organizations and groups.[11]

power bases

The differing sources or bases of power within an organization.

Table 1-1 French and Raven's Six Bases of Power

Base	Definition
Reward power	The capability of controlling the distribution of rewards given or offered the target.
Coercive power	The capacity to threaten and punish those who do not comply with requests or demands.
Legitimate power	Authority that derives from the power holder's legitimate right to require and demand obedience.
Referent power	Influence based on the target's identification with, attraction to, or respect for the power holder.
Expert power	Influence based on the target's belief that the power holder possesses superior skills and abilities.
Informational power	Influence based on the potential use of informational resources, including rational argument, persuasion, or factual data.

Source: French and Raven (1959).

Of the bases of power listed in Table 1-1, the first three are typically conferred on an individual by an institution or organization. They are the types of power that managers often have been given or what have been called *position power*. But, as the table indicates, they are not the only bases of power. Leaders have the opportunity to influence others through the last three types shown in the table: referent, expert, and informational power. In other words, leaders can influence others through their credibility, relationships, knowledge, and expertise. This is called *personal power*, or the influence a leader derives from being seen by others as likable and knowledgeable. As we will discuss later in this book, our communication behaviors help us to establish our credibility with others as well as build positive, productive relationships. In fact, leadership can be viewed as being a multidirectional influence relationship as compared with management, which is a unidirectional authority relationship.[12] The changes in organizational realities discussed earlier, particularly those that require employees to interact with one other, often unfamiliar individuals, both within and outside of the organization, cope with constant change, and integrate different systems that may mutually affect one another.[13] In this type of setting, leadership may depend less on individual, heroic actions, our common stereotype of a leader, and more on relational behaviors.[14] Such activities include creating an effective team: "activities intended to construct the social reality of team by creating an environment where positive outcomes of relational interactions can be realized."[15] (The concept of social construction of reality is explained next.)

Through communication we also express and demonstrate our knowledge base and expertise, important aspects of leadership influence. Interestingly, studies have shown that power demonstrated through expertise and knowledge have the strongest correlation with performance and satisfaction, whereas the use of coercive power is the least effective reason for compliance and has negative correlations with organizational effectiveness.

? **Critical** Thinking

Identify a situation in which differences in power exist between the communicators. How do these differences affect the rules or expectations regarding how communication occurs in that situation? Have you seen instances where people failed to heed those rules or expectations? What was the outcome?

Leaders also differ from managers in another important way. The overriding function for management is to provide order and consistency in organizations, whereas the primary function of leaders is to produce change and movement.[16] Leaders change the way people think about what is possible[17] and they do so primarily through by shaping behaviors and framing reality and change communicatively.[18] Table 1-2 distinguishes the activities of managers and leaders. It is important to note that, according to Kotter, the functions of both managers and leaders are important for the success of an organization.

Table 1-2 Functions of Management and Leadership

Management	Leadership
Produces Order and Consistency	*Produces Change and Movement*
Planning and Budgeting	**Establishing Direction**
• Establish agendas	• Create a vision
• Set timetables	• Clarify the big picture
• Allocate resources	• Set strategies
Organizing and Staffing	**Aligning People**
• Provide structure	• Communicate goals
• Make job placements	• Seek commitment
• Establish rules and procedures	• Build teams and coalitions
Controlling and Problem Solving	**Motivating and Inspiring**
• Develop incentives	• Inspire and energize
• Generate creative solutions	• Empower subordinates
• Take corrective action	• Satisfy unmet needs

Source: Adapted from J. P. Kotter. (1990). *A Force for Change: How Leadership Differs from Management.* (New York, NY: Free Press): 3–8.

plurality

Because people in communication mutually construct the meanings they have for situations and each other, multiple interpretations of any situation always exist, and no one person can control those interpretations.

Effects of globalization also reinforce the importance of communication. Therefore, it is imperative to have an understanding of cultural differences, which may affect communication effectiveness. **Plurality** refers to the fact that people in communication mutually construct the meanings they have for situations and each other. Plurality means that there are always multiple interpretations of any situation and that no one person can control those interpretations, try as he or she might. Recognition of the reality of plurality requires that we be open to or willing to listen to the voices and opinions of others if there is any hope of achieving something approaching shared understanding. This ability can be hindered by our own cultural understandings. For example, in the U.S., the emphasis on individualism has resulted in the assumption that the key purpose of communication is to express one's self; our opinions, feelings, ideas, goals. A more collective focus would place the emphasis on understanding others, a focus that better enables one to create successful communication strategies that include all contextual elements of a situation.

In the workplace, attempting to move toward shared understanding is, of course, important if we are to achieve organizational and personal goals. Unfortunately, our common understandings of communication and the notion of reality itself often gets in the way of fully appreciating and accounting for plurality. (The concept of plurality is based in a social constructionist approach, which is discussed later in this chapter.)

Advances in technology have also greatly affected communication within organizations. The spread and general pervasiveness of electronic and digital communication have made it more difficult for organizations to control the reception of messages sent intentionally—and more and more often, unintentionally—to both internal and external audiences. University programs' valorization of "hard skills" over those considered "soft skills," i.e., communication, has led to a general lack of appreciation for and understanding of such simple tasks as how to select the appropriate media for a message. (By the way, this distinction between "hard skills" and "soft skills" is a gendering of language use that implies "hard skills" is a masculine activity, while subordinating "soft skills" to the feminine realm of activity.) Thus, a general state of "mindlessness" often drives many of the decisions about which media to use for particular purposes, situations and the organizational level, leading to miscommunication, lower productivity, and damaged morale. Choices such as media selection are only the tip of the iceberg. In fact, at the heart of many organizational problems is a lack of mindful, knowledgeable consideration and planning of communication.

Evolution of Our Understanding of the Communication Process

Over time, the definition of what constitutes communication and how it occurs has evolved. Our commonsensical views of communication, though, often have not followed suit. If you ask a room full of people to define communication, most will say something like "It is the transfer of information from one person to another." This is an excellent model for communication and was, in fact, one of the first. However, our views of communication have changed with time to give us a more complex view of its process and function. An understanding of communication as an informative process, for example, ignores the effects of distortion on information transfer or the multiple possible interpretations that a receiver might make of a message. Because of the effects of globalization in terms of the increasing diversity of the workforce and the effects and interdependencies of international and multinational corporations, most of us now recognize, to some degree at least, that people of different cultures interpret the world differently. Consequently, this view of communication—as a simple process of transmission of information—is no longer considered useful in thinking about how communication between two or more people occurs. This becomes clearer when one recognizes that the transmission of information model best describes the way that machines communicate, that is, data transmission. Even though many scientists like to think of humans as being analogous to machines, this is not at the current moment true. People have the capability for high levels of adaptability and their sensory capacities and differing experiential knowledge lead to unpredictable adaptations and interpretations beyond current machine capabilities.

Furthermore, in a business setting, much of the communication that occurs is not merely informative; it is almost always persuasive by its very nature. To put it rather bluntly, we are almost always attempting to "sell" something in organizational settings—if nothing more than ourselves—to someone else. Selling ourselves and influencing others involves yet another important consideration—our credibility, maintaining it and enhancing it—often through our communication practices. And these practices are not relegated to what we write or say. Our communication practices also involve nonverbal cues. In fact, in face-to-face communication situations, some researchers claim that more than 90 percent of the available information is transmitted nonverbally. If we ignore nonverbal communication, we may be transmitting information to others that we do not intend to transmit or that does not align with our oral message, creating further confusion. Consequently, much of the communication that takes place in a professional setting has little to do with simply transmitting information but a great deal to do with managing the impressions we make on others.

We also may underestimate the contested nature of meaning in organizational settings. Studies have shown that much organizational communication is characterized by ambiguity, deception, and diversity of viewpoints rather than shared meaning.[19] In fact, some researchers view organizational cultures as contested political domains in which the possibility for genuine dialogue and the arrival at shared meanings is often seriously impaired.[20]

For these reasons, it is imperative to develop a more sophisticated understanding of communication, its purposes, and its processes if we are going to be successful in today's complex and rapidly changing business environment.

The Social Construction of Reality and Its Effects on Conceptualizing Communication

Another more recent development that has placed communication at the center of interest in organizational settings is the development of what is called the *social construction of reality*. Until the late 1960s, it was generally accepted that human beings could easily study and grasp the meaning of objects and processes in our world. In their book *The Social Construction of Reality*, Peter L. Berger and Thomas Luckmann introduced a different view of reality, arguing that all knowledge, including the most basic, taken-for-granted commonsense knowledge of everyday reality, is derived from and maintained by social interactions.[21] In plain language, people create their cultures—their "reality"—through communication practices, if we include the symbolic aspects of artifacts, stories, clothing, ways of thinking, acting, and talking, etc. In other words, when particular groupings of people interact—families, tribes, communities, and cultures—they do so with the understanding that their respective perceptions of "reality" are related because they share similar experiences and values. As they act on this understanding over time, their common knowledge of "reality" becomes reinforced, a process that is largely invisible to the participant because he or she naturalizes the experience, i.e., it seems "normal" to them. Socially constructed "reality" is an ongoing, dynamic process; reality is reproduced by people acting on their interpretations and their knowledge of it. A **social construction**, or **social construct**, is any phenomenon "invented" or "constructed" by participants in a particular culture or society, existing because people agree to behave as if it exists or to follow certain conventional rules. One example of a social construct is social status; that is, individual persons do not have greater status than others unless it is socially conferred. One can see that a Mercedes has the same function as a Hyundai, for instance, transporting an individual to work, school, or shopping, but culture confers greater status to the Mercedes, which then attaches to the individual. From a functional perspective, however, each vehicle is generally equal; only cultural meanings enable us to believe that someone who drives a Mercedes is better than someone who drives a Hyundai. Another example of social construction is the use of money, which has worth only because society has agreed to treat it as valuable. Otherwise, it is simply paper.

social construction or social construct

Any phenomenon "invented" or "constructed" by participants in a particular culture or society and existing because people agree to behave as if it exists or to follow certain conventional rules.

The importance of communication comes at the beginning of the process—actors *interacting* to form mental representations, which become habituated—and continues to the end when these mental representations and roles are institutionalized in practice. This process of creating social reality is one of *meaning making*.

The theory of the social construction of reality might be better understood by comparing it to the natural sciences and their focus of study, the natural world and the universe. For example, it is known that water freezes at 32 degrees Fahrenheit, that light travels at 186,000 miles per second in a vacuum, and the normal body temperature of a human being is 98.6 degrees. These are the laws of nature that we all generally accept as fact (although "miles" and "degrees" are also human constructs for something we perceive in nature). However, when we look at the social sciences, we see that the behaviors and values of human beings across the world vary, that is, cultures differ in their values, belief systems, and social practices. A social constructionist perspective understands that these values, beliefs, and cultural practices are created and reinforced through communication thought broadly, as the use of symbols and symbol systems to create meaning, that is, create our cultural and social realities. This perspective aligns with the effects of globalization in that interactions among different cultures reveals the differing social "realities" in which each operate. In the U.S., the individual is the center of our understandings, for example, whereas in a more collectivist culture, the group is the center. These social "truths" create distinctively different ways of understanding, interacting, and behaving in the world. Consequently, a social constructionist view enables us to move away from an ethnocentric view of the world to one where many social realities are valid and deserving of our recognition and appreciation.

Figure 1-1 The Natural World vs. Social Reality

© Robyn Walker

The primary reason that a social constructionist view is significant for leaders or potential leaders is because it provides a powerful basis for understanding and marshaling influence through communication within an organization through strategic assessment and planning of messaging. In other words, such a perspective provides greater potential empowerment of the individual as compared with traditional leadership theory, which has often viewed leadership as a trait, style, or characteristic inherent in an individual. This latter view focuses on a particular individual's psychological and/or cognitive makeup. A social constructionist view, on the other hand, recognizes that leaders are more involved with the management of meaning, often through the practice of framing or defining events in particular ways. However, meaning making involves the receivers of the message as well because they may or may not accept the message framing that is offered. This problem thus leads to the importance of recognizing the context of a communicative event and adapting messages so as to better ensure their intended reception by the audience. Dealing with these challenges is the realm of a strategic approach to communication.

A social constructionist view enables us to see that leadership is co-constructed, it is a product of sociohistorical and collective meaning making, and is negotiated on an ongoing basis through complex interactions among leadership actors, be they designated by the organization or by emergent leaders or followers. With this understanding, the importance of a strategic approach to communication becomes much clearer. Leadership is achieved—or not—through the processes of communication with others. Through your words and actions, you have the potential to demonstrate leadership by maintaining existing realities or creating new realities for coworkers, customers, clients, and the general public for your organization and its activities. (The rules of reality construction for leaders are provided in Figure 1-2). This textbook will provide you the tools to shape those realities while also recognizing the contributions to leadership of those who take a more psychological and cognitive approach to the phenomenon.

How to Analyze Case Studies

A business case study is a description of an opportunity or problem faced by an individual, a manager, an executive, or an entire organization that students are asked to read, analyze, and respond to either orally or in writing. Case studies are beneficial because they provide students an opportunity to apply the knowledge they have gained, an activity that leads to and demonstrates a higher level of knowledge acquisition.

Figure 1-2 The Rules of Reality Construction

> **Rule 1: Control the Context**
> Leaders often cannot control events, but they can control how events are interpreted.

> **Rule 2: Define the Situation**
> Framing reality means defining "the situation here and now" in ways that connect with others.

> **Rule 3: Apply Ethics**
> "Reality" is often contested. Framing a subject is an act of persuasion, one imbued with ethical choices.

> **Rule 4: Interpret Uncertainty**
> The uncertainty of the situation opens it up for interpretation and provides an opportunity for the more verbally skilled to emerge as leaders.

> **Rule 5: Design the Response**
> Leadership is a design problem. Leaders must figure out what leadership is and through their actions persuade themselves and others that they are doing it.

> **Rule 6: Control Spontaneity**
> Think strategically then respond.

Source: Adapted from Fairhurst, G. T. (2011). *The Power of Framing: Creating the Language of Leadership.* San Francisco, CA: John Wiley & Sons.

Application enables students to better understand how the knowledge provided in a text can be used in real-world situations and thus enables them to learn more about issues they may deal with in organizational settings. In addition, case studies enable students to practice critical and analytical thinking, both higher-order cognitive abilities needed to be a strategic communicator and businessperson.

This text provides both fictional case studies and those based on field and library research. Fictional case studies are often shorter and are useful for introducing concepts to students, whereas field or library case studies are based on actual events and often provide greater detail, depth, and complexity. Because of this, they are useful for higher-order application of text concepts and principles.

Case study analysis first involves reading the case carefully, taking notes, and then analyzing the information to determine the key problems or opportunities involved in the situation, as well as the preferred outcome. All of these aspects are necessary to identify the proper course of action.

Initial Analysis

Analysis involves a simple process of asking the right questions and coming up with the right answers. In order to analyze a case study well, begin by asking and answering the following questions:

1. Who is the decision maker in this case, and what is his or her position and responsibilities?

2. What appears to be the issue(s) of concern (problem, challenge, or opportunity) and its significance for the organization? Ranking the issues in order of their importance can help to identify the best solution.

3. Why or how has the issue arisen? The goal is to identify the cause and effect of the issue identified, which again may help to identify a solution or recommendation.

4. When does the decision maker have to decide, resolve, act, or dispose of the issue? How urgent is the situation?

5. Who is affected most by the issue? It often is helpful to rank stakeholders in order of most affected, since this ranking can help you determine the best solution.

6. What are the constraints regarding the type of decision that might be made? Identifying constraints can often help you determine the best solution as well.

Identification of Solutions and Recommendations

Once you have completed the analysis of the situation and identified the key issues, their causes, and the stakeholders who will be most affected, you are in a position to best identify appropriate solutions and recommendations. But further analysis is needed, since a list of possible solutions must be generated and each assessed for its ability to lead to the desired outcome identified earlier in the analysis.

Once this final analysis is completed and the best solution is identified, a plan for implementing and communicating the solution to appropriate stakeholders must be completed — the last step in the process.

How This Book Is Organized

This book is divided into two parts. The first deals with the steps involved in formulating personal communication strategies in the workplace. The second discusses how strategy can be applied at both the personal and the organizational level, with a greater focus on the deployment of tactics or skills.

Another unique feature of this textbook is that it integrates information from various fields of communication research and practice. This approach may be somewhat controversial because these diverse fields have different ontological perspectives and theoretical foundations. However, the purpose for doing so is not to lessen the distinctiveness of these fields or the importance of their contribution to our understanding of communication but is necessary for a strategic approach to communication in an organizational setting. It thus provides a more streamlined, coherent method for potential business leaders to apply the findings from these areas without years of study. You will thus find discussions that are drawn from the fields of rhetoric, composition, and interpersonal, group, and organizational communication. The text also integrates personal communication strategies with discussions of topics from the areas of management and corporate communication. Management communication skills are those that are needed to effectively interact with others and to manage and influence groups; corporate communication skills are those abilities that are needed to lead organizations and address a broader community.

Part 1: The Strategic Process

- **Foundations of Communication (Chapter 2):** This chapter discusses foundational principles of communication that are helpful in developing a more sophisticated understanding of the process of communication, such as communication models, perception, and self-concept. It also discusses challenges to the practice of strategic yet ethical communication and techniques for overcoming these challenges.

- **Step One: Identify the Purposes of Communication (Chapter 3):** The first step in the strategic communication process is to identify the purposes of your communication and then devise a communication strategy that effectively achieves those purposes. The four purposes of business communication are to inform, to persuade and influence, to convey goodwill, and to establish credibility. Not only is it important for the communicator to know his or her purpose or purposes, but also it is expected that the purpose will be apparent to the audience for the message, generally from the beginning of that message. In other words, business audiences generally want to know immediately what your message is about and why they should pay attention to it.

- **Step Two: Analyze the Audience (Chapter 4):** The second step in the strategic communication process is to conduct an audience analysis. All good communication should be driven by and focused on your audience or stakeholders: their interests, needs, expectations, and concerns. In other words, effective messages should be audience centered.

- **Steps Three and Four: Consider the Context and Select a Channel of Communication (Chapter 5):** The third and fourth steps in the strategic communication process have to do with considering contextual issues, such as organizational culture, communication climates, and communication flow within an organization and then choosing the appropriate channel and medium for communicating your message.

Business Communication Process Steps and Strategies

Process Steps	Corresponding Strategy
1. Identify the Purposes	▪ Inform ▪ Persuade ▪ Convey and maintain goodwill ▪ Establish and maintain credibility or reputation at the organizational level
2. Analyze the Audience	▪ Achieve audience focus
3. Consider the Context	▪ Make contextual adjustments
4. Select the Channel(s) & Media	▪ Select the appropriate channel(s)/media

Part 2: Communication Tactics for Differing Channels and Contexts

- **Communicating in Writing (Chapter 6):** This chapter discusses the different types of written messages—routine or informative, bad news, and persuasive—and provides tactics for creating them. It also discusses special considerations for electronic messages and provides a discussion of proposals and formal report formats.

- **Communicating in Oral Presentations (Chapter 7):** This chapter discusses oral, nonverbal, and visual considerations and tactics for preparing and delivering effective oral presentations, including dealing with question-and-answer sessions.

- **Communicating with Employees (Chapter 8):** This chapter opens with a discussion of interpersonal communication issues, such as interpersonal styles, nonverbal communication, and effective listening techniques. It then puts these considerations and tactics to work in discussions of specific employee communication situations, such as providing feedback and conducting performance appraisals.

- **Communicating during the Employment Process (Chapter 9):** This chapter addresses elements of communication as they are applied in the processes of both applying for jobs and screening potential employees and hiring them. The job application process involves researching potential employers, preparing application materials, preparing for and performing interviews, and following up with employers. The hiring process includes writing job descriptions, screening applicants' employment messages, writing or gathering interview questions, interviewing applicants, and communicating a decision to those applicants. It also includes a discussion of preparing for, managing, and following up on meetings, including the use of video and teleconferencing.

- **Communicating in and Leading Groups and Teams (Chapter 10):** This chapter discusses issues involved in group communication, including the team formation process, individual roles within groups, conflict resolution, decision-making, and ensuring that process losses do not occur.

- **Strategic Organizational Communication (Chapter 11):** This chapter discusses the importance of creating a strategic plan for communicating with both internal and external audiences. Internal audiences are typically employees whereas external audiences include clients and customers, suppliers, news media, investors, and the public at large.

At the end of the text, you will also find appendices that address common writing problems and provide commonly used templates for business writing.

Summary

The concept of strategy originated with the military and has been adapted to business applications. Formulating strategy involves looking at the overall picture of an organization, including its goals, and formulating a plan to achieve those goals. In terms of communication, strategy may be applied at the personal as well as the organizational level. In other words, individuals may analyze organizational situations and formulate communication strategies for achieving their personal goals; they may also look at organizational situations and formulate communication strategies for achieving organizational goals. Tactics are then selected to enact that strategic plan.

Becoming a strategic communicator has become more important with recent trends in the business world. One trend is the process of globalization, which has created a more competitive business environment as well as the need to work with people and organizations from other cultures. Leadership has become more important because it is through the process of influencing others that many of these tasks are accomplished. In addition, our understanding of the process of communication has become more sophisticated. We now know that communication is not simply the task of transferring information. Because of our differences, we interpret information in different ways, thus messages may become distorted or misunderstood. Communication in the workplace is also multipurpose: We must maintain and often continually enhance our credibility or self-image if we are to successfully influence others. This is accomplished not only through our oral and written messages, but also through our nonverbal practices. Lastly, the power of language to create our social realities is finally getting the recognition it deserves. From a leadership perspective, this understanding provides opportunities to shape others' understanding of organizations and their activities.

Key Terms

strategy **3**	management **5**
tactics **3**	power bases **6**
mindfulness **4**	plurality **7**
leadership **5**	social construction or social construct **9**

Discussion Questions

1. Name and discuss the three reasons why a strategic approach to communication is particularly important today.
2. What is the difference between strategy and tactics?
3. Describe the difference between a manager and a leader. What are the differences in the types of power that they generally hold? Why do these differences make a strategic approach to communication important or useful?
4. In your own words, describe the meaning of the term *social construction of reality*. What are some examples of social constructions that you are commonly exposed to or accept?
5. What is the meaning of *plurality*? What effect does this understanding have on the way that you communicate with others if you wish to be successful in that communication?

Applications

1. Conduct research on the effects of globalization on organizations, focusing on communication issues. Write a report that summarizes your findings and provide recommendations to today's leaders and managers in terms of best communication practices.
2. Conduct research on leadership and communication. Write a report in which you summarize your findings and set goals for yourself in terms of the leadership communication skills you would like to improve or enhance. A well-written goal should be specific, measurable, attainable, and time bound. An example is "I will create a communication strategy to persuade my boss to promote me to manager by the end of 2011 and implement it successfully."

Endnotes

1. Veil, S. (2011). Mindful learning in crisis management. *Journal of Business Communication*, 48(2): 16–147.

2. *Mindful* Staff. (2014, Oct. 8). What is mindfulness?. *Mindful*. Retrieved May 31, 2017 from *https://www.mindful.org/what-is-mindfulness/*.

3. Good, D.J., & Lyddy, C.J., et al. (2016, Jan.). Contemplating mindfulness at work: An integrative review. *Journal of Management*. 42 (1). Boyatzis, R.E., & McKee, A. (2005). *Resonant Leadership: Renewing Yourself and Connecting with Others Through Mindfulness, Hope, and Compassion*. Boston: Harvard Business School Press, and Carroll, M. (2007). *The Mindful Leader: Ten Principles for Bringing Out the Best in Ourselves and Others*. Shambhala Publications. ISBN 9781590303474.

4. Good, D.J., & Lyddy, C.J., et al. (2016, Jan.). Contemplating mindfulness at work: An integrative review. *Journal of Management*. 42 (1) and Schultz, P. (2015). "Mindfulness, work climate, and psychological need satisfaction in employee well-being." *Mindfulness*. 6, 971–985. doi:10.1007/s12671-014-0338-7.

5. Schultz, P. (2015). "Mindfulness, work climate, and psychological need satisfaction in employee well-being." *Mindfulness*. 6, 971–985. doi:10.1007/s12671-014-0338-7.

6. Lampe M (2012). Mindfulness-based business ethics education. *Academy of Educational Leadership Journal*. 16 (3).

7. Thomas, G.F. & Stephens, K.J. (2015). An introduction to strategic communication. *International Journal of Business Communication* 52(1) 3–11. DOI: 10.1177/2329488414560469

8. Kanter, R. M. (1989). The new managerial work. *Harvard Business Review*, 67, 85–92.

9. Keys, B. & Case, T. (1990). How to become an influential manager. *Academy of Management Executive*, 4, 38–50, p. 38.

10. Keys, B. & Case, T. (1990). How to become an influential manager. *Academy of Management Executive*, 4, 38–50, p. 39.

11. French, J. R. P. & Raven, B. (1959). The bases of social power. In D. Cartwright (Ed.), *Studies in social power*. Ann Arbor, MI: Institute for Social Research.

12. Rost, J. C. (1991). *Leadership for the Twenty-First Century*. New York: Praeger.

13. Marion, R. & Ulh-Bien, M. (2001). Leadership in complex organizations. *Leadership Quarterly*, 12 (4), 389–418.

14. Carmeli, A., Ben-Hador, B., Waldman, D. A. & Rupp, D. E. (2009). How leaders cultivate social capital and nurture employee vigor: Implications for job performance. *Journal of Applied Psychology*, 94 (6): 1553–1561; Fletcher, J. K. (1999). *Disappearing Acts: Gender, Power and Relational Practices at Work*. Cambridge, MA: The MIT Press; Fletcher, J. K. & Kaeufer, K. (2002). Shared leadership: Paradox and possibility. In C. L. Pearce & J. A. Conger (Eds.) *Shared Leadership: Reframing the Hows and Whys of Leadership* (pp. 27–45). Sherman Oaks, CA: Sage Publications; Pearce, C. L. & Conger, J. A. (2002); Tsui, A. S., Pearce, C. L., Porter, L. W., Tripoli, A. A. (1997). Alternative approaches to employee-organization relationship: Does investment in employees payoff? *Academy of Management*, 40 (5): 1089–1121; Williams, M. (2007). Building genuine trust through interpersonal emotion management: A threat regulation model of trust and collaboration across borders. *Academy of Management*, 32 (2): 595–621.

15. Fletcher, J. K. (1998). Relational practice: A feminist reconstruction of work. *Journal of Management Inquiry*, 7 (2): 163–186, p. 169.

16. Kotter, J. P. (1990). *A Force for Change: How Leadership Differs from Management*. New York: Free Press.

17. Zaleznik, A. (1977). Managers and leaders: Are they different? *Harvard Business Review*, 55, 67–78.

18. Higgs, M. & Rowland, D. (2005). All changes big and small: Exploring approaches to change and its leadership. *Journal of Change Management*, 5 (2): 121–152; Rowland, D. & Higgs, M. (2008). Sustaining change: Leadership that works. Chichester: Jossey-Bass.

19. Weick, K. (1979). *The Social Psychology of Organizing* (2nd ed.). Reading, MA: Addison-Wesley; Eisenberg, E. M. (1984). Ambiguity as strategy in organizational communication. *Communication Monographs*, 51, 227–242; Conrad, C. (1985). Chrysanthemums and swords: A reading of contemporary organizational communication theory and research. *Southern Speech Communication Journal*, 50, 189–200.

20. Frost, P., Moore, L., Louis, M., Lundberg, C., & Martin, J. (1991). *Reframing Organizational Culture*. Newbury Park, CA: Sage Publications.

21. Berger, P. L. & Luckmann, T. (1967). *The Social Construction of Reality: A Treatise in the Sociology of Knowledge*. Harpswell, ME: Anchor.

© pressmaster / bigstockphoto.com

Chapter 2

Foundations of Communication

After reading this chapter, you will be able to

- *Approach communication from a more sophisticated perspective, one that underscores the importance of a strategic yet ethical approach.*

- *Understand the process of perception, how it affects the way we interpret information, and its importance in developing a strategic approach.*

- *Understand the importance of self-awareness as a foundational element of effective communication and its connection to understanding others, a key element of a strategic approach.*

- *Identify some of the obstacles to strategic and ethical communication, including how perception can affect the way we think and our ability to gather, analyze, and evaluate information (i.e., the critical-thinking process that is imperative for strategic communication).*

Case Questions

1. What unexplored assumptions about the social reality at California Design, Inc. may have contributed to the situation that Lara now faces?
2. How might differing perceptions of the situation by those involved have contributed to the creation of this situation?
3. What are the implicit understandings of those involved in this situation regarding how communication works, that is, their preferred communication model? How might understanding and applying a different, more accurate communication model help to avoid or minimize this situation?
4. What is or should be leadership's or management's role? Who solves, or should solve, these problems and how?

The Case of California Design, Inc.

California Design, Inc. is a small company started in 1990 by Clarence Ross, an interior designer. Throughout the housing boom of the early 2000s, the company grew exponentially, adding designers, a sales consultant group, and a manufacturing facility. The company has survived the Great Recession by marketing its services to wealthy clients less affected by the country's economic decline, but it did freeze hiring in the late 2000s and is now short staffed in all of its key departments.

Lara Adams is an interior designer at California Design who joined the firm in 2015. She is frustrated by the frequent communication mix-ups that occur, largely, she believes, due to the increased time pressures on remaining personnel caused by staffing shortages. Today, for instance, she has received an e-mail that informs her the sales department has failed to cancel one of her design consultations with a client. This means that Lara is double booked for her 2 p.m. time slot.

The company's policy is to contact clients to confirm their appointments two days before the scheduled date and time. If the client cannot be contacted or does not respond to calls and messages from the sales department, then the appointment is dropped by the designers' administrative assistant and the time slot is filled with a client who has missed an appointment in the past and has requested a place on a waiting list for last-minute openings.

However, this policy was not followed in the case of client Alfonzo Rio. Sales consultant Louis Freeman writes that Alfonzo contacted him to confirm the appointment and that confirmation was not passed on to Lara or the department's administrative assistant.

Lara is doubly frustrated because she has ordered a custom chaise for another customer through the company's in-house manufacturing facility. The order was submitted two weeks ago, and manufacturing confirmed that the chaise would be completed and delivered this afternoon. She has just gotten off the phone with the angry client who called to loudly complain because she had received an automated e-mail notification that the scheduled delivery of the chaise had been delayed a week. The client had planned a social event at her home this weekend with the understanding that her redesigned living room would be completed. She is now demanding some type of compensation for the company's failure to uphold its contractual obligation.

This isn't the first time that these problems have occurred and been dumped in Lara's lap to resolve. She is so frustrated that she wants to eliminate the waiting list for clients to avoid these sorts of mix-ups and to stop ordering product through the company facility. Both of these moves would involve lost revenues for the company but would make Lara's life easier and would potentially improve customer satisfaction.

Strategic Communicators

To be a strategic communicator requires a number of skills and abilities as well as certain knowledge; some might say it even requires a certain mindset. This knowledge includes principles and concepts that are considered the foundation of effective communication, including a high level of self-awareness; an ability to understand other people (who often have differing experiences, values, and interests from our own, including cultural differences); a basic knowledge of the complexity of the communication process itself; and the ability to think critically—to analyze and evaluate situations and to use that information to formulate effective communication strategies. Because of the importance of communication in today's global organizations, it is easy to see why the requirements for strategic communicators closely mirror the competencies for globally literate leaders.[1]

- **Personal literacy.** Understanding and valuing yourself (i.e., self-awareness and self-esteem).
- **Social literacy.** Engaging and challenging other people (which requires an understanding of those others in order to be effective).
- **Business literacy.** Focusing and mobilizing your organization (which requires an understanding of the business environment as well as the organization's culture and processes).
- **Cultural literacy.** Valuing and leveraging cultural differences.

All of these capacities are founded on the ability and willingness to continuously observe and analyze the social realities with which we interact and of which we are a part; in other words, we must be open to continually learning about our environment so as to better engage with it. Before discussing these issues from the perspective of communication—self-awareness, understanding others, and understanding cultural issues—let's begin with a discussion of how concepts of communication have developed over time so that we may gain a greater understanding of how communication operates. (Understanding the business environment and organizational culture and communication processes will be discussed in Chapter 5.)

Models of Communication

How would you define communication? Without looking ahead, take a moment and write down a short definition or say it aloud.

Odds are that you came up with something like "conveying information to other people," perhaps with a bit more elaboration. Pat yourself on the back if you used this definition because you exemplify a theorist of communication, identifying one of the first models used to describe the process. In Chapter 1, we learned the definition of what constitutes communication and how it occurs has evolved over time. This section will provide an overview of the different ways of thinking about communication and how they developed. We'll end with the dialogic model, which is the foundation for this textbook because it best addresses the challenges of working with diverse groups and individuals than some of the more traditional models.

The purpose of this discussion is to show that how we think about communication has become more nuanced and complex just as our world has become more complex. To be an effective strategic communicator, the way we think about communication and its processes should reflect this understanding. Becoming familiar with the models of communication also helps us better understand our own personal style and whether or how it may need to be adjusted to improve our communication competence. The models of communication we will cover in this chapter are (1) information transfer, (2) transactional process, (3) strategic control, and (4) dialogic process.

Communication as Information Transfer

Communication as information transfer, as was discussed in Chapter 1, assumes that one person can transmit the information in his or her head to another without distortion or personal interpretation (see Figure 2-1). We now know that this approach to communication ignores the effects of distortion on information transfer or the multiple possible interpretations that a receiver might apply to a message. Because of the effects of globalization, the increasing diversity of the workforce and the influence and interactions of international and multinational corporations, most of us know that people of different cultures interpret the world differently. Even people from the same culture may have multiple interpretations of the same event, depending on their worldview, value system, and life experiences. This model also does not adequately account for the power of nonverbal communication. Consequently, this model of communication is no longer considered useful in thinking about how communication occurs; it more accurately describes communication between machines in the form of electric impulses.

Figure 2-1 Information Transfer Model of Communication

Human communication attempts to do more than simply transfer information. As Chapter 3 will discuss in more detail, there are several purposes for communicating in a business environment—to create and maintain relationships, to establish and maintain our credibility, and to persuade and influence others—and these are all the more important because of the political nature of many organizations. Organizations should also establish communication plans to achieve similar goals of:

- Maintaining effective relationships with employees to enhance productivity and morale and longevity of employment
- Supporting effective relationships with external stakeholders to sustain sales, growth, and profitability
- Sustaining and enhancing their reputations with all organizational stakeholders, including the public at large.

Because of these potential challenges—differing perspectives and a variety of purposes—it is often beneficial to analyze important or new communication situations so as to better adapt to those situations before proceeding with critical communication tasks.

Communication as Transactional Process

Model 2, communication as transactional process, acknowledges that both senders and receivers are active and simultaneous interpreters of messages (see Figure 2-2). One advantage of this model over the information-transfer approach is that it acknowledges the importance of feedback, particularly the nonverbal type, in meaning making. In other words, receivers are not passive objects who simply receive a message, like a machine; they also bring their own observations and experiences to the interpretation of the message, creating opportunities for misunderstanding of the intent.

However, this model of communication also has received criticism for its emphasis on achieving shared meaning. Therefore, it is most usefully applied in interpersonal relationships in which shared meaning is the goal, those involving friends, families, and intimate partners.

Figure 2-2 Transactional Process Model of Communication

This goal is often not the case in organizations, however. studies have shown that much organizational communication is characterized by ambiguity, deception, and diversity of viewpoints rather than shared meaning.[2] In fact, some researchers view organizational cultures as contested political domains in which the possibility for genuine dialogue is often seriously impaired.[3] Consequently, this model is generally not the best to apply because it doesn't recognize the competitive, political nature of many organizations. In fact, management professor Kathleen Reardon (2005) goes so far as to claim that it's "all politics" in organizations. "In any job, when you reach a certain level of technical competence, politics is what makes all the difference with regard to success. At that point, it is indeed all politics. Every day brilliant people take a backseat to politically adept colleagues by failing to win crucial support for their ideas."[4] This political climate is often the result of reward systems that focus solely on individual performance to the neglect of team achievement; employees are rewarded for competing against each other, sometimes using destructive interpersonal tactics to gain personal advantage. This setting makes it even more important to understand how to be strategic in our communication. We need to understand the workings of power within an organization—who has it and who doesn't—to enable us to better negotiate those power networks by observing and listening to others; fostering and managing important relationships; and analyzing different organizational contexts so as to better adapt to these political landscapes. Doing so, according to Reardon, also involves the ability to be persuasive and influential, the basic mark of a leader, as you may recall from the discussion of leadership in Chapter 1.

Communication as Strategic Control

Model 3, communication as strategic control, assumes that communication is a tool that individuals use to control their environment and thus it recognizes the play of power and politics within an organizational setting. From this perspective, a competent communicator chooses strategies appropriate to the situation and accomplishes multiple goals. The major criticism of this approach is its recognition that people should not be expected to communicate in any objectively rational way. Instead, communication choices are personally, socially, politically, and ethically motivated. In extreme cases, this model could lead to communicative practices that ignore the goals of clarity and honesty when it is in the communicator's best individual interest to do so.[5] In other words, an "ends justifies the means" approach might take hold in which concern about damage to others (and oftentimes one's own credibility) takes a back seat to short-term personal goals. In addition to these potentially ethical issues, an overly self-interested approach may lead us to ignore the larger "political" elements at work in many organizations, sometimes at our own peril. An example would be an individual who believed he or she was right and focused on proving it, but in the process, alienated his or her colleagues and caused so much trouble for management that the person became marginalized or was ultimately let go. Because of the limitations of the strategic control approach, there is a need for a model of communication that recognizes the interdependency of human beings in most organizational situations to help balance the pursuit of short-term personal gain.

It is important to make a distinction between a model of communication as strategic control and a strategic communication approach. A strategic communication approach, as discussed in Chapter 1, involves recognition of the various stakeholders to a communication event and the possibility of miscommunication. The goal is to adjust the message so as to better align it for all stakeholders' understanding, the goal being message management and influence rather than control of others. To put it more bluntly, strategic messaging recognizes the challenges of communicating clearly with others and attempts to ameliorate some of those challenges. It is a conscious thinking and planning process that attempts to account for the obstacles to clear communication with a long-term perspective. This view might be better understood by considering the next communication model.

Communication as Dialogic Process

Model 4, the dialogic model, mitigates against many of the problems associated with the previously discussed approaches. It goes beyond the information-transfer model to focus on the contribution of the "receiver's" perspective to an interpretation and course of action jointly decided upon. In other words, the sender and receiver are jointly creating social reality. This perspective is critically important to the strategic communicator because the focus of a good strategic communicator is not on himself or herself but rather on the audience, organizational stakeholders, and the context within which communication takes place. Audience analysis, combined with an examination of the communication context, should generally drive strategy and message formulation, rather than our own sometimes narrow self-interest. A skilled strategic communicator can achieve both his or her personal goals as well as those of the group through such analysis. This strategic approach is long term in its temporal orientation as opposed to short term, a tactical view.

dialogic model of communication

This model of communication takes other people's points of view into account, acknowledging that the speaker and the listener may have different perspectives.

dialogue

A conversation among two or more persons. From the dialogic perspective, that dialogue would be characterized by such attributes as trust, lack of pretense, sincerity, humility, respect, directness, open-mindedness, honesty, concern for others, empathy, nonmanipulative intent, equality, and acceptance of others as individuals with intrinsic worth, regardless of differences of opinion or belief.

monologue

Talking to oneself. From a dialogic perspective, a monologue is characterized by such qualities as deception, superiority, exploitation, dogmatism, domination, insincerity, pretense, personal self-display, self-aggrandizement, judgmentalism that stifles free expression, coercion, possessiveness, condescension, self-defensiveness, and viewing others as objects to be manipulated.

The **dialogic model of communication** also attempts to deal with the contested nature of communication that is ignored by the transactional model by acknowledging that differences of perspective may exist between communicators. In other words, it doesn't assume that meaning or even the goal of communication is shared but instead recognizes the interplay between the difference and similarity of those involved in the communication process and thus better enables the communicator to take steps to attempt to negotiate difference. Finally, it also attempts to moderate the ethical problem of the strategic model by acknowledging that we are not isolated individuals; rather, we live in groups and communities and our actions affect others. According to Dean C. Barnlund (1986), communication is inherently ethical. Privately, human beings are "free to invent whatever meaning they can. But when [people] encounter each other, a moral issue invades every exchange because the manipulation of symbols always involves a purpose that is external to, and in some degree manipulative of, the interpreter of the message."[6] Barnlund's statement recognizes the socially constructed nature of reality—human beings create meaning through communication—and the possibility that a strategic approach to communication may go awry in an ethical sense through manipulation, deception, or the withholding of information or by holding onto other theories about the communication process that may ignore the complexity of the communication environment and process.

According to the dialogic model, the strategies that we use to communicate must consider how our messages affect others' perception of us as well as the effect of our communication on others. This model implicitly recognizes the growing importance of interpersonal relationships on our own success and happiness in the workplace, as well as our personal lives, as the boundaries between these two have become blurred with the proliferation of technology—cell phones, laptops, e-mail, the Internet, and so on.

Communication understood as **dialogue** is characterized by such attributes as trust, lack of pretense, sincerity, humility, respect, directness, open-mindedness, honesty, concern for others, empathy, nonmanipulative intent, equality, and acceptance of others as individuals with intrinsic worth, regardless of differences of opinion or belief.[7] This attitude contrasts with the understanding and practice of communication as **monologue**, which is characterized by such qualities as deception, superiority, exploitation, dogmatism, domination, insincerity, pretense, personal self-display, self-aggrandizement, judgmentalism that stifles free expression, coercion, possessiveness, condescension, self-defensiveness, and viewing others as objects to be manipulated.[8] Communication as monologue means that the communicator is essentially talking to himself or herself, ignoring the effects that communication has on others, or worse, using communication to control others for his or her own needs. Communication as monologue is an **egocentric** process in which little or no concern or empathy is shown for the desires or feelings of others. This mindset can be compared with a strict strategy as control approach to communication.

egocentric

Concerned with the self rather than others or society.

To better demonstrate the differences between a monologue and a dialogue, Barnlund (1986) offers three types of communication. The first type comprises messages whose intent is to coerce others. Meaning is controlled by choosing symbols that so threaten the interpreter of the message that he or she becomes incapable of, and blind to, alternative meanings.[9] Second, there are messages of an exploitative sort in which words are arranged to filter the information, narrow the choices, and obscure the consequences so that only one meaning becomes attractive or appropriate.[10] Both of these types can be the result of the use of information transfer and strategy as control models of communication. The third type involves what Barnlund calls "facilitative" communication in which words are used to inform, enlarge perspective, deepen sensitivity, remove external threat, and encourage independence of meaning.[11] "The values of the listener are, in the first case, ignored, in the second, subverted, in the third, respected."[12] Barnlund's distinctions about the intent of communication is another illustration of its use to create social reality.

As we will discuss in the next chapter, facilitative communication can be beneficial in achieving two important purposes of communication in organizations: establishing and maintaining relationships (i.e., conveying goodwill), and establishing and maintaining credibility as a person respectful of others.

The dialogic model differs from the earlier models of communication, particularly the information transfer and strategy as control models, in which other people are sometimes viewed as objects to be acted upon, communicated to, ordered, and controlled.[13] (Figure 2-3 compares the four models of communication discussed in this section.) In contrast, the dialogic model perceives others as *interdependent* partners capable and deserving of their own voice to influence the organizational dialogue. The dialogic model thus is considered an index of the ethical level of communication to the degree that participants in communication display the attributes of dialogue.[14]

Figure 2-3 Comparison of Four Models of Communication

Model of Communication	Primary Characteristics	Disadvantages
Information Transfer	Transmissional	Lacks recognition of barriers to communication and what the other brings to the interaction
Transactional Process	Simultaneous interpretation	Focuses on achieving shared meaning without due recognition of contested domain of organizations
Strategic Control	Control the environment	Can evolve to manipulation and deception of others
Dialogic	Recognition of the other and plurality of interpretation	Challenging to cope with the complexity of social realities

Even though this recognition of our interdependence with others may seem like commonsense in terms of our understanding, it may not as easily be practiced. That's because people in the United States tend to have an individualistic perspective in which the focus is on looking out for and valorizing the self rather than focusing on the well-being of the group, a more collectivist orientation.

Another reason that the dialogic model is potentially most useful has to do with the changes in the business environment due to the process of globalization. Thus, **plurality** often exists within these organizations. Plurality means that there are always multiple interpretations of any situation and that no one person can control those interpretations, try as he or she might. Recognition of the

plurality

The recognition that there are multiple different interpretations of any situation and that no one communicator can control all these interpretations.

Responsible Communication

One ethical problem that is exposed by the dialogic model of communication is what is termed *moral exclusion*. According to Susan Opotow (1990), moral exclusion occurs when the application of moral values, rules, and fairness is not considered necessary for particular individuals or groups. The practice of moral exclusion results in individuals being perceived as nonentities, expendable, or undeserving. The result is that harming such individuals becomes acceptable, appropriate, or just. One glaring example of moral exclusion is some U.S. policy makers' inferences that all Muslim people are potential terrorists. The error of this assumption can be made clear through a simple syllogism: all Christians are potential terrorists.

Persons who are morally excluded are thus denied their rights, dignity, and autonomy. In her analysis, Opotow identifies several dozen ways in which moral exclusion is manifested; of those, many involve communication and language use. For example, showing your belief in your superiority or the superiority of your group by making unflattering comparisons to other individuals or groups is one manifestation of moral exclusion. Another example of language use to morally exclude others is by characterizing them as lower life forms or as inferior beings. Other examples of moral exclusion include

- placing the blame for any harm on the victim;

- justifying harmful acts by claiming that the morally condemnable acts committed by "the enemy" are worse;

- misrepresenting harmful behaviors by masking or conferring respectability on them through the use of neutral, positive, technical, or euphemistic terms to describe them; and

- justifying harmful behavior by claiming that everyone is doing it or that it is an isolated case.

Question for Thought

- Can you think of recent examples in the news of the use of moral exclusion? In these examples, how has moral exclusion been used to manipulate meaning for others?

---

reality of plurality requires that we be open or willing to listen to the voices and opinions of others if there is any hope of achieving something approaching shared understanding. In the workplace, attempting to move toward shared understanding is, of course, important if we are to achieve organizational and personal goals and demonstrate our full leadership potential.

intercultural communication

The exchange of information among people of different cultural backgrounds.

Therefore, the dialogic model of communication is compatible with many of the concerns and goals of intercultural communication. **Intercultural communication** is the exchange of information between individuals who are unalike culturally.[15] The most effective way to deal with the challenges posed by conducting business across cultures is to be open to what may be learned about another culture and how that knowledge can be applied to communicate more effectively with its members. In this regard, plurality and its requirement of openness to the opinions of others help us to practice more effective intercultural communication. (Cultural differences are discussed in more detail in Chapter 4.)

The characteristics of dialogue overlap with much of the research on intercultural sensitivity. For example, several studies have identified empathy, understanding of others, valuing of difference, adaptability, and being nonjudgmental and open-minded as elements of intercultural competence.[16]

Perception

perception

Awareness of the elements of the environment made possible through our senses.

Hopefully, with the discussion of social reality in the previous chapter, you are more aware of the possibility that your perceptions of reality may differ from those around you. For example, if you have had an argument with a friend or family member, chances are it was based on different perceptions of a particular situation. **Perception** is closely linked to the notion of the social constructionist nature of reality, which was discussed in Chapter 1. Some would say that because of our experiences, beliefs, and values, it is impossible to comprehend what is really "out there" because everything is interpreted or filtered through our unique personal experiences and cultural beliefs. Because we all have different life experiences, value systems, worldviews, and beliefs, we may perceive reality differently. Even common barriers such as our mood and distractions such as noise, stress, and tiredness can affect what and how we perceive. These differences in perception can be enormous obstacles to effective communication, especially if we are not aware of them. These differences become even more important with the increased diversity of the workplace and the increased internationalization of business activities—that is, globalization.

The perceptual process reveals how differences in judgments of reality may occur. The first step in the process of perception is the receipt of information through our senses (see Figure 2-4). This sensory data is then selected and organized into a pattern from which we infer meaning. Selection is the way that we pay attention to sensory cues. It is often not a conscious process, and it is *selective*, which means that we generally pay attention only to some cues, not all of them. Obviously, then, selection can lead to misunderstanding if we are communicating with someone who is paying attention to different cues than we are. You have probably had myriad conversations in which you asked your companion, "Did you see that?", and the response was, "No, I was paying attention to *X*." This is the process of selection at work.

Figure 2-4 Steps in the Perceptual Process

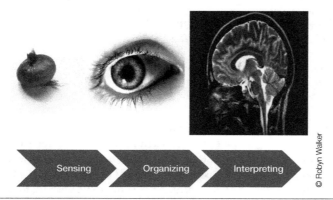

© Robyn Walker

Misunderstanding can also arise at the organization level of the perceptual process because we may fit the information into patterns that differ from the way that others see things. You have probably done exercises in class or elsewhere where you have been shown a diagram similar to the one in which some people see the face of a beautiful woman while others see the face of a crone.

During the perceptual process, misunderstanding may occur based on the inferences we draw from the previously mentioned patterns. You have certainly had the unwinnable argument: "I think the movie was excellent because [fill in the blank here]," while your companion replied something like, "You've got to be kidding! That was the biggest disappointment of the century!" Because of differing values, experiences, and tastes, the inferences that we draw from stimuli may be unlike those of others and, if these inferences are not questioned, can create misunderstandings. These sorts of inferential errors are more likely in a world that is characterized by diversity of cultural backgrounds and demographic differences.

Because our opinions may often differ from others, it is not useful to try to ascertain who is right or wrong because it may simply depend on a matter of taste, values, beliefs, or personal preferences. We have all had experiences where our perceptions differ from others, a recognition that creates a problem for our more commonsense understanding of the process of communication—the basic assumption that just because we communicated information, it was successfully received as we intended it and that meaning was shared.

Perceptual differences may lead to additional problems, such as those having to do with stereotyping, attribution, impression formation, and culture. **Stereotyping** is not necessarily a bad thing. On the one hand, it can be a label for a process of making sense out of what we perceive by categorizing or generalizing about it. On the other hand, it can be an oversimplified way of labeling people

stereotyping

A standardized mental picture that is held in common by members of a group and that represents an oversimplified opinion, prejudiced attitude, or uncritical judgment.

with the intention of denigrating them in some way. This can be particularly problematic when dealing with people of other cultures. One type of stereotype that can be formed when interacting with people of other cultures is **projected cognitive similarity**, which is the tendency to assume others have the same norms and values as your own cultural group.[17] Research has shown that when an aggressive style of communication is exhibited in intercultural team decision making, people of East Asian cultures are less participatory, since this style contrasts with their own norms of politeness and modesty.[18] A second stereotype common to intercultural interactions is the **outgroup homogeneity effect**, which is the tendency to think members of other groups are all the same.[19] Although there are cultural tendencies, this belief denies the variation among individuals of any cultural group and can detract from the development of positive working relationships.

A second type of perceptual inference is called an **attribution**. When we form an attribution, we develop a "theory" for another's behavior. Attribution can also apply to how others see us. For example, if we are late to arrive at work, our boss may think we have a poor work ethic, when we simply had a flat tire that delayed us that day. If we are not aware of these perceptual problems, then we can find ourselves in serious problems at work by discriminating against others, damaging relationships, and doing things that damage our own credibility or image.

projected cognitive similarity

The tendency to assume others have the same norms and values as your own cultural group.

outgroup homogeneity effect

The tendency to think members of other groups are all the same.

attribution

The assignment of meaning to other people's behavior.

? Critical Thinking

What are some of the common stereotypes that you hold? Can you identify persons or situations in which those stereotypes do not hold? How might you gain more accurate knowledge about those persons you tend to stereotype?

impression formation

The process of integrating a variety of observations about a person into a coherent impression of that person.

A similar concept is **impression formation**. Basically, impression formation is the process of integrating a variety of observations about a person into a coherent impression of that person. Again, understanding this principle is important for the strategic communicator because we also attempt to manage the impression that others form of us. Today, for example, did you worry about your choice of clothing and how it might affect how others saw you? Did you worry about the state of your hair or whether you might have bad breath? Our ability to manage the impressions we make on others depends on our ability to see ourselves as others might see us.

Perceptions may also differ by culture. The increased interdependence of people around the world and diversity in the workplace requires recognition of the contested perceptual nature of reality and our interpretation of it. It thus requires openness to others' views and opinions if we are to communicate effectively to reach anything approaching shared meaning. Unfortunately, the process of maturation may lead us to develop a sense that our identities are complete and fully formed. This process, and other psychological aspects, can lead to the perception by others that we have become a "closed system," unable to learn, change, and adapt to our often rapidly evolving social realities.

Understanding the role of perception in communication is critical for strategic communicators. Without this recognition, we may assume that others are perceiving reality just as we are, and if this assumption is in error, miscommunication is likely. Misunderstanding may be introduced during each of the steps in the perceptual process, and thus we may need to adjust our communication to lessen the occurrence of these problems. This adjustment relies on our ability to observe situations, analyze what is happening, and then make intentional choices about how best to manage the communication process. Finally, it is important to recognize that people make judgments about us based on our communication practices; this understanding gives us power to actively shape those perceptions. But as the dialogic model illustrates, this ability must demonstrate respect for others, avoiding the use of negative interpersonal tactics and intentions, such as manipulation and deception.

> **?** **Critical** Thinking
>
> *Have you experienced a situation in which people perceived a situation in different ways? What could have contributed to these differences in perception?*

Self-Awareness and Communication

A discussion of perception naturally leads to a look at self-concept and self-awareness. This is because how we perceive ourselves plays a critical role in communication. Our self-concept and awareness of it are important to effective strategic communicators for several reasons. First, to be effective, we must know ourselves, our strengths and our weaknesses, so that we can leverage our strengths to better achieve our career goals and work on eliminating our weaknesses so that they don't become a stumbling block to that achievement. Second, our self-concept affects how we interact with others. These two reasons are interconnected. In the political climate of many business organizations, other people will be making observations and judgments about us regarding our strengths and weaknesses, and our ability to talk about both intelligently can help to enhance our credibility. In other words, today's complex business environment requires that we take steps to become more **self-reflexive** in our communicative actions. Leveraging our strengths and minimizing our weaknesses can also help to create productive work relationships that enable us to influence others and successfully navigate political terrains.

self-reflexive
Having an accurate image or reflection of one's self.

Self-Concept

Self-concept is how we think about ourselves and describe ourselves to others. It is often the product of our experiences and, to some degree, the result of our interpretation of the messages that others send us. In other words, communication is foundational in the forming of our self-concept; people are the products of how others treat them and of the messages others send them. Dean Barnlund (1970) introduced the idea that individuals "construct" themselves—or their identities—through the relationships they have, wish to have, or perceive themselves as having. Barnlund developed the idea that "six persons" are involved in every two-person communication. These six persons emerge from the following:

self-concept
How we think about ourselves and describe ourselves to others.

- How you view yourself.
- How you view the other person.
- How you believe the other person views you.
- How the other person views himself or herself.
- How the other person views you.
- How the other person believes you view him or her.

Barnlund's model emphasizes the relational nature of communication and the centrality of the self and our perception of the self in communication. It also implicitly recognizes not only the socially constructed nature of reality, but also our social identities. That is, identity creation is an on-going process of reality construction. Perception is key in this process. From Barnlund's model comes the notion of the **self-fulfilling prophecy**, or the idea that you behave and see yourself in ways that are consistent with how others see you.[20] With this understanding, it should be obvious that, depending on our relationship and the situation, some people have differing expectations of us and will see us in ways that are different from how others see us. For example, friends and family may have an emotional attachment to us that makes us feel special, accomplished, and well loved. This emotional attachment is important for the development of self-esteem. However, those who do not

self-fulfilling prophecy
The idea that we see ourselves in ways that are consistent with how others see us.

have that strong emotional attachment—teachers, employers, new acquaintances, and strangers, among others—may see us in a different light, one in which they see our positive attributes as well as those areas that might be improved; in fact, they may focus on the negative, creating a perception that is very different from who we prefer to believe we are.

Depending on our experiences and relationships, our self-concept thus may be positive or negative, accurate or inaccurate. And how you view yourself can make a big difference in your ability to communicate and achieve your purposes.

Self-Awareness and Emotional Intelligence

self-awareness

An understanding of the self, including one's attitudes, values, beliefs, strengths, and weaknesses.

intrapersonal communication

One's communication with oneself, including memories, experiences, feelings, ideas, and attitudes.

intrapersonal intelligence

The ability to form an accurate model of oneself and to use this model effectively.

reflexivity

The capacity for reflection.

interpersonal intelligence

The ability to understand others.

For this reason, it is important to develop high levels of **self-awareness** or an understanding of the self, including your attitudes, values, beliefs, strengths, and weaknesses. Self-awareness is developed in two ways: by communicating with oneself and by communicating with others. Communication with ourselves is called **intrapersonal communication**, which includes "our perceptions, memories, experiences, feelings, interpretations, inferences, evaluations, attitudes, opinions, ideas, strategies, images, and states of consciousness."[21] According to Gardner and Krechevsky (1993), **intrapersonal intelligence** is the capacity to form an accurate model of oneself and to be able to use that model to operate effectively in life. Intrapersonal intelligence is developed by reflecting on our thoughts and actions to understand what motivates those thoughts and actions. Another word for this process is **reflexivity**.

Intrapersonal intelligence is a correlative ability to **interpersonal intelligence**.[22] Interpersonal intelligence is the ability to understand other people: what motivates them, how they work, and how to work cooperatively with them. Essentially, Gardner and Krechevsky claim that we must have self-awareness in order to understand others. For example, if our self-concept does not match the perception that others have of us, then we may misinterpret their responses to our messages. We may also misinterpret the way that our communication is interpreted by others. For instance, we may believe that we are highly reliable; however, others may believe the opposite about us. This commonly happens in student teams in which a member is commonly late for meetings and with assignments but is able to rationalize that behavior in positive ways, whereas others begin to mistrust the person's reliability. Such contradictions in perception held by others can obviously negatively impact our ability to work with others. Furthermore, if we are unaware of these contradictions, then we are unable to change our communicative behaviors, both verbal and nonverbal, to better correspond with the message we want to send about ourselves. In addition, it is important that the messages we send through our actions correspond to those we send orally and in writing because people are more likely to believe the nonverbal communication cues. A third problem that may occur due to a lack of self-awareness is that we may not recognize differences in others; we may project our self-understanding onto them. This latter issue is a particular problem in diverse cultural settings and can negatively affect our ability to communicate as well as to demonstrate recognized leadership behaviors.

self-esteem

How we like and value ourselves and how we feel about ourselves.

The second part of self-concept is **self-esteem**, or how we feel about ourselves and how well we like and value ourselves. Perception and communication are both affected by self-esteem. In the contemporary business world, high levels of self-awareness and self-esteem may help us be more open to the opinions and perspectives of others—the basis of dialogic communication.

Without high levels of self-awareness and self-esteem, we may feel threatened when we meet others who are different from us, and that feeling may get in the way of our ability to be open to listening to and considering others' perspectives and opinions. A high level of self-esteem also is important because we must be willing to admit that perhaps we don't know everything; we always have opportunities to learn. According to Evered and Tannenbaum (1992), in order to engage in dialogue we must be able to take "the stance that there is something that I don't already know." We must be able to engage with others "with a mutual *openness* to learn," rather than becoming defensive or closed to other opinions.[23]

It is important to recognize that *both* self-awareness and self-esteem are needed for effective communication with others. One if the criticisms of today's youth, for instance, is that due to parenting practices in the 2000s, many have a sense of entitlement. This might be considered the result of a high level of self-esteem without a correlative level of self-awareness, which involves recognition of others' perception of our self. That is, we may have high levels of self-esteem and fail to recognize some of the weaknesses that others may perceive about us. This lack of recognition of others' perspectives can lead to problems in communication and perceptions about our social "reality."

A related concept and outgrowth of Gardner's and others' work in the area of intrapersonal and interpersonal intelligence is that of **emotional intelligence**. Emotional intelligence refers to an assortment of non-cognitive skills, capabilities, and competencies that influence a person's ability to successfully cope with environmental demands and pressures. Studies indicate that high levels of emotional intelligence are better indicators of job performance than academic IQ.[24]

Emotional intelligence consists of five dimensions:

- **Self-awareness**, or the ability to be aware of what you are feeling.
- **Self-management**, or the ability to manage your emotions and impulses.
- **Self-motivation**, or the ability to persist in the face of setbacks and failures.
- **Empathy**, or the ability to sense how others are feeling.
- **Social skills**, or the ability to handle the emotions of others.

emotional intelligence
The assortment of non-cognitive skills that influence our ability to cope with the pressures and demands of the environment.

In addition to self-awareness, empathy, and social skills, emotional intelligence involves emotional control, or the ability to delay gratification and resist impulses, which can greatly affect our career success and our ability to communicate with others. Studies have shown that those who were able to resist temptation as small children are more socially competent as adolescents.[25] They were more personally effective, self-assertive, and better able to cope with life's frustrations. They were less likely to be negatively affected by stress or to become disorganized when pressured; they embraced challenges, were self-reliant and confident, trustworthy and dependable, and took initiative. More than a decade later, they were still able to delay gratification. Those who were less able to delay gratification were more likely to shy away from social contacts, to be stubborn and indecisive, to be easily upset by frustrations, to think of themselves as unworthy, to become immobilized by stress, to be mistrustful and resentful about not getting enough, to be prone to jealousy and envy, and to overreact to irritations with a sharp temper, thus provoking arguments.

The role of emotional intelligence is still debated among researchers, but it is generally acknowledged to be an important construct when thinking about leadership abilities. The underlying premise of the construct is that those who are more sensitive to their own emotions and the impact of their emotions on others will be more effective leaders.

Cultural Intelligence

A similar construct, cultural intelligence, is particularly relevant in today's diverse business world and for global leaders. There are three elements of cultural intelligence:

- **Cognitive knowledge:** The possession of a wide-ranging information base about a variety of people and their cultural customs.
- **Motivation:** Healthy self-efficacy, persistence, goals, value-questioning, and integration.
- **Behavioral adaptability:** The capacity to interact in a wide range of situations, environments, and diverse groups.[26]

The Global Literacy Competence (GLC) Model offers a road map to begin to conceptualize the stages of cultural intelligence development (see Figure 2-5).[27] The competencies that are described in Figure 2-6 are consistent with emotional intelligence work. The GLC assumes that ascending to a higher level of global leadership function is not only possible but also is required for excellence in a cross-cultural environment.

Figure 2-5 Global Leadership Competency Model

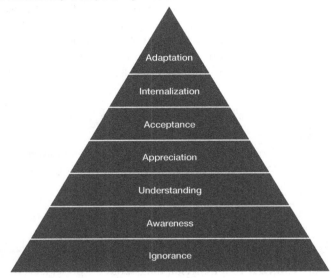

Source: Chin, C. O., Gu, J. & Tubbs, S. (2001). Developing global leadership competencies. *Journal of Leadership Studies*, 7(4), 20–35.

Figure 2-6 Levels of Global Communication Competence

Level	Description
Awareness	This is the novice stage; with exposure come vague impressions. They are brief sensations of which people are barely conscious. At this level, there is little or no sense-making, but a dawning awareness of something different and possibly interesting, strange, frightening or annoying.
Understanding	At this stage individuals begin to exhibit some conscious effort to learn why people are the way they are and why people do what they do. They display interest in those who are different from themselves. Sanchez et. al. (2000) refers to this as the "transition stage." This is a stage whereby the individual collects information through reading, observation and real experiences as well as by asking questions to learn more about the new cultural phenomenon.
Appreciation	Individuals begin to take a "leap of faith" and experience a genuine tolerance of different points of view. Through understanding the basic differences as well as areas where one thinks, acts, and react similarly, a positive feeling toward the "new" cultural phenomenon begins to form. Individuals not only put up with the "new" culture but also display a genuine appreciation of and, in some cases, preference for certain aspects of the "new" culture.
Acceptance	In this stage, the possibility of interaction between cultures increases appreciably. People are more sophisticated both in terms of recognizing commonalities and in terms of effectively dealing with differences. At this stage, there is the willingness to acquire new patterns of behavior and attitudes. This is a departure from the ethnocentric notion that "my way is the best way and the only way."
Internalization	At this stage, the individual goes beyond making sense of information and actually embarks on a deliberate internalization process with profound positive feelings for the once unknown cultural phenomenon. At this stage, there is a clear sense of self-understanding leading to readiness to act and interact with the locals/nationals in a natural, appropriate and culturally effective manner.
Adaptation	Cultural competence becomes a way of life. It is internalized, to the degree that it is out of one's consciousness, thus becomes effortless, and second nature. Individuals at this level display and possess the (1) capacity for gathering knowledge about different cultures, (2) drive or motivation, and (3) behavioral adaptability—the capacity to act effectively based upon their knowledge and motivation.

Source: Chin, C. O., Gu, J. & Tubbs, S. (2001). Developing global leadership competencies. *Journal of Leadership Studies*, 7(4), 20–35.

The developers of the GLC model challenge the application of Western cultural idiosyncrasies, such as American individualism, which they believe are counterproductive in many cultural settings, particularly Asia.[28] They are supported by the findings of the GLOBE researchers, which are discussed more in Chapter 4. The model is also consistent with contingency theory, which assumes that as context changes, so must the behaviors of leaders.[29] That is, for leaders working abroad, the context is very different from their home country's cultural context. (Context is discussed in more detail in Chapter 5.) This notion is in accord with that of mindfulness, which was discussed in the previous chapter in that we should attempt to be more aware of the present moment rather than unthinkingly bringing thoughts and concepts from past experiences that may not strictly apply to our present situation.

? Critical Thinking

Using an Internet search engine, search for Web sites that offer free self-assessments of emotional intelligence, and cultural intelligence. After completing the self-assessments, consider the steps you might take to improve your competence in these areas.

Needed Skills for Strategic and Ethical Communication

We have already explored how a lack of understanding about the potential complexity of communication processes in different situations can lead to strategy errors and even unethical practices. Another practical challenge is posed by the sheer amount of information with which we are bombarded each day. More information has been produced in the last 30 years than in the previous 5,000. A single edition of the *New York Times* contains more information than the average person was likely to be exposed to in an entire lifetime in seventeenth-century England.[30] In fact, more information is generated worldwide in a twenty-four-hour period than you could process and absorb in all your years on Earth. With the increasing use of the Internet, we are approaching a point at which more information will be generated in one hour than could be processed and absorbed in a lifetime.[31]

The corresponding overload affects our ability to gather, analyze, and identify information on which to base sound decisions and communication strategies. It thus requires that we become aware of the subconscious processes we use to process information that may lead us to faulty decisions. Again, this notion is in line with the practice of mindfulness and importance of reflexivity.

It also requires that we spend some time developing our critical-thinking abilities because analysis is the basis of strategic thinking, or the ability to formulate communication strategy. This is particularly a problem in today's educational environment in which students are commonly taught to test well, not necessarily to think well. In his book *Academically Adrift: Limited Learning on College Campuses*, Richard Arum reveals the results of a study that followed 2,322 traditional-age students for a four-year period and examined testing data and student surveys at a broad range of twenty-four U.S. colleges and universities, from the highly selective to the less selective. The study found that 45 percent of students made no significant improvement in their critical thinking, reasoning, or writing skills during the first two years of college. After four years, 36 percent showed no significant gains in these so-called higher-order thinking skills.[32] Students majoring in business, education, social work, and communications showed the least gains in learning.

Higher-order thinking skills needed for strategic thinking go beyond rote learning or memorization of concepts. Rote learning or memory of learned materials is needed for understanding, but higher-order learning also includes the ability to comprehend, apply, analyze, synthesize and evaluate information, the latter three abilities being part of critical thinking (see Figure 2-7).[33]

Figure 2-7 Categories in the Cognitive Domain of Bloom's Taxonomy

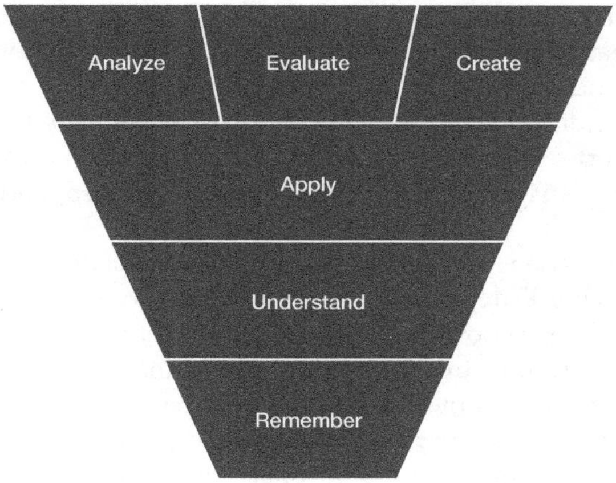

Source: Krathwohl, D. R. (2002). A revision of Bloom's taxonomy: An overview. *Theory into Practice*, 212–218.

The ability to learn and think well is also needed for living in our more complex and rapidly changing world, in which "the work of the future is the work of the mind, intellectual work, work that involves reasoning and intellectual discipline."[34] Because of the rapidly changing world we now live in, well-regarded management writer Peter Senge has called for a need to develop "learning organizations."[35] In these types of organizations, leadership is decentralized so as to enhance the capacity of people to work productively toward common goals. Senge's basic rationale for such organizations is that in situations of rapid change, only those that are flexible, productive, and adaptive will excel. To create such an organization, people must have the capacity to learn, and to learn, they must have a structure and culture that is conducive to reflection and engagement. (Organizational culture will be discussed in more detail in Chapter 5.)

There are several obstacles to thinking well and good decision making, including perceptual mindsets and certain thinking styles.

Perceptual Mindsets

perceptual mindsets
Our cognitive and psychological predispositions to see the world in a certain way.

As discussed earlier, the process of perception is often overlooked in the course of human meaning making, and the unique ways that individuals organize and interpret information are shaped by their values and experiences. These psychological and cognitive predispositions are called **perceptual mindsets**, which can pose another challenge to evaluating information well. These biases, preconceptions, and assumptions can get in the way of our ability to make effective decisions and to solve problems. Because of our mindsets, we are prepared to receive only certain messages and to ignore others. To put it bluntly, we are conditioned to view the world narrowly. One example might be our choice to affiliate with a political party. We may so closely identify with the party's platform that we are unable to listen to others with different political affiliations and to be open to ideas that may provide viable solutions. Another way to think about this phenomenon as previously discussed is that we have essentially become a "closed system," unable to learn or adapt to changing situations. One outcome of this phenomenon at the cultural level is the polarization that currently characterizes American political discourse and paralyzes decision making at the highest levels of government.

Our mindsets are affected by several practices that limit our ability to consider information thoroughly and objectively. These include confirmation bias, false dichotomies, and inferential errors.

Confirmation Bias

Confirmation bias is a tendency to distort information that contradicts our currently held beliefs and attitudes.[36] Confirmation bias exhibits itself in group communication situations and also affects our individual decision making.

In groups, research indicates a strong tendency among members to "show interest in facts and opinions that support their initially preferred policy and take up time in their meetings to discuss them, but they tend to ignore facts and opinions that do not support their initially preferred policy."[37]

For individuals, confirmation bias can also distort evidence that disconfirms our viewpoints and perceptions. This process is called *self-confirmation*.[38] Women, for example, often have to deal with self-confirming beliefs of supervisors and colleagues.[39] In other words, women may believe they must conform to stereotypes by acting in accommodating, unassertive ways; they may have more difficulty being taken seriously by others and thus receive fewer promotions and raises. However, refusing to accept these stereotypes may also have negative consequences. In some cases, assertive women may be judged as too aggressive and uncooperative, and thus they may be deemed undeserving of promotion or advancement. Women leaders must thus find a way to negotiate what is called this "double bind." Research shows that adopting an androgynous communication style—one that is assertive in certain situations and more accommodative in others may help resolve this problem.

To combat confirmation bias, Rothwell suggests the following:

1. Actively seek out disconfirming information and evidence.
2. Vigorously present and argue disconfirming evidence to others or the group.
3. Play devil's advocate.
4. Gather allies to challenge confirmation bias. [40]

> **confirmation bias**
>
> A tendency to distort information that contradicts the beliefs and attitudes we currently hold.

False Dichotomies

Dichotomous, either–or thinking is the tendency to see the world in terms of black and white or opposites. Either–or thinking often leads us to describe situations in the language of extremes. Such thinking is typically false because there are almost always more than two possibilities in our complex world. In these cases, we have created a **false dichotomy**, which blinds us to other possibilities.

The bell-shaped curve is an example of an alternate view—one in which there are numerous possibilities along a certain range. In a bell curve, if specific information is gathered from a random group of individuals, the data tend to bunch up in the middle. However, someone who applies either–or thinking would focus on the few individuals or situations that lie at the extreme ends of the spectrum and ignore the more numerous cases in the middle.[41] Such thinking can lead to poor decisions because it may ignore the bulk of the most valid information available on the subject.

To avoid the pitfalls of false dichotomies, you should

1. Be suspicious of absolutes. Look for alternatives to the one or two suggestions recommended.
2. Employ the language of qualification. Speak in terms of degrees by using such terms as *sometimes, rarely, occasionally, mostly, usually,* and *moderately.*[42]

> **false dichotomy**
>
> A dichotomy that is not jointly exhaustive (i.e., there are other alternatives) or that is not mutually exclusive (i.e., the alternatives overlap). A false dichotomy may be the product of either–or thinking.

Inferential Errors

Inferences are conclusions about the unknown based on the known. We draw inferences from previous experiences, factual data, and predispositions. Because of this tendency, inferences are guesses varying from the educated to the uneducated.

Making inferences is not necessarily a negative practice, as was discussed in the previous section on perception. We could not function on a daily basis without making inferences. However, the

> **inference**
>
> A conclusion about the unknown based upon the known.

principal problem with inferences is that we are often unaware that we are making them and thus rarely question their accuracy.

The two general sources of inferential errors are (1) a faulty information base or misinformation and (2) a seriously limited information base.[43] However, more specific sources of inferential errors exist. These are vividness, unrepresentativeness, and correlation.

Vividness Graphic, outrageous, shocking, controversial, and dramatic events draw our attention and tend to stick in our minds. We tend to overvalue vivid, concrete information and undervalue abstract, statistical information. Statistical information tends to be dry and lifeless because it leaves out of the equation representations of people and the real consequences of decisions on their lives. This is important to remember when it comes to communicating information to others: We remember vivid images much better than abstractions. If we are not aware of this, it can skew our ability to make good decisions.

Unrepresentativeness When we make a judgment, we tend to assess its accuracy based on our knowledge of information in a general category. However, if the information is not representative or does not agree with that general information, our inference will be incorrect. It is thus a good idea to ask whether information was derived from a representative sample or whether the sample size was too small or not inclusive enough to be considered representative. Unrepresentative samples can lead to overgeneralizing.

correlation

A consistent relationship between two or more variables.

Correlation A **correlation** is a consistent relationship between two or more variables. An example of a positive correlation is that as you grow older, your ears grow larger. In this case, a correlation exists between age and ear size. However, a correlation is not necessarily a cause—that is, old age does not cause larger ears, but growth processes do. Another common correlation is that the death penalty decreases the instance of crime. However, no significant evidence exists that this is the case. In fact, Stephen Jay Gould finds that "the vast majority of correlations in our world are, without a doubt, noncausal."[44]

To avoid the problems associated with inferential errors, ask the following questions:

1. Is the evidence sufficient to draw the inference?
2. Is the evidence the best available?
3. Is the evidence recent?
4. Is the evidence relevant to the inference? Does it really prove the claim?
5. Is the evidence one-sided? Is there contradictory information?
6. Can you verify the facts? How do you know that what is said is actually true?
7. Are the sources of the information reliable?
8. Are the sources of the information authorities for the subject? Are the authorities trustworthy or biased?
9. Is the statistical sample representative of the whole? Is the sample size adequate?
10. Is the example typical or is it an exception?
11. Is the relationship only a correlation or is it causal?[45]

Other Perceptual Errors

In additional to perceptual mind-sets, other common barriers exist that can contribute to inaccurate perceptions. Beware of the following:

- **Oversimplifying.** People tend to prefer simplicity over complexity because it takes less effort.
- **Imposing consistency.** Because we look for patterns, we may impose consistency where it doesn't exist.

■ **Focusing on the negative.** People tend to focus more on the negative than the positive. Experiments have shown that if just one negative characteristic is included in a list of personal attributes, people will rank the person being described significantly lower than if the negative characteristic wasn't included.

■ **Making a fundamental attribution error.** When other people fail, we assume it was their fault—but when they succeed, we assume it was the situation that determined their success.

■ **Exhibiting a self-serving bias.** Similar to the fundamental attribution error, we assume that our successes result from our personal qualities but that our failures result from circumstances beyond our control.

Thinking Styles

In addition to perceptual challenges, the way we process information can affect our ability to think well and make good decisions. For example, we can process information in one of two ways: We can absorb it like a sponge, or we can filter it. Perhaps the more common way of processing information is by absorbing it. This process is passive and requires little thinking. Although the advantage of this process is that it enables you to absorb a lot of information, the disadvantage is that it provides you with no method to decide whether information is valid or useful.

In contrast, the filter method provides you a way of processing information more actively, effectively giving you a choice in what you absorb and what you ignore. Using the filter model requires that you ask questions about the material being presented. Your mission is to critically evaluate the material and formulate personal conclusions based on that evaluation. In other words, critical thinking should be applied. **Critical thinking**, as defined by the National Council for Excellence in Critical Thinking, is as follows:

> *The intellectually disciplined process of actively and skillfully conceptualizing, applying, analyzing, synthesizing, and/or evaluating information gathered from, or generated by, observation, experience, reflection, reasoning, or communication, as a guide to belief and action. In its exemplary form, it is based on universal intellectual values that transcend subject matter divisions: clarity, accuracy, precision, consistency, relevance, sound evidence, good reasons, depth, breadth, and fairness. It entails the examination of those structures or elements of thought implicit in all reasoning: purpose, problem, or question-at-issue, assumptions, concepts, empirical grounding; reasoning leading to conclusions, implications and consequences, objections from alternative viewpoints, and frame of reference.[46] (www.criticalthinking.org, 2009)*

critical thinking

The intellectually disciplined process of actively and skillfully conceptualizing, applying, analyzing, synthesizing, and/or evaluating information gathered from, or generated by, observation, experience, reflection, reasoning, or communication as a guide to belief and action.

Critical thinkers actively seek alternative hypotheses, explanations, conclusions, and sources and are open to them. They endorse a position only to the extent that the information justifies it. They are well-informed and consider seriously points of view other than their own.[47]

There is also an ethical component to critical thinking. In other words, critical thinkers communicate a position honestly and clearly: theirs as well as that of others. This means that they are reflectively aware of their own basic beliefs and care about the dignity and worth of every person. It requires that they discover and listen to others' views and reasons, avoid intimidating or confusing others with their critical-thinking prowess, and take into account others' feelings and level of understanding. You should notice by now that this ethical component mirrors some of the concerns of the dialogic model.

In addition, to be a critical thinker requires that we are able to deal with ambiguity. When evaluating information, it is helpful to recognize that no single correct answer exists for many contemporary issues. Because our world is a complex place, many points of views and perspectives have valid points. Depending on the broader goal or a person's value system, choosing the best solution can be a difficult process.

Emotions can get in the way of our ability to evaluate information fairly and accurately. Emotions can also get in the way of our ability to be open to all the relevant information and to weigh that information as objectively and thoroughly as it deserves, especially if the information doesn't correspond with our core values and beliefs. In other words, our self-concept or identities can get in the way of our ability to think critically.

Finally, it is important to ask, "Who cares?" Because we are human beings, we often have personal interests at stake in the arguments that we make. Therefore, it is useful to ask yourself the following: Who will benefit from certain perspectives or proposals? Is the information that is presented colored by that perspective? Is this a one-sided argument? If so, what is the other side of the issue, and does it offer information potentially valuable for good decision making?

Learning how to evaluate information critically can help us to better gather information on which to base decisions that may affect our career and life choices. Such skill is critical to being a strategic communicator. It can also help us to achieve a critical goal of business communication: establishing our credibility by highlighting our cognitive abilities, a common characteristic of those recognized as leaders.

However, as should be clear from this discussion, to be able to communicate well in a diverse, complex, and rapidly changing world, we must have an accurate self-concept, relatively high levels of self-esteem, and a critical mind-set. The work of today's leader is thus, in part, to also pursue these goals in self-development.

Summary

Three models have historically been used to explain the communication process. They are communication as information transfer, communication as transactional process, and communication as strategic control. A fourth model, the dialogic model of communication, better meets the needs of today's organizations because it recognizes the growing importance of interpersonal relationships on our own success and happiness in the workplace as well as in our personal lives. According to the dialogic model, the strategies that we use to communicate must take into account how our messages affect others' perception of us as well as the effect of our communication on others. The dialogic model also highlights the inherently ethical nature of communication and helps address the challenges of communicating with others from different cultures.

Perception involves the use of our senses to interpret our surroundings. Because the perceptual process is based on interpretation, it introduces opportunities for misunderstanding as we communicate with others. It is thus foundational to an understanding of the communication process. It is also important to understand that others may perceive us in ways that we do not intend; for this reason, it is important to be sensitive to those interpretations and to use our strategic-communication skills to ensure that we are being perceived as we intend or hope. The way that we think about ourselves and an awareness of the self in terms of understanding are also important to our communication abilities. It is through self-understanding that we begin to understand others, a critical part of the dialogic model that is the foundation of this text.

However, perceptual mindsets and our thinking style can get in the way of our ability to be strategic yet ethical communicators. Our perceptual mind-sets are affected by several practices that limit our ability to consider information thoroughly and objectively. These include confirmation bias, false dichotomies, and inferential errors. In addition to perceptual challenges, the way that we process information can affect our ability to think well and make good decisions. We can process information in one of two ways: We can absorb it like a sponge, or we can filter it. The filter method provides you a way of processing information more actively, effectively giving you a choice in what you absorb and what you ignore. Using the filter model requires that you ask questions about the material being presented. Your mission is to critically evaluate the material and formulate personal conclusions based on that evaluation. In other words, critical thinking should be applied.

Key Terms

dialogic model of communication **21**

dialogue **21**

monologue **21**

egocentric **22**

plurality **22**

intercultural communication **23**

perception **23**

stereotyping **24**

projected cognitive similarity **25**

outgroup homogeneity effect **25**

attribution **25**

impression formation **25**

self-reflexive **26**

self-concept **26**

self-fulfilling prophecy **26**

self-awareness **27**

intrapersonal communication **27**

intrapersonal intelligence **27**

reflexivity **27**

interpersonal intelligence **27**

self-esteem **27**

emotional intelligence **28**

perceptual mindsets **31**

confirmation bias **32**

false dichotomy **32**

inference **32**

correlation **33**

critical thinking **34**

Discussion Questions

1. Explain each of the four models of communication and what distinguishes them, including their strengths and weaknesses. Why might the dialogic model better meet the needs of today's workplace?

2. Identify examples of moral exclusion and describe the intent and effect of their use. Based on this analysis, discuss whether such practices are ethical. Support your response with evidence.

3. How have differing perceptions affected your communication with others? What steps might you take to avoid misunderstandings created by perceptual differences?

4. What are three different errors that may occur due to our perceptual mind-sets? How might these be avoided?

5. What are some examples of black-and-white, or dichotomous, thinking from recent news reports or opinion columns you have seen or read? What other possibilities might exist to broaden the views or options presented in these reports?

6. What are the benefits of thinking critically?

Applications

1. Use a SWOT (strengths, weaknesses, opportunities, threats) analysis to determine your career goals. This is an exercise in analysis, evaluation, and, ultimately, strategic thinking. First, identify the opportunities available to you and their corresponding possible risks; second, identify your strengths and weaknesses; third, identify the resources available to you to attain these opportunities; and fourth, match the opportunities available to you with those that are attainable. From this analysis should emerge an attainable career goal. It should also help you to identify personal characteristics that you might leverage in a career search as well as those liabilities for which you might set goals to eliminate or reduce.

2. Using the Internet, search for free online self-assessments of emotional intelligence, locus of control, leadership traits, and self-monitoring. One place to start is at *www.queendom.com*. After completing the assessments and reading the results, summarize them and then write three goals for self-improvement for each personality measure, including your plan for achieving each of them.

3. Using YouTube, identify examples of persons who you think exemplify a leader. Make a list of your observations: What does the person do that exemplifies leadership? You might look at the way he or she speaks, looks, or behaves. From this list, what traits of a leader did you infer from your observation? What did you notice about the way this person communicated? Set some personal goals for yourself to help you to begin to incorporate the traits you identified in your own communication practices.

4. Choose a culture that differs from your own and then describe your beliefs and attitudes about and perceptions of this culture. Now conduct research to find out as much about the culture and its values, beliefs, and practices as you can. You may also wish to interview someone from this culture, if the opportunity is available. After learning more about the culture, what misperceptions did you hold about it? Has your researched changed your attitudes and beliefs about the culture?

Endnotes

1. Rosen, R., Digh, P., Singer, M., & Phillips, C. (2000). *Global Literacies: Lessons on Business Leadership and National Cultures.* New York: Simon & Schuster.

2. Conrad, C. (1985). Chrysanthemums and swords: A reading of contemporary organizational communication theory and research. *Southern Speech Communication Journal*, 50, 189–200; Eisenberg, E. M. (1984). Ambiguity as strategy in organizational communication. *Communication Monographs*, 51, 227–242; Weick, K. (1979). *The Social Psychology of Organizing* (2nd ed.). Reading, MA: Addison-Wesley.

3. Frost, P., Moore, L., Louis, M., Lundberg, C., & Martin, J. (1991). *Reframing Organizational Culture.* Newbury Park, CA: Sage Publications.

4. Reardon, K. K. (2005). *It's All Politics: Winning in a World Where Hard Work and Talent Aren't Enough.* New York: Doubleday.

5. Conrad, C. (1985). Chrysanthemums and swords: A reading of contemporary organizational communication theory and research. *Southern Speech Communication Journal*, 50, 189–200; Okabe, R. (1983). Cultural assumptions of east and west: Japan and the United States. In B. Gudykunst (Ed.), *International Communication Theory* (pp. 212–244). Newbury Park, CA: Sage Publications.

6. Barnlund, D. C. (1986). Toward a meaning-centered philosophy of communication. In J. Stewart (Ed.), *Bridges Not Walls: A Book About Interpersonal Communication* (pp. 36–42). New York: Newbury Award Records.

7. Larson, C. U. (2004). *Persuasion: Reception and Responsibility* (10th ed.). Belmont, CA: Wadsworth/Thomson Learning, p. 36.

8. Ibid., p. 36.

9. Barnlund, 1986, p. 41.

10. Ibid.

11. Ibid.

12. Ibid.

13. Eisenberg, E. M., & Goodall, Jr., H. L. (1993). *Organizational Communication: Balancing Creativity and Constraint*. New York: St. Martin's Press.

14. Larson, 2004, p. 36.

15. Rogers, E. M., & Steinfatt, T. M. (1999). *Intercultural Communication*. Prospects Height, IL: Waveland Press.

16. London, M. & Sessa, V. I. (1999). *Selecting International Executives: A Suggested Framework and Annotated Bibliography*. Greensboro, NC: Center for Creative Leadership; Kuhleman & Stahl, 1996, 1998, reported in Stahl, G. K. (2001). Using assessment centers as tools for global leadership development: An exploratory study. In M. E. Mendenhall, T. M. Kuhlmann, & G. K. Stahl (Eds.), *Developing Global Business Leaders: Policies, Processes, and Innovations* (pp. 197–210). Westport, CT: Quorum.

17. Varner, I. & Beamer, L. (2009). *Intercultural Communication in the Global Workplace*. Thousand Oaks, CA: Sage.

18. Aritz, J. & Walker, R. (2012). The effects of leadership style on intercultural group communication in decision-making meetings. In P. Heynderickx, S. Dieltjens, G. Jacobs, P. Gillaerts, & E. D. Groot (Eds). *The Language Factor in International Business: New Perspectives on Research, Teaching and Practice*. Bern: Peter Lang.

19. Varner, I. & Beamer, 2009.

20. Wood, J.T. (1997). *Communication Theories in Action*. Belmont, CA: Wadsworth.

21. Shedletsky, L. J. (1989). The mind at work. In L. J. Shedletsky (Ed.), *Meaning and Mind: An Intrapersonal Approach to Human Communication*. Bloomington, IN: ERIC and the Speech Communication Association.

22. Gardner, H., & Krechevsky, M. (1993). *Multiple Intelligences: The Theory in Practice*. New York: Basic Books.

23. Evered, R., & Tannebaum, R. (1992). A dialog on dialog. *Journal of Management Inquiry*, 1, 43–55, p. 45.

24. Robbins, S.P. (2001). *Organizational Behavior* (9th ed.). Upper Saddle River, NJ: Prentice Hall.

25. Schoda, Y., Mischel, W. & Peake, P.K. (1990). Predicting adolescent cognitive and self-regulatory competencies from preschool delay of gratification. *Developmental Psychology*, 26, 978–986.

26. Earley. P. C., & Ang, S. (2003) *Cultural Intelligence*, Stanford University Press: Stanford, CA.

27. Chin, C. O., Gu, J. & Tubbs, S. (2001). Developing global leadership competencies. *Journal of Leadership Studies*, 7(4): 20–35.

28. Ibid.

29. Ibid.

30. Wurman, R. (1989). *Information Anxiety*. New York: Doubleday, 1989.

31. Davidson, J. (1996). The shortcomings of the information age. *Vital Speeches*, 62, 495–503.

32. Rimer, S. (2011). Study: Many college students not learning to think critically. *The Hechinger Report*. Retrieved Feb. 1, 2013, from *http://www.mcclatchydc.com/2011/01/18/106949/study-many-college-students-not.html#storylink=cpy*.

33. Krathwohl, D. R. (2002). A revision of Bloom's taxonomy: An overview. *Theory into Practice*, 41(4): 212–218.

34. Paul. R. (1993). *Critical Thinking: What Every Person Needs to Survive in a Rapidly Changing World* (3rd ed.). An anthology on critical thinking and educational reform. Tomales, CA: Foundation of Critical Thinking Press, p. 13.

35. Senge, P. (1990). *The Fifth Discipline*. New York: Doubleday Business.

36. Hunt, M. (1982). *The Universe Within: A New Science Explores the Human Mind*. New York: Simon and Schuster.

37. Janus, I. (1983). *Groupthink: Psychological Studies of Policy Decisions and Fiascos*. Boston MA: Houghton Mifflin, p. 10.

38. Postman, N. (1976). *Crazy Talk, Stupid Talk*. New York: Dell.

39. Haslett, B., Geis, F. L., & Carter, M. R. (1992). *The Organizational Woman: Power and Paradox*. Norwood, NJ: Ablex Publishing.

40. Rothwell, J. D. (1998). *In Mixed Company: Small Group Communication* (3rd ed.). Fort Worth, TX: Harcourt Brace College Publishers. p. 186.

41. DeVito, J. (1989). *The Interpersonal Communication Book*. New York: Harper and Row.

42. Rothwell, 1998, p. 188.

43. Ibid.

44. Gould, S.J. (1981). *The Mismeasure of Man*. New York: W.W. Norton, p. 241.

45. Rothwell, 1998, p. 202.

46. Scriven, M., & Paul, R. (1987). Critical thinking defined. Presented at the 8th Annual International Conference on Critical Thinking and Education Reform, Summer 1987. Retrieved Feb. 1, 2013, from *http://www.criticalthinking.org/pages/defining-critical-thinking/766*.

47. Ennis, R.H. (2002). A super-streamlined conception of critical thinking. Retrieved June 29, 2009, from *www.criticalthinking.net/*.

A Philosophy of Dress: *Rebuilding Trust in the Brooks Brothers Brand (A)*

Introduction

On the largest shopping day of 2001, Claudio Del Vecchio, CEO of Retail Brand Alliance, read the headlines of major newspapers from the U.S. and his native Europe which stated that his company had just acquired Brooks Brothers from the struggling discount retailer Marks & Spencer. As a long-time customer who grew up wearing Brooks Brothers suits, Del Vecchio knew that the company had lost its identity during a series of takeovers in the 1980s. For over a century and a half, Brooks Brothers was the most profitable menswear retailer in the U.S., and many industry experts now questioned whether the firm would survive. As Del Vecchio reviewed the morning papers, he pondered how he could recapture the trust of customers by restoring the core Brooks values of quality, great value, and exceptional customer service and position the company for strong future growth.

The Making of a Dynasty

In 1977 the *Washington Post* wrote, "The Brooks look is a moral trust maintained from one decade to the next, because generation after generation has trusted the company with an unquestioning faith that they give to virtually no other institution in modern life."[1] Since its inception in 1818, Brooks Brothers has conducted business built on a philosophy of dress that captures the American ideals of upward mobility, accomplishment, and class. The company captured this idea in a 1980s advertisement that stated Brooks Brothers is not for the rich but for the successful.[2]

Brooks Brothers' monumental success is attributed to its foundational attributes of quality, value and customer service. As a vertically integrated company, management held the view that by controlling all aspects of the production process, Brooks was able to provide value to the customer by producing a superior quality product at a price others would charge for an inferior good.

In a sense, the retailer's commitment to the customer is legendary. Historically, Brooks never had a design team. Management made merchandising decisions based on the input of the sales associates because they knew the customers best. The friendship, as Brooks would describe it, between the customer and the sales associate was the key reason that customers made Brooks Brothers *their* store and made Brooks a staple at every major event (or daily activity) including weddings, job interviews, and Presidential Inaugurations.

Sworn Symbol of Style

Brooks Brothers adopted the symbol of the Golden Fleece in 1850. The symbol has endured and continues to signify Brooks' quality and heritage. The birth of the Golden Fleece symbol came on January 10, 1430 when Philip the Good, Duke of Burgundy, established an order of Knighthood in honor of his bride, Isabella of Portugal. The Knighthood was named The Order of the Golden Fleece. In homage to Isabella, 31 Knights of the Order took an oath to guard the Church and the glory of the saints. "The Lamb of God, suspended at each Knight's heart, symbolized at once both gentle humility and the woolen fabrics to which so much of Burgundian wealth was owed. Since the days of chivalry, a ram or lamb, suspended by a ribbon, has often been the symbol of the woolen trades." These natty Knights set the European

---

This case was prepared by Research Assistants Jared M. Johnson and Christopher C. Stevenson under the direction of James S. O'Rourke, Concurrent Professor of Management, as the basis for class discussion rather than to illustrate either effective or ineffective handling of an administrative situation. Information was gathered from corporate as well as public sources.

1. Cooke, John William. *Generations of Style*. New York, NY: Brooks Brothers, 2003, p. 11.
2. *Ibid*, p. 28.

medieval standard for chivalric style.[3] This is the style and substance that Brooks Brothers embodied in selecting the Golden Fleece emblem. The sanctity of the Brooks' symbol has swayed with the whims of corporate steering, yet has not snapped.

The Early Years

Henry Sands Brooks opened his first store on April 7, 1818 on Cherry Street in New York City at the age of 46. His mission was "to make and deal only in merchandise of the best quality, to sell it at a fair profit only, and to deal only with people who seek and are capable of appreciating such merchandise." Before his death in 1833, Mr. Brooks' sons were taught the ways of the business and they subsequently named it "Brooks Brothers."[4]

Brooks was one of the first clothing manufactures to sell "off the rack" merchandise. Traditionally, people had their fine clothing custom produced. The rich had a personal tailor that could complete a garment relatively quickly. Those without such resources had limited wardrobes made of coarse materials for durability. Off the rack clothing was less expensive to produce than custom clothing, thus affording a greater number of people access to comfortable, quality clothing. This merchandise was frequently displayed inside-out to showcase quality workmanship. Soon Brooks developed a reputation for excellent customer service and quality menswear. Like Americans, many immigrants who arrived in New York knew the road to opportunity was traveled much easier in an original Brooks Brothers suit.[5]

To assure that the best fabrics were used in the merchandise, Brooks Brothers developed strong relationships with a select group of cotton and wool producers in Britain. In the late nineteenth century, the cotton used in the classic oxford was originally purchased in England then processed at mills in Scotland. From there, the fabric was transported to New York where Brooks constructed its clothing.[6]

Brooks prided itself on bringing innovation in an array of offerings to the market. Some of the American classics that can be credited to Brooks Brothers include:

Sack Suit: First introduced in 1900, this suit has undergone very little change in the last 50 years. Known for its comfortable features such as the natural shoulders and straight lines, *The New Yorker* boldly labeled the classic American suit a "philosophy in dress."[7]

Seersucker: Introduced to the American public in 1830, this lightweight, breathable cotton has been a perennial summer staple ever since.[8]

Button-down Polo Shirt: The classic button collar dress shirt was introduced to the American market after John Brooks watched a British polo match. During the event, he noticed that buttons were used to prevent the riders' collars from flapping in the wind. Soon after, Brooks introduced a dress shirt with a soft collar and buttons and the creation became one of the greatest success stories in U.S. fashion.[9]

Repp Tie: "The traditional ties of the American businessman" hit the U.S. market in the 18th century after being discovered in England. Originally, the regimental rep was designed to represent whatever British regiment a gentlemen served in, and each had its own distinctive stripe and coloration.[10] Because of strict standards of quality, Brooks only used the finest silk and all ties were hand-sewn with a special slip stitch. This guaranteed durability and allowed the tie to relax under the pressure of the knot, so it would lie flat.[11]

BrooksEase: As business required greater travel, customers demanded a cool suit that would still look sharp after being in a garment bag or wedged in an economy class seat. Brooks exceeded expectations by offering suit separates. The company not only created a technologically advanced fabric that resisted wrinkles

---

3. "Golden Fleece." Encyclopedia M ythica from Encyclopedia Mythica Online. *http://www.pantheon.org/articles/g/golden_fleece.html.* [Accessed April 17, 2005]

4. Cooke, John William. *Generation of Style.* New York, NY: Brooks Brothers, 2003,p. 20

5. *Ibid*, p. 5

6. *Ibid*, p. 28

7. *Ibid*, p. 30

8. "The Seersucker Story." Brooks Brothers [Internet]. *www.brooksbrothers.com/catalogview.* [Accessed April 17, 2005]

9. "Our Heritage." Brooks Brothers [Internet]. *www.brooksbrothers.com/aboutus/heritage.* [Accessed April, 17, 2005]

10. Molloy, John T., John T. Molloy's New Dress for Success. New York, NY: Warner Books, Inc., 1988.

11. Cooke, John William. *Generations of Style.* New York, NY: Brooks Brothers, 2003, p. 30.

but also developed a system of dying fabrics that guaranteed customers exact colormatches.[12]

A Company that Knows Adversity

World War II posed considerable challenges for Brooks as the government drafted laws limiting the availability of materials for clothing and shoes. For example, pants could be neither cuffed nor pleated and double-breasted suits were not allowed because the excess fabric could be used for military uniforms and bandages. In addition, the vastly limited trans-Atlantic trade prevented Brooks from carrying much of its customary British fabrics.[13]

By the end of the 1940s, Brooks Brothers had escaped an extraordinarily tough retail environment, but not without cost. Winthrop Brooks, the company's president at the time, sold the retailer to Garfinkle & Co. Winthrop was quick to calm the fears of the Brooks loyalists by stating that the Brooks family would still hold key leadership positions and British imports would continue to increase. Moreover, newly appointed CEO John C. Wood was eager to communicate his commitment to quality and innovation. Although not all of Wood's new fashion ideas, such as removing the button from behind the collar of the Polo Shirt, were well received, he was quick to revert back to the classics that created such an affinity for the label.[14]

During the early part of the 1960s Americans had a renewed sense of optimism. President John F. Kennedy, clad in the traditional Brooks Brothers Sack Suit, became the model of the American "can-do" attitude through the introduction of the space program and the avoidance of catastrophe during the Cuban Missile Crisis. As the decade of the 1970s rolled in with its anti-establishment ideologies, fashion trends changed considerably. The traditional wool and cotton classics gave way the polyester leisure suit and the Brooks look was no longer in vogue with America's younger generation. Although Brooks had a history of not selling trend, it had to respond to the demands of its younger clients: the solution was an introductory line aimed at the young executive called Brooksgate. This line of suits featured wider lapels and a lowercut.[15]

Brooks' legacy of being the most profitable menswear provider in history made it a take-over target in the "winner-take-all" mergers and acquisition era of the 1980s. In the early part of the decade, Allied Stores purchased all of Garfinkel's holdings and had the aspirations of rapidly expanding Brooks Brothers. Brooks Brothers CEO, Frank Reilly, who began working at the company in the 1950s, understood the monolithic Brooks' culture that seemingly existed in a "time warp" but also knew the benefits of expansion. Under the leadership of Reilly, the company launched its first women's catalog and continued to have success with the Brooksgate line. As the decade progressed, fashion trends began to turn away from the classics such as the sack suit and aimed for individual expression and masculinity. Italian designers and their "power suits" represented the latest threat to Brooks' strength of "deal[ing] in conservative clothing."[16]

Robert Campeau, a short-lived acquisition icon of the 1980s, purchased Allied Stores in 1984 with a no-money down loan. Concerned with other buy-out targets, Campeau left Brooks alone until he sold it 14 months later to raise an additional $750 million to buy Federated Department stores.[17] The company was sold to Marks & Spencer, a discount retailer based in the United Kingdom.

A Downward Spiral

Marks & Spencer had big dreams for Brooks Brothers. Market analysts believed that the company paid too much for the famed menswear producer. Known for selling high turnover women's wear, Marks & Spencer had little knowledge of the high-end men's market and had no acquisition experience. More to the point, the company's leadership did not subscribe to the idea that a company could be successful by selling to customers who only shopped a couple of times per year.[18] What Marks & Spencer's management forgot was that these individuals would buy a number of suits, shirts, and ties when they visited the store. Clearly, Brooks Brothers was on the verge of a life-or-death battle.

12. Glassmoyer, Michael. Personal Interview. April 1, 2005
13. *Ibid*, p. 67
14. *Ibid*, p. 67
15. *Ibid*, p. 99
16. *Ibid*, p. 116
17. *Ibid*, p. 120
18. *Ibid*, p. 122

Determined to make the acquisition work and prove dissenting analysts wrong, Marks & Spencer launched a series of new initiatives to modernize the perceived archaic business model of the famed men's retailer. Some of the plans to increase the competitiveness of Brooks Brothers included:

Marketing: Historical Brooks Brothers advertising focused on the firm's heritage, quality products, and innovations in the clothing. Catalogs featured traditionally dressed models sporting a sack suit and Repp tie. In an attempt to attract a younger client base in an age defined by the mantra of "if you've got it, flaunt it," Marks & Spencer's twenty-something models posed with slick hair, a bold shirt, and a slightly arrogant smirk.[19] In addition, Brooks Brothers' ads appeared in trendy magazines such as *GQ* and with pictures that featured models with loosened ties and partially unbuttoned shirts.[20]

Stores: Brooks Brothers was thought of as a store people aspired to shop at, thus the retail space had an intended exclusive feel. To appeal to a wider audience, Marks & Spencer began changing the environment of the stores and started with complete remodeling of the flagship. Inserted in place of the tremendously popular "shirt wall" were escalators. The century-old fixtures and memorabilia were replaced by a more contemporary motif.[21]

Brooks Brothers launched two new series of stores. The first was a smaller mall store that featured an amended variety of main stores' selections. Second, Brooks introduced the outlet concept in 1991. These stores allowed the company to reach a segment of the market that normally would not shop in areas where the major Brooks Brothers were located. In addition, stores and factories had a place to send products that were overproduced.[22]

Inventory Monitoring: Brooks Brothers was admittedly behind in the area of technology. Marks & Spencer implemented its IT infrastructure, which was designed to monitor large volume inventory changes, into all Brooks stores. Consequently, management became more interested in monitoring the number of individual items instead of the cost of these "improvements" (i.e. a reduction of floor personnel who were essential in maintaining relationships with customers).[23]

Trend: Historically, Brooks played the role of the innovator but the 1990s trend of business casual forced the company to compete, for the first time, with other makers from the role of the underdog. In order to make the label trendier, Marks & Spencer hired Brooks' first design team. As Brooks Brothers became more hip to challenge brands such as J. Crew and Banana Republic, its long-time relationships with a loyal customer base became even more fractured.[24] Traditionally, when contemplating new merchandising decisions, management would present ideas found in Britain to sales associates with the question, "Would it sell?" Sales associates, because they best knew the client, had the most input into the company's selection.[25]

Efficiency: The Marks & Spencer business model was built on turnover and low cost. Thus, it was believed that Brooks Brothers had to become more efficient in terms of production and consolidate its offerings to increase profitability. To accomplish this end, Brooks closed its suit production facility, vastly expanded the number of suppliers, outsourced the production of garments, and limited the sizes and varieties of goods. This was a major shift from the traditional model of maintaining long relationships with select suppliers, controlling all aspects of production, and maintaining a healthy selection of goods to fit virtually any man who entered a store.[26]

---

19. *Ibid*, p. 123

20. Glassmoyer, Michael. Personal Interview. April 1, 2005.

21. *Ibid*, p. 131

22. Cooke, John William. *Generations of Style*. New York, NY: Brooks Brothers, 2003, p. 125

23. *Ibid*, p. 130

24. Aoki, Naomi. "An Alteration at Brooks Brothers." *Boston Globe*, November 12, 2003; [cited 2005 April 1].
    Available from: *http://bidtxt.whenu.com/*.

25. Cooke, John William. *Generations of Style*. New York, NY: Brooks Brothers, 2003, p. 131

26. *Ibid*, p. 134

Innovation: Prior to the acquisition, Brooks Brothers terminated its Brooksgate clothing and was researching a suit separates offering as the new introductory line. Marks & Spencer had already established such a line and was able to refine the technology to meet the Brooks Brothers quality standard. This worsted wool fabric was able to remain virtually wrinkle free whether trapped in economy class on an airplane or packed away in a suitcase.[27]

After spending $750 million on acquiring the legendary retailer and investing over $1 billion into the business, Marks & Spencer put Brooks Brothers up for sale.[28] Although Marks & Spencer made significant contributions to Brooks Brothers such as the development of the BrooksEase suit, many needed improvements in the IT infrastructure, and introducing business casual merchandise, they simply did not understand the Brooks model of business and corporate culture. In November of 2001, Brooks Brothers was acquired by Retail Brand Alliance for $225 million.[29]

Retail Brand Alliance

Privately owned by CEO Claudio Del Vecchio, Retail Brand Alliance is the parent of mid-market professional women's retailers Casual Corner and Petite Sophisticate. Del Vecchio got his business education working under the tutelage of his father who is the founder of the Italian eye-wear manufacturer Luxotica. In the early 1980s the younger Del Vecchio moved to the U.S. to run Luxotica's American operations and subsequently bought U.S. Shoe in the 1990s to acquire LensCrafters. The plan was to keep LensCrafters under Luxotica and sell the shoe business and U.S. Shoe's women's clothing business, Casual Corner. Although the shoe company sold with ease, Casual Corner was a struggling business. Del Vecchio decided to purchase Casual Corner from his father, leave Luxotica, and devote his attention to reviving the ailing women's brand. With a hands-on nurturing approach and patience, Del Vecchio rebuilt Casual Corner under the parent company Retail Brand Alliance.[30]

The Day After Thanksgiving

Claudio Del Vecchio is a long-time Brooks Brothers customer. Lamenting about the fact that Brooks Brothers had deteriorated to a commoditized brand competing with Banana Republic and Bachrach, Del Vecchio knew he must rebuild the trust given by so many to the brand. Recalling the days when people aspired to wear Brooks Brothers clothing, he knew that the retailer must return to its core of quality, value, and excellent customer service. The previous owners completely changed the formula that made Brooks Brothers America's most profitable retailer for so long. Del Vecchio was responsible for developing a plan to return the company to its heritage and prove to the public that Brooks Brothers is worthy of their trust.

Discussion Questions

1. Who are the key stakeholders in Brooks Brothers? How will an attempt to restore the brand to its former glory affect each of these stakeholders?

2. What are the major components of the brand, and how can Brooks Brothers restore these to their former strength?

3. How should Brooks Brothers communicate their new business strategy with the customer? Inside the company? To the public?

4. Do Retail Brand Alliance and Del Vecchio have the experience that it takes to run a high-end luxury retail menswear company? What are the differences between Casual Corner and Brooks Brothers?

5. What should Brooks Brothers do with the changes that Marks and Spencer contributed to the firm? Should Brooks Brothers close down the outlet stores?

27. Glassmoyer, Michael. Personal Interview: April 1, 2005

28. Cooke, John William. *Generations of Style*. New York, NY: Brooks Brothers, 2003, p. 134.

29. Aoki, Naomi. "An Alteration at Brooks Brothers." *Boston Globe*, November 12, 2003; [cited 2005 April 1]. Available from: *http://bidtxt.whenu.com/*.

30. Cooke, John William. *Generations of Style*. New York, NY: Brooks Brothers, 2003, pp. 143–145.

Chapter 3

Step One: Identify the Purposes of Communication

The Case of Barnaby Consulting Corp.

Lincoln Frazer, director of recruiting for Barnaby Consulting Corp., has just come from a meeting with the directors of marketing and human resources. Marketing Director Martha Reynolds called the meeting to report that several clients have recently complained about the interpersonal skills of Barnaby's consultants. To help eliminate this problem, Martha has asked the human resources and recruiting directors to review their practices to make sure that Barnaby is hiring consultants with the needed skills to communicate with clients well and make sure that current consultants have sufficient training in building and maintaining excellent customer relations.

Barnaby Consulting Corp., a "boutique" firm, provides consulting services in the area of virtual management. Virtual management, brought about by the rise of the Internet, globalization, outsourcing, telecommuting, and virtual teams, is the management of widely dispersed groups and individuals, perhaps without ever meeting them face to face. Because of this, team leaders face challenges of coordinating work across different time zones and physical distance, of establishing effective working relationships in the absence of face-to-face communication, and of dealing with choices of appropriate technology and its use. In global virtual teams, the added dimension of cultural differences impacts a team's functioning. Barnaby's consultants' role is to provide solutions to clients to address these multifaceted challenges.

The challenge of identifying consultants with excellent communication skills is no news to Frazer. Because of young people's reliance on technology as a primary means of communication, Frazer has noticed a decline in their skills at and comfort with communicating face to face. This lack can impede their ability to maintain the reputation of Barnaby in their interactions with clients and to build the long-lasting relationships upon which many organizations depend for future business.

After reading this chapter, you will be able to

- *Identify the four purposes of business communication: to inform, to convey goodwill, to establish credibility, and to persuade and influence.*

- *Begin to apply the four purposes of business communication in your communication practices through greater knowledge, self-awareness, and critical-thinking abilities.*

Case Questions

1. What is the role of communication in establishing the credibility of an employee? How does this credibility contribute to the overall reputation of the employer?

2. What is the role of communication in establishing long-term relationships with clients and customers? How does this take place in practice?

3. What is the role of credibility and trusted relationships in a firm's ability to influence its customers, clients, and other stakeholders?

Four Purposes of Communication

This chapter deals with the first step in strategy formulation: identifying the purpose(s) of your communication so that you can more effectively plan and formulate your messages. Note that being an effective strategic communicator requires knowledge and specific skills: (1) self-awareness, (2) the willingness and ability to understand others, and (3) the ability to think critically. These were discussed in Chapter 2.

More than 2,000 years ago, Greek philosopher and writer Aristotle (384–322 B.C.E.) identified three purposes of communication: to inform, to persuade, and to entertain. Although entertainment is the purpose of much of the communication that occurs in American culture today, it is not emphasized in communication for business purposes. In fact, communication intended to entertain can have a negative effect on the relationship you have with others, or it can damage your credibility. For example, if you use humor in oral presentations or e-mail messages at work, you take the risk of offending others who might not share your sense of humor or of creating an image of yourself as unprofessional. Some attempts at humor may even violate the law if they are considered racist, sexist, ageist, or otherwise discriminatory of others.

For these reasons, entertainment will not be considered one of the foundational purposes of communication in organizational settings. However, four purposes of communication still exist in the professional workplace:

- To inform
- To convey goodwill
- To establish credibility
- To persuade and influence

These purposes apply to the individual, although similar concepts are relevant to organizations under different terms, including reputation management, public relations, and marketing. These will be discussed in more detail in Chapter 11.

Many authors group the purpose of credibility and goodwill into a single category, but these have been separated in this text to emphasize the importance of both to effective individual communication and to help you better understand their nuances. Figure 3-1 illustrates how these four purposes of business communicate often overlap in practice and achievement.

Figure 3-1 The Four Purposes of Business Communication

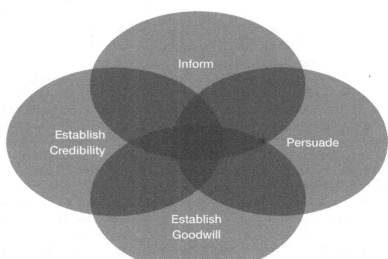

Communicating to Inform

When asked the purpose of communication, most of us respond with one simple answer: to inform. Our common sense tells us that we communicate to tell someone about something. To inform is to pass on information. In the world of work, you are informing when you explain something to your colleagues, your employees, or your customers and clients. If you tell an employee how to write a report, you are informing; if you tell a customer how to fill out a form, you are informing. You also inform when you tell another person what happened. Perhaps you received a phone call from a customer who is angry about his or her service, and you need to describe the call to your supervisor to learn what to do next. This situation is another example of communicating to inform.

Because most of us have been using the model of communication as information transfer for much of our lives, we assume we are experts at informing. Therefore, little space will be devoted to the purpose of communicating information in this text, although all the steps of strategy formulation can be applied to informative messages. For example, you should analyze your audience to make sure that you are delivering the information that it needs and wants, consider the context of the communication, and use the channel or medium of communication that is best suited for your purpose and your audience's preferences. These strategic issues will be discussed more in the chapters that follow.

Another way to think about informing is that it often is the goal of *routine* messages, such as sending an e-mail to colleagues to remind them of a meeting, passing on information about a new procedure, or updating a client on the status of an order. Tactical considerations for writing routine messages will be discussed in more detail in Chapter 6.

Communicating to Convey Goodwill

According to *Merriam-Webster's Collegiate Dictionary*, **goodwill** has three definitions: "1. friendly disposition; kindly regard; benevolence. 2. cheerful acquiescence or consent. 3. an intangible, salable asset arising from the reputation of a business and its relations with its customers." For those of you who have taken accounting courses, you are probably familiar with the third definition of goodwill; in business contexts, goodwill is considered an asset having to do with how others regard the organization. As a purpose of business communication, goodwill can be thought of as the ability to create and maintain positive, productive relationships with others and can be viewed as an intangible asset as well.

goodwill
In the business communication context, the ability to create and maintain positive, productive relationships with others.

Conger has studied how individuals use language to motivate people, often considered the role of a leader. His research indicates that people with high credibility on the relationship side, that is, goodwill, have demonstrated that they can be trusted to listen and to work in the best interests of others. Recognition of the value of conveying and maintaining goodwill in organizational settings is one important way of compensating for one of the weaknesses of the strategic control model: narrowly pursuing your own interests without regard to others.

If you have work experience, you understand the practical value of relationships in organizational settings. Establishing and maintaining relationships with others, or **networking**, is one of the most successful forms of job hunting, for example. Likewise, the best form of advertisement is word of mouth, not only because it is inexpensive, but also because people are more likely to trust the judgment of those they already know. When working with others or in groups, people are more likely to cooperate with those they know, like, and trust.

networking
Establishing and maintaining relationships with others.

Having a positive relationship with another person or being an expert in a relevant field often enables us to be more successful at persuasion. As long ago as the middle of the fourth century B.C.E., Aristotle made this assertion in *On Rhetoric*. For Aristotle, the problem of communication essentially boiled down to seeing the available means of persuasion in each particular case. According to Aristotle, to persuade successfully, communicators must know the extent to which they enjoy the trust, respect, and affection of the people with whom they are communicating. Aristotle recognized that the importance of the character of the speaker (or writer) is a legitimate concern in effective communication.

From an organizational perspective, relationships can play an important role in producing effective supervision, promoting social support among employees, building personal influence, and ensuring productivity through smooth work flow. The need for good interpersonal relationships in organizations is particularly important from both the standpoint of the individual, who requires social support in an increasingly turbulent world, and the standpoint of the organization, which must maintain high levels of cooperation among employees to meet customer demands and remain competitive.

Trust

As discussed in Chapter 1, the recent flattening of organizational hierarchies and resulting interdependence of work tasks among employees, as well as the increasing diversity of the workplace, requires corporate cultures of trust built on respect for differences and mutual cooperation. Informal interpersonal relationships and communication networks are the most dynamic sources of power in organizations today.[1] (Communication networks are discussed in more detail in Chapter 5, "Steps Three and Four: Consider the Context and Select Channels of Communication.") In contrast, more formal relationships are slower and less trustworthy sources of information. Most decision makers rely heavily on verbal information from people they trust.

trust

The confidence that others' intentions are good.

Interpersonal skills and the ability to work well in a team are frequently cited as the top characteristics that recruiters find most attractive in prospective employees. These skills and abilities are founded on trust. **Trust** can be understood as the confidence that our peers' intentions are good.[2] In other words, we must believe that those with whom we work will not act opportunistically or take advantage of us and others to narrowly pursue their own self-interest.

Studies indicate that trust is a complex concept consisting of five components: integrity, competence, consistency, loyalty, and openness (see Figure 3-2).[3] *Integrity* refers to a person's ethical character and basic honesty. To feel that our peers are *competent*, we must be convinced that they have the technical knowledge and interpersonal skills required to perform their jobs. If you don't believe

Figure 3-2 The Five Components of Trust

a coworker is competent, then you are unlikely to depend on that person or respect his or her opinion on work-related matters. We are more able to trust those who appear *consistent* in their behavior or who are reliable, predictable, and demonstrate good judgment. We tend to trust others who are *loyal* and willing to protect and help others to save face. Finally, we tend to trust those who are *open*; conversely, we find it difficult to trust those who appear evasive, deceptive, or secretive.

Interpersonal Communication Styles

Additional factors affect our ability to forge the relationships businesspeople depend on: valuing relationships, assertiveness, and active listening.[4] The first step in building interpersonal relationships at work is learning to *recognize the importance of relationships* in business, if you haven't already done so. For many individuals, interpersonal communication *is* the work, particularly among managers and leaders.

The importance of *assertiveness* becomes obvious when you consider alternative communication styles. On one hand, the avoiding, passive-aggressive individual whines, complains, and frets about problems at work but says nothing when asked directly what is wrong.[5] This strategy, known as **avoidance**, is defined as a conscious attempt to avoid engaging with people in the dominant group.[6] Avoidance is also considered *passive*, an attempt to separate by having as little to do with the dominant group as possible. The result of an avoiding, passive approach is a consistent inability to raise and resolve problems, needs, issues, and concerns.

At the other extreme, aggressive individuals sabotage their ability to meet their needs and to establish supportive relationships by creating defensiveness and alienating others.[7] **Aggressiveness** is a series of behaviors and characteristics that include hurtful expressiveness, self-promotion, attempts to control others, and argumentativeness.[8] Aggressive individuals, also described as argumentative, are not only more aggressive but also more insecure and less likely to be well regarded or happy at work.[9]

In contrast to avoidance and aggression, **assertiveness** is defined as "self-enhancing, expressive communication that takes into account both the communicator's and others' needs."[10] Assertiveness clearly involves articulating what you want from others in terms of behavior while remaining sensitive to the effect of your words and actions on others. It is direct but not attacking or blaming. Assertiveness is associated with positive impressions and overall good quality of work experience.

Like assertiveness, *listening* is a learned skill and one that very few individuals ever master. Talking to someone who really knows how to listen actively makes you feel valued, important, and free to speak your mind.[11] (Active listening is discussed in more detail in Chapter 8, "Communicating with Employees.") In an ideal communication situation, assertiveness and active listening go hand in hand as people are able to express their own perceptions and desires and at the same time attend to those of others. As you may recognize, these two skills are the foundation of the dialogic model of communication introduced in Chapter 2. They are also important if we are to influence others or to demonstrate leadership.

avoidance

The strategy of knowingly avoiding engagement with those in the dominant group.

aggressiveness

Asserting one's rights and needs at the expense of others through hurtful expression, self-promotion, attempts to control others, and argumentativeness.

assertiveness

Self-enhancing, expressive communication that takes into account one's own needs as well as those of others.

Communicating to Establish Credibility

Aristotle recognized that the importance of the character of the speaker—or writer—is a legitimate concern in effective communication. In our time, when the facts are often complex and hard to determine for ourselves—and when television, cell phones, video, the Internet, and other technologies bring speakers "up close and personal" for our inspection—the importance of credibility has been magnified several times beyond that of ancient Greece.

Credible people demonstrate that they have strong emotional character and integrity; they are known to be honest, steady, and reliable. Credibility is akin to reputation at the organizational level. Sophisticated customers do not make financial decisions based solely on an organization's competitive advantage in the marketplace.[12] Instead, customers are increasingly sensitive to a company's reputation. In fact, public relations developed as a functional area to manage the reputations of companies.

Just as an organization understands that its reputation and image can affect its successful continuation, savvy employees are aware that these same concepts can be applied in their own careers. One study indicates that 92 percent of more than 2,300 executives said that if a person loses credibility with them, it would be very difficult to gain it back.[13]

To make matters worse, most managers overestimate their own credibility considerably.[14] In the worst-case scenario, they may revert to the old command-and-control style of leadership, which studies have shown damages productivity and morale in skilled, well-educated workers and creates frustrated, silenced employees who steal all the pencils and sabotage the company's computer system. Not understanding or ignoring the importance of credibility may ultimately lead to a Machiavellian game of terror and threats in which strong tactics of domination and control are used to gain influence rather than softer, less-destructive methods.

Factors that help to build credibility include the following (Figure 3-3):

- Expertise and competence.
- Personal ethics and integrity, or trustworthiness.
- Control of emotions.
- Development and maintenance of a professional image.

Figure 3-3 **Factors that Help Build Credibility**

Expertise and Competence

Clearly, your relevant knowledge and ability to perform your job well affect your credibility. Skill levels and competency are also important for the effective functioning and performance of small groups and teams. Attitude and personality characteristics can also improve your reputation as a competent, conscientious employee. For example, those who complain without offering solutions to the problem are perceived more negatively than those who discuss problems in terms of their solutions. The former may be seen as "whiners," whereas the latter become known as problem solvers. These perceptions contribute to your overall image within a company and may help or detract from your ability to establish yourself as a leader.

Competence also extends to communication skills. Speaking correctly and being articulate generally enhance our credibility by indicating to others that we are well educated and intelligent. The same goes for our written communication. If our written messages are full of errors, then we may be perceived as undereducated, lazy, or not detail oriented. All of these negative judgments can affect our credibility. For example, a résumé or letter with a grammatical error may eliminate a job applicant from further consideration. Likewise, consistent problems producing correct writing or speaking articulately may eliminate an employee from a position working with external audiences, where his or her communication skills may negatively affect the reputation of the organization.

This recognition provides an opportunity for those who can communicate well in today's competitive business environment. In other words, one way you can positively distinguish yourself from others is by demonstrating excellent communication skills. Employees who can write clearly and speak articulately can create a better impression of a firm with customers, suppliers, and outsiders than can any public relations program.

? **Critical** Thinking

What competencies and areas of expertise do you possess that can help you build your feelings of confidence as well as your credibility with professional audiences? What skills in communication can help you do the same?

Effective communication skills have become crucial for both personal performance and organizational productivity. With the proliferation of personal computing, more and more employees at all levels in the company are producing written messages that represent an organization, and the quality of this material can have a significant effect on both perceptions and performance. Technology has also created a problem of exposure. Voice mail, e-mail, text messaging, blogs, social media, audio/video conferencing, and other technologies expose businesses to an ever-growing array of diverse audiences.

E-mail is a particular problem because of its wide use. "Your company's voice is often judged by what pops into your client's inbox. That first impression better be a good one," says one executive.[15] Another says, "If I get an e-mail that's full of errors and I know nothing else about you, there's no reason for me not to think you'll handle my business in the same way you handled that writing."[16]

? **Critical** Thinking

Discuss your greatest challenges in achieving grammatical correctness and precise word choice in your written and oral communication. Have these affected your confidence or your credibility with your communication audiences? Have you taken steps to become more correct and thus more confident in your written and oral communication? If not, what steps might you take?

Personal Ethics and Integrity

In addition to interpersonal skills and the ability to work in teams, personal ethics and integrity are among the top five characteristics sought by recruiters. The attractiveness of ethical employees may be a result of the continuing problems of unethical and illegal practices by U.S. businesses. This renewed concern with ethics began in the 1990s and early 2000s due to the illegal accounting practices of such companies as Enron, WorldCom, and Tyco, and has continued today with the recent concerns about the legality and ethics of the practices of the world's largest financial institutions, practices that have resulted in the most severe recession since the Great Depression of the 1920s.

The causes of such unethical behavior have been widely studied. For example, Lehman and DuFrene claim unethical behavior stems from a number of causes, including the following:

- Excessive emphasis on profits by managers. According to former Federal Reserve Chairman Alan Greenspan, "infectious greed" ultimately pushed companies such as Enron, Global Crossing, and WorldCom into bankruptcy. Greed has also been blamed for the debacle in the financial sector in the early 2000s.
- A misplaced sense of corporate loyalty may cause an employee to do what seems in the best interest of the corporation, even if it is illegal or unethical.
- An obsession by employees to gain personal advancement.
- An expectation that illegal or unethical actions will not be caught.
- An unethical tone set by top management.
- Uncertainty about whether an action is wrong.
- Unwillingness to take a stand for what is right.

Eisenberg and Goodall claim that another possible related reason for unethical communication behavior may be the increased pressure to compete. The increasing complexity of organizations may also lead to lies or distortion, turf building, and cover-up.[17]

Terence Mitchell and William Scott attribute unethical behavior to the United States' "ethic of personal advantage." This ethic has three themes:

1. A present versus future orientation
2. An instrumental as opposed to a substantive focus
3. An emphasis on individualism contrasted with community

Other scholars agree with this assessment. For example, Eisenberg and Goodall state that the "greatest weakness of businesspeople in the past two decades has been short-term thinking, or the willingness to trade off long-term value for immediate gain."[18]

Likewise, in his study of the Los Angeles riots, Michael Lerner contends that the looters were merely "living out the cynical American ethos." Lerner claims that we live in a culture of looting in which the highest goal is to "look out for number one" and to "get what you can when you can."[19] This assessment echoes that of Mitchell and Scott, who advance the case that unethical behavior is caused in part by an emphasis on individualism and instrumentalism.

> *Any cost to others is acceptable as long as you don't get caught or don't hurt your own future chances.... Within this ethos, concern for the future—of the planet, of one's own country or even of one's own children—seems naive and silly, something to be left to "do-gooders." The ethos of looting is the "common sense" of the society.*[20]

The unethical practices of corporations and their employees can have far-reaching consequences. Those affected by the decisions, the *stakeholders*, can include people inside and outside the organization. Financial markets can suffer from an erosion of public confidence. With globalization, this erosion has negative repercussions for the entire world, as evidenced by the world financial crisis early in the 21st century from which economies are still attempting to recover.

Leaders may unintentionally make unethical decisions because they lack the necessary knowledge, skills, and experience. Not understanding how to go about making ethical decisions can be an issue, as can ignorance of ethical perspectives that can be applied to ethical dilemmas. Table 3-1 provides a list of milestones for developing ethical competence.

Table 3-1 Milestones for Assessing Ethical Competence

Greater self-awareness	Greater self-understanding should help you develop a clearer grasp of your values and moral blind spots.
Greater self-confidence	Greater self-confidence should help you shoulder the heavier ethical burdens that come with increased responsibility.
Stronger character	Character consists of displaying admirable qualities in a variety of settings.
Healthy moral imagination	Expanding ethical capacity will make you aware of a wider array of ethical problems and help you develop creative solutions grounded in moral principles.
Sounder moral reasoning	Rejecting faulty assumptions, gathering information, building arguments, and taking a systematic approach to problem solving are part of reasoned ethical decision making.
Greater resistance to outside pressure	Resisting group, organizational, and cultural pressures to set aside moral principles is an integral part of a moral bearing.
Better follow-through	Holding good values and making choices based on those values leads to more ethical decision making.
Healthier ethical climate	Expanding ethical capacity means working to change the climate of your small group, organization, and community for the better.

Source: Adapted from Johnson, C., & Hackman, M. Z. (2002). "Assessing Ethical Competence."
Paper presented at the meeting of the National Communication Association, Atlanta (November).

As the information in the table implies, integrity is the ability to adhere to a strong set of moral or ethical principles regardless of the situation or the pressures that come to bear. Leaders with integrity inspire confidence that they can be trusted to do what they say they are going to do. They are loyal, dependable, and not deceptive.

Making and implementing ethical decisions takes both critical thinking and communication skills. (Chapter 2 explained steps in the critical thinking process.) In addition to displaying integrity, you can do something to ensure that your communication is ethical. Putting ethical practices first will not only benefit your employer, colleagues, clients, and customers but also enable you to maintain your credibility and create a reputation of fairness and good judgment that can enhance your ability to communicate and succeed in your career goals over the long term, the orientation of a strategic perspective.

In Table 3-2, you will find the "Nine Commandments" of the National Communication Association that help to ensure ethical communication practices.

As we have discussed, communication is inherently ethical. This is because whenever people interact with one another, ethics invades every exchange because the manipulation of symbols involved in language use also involves a purpose that is external to, and in some degree manipulative of, the audience for or interpreter of the message.[21] Communication can be intended to prevent, restrict, or stimulate the cultivation of meaning. In the first case, messages can be intended to coerce others by choosing symbols that are threatening to the audience or interpreter of the message. The values of the listener are ignored in this type of communication. In the second, messages can be intended to exploit by arranging words to filter information, narrow the choices, or obscure the consequences so that only one meaning becomes attractive or appropriate. The values of the listener are subverted in this type of message. Finally, messages can be facilitative. In such communication, words are used to inform, enlarge perspective, deepen sensitivity, remove external threat, or encourage independence of meaning.[22] The values of the listener are respected in this type of interaction.

Just as certain communicative behaviors are considered ethical, it is easy to identify those that are considered unethical. W. Charles Redding (1991) has developed the typology of unethical messages in organizations shown in Table 3-3.

Table 3-2 The National Communication Association Credo for Communication Ethics

Questions of right and wrong arise whenever people communicate. Ethical communication is fundamental to responsible thinking, decision making, and the development of relationships and communities within and across contexts, cultures, channels, and media. Moreover, ethical communication enhances human worth and dignity by fostering truthfulness, fairness, responsibility, personal integrity, and respect for self and others. We believe that unethical communication threatens the quality of all communication and consequently the well-being of individuals and the society in which we live. Therefore, we, the members of the National Communication Association, endorse and are committed to practicing the following principles of ethical communication:

- We advocate truthfulness, accuracy, honesty, and reason as essential to the integrity of communication.
- We endorse freedom of expression, diversity of perspective, and tolerance of dissent to achieve the informed and responsible decision making fundamental to a civil society.
- We strive to understand and respect other communicators before evaluating and responding to their messages.
- We promote access to communication resources and opportunities as necessary to fulfill human potential and contribute to well-being of families, communities, and society.
- We promote communication climates of caring and mutual understanding that respect the unique needs and characteristics of individual communicators.
- We condemn communication that degrades individuals and humanity through distortion, intimidation, coercion, and violence, and through the expression of intolerance and hatred.
- We are committed to the courageous expression of personal convictions in pursuit of fairness and justice.
- We advocate sharing information, opinions, and feelings when facing significant choices while also respecting privacy and confidentiality.
- We accept responsibility for the short- and long-term consequences of our own communication and expect the same of others.

Table 3-3 Typology of Unethical Messages

Type	Examples
Coercive	An employee criticizes the boss's "pet" development program in a meeting and is fired on the spot for her remarks.
Destructive	A supervisor makes a sexist joke at the expense of an employee.
Deceptive	Federal Aviation Administration employees falsify employee work records to justify the firing of air traffic controllers during their strike.
Intrusive	Electronic surveillance of employees is conducted through hidden video cameras.
Secretive	Some investment firms suppressed information about the value of commercial mortgage-backed securities.
Manipulative or Exploitative	Management threatens union members with a plant closing if they don't ratify a contract.

Source: Adapted from Redding, W. C. (1991). "Unethical Messages in the Organizational Context."
Paper presented at the Annenberg Convention of the ICA, Chicago.

Responsible Communication

Have you been on the receiving end of the types of unethical messages listed in Table 3-3? How did you feel? What might be appropriate responses to such unethical communication practices?

Messages can be used to harm or mislead others. In particular, persuasive messages always contain the potential for unethical practices. This is because persuasion involves the following:

- a person or group attempting to influence others by altering their beliefs, attitudes, values, and overt actions;

- conscious choices among ends sought and means used to achieve those ends; and

- a potential judge (any and all receivers of the message).

Because of the potential for unethical communication practices, both senders and receivers of messages hold responsibilities. Responsible communicators exercise critical thinking to carefully analyze claims, assess probable consequences, and weigh relevant values.[23] In addition, responsible communicators exercise the ability to respond and are responsive to the needs and communication of others in sensitive, thoughtful, and fitting ways.[24] More specifically, both parties in an interaction bear mutual responsibility for active participation, which occurs through two steps: reasoned skepticism and appropriate feedback.

Reasoned skepticism involves actively searching for meaning, analyzing and synthesizing information, and judging its soundness and worth. **Appropriate feedback** requires that you are honest and reflect your true understanding and judgments. However, such feedback should also be appropriate for the subject, audience, and occasion or context—primary elements of business communication strategy.

reasoned skepticism

The process of actively searching for meaning, analyzing and synthesizing information, and judging the worth of that information.

appropriate feedback

Feedback that is honest, reflects the communicator's true understanding and judgment, and is appropriate for the subject, audience, and occasion or context.

Emotional Control

Employees are expected to maintain a professional demeanor while in the office or when they represent their office in the field. Part of our ability to accomplish that goal often has to do with our ability to control our emotions as discussed in the previous chapter. According to a study done by the University of Missouri at Columbia, "many employees do not want their coworkers to express any type of strong emotion—positive or negative."[25] In this study, the employees were asked to describe situations in which they believed their coworkers acted appropriately and inappropriately. The consensus of the employees was that negative emotion should never be expressed, and positive emotion should be shown in moderation.

Expressions of negative emotions, such as fear, anxiety, and anger, tend to be unacceptable except under fairly specific conditions. For example, verbalized anger is direct, aggressive, and intentional. When people allow anger to control their communication, the results are generally unproductive. Outbursts of anger tend to make others uncomfortable, especially when irrational forms of anger are exhibited. If construed as harassment in the workplace, excessive displays of anger can lead to disciplinary measures. Outbursts of anger may also be interpreted by others as a sign of a lack of self-control, which might negatively affect our credibility. Not only can negative emotions be conveyed verbally and nonverbally, but they can also be communicated in writing. As will be discussed in Chapter 6, tone is particularly important to consider when writing because of the prevalence of e-mail for communication in many organizations. Just as tone of voice can convey emotions, so can tone in writing.

Developing a Professional Image

All the aspects of credibility discussed thus far help us cultivate a professional image: our expertise and competence in a variety of job skills, our integrity, and our ability to control our emotions. Our communication skills, both written and oral, can enhance our image as professionals. Personality traits can also contribute to a more credible and professional image. If we show ourselves to be dependable, reliable, careful, thorough, able to plan, organized, hardworking, persistent, and achievement oriented, we are more likely to be perceived as professional and competent.

Our appearance—dress, body type, and posture—also communicates to others. Every time you walk into a room, your appearance communicates who you are even before you speak.[26] For example, in most organizational cultures, it would not be appropriate for the company president to walk into a business meeting wearing flip flops and shorts. On the other hand, a fishing guide would not show up for work in a three-piece suit. Dressing appropriately for a particular situation or context can affect whether others perceive us as professional and credible. It also sends the message that we are a part of the group, because we understand and respect its norms for behavior. This message can help you in the relationship area of communication (goodwill) as well.

impression management

The attempt to control the impression of ourselves that we present to others in any communication situation

Some people are better able to consciously cultivate a professional image. **Impression management** is the control of communication information through a performance. In impression management, people try to present an "idealized" version of themselves to reach desired ends. The idea that self-presentation is a kind of performance comes from the work of Erving Goffman, who described everyday interactions using a theatrical lens. In other words, he viewed individuals as "actors" and interaction as a "performance" shaped by the context and situation and constructed to provide others with "impressions" consistent with the actor's desired goals.

We all attempt to manage the impressions we make to varying degrees in various situations. For example, when you are with your friends, you probably try to dress and act like them so as to be seen as part of the group. When you go on a date, you are likely to be on your best behavior to reduce the risk of doing or saying something that may not be viewed as attractive by the other person. In small-group situations, you often hold back during the forming stage of the group process for the same reason—so as not to leave a lasting, potentially negative first impression.

Three essential types of communication are used to manage impressions: manner, appearance, and setting.[27] Manner includes both verbal and nonverbal communication. Manner, for example, might be seen as indifferent, silly, businesslike, intelligent, immature, friendly, warm, or gracious. Manner might be considered an indication of attitude. Our appearance may suggest a role we play, a value we hold, our personality, or how important we view the communication setting. Setting includes your immediate environment as well as public displays of who you are (your car, your electronic devices, your clothing choices, your jewelry).

In addition to manner, appearance, and setting, those who aspire to leadership positions or greater influence might give some thought to the traits they display. The trait approach to leadership was one of the first systematic attempts to study leadership. Trait theory has ebbed in its popularity over the years, but more recent studies have shown that personality traits are strongly associated with individuals' perception of leadership.[28] The traits associated with leadership that have been most commonly identified by these studies are the following:

- **Intelligence**. Zaccaro, Kemp, and Baker (2004) found support for the finding that leaders tend to have higher intelligence than non-leaders. Having strong verbal ability, perceptual ability, and reasoning appears to make one a better leader.

- **Self-confidence**. Self-confidence can help us establish our credibility and have the assurance needed to influence others.

- **Determination**. Determination is the desire to get the job done and includes such characteristics as initiative, persistence, dominance, and drive. People with determination are willing to assert themselves, are proactive, and have the capacity to persevere when faced with obstacles.

- **Integrity**. As already discussed in a previous section of this chapter, integrity is the quality of honesty and trustworthiness.

- **Sociability**. Sociability includes such characteristics as being friendly, outgoing, courteous, tactful, and diplomatic. Social leaders have good interpersonal skills and create cooperative relationships with others.

Knowledge of leadership traits can help us assess our strengths and weaknesses in these areas and provide us the opportunity to make changes that increase the potential impact of these traits or better manage the impressions that we make through our communication practices.

Effectively managing the impression we make requires us to be participants in our communication with others as well as an observer of that process. In other words, we must be able to assume a detached view of ourselves so that we can effectively perceive how others are responding to us and adjust our communicative behavior if necessary to improve our ability to communicate with them. As discussed in Chapter 2, self-awareness and perception are important parts of communication because they affect the way we understand ourselves, events, and others, and how others do the same.

The activity of observing ourselves in communicative situations is called *self-monitoring*. **High self-monitors** are those individuals who are highly aware of their impression-management behavior.[29] On the other hand, **low self-monitors** communicate with others with little attention to how others respond to their messages. They have little idea about how others perceive them and know even less about how to interact appropriately with others.

Impression management, or managing how others perceive us, can help us achieve our goals through our communication practices, particularly in the image-conscious business world. When we use language that is appropriate for the occasion or situation; when we use nonverbal communication to demonstrate understanding or empathy, self-confidence, and other leadership traits; and when we wear clothing that is within appropriate guidelines for the situation, we increase the likelihood that we will be viewed as credible and professional, which can better enable us to achieve our goals.

Impression management is one aspect of a natural and productive process called **anticipatory socialization** through which most of us develop a set of expectations and beliefs concerning how people communicate in particular occupations and in formal and informal work settings.[30] The communication course you are now enrolled in—as well as some of the other university courses you are now taking—is part of that process. Any internships or other job-related activities you may have also contribute to that process. In fact, learning how to work in a position probably begins in early childhood.

Because the anticipatory socialization process probably begins in childhood, it is also a part of our self-concept. Most discussions of anticipatory socialization recognize that, as people mature, they use the information they gather about jobs from their environment to compare against their self-concept. This comparison helps them make judgments about choosing occupations and specific jobs.[31] This process may be likened to an informal and ongoing self-inventory to determine career opportunities that best match an individual's skills and attitudes. It might also be compared with the social construction of our identities as we use outside information to define and determine who we are.

Some people believe that impression management is unethical or deceptive. Another view is that impression management is necessary for successful communication in specific situations. It relies on the ability to develop an awareness of the appropriate behavior, communication practices, and self-presentation for a particular occasion or situation and adjust to meet those expectations to better ensure successful communication outcomes.

Impression management can help others and ourselves save face or avoid embarrassment. When we act in ways that are appropriate to the situation, we are respecting the expectations of others. In these cases, impression management is a matter of politeness.

Like many matters of communication, the ethics of impression management come down to intent. Behaviors and presentation style that attempt to deceive or mislead others can be judged as unethical. That is another reason why the dialogic model can be helpful: Our actions must be guided by consideration of others and their effects on them. Even in their least offensive form, actions to manage the impression we make may be seen as superficial, pretentious, lacking integrity, or as "sucking up" by others. Having a strong sense of personal integrity and conviction in our beliefs can help offset these types of judgments. As discussed earlier, attempting to judge our actions from the viewpoint of others can be a helpful guide in determining their effectiveness and appropriateness to a situation.

high self-monitors

People who are highly aware of their impression-management behavior and efforts.

low self-monitors

People who have little awareness about how others perceive them and little knowledge about how to interact appropriately with others.

anticipatory socialization

The process we use to develop a set of expectations and beliefs about how people communicate in various formal and informal work settings.

Communicating to Persuade and to Influence

Although we may believe that most of our communication is intended to inform others, in the business world almost all communication is persuasive. In other words, you are trying to get another person to do or believe something. In business, you are almost always selling: selling your ideas, yourself, your products, your services, or your organization and its mission. Selling and persuading are nearly synonymous in the business world. You may be trying to persuade your supervisor to give you a raise, you may be attempting to persuade a colleague to change a portion of a project on which you are both working, or you may be trying to sell a customer your company's service or product. All of these are examples of persuasion at work. Persuasion is known by a number of terms, including *motivation*, *influence*, and *leadership,* depending on the context of the communication. (*Influence* is an interpersonal communication term and will be discussed in more detail later in this section.)

To succeed at persuasion, you must generally give the person you are communicating with good reason to do or believe what you want them to. That is one reason why it is important to identify your purposes before you communicate in the workplace. If you believe you are only informing, then you may fail to provide the good reasons or evidence necessary to persuade, if that is indeed your primary purpose.

Evidence consists of a variety of types of information, such as facts, anecdotes, examples, and statistics. These types of evidence and their usage are discussed in more detail in Chapter 6.

Conveying goodwill, establishing positive relationships, as well as establishing our credibility, helps to make our goal of persuasion much easier.

? Critical Thinking

Think about a time that you were unsuccessful at persuasion. Why were you unsuccessful? In retrospect, in terms of your communication approach what could you have done differently to have improved your chances of succeeding?

Conger's Multistep Model of Persuasion

According to Conger, persuasion is a difficult and time-consuming activity, but it is a necessary skill in today's business environment because the old "command-and-control" managerial model now often results in poor or unwanted outcomes.

> *"The day when you could yell and scream and beat people into good performance is over. Today you have to appeal to them by helping them to see how they can get from here to there by establishing some credibility and by giving them some reasons and help to get there. Do all those things, and they'll knock down doors."* [32]

According to Conger, there are four essential steps to effective persuasion: establish credibility, provide a frame for common ground, provide evidence, and connect emotionally.

1. **Establish credibility.** For Conger, credibility has two aspects: expertise and relationships, or goodwill, using the terminology of this text. People are considered to have high levels of expertise if they have a history of sound judgment or have proven themselves knowledgeable and well informed about their proposals.[33] As for relationship, people with high credibility have demonstrated *over time* that they can be trusted to listen and to work in the best interest of others.[34]

2. **Provide a frame for common ground.** To strengthen the appeal of your proposal to others, you must first identify its tangible benefits to the people you are trying to persuade. To do this, you must thoroughly understand your audience and its needs and concerns.

3. **Provide evidence.** Effective persuaders should use a variety of types of evidence—numerical data, examples, stories, metaphors, and analogies—to make their positions come alive[35] and to support their claims.

4. **Connect emotionally (convey goodwill).** In our culture, we may like to believe that people make decisions based on reason, but emotions are always at play.[36] In fact, Conger claims that emotions play a primary role in persuasion. To connect emotionally with an audience, Conger suggests that the communicators

    (a) show their own emotional commitment to the proposal being made—they must show conviction and even passion—and

    (b) adjust their arguments to their audience's emotional state. However, in showing their own emotional commitment to their proposal, communicators must use some restraint to maintain credibility.

Conger attempts to conceptualize our understanding of persuasion from that of simply convincing and selling, which might veer off into a monologue involving manipulation and even coercion, to that of learning and negotiating. Unlike what you may have been taught in previous composition courses, persuasion is generally not easily accomplished in a single moment in time, with the presentation of an argument or evidence, but rather it involves the stages of discovery of information, preparation, and dialogue. Dialogue must happen before and during the persuasive process. "A persuader should make a concerted effort to meet one-on-one with all the key people he or she plans to persuade."[37] In some cases, through this dialogue, effective persuaders may find that they need to adjust their positions to better achieve their goals. This approach supports and underscores the importance of using the dialogic model, discussed in Chapter 2, to achieve our communication purposes. Conger's model also emphasizes the interdependence of the purposes for communication to successful persuasion: To be successful, one must also establish his or her credibility, convey goodwill, and establish a relationship built on trust. He or she must know his or her audience and focus on its concerns and interests.

Conger's model recognizes the complexity of communication and, more specifically, persuasion, particularly in political environments in which participants have varying interests and resources are often limited, thereby, revealing the value of a strategic, yet ethical approach.

Interpersonal Communication and the Role of Influence

In Conger's model, interpersonal communication is critical to effective persuasion. Here we can see the usefulness of applying concepts from differing communication perspectives to actual practice. In interpersonal and small-group communication situations, persuasion is often referred to using another term: **influence**. The definition of *influence* is very similar to that of persuasion: It is the power that a person has to affect other people's thinking or actions.[38] Recall the Chapter 1 discussion of the differing bases of power. Some have legitimate or position power (managers) while others must rely on personal power to influence others (leaders). (Note: managers may also be leaders.)

In the area of interpersonal influence, one area of research focuses on **compliance-gaining** and **compliance-resisting** behaviors. Compliance-gaining is defined as those attempts made by a communicator to influence another to "perform some desired behavior that the [other person] otherwise might not perform."[39] Compliance-gaining occurs whenever we ask someone to do something for us. For example, we may ask our supervisor to give us a raise or promotion or a coworker to switch days off with us. Like Conger's view that effective persuasion takes time and may consist of several stages, research into compliance-gaining shows that its success also often involves a series of attempts. In other words, think of persuasion or influence as a process best approached with thought and planning rather than as a one-time event.

Research on compliance-gaining indicates that people generally prefer socially acceptable, reward-oriented strategies.[40] In other words, people are more apt to be persuaded or influenced if they are offered some kind of reward or benefit for doing so. Conversely, people do not respond well to negative, threatening, or punishing strategies used to gain compliance. This is where some

influence

The power to affect the thoughts or actions of others.

compliance-gaining

Attempts made by a communicator to influence another person to do something that the person otherwise might not do.

compliance-resisting

The refusal to comply with another person's attempts at influence.

scholars draw the line for the similarities between persuasion and influence: specifically, actions aimed at compliance-gaining. Compliance-gaining behaviors that rely on coercion and threats can be seen as abuses of power rather than the ethical pursuit of persuasion or influence. Studies indicate that as more resistance is encountered, compliance-gaining efforts generally move from positive tactics to more negative ones. At this point, compliance-gaining efforts may move from ethical attempts to influence to coercion.

Compliance-resisting is defined as the refusal to comply with influence attempts.[41] When resisting requests, people tend to offer reasons or evidence to support their refusal.[42] People who are more sensitive to others and who are more adaptive are more likely to engage in further attempts to influence.[43] They may address some of the obstacles they expect when they initiate their request and adapt later attempts to influence by offering counterarguments.

For example, if you are preparing to ask your supervisor for a raise, you might consider some of the reasons he or she might refuse. Your supervisor might respond by saying money isn't available, you don't deserve a raise compared to your peers' contributions, or you have not performed in such a manner as to deserve a raise. In such a case, a person who is adaptive and sensitive to his or her audience's needs and concerns will respond with information or evidence intended to counter these claims.

interpersonal dominance

The relational, behavioral, and interactional state that reflects the actual achievement—by means of communication—of influence or control over another person.

Another term that is closely related to compliance-gaining is **interpersonal dominance**, which is defined as "a relational, behavioral, and interactional state that reflects the actual achievement of influence or control over another via communicative actions."[44] The term *dominance* often carries a negative connotation, especially when the objective is to control others, but Burgoon argues that dominance may comprise positive qualities, as well, including aspects of social competence.

Interpersonal dominance is better understood by examining its four dimensions. *Persuasiveness and poise* refer to a person's ability to act influentially and to behave with dignity. *Conversational control and panache* refer to the individual's presence and expressiveness. *Task focus* refers to an individual's ability to remain focused on the task at hand. *Self-assurance* refers to a person's level of confidence and ability to avoid either arrogance or timidity. These dimensions also coincide with the traits that we associate with leaders and can be applied in interpersonal, group, and public-speaking situations.

? Critical Thinking

The construct of interpersonal dominance can be a useful one in thinking about yourself as a leader as it is similar to some of the elements identified by trait approaches to leadership. Identify someone who projects all of the characteristics of interpersonal dominance. Can you imagine what it would sound like, look like, and feel like to be that person? Can you incorporate some of these elements into your own communication practices?

The flattening of organizational hierarchies over the last few decades and the resulting interdependence of work tasks among employees have resulted in a greater need for excellent interpersonal skills. Because of these changes, Bernard Keys and Thomas Case claim that "influence must replace the use of formal authority in relationships with subordinates, peers, outside contacts, and others on whom the job makes one dependent."[45] This means that because positional authority is no longer sufficient to get the job done, a web of influence or a balanced web of relationships must be developed. "Recently managers have begun to view leadership as the orchestration of *relationships* among [sic] several different interest groups—superiors, peers, and outsiders, as well as subordinates."[46]

Just as managers must learn how to foster and orchestrate relationships between people, often through the process of influence, so must subordinates. According to Keys and Case, of the types of influence that subordinates use on superiors, **rational explanation**, which includes some sort of formal presentation, analysis, or proposal, is the most frequently used. It usually involves the presentation of evidence. A host of other tactics—such as arguing without support and using persistence and repetition, threatening and manipulation—were not found to be effective. In fact, Keys and Case found that subordinates who used these tactics usually failed miserably. Nevertheless, no one influence tactic will be best in all situations; instead, subordinates must learn to tailor their approaches to the audiences they are attempting to influence and the objectives being sought, an underlying principle of strategic communication.[47]

Similarly, Riley and Eisenberg claim that the primary skill individuals must cultivate in managing their bosses is advocacy—the process of championing ideas, proposals, actions, or people to those above them in the organization. Advocacy requires learning how to read your superior's needs and preferences and designing persuasive arguments that are most likely to accomplish your goals. (Analyzing audiences is discussed in Chapter 4, "Step Two: Analyze the Audience.") Successful advocacy involves the following considerations:

1. **Plan (strategize).** Think through a communication strategy that will work.

2. **Determine why your boss should care or analyze your audience.** Connect your argument to something that matters to your boss such as a key objective or personal value.

3. **Tailor your argument to the boss's style and characteristics.** Adapt your evidence and appeal to those things that are persuasive to your boss, not those things that are persuasive to you.

4. **Assess your audience's prior technical knowledge.** Do not assume too much about your boss's level of knowledge and vocabulary or jargon.

5. **Build coalitions.** Your arguments need the support of others in the organization.

6. **Hone your communication skills.** An articulate, well-prepared message is critical to building your credibility with your boss.

Building coalitions is one way to influence others if you do not have a position of power. Building coalitions involves identifying like-minded individuals in your organization and developing trusted relationships with them. The value and importance of establishing a positive relationship with your audience and others involves the third purpose of business communication—goodwill.

rational explanation

Explanation that includes some sort of formal presentation, analysis, or proposal and usually involves the presentation of evidence.

? Critical Thinking

Discuss your own application of the four purposes of business communication. Do you agree that you generally should consider and apply all four in business contexts? Why or why not?

Summary

The purposes of business communication are to inform, persuade and influence, convey goodwill, and establish credibility. These purposes should be considered whether you are planning to communicate in writing, in person, using the phone, or via e-mail or other electronic media. It is also important to recognize that most business communication is generally not intended solely to achieve one purpose. Because most business communication includes some aspect of sales or persuasion and successful persuasion also often depends on your relationship with your audience—that is, goodwill and your credibility—you should pay attention to achieving all four purposes in many, if not all, of your messages.

Your ability to establish credibility and create and maintain relationships with others depends a great deal on how others perceive you. Consequently, to be an effective communicator, you must have a large measure of self-awareness as well as insight into how others perceive and respond to you. If you become aware of weaknesses in certain areas that may negatively affect your abilities to communicate with others and ultimately your attainment of career goals, then you have an opportunity to change for the better.

Key Terms

goodwill **46**

networking **46**

trust **47**

avoidance **48**

aggressiveness **48**

assertiveness **48**

reasoned skepticism **54**

appropriate feedback **54**

impression management **55**

high self-monitors **56**

low self-monitors **56**

anticipatory socialization **56**

influence **58**

compliance-gaining **58**

compliance-resisting **58**

interpersonal dominance **59**

rational explanation **60**

Discussion Questions

1. What characteristics do you look for to determine the credibility of your coworkers, classmates, or other speakers? What strategies can speakers use to establish credibility?
2. Instructors use a variety of compliance-gaining tactics in the classroom. What are some of these tactics? What are some strategies that students use to resist instructors' compliance-gaining efforts? Have you seen examples of these tactics used in the workplace or in other organizations of which you are a part? Were they effective? If so, why?
3. What are the five components of trust? What role do these components play in your relationships with family members? Friends? Coworkers?
4. What are the elements of credibility? How have you seen each one applied in your organization (this might also be a student organization to which you belong)? How might they be applied better?
5. Are you aware of your own impression-management practices? How do you manage the impressions you make in differing contexts or situations?

Applications

1. Observe a live or recorded speech or oral presentation in which the speaker is attempting to persuade. How credible was the speaker? What did he or she say or do that enhanced or detracted from his or her credibility? How effective was the speaker in conveying goodwill or establishing a relationship with his or her audience? What did the speaker say or do that helped to build or detracted from his or her goodwill? Finally, how persuasive was the speaker? What did he or she say or do that supported or detracted from the talk's persuasiveness? How did the speaker's credibility or ability to convey goodwill affect his or her persuasiveness?

2. Find a persuasive business message at least one page long. Do the content and appearance of the document enhance or detract from the writer's credibility? Did the writer use language or style to establish or maintain a relationship with the reader? If so, how? Were there words or phrases that detracted from the writer's goodwill? How successful was the writer in his or her attempts to be persuasive? What contributed to that success or detracted from it?

3. Observe a group or watch an episode of a television show, such as *Survivor*, that focuses on group dynamics. Identify group members and then analyze their behaviors, looking for clues to their level of emotional intelligence and their ability to self-monitor. How do these behaviors affect their membership in and relationship to others in the group?

4. Find a reality television show or a video posted on YouTube in which a participant in a group situation exhibited a low ability to self-monitor. In other words, the person failed to successfully manage the impression he or she was making on others. What was the effect on others? If decision making was involved, what was the effect on the quality of the decision-making process?

5. Begin to visualize yourself as a leader or as a more effective leader. Create a list of the communication behaviors—written, oral, and nonverbal—that are involved in the successful creation of this role for yourself. For each item in the list, write an affirmative statement that details how you will enact that behavior in future interactions when leadership is appropriately enacted or applied.

6. If you currently are employed or have work experience, consider your manager's behavior. How did he or she approach the four purposes of business communication? What did the manager do well? What steps might he or she have taken to improve achievement of the purposes of business communication? Based on this analysis, what behaviors should you avoid? Adopt? Why?

Endnotes

1. Kanter, R. M. (1989). The new managerial work. *Harvard Business Review*, 67, 85–92.

2. Lencioni, P. M. (2002). *The Five Dysfunctions of a Team*. San Francisco: Jossey-Bass.

3. Robbins, S. P. (2001). *Organizational Behavior* (9th ed.). Upper Saddle River, NJ: Prentice Hall.

4. Eisenberg, E. M., & Goodall, Jr., H. L. (1993). *Organizational Communication: Balancing Creativity and Constraint*. New York: St. Martin's Press, p. 252.

5. Ibid.

6. Pearson, J. C., Nelson, P. E., Titsworth, S., & Harter, L. (2003). *Human Communication*. New York: McGraw-Hill, p. 214.

7. Eisenberg, E. M. & Goodall, Jr., H. L. 1993, p. 252.

8. Orbe, M. P. (1996). Laying the foundation for co-cultural communication theory: An inductive approach to studying "nondominant" communication strategies and the factors that influence them. *Communication Studies*, 47, 157–176, p. 170.

9. Infante, D., Trebling, J., Sheperd, P., & Seeds, D. (1984). The relationship of argumentativeness to verbal aggression. *Southern Speech Communication Journal*, 50, 67–77.

10. Orbe, 1996, p. 170.

11. Eisenberg & Goodall, 1993, p. 252.

12. Eisenberg & Goodall, 1993.

13. Pagano, B., Pagano, E., & Lundin, S. (2003). *The Transparency Edge: How Credibility Can Make You or Break You in Business*. New York, NY: McGraw-Hill.

14. Conger, J. (1998). The necessary art of persuasion. *Harvard Business Review*, 76, 84–95.

15. Moerke, A. (2004). Business writing brush-up. *Sales and Marketing Management*, 156 (5), 63.

16. Ibid.

17. Eisenberg & Goodall, 1993, p. 333.

18. Ibid.

19. Lerner, M. (1992, May 14). Looters living out the cynical American ethos. *Los Angeles Times*, B7.

20. Ibid.

21. Barnlund, D. C. (1986). Toward a meaning-centered philosophy of communication. In J. Stewart (Ed.), *Bridges Not Walls: A Book About Interpersonal Communication* (pp. 36–42). New York: Newbury Award Records, p. 40.

22. Barnlund, 1986, p. 41.

23. Larson, C. U. (2004). *Persuasion: Reception and Responsibility* (10th ed.). Belmont, CA: Wadsworth/Thomson Learning, p. 29.

24. Ibid.

25. Dealing with emotions in the workplace (2002, November). *USA Today Magazine Online*. Retrieved December 13, 2003, from *http://www.findarticles.com/cf_dls/m1272/2690_131/94384310/p1/article.jhtml*, p. 1.

26. Buhler, P. (1991). Managing in the 90's. *Supervision*, 52, 18.

27. Wiggins, J. A., Wiggins, B. B., & Vander Zanden, J. (1993). *Social Psychology.* (4th ed.). New York: McGraw-Hill.

28. Bass, B. M. (1990). *Bass and Stogdill's Handbook of Leadership: A Survey of Theory and Research*. New York: Free Press; Bennis, W. G., & Nanus, B. (1985). *Leaders: The Strategies for Taking Charge*. New York: Harper & Row; Kirkpatrick, S. A., & Locke, E. A. (1991). Leadership: Do traits matter? *The Executive*, 5, 48–60; Lord, R. G., DeVader, C. L., & Alliger, G. M. (1986). A meta-analysis of the relation between personality traits and leadership perceptions: An application of validity generalization procedures. *Journal of Applied Psychology*, 71, 402–410; Nadler, D. A. & Tushman, M. L. (1989). What makes for magic leadership? In W. E. Rosenbach & R. L. Taylor (Eds.), *Contemporary Issues in Leadership* (pp. 135–139). Boulder, CO: Westview; and Zaleznik, A. (1977). Managers and leaders: Are they different? *Harvard Business Review*, 55, 67–78.

29. Snyder, M. (1979). Self-monitoring processes. In L. Berkowitz (Ed.), *Advances in Experimental Social Psychology*. New York: Academic Press.

30. Jablin, F. M. (2001). Organizational entry, assimilation, and disengagement/exit. *The New Handbook of Organizational Communication* (pp. 732–818). Thousand Oaks, CA: Sage Publications.

31. Ibid.

32. Conger, 1998, p. 86.

33. Ibid., p. 88.

34. Ibid.

35. Ibid., p. 92.

36. Ibid., p. 93.

37. Ibid., p. 89.

38. Pearson, J. C., Nelson, P. E., Titsworth, S., & Harter, L. (2003). *Human Communication.* New York: McGraw-Hill.

39. Wilson, S. R. (1998). Introduction to the special issue on seeking and resisting compliance: The vitality of compliance-gaining research. *Communication Studies,* 49, 273–275, p. 273.

40. Miller, G. R., Boster, F. J., Roloff, M. E., & Seibold, D. (1977). Compliance-gaining message strategies: A typology and some findings concerning effects of situational differences. *Communication Monographs,* 44, 37–51.

41. Pearson et al., 2003.

42. Saeki, M., & O'Keefe, B. (1994). Refusals and rejections: Designing messages to serve multiple goals. *Human Communication Research,* 21, 67–102.

43. Ifert, D. E., & Roloff, M. E. (1997). Overcoming expressed obstacles to compliance: The role of sensitivity to the expressions of others and ability to modify self-presentation. *Communication Quarterly,* 45, 55–67.

44. Burgoon, J. K., Johnson, M. L., & Koch, P. T. (1998). The nature and measurement of interpersonal dominance. *Communication Monographs,* 65, 308–335, p. 315.

45. Keys, B., & Case, T. (1990). How to become an influential manager. *Academy of Management Executive,* 4, 38–50, p. 38.

46. Ibid., p. 39.

47. Keys & Case, 1990.

Cable News Network: *CNN Apologizes to the Chinese People*

Introduction

On April 9, 2008, during the evening broadcast of *The Situation Room*, Wolf Blitzer asked Jack Cafferty to comment on the United States' relationship with China. Cafferty responded:

> "I don't know if China is any different, but our relationship with China is certainly different. We're in hock to the Chinese up to our eyeballs because of the war in Iraq, for one thing. They're holding hundreds of billions of dollars worth of our paper. We are also running hundreds of billions of dollars' worth of trade deficits with them, as we continue to import their junk with the lead paint on them and the poisoned pet food and export, you know, jobs to places where you can pay workers a dollar a month to turn out the stuff that we're buying from Walmart. So I think our relationship with China has certainly changed...I think they're basically the same bunch of goons and thugs they've been for the last 50 years."

Over the next month and a half, thousands of Chinese Americans organized outside of CNN studios across the U.S. demanding an apology from Cafferty and CNN. CNN responded with silence, clarifying statements and thin apologies, all of which served to fuel negative opinion and ultimately elevate the story to international headlines.

Jack Cafferty and *The Situation Room*

Mr. Jack Cafferty is a veteran of New York nightly news with more than twenty years of experience covering the world's financial and capital news. He started his career in Reno, Nevada, in 1960. Before joining CNN, he was a news anchor at New York's WB-11, WNYW-TV, and Fox 5 News. At CNN, he was a co-host on *American Morning*, a host of the business show *In the Money* and an anchor on *Before Hours*, CNN's former morning program. Mr. Cafferty is based in the network's New York bureau and has received various distinctions in his career including an Edward R. Murrow Award, and Emmy Award and the New York Associated Press State Broadcasters Award.[1]

Mr. Cafferty has provided insights and commentary to *The Situation Room* since 2005. Hosted by CNN's main political anchor Wolf Blitzer, *The Situation Room* is modeled after the White House Situation Room and aims to integrate traditional news gathering techniques with innovative online resources. This political newscast show runs in a three-hour block weekly and an hour block on Saturdays, covering politics, security and international news.

Mr. Cafferty has been described by many as someone who "sounds off" and "tells it like it is" with a curmudgeon-like persona. Controversy is not something new for Mr. Cafferty. On the night before the 2006 midterm elections he called Donald Rumsfeld, then Secretary of Defense, "an obnoxious jerk and war criminal." After phone calls from the Pentagon to CNN staffers in Washington D.C., CNN's president and executive producer of *The Situation Room* urged Cafferty to recant his comments on-air. Following these protestations, Cafferty told CNN viewers "You know, I've stepped over the line."[2]

This case was prepared by Research Assistants Takashi Doi, Anielka Munkel, and Phillip Morley under the direction of James S. O'Rourke, Concurrent Professor of Management, as the basis for class discussion rather than to illustrate either effective or ineffective handling of an administrative situation. Information was gathered from corporate as well as public sources.

1. CNN. "Anchors/Reporters - Jack Cafferty." *CNN.com*. 01 May 2009
   <*http://www.cnn.com/CNN/anchors_reporters/cafferty.jack.html*>.
2. Time Inc. "CNN's Jack Cafferty Mouths Off." *TIME.com*. 15 Sept. 2007. 01 May 2009
   <*http://www.time.com/time/nation/article/0,8599,1662283,00.html*>.

CNN Worldwide

Founded by Ted Turner in 1980, Cable News Network (CNN) was the world's first 24-hour cable television news channel.[3] From its headquarters in Atlanta, the network has expanded around the world, becoming a global brand that offers targeted regionalized services to international audiences worldwide. With 40 news bureaus, its news service is available to over 2 billion people in more than 200 countries in seven different languages.[4]

CNN became an alternative to the traditional morning and evening news cycle that had dominated television news since its inception by providing around-the-clock news reports and updates. Events that brought global attention to the network include its live coverage of the Gulf War in 1991, the attacks of September 11, 2001, and the United States presidential elections in 2008.

According to the Nielsen Ratings, CNN is America's number one cable news network.[5] In terms of news gathering resources, it ranks second only to Britain's BBC News. Today the CNN brand comprises nine cable and satellite television networks; five websites, including *CNN.com*, the first major news and information website; one private place-based network; two radio networks; wireless devices that provide news and information to mobile devices; and CNN Newssource, the world's most extensively syndicated news service.[6] CNN's main slogan is "The Most Trusted Name in News."

CNN in China

CNN is one of 30 foreign media companies that have an agreement with the Ministry of Industry and Information Technology (MIIT) to broadcast in China. While the agreement allows these companies to broadcast within the country, CNN has reported that the agreement requires their broadcast signal to pass through a Chinese-controlled satellite, allowing the Chinese authorities to control which content is delivered to television viewers.[7] Furthermore, CNN's reach is restricted in China; only certain hotels, offices and housing developments that are open to foreigners are able to carry the broadcast. Given this regulatory environment, very few Chinese residents have access to CNN's television programming.

However, CNN's reach into China is growing through CNN's web site, *cnn.com*. According to Alexa, 72.4% of *cnn.com* visitors are from the United States, while 2.8%, the third highest percentage, are from China.[8] Comparatively, the British Broadcasting Company's website *bbc.co.uk* attracts 2.0% of its total visitors from China.[9] To strengthen its appeal to Chinese readers, the BBC has recently launched a Chinese language edition of its website.

While the BBC's English edition is available within China, their new Chinese language edition is banned within China. According to the China Internet Network Information Center, the number of Internet users in China grew 42% to 298 million from 2007 to 2008 with 91% using a broadband connection.[10] With the number of Internet users in China growing rapidly, it is likely that the number of Chinese citizens consuming foreign media will increase.

CNN Criticized for Tibet Photo

In the weeks leading up to Mr. Cafferty's comments on China, CNN was already embroiled in controversy over its reporting. On March 15, 2008, CNN published an article on its website titled, "Report: 100 Dead in Tibet Violence." This article included a photo that showed two unarmed people crossing a road with two Chinese military vehicles approaching. Criticism was not focused on what the photo showed, but what it did not show. Internet bloggers found the original photo by Getty Images and determined that CNN had cropped out an important part of the photo, a

3. "CNN." *New Georgia Encyclopedia.* 30 Jan. 2004. 01 May 2009 <http://www.georgiaencyclopedia.org/nge/Article.jsp?id=h-2643>.

4. CNN. "CNN News at a Glance - Overview." *CNN.com.* 01 May 2009 <http://www.cnnasiapacific.com/factsheets/?catID=9>.

5. The Project for Excellence in Journalism. "The State of the News Media 2007: An Annual Report on American Journalism." *Journalism.org.* 01 May 2009 <http://www.stateofthenewsmedia.org/2007/narrative_cabletv_audience.asp?cat=3&media=6>.

6. CNN. "CNN News at a Glance." *CNN.com.* 01 May 2009 <http://www.cnnasiapacific.com/factsheets/?catID=9>.

7. "China raises pressure on CNN over remarks." *Nytimes.com* 17 Apr. 2008. 01 May 2009 <http://www.iht.com/articles/2008/04/17/business/cnn.php>.

8. Alexa. "CNN.com." *Alexa.com.* 01 May 2009 <http://www.alexa.com/data/details/traffic_details/cnn.com>.

9. Alexa. "Bbc.co.uk." *Alexa.com.* 01 May 2009 <http://www.alexa.com/data/details/traffic_details/bbc.co.uk>.

10. "China tops world in Internet users" *CNN.com.* 14 Jan. 2009. 01 May 2009 <http://edition.cnn.com/2009/TECH/01/14/china.internet/index.html>.

group of Tibetan rioters throwing objects at the vehicles. This created a wave of criticism that spread virally across Internet forums and blogs. Critics held this photo as evidence in their claim that CNN held a bias against China.

Five days after the article was published, a 23-year old student at Beijing's Tsinghua University launched the anti-CNN.com website to collect and publish distorted reports from CNN and other Western media outlets. In the first few days of the website being online, the site received more than 2,000 posts by visitors.[11] CNN later responded with a statement on their website refuting allegations of bias in its coverage of events in Tibet (See Appendix A).

However, criticism of CNN's coverage did not end there. Web sites and theme songs criticizing CNN were created. The slogan "don't be too CNN," which means "don't be too biased" or "don't ignore the truth," went viral, and two songs lampooning CNN became popular on China's Internet. Both songs were titled "Don't Be Too CNN." "Why do you rack your brains in trying to turn black into white? Don't be too CNN," claimed one online singer Murong Xuan.

The Fallout

National Response

Five days after his initial comments on China, Cafferty clarified his position stating: "Last week, during a discussion of the controversy surrounding China's hosting of the Olympic Games, I said that the Chinese are basically the same bunch of goons and thugs they have been for the last 50 years. I was referring to the Chinese government, and not to Chinese people or to Chinese-Americans." CNN also issued a written statement two days later: "CNN would like to clarify that it was not Mr. Cafferty's, nor CNN's, intent to cause offense to the Chinese people, and [CNN] would apologize to anyone who has interpreted the comments in this way."[12] However, the Chinese American community viewed the apologies as insufficient. Following these statements, the U.S. Legal Immigrant Association started an online petition demanding a formal apology from CNN. Ultimately, the petition was signed by more than 45,000 people.[13]

On April 19, thousands of Chinese Americans gathered at CNN studios in Los Angeles, California, demanding that Cafferty "openly apologize" and be removed from the air permanently.[14] A letter taped to a door of the bureau stated, "If our demands are not taken seriously, we shall unite more public support to fight against such racial prejudice."[15] A second letter slid under the bureau's door criticized CNN's coverage of unrest in Tibet and the anti-Chinese protests that followed the running of the Olympic torch in advance of the Summer Olympic Games in Beijing.

In New York, on April 24, 2008, beautician Liang Shubing and teacher Li Lilan filed a lawsuit against Cafferty and CNN, seeking $1.3 billion in damages for "violating the dignity and reputation of the Chinese people."[16] The amount represented $1 for each Chinese person worldwide. Meanwhile, protests continued on April 26 at CNN's headquarters and its San Francisco bureau.

CNN's Website Targeted

Negative reaction surged after CNN's statement supporting Cafferty's reporting. On April 16, 2008, CNN's website, *cnn.com*, experienced problems that prevented users from accessing the site in what appeared to be a "Distributed Denial of Service (DDOS)" attack conducted by the Chinese hacker group using the name "Revenge of the Flame." People in certain Asian markets, including Japan, South Korea, Hong Kong and mainland China, were temporarily unable to access *cnn.com* due to the countermeasures taken by CNN to limit the extent of the attack.[17]

11. People's Daily Online. "CNN: What's wrong with you? (2)" *People's Daily Online*. 03 Apr. 2008. 01 May 2009 <*http://english.people.com.cn/90001/90776/90883/6386009.html*>.

12. CNN. "Transcripts." *CNN.com*. 14 Apr. 2008. 01 May 2009 <*http://transcripts.cnn.com/TRANSCRIPTS/0804/14/sitroom.03.html*>.

13. CNN. "China demands apology from Cafferty." *CNN.com*. 15 Apr. 2008. 01 May 2009 <*http://www.cnn.com/2008/WORLD/asiapcf/04/15/cnn.china/*>.

14. CNN. "CNN commentator's comments draw protests." *CNN.com*. 19 Apr. 2008. 01 May 2009 <*http://www.cnn.com/2008/US/04/19/cnn.china/*>.

15. CNN. "CNN commentator's comments draw protests."

16. International Business Times. "CNN Faces $1.3 Bln Lawsuit - $1 per person in China." *International Business Times*. 24 Apr. 2008. 01 May 2009 <*http://www.ibtimes.com/articles/20080424/cnn-time-warner-lawsuit-china-media.htm*>.

17. Fowler, Geoffrey A. "CNN's Coverage of China is Raising Hackles" *The Wall Street Journal* 19 Apr. 2008. 01 May 2009 <*http://online.wsj.com/article/SB120856947042728137.html?mod=googlenews_wsj*>.

Trust in Media Companies

Trust in media companies worldwide has continued to decline since 2005. In Edelman's 2009 report on credibility and trust, the 2009 Edelman Trust Barometer, the report found a sharp decline of trust in television news. The credibility of television news declined from 49% to 36% and the credibility of newspaper articles fell from 47% to 34% from 2008 to 2009.[18] Among North America, Asia Pacific, Europe and Latin America, North America showed the lowest level of trust in media companies. In 2008, the Edelman report stated that CNN was the most relied-on news source. Globally, CNN, BBC and Google are the most relied-on news sources for information about a company (25%, 17%, and 9%, respectively).[19]

Similarly, trust in digital media sources for news about companies in 2008 followed the downward trend for all media, with free content sources (such as Wikipedia and Web portals) and social networking sites (such as MySpace and Facebook) declining globally among 35-to-64 year-olds from 38% to 27%, and 20% to 15%, respectively. Among 35-to-64-year-olds, search engines emerged as the most trusted of all digital channels (35%), with markedly lower levels of trust for business (19%) and non-business (16%) blogs.[20]

The Chinese American Community

The number of Chinese-Americans in the United States has grown steadily over the past ten years. As of 2007, there are over 3.5 million Chinese-Americans living in the United States, or 1.2% of the total population. From 2000-2007, the Chinese-American population has increased by 29%. Furthermore, over 2 million Chinese Americans speak Chinese, the third most-spoken language in the United States.[21] In a recent survey of Internet-savvy Chinese Americans, 61% of respondents indicated they rely on Chinese language media for their information. Additionally, the survey found that 69% of Chinese Americans reported a post-graduate degree with a median household income of $55,600 annually.[22]

U.S. Trade Relations with China

Less than a year earlier, on August 15, 2007, Mattel, the world's largest toy company, announced the biggest recall in its history. The company recalled 436,000 Chinese-made die-cast toy cars that were found to be covered in lead paint.[23] Ultimately, this recall of lead-covered toys not only affected Mattel, but later occurred throughout the toy industry. In addition to toys, a series of additional recalls occurred against products manufactured in and exported from China, including contaminated pet food ingredients, children's jewelry, defective tires and tainted toothpaste.

With public concern over the safety of Chinese-made products, in November of 2007, an "action plan" on the safety of imported goods was created by President George W. Bush, calling for improved certification of imports, greater efforts to keep tainted goods from being shipped to America and for American training to help other countries build up their safety-inspection capabilities.[24]

However, after pressing China to step up efforts to police the safety of its food and other exports, the Bush administration found Chinese leaders pushing back, with demands for American commitments to ensure the safety of American food and goods. During the summer of 2007, China proposed extensive new import inspections for American-made medical equipment such as patient monitors and surgical implants, but did not impose the same rules on domestic rivals.[25] These trade issues between the U.S. and China produced a wave of negative

18. Edelman. "2009 Edelman Trust Barometer." *Edelman.com*. 01 May 2009
    <http://www.edelman.com/trust/2009/docs/Trust_Book_Final_2.pdf >.

19. Edelman. "2008 Edelman Trust Barometer." *Edelman.com*. 01 May 2009
    <http://www.edelman.com/TRUST/2008/TrustBarometer08_FINAL.pdf>.

20. Edelman. "2009 Edelman Trust Barometer." <http://www.edelman.com/trust/2009/docs/Trust_Book_Final_pages.pdf>.

21. "Chinese American" *Wikipedia, The Free Encyclopedia*. 01 May 2009. Wikimedia Foundation, Inc.
    <http://en.wikipedia.org/wiki/Chinese_American>.

22. Global Advertising Strategies. <http://www.ethnicusa.com/en/market_data/research_prod/index.php?id4=452>.

23. Story, Louise, and David Barboza. "Mattel Recalls 19 Million Toys Sent From China." *Nytimes.com* 15 Aug. 2007. 01 May 2009
    <http://www.nytimes.com/2007/08/15/business/worldbusiness/15imports.html?_r=1>.

24. Weisman, Steven. "China Resisting Pressure on Product Safety." *Nytimes.com* 06 Dec. 2007. 01 May 2009
    <http://www.nytimes.com/2007/12/06/world/asia/06cnd-trade.html>.

25. Weisman, Steven. "China Resisting Pressure on Product Safety."

media coverage (both print and television) on China and Chinese-made products.

China's Foreign Ministry Demands an Apology

Following CNN's statement on April 16, 2008, the Chinese government responded to CNN's handling of the issue. Senior Foreign Ministry spokesman Liu Jianchao summoned Jaime FlorCruz, CNN's bureau chief in Beijing, to the ministry to voice its disapproval. Specifically, the spokesman told FlorCruz that the ministry did not view CNN's statement about Cafferty's comments as an apology, and that CNN had not done enough to ease its concerns over Mr. Cafferty's behavior.[26] With increasing criticism and the intervention of the Chinese government, Cafferty's comments were elevated to international headlines. How should CNN respond to the Chinese Foreign Ministry and, more importantly, how should CNN respond to its viewers?

Timeline of Events

April 9, 2008 Wednesday	Jack Cafferty, during the broadcast of CNN's The Situation Room, is asked to comment on the United States' relationship with China. Cafferty responds: "I think they're basically the same bunch of goons and thugs they've been for the last 50 years."[27] The remark sparks a firestorm of criticism among the Chinese American community.
April 14, 2008 Monday	Jack Cafferty clarifies his remarks: "Last week, during a discussion of the controversy surrounding China's hosting of the Olympic Games, I said that the Chinese are basically the same bunch of goons and thugs they have been for the last 50 years. I was referring to the Chinese government, and not to Chinese people or to Chinese-Americans."[12]
April 15, 2008 Tuesday	At its weekly news conference, the Chinese Foreign Ministry demands an apology from CNN saying Cafferty's comments reflect his "ignorance and hostility toward China." By the afternoon, nearly 45,000 people sign an online petition condemning his statements as "racist" and "despicable."[13] The petition demands that CNN discipline Cafferty and apologize to the Chinese people.
April 16, 2008 Wednesday	China's Ministry of Information department summons CNN's bureau chief in Beijing to deliver a near identical protest. CNN issues a statement saying that Mr. Cafferty's comments represent his "strongly held" opinion of the Chinese government, not the Chinese people. The network adds, "It was not Mr. Cafferty's nor CNN's intent to cause offense to the Chinese people," and says CNN "would apologize to anyone who has interpreted the comments in this way."[28]
April 17, 2008 Thursday	Tech-oriented web sites in Asia report calls from hacker groups in China for denial-of-service attacks to be launched against the CNN web site over the network's coverage of unrest in Tibet and Cafferty's comments.
April 19, 2008 Saturday	Thousands of Chinese Americans gather to protest in Los Angeles outside of CNN studios on Sunset Boulevard.
April 24, 2008 Thursday	In New York, beautician Liang Shubing and teacher Li Lilan file a lawsuit against Cafferty and CNN, seeking $1.3 billion in damages for "violating the dignity and reputation of the Chinese people."[16]
April 26, 2008 Saturday	Hundreds protest in front of CNN headquarters in Atlanta, Georgia. An estimated 5,000 Chinese Americans gather in San Francisco to protest Jack Cafferty's controversial remarks.

26. Drew, Jill. "China Spurns Apology, Keeps Pressure on CNN." *Washingtonpost.com* 18 Apr. 2008. 01 May 2009 <*http://www.washingtonpost.com/wp-dyn/content/article/2008/04/17/AR2008041701599.html*>.

27. CNN. "Transcripts." *CNN.com*. 09 Apr. 2008. 01 May 2009 <*http://transcripts.cnn.com/TRANSCRIPTS/0804/09/sitroom.03.html*>.

28. Thomson Reuters. "CNN tells China it didn't mean to cause offence." *Reuters.com*. 16 Apr. 2008. 01 May 2009 <*http://www.reuters.com/article/entertainmentNews/idUSPEK25277120080416*>.

Discussion Questions

1. What are the critical issues in this case and who are the stakeholders?
2. To what extent did CNN's role as a news company hinder its ability to deal with the issue effectively?
3. How could CNN better support their mission to be "The Most Trusted Name in News?"
4. To what extent should a news company stand behind the opinions of its journalists?
5. What long-term implications will this event have on CNN's worldwide reputation and future business?

Appendix A

CNN Statement on Tibet Coverage

(CNN) — CNN has been singled out for criticism for our coverage of events in Tibet through an anti-CNN.com Web site and elsewhere. We have provided comprehensive coverage of all sides of this story, but two specific allegations relate to pro-Tibetan bias. We would like to take this chance to respond to them:

Allegation 1: CNN intentionally cropped an image in order to remove Tibetan protesters throwing stones at Chinese trucks.

CNN refutes all allegations by bloggers that it distorts its coverage of the events in Tibet to portray either side in a more favorable light. We have consistently and repeatedly shown all sides of this story. The one image in question was used wholly appropriately in the specific editorial context and there could be no confusion regarding what it was showing, not least because it was captioned: "Tibetans throw stones at army vehicles on a street in the capital Lhasa." The picture gallery included in Tibet stories includes the image.

We have also published images showing violence by Tibetans against the Chinese. A March 18 story shows Tibetan youths attacking a Chinese man.

Additionally, we have published video from the Chinese media apparently showing Tibetans attacking Chinese interests in Lhasa.

Allegation 2: CNN referred to Tibet as a "country."

CNN's policy is to refer to Tibet as "Tibet Autonomous Region of China." In our dozens of stories on the topic to date, we are aware of only two instances where it was incorrectly referenced as a country.

CNN's reputation is based on reporting global news accurately and impartially, while our coverage through the use of words, images or video always reflects a wide range of opinions and points of view on every story.

Source: *CNN.com*. 28 Mar. 2008.
< *http://www.cnn.com/2008/US/03/28/tibet.statement/>*.

© Savol_67 / bigstockphoto.com

Chapter 4

Step Two: Analyze the Audience

The Case of Speedy Travel Inc.

Sheila Markham let out a long sigh as she sat looking at her computer screen. She had been hired four months ago by Speedy Travel, whose key target market was college students, to increase its sales. Her investigation of the company and its competitors led her to the conclusion that the small full-service firm needed to update its distribution methods and change its product offerings to better suit the desires of its customers. Although most of Speedy Travel's traditional market had been students from the local college, it had failed to transition to a solid Internet presence, where most young people made their travel arrangements. Its "product line" consisted primarily of package tours, whereas young people tend to prefer making their own travel arrangements. Worse yet, it seemed that the company had adopted a "bad" business model since it relied almost solely on new customers, a new student population, rather than building repeat business. This made the challenge of marketing and sales even more difficult. Another market that was being missed was the growing diversity of the student population attending the nearby university, which had the highest international student population of any in the country.

Speedy Travel was family-owned and had been since its start thirty-five years ago. At that time, the company's business model had made it a success, but with little change since then, the agency was struggling. Sheila had spent enough time with management to know that its members believed the problem wasn't the business but was with the customer.

Somehow, though, she needed to find a way to persuade management to adopt her suggested changes, regardless of the anticipated resistance she believed her message would receive.

After reading this chapter, you will be able to

- *Use a variety of frameworks to analyze business audiences to identify their values, preferences, interests, attitudes, and concerns.*

- *Discuss general types of business audiences and their needs.*

- *Describe the differences between messages that focus on the audience's needs and expectations and those that are conveyed from the writer's or speaker's perspective.*

Case Questions

1. What are the interests of Sheila's audience, Speedy's management team? What are its concerns? What objections might it have to Sheila's proposal?
2. How might Sheila best address her audience's concerns and objections? To what shared interests might she appeal in her message?
3. Would the way the message is structured make a difference in terms of its success? If so, what issue(s) should Sheila address first? Second? Third? Why?
4. What sales message might Sheila provide in terms of identifying the benefits of a new marketing strategy?

Analyze the Audience

On its face, audience analysis may appear to be a simple task. But think about it: To truly see the world from another's perspective would require that one have the ability to leave one's own body and mind behind for a time and occupy those of another. Does that seem like a practical exercise? If not, then what tools are available for us to understand another person and how he or she sees and experiences the world? This chapter will present various methods for thinking about the audience so as to help you get a better sense of its concerns, needs, knowledge, and questions.

Understanding how others both differ from and are similar to us are necessary skills for effective communication. To be persuasive, for example, we often need to know the common goals that we and our audience share in order to positively frame or begin a discussion. But differences are also important; recognition of differences may be the first step in "getting out of our bodies" so that we might imagine what it might be like to be another person. This can be a challenging activity if we have limited life experience or lack the ability to empathize with others. It can be potentially even more challenging in an individualist culture such as the United States, where we tend to privilege self-interest and are thus primarily focused on ourselves and our own needs, particularly in a competitive workplace. As Chapter 2 discussed, other factors, such the tendency to assume others have the same norms and values as ourselves, what is called *projected cognitive similarity*, or the tendency to think members of other groups are all the same—the *outgroup homogeneity effect*—make it more challenging to understand others, particularly if we are unaware of these tendencies. Some people have an advantage in their ability to see the world through others' eyes. Those who are not in a privileged position in society often are provided the perspective of those with power through media, schools, and other institutions. They also must operate in the world of those who have more power and privilege, so they have a greater opportunity to understand how that world works. "Border" persons, or those who must navigate two or more cultures, may have more insight into others' differences because they must be able to live in and navigate differing realities or worldviews. On the other hand, those who have privilege may have a greater challenge in recognizing how others differ because that privilege—and potential difference—is often invisible to them and taken for granted.

Learning how to see through another's eyes—to *empathize*—can be a difficult yet important skill in communicating successfully with others in the workplace as well as in our personal lives. Without the ability to empathize with others and understand their views and feelings, we are unable to successfully enact a dialogic model of communication.

When you are crafting important business messages or messages to new audiences, you should analyze your audience. Such an analysis is the basis for deciding the appropriate channel or medium to use, the content of the message, the organization, and the tone and style. This analysis might also help to determine whether a message should even be sent or, if so, when to do so. Therefore, analysis is critical for successful communication. As this discussion attempts to reveal, analyzing audiences can be particularly challenging, so this chapter provides a variety of lenses to apply to identify your audience's interests and concerns.

To learn more about others, we can converse with those who are different from ourselves and ask such simple questions as "What do you care about?" and perhaps, more tellingly, "What are your fears?" We can also spend time in other cultures—even those that exist in our own country, state, and city—proactively learning how they differ from our own (Please review the elements of Global Communication Competence presented in Chapter 2). Learning the different experiences and perspectives of those with different demographic characteristics can be as simple as having an openness and interest in learning more about those in our immediate circle. This chapter discusses the following lenses through which you might gain a better understanding of your audience:

- The audience's demographics, including age, ethnicity, socioeconomic status, and education level. Special attention is given to generational differences, culture, and personality types.

- Its knowledge of your company, product, service, or the situation; its interests in and attitudes about the topic of your message; and its concerns, reservations, or questions about the topic of your message.
- Types of business audiences.

Your audience's preferences and interests should always guide the decisions you make as a strategic communicator. The most successful messages construct win–win situations for both you and your audience. That's because such messages generally ensure quicker agreement and better relationships. Therefore, it is of critical importance to spend time analyzing your audience in order to achieve this goal.

Audience Demographics

If you have taken marketing courses, then the term **demographics** is probably a familiar one. Demographics are the statistical data about a particular population, including its age, gender, ethnicity, income, education level, and so on. Marketing and business communication have a great deal in common because both fields are generally concerned with sales or persuasion. Just as you should consider a potential market's characteristics before you can go about creating a successful marketing plan or campaign, you should also consider a potential audience's characteristics before creating a message to ensure the best chance of success.

demographics

The statistical data about a particular population, including its age, income, education level, and so on.

For example, if you are marketing home-health products to seniors, then you would consider the preferences of older people regarding advertising media, product distribution, and pricing. In the selection of an advertising medium, for instance, you would be more likely to select the local newspaper for a senior market than for a product aimed at young adults. Older people are more likely to read the local newspaper than teenagers and college students.

When crafting messages intended for an older audience, you would probably create messages with a more formal tone and avoid the use of slang words that may not be familiar to its members. When considering visual presentation of a written message intended for older people, you might select larger font sizes to make the message more readable and include illustrations of older people so they can more easily identify with the message you are sending.

We should also consider our audience's ability to identify with the content of our messages. As mentioned above, it is easier for people to identify with messages that contain images of people like themselves. Likewise, using examples and anecdotes that are easier for your specific audience to identify with or relate to can help make your communication more effective. If you are writing messages aimed at persuading a female audience to purchase your company's automobile, for example, you would probably focus on the vehicle's reliability and safety. In contrast, if your audience is male, then you might instead focus on the vehicle's performance as an attractive feature. Rural audiences or persons employed in the construction trades might simply prefer a different model—a pickup truck—as compared with the sedan or the sports utility vehicle that is marketed to suburbanites.

Your ability to provide the appropriate amount of information for your particular audience can affect your ability to fulfill your intended communication purposes, the first element of communication strategy discussed in Chapter 3, "Step One: Identify the Purposes of Communication." If you don't provide sufficient or relevant information aimed at meeting your audience's specific needs, then you will be less able to fulfill your purposes of informing, persuading, conveying goodwill, and establishing your credibility. For these reasons, the elements of communication strategy are interdependent, meaning they depend on each other for the success of your messages.

? Critical Thinking

Identify an audience, an individual or group with whom you find it difficult to communicate. Describe the audience. What are its demographic features? What are its needs in the particular context in which you communicate with it? Concerns? Expectations? How might taking these elements into consideration help you to communicate with this audience more successfully?

Generational Differences

Generational differences fall under the category of *demographics*, but because they have been the focus of much research and writing recently, a separate discussion has been devoted to them here. Generational differences have become of particular interest to organizations because it has been shown that problems formerly associated with employee loyalty and work ethics can be ascribed to generational differences. Sixty-five percent of respondents say that generational gaps make it difficult to get things done in an organization; problems that include lack of communication, differences in values, and tension between change and stability.[1] Thus, understanding generational differences can be particularly helpful to those already in or aspiring to be in leadership positions.

There are four generations that may be found in today's workplace: traditionalists, or those born before 1946; baby boomers, or those born between 1946 and 1964; Gen Xers, those born between 1965 and 1981; and millennials, those born after 1982.

- **Traditionalists.** Forged by war and depression, this generation honors hard work, respects leaders, and maintains loyalty to institutions. In return, its members expect to receive a job for life. Weaned on deprivation and duty, they prefer to save their money and defer gratification and rewards until retirement.

- **Baby boomers.** Boomers have had to compete with their generational colleagues for limited openings all the way up the hierarchy. They have learned political skills and how to read their bosses. And yet they have been called the "me" generation because their parents spoiled them and, from the beginning of the television age, advertisers have catered to them. Basically optimists, they have taken to heart a message from their parents and from various cultural icons of the 1960s: Make the world a better place.

- **Generation Xers (or nexters).** These are the so-called latchkey kids, fending for themselves after school and the first to experience—in great numbers—divorcing parents and one-parent families. They have learned to be resourceful and independent. Most have created surrogate "families" through networks of close, reliable friends. Having seen mergers and downsizing devastate people they care about over the years, they tend not to trust companies or the individuals who manage them.

- **Millennials (or Generation Y).** The front end of this cohort has just recently started entering the full-time workforce. "Techno-savvy"—they have always known computers—they arrive at the workplace fully expecting to have input in all decisions affecting their work because they were often the center of attention in their families. Millennials grew up immersed in diversity at school, on TV, and via the World Wide Web, so they accept working with many cultures, races, and lifestyles. Because of the structure in their families, they also expect structure in the workplace.

Understanding these generational differences can help the strategic communicator identify the values and expectations of a particular audience and formulate messages that take those values into account.

Culture

If we assume that others have the same experiences, beliefs, and values as ourselves, then we suffer from what is called **ethnocentrism**. Ethnocentrism is the belief that our own cultural background, including ways of analyzing problems, values, beliefs, language, and verbal and nonverbal communication, is correct. This belief can lead to an ignorance about and insensitivity to others that, as has been discussed, can negatively affect our ability to communicate with others.

Culture has an important effect on communication. **Culture** is defined as the learned beliefs, values, rules, norms, symbols, and traditions that are common to a group of people. It is a way of life, customs, and script for a group of people.[2]

In the United States, the study of culture began in earnest in the 1960s with research on ethnic and racial identities and has since expanded to look at differences among people of different countries, societies, and regional groups. In the past few decades, many studies have focused on identifying and classifying the basic values of different cultures. Each has produced greater understanding of cultural differences, but each also has its limitations and critics. However, understanding these concepts can provide us some insight into cultural differences and how they may affect our communication effectiveness.

ethnocentrism

The belief that your own cultural background—including its ways of analyzing problems, values, beliefs, language, and verbal and nonverbal communication—is correct and that other cultures are somehow inferior.

culture

The learned beliefs, values, rules, norms, symbols, and traditions that are common to a group of people.

The GLOBE Studies

The GLOBE (Global Leadership and Organizational Behavior Effectiveness) research program has involved more than 160 investigators who have used quantitative methods to study the responses of 17,000 managers in more than 950 organizations representing 62 different cultures. The researchers divided the data from the sixty-two countries into ten regional clusters and identified nine cultural dimensions: uncertainty avoidance, power distance, institutional collectivism, in-group collectivism, gender egalitarianism, assertiveness, future orientation, performance orientation, and humane orientation.[3]

- **Uncertainty avoidance.** This dimension refers to the extent to which a cultural group relies on established social norms, rituals, and procedures to avoid uncertainty.
- **Power distance.** This dimension refers to the degree to which members of a cultural group expect and agree that power should be shared unequally.
- **Institutional collectivism.** This dimension describes the degree to which a cultural group encourages institutional or societal collective action. It is concerned with whether cultures identify with broader societal interests rather than with individual goals.
- **In-group collectivism.** This dimension refers to the degree to which people express pride, loyalty, and cohesiveness in their groups or families.
- **Gender egalitarianism.** This dimension measures the degree to which a cultural group minimizes gender role differences and promotes gender equality.
- **Assertiveness.** This dimension refers to the degree to which people in a culture are determined, assertive, confrontational, and aggressive in their social relationships.
- **Future orientation.** This concept refers to the extent to which people engage in future-oriented behaviors such as planning, investing, and delaying gratification.
- **Performance orientation.** This dimension describes the extent to which a cultural group encourages and rewards its members for improved performance and excellence.
- **Humane orientation.** This dimension refers to the degree to which a culture encourages and rewards people for being fair, altruistic, generous, and caring to others.

The United States falls into the Anglo cluster, which also includes Canada, Australia, Ireland, England, South African whites, and New Zealand. These countries are high in performance orientation and low in in-group collectivism. This means that people in these countries tend to be competitive, results-oriented, and less attached to their families and other groups as those in other countries. The other nine regional clusters identified by the GLOBE studies are Confucian Asia, Eastern Europe, Germanic Europe, Latin America, Latin Europe, Middle East, Nordic Europe, Southern Asia, and Sub-Saharan Africa. Table 4-1 provides a classification of the cultural clusters with regard to how they scored on each cultural dimension.

Table 4-1 Cultural Clusters Classified on Cultural Dimensions

Cultural Dimension	High-Score Clusters	Low-Score Clusters
Assertiveness Orientation	Eastern Europe Germanic Europe	Nordic Europe
Future Orientation	Germanic Europe Nordic Europe	Eastern Europe Latin America Middle East
Gender Egalitarianism	Eastern Europe Nordic Europe	Middle East
Humane Orientation	Southern Asia Sub-Saharan Africa	Germanic Europe Latin Europe
In-group Collectivism	Confucian Asia Eastern Europe Latin America Middle East Southern Asia	Anglo Germanic Europe Nordic Europe
Institutional Collectivism	Nordic Europe Confucian Asia Latin Europe	Germanic Europe Latin America
Performance Orientation	Anglo Confucian Asia Germanic Europe	Eastern Europe Latin America
Power Distance	No clusters	Nordic Europe
Uncertainty Avoidance	Germanic Europe Nordic Europe	Eastern Europe Latin America Middle East

Source: Adapted from House, R. J., Hanges, P. J., Javidan, M., Dorfman, P. W., & Gupta, V. (Eds.). 2004. *Culture, Leadership, and Organizations: The GLOBE Study of 62 Societies* (Newbury Park, CA: Sage Publications).

Although the GLOBE study has generated a great deal of data from many sources, it has received some criticisms. It does not provide a clear set of assumptions or propositions that form a single theory about the way that culture relates to leadership. It also measures a broad variety of characteristics that are difficult to identify as a set of universal attributes in isolation from the context in which they occur.

Hofstede's Cultural Dimensions

Perhaps the most referenced study of culture is the research of Geert Hofstede. Hofstede analyzed questionnaires obtained from more than 100,000 respondents in more than 50 countries and identified five major dimensions on which cultures differ: power distance, uncertainty avoidance, individualism–collectivism, masculinity–femininity, and long-term versus short-term orientation.[4] (The more recent GLOBE study identified similar dimensions but developed additional cultural categories.)

- **Power distance.** The extent to which less powerful people expect and accept the fact that power is unequal. People in Malaysia, Panama, Guatemala, the Philippines, and Mexico are most accepting of power distance, while Austrians, Israelis, Danes, New Zealanders, and the Irish are the least accepting. The United States also was shown to have greater equality among different societal levels.

- **Individualism versus collectivism.** In **individualistic culture,** the autonomy of the individual is of paramount importance, whereas commitment to the group is most important in **collectivist culture.** The individualism–collectivism continuum is thought by some scholars to be the most important dimension that distinguishes one culture from another.[5]

  The United States ranks number one in individualism. Venezuela is the most collectivist of countries, with Mexico, Thailand, Singapore, and Japan also ranking on the collectivist side of the continuum.[6] Approximately 70 percent of the world's population lives in collectivist cultures.[7] Table 4-2 summarizes the characteristics of individualistic and collectivist cultures.

individualistic culture

A culture with an "I" focus in which competition, not cooperation, is encouraged and individual initiative and achievement are highly valued.

collectivist culture

A culture in which cooperation rather than competition is encouraged and in which individual goals are sacrificed for the good of the group.

Table 4-2 Characteristics of Individualist versus Collectivist Cultures

Individualistic Cultures	Collectivist Cultures
■ Value individual freedom; place "I" before "we."	■ Value the group over the individual; place "we" before "I."
■ Value independence.	■ Value commitment to family, tribe, and clan.
■ Value competition over cooperation.	■ Value cooperation over competition.
■ Value telling the truth over sparing feelings.	■ Value "saving face" by not causing embarrassment.
Examples: United States, Australia, Great Britain, Canada, Netherlands	Examples: Venezuela, Pakistan, Peru, Taiwan, Thailand

- **Masculinity versus femininity.** In this dimension, masculinity indicates distinct gender-based roles in the culture, whereas a feminine culture implies blurring between the roles of men and women. Consequently, Middle Eastern cultures are masculine while Scandinavian countries are feminine. The United States also ranks fairly high in masculinity.

- **Avoidance of uncertainty.** This dimension has to do with a cultural group's tolerance for uncertainty and ambiguity. The United States has a relatively low avoidance of uncertainty.

- **Long-term versus short-term orientation.** Values associated with long-term orientation are thrift and perseverance; values associated with short-term orientation are respect for tradition, fulfilling social obligations, and protecting one's "face." The United States falls within the long-term orientation.

Because of the saliency of the individualist–collectivist distinction, two additional concepts related to this distinction have been developed. These are low- versus high-context cultures and face negotiation theory.

Low-versus High-Context Cultures Anthropologist Edward T. Hall gave us another way to look at cultural difference in terms of high and low context. Individualist and collectivist cultures emphasize different kinds of communication. People in collectivist cultures pay a great deal of attention to the context of the communication rather than the explicit, transmitted code or words. For example, in Japan, Korea, China, and Arab and Latin American countries, a good deal of time is spent in relationship building—formal communication and getting acquainted—before business takes place and intentions are stated. Table 4-3 shows examples of low- versus high-context cultural characteristics.

In contrast, low-context cultures pay more attention to the explicit code or words than to the context. In the United States, Switzerland, Germany, and Scandinavian countries, people get to the point and clearly state what they want.

These cultural differences also can affect how people perceive verbal and nonverbal cues. Those in low-context, individualistic cultures tend to pay more attention to verbal skills, whereas those from high-context, collectivist cultures tend to pay more attention to nonverbal skills.

Table 4-3 Characteristics of Low- and High-Context Cultures

Low-Context	High-Context
Northern Europe, North America	**Japan, Saudi Arabia, Mediterranean Europe, Latin America**
■ Less formality	■ Very formal
■ Direct, explicit communication	■ Indirect, implicit communication
■ Getting right to business	■ Building a relationship and trust before conducting business
■ Needing larger personal space	■ Being comfortable with little personal space (Latin America, Saudi Arabia)

Regional cultures within the United States also display these differences. For example, African American cultures tend to be more collectivist and high context than do those of whites of European descent, and working-class people tend to be more collectivist and high context than white-collar professionals.

A strategic communicator isn't limited by his or her cultural predilections, however. Instead, he or she learns to pay attention to both verbal and nonverbal skills, as well as the context in which communication takes place, because these all provide vital information about differing situations and the people involved in them.

Face Negotiation Theory Face negotiation theory is a theory first postulated by Stella Ting-Toomey in 1985 to explain how different cultures manage conflict and communicate. The theory has gone through multiple iterations since that time and was updated most recently in 2005. In essence, the theory explains that the root of conflict is based on identity management on an individual and cultural level. The various facets of individual and cultural identities are described as *faces*. **Faces** are the public images of an individual or group that the society sees and evaluates based on cultural norms and values. Conflict occurs when a group or individual's face is threatened. This can occur in two directions: embarrassing another can make individuals of certain cultures uncomfortable since this entails a potential act of impoliteness. Conversely, saving one's own face, or avoiding embarrassing one's self, can also be a concern.

faces

The public image of individuals, or groups, that their society sees and evaluates based on cultural norms and values.

Many different strategies and factors affect how cultures manage identity. Ting-Toomey argues that the face of the group in collectivist cultures is more important than the face of any individual in that group. In individualist cultures, the face of the individual is more important than the face of the group. Furthermore, there are small and large power distances associated with each culture. A small-power-distance culture believes that authority is earned, power is distributed equally, and everyone's opinion matters. The individual is highly valued, as in the United States, for example. In large-power-distance cultures, authority is inherited, power is from top to bottom, and the boss is infallible. The good of the group is valued.

? Critical Thinking

Identify an audience from a different culture than your own. What cultural differences might affect the content of or your approach to a message intended for that audience?

Gender

Gender is a social construction in that based on our biological sex, we are typically taught to conform to certain gender stereotypes as we grow up. For example, males are often taught to avoid crying and certain other emotional displays, although shows of anger may be considered appropriate. They may be taught that men are tough, strong, and competitive. As such, they are often discouraged from playing with dolls, wearing pink clothing and makeup, and pursuing certain occupations, such as nursing, teaching, and social work.

Girls are often socialized to be just the opposite: soft, caring, and collaborative. In fact, some say that men and women live in different worlds; experiencing their own culture or social reality. To the extent that this is the case, it is important to recognize these differences and how they extend to ways of communicating. Table 4-4 below illustrates some of the common communication styles associated with each gender in terms of their culturally defined weaknesses and strengths.

Table 4-4 Strengths and Weaknesses of Gendered Communication

Gender	Communication Strengths	Communication Weaknesses
Feminine	■ Ability to read body language and pick up nonverbal cues. ■ Good listening skills. ■ Effective display of empathy.	■ Overly emotional. ■ Meandering – won't get to the point. ■ Not authoritative.
Masculine	■ Commanding physical presence. ■ Direct and to-the-point interactions. ■ Effective display of power.	■ Overly blunt and direct. ■ Insensitive to audience reactions. ■ Too confident in own opinion.

Source: Goman, C. K. (2016, May). Is your communication style dictated by your gender? *Forbes Magazine.* Retrieved June 7, 2017 from *https://www.forbes.com/sites/carolkinseygoman/2016/03/31/is-your-communication-style-dictated-by-your-gender/#4c35301aeb9d.*

Because of these gendered expectations, people in the workplace are continuously—and often unconsciously—assessing your communication style for two sets of qualities: warmth (empathy, likeability, caring) and authority (power, credibility, status).[8] This can introduce challenges for those who do not strictly adhere to these gendered stereotypes. A particular challenge is presented to women who wish to be considered as leaders, since the male communication style is generally associated with our cultural ideals about leadership. This challenge is called "the double bind," which means that if women use a feminine communication style, they may be considered too weak to be a leader but if they use a masculine style, they are considered too aggressive. Thus, they are often placed in a no-win situation.

Responsible Communication

Language can be used to exclude, denigrate, and discriminate against others. Language can also be used in more subtle ways that ignore or minimize the contributions of one sex in society. Such language use can be considered sexist and should be avoided in the professional workplace.

The following are specific guidelines for avoiding sexist language use:

1. Replace *man* or *men* as words or in expressions. For example, instead of *man* use *human being*, *person*, or *individual*.

2. Use gender-neutral terms when possible to designate occupations, positions, and roles. For example, instead of *businessman* use *business owner*, *manager*, *executive*, *retailer*, and so on.

3. Refer to members of both sexes by parallel terms, names, or titles. For example, instead of *man* and *wife*, use *husband* and *wife*. Rather than using *men* and *ladies*, use *men* and *women*.

4. Avoid the third-person singular masculine when referring to an individual who could be of either sex. Instead of saying, "When a manager holds a meeting, he ...," use the plural form of the pronoun when speaking generally, or the name of the person and the appropriate pronoun when communicating specifically. For example, "When managers hold meetings, they ..." or "When our manager, Ms. Johns, holds a meeting, she ..."

5. Avoid language that disparages, stereotypes, or patronizes either sex. Avoid referring to adult females as *girls* or unmarried women as *spinsters* or *old maids*, for example. In addition, you should avoid terms such as *womanly*, *manly*, *feminine*, or *masculine* in ways that stereotypically associate certain traits with one sex or another.

6. Become aware that some individuals do not identify with either sex or dominant gender and prefer the use of gender neutral terms and titles. The best way to deal with this situation is simply to ask the person what is preferred.

Interestingly, a recent study by the Ketchum Leadership Communication Monitor, shows that women perform better on almost every leadership attribute; still, most people—54 percent—look to men to better navigate the uncertainty of our times. See Figure 4-1 below.

Figure 4-1 Leadership Attributes by Gender

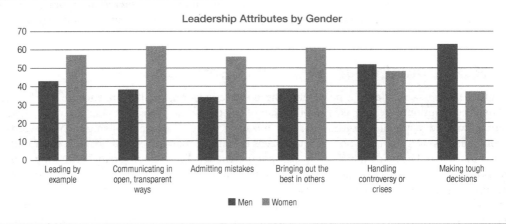

Source: Ketchum Leadership Communication Monitor (2014). Retrieved June 6, 2017 from *https://www.ketchum.com/leadership-communication-monitor-2014.*

As the Ketchum study indicates, a feminine style of communication is preferred in collaborative environments where listening skills, inclusive body language, and empathy are more highly valued, while a masculine style fits better where people are expected to take charge. Men are also judged to be better at monologue, women at dialogue.[9]

Not only are speaking styles different between the genders, so are nonverbal cues. Women generally display more "warm" body language cues. They are more likely to focus on those who are speaking by orienting head and torso to face participants. They lean forward, smile, synchronize their movements with others, nod and tilt their heads.[10]

Men send more "status" signals through an array of dominant behaviors, such as side-to-side head shaking, anger and disgust expressions. They stand tall or they sprawl, sitting with their legs spread or widely crossed, their materials spread out on a conference table, and their arms stretched out on the back of a chair.[11]

In all cases, a communication style turns into a weakness when overdone or used in the wrong context. A female's collaborative approach can come across as submissive and a male's directness can be taken as callousness. Men come across as too aggressive when their expansive postures infringe on other people's personal space, when they have a "death grip" handshake, and when they emphasize status cues to the point where they look haughty and uncaring. Women are viewed as weak or passive when they are unnecessarily apologetic, when they smile excessively or inappropriately, and when they discount their own ideas and achievements.[12] Differing organizational cultures also exhibit preferences for certain styles of communication. This issue will be discussed in more detail in Chapter 5.

Dealing with these differences in the workplace can be challenging. For example, since men tend to prefer giving advice rather than listening for empathy, the listener should clarify the speaker's desires: "Do you want me to listen or give you advice?" is the appropriate question to ask in this case.

In decision-making situations, you should express your intent clearly. Do you want to seek consensus or gather input regarding a decision that you will make?

Likewise, in conflict situations, men tend to argue more and find it interesting to disagree, while women more often seek agreement and see disagreement as more threatening to relationships. To better deal with these differing expectations, it is important to recognize the value of conflict and allow yourself and others to take a strong position. Reframing the conflict as an opportunity and staying away from personal attacks and blaming can make disagreements more comfortable.

Professional Jargon and Plain Language Use

Another issue to consider is a person's background, education, or specialization. It has become somewhat commonplace to make fun of the jargon used in some professions that assume everyone has the same educational background or specialization. Search the Internet using such keywords as "worst business jargon," and you will find dozens of phrases that are termed obscure, meaningless, and otherwise to be avoided, including "core competencies," "low-hanging fruit," "thinking outside the box," etc. Such terms are often simply considered annoying because of their overuse, but other terminology use, often by specific industries, can simply be meaningless to outsiders. Settings that have received common criticism for obscure or meaningless language use are the government, science, law, and investment banking. (Please see Figure 4-2 for examples of field specific jargon use.) In other words, without specialized education or knowledge of these fields, it can be challenging to understand what is being communicated.

Figure 4-2 Examples of Field-Specific Jargon Use

Investment Banking	"In our balanced portfolios, over half of our fixed-income exposure is in non-core bond funds, including actively managed unconstrained/absolute-return-oriented, flexible multi-sector, and global bond funds. These positions benefited greatly from rising interest rates and added significant value, when compared to core bonds. Gains were in the 5% to 10% range versus 2.5% for the core bond index. Looking ahead to 2017, we think these strategies should again meaningfully outperform core bonds, although 2016's returns will likely not repeat."
BioTech	"How did those IQs go on that new bioreactor? Jake told me that the DCS has to go through final tweaking before they can do the PQs. To make it worse, the FDA is in here this week, and our department is still trying to recover from the last two 483s—I'm on my way to sort through the resulting stack of batch records right now. I don't know when I'll manage to get to that work on the CMC section for the new BLA. ..."
Law	"I am herewith returning the stipulation to dismiss in the above entitled matter; the same being duly executed by me."

To deal with this problem, the federal government has mandated the use of **plain language** by its employees. Plain language (also called Plain English) is communication your audience can understand the first time it reads or hears it. Language that is clear in meaning to one set of readers may not be to others, so it is very important to analyze your audience to ensure its understanding of your message. Common writing techniques that can help you achieve this goal are the use of:

plain language
Communication your audience can understand the first time they read or hear it.

- Logical organization with the reader in mind.
- "You" and other pronouns.
- Active voice.
- Short sentences.
- Common, everyday words.
- Easy-to-read design features.

Audience Knowledge, Interests, Attitudes, and Concerns

A macro-level analysis of an audience's demographic features can provide valuable insights into its values and beliefs. This knowledge may help us decide the best way for communication to occur as well as determine message content, organization, tone, and style. A micro-level audience analysis can be helpful in providing us even more specific guidance regarding the content of our messages. Such micro-level analysis includes a questioning of our audience's knowledge about our topic, as well as its interests, attitudes, and concerns.

Knowledge

Your audience's knowledge about the topic of your message should be considered before crafting it. For example, if you are communicating to your coworkers about a product on which all of you have been working for the past six months, it is probably safe to use acronyms related to the product and your company because you can assume that your audience is knowledgeable about the meanings of those abbreviations. However, if you are crafting messages for new customers, then you should avoid the use of acronyms because they are probably not familiar with their meaning. If you ignore this fact, your message will probably not be as successful in clearly communicating the information you intended.

Likewise, when communicating with audiences who lack knowledge of a product, service, or situation, you should provide more explanation or information. One common characteristic of inexperienced business communicators is that they are often unable to recognize the difference between their knowledge of a particular topic and that of their audience.

As stated earlier, your ability to provide the appropriate amount of information for your particular audience can affect your ability to fulfill your intended communication purposes. Without adequate or relevant information aimed at meeting your audience's needs and expectations, you are less likely to fulfill your purposes of informing, persuading, conveying goodwill, and establishing credibility.

Interests and Attitudes

As discussed in the earlier section "Audience Demographics," providing information that your audience is interested in and can relate to is one of the strategies of successful business communication. In an oral presentation, for instance, if you focus on information that does not address your audience's interests, then you are likely to lose its attention and fail at your communication purpose. The examples and content you provide in an oral presentation aimed at college students should differ significantly from those you might use in a presentation delivered to college administrators, even if the purposes are similar (for example, to persuade, inform, establish credibility, or convey goodwill).

Likewise, it is important to consider the attitudes of your audience toward the topic of your message in formulating a successful communication strategy. If your audience is reluctant to agree with the content of your message or the position you present, then give some thought to how to present your message in a way that might overcome this reluctance.

common ground

The interests, goals, and commonalities of belief that the communicator shares with the audience.

One tactic is to think about the beliefs, values, or goals that you and your audience have in common. If you can begin your message by establishing agreement that you and your audience share the same interests or goals, then you are showing that you and your audience share some commonalities of belief that should reduce resistance to the content and purpose of the remainder of your message. This tactic, which is referred to as establishing **common ground**, is generally effective in situations where your purposes include persuading and conveying goodwill. Another useful tactic is to focus your message on the benefits to your audience. Doing so will likely ensure a positive reception for your message. Again, this tactic is often used when your purposes are to persuade and convey goodwill.

Concerns and Questions

You are unlikely to be successful in attempts to persuade and convey goodwill if you do not effectively address your audience's concerns and questions. What is more frustrating than receiving a message that leaves you with many of your questions unanswered or your concerns completely ignored? Such lapses in communication can negatively affect the relationship the communicator has with his or her audience, as well as his or her credibility. Such lapses can also negatively affect morale and productivity, both of which may affect a company's bottom line.

In oral presentations, this situation can create problems for the presenter, particularly if he or she is attempting to persuade or influence. In an ideal situation, the presentation would accomplish that goal. However, if presenters are not attentive to the questions, concerns, and objections their audiences might have, then they may find themselves back at square one when the question-and-answer session begins. Ideally, in these situations, a presenter would have anticipated all of the audience's questions, concerns, and objections and answered or eliminated them during the presentation. This is true of written messages as well.

Types of Business Audiences

Another way to identify an audience's concerns is to think about its role within the organization. Business audiences are often quite different from those you may be familiar with in your academic experience. For example, most writing in school is intended for a teacher, who knows a great deal about the subject and who is required to read or listen to your message. However, this situation may not be true in the workplace. You may communicate with audiences who have little understanding of your topic, and it is very likely that you will write or speak to people who are not obliged to spend time reading or listening to your messages, such as potential customers. For these reasons, it is important to consider their interests and concerns if we are to achieve a greater likelihood of success in our communication attempts.

Another difference between communication in an academic setting and in the workplace is that you may be communicating with a variety of people rather than a single person. If you are communicating with several or many people, they may have varying knowledge and needs. They may also differ in the strategies they use and skills they have for listening, reading, and processing information.

According to a typology devised by Olsen and Huckin, in the workplace you will generally be communicating with five types of audiences: (1) managerial, (2) nonexperts, (3) expert, (4) international or multicultural, and (5) mixed.

Managerial Audiences

Managers are often the most important audiences you will communicate with because they have decision-making ability and power over your future. According to Henry Mintzberg, managers fulfill three types of roles that affect the way they communicate: *interpersonal, informational,* and *decisional.* (Note: Mintzberg does not distinguish between managers and leaders.) The primary managerial role is interpersonal. Managers must lead and motivate a group of employees and often communicate with external audiences such as suppliers, clients, and other departments. In this role, managers are also expected to disseminate information to these various audiences. Finally, managers must use information to make decisions that affect the various audiences with which they interact.

Because of the demands of these various roles, managers often have to deal with enormous time pressures. They have little time to listen or read carefully. Mintzberg's study found that 50 percent of the activities that executives engaged in lasted less than nine minutes. Many also treat message processing as a burden to be dispensed with as quickly as possible.

To ensure that your messages are received by managers, you can use a few tactics. You can, for example, put key information up front where it is easily accessible. James Souther studied how managers read reports and found that all of them read the executive summary and most read the introduction, background, and conclusions sections. Only 15 percent read the body of the report. In general, managers look for the "big picture" and tend to ignore details.

Nonexpert Audiences

Nonexpert audiences may be the most difficult to address because they know little about a subject and will need more details. (Managers are also often nonexperts, but they often ignore details unless they are micromanagers or specialists.) If you are communicating with a customer or client or perhaps a fellow employee from another department, then you are probably communicating with a nonexpert audience.

The problem with communicating with a nonexpert audience is that you probably think like a specialist. (Please see discussion of "Professional Jargon and Plain Language.") In other words, you may think about your topic differently than a nonexpert and use different terminology than he or she might when discussing that topic. In addition, you may have difficulty identifying exactly what a nonexpert audience doesn't know because you are so familiar with the topic.

As with managers, there are strategies you can use to communicate with nonexpert audiences. These include the following:

1. Use a conventional mode of presentation.
2. Refer to common knowledge as much as possible without distorting the meaning of your message.
3. Provide an overview at the beginning of the message that explains what it is about and what it will cover.
4. Provide appropriate background information.
5. Include lots of definitions and explanations. For more complex concepts, you can incorporate examples, illustrations, and analogies to aid in clarifying their meaning.

Expert Audiences

Expert audiences are those who know as much about the topic as you do. Generally, expert audiences, who may be your peers, speak the same language as you do—that is, they understand the jargon associated with your profession. They also understand the same concepts, so you don't need to provide as much explanation and examples. In other words, they can fill in the gaps by making inferences about material that is common knowledge to both of you.

Strategies for communicating with expert audiences include the following:

1. Use standard technical terms.
2. Use a conventional format.
3. Emphasize data and display it in standard ways using graphs, tables, equations, and so on.
4. Make your points clear and easy to find.
5. Do not overstate your claims, because doing so may undercut your credibility.

International or Multicultural Audiences

The global economy and the growing diversity of the workplace mean that we will likely communicate with audiences whose first language may not be English and who have differing cultural interpretations of symbols and behaviors. When communicating with people whose first language may not be English, you should

1. Avoid long or complicated sentences, because this may be more difficult for them to follow and comprehend.
2. Avoid slang, colloquial, or other idiomatic vocabulary uses. Such sayings as "in the ballpark," "under the weather," and "do an end run" may be interpreted literally by nonnative speakers of English, which will obviously cause confusion in terms of meaning.

Mixed Audiences

Even more difficult to communicate with are audiences who are composed of a variety of people: managers, nonexperts, experts, and nonnative speakers, or some combination of these. For example, you may be writing marketing literature that will be read by experts, nonexperts, and nonnative speakers or speaking to a group composed of the same individuals. There are two strategies for dealing with mixed audiences:

1. "Layer" a written message so that different sections are aimed at different audiences.
2. "Democratize" your message so that all audiences can understand all parts of it.

An example of the layered approach is a formal report. Such a report might include an executive summary, background information, and recommendation sections aimed at managers, while the body and appendices contain the details needed by specialists who are charged with implementing the report.

However, if you are speaking to a mixed audience, you may wish to use the democratic strategy. In this case, you aim your message primarily at the most important audience, but you add information in appropriate places that is needed for understanding by the other audiences. Although this approach is similar to the layered one, it differs in that you add examples, definitions, and explanations throughout the message that are needed for understanding by all audiences.

Audience-Centered Messages

One of the most common manifestations of communication that does not consider the needs, concerns, and interests of its audience is **self-centered communication**. Although some of the reasons for self-centered communication might be cultural as well as developmental—that is, the psychological maturity of the writer or level of self-awareness—another cause is our lack of awareness about our own message-formulation process.

self-centered communication

Communication that fails to consider the needs, concerns, or interests of its audience.

In the first draft of a written message, for example, many of us write to ourselves in an attempt to figure out what we want to say. Such documents may begin without identifying a purpose or topic; in this process, we are often writing to identify the purpose or topic of our message for ourselves. This process may also be applied to oral presentations if we tend to work from a written script.

In this stage of the process, beginning ideas may be general, abstract, or somewhat unrelated to the topic at which we eventually arrive. In addition, such writing is generally not well organized. Paragraphs may cover several topics; they may lack topic sentences, or the topic may not be clearly stated. But as we continue to write, we usually narrow our topic and then *voila!* We discover our purpose for writing. It is at this point that we may stop the process. But we have only discovered the topic of our communication for ourselves; it has been a writing exercise that was intended to clarify our own thinking. The next step—and the step that is often missed or skipped—is to transform that information into a message that is intended for an audience.

Much writing for school assignments, particularly essay exams, follows this process and can be described as *self-centered* writing. The writer begins to write about a general topic, perhaps making some detours along the way into related topics. In essay exams, the goal is often to get down on paper as many relevant ideas as possible—often in no particular order—to demonstrate to the teacher that you remember all the topics he or she discussed in class.

In this case, the teacher is required to read this jumble of thoughts as part of his or her job and interpret whether the jumble is adequate coverage of the topic. However, businesspeople are not required to interpret such jumbles—they often don't have the time—and this is when it is important to recognize the difference between self-centered and audience-centered message formulation.

As indicated earlier, a self-centered message is generally the first draft of a message. The writer is writing to discover what he or she wants to say. But in doing so, several problems may emerge. One problem that often characterizes self-centered messages is that the main topic comes at the end. The message may also skip important information or provide it in an illogical order.

The following steps should be applied to change self-centered messages to **audience-centered communication**:

1. Check whether the message should be turned upside down: Is the main topic or point at the end? If so, put it at the beginning of the second draft.
2. Eliminate any information that is not relevant to the main topic or its sub-points.
3. Organize what remains into a logical order.
4. Elaborate on any points that need additional explanation.
5. Proofread for correctness.

A self-centered process for message formulation and delivery can also occur when creating oral presentations, so it also is important to adjust planning and preparation to achieve greater audience focus.

Application of Audience-Centered Communication

Résumés and application letters are excellent examples of the importance of audience-centered content and organization. As you plan for job-application messages you should always begin with an analysis of your audience's needs, interests, questions, and concerns. Prospective employers want to know whether you can do the job they have to offer. To put it bluntly, they want to know what you can do for them. Employers are not offering jobs with the main objective of fulfilling your needs. Therefore, résumés and cover or application letters need to be focused on showing that you have the skills and experience for which they are looking. Employers want to know that you are the best-qualified applicant for the job.

In terms of purposes, then, employment messages are persuasive. But it is important to remember that successful persuasion also often relies on our ability to establish credibility and a trusting relationship with our audience, so it is important to provide evidence to support the claims that we make about ourselves in order to be persuasive and establish credibility. Fortunately, it is often fairly easy to discover what an audience's needs are when creating employment messages. These are generally found in the job description or job posting. We then just need to identify those skills or characteristics that the employer is looking for, match them with our own, and make this match apparent and persuasive to our audience, the prospective employer.

The application letter in Figure 4-3 is a response to a job advertisement that asks for applicants who have a bachelor's degree in marketing and proven sales experience, as well as evidence of the ability to self-motivate. Ask yourself whether the letter focuses on providing the information an employer would need to make a decision about whether the writer is qualified for the position of customer service representative. How might the letter be improved?

In your analysis, you should have noticed that it is not apparent that the applicant knows what the job qualifications are, nor does the letter clearly state that the applicant has those qualifications. More specifically, it does not provide evidence that shows that the applicant has the qualifications

audience-centered communication

Communication that considers the needs, concerns, and expectations of the audience.

for which the employer is looking. Rather than focusing on discussing the issues in which the reader is interested, it addresses only what the writer enjoys and wants. This letter is an extreme case of a message that is self-centered rather than audience-centered. The letter in Figure 4-4 is a better example of an audience-centered message.

In the second letter, the writer does the following:

1.   She addresses the specific skills that will help her perform the job of customer service representative.

2.   She states how her skills will contribute to the company's goals. This tactic, which focuses on the benefits that the writer provides, is a common one in persuasive messages.

3.   She has organized her information into short, concise paragraphs devoted to a single sub-point, which makes it easy for the reader to skim. The document's organization also attends to the reader's needs.

4.   She provides the most important information first to emphasize it. Typically, relevant work experience is the most persuasive evidence a job applicant can present to employers.

5.   She ends with a proactive statement that indicates high interest in the job, as well as initiative.

Figure 4-3 Self-Centered Employment Letter

Leona Frey
4234 Meadowlark Lane
Nashville, TN 78000

January 15, 2018

Juanita Ramos, Sales Manager
Nashville Digital Products, Inc.
1237 34th Street East
Nashville, TN 78001

Dear Ms. Ramos:

I am applying for the entry-level sales position you advertised on the JOBS Web site. I believe the position will suit my personality and provide me the opportunities for which I am looking.

I am a fun-loving person who enjoys interacting with others. I believe the sales position you are offering would enable me to meet a lot of new people. As the social chair of my sorority, I excelled at creating fun ways for others to meet and interact.

I am looking for a position that will take advantage of my people skills and provide me opportunities for rapid promotion and pay raises. For those reasons, I believe your company will find me a good match for its needs.

Sincerely,

Leona Frey

? Critical Thinking

Do you write to yourself to discover what it is you want to write? If so, have you recognized that this is just the first draft and that you may now need to edit the document heavily for others to read? Have you read writing that was clearly written from the writer's perspective and did not consider the reader? What were your reactions?

Figure 4-4 Example of an Audience-Centered Employment Letter

Leona Frey
4234 Meadowlark Lane
Nashville, TN 78000

January 15, 2018

Juanita Ramos
Nashville Digital Products, Inc.
1237 34th Street East
Nashville, TN 78001

Dear Ms. Ramos:

I am applying for the entry-level sales position you advertised on the JOBS Web site. I am well qualified for the position, since I have the experience, education, and personal characteristics you are seeking.

My experience working for Morris Electronics as a salesperson will enable me to quickly become a productive member of your team. At Morris, I used my interpersonal skills successfully to become the top salesperson in the store twice in my first six months there.

I will complete my bachelor's degree in marketing this May. My education has provided me much useful knowledge that I can apply as a sales representative for your company. My courses in marketing, customer service, and business communication have provided me an excellent understanding of sales techniques, and practice in the communication skills necessary to satisfy your business clients.

I am hard-working and have excellent time-management skills. While taking a full load of courses, I worked part time or interned during my entire college career. I was still able to participate in the Student Marketing Organization, eventually being elected president, and to maintain a 3.5 cumulative grade point average.

I will call you in a week to make an appointment to talk to you in more detail about how I might contribute to the continuing success of Nashville Digital.

Sincerely,

Leona Frey

Summary

A second critical component of communication strategy formulation is the analysis of your audience or audiences. If your message is not tailored to take into account your audience's perspective as well as its knowledge, interest, needs, and expectations, then it will likely not succeed in fulfilling its purposes. As simple as audience analysis appears, though, it can be difficult to perform effectively because we often have difficulty understanding that others differ from us in many important and perhaps subtle ways. Because of the strong emphasis on the individual in American culture, we may be egocentric and ethnocentric, which means we have difficulty empathizing with or understanding others and their cultural differences. To overcome this tendency, a systematic method for analyzing audiences should be applied. When analyzing an audience, you should consider the following characteristics:

- Its demographics, including age and generational differences, ethnicity, socioeconomic status, education level, and culture (including regional differences), if appropriate.
- Its knowledge of your company, product, service, or the situation—the topics—you address in your message.
- Its interests in and attitudes about the topic of your message.
- Its concerns, reservations, or questions about the topic of your message.

Writing to business audiences differs dramatically from writing to an academic audience or teacher. Teachers are obliged to read your writing; they often are knowledgeable about the topic of your messages. However, this is not always true in a business setting, where people often face enormous time pressures. Because of these differences, you can use strategies to communicate more effectively with the various types of business audiences: managerial, nonexpert, expert, international or multicultural, and mixed.

It is important to recognize the difference between communication that is aimed at meeting your audience's needs and that is formulated from the perspective of the writer or the speaker. In the process of developing a message, we often create messages that help us to solve a problem or decide what we want to communicate. It is important to remember that this message probably is not structured in such a way as to best meet our audience's needs; it may also fail to contain the information for which the audience is looking. It is important to understand our own process for formulating messages so that we can take the necessary steps to create audience-centered communication.

Key Terms

demographics **72**

ethnocentrism **74**

culture **74**

individualistic culture **76**

collectivist culture **76**

faces **77**

plain language **80**

common ground **81**

self-centered communication **84**

audience-centered communication **85**

Discussion Questions

1. When you are communicating with friends, what demographic issues might affect the way that you deliver your message and its content? What are their expectations regarding the content and delivery of messages that you convey to them, and how do you meet those expectations? How might you better meet their expectations?

2. When communicating with your instructors, what demographic issues might affect the way that you deliver your message and its content? What are their expectations regarding the content and delivery of messages that you convey to them, and how do you

   meet those expectations? How might you better meet their expectations?

3. If you work as a supervisor or manager, what demographic issues might affect the way that you deliver your message and its content? What have been the expectations of your team or employees regarding the content and delivery of the messages that you convey to them? How did you meet those expectations? How might you better meet them?

4. If you work or have worked part time, what demographic issues might affect the way that you deliver your message and its content? What have been the

expectations of your supervisor regarding the content and delivery of the messages that you convey to him or her? How did you meet those expectations? How might you better meet them?

5. When you are applying for an internship or job, what are employers' expectations regarding the content and delivery of your employment messages? How can you meet these expectations?

Applications

1. Using an Internet search engine, identify an organization that was faced with a problem and needed to communicate to various audiences who held different interests that might affect the way the organization deals with the problem.
   a. Identify each audience that held an interest in the decision.
   b. Identify each audience's interests, expectations, beliefs, and concerns.
   c. Assess the effectiveness of the organization's messages in meeting each audience's concerns and addressing them in a satisfactory manner.
   d. In those cases in which the organization might have done a better job in addressing the audience's interests, explain how it might have better accomplished this task.

2. Your company is planning to announce a series of layoffs that will affect 10 percent of your employee population. Write an analysis that addresses the following issues:
   a. What audience concerns and questions would you need to address to attain the maximal communication outcome?
   b. To which purposes of communication would you need to attend?
   c. At what type of audience would the message be aimed?
   d. What would be the focus and content of your strategy to effectively communicate this decision to employees?

3. Using an Internet job search Web site, identify potential positions for which you might apply on graduation. Review the job advertisements to identify the types of applicant qualifications and experience for which the organizations are looking. Choose one advertisement for which your skills best meet the organization's needs. Write an application letter that demonstrates that you understand the organization's needs and are qualified to fulfill them.

4. Identify a culture different from your own and use an Internet database to research the beliefs, values, attitudes, and practices of its people. Write an essay in which you discuss these characteristics and compare them to those of your own culture. How might these differences affect your communication with people of this culture? What similarities do you hold that might provide opportunities for establishing common ground?

5. Interview a working professional in your intended field to discover how business people's concerns, expectations, and communication practices differ from those of college students. Write an essay that discusses the results of your interview and concludes with a list of goals you intend to pursue to adjust your communication practices—written, oral, and nonverbal as well as those involving the use of technology—to better meet the expectations of the professional workplace.

Endnotes

1. Lancaster, L. C., & Stillman, D. (2002). *When Generations Collide: Who They Are. Why They Clash. How to Solve the Generational Puzzle at Work*. New York: HarperBusiness.

2. Gudykunst, W. B., & Ting-Toomey, S. (1988). *Culture and Interpersonal Communication*. Thousand Oaks, CA: Sage Publications.

3. House, R. J., Hanges, P. J., Javidan, M., Dorfman, P. W., & Gupta, V. (Eds.) (2004). *Culture, Leadership, and Organizations: The GLOBE Study of 62 Societies*. Thousand Oaks, CA: Sage Publications.

4. Hofstede, G. (1980). *Culture's Consequences: International Differences in Work-Related Values*. Beverly Hills, CA: Sage.

5. Hui, C. H., & Triandis, H. C. (1986). Individualism-collectivism: A study of cross-cultural research. *Journal of Cross-cultural Psychology*, 17, 225–48.

6. Hofstede, G. 1980.

7. Triandis, H. (1990). Cross-cultural studies of individualism and collectivism. In J. Berman (Ed.), *Cross-cultural perspectives*, (pp. 41–133). Lincoln, NE: University of Nebraska Press.

8. Goman, C. K. (2016, May). Is your communication style dictated by your gender? *Forbes Magazine*. Retrieved June 7, 2017 from *https://www.forbes.com/sites/carolkinseygoman/2016/03/31/is-your-communication-style-dictated-by-your-gender/#4c35301aeb9d*.

9. Ibid.

10. Ibid.

11. Ibid.

12. Ibid.

APPLE: *A Case Study in External Communication**

Introduction

As soon as the news of the Apple iCommunicator surfaced, David and Mary Jones** eagerly bought two and switched to AT&T, the iCommunicator's exclusive wireless carrier in the United States.

Several weeks later, after a hectic morning in the office, David drove home to meet Mary for lunch. "Hey, David, I wasn't expecting you to be home for lunch today. How's work?" Mary warmly greeted her husband and proceeded to set the dining table.

"It's fine—mundane as usual," David replied. "But my iCommunicator keeps dropping Internet connections and calls. My calls have dropped multiple times during important conference calls, and if I try to view a web page for more than a minute, it loses its connection," David sighed as he immediately went to the couch and took off his shoes to relax.

Mary had not experienced any problems with her own iCommunicator and wondered if David had somehow received a defective product. She placed a plate of pasta on the dining table and responded, "I'm sorry to hear that; I haven't had any problems with my iCommunicator. You should give AT&T a call and we'll get it figured out."

After lunch David called AT&T and was connected to a customer service representative who said, "We have been receiving a large number of calls regarding the connectivity problems with the iCommunicator. The problem is with the iCommunicator itself and not AT&T, but I apologize for the inconvenience."

David called Apple Customer Service next. "Hello, I am having problems with my new iCommunicator. My calls keep dropping and I keep getting disconnected when I try to access Internet sites. This is a recurrent problem." Bill, a customer service representative, responded, "Mr. Jones, the problem you are experiencing with your iCommunicator is also being experienced by other customers. However, you can solve the problem by getting a special plug-in for your iCommunicator."

Astonished by the customer service representative's comment, David asked, "How would a plug-in prevent my calls from being dropped and solve my other connectivity problems?" Bill continued, "Like most mobile devices, iCommunicators have antennas. The antenna is located on the lower left corner of the iCommunicator. It is sensitive when tightly gripped, and a plug-in by-passes that problem. You may also return the device, but there will be a 10% restocking fee."

David couldn't contain himself. "What are you talking about? The iCommunicator has a defective design. You sold me this defective device. And, now you expect me to pay a restocking fee? This is ridiculous! Apple intentionally misrepresented the iCommunicator. Why would I want a device that doesn't work?"

Discussion of the Problem

Apple launched the iCommunicator about two months ago into a highly demanding environment. Prior to the product's actual unveiling at Apple's Worldwide Developers Conference (WWDC) in San Francisco six months ago, there was widespread speculation about the new device. Two prototypes of iCommunicators were "leaked" to the media, garnering much public attention and exposure, resulting in widespread anticipation of the device's release.

The iCommunicator is similar to a tablet but has two additional features:

1. When using the telephone mode, the image of the recipient of the call is projected as a hologram, so the callers can have a conversation as if they are talking to each other face-to-face.

This Case was originally written by Jenny Lee, Ian McCarthy, Andrew Nguyen, and Robbie Reid, as an assignment for a course taught by Dr. Robyn Walker at the USC Marshall School of Business. Written April 25, 2012, used by permission of the USC Marshall School Case Study Initiative.

* This case describes a hypothetical problem involving Apple, which is provided as an example of the types of communication problems that could occur if a company launches a defective product and doesn't respond in a way that is expected by the public. Although the case may resemble a problem that Apple has already experienced, it should be viewed within the context of the product that is described in the case.

** Fictional names used to personify the situation and illustrate the type of issues some in this position would experience.

2. When searching websites, the pages are projected as holograms and the user can move text, images, etc. just with the wave of a hand or finger.

On the pre-order launch date, Apple received more than 100,000 pre-orders for the iCommunicator within the first 24 hours, which was one of the largest pre-orders that Apple had ever received on a single day. After a month, Apple had sold more than 500,000 iCommunicators, even considering its $5,000.00 price tag.

Within week of the launch, customers reported connectivity issues and image problems. They said that if they touched the antenna located on the outside of the phone in two places when in use, the images and sound would become blurred.

They also reported that the device would drop signals when tightly held in a particular way. Although the antennas on mobile devices fluctuate in signal strength, it is evident that hardware designers at Apple had failed to take this into consideration when drafting design plans for the iCommunicator.

The problem has been featured on many blogs and on proprietary online forums. Given the environment of high expectations from consumers, the price of the device, and high sales volume, Apple could have expected much scrutiny from the customers once the product was released. Many companies facing a similar situation would have taken extreme measures to ensure the product performed to their standards. What did Apple do?

Apple's Response to the Problem

Apple acknowledged that the device had connectivity problems but insisted that the problem was common to all mobile devices. Additionally, Apple issued a press release that compared the iCommunicator's reception to that of smart phone devices, including RIM's Blackberry. The press release also mentioned that connectivity problems were common and simply a "fact of life." However, it was evident that the connectivity problem was caused solely by the way the device was designed, a problem unique to the Apple iCommunicator.

Additionally, Apple announced a press conference, which led to speculation of a fix for the problem, or perhaps replacement of devices to satisfy customers and improve the company's reputation. Instead, the company simply reiterated, "We're not perfect. Devices are not perfect. We all know that. But we want to make our users happy."

Because of problems with signal strength (the phone displayed four bars when it should have been displaying only two), Apple announced that it would adopt AT&T's recommended formula to calculate the number of bars to be displayed. While the signal strength would remain the same, the iCommunicator's bars would accurately report signal strength and provide users with a better indication of the reception in a given area.

Consumer Reports then released information that indicated that a plug-in could mitigate the connectivity problems. And, within a week Apple offered free plug-ins. However, it was a temporary fix to a problem that would eventually recur (perhaps, even within several months).

Lastly, Apple offered consumers the option to return their device if they were ultimately not satisfied; however, Apple would charge a 10% restocking fee if customers didn't return them within 30 days of purchase.

Public's Reaction

Apple received serious backlash from the general public in response to the connectivity problem. Since the iCommunicator was a highly anticipated, not to mention expensive product, people expected great performance from their new mobile device. As a result, iCommunicator customers fall into three categories:

1. *People who are indifferent to the lack of connectivity*
   A large percentage of people (about 40%) have not waivered on their decision to immediately purchase the iCommunicator, even after being informed of problems related to connectivity. According to A. M. Sacconaghi, Jr. (an analyst with Sanford C. Bernstein & Company), the question of why someone would purchase an expensive device that does not operate to its fullest potential is quite simple. They do so because, "It's iconic, it's cool, it's the *it* device and people want it."

2. *People who have planned to postpone buying the iCommunicator until the connectivity problem is fixed*
   This group consists of people who still plan to buy the device (about 30%), but not until the flaw is fixed and the device can fully function. This public reaction is somewhat negative, but not enough to fully deter one from buying the product. Bruce Namerow, owner of a web consulting company in Washington says, "I'll buy it the day Apple fixes it. I don't see how they can sell a device that has such problems. That to me is unbelievable."

3. *People who will cut ties with AT&T and Apple because of how the problem was handled*

People within this group (about 30%) were so negatively affected that they blamed Apple and AT&T for the problem and vowed never to do business with either company again.

Given that the bottom-line purpose of a mobile device is to make calls and connect seamlessly with the Internet, and that this industry is highly competitive with many players, Apple is faced with a communication challenge moving forward. And, with so many challenges, Apple must make decisions about how to move forward if it wants to save its brand image and customer loyalty.

Discussion Questions

1. What steps did Apple take to address the iPhone antenna issue?

2. Do you think Apple's communication with the public was effective? If not, what would have been your recommendations?

3. Will Apple's communication with the public ultimately affect its brand image and customer loyalty?

4. Do you think Apple knew about the antenna problem beforehand? If so, would it have been better to postpone the release of the product or go ahead with its debut, knowing the problem would surface?

5. What can Apple do to turn this negative experience into a positive one?

Sources

Apple. "Apple – Press Info – Statement by Apple on iPhone 4 Pre-Orders." *Apple.* Apple Media, 16 June 2010. <*http://www.apple.com/pr/library/2010/06/16Statement-by-Apple-on-iPhone-4-Pre-Orders.html*>.

Apple. "Apple – Press Info – iPhone 4 Sales Top 1.7 Million." *Apple.* Apple Media, 28 June 2010. <*http://www.apple.com/pr/library/2010/06/28iPhone-4-Sales-Top-1-7-Million.html*>.

Chen, Jason. "iPhone 4 Loses Reception When You Hold It By The Antenna Band?" *Gizmodo. Gizmodo.com*, 24 June 2010. <*http://gizmodo.com/5571171/iphone-4-loses-reception-when-you-hold-it-by-the-antenna-band*>.

Golijan, Rosa. "The Tale of Apple's Next iPhone." *Gizmodo. Gizmodo.com*, 4 June 2010. <*http://gizmodo.com/5520471/the-tale-of-apples-next-iphone*>.

Parker, Philip M. *The 2011-2016 World Outlook for Mobile Phone Handsets.* Publication. ICON Group International, Inc., 20 Jan. 2011.

Ritchie, Rene. "Steve Jobs: BlackBerry, Android, Windows Mobile Have Antenna Problem Too." *IMore.com.* 26 July 2010. Web. <*http://www.imore.com/2010/07/16/steve-jobs-blackberry-android-windows-mobile-antenna-problem/*>.

Wolverton, Troy. "Another Next-generation iPhone Surfaces, This One in Vietnam." *MercuryNews.com.* Mercury News, 23 May 2010. <*http://www.mercurynews.com/ci_15072831?source%3Dmost_viewed.20F88DA3D7D369F5BB-70F372987EAE1F.html*>.

© Rawpixel.com / bigstockphoto.com

Steps Three and Four:
Consider the Context and Select
a Channel of Communication

After reading this chapter, you will be able to

■ *Recognize the importance of considering context as part of the strategic communication process.*

■ *Analyze the context of a communication situation to identify factors that need to be taken into account when formulating a message.*

■ *Learn about the elements that affect the quality of communication that occurs within an organization, including corporate culture and structure, as well as formal and informal communication networks.*

■ *Select a channel and medium that will best help you fulfill your purpose(s) for communicating and properly engaging with your audience(s).*

Case Questions

1. Why is working virtually potentially more problematic than working in an organizational environment in which members can occasionally meet face to face?
2. If you were leader of this virtual team, what would you do to build a culture of trust among its members?
3. What additional concerns might need to be addressed when attempting to create a communication strategy that accounted for cultural differences and that would make all feel included and appreciated?

The Case of the Virtual Team

Jennifer was frustrated. She had submitted her contribution to the software project on which she was working electronically to her team four days ago and had heard nothing from anyone since. Enough was enough. She keyed in the message: "Are you not in the … assignment anymore?" and pressed the Send key.

In fact, in the past three months, Jennifer estimated that she accounted for more than 50 percent of the communications for the team. This lack of responsiveness was one of the challenges of working in a virtual team, with members scattered across the globe. Jennifer was part of a project management team responsible for creating smartphone apps that would be compatible with phone technologies used worldwide. Team members were located in East Asia, Europe, and South America. Although they worked for the same company, TekTron, their native languages were different as well as their cultural values. These differences created challenges in regard to team members' expectations about communication, time, and relationships.

These differences and their effect on the team had not been well addressed by company management. It had also led Jennifer to believe that she couldn't rely on her team members; it had damaged her ability to trust.

Contextual issues—particularly those dealing with organizational context—and channel-choice considerations are both elements of the strategic communication process that can be applied at both the individual (personal) and corporate levels. You should consider these issues when strategizing personal messages; the consideration of these issues should also be done at the corporate level to create an effective communication plan for an organization. Potential leaders and managers will thus read the following information with both goals in mind.

Organizational Context

"Communication is the lifeblood of any organization, big or small," says Ronald Gross, head of Censeo Corporation, a Maitland, Florida, human resources consulting firm.[1] However, a company's policies, programs, and structures can support or interfere with good communication. The context within which communication occurs can also affect how, what, when, and whether we should communicate. The corporate culture of an organization also can affect the quality of communication that occurs within it. This section discusses these issues in addition to the types of communication networks that exist in organizations, formal and informal.

Context Defined

Context is the situation or setting in which communication occurs. Context can influence the content, the quality, and the effectiveness of a communication event.

There are several ways to think about context in terms of communication. For example, the discipline of communication itself arranges its areas of research and study by context: intrapersonal communication, interpersonal communication, small-group communication, public speaking, organizational communication, and mass communication. The differences among these communication situations will affect your choices of the most appropriate oral, nonverbal, or written codes. This textbook draws on all of these differing contexts and situates them within a broader one—that of the organization and what is termed strategic communication. Organizational context is the situation (e.g., the corporation, the accounting firm, the manufacturing plant, the not-for-profit) in which communication takes place. Social rules, modes of behavior, type of dress, language style, nonverbal communication, communication media choice, and topics of discussion are all affected by where and under what circumstances they occur within an organization.

context
The situation or setting in which communication occurs.

Context as a Strategic Issue

Context is developed within an organization through the process of individuals interacting. What that means is that context is not something "out there"; it is something that is being created and re-created all the time in organizations (and other settings) primarily through communication practices as thought broadly. That means that communication includes oral, written, and nonverbal elements, such as symbols, artifacts, behaviors, and so on. Creating a common context in the minds of communicators is a product of repetitive exposure to people in certain roles under similar circumstances and in comparable settings. (This understanding aligns with the social construction of reality theory that was discussed in Chapter 1.) Through repeated experience, a series of probable interpretations of symbols, messages, behaviors, artifacts, and so on becomes the norm while other interpretations are ignored or given less credence. Context is important for helping us understand the meaning of communication behaviors within a particular situation, but it also is often overlooked because of this process of context creation: It is so much a part of our reality that we often have difficulty seeing it and thus analyzing it. In other words, we cannot get outside our "box" to see things as a newcomer or an outsider might.

Trained mindlessness describes this condition, which also might be termed a lack of strategic focus. Trained mindlessness might even be part of the organization's culture. Individuals who follow the same routine every day without change may become "mindless experts" who concentrate on the end result and pay little attention to the process or changing contextual issues. The problem is that such individuals are not attentive to the task environment or the context and thus do not notice things out of the ordinary.[2] Such indifference to the environment or the context of a situation may affect not only the organization at a strategic level but also our ability as individuals to act strategically in terms of our communication.

The importance of developing a sensitivity to context has become a requirement for leaders, too. In *In Their Time: The Greatest Business Leaders of the Twentieth Century*, Tony Mayo notes that business opportunities emerge when environmental factors and individual action come together. Environmental factors create specific and sometimes unique contexts for business. Within this contextual framework, some individuals envision new enterprises or new products and services, while others see opportunities for maximizing or optimizing existing businesses, and still others find opportunities through reinvention or recreation of companies or technologies that were considered stagnant or declining.

contextual intelligence

The awareness of and ability to adapt to the context.

This awareness of and ability to adapt to the context is called **contextual intelligence**. This ability to "seize the zeitgeist" of the time moves to the fore the study of situational context and places a secondary focus on developing individual characteristics of leadership.[3]

adaptive capacity

The ability to change one's style and approach to fit the culture, context, or condition of an organization.

The ability to succeed in multiple contexts is based on what Warren Bennis and Robert Thomas in *Geeks & Geezers* called **adaptive capacity** —the ability to change one's style and approach to fit the culture, context, or condition of an organization.[4] Success in the twenty-first century will require leaders to pay attention to the evolving context.

Dimensions of Context

As discussed, all communication occurs within a particular context or situation. For this reason, it is important to spend some time analyzing the context, situation, or environment in which communication takes place to formulate an effective strategy to suit that particular set of circumstances.

There are several dimensions to context, including the physical, social, chronological, and cultural. The *physical* context or setting can influence the content and quality of interaction. For example, if you were to ask your boss for a raise, the effect of the setting might dramatically affect your chances for success. How might the following settings affect the success of such an interaction, how it might take place, or whether it should take place: In the boss's office? At a company picnic? Over lunch at a restaurant? In your work area with others observing?

The *social context* refers to the nature of the relationship between the communicators as well as who is present. In the same situation mentioned above, imagine how the relationship between your manager and yourself might affect your request for a raise if

- You and the manager have been friends for several years, as opposed to a situation in which you and your manager have no personal relationship.

- You are the same age as your manager, *or* she or he is fifteen years older (or younger) than you.

- You and the manager have gotten along well in the past, compared to a situation in which you and the manager have been involved in an ongoing personal conflict.

The *chronological context* refers to the ways time influences interactions. For example, how might the time of day affect the quality of an interaction? How might the communicator's personal preferences regarding time affect communication and its success? Is it a busy time of year for employees and managers? Has there just been a major layoff, downsizing, or profit loss? In this last case, you might want to put off your request for a raise until conditions improve.

The *cultural context* includes both the organizational culture as well as the cultural backgrounds of the people with whom you may be communicating. **Organizational culture** refers to a system of shared meanings and practices held by members that distinguish the organization from other organizations. Organizational culture can affect the means and style of communication that takes place in an organization. (Organizational culture is discussed more fully in the following section.)

A person's cultural influences also can affect the kind and quality of communication that takes place, and they can help determine approaches that will be more effective. For example, young people have different expectations than seniors, Latinos have different expectations than Asians, Californians have different expectations than people from the Midwest or East Coast, and men may communicate differently than women. (Several approaches to cultural values were discussed in Chapter 4, "Step Two: Analyze the Audience.")

Environmental factors may also affect what should be communicated and how. For example, if the economy is doing poorly, then some messages may be inappropriate or may have little chance for success. If you work in a highly litigious environment or one that is strongly regulated, then constraints may exist for what you can communicate and how. Larger social, political, or historical events may affect whether certain messages are appropriate or have a chance of success.

organizational culture

The system of shared meanings and practices within an organization that distinguish it from other organizations.

Organizational Culture

Organizational culture "provides an immediate, familiar outline of what you should pay attention to and the constraints within which you should steer your actions."[5] Organizational culture is "a pattern of shared basic assumptions that the group learned as it solved its problems of external adaptation and internal integration and which has worked well enough to be taught to new members as the correct way to perceive, think, and feel in relation to these problems."[6] As should be recognized after the discussion of social reality, organizational culture is the creation of communication behaviors that are patterned by management and adopted by employees. Individual members' socialization into that culture determines what they can and cannot do.[7] Organizational structure and policies that affect organizational culture affect the quality of communication within an organization and vice versa. For example, a culture that is built around a hierarchical organizational structure will likely have a top-down communication flow. A flatter organizational structure may better promote communication flow in all directions: down, up, and horizontally. This process is iterative in that the structure, culture, and communication inform and maintain each other. The culture of a business provides part of the *context* (explained in the previous section) for interpreting the meaning of everyday organizational life as well as determining what are considered appropriate messages and the proper or expected ways to convey them.

Zappos, an online retailer, is a good example of an organization whose reputation relies upon its message about its unique corporate culture: Its number one core value is to "deliver WOW through service" to its customers. The use of "WOW" is just one clue to Zappos's unique culture. Other values include "create fun and a little weirdness," "do more with less," "build open and honest relationships," and "be humble." Compare these values with the type of culture that you might find in an investment banking firm where competition, individualism, and the drive for profits and bonuses would likely be key elements and it should be easy to see how culture might affect how communication occurs and what is expected and accepted within an organization in terms of behaviors.

Research suggests that there are seven primary characteristics that, when taken as a whole, capture the essence of an organization's culture.[8] These are:

1. **Innovation and risk taking**, or the degree to which employees are encouraged to innovate and take risks.

2. **Attention to detail**, or the degree to which employees are expected to exhibit precision, analytical skills, and attention to detail.

3. **Outcome orientation**, or the degree to which management focuses on results or outcomes rather than on the techniques and processes used to achieve these outcomes.

4. **People orientation**, or the degree to which management decisions consider the effect of outcomes on people within the organization.

5. **Team orientation**, or the degree to which work activities are organized around teams rather than individuals.

6. **Aggressiveness**, or the degree to which people are aggressive and competitive rather than easygoing.

7. **Stability**, or the degree to which organizational activities emphasize maintaining the status quo rather than focusing on change.

Each characteristic is listed in Table 5-1 and exists on a continuum from low to high. Appraising the organization on each of these characteristics can provide a picture of the organization's culture.

More generally speaking, the culture of business can be characterized as typically having a bias toward action, a demand for confidence, and a results orientation.[9] The culture of business can be seen in everyday office interactions. Being knowledgeable about an organization's culture can help you gauge the type and quality of communication that takes place as well as whether you are a good match with an organization. For example, do people wear T-shirts and shorts or suits to work every day? Does the organization have an "open door" policy or are you expected to obey the hierarchical ordering of management when communicating concerns? Does the office have an open floor plan or do employees have private offices? The first situation in each of these cases probably signals that the culture is less formal in terms of its expectations and communication patterns while the second situation may indicate a culture that is more formal in terms of its expectations regarding punctuality and communication choices and behaviors.

Table 5-1 Primary Characteristics of Organizational Culture

1. The degree to which employees are encouraged to be innovative and take risks.
2. The degree to which employees are expected to exhibit precision, analysis, and attention to detail.
3. The degree to which management focuses on results or outcomes rather than on the techniques and processes used to achieve those outcomes.
4. The degree to which management decisions consider the effect of outcomes on people within the organization.
5. The degree to which work activities are organized around teams or groups rather than individuals.
6. The degree to which people are aggressive and competitive rather than easygoing and cooperative.
7. The degree to which organizational activities emphasize maintaining the status quo compared to promoting change.

Source: O'Reilly, III, C. A., Chatman, J., & Caldwell, D. F. (1991). "People and Organizational Culture: A Profile Comparison Approach to Assessing Person–Organization Fit," *Academy of Management Journal*, September: 487–516.

Various attempts have been made to categorize organizational culture types. One such schema, the Organizational Culture Inventory developed by Robert A. Cooke, identifies three:

- Constructive
- Passive-Defensive
- Aggressive-Defensive

Please note that these three types align with the interpersonal communication styles of individuals discussed in Chapter 3. Thus, reliance on a particular interpersonal style within an organization can be a reliable clue as to its culture. From a leader perspective, then, it is important to reflect on your own interpersonal style and to consider whether it is the style you want to be reflected in the organizational culture. Each culture and its attributes are discussed next.

Constructive Culture

The cultural norms of a Constructive Culture are:

- Achievement
- Self-Actualization
- Human-focused encouragement
- Affiliation[10]

Organizations with Constructive cultures encourage members to work to their full potential, resulting in high levels of motivation, satisfaction, teamwork, service quality, and sales growth. Members must balance expectations for taking initiative and thinking independently with those for consensus and power sharing. They are expected to participate without taking over and to voice unique perspectives and concerns while working toward agreement.

Constructive cultural norms are evident in environments where quality is valued over quantity; creativity is valued over conformity; cooperation is believed to lead to better results than competition; and effectiveness is judged at the system level rather than the component level. Of the four Constructive cultural norms, Achievement is the most task-oriented. As a result, Achievement is often confused with other, less effective, task-oriented norms such as Perfectionism and Competition, norms of the Aggressive-Defensive culture type (see below). Achievement cultures are unique, however, in that they emphasize setting and attaining challenging but realistic goals that are based on improving an individual's performance (as opposed to setting impossible goals and focusing on outperforming others). In other words, members of Constructive cultures are expected to pursue self-set goals based on their own relevant strengths and interests. In this regard, Constructive cultures are focused on nurturing individual strengths rather than attempting to force individuals to fit into organizationally defined performance norms. In fact, Constructive cultures support individuals in resisting conformity. Such cultures are more common in newer industries, such as technology.[11]

Passive-Defensive Culture

The norms of a Passive-Defensive Culture are:

- Seeking approval
- Maintaining conventions
- Supporting dependency
- Avoiding conflict[12]

Little needs to be said about such norms as their negative implications would seem to be obvious. But for clarity's sake, a brief explanation will be provided. Members of organizations with Passive-Defensive cultures feel pressured to think and behave in ways that are inconsistent with the way they personally believe they should behave in order to be effective. Members are expected to do whatever it takes to please others (particularly superiors) and avoid interpersonal conflicts. Personal beliefs, ideas, and judgment take a back seat to rules, procedures, and orders—all of which are to be followed without question. As a result, organizations with Passive-Defensive cultures experience quite a bit of unresolved conflict and turnover and their members report relatively low levels of motivation and satisfaction.

Passive-Defensive cultural norms tend to emerge in organizations where scientific management principles are practiced. Such organizations rely on a high degree of structure, standardization, and control to ensure reliable and consistent output. This management approach was moderately successful during the Industrial Era (when the external environment was relatively stable and competition was limited); however, it renders today's organizations ineffective in terms of responding to customer needs and keeping up with dynamic and changing competitive markets.[13] A common example of a Passive-Defensive culture might be that of a business school with an overreliance on scientific explanations of behavior, which tend to treat individuals as if they were machines without feelings or unique abilities and needs. Passive-Defensive cultures also are common in government and highly regulated industries. Passive-Defensive cultures also are understood as being "bureaucratic."

Passive-Defensive cultural norms are based on "Theory X" assumptions regarding the management of people and work. As described by Douglas McGregor, Theory X managers assume:

- The average person dislikes work and, if possible, will avoid it;
- The way to motivate people to perform is through coercion, tight controls, strict direction, and punishment;
- People seek security and therefore prefer to be directed and avoid responsibility.[14]

In this type of culture, expectations that promote conventional and avoidance behaviors are supported when managers:

- Ignore tasks that are done particularly well by direct reports.
- Fail to work with employees to correct problems or mistakes.
- Criticize people when they make mistakes or experience problems.
- Respond to inadequate performance by assigning undesirable tasks or administering some other form of punishment.[15]

Given these assumptions, the dominant belief in Passive-Defensive cultures is that a high degree of structure, standardization, regulation, and control are necessary to ensure reliable productivity.

Aggressive-Defensive Culture

The Aggressive-Defensive cluster includes cultural norms that reflect expectations for members to approach tasks in forceful ways to protect their status and security.

The Aggressive/Defensive cultural norms are:

- Oppositional
- Focus on power attainment and maintenance
- Competitive
- Perfectionism[16]

Like the Passive-Defensive Culture, the Aggressive-Defensive cultural norms would appear to need little exposition to demonstrate their negative effects on morale and productivity. However, since these cultures are still being mindlessly produced and promoted, discussion will be provided for clarity's sake. Organizations with Aggressive-Defensive cultures encourage members to *appear* competent, controlled, and superior—even if, in fact, they lack the necessary knowledge, skills, abilities, or experience. Those who seek assistance, admit shortcomings, or concede their position are viewed as incompetent or weak. The constant pressure to maintain the facade of perfection and expertise comes at the expense of members' health, motivation, teamwork, and the way in which customers or clients are treated.

Aggressive-Defensive cultural norms tend to be pervasive in organizations that operate in fast-paced environments, that are instituting or have recently gone through downsizing, or that emphasize traditional approaches to quality control. An obvious example would be the investment banking industry, other sales-based organizations, and some entrepreneurial endeavors. Organizations with Aggressive-Defensive cultures tend to place relatively little value on people (whether they be employees, stockholders, or customers) and operate on the philosophy that the road to success is through finding errors, weeding out "mistakes," and promoting internal competition. While the decisions and strategies implemented by these organizations may help them to achieve short-term gains, they typically come at the cost of longer-term success and survival.

Expectations for Aggressive-Defensive behaviors are promoted by factors involving goal setting, job insecurity, and disempowerment at the member/job level; use of punishment and sources of power at the manager/unit level; as well as cultural values and disrespect for members at the organizational level.

Aggressive-Defensive norms are built upon a value structure whereby management puts its own interests before those of its key constituents—its customers, employees, suppliers, and even stockholders. Members place priority on doing what is best for themselves over the long-term best interests of their organization. Previous organizational successes (due to prior leadership, technological patents, or good business strategies) fuel the arrogance and short-term orientation of management and allow Aggressive-Defensive organizations to continue to appear effective—at least for a while.[17] However, as shown by John Kotter and James Heskett's study of 207 organizations (and consistent with research based on the OCI), this type of value structure prevents organizations from effectively adapting to changes in their environments and ultimately has a negative impact on their financial performance.[18] An example might be the financial debacle of 2006 that led to the Great Recession. Other organizations that may adopt an Aggressive-Defensive culture are the military and police institutions.

More specifically, organizations with strong Aggressive-Defensive cultures value *confrontation and competition* over cooperation and teamwork; they value *criticism and overconfidence* over learning and reasonable risk-taking; they value what is *impossible* as opposed to what is attainable; and they value their *financial* assets over their people. An excellent illustration of these values in action is provided by a description of Drexel Burnham Lambert's Beverly Hills office under the management of Mike Milken:

> As their power grew and the volume of their deals skyrocketed, Mr. Milken's band of traders took on a superhuman aura—a tight-knit group working 16-hour days under extreme pressure and loving every minute of it…Mr. Milken set the tone, badgering traders for not squeezing the most out of a trade, hectoring employees who tried to leave after only 12 hours of work…Even when Mr. Milken himself briefly keeled over at his desk on the trading floor in 1981, his brother and coworker Lowell came over, viewed the unconscious body, and simply returned to his office. The message was clear: Keep working.[19]

It should be noted that organizations may exhibit some combination of these cultures. For example, an organization may promote a Passive-Defensive culture externally and an Aggressive-Defensive culture internally. An example might be that of a business school that seeks approval from students, parents, and hiring institutions but promotes a competitive environment for employees.

Communication Climates

Although what constitutes a healthy organizational culture can be debated, one description of a good organization includes communication behaviors and attitudes seen in the following list.[20] Good organizations are places where authentic (as opposed to pretentious) people:

- Listen well.
- Respect the validity of others' experience.
- Feel free to be assertive.
- Have a clear sense of direction and control.
- Get good feedback about their performance.
- Feel valued as intelligent human beings.[21]

In addition, good organizations provide opportunities for employees to voice their opinions and concerns, encourage conversations that are simultaneously supportive and critical, promote a positive experience of work, and are able to remain profitable in a competitive marketplace. Many of the characteristics of good organizations are obviously elements of communication, including the ability to listen well, provide good feedback, and communicate assertively yet respectfully with others, while others are behaviors that communicate through nonverbal means.

Such organizations have also been described as having a **supportive communication climate**, which aligns with the Constructive Culture discussed earlier.[22] An organization that exhibits a supportive communication climate is one in which you feel free from threat. You perceive that although the content of your communication may be evaluated and even rejected, no one is passing judgment on your personal worth. In the absence of threat, and perceiving that others are open and honest, you freely express your opinions and feelings, trust others, and are open to them.

In contrast, unhealthy work conditions include

- Authoritarian and detailed supervision.
- Tasks characterized by restrictions on employees' abilities to use resources.
- Work-production systems that do not provide opportunities to contribute initiative, responsibility, or personal knowledge to the job.
- Limited opportunities for employees to exercise influence in the planning and organizing of tasks.
- Tasks that deprive the individual of the self-determination of work rate and methods for carrying out the work.
- Tasks that limit human contacts during work.[23]

Such an organization can be characterized as one that does not value its employees as intelligent human beings and does not trust them to make responsible, knowledgeable decisions. Although these characteristics may appear to have little to do with communication, they do concern a characteristic that is necessary for effective communication: trust.

Just as healthy organizations are characterized as having supportive climates, unhealthy ones are characterized as having **defensive communication climates**. A defensive communication climate is one in which you feel threatened. As should be apparent by the discussion of organizational culture provided in the previous section, defensive communication behaviors are characteristic of both Passive-Defensive and Aggressive-Defensive cultures. You perceive that your communication can be used against you, carefully edit your comments to protect yourself from real or anticipated threat, and mistrust others and thus are closed to them. Table 5-2 distinguishes those behaviors that characterize defensive and supportive organizational climates.

supportive communication climate

An organizational climate in which individuals do not feel threatened.

defensive communication climate

An organizational climate in which individuals feel threatened.

Table 5-2 **Characteristics of Defensive and Supportive Organizational Climates**

Defensive	Supportive
1. Evaluation. To pass judgment on another.	1. Description. Nonjudgmental. To ask questions, present feelings, refrain from asking the other to change his or her behavior.
2. Control. To try to do something to another; to try to change behavior or attitudes of others.	2. Problem orientation. To convey a desire to collaborate in solving a mutual problem or defining it; to allow the other to set his or her goals.
3. Strategy. To manipulate another; to engage in multiple or ambiguous motivations.	3. Spontaneity. To express naturalness, free of deception; straightforwardness; uncomplicated motives.
4. Neutrality. To express a lack of concern for the other; the clinical, person-as-object-of-study attitude.	4. Empathy. To respect the other person and show it; to identify with his or her problems; to share his or her feelings.
5. Superiority. To communicate that you are superior in position, wealth, intelligence, and so on, to arouse feelings of inadequacy in others.	5. Equality. To be willing to enter into participative planning with mutual trust and respect; to attach little importance to differences of worth, status, and so on.
6. Certainty. To seem to know the answers and be dogmatic, wanting to win an argument rather than solve a problem; seeing one's ideas as truths to be defended.	6. Provisionalism. To be willing to experiment with your own behavior; to investigate issues rather than taking sides; to solve problems, not debate.

Source: Gibb, J. (1961). "Defensive Communication," *Journal of Communication*, 11, 141–148.

Most organizations are a combination of these characteristics. Therefore, the ability to be strategic in our communication practices is helpful, at least in the United States where competition is common in many organizations, if only in performance appraisal and compensation policies which, as extrinsic motivators, may count most in fueling individualistic behaviors.

As should be apparent by this discussion, the communicative behaviors of leaders and followers create and maintain organizational cultures. A mindful actor would be cognizant of this process and would take steps to ensure the creation of a culture that best supports short-term as well as long-term success of the organization and its stakeholders. Unfortunately, many of today's leaders do not have the requisite knowledge of communication and culture creation necessary to maximize organizational performance. Today's business environment also contributes to this problem with its focus on short-term outcomes rather than having a long-term process orientation, particularly those processes associated with effective communication. This discussion potentially gives you an advantage in the workplace.

? Critical Thinking

Identify a group or an organization in which you have been involved. Was its communication climate defensive or supportive? What aspects of the group or organization characterized its communication climate as such? If you are a leader, what can you do to improve the communication climate where you work?

Formal Communication Networks

An organization's formal communication network is typically reflected in its structure or organizational chart. Such charts summarize the lines of authority; each position in the hierarchy represents a link in the chain of command, and each line represents a formal channel for the transmission of official messages. Information may travel three ways in an organization: down, up, and horizontally.

- **Downward flow.** Organizational decisions are usually made at the top and then flow down to the people who will carry them out. Most of what flows downward is intended to maintain the formal organizational culture and the company's overall profitability.

- **Upward flow.** Because the employees who perform the work of the organization often have the most information, managers should have access to their feedback to improve processes, productivity, morale, decision-making, and, ultimately, organizational profitability or sustainability. Because upward communication may be less formalized than downward flow, it "has to be constantly fostered and reinforced, so that people see it's something that's valued."[24]

- **Horizontal flow.** Communication also flows within and between departments. This information helps departments and employees share and coordinate their activities to improve productivity and the quality of decision-making.

Network communication flow can be an indicator of corporate culture. For example, if most communication is downward, the organization is generally more hierarchical and formal in its culture and thus likely to be more bureaucratic. In contrast, an organization that provides formal mechanisms for upward horizontal flow and acts on the information provided is likely to be less formal and more egalitarian as in a Constructive Culture.

From a communication perspective, effective leaders and managers should assess the formal communication network to see where there are gaps in communication that might negatively affect the overall health of the organization. (The steps in organizational communication strategy formulation are discussed more in Chapter 11.) On an individual level, assessing and understanding the flow of communication within an organization can help you better strategize your own communication practices.

Informal Communication Networks

Every organization also has an informal communication network—the "grapevine"—that supplements formal channels. Most of this information is conveyed through casual conversations between employees. Although these conversations may also deal with personal matters, 80 percent of the information that travels through the grapevine deals with business.

Savvy managers will pay a great deal of attention to the informal communication network within an organization and will use it to disseminate accurate information to employees. If ignored, the informal communication network is another means by which managers can lose control of the flow of information within an organization, causing other problems such as poor morale or distrust.

However, awareness of the informal communication network should be tempered with recognition of the need for flexibility. Organizations must be flexible to remain competitive. Strict rules and procedures can be a hindrance to this needed flexibility in the current business climate, which is characterized by the constant of change. Without the time to formalize some relationships, their effectiveness often depends on the trust that can develop over time among employees.[25]

One way to provide more control over the informal communication network is to constantly update employees on changes in company policies, practices, earnings perspectives, and product and service lines and to encourage an open flow of communication upward. Good formal communication can help to minimize the potential negative effects of the grapevine.

Choosing a Communication Channel and Medium

Broadly speaking, four channels of communication exist: written, oral, nonverbal, and visual. However, these broad categories can be broken down further. For example, written communication can be disseminated using a variety of media or forms, including memos, letters, e-mails, instant or text messaging, faxes, press releases, company Web sites, wikis, blogs, blog applications, and reports. Oral communication can also use various media or forms such as face-to-face or interpersonal, telephone, voice messages, teleconferences and videoconferences, speeches, meetings, and podcasts. Typically, nonverbal communication supplements oral forms, but it shouldn't be underestimated because most communication in face-to-face situations is nonverbal. Similarly, visual communication supplements both written and oral forms of communication in the form of diagrams, photographs, charts, tables, video, and artwork.

Channel choice might be influenced or informed by earlier steps in the strategic communication process. For instance, purpose of communication might affect channel choice; in a situation in which the purpose is primarily to establish relationship or convey goodwill, a face-to-face meeting might be the best choice to achieve this goal. Audience analysis might yield information that indicates it prefers a particular medium of communication such as e-mail or phone discussions. Similarly, an examination of organizational context issues might indicate that written memos are still the conventional medium for communicating with staff in a particular organization, whereas text messaging is the preferred mode in others.

Figure 5-1 lists additional issues that might be considered when selecting the channel and medium that best suits a particular communication situation.

These considerations are discussed in more detail in the following sections.

Figure 5-1 Channel Selection Considerations

Richness versus leanness	Cost
Need for interpretation (ambiguity)	Amount of information conveyed
Speed of establishing contact	Permanent record
Time required for feedback	Control over the message

Richness versus Leanness

Some channels of communication provide more information than others. Generally, the richest channels of communication provide nonverbal information in addition to that provided in written or oral form. For this reason, the richest channel of communication is face-to-face, or what is often called *interpersonal communication*. Face-to-face communication provides participants a rich source of information, including vocal cues, facial expressions, bodily movement, bodily appearance, the use of space, the use of time, touching, and clothing and other artifacts.

In addition, face-to-face communication provides opportunities to facilitate feedback and establish a personal focus. These aspects also contribute to the richness of interpersonal communication as a channel of communication.

Face-to-face communication is particularly useful for job interviews in which the prospective employer is presumably interested in gathering as much information as possible from applicants. Similarly, personnel issues involving an individual may best be explored in a face-to-face communication situation because this mode might provide more information about the person's feelings, attitudes, or nonverbal clues to issues that are preventing him or her from functioning at the highest possible level.

Other channels of communication that provide access to nonverbal information are oral presentations, meetings, and group work. This is true regardless of whether this communication is mediated or not. In other words, presentations might take place using Skype, podcasts, video-conferencing, or other technology that allows audiences to view speakers who are not in the same place. Similarly, presentations might be recorded and viewed at a later time. Opportunities for checking the accuracy of interpretation of information may be more limited in these situations, though, because one person may more easily exercise control over the exchange of information.

Voice communication also provides some nonverbal information—much less than communication that enables us to view another's facial expressions, body language, clothing, and other artifacts, but potentially more than is provided by written communication. However, even some nonverbal information such as emotions can be communicated via e-mail and text messaging. Even in more formal types of written communication, such as paper memos and letters, tone can be communicated and can be an indicator of the writer's attitude or mood, and emoticons can be used in less formal types of writing, such as text and e-mail messages.

Perhaps the leanest medium of communication is a text or instant message. Lean media are useful for sending routine simple messages, such as short responses to queries or meeting times. However, they should not be used for persuasive purposes, more complex messages, or when establishing credibility or goodwill is the focus. They can maintain credibility and goodwill, however, to some degree, after these have been established. Similarly, they can damage credibility and goodwill, so even when using this lean medium some care should be taken.

Need for Interpretation

Some channels of communication are more ambiguous or leave more room for interpretation of the message being sent than others. Nonverbal communication may be the most ambiguous channel of communication because it requires the audience to interpret almost the entirety of the message. Nonverbal communication is difficult to interpret for a variety of reasons, mainly because it is not generally considered a coded language. Because of this, one nonverbal code may communicate a variety of meanings. For example, you may stand close to someone because you are in a crowded room, are having difficulty hearing him or her, or are attracted to the person. Studies indicate that receivers of nonverbal cues can often only guess about the meaning of those cues.[26]

Similarly, nonverbal communication can be difficult to interpret because a variety of codes may communicate the same meaning. This problem is particularly apparent when cultural differences come into play in a communication situation. In a public speaking situation, for example, you might show respect for the speaker by looking directly at him or her, whereas in some cultures listeners show respect when they avert their eyes from the speaker.

A third issue that may affect a person's ability to interpret nonverbal codes accurately is intentionality. Some nonverbal codes are sent intentionally, and others unintentionally. If you smile at a friend, you are intentionally showing him or her that you are glad to see that person. However, the same nonverbal cue may be sent unintentionally yet interpreted as intentional. You might be thinking about a pleasant experience you had the night before and unintentionally smile. But if this occurs while you are walking down the street, the stranger approaching you may interpret this unintentional signal as an intentional cue of interest in him or her.

For this reason, face-to-face communication may be more ambiguous than other channels of communication. Furthermore, depending on our sensitivity to nonverbal communication codes, we may overreact to certain nonverbal messages; conversely, we may be only somewhat aware or completely unaware of such information. Culture may play a role as well. The United States tends to be what is termed a "low-context" culture, which means that we tend to pay less attention to the contextual features of a situation and focus more on the verbal aspects, or what is said.

Written communication has the potential to be the least ambiguous channel of communication, particularly if it is prepared by a highly skilled writer who is able to precisely encode such a message. Such a writer must understand his or her purposes and audiences and have an excellent command of the language and its correct usage. For this reason, many official or legal messages such as contracts are delivered in the form of written documents. Similarly, instructions are often provided in written form, which also serves as a record that can be skimmed to quickly provide the needed information.

However, written communication can also become ambiguous when sending text messages, instant messaging, or using such social media as Twitter. One reason is that the abbreviations used for words or phrases may be unknown to some readers. Therefore, the audience's knowledge of such jargon should be considered when using these media.

Speed of Establishing Contact

Another important consideration, particularly in the business world, is the time it will take for a message to be delivered. As the old saying goes, time is money. For this reason, electronic forms of communication have become popular. Using the telephone, writing an e-mail or text message, using blogs and blog applications (such as Twitter) or other social media such as Facebook or LinkedIn, posting to wikis, Skyping, using virtual team applications, or sending a fax are nearly instantaneous channels of communication. In contrast, sending a written message or package by mail may take days. If you wish to communicate with someone who lives or works in another state or nation, then it may take days or even weeks to arrange a face-to-face meeting. For these reasons, electronic channels of communication have become extremely useful in the modern workplace. More and more companies are creating shared digital spaces or virtual teams where employees who are located in different areas of the country and even the world collaborate electronically to get their work done. Even communication within the same building is often conducted electronically through e-mail—the preferred method in most organizations—or text messaging.

Time Required for Feedback

Just as we may need to contact someone immediately, we may also need a response from that person just as rapidly. The most rapid forms of communication, as explained above, are generally electronic. However, depending on the person with whom you are communicating, his or her personality, and your relationship, communicating with a person via an electronic channel does not guarantee prompt feedback. In other words, corporate cultures and individuals may have preferences for specific communication channels or mediums and differing communication practices.

As mentioned earlier, much communication now occurs in organizations using e-mail, while some individuals may prefer face-to-face communication and thus may be more responsive to messages delivered using this medium. Others may prefer the telephone or electronic means. It is important to consider corporate and industry practices as well as the preferences of individuals to ensure the most prompt response to your messages. For example, if you are attempting to communicate with individuals working in a large shipping facility, they may not have real time access to computers or smartphones. Instead, they may communicate using radios or interpersonally.

Cost

Many channels of communication are relatively inexpensive for business users. Mail, e-mail, text messages, telephones, faxes, wikis, blogs and blog applications, social media, videoconferencing and teleconferencing tools, and Skype are generally considered inexpensive forms of communication. These tools have made it much less expensive for stakeholders both inside and outside organizations to communicate with each other, regardless of their location. Still, there are times when it may be appropriate to choose the greater expense of arranging a face-to-face meeting. Such cases might include introducing members of a virtual team who will be working on an important project for some time, interviewing job applicants for key positions, or meeting with important clients or accounts. The benefits of establishing rapport in these instances are expected to offset the increased costs of such arrangements.

Amount of Information Conveyed

The best channel for conveying large amounts of information is generally a written one. One reason is that most of us are generally poor listeners. Studies indicate that we retain only 10 percent or so of what we hear. Therefore, if you want people to have the opportunity to process and remember the information you have to deliver, particularly if the message is long or complex, then it is generally best delivered using a written channel.

You can see this channel-choice consideration practiced in everyday news delivery. If you want more information about what is happening in your community, state, country, or the world, you will probably read a print or electronic version of a newspaper or newsmagazine or visit an Internet news site. If you want less information about these issues or have less time, then you might watch or listen to a television newscast or listen to a radio news program on your way to work. Typically, less information is delivered by these electronic, oral channels, because they appeal to people who do not have much time or do not wish to invest much time in such information, who have shortened attention spans, or who do not like to read. These media generally deliver less information about the topics they address, although the Internet is making these distinctions less important as more news is delivered online in a variety of formats.

Regardless of whether the information is delivered electronically or on paper, though, if you have a fairly large quantity of complex or detailed information to deliver, a written communication channel is generally the best because it provides readers the opportunity to take the time necessary to process that information, often at their own convenience.

There are times, though, when a written channel may not be sufficient for delivering complex information; one example is training. Although more and more training programs are being delivered online, some situations may require a two-channel delivery system to provide trainees written materials as well as face-to-face instruction to ensure that information is understood and to answer participants' questions. The two-channel approach might also be used for important or persuasive messages. For example, an e-mail, memo, report, or proposal might be provided and then followed up with a meeting or oral presentation, or vice versa, depending on the communication goals. In addition, performance appraisals and reprimands are typically delivered both face-to-face and in writing. In this instance, the face-to-face meeting is intended to maintain rapport while the written message serves as a record of the exchange.

Need for a Permanent Record

Businesspeople are often involved in situations where they must keep records of what occurred during various work activities throughout the day or week. These situations include the need to record what occurred at a department meeting, an employee's work history, the findings of an audit of a client's financial records, and an employee's travel expenses. Most legal documents, including contracts, use the written channel of communication for this reason: the need to maintain a record. E-mail messages and other electronic forums such as Web sites, social networking sites, and blogs, if stored and backed up properly, can also serve as a record. This ability is not only a benefit, though; it can have very negative consequences for those who take advantage of the spontaneity of these electronic communication tools without taking the time to consider the strategic issues mentioned in this text. In other words, it is important to consider the impact of the message on the audience as well as to consider whether it might negatively affect our own credibility or relationship with the receiver. In the worst case, it may have much more negative consequences, such as losing our job if we anger a client, present a negative image of the company to the public, or reveal company information that is intended to remain internal to the organization.

Control over the Message

Written channels of communication are often the best choice when you wish to maintain greater control of the message that you send. The reason? If information is presented orally and interpersonally, you have a greater chance of persons who disagree with you speaking out and potentially derailing or confusing the message. That is why many negative messages are sent using a written channel of communication.

For example, if you must tell a job applicant that he was not selected for the position for which he recently interviewed, you can maintain control over the act of delivering that information by doing so in the form of a letter or a well-written e-mail message. Although calling the person to deliver the message might exhibit greater goodwill on your part because you have taken the time to interact using a channel that enables you to send nonverbal codes (vocal cues), you also risk a situation that might spin out of control if the person does not take the news well or wishes to take more of your time to find out why he or she was not selected. In this case, you also may be put in a position to explain the decision more fully. However, by sending a polite letter or e-mail, you are able to convey the same basic message without the risk of losing control of the situation or your time. But even this selection matters. If you send an e-mail rather than a letter, you are more likely to be contacted by the receiver, so you should consider whether you want to encourage further interaction on the matter. If not, a letter might be a better choice.

Similarly, in crisis situations, some companies refuse to speak to the news media for fear of losing control of the message or releasing information that may be damaging. These situations may be handled by using the written communication channel to send a press release to the media or post a message to the public on the company Web site. The press release delivers information but does not provide an opportunity for the receiver to question the communicator and for the communicator to potentially lose control of the message that the company intends to convey. Oral channels of communication are often riskier because they expose the speaker to differences of opinion, conflict, and personalities that may be difficult to control. On the other side, conflict situations demand greater control of the nonverbal elements of communication and thus expose the communicator to risk in terms of unintentionally sending a negative message. One common example occurs in legal situations in which the defendant may not "appear" to be sorry for his or her actions and this lack of remorse may affect sentencing.

However, if one of the primary purposes of the message is to convey or maintain goodwill, then it is generally better to deliver the bad news face-to-face. Table 5-3 provides a summary of the proper use of differing media within an organizational context.

Table 5-3 Use of Communication Media

Medium	Best Uses
Memo	■ Simple, routine messages ■ Confirming policies ■ Distributing to a large, internal audience ■ Providing information when a response isn't required ■ Communicating with an external audience
Letter	■ Conveying formality ■ Providing a written record ■ Writing a complaint ■ Communicating condolences or thanks ■ Sending brief, impersonal, or routine messages
E-mail	■ Providing a hard copy ■ Sending a visual display of information ■ Simple, routine messages ■ Confirming policies ■ Distributing to a large, internal audience
Fax	■ Communicating general information about a company and its products or services
Web page	■ Sharing information with large audiences in an economical fashion ■ Inspiring and motivating others ■ Demonstrating products or training
Oral presentation	■ Introducing a persuasive message or following up on one when goodwill and credibility are especially important ■ Delivering bad news to a large audience when goodwill and credibility are especially important
Face-to-face	■ Communicating confidential information ■ Negotiating ■ Promoting or firing an employee ■ Communicating personal warmth or care ■ Reading nonverbal communication cues
Telephone	■ Providing quick feedback or response ■ Sending confidential information ■ Confirming
Voice mail	■ Informing when feedback isn't needed ■ Confirming ■ Sending a simple message
In-person meetings	■ Decision making and problem solving ■ Inspiring and motivating others
Videoconferencing	■ Making a personal connection with a large audience ■ Training ■ Decision making and problem solving

New Media and the Organization

As discussed earlier, rapid technology changes have made communication cheaper and faster for organizations, providing more avenues for connecting with employees, suppliers, and current and potential customers. People who use the Internet to share relevant video contribute to the capture of a marketing advantage for their companies.[27] On a macro level, "the use of social networking sites or even Internet-based virtual worlds such as Second Life may become important for organizations to establish their brands, especially among young people."[28] The business networking and blogging application Twitter and others like it are growing in popularity and usefulness in the business realm. Likewise, Facebook has become an important marketing tool for many organizations. A number of authors indicate that Web-based training and education, once seen only in the most progressive organizations, should be expected by nearly everyone entering the workforce or hoping to advance.[29]

Although the benefits of new media should be considered by organizations, it is also important to be aware of the potential risks, such as the damage that hurtful or misunderstood words sent via mediated channels can cause in organizational environments.[30] Other research emphasizes the pitfalls of overreliance on technology and the importance of developing communication management skills to avoid burnout. Such skills include the ability to prioritize mediated communication tasks, learning to disconnect from work by turning off cell phones during nonbusiness hours, and only checking e-mail at several designated times during the work day.[31]

The sections that follow discuss both the benefits and the potential risks involved in the use of new technologies, specifically the most used media in organizations today—e-mail—as well as the burgeoning world of social media.

E-mail

More information is probably available on e-mail than any other technology because it has been around for some time and is relied on by many organizations as a primary medium of communication among employees, customers and clients, and the public. In fact, 98 percent of business-to-business communications employ e-mail.[32] E-mail provides several advantages to organizations, but its extensive use also exposes organizations to several potential challenges.

Benefits of E-mail

E-mail is a highly effective communication medium that is central to the way that organizations function, enabling virtual teams, working at home, and collaboration in many forms.

- **Knowledge sharing and communication networks.** E-mail is a core communication technology for the creation, distribution, and application of knowledge in organizations. In a survey of e-mail users, respondents commented that e-mail had improved teamwork and information flow and allowed information to be shared with multiple coworkers. The researchers also found that the majority of respondents reported that the net effect of e-mail is improved organizational communication.[33]

- **External communications and image.** Prompt response to external e-mails and professional language are as important for maintaining external relationships as they are for communication between employees.

Challenges of E-mail

However, the growing dependence on e-mail also invites problems. The average corporate user receives 126 e-mail messages a day, a 55 percent increase since 2003.[34] Twenty percent of an employee's eight-hour day is spent working with e-mail,[35] and knowledge workers spend one to two hours a day managing e-mail.[36]

This trend poses a number of challenges to organizations and individuals alike. The literature on e-mail use in organizations reveals four major concerns:

1. **Individual e-mail efficiency**—the time spent handling e-mail and time recovering from e-mail interruptions to work flow.

2. **Individual e-mail pressure**—anxiety caused by e-mail volumes and the perceived need to respond to e-mails quickly.

3. **Organizational e-mail effectiveness**—using e-mail to support effective decision making and knowledge sharing, as well as improving business processes that depend on e-mail.

4. **Organizational risk**—the risk of litigation resulting from unguarded comments made by an employee in an e-mail and regulatory action resulting from the deletion of e-mail.

E-mail may cause stress because of its speed, recordability, use of multiple addresses, processing, routing, and lack of social and conversational cues[37] (see Table 5-4). E-mail may encourage an inhospitable working environment, isolation, and inconsiderate behavior. Close supervision and rigid performance monitoring contributes significantly to job pressure, and e-mail may be an instrument of harassment and bullying and has been shown to escalate disputes. Even those who do not receive a specific e-mail may be affected because others within the organization are affected by that e-mail and are themselves affected by other e-mails that, in aggregate, can create a climate of stress within an organization.

Table 5-4 E-mail Characteristics

E-mail Characteristics	Anticipated Effect	Negative Personal or Organizational Consequences
Speed and convenience	Increased number of messages and increased expectation of response speed	Work overload, errors
Recordability	Increased potential for control	Resentment, reduced autonomy
Multiple addressability, processing, and routing	Communication manipulation	Potential harassment, possible litigation
Lack of social cues	Weakened interpersonal bonds; lowered commitment	More misunderstanding, lower decision quality, context, escalation of disputes
Lack of conversational cues	Focus of attention on internal (negative) states	Greater susceptibility to negative affect (mood) and negative evaluations

Source: Taylor, J. R., Flanagin, A. J., Cheney, G., & Seibold, D. R. (2001). "Organizational Communication Research: Key Moments, Central Concerns, and Future Challenges." In W. Gudykunst (Ed.), *Communication Yearbook* 24 (pp. 99–138). Newbury Park, CA: Sage.

In fact, according to one report, more than one-third of workers suffer from "e-mail stress."[38] Self-reported e-mail checking suggests more than one-third of workers check their e-mail inbox every fifteen minutes, but monitoring software reveals that workers actually check e-mail more regularly, some as often as forty times an hour. E-mail is a problem for employees, who are overwhelmed by the volume, lose important items, and feel pressured to respond quickly, often within seconds.[39] However, the sources of e-mail pressure extend beyond overload and include e-mail interruptions to work, unclear priorities, lost e-mail, unclear timescales, inappropriate language, and inappropriate use of the medium.

The proliferation of e-mail use has also created problems for organizations. Although unwanted e-mails or spam is undoubtedly a problem, it is intra-organizational e-mail that consumes employees' time and intellectual bandwidth. At 3M:

■ 16 percent of e-mails received were copied unnecessarily.

■ 13 percent of e-mails received were irrelevant or untargeted.

■ 41 percent of e-mails received were for information purposes.

■ Only 46 percent of actionable e-mails received stated what action was expected.

- 56 percent of employees agreed e-mail is used too often instead of phone or face-to-face communication.
- Only 45 percent of employees said their e-mails were easy to read.[40]

In fact, it is estimated that e-mail overload cost the U.S. economy nearly $1 trillion in 2010.[41]

In addition, e-mails create a permanent written record that can be obtained and used in a lawsuit against individuals or their company. What might seem like a private communication can be obtained and interpreted by lawyers suing a company as key evidence of admissions, breach of contract, tortious wrongdoing, or improper motive. Seemingly innocuous comments can come back to haunt an organization, possibly many years later. Deleting an e-mail is not equivalent to shredding: E-mail is semi-permanent. Deleting or tampering with e-mail can come under "spoliation" and is also illegal.[42]

To address these issues, companies should take two steps:

1. Assess e-mail usage, develop policies and procedures, and communicate them clearly to employees. Surveys of business partner relationships, such as customers and supplier satisfaction, should include a section on communications effectiveness and address e-mail competence in particular.

2. Develop training programs to ensure that e-mail is used properly and messages are well written. Such programs should also provide methods for employees to better manage e-mail and reduce stress.

E-mail can increase speed of communication among organizational stakeholders, but organizations need to take steps to ensure that they have policies in place to maintain productivity levels and protect themselves against legal threats.

Social Media

Over the last two years alone, social media have dramatically transformed the pace at which information is shared—and the information being shared isn't just social. Millions of employees use Facebook, Twitter, blogs, wikis, and other applications to communicate with one another and the world. Many companies—79 percent of the Fortune Global 100 alone—use social media to communicate with customers and allow customers to in turn generate their own content through product reviews, blog entries, and other messages about the organization. Corporate blogs, applications like Yammer, and intranet discussion boards have accelerated the flow of information inside companies as well.

Four common types of social media used by organizations are described below:

- **Social networking:** Social network sites are for groups of people who share common interests or activities. Facebook and Google+ are social networking sites with which most of us are familiar, while LinkedIn is a professional networking site. Organizations are now taking advantage of these sites to market their products and services and communicate with customers.

- **Wikis:** Like social networking sites, wikis are developed collaboratively by a community of users with one additional feature: Users can add and edit content. You are probably familiar with Wikipedia, which is a free, Web-based, collaborative, multilingual encyclopedia project supported by the nonprofit Wikimedia Foundation. Organizations can create their own wikis that enable workgroups to communicate online, write collaboratively, and manage schedules.

- **Blogs:** A blog is a Web site on which an individual or group of users can share content and record opinions and information on a regular basis. Companies commonly use blogs either internally to communicate with employees or externally to communicate with customers.

Successful blogs provide an avenue for customers to engage interactively with thought leaders in an organization with the goal of developing relationships. One downside of blogs, however, is that this interactive element does not always result in positive comments.

- **Microblogs:** A microblog is used for short messages where quick delivery is important. For example, Twitter, a popular microblogging tool, allows for only 140 characters per message. To take advantage of Twitter, many organizations have designated official "tweeters" to communicate with customers: Ford Motors, General Motors, Honda, Jet Blue, Southwest Airlines, Marriott International Hotels, the list goes on. The official "tweeter" at Ford Motors, Scott Monty, head of social media, said the use of Twitter is "part of a larger social media strategy to humanize the Ford brand and put consumers in touch with Ford employees."[43] At Xerox, all employees are required to attend Twitter training to better enable them to manage the brand. As this statement demonstrates, microblogging has become another important communication tool in organizations.

According to *BusinessWeek*'s Corporate Executive Board, 71 percent of companies plan to increase their investments in social media—but only a third have guidelines for how it should be used. This development points to a series of internal and external risks that companies should move fast to manage as employees' use of social media accelerates.

Risks from Internal Communications

Even purely internal use of social media can present real risks to companies. Information simply flows faster through this medium—it's faster than the grapevine—and may have more credibility and impact. The question that organizations need to address is, when can that fast flow of information cause problems?

- **Secrets are harder to protect**. Know that material information about company plans and strategies will flow down through the organization faster. Be sure that key employees know just how slippery this slope is.

- **Compensation isn't confidential any more**. Assume that information about employee compensation will no longer stay with the employee. Disparities in pay, benefits, and work arrangements will be rapidly exposed and compared among employees.

- **Strategic actions may be signaled in advance**. If employees are asked to implement strategic actions, those strategies will be almost impossible to conceal from those outside the organization. Organizations will need to anticipate leaks and be prepared for quick action if and when they occur.

- **Inconsistencies within an organization may be exposed**. Different departments within organizations inevitably take different positions regarding customers, employees, and regulators. The blogosphere will quickly reveal these inconsistencies for all to see. When information is flowing more freely than ever before, managers will need to take steps to ensure that all company positions are in harmony.

Risks from External Communications

When employees use external social media—blogs, Twitter, Facebook, and so on—they can easily harm the company, sometimes without even knowing it. A few examples include the following:

- **Premature release of new product information**. Employees commonly leak pictures or descriptions of a new product before its official release. Even a casual tweet revealing the location of a key employee can signal new product or business development activity before it is ready for public release.

- **Exposure of company problems**. Employee "venting" is ubiquitous on Facebook and Twitter. In some cases, that frustration is an indictment of the company's own products, services, or, perhaps most commonly, management culture.
- **Harassment**. Social media almost immediately gave rise to claims of workplace harassment—a superior using Facebook or another medium to make unwanted advances.

Companies need a plan to manage fast-evolving social media risks. Because so few companies have taken even initial steps in this area, the best approach is to start with a basic checklist:

- Develop a policy on the use of social media, both internally and externally.
- Work with the legal department to create records-retention policies for social media and make sure employees are aware of them.
- Partner with the corporate communications department to monitor the organization's brand in social media.
- Work with the information systems department to incorporate secure social media in the organization's information technology (IT) road map.
- Understand employees' workflows to build awareness about proper use of social media and effective information protection.

Employees also need to be aware of the risks of social media. Employees should not broadcast confidential company information on social network sites and should be careful about expressing their opinions about the company, their manager, or their colleagues on the Internet if they don't want to risk reprimands or dismissal.

Summary

- The context of communication should be considered when formulating a message. Context includes various internal and external environmental factors. The culture of the corporation as well as the communication climate can affect whether messages are communicated and how they are conveyed. For those interested in organization-wide planning, it is helpful to understand the flow of communication in an organization, both formal and informal networks.

- After considering the context for communicating and the organizational culture in which you will communicate, you are in a better position to select the appropriate channel and media to convey your message. Broadly, the four channels of communication are written, oral, nonverbal, and visual. There are a number of media from which to choose to communicate using written and oral channels.

- The choice of medium can be influenced by knowledge gained during earlier steps in the strategic communication process. In other words, the purpose of communication, the audience, and the context might inform media choices. Other factors to consider include the amount of complex information you wish to convey. Or you might select a written channel because this also serves as a record to which the receiver can refer back and because the information is less costly to deliver using your company mail service. Likewise, you might select an oral channel to communicate with your colleague in the next office because you want the additional information it provides ("richness" in the form of nonverbal communication), and you also desire immediate contact and feedback.

- The proliferation of new media has presented new opportunities and benefits to organizations as well as led to new challenges and threats. In recent years, e-mail in particular has proliferated in organizations and has led to increases in productivity as well as greater costs to organizations and stress to employees. Social media presents the next challenge to organizations in terms of creating effective programs to monitor and manage its use. Training employees in effectively and appropriately using new media and implementing company policies can greatly alleviate some of the potential challenges they create.

Key Terms

context **94**

contextual intelligence **95**

adaptive capacity **95**

organizational culture **96**

supportive communication climate **101**

defensive communication climate **101**

Discussion Questions

1. As a current or future leader, what can you do to create supportive communication climates in your department and organization?

2. You want to ask your supervisor for a raise. How might context effect your decision about when and how to deliver this message? What channel and medium of communication would you use and why?

3. You are the salesperson for a company and have unknowingly sold faulty product to a dozen customers. Are there contextual or environmental factors that might affect the delivery of this message? What is the best channel and medium of communi-

cation for dealing with this problem and why? Would you use more than one channel? If so, in what order?

4. You are the owner of a midsized company, and one of your managers has been arrested for fraud. Are there contextual and environmental factors that might potentially affect the delivery of this message? With what audiences would you wish to communicate? What is the best channel and medium of communication for each audience and why?

5. How do you feel about e-mail monitoring practices? Are there ethical concerns involved in such a decision? If so, what are they?

Applications

1. Identify an organization of which you are a part. This organization can be your workplace or a church, sports, or university organization in which you participate. Identify the formal communication network the organization uses and consider the following questions:

   ■ Does it primarily use upward, downward, or horizontal flow or some combination of these?

   ■ Does it use its formal communication network as effectively as it might?

   ■ What role does the grapevine play in this organization?

   ■ What are its favored channels or media of communication? Are these effective or not, and why?

   Based on your analysis, write an informal report summarizing the use of formal and informal network channels in the organization and provide recommendations for improving their use.

2. Identify an organization of which you are a part. This organization can be your workplace or a church, sports, or university organization in which you participate. Identify and analyze the media that are typically used to communication in the organization. If possible, try to identify the audiences who typically use each medium and for what purpose. Then write an informal report that summarizes your findings and provides recommendations for improving the use of media in your organization. Explain why your recommendations will improve communication based on channel choice considerations.

3. Conduct research on organizational policies regarding e-mail use in the workplace. Write a report to your supervisor that summarizes your findings and presents recommendations for implementing an e-mail use policy in your organization.

4. You are the marketing manager of your organization. Conduct research on the uses of social media by organizations for marketing aims and write an informal proposal to the president of the company in which you report your findings and recommend actions for the use of social media for marketing purposes based on those findings.

5. Conduct research on e-mail monitoring policies in organizations. Use the information you have found to write a report to your manager, either recommending that an e-mail monitoring practice be instituted by the firm or avoided. Use your research to support your recommendation.

Endnotes

1. Wessel, H. (2003, February 12). Speaking their piece: Feedback from workers plays a major role in the vitality of a company. *Orlando Sentinel*, G1.

2. Veil, S. (2011). Mindful learning in crisis management. *Journal of Business Communication*, 48 (2): 116–147.

3. Mayo, T. (1980). *In Their Time: The Greatest Business Leaders of the Twentieth Century*. Boston: Harvard Business School Press.

4. Bennis, W., & Thomas, R. J. (2002). *Geeks and Geezers*. Boston: Harvard Business Review Press.

5. Weick, K. E., & Sutcliffe, K. M. (2001). *Managing the Unexpected: Assuring High Performance in an Age of Complexity*. New York: Jossey-Bass, p. 146.

6. Schein, E. H. (1992). *Educational Culture and Leadership*. New York: Jossey-Bass, p. 12.

7. Boreham, N., & Morgan, C. (2004). A sociocultural analysis of organisational learning. *Oxford Review of Education*, 30 (3), 307–326, p. 309.

8. Chatman, J. A., & Jehn, K. A. (1994). Assessing the relationship between industry characteristics and organizational culture: How different can you be? *Academy of Management Journal*, 37, 522–553; O'Reilly, C. A., III, Chatman, J., & Caldwell, D. F. (1993). People and organizational culture: A profile comparison approach to assessing person-organization fit. *Academy of Management Journal*, 34, 487–516.

9. Peters, T., & Waterman, R. (1982). *In Search of Excellence*. New York: Harper and Row.

10. Organizational Culture Inventory Guide (n.d.). *The Aggressive/Defensive Cluster*. Retrieved June 12, 2017 from *www.survey-server2.com/ocikituniversity/agressive_overview.asp*.

11. Ibid.

12. Ibid.

13. Ibid.

14. McGregor, D. (1960). *The Human Side of Enterprise*. New York: McGraw-Hill.

15. Organizational Culture Inventory Guide, n.d.

16. Ibid.

17. Ibid.

18. Kotter, J. P. & Heskett, J. L. (1992). *Corporate culture and performance*. New York: Free Press.

19. Organizational Culture Inventory Guide, n.d.

20. Spencer, D. (1986). Employee voice and employee retention. *Academy of Management Journal*, 29, 488–502.

21. Ibid.

22. Gibb, J. (1961). Defensive communication. *Journal of Communication*, 11, 141–148.

23. Eisenberg, E. M., & Goodall, Jr., H. L. (1993). *Organizational Communication: Balancing Creativity and Constraint.* New York: St. Martin's Press.

24. Wessell, 2003.

25. Eisenberg & Goodall, 1993, p. 235.

26. Motley, M. T., & Camden, C. T. (1988). Facial expression of emotion: A comparison of posed expressions versus spontaneous expressions in an interpersonal communication setting. *Western Journal of Communication,* 52 (1), 1–22.

27. Moran, G. (2007, July). Now see this: Online video can breathe new life into your business. *Entrepreneur,* 35 (7), 30.

28. Schramm, J. (2007, September). Internet connections. *HRMagazine,* 52 (9), 176.

29. Education. (2005, November). *Inc., 27* (11), 147–148.

30. Lyons, D. (2005, November 14). Attack of the blogs. *Forbes,* 176 (10), 128–138.

31. *HR Magazine.* (2006). Technology spurring stress, decreasing productivity. *HR Magazine,* 51 (5), 14.

32. Taylor, J. R., Flanagin, A. J., Cheney, G., & Seibold, D. R. (2001). Organizational communication research: Key moments, central concerns, and future challenges. In W. Gudykunst (Ed.), *Communication Yearbook 24* (pp. 99–138). Thousand Oaks, CA: Sage.

33. Tassabehji, R., & Vakola, M. (2005). Business e-mail: The killer impact. *Communications of the ACM,* 48 (11), 64–70.

34. Radicati Group. (2007). Addressing information overload in corporate e-mail: The economics of user attention. White paper (April). Retrieved October 5, 2007 from *www.radicati.com.*

35. Davenport, T. (2005). *Thinking for a Living.* Harvard Business School Press.

36. Cain, M. (2006). Who needs training on e-mail? Gartner Research, July 2006, ID no. G00141290.

37. Taylor et al., 2001.

38. N. A. (2007). One in three workers suffers from 'e-mail stress.' *Daily Telegraph,* (13 August), Retrieved August 14, 2007, from *http://www.telegraph.co.uk/news/main.jhtml?xml=/news/2007/08/13/ne-mail113.xml.*

39. Jackson, T., Burgess, A., & Edwards, J. (2006). Simple approach to improving e-mail communication. *Communications of the ACM,* (June 2006), 49 (6), 107–109.

40. Jackson et al., 2006.

41. Spira, J. (2011). Information overload: None are immune. *Information Management,* 21 (5), 32.

42. Sinrod, E. (2004). Where's my e-mail? The legal implications of disappearing e-mail. *Journal of Internet Law,* (September) 8 (3), 23–24.

43. Ford Media. (2009). Allure of social media helps Ford reach new customers. Retrieved March 28, 2013 from *http://media.ford.com/article_display.cfm?article_id=30634.*

Johnson & Johnson: *A Dispute with the American Red Cross*

"Our primary goal is simply to restore the long-standing legal boundaries that the American Red Cross and Johnson & Johnson have observed around the Red Cross trademark for more than 100 years. It is now appropriate to let the judicial process take its course."[1]

Johnson & Johnson Statement on Litigation with the American Red Cross, September 20, 2007

As Vice President of Corporate Communications at Johnson & Johnson, Ray Jordan was well aware that suing a nationally renowned humanitarian organization like the American Red Cross had the makings of a communications nightmare. Nevertheless, after repeated attempts to negotiate with the non-profit, Johnson & Johnson was left little choice but to file suit in the hope of restoring longtime cooperation between the two organizations.

Legal Issues

On August 8, 2007, Johnson & Johnson officially filed a lawsuit against the American Red Cross and four of their licensing partners for trademark violations in their use of the red cross emblem. Following more than a century of cooperation between both entities in marketing the symbol, the American Red Cross recently began licensing the trademark to its partners for use on consumer retail products, including baby mitts, nail clippers, toothbrushes, and humidifiers.

Upon discovering that the American Red Cross had authorized usage of the red cross emblem to licensed partners, management at Johnson & Johnson saw potential for the non-profit's products to compete with their own healthcare lines whose products bore the same emblem. Mindful of how neither party stood to benefit from a publicized lawsuit, Johnson & Johnson opted to file suit against the American Red Cross only after the non-profit rejected offers for mediation following months of attempted dialogue.

With the intention of restoring the legal boundaries surrounding usage of the red cross emblem, Johnson & Johnson and Johnson & Johnson Consumer Companies, Inc. filed a civil complaint on August 8, 2007, in the United States District Court, Southern District of New York, against the American National Red Cross. Additional defendants named in the suit include the commercial licensees of the American Red Cross, namely Learning Curve International, Inc.; Magla Products, LLC.; Water-Jel Technologies, Inc.; and First Aid Only, Inc.[2]

In a company statement on August 9, Johnson & Johnson officials commented on the suit brought before the American Red Cross saying, "both Johnson & Johnson and the American Red Cross have long-held separate and distinct rights to the use of the Red Cross Design trademark."[3] According to the press release issued

This case was prepared by Research Assistants Jennifer Galano, Christopher Schlax, and Anthony Wang under the direction of James S. O'Rourke, Concurrent Professor of Management, as the basis for class discussion rather than to illustrate either effective or ineffective handling of an administrative situation. Information was gathered from corporate as well as public sources.

1. "Johnson & Johnson Statement on Litigation with the American Red Cross." 20 September 2007.
   http://www.jnj.com/news/jnj_news/20070920_191937.htm.

2. "Johnson & Johnson Statement on Civil Complaint against the American National Red Cross and Commercial Licensees."
   9 August 2007. *http://www.jnj.com/news/jnj_news/20070809_081717.htm.*

3. Ibid.

by the American Red Cross, Johnson & Johnson demanded that the following actions be taken by the non-profit in accordance with the lawsuit:

- Permanently abandon usage of the red cross emblem on first aid and emergency kits placed in the retail marketplace.
- Deliver to Johnson & Johnson the inventory of commercially licensed products bearing the red cross symbol for destruction.
- Remit to Johnson & Johnson the profits from the sale of these products, as well as the related interest on the proceeds.
- Pay punitive damages to Johnson & Johnson.[4]

Johnson & Johnson Corporate History

After having considered various practical uses for the research conducted by antisepsis advocate Joseph Lister, Robert Wood Johnson joined with his two brothers in 1885 to create a line of ready-to-use surgical dressings. The company produced its first products in 1886 and officially incorporated as Johnson & Johnson one year later, with Robert Wood Johnson serving as president of the company. Upon his death in 1910, his brother, James Wood Johnson, assumed control of the company until 1932, at which point Robert Wood "General" Johnson II took direction. He is credited with having written the famous Johnson & Johnson Credo, which outlines the company's core values and commitment to corporate social responsibility.

Since the early twentieth century, the company has diversified into a broad array of product lines and has operated on the principle of decentralized management, ever mindful of their accountability to customers, employees, communities, and shareholders. Under the leadership of current Chief Executive Officer William C. Weldon, Johnson & Johnson comprises more than 250 operating companies across the globe and ranks as a market leader among major healthcare and pharmaceutical entities, such as Merck and Pfizer. The company is organized into the Consumer, Pharmaceutical, and Medical Devices and Diagnostics business segments, which produce popular brands like Band-Aid, Tylenol, Neutrogena, and Splenda.

The American Red Cross

The American Red Cross is a humanitarian organization dedicated to providing emergency help, disaster relief, and educational training in the United States as part of the International Federation of Red Cross and Red Crescent Societies. Famed nurse Clara Barton organized the first successful Red Cross Society in the United States in 1881, which was granted official status upon the ratification at the Geneva Conventions. In accordance with its humanitarian mission, the American Red Cross began selling first aid kits in 1903 and gained public favorability by caring for wounded soldiers during the First and Second World Wars.

Currently, the American Red Cross is supported by community donations and the efforts of more than one million volunteers and thirty thousand employees who aid in providing relief to the afflicted. The non-profit is also the largest supplier of blood and blood products to more than three thousand hospitals across the nation

The role of senior management and board of directors of the American Red Cross was clarified in United States legislation during the aftermath of Hurricane Katrina. In accordance with this legislative initiative, the new Chief Executive of the American Red Cross, Mark W. Everson, was elected in April 2007.

The Red Cross Symbol

As determined by representatives of sixteen nations to an 1863 humanitarian aid conference in Geneva, medical personnel of any country who were volunteering to care for the "wounded of armies"[5] should wear an easily recognizable symbol. The symbol of a red cross on a white background, an inversion of the red flag of Switzerland that bears a white cross, was chosen as the emblem to honor the Swiss origin of this plan.

The American Red Cross looks to a federal criminal statute to protect the emblem, as opposed to a federally issued trademark to claim ownership of the red cross emblem. This is not unique, as other icons, such as Smokey Bear, the Olympic Rings, and the 4-H Club insignia, are also protected under United States criminal provisions.[6]

---

4. "American Red Cross Defends Use of Emblem and Mission." 10 August 2007. *http://www.redcross.org/pressrelease/0,1077,0_314_6907,00.html.*

5. American Red Cross: Clara Barton Chapter. "Clara Barton in Dansville." *http://www.redcrossclara.com/History.html.*

6. Stearman, Jennifer, Andrea Morisi, Heather Angus. "Protecting Our Emblem: M ark of the Red Cross." Legal Times. 1997. *http://www.redcross.org/logos/legtimes.html.*

The American Red Cross began using the red cross emblem in 1881, six years before Johnson & Johnson began using the emblem in 1887. The non-profit was granted its Charter in a congressional bill in June 1900. A 1905 amendment gave the American Red Cross the use of the emblem, and specifically stated that "in carrying out its purposes under this [charter], [the Red Cross] may have the use, as an emblem and badge, a Greek red cross on a white ground…" The Charter grants the Red Cross "to conduct other activities consistent with" its Charter purposes.[7]

In the 1905 Charter amendment, Congress expressed their intention for the Red Cross to have exclusive use of the emblem. These rights were confirmed by the U.S. Patent and Trademark Office, which specifically reserved an application serial number for the Red Cross to register its emblem in "every" class of goods and services.

Concurrent with the issuance of the Charter amendment, however, several entities were already using the red cross symbol as their own trademark, including Johnson & Johnson. The 1900 congressional bill did not prohibit these earlier uses. In 1910, Congress formally established that "lawful use of the Red Cross name and emblem that began prior to January 5, 1905, could continue, but only if that use was for the same purpose and for the same class of goods."[8]

By 1942, more than two hundred companies had claimed that their ownership of the red cross symbol predated the January 5, 1905 amendment. Since then, however, the number of entities using the red cross symbol has reduced to twenty-one companies.[9]

Johnson & Johnson: A Public Statement

In anticipation of a public announcement by the American Red Cross that would officially acknowledge the lawsuit, Johnson & Johnson was poised to respond to the negative media coverage that would inevitably follow release of the news. Thus, the company issued a statement on August 9, 2007, in which it expressed a great respect for the relief efforts that the American Red Cross has provided to hundreds of humanitarian initiatives over the decades. To that end, Johnson & Johnson has remained an advocate for the mission of the American Red Cross through philanthropic aid, "consistently supporting the organization through cash donations, product donations, and employee volunteering."[10]

The statement notes that Johnson & Johnson began using the red cross emblem and written "red cross" trademarks in 1887, which predates the formal charter of the American Red Cross. After more than one hundred years of exclusive rights to use the red cross design on commercial products, such as first aid kits and wound-care products, Johnson & Johnson denounces the non-profit's campaign to use the design in retail initiatives outside of traditional relief services. The statement says that the distribution of consumer goods bearing the symbol by American Red Cross "is in direct violation of a Federal statute protecting the mark, as well as in violation of our longstanding trademark rights."[11]

Communication Issues

Johnson & Johnson: Strategies

According to Ray Jordan, Vice President for Corporate Communications at Johnson & Johnson, the public relations consequences of taking a major humanitarian organization to court would be akin to a "nuclear holocaust."[12] Thus, Johnson & Johnson was disinclined to issue a press release announcing the suit against the American Red Cross and prepared a company statement as a precaution against potential backlash from the non-profit. The supposition that the humanitarian organization would also avoid media coverage of the suit was crushed once the American Red Cross issued a press release the evening after having been notified of the lawsuit.

---

7. *http://www.redcross.org/pressrelease/0,1077,0_489_6910,00.html*

8. Stearman, Jennifer, Andrea Morisi, Heather Angus. "Protecting Our Emblem: Mark of the Red Cross."

9. Ibid.

10. "Johnson & Johnson Statement on Civil Complaint against the American National Red Cross and Commercial Licensees." 9 August 2007. *http://www.jnj.com/news/jnj_news/20070809_081717.htm.*

11. Ibid.

12. Telephone conference with Ray Jordan, Johnson & Johnson. New Brunswick, NJ. 1 October 2007.

American Red Cross: Response

According to Carrie Martin of the American Red Cross public relations department, the non-profit was shocked that Johnson & Johnson had initiated a legal battle over reclaiming usage of the emblem. A press release was prepared by the American Red Cross to defend their use of the symbol and was broadcast across public newswires the evening following notification of the lawsuit.

Martin would go on to give 25 media interviews in the next 48 hours, which included correspondence with newspapers from Moscow, Paris, and London. She wanted to make it clear that the American Red Cross was using the symbol to fulfill the mission given to the group by Congress, "helping the country prepare for emergencies."[13] Since the terror attacks of September 11, 2001, the American Red Cross feels that marketing preparedness kits through retailers is a natural extension of their mission and, thus, legitimizes usage of the red cross symbol on consumer products. Martin also stated that taking the products off the shelves as the lawsuit states would be a "disservice to consumers."[14]

As described in the August 8, 2007, Associated Press wire story, many of the products in question were supplements to health and safety kits issued by the American Red Cross, which directed the $10 million of profits from sales to disaster relief efforts. American Red Cross President and CEO Mark Everson expressed confidence that the non-profit would prevail in the lawsuit, as well as his hope that "the courts and Congress will not allow Johnson & Johnson to bully the American Red Cross."[15] Everson also implied that the repossession and destruction of products "that J&J wants to take away from customers" would cause Americans to lose a degree of security when faced with an emergency.

Johnson & Johnson: Reaction

Johnson & Johnson was surprised at the aggressive tone of the newswire message issued by the American Red Cross, as it essentially pitted the non-profit against the company when, as Jordan noted, the company viewed the American Red Cross as "a longtime partner."[16] According to the August 8, 2007, press release by American Red Cross President and CEO Mark Everson, "for a multi-billion dollar drug company to claim that the Red Cross violated a criminal statute that was created to protect the humanitarian mission of the Red Cross — simply so that J&J can make more money — is obscene."[17] Jordan recognized that the American Red Cross evidently did not share the same desire to minimize the degree of media coverage surrounding the lawsuit. He noted that articles in *The New York Times* and the *The Wall Street Journal* discussing the American Red Cross news release presented a more "balanced" and unbiased view of the lawsuit.[18] Consequently, Jordan stated that "we were not inclined to take off the gloves" by engaging in a public relations battle with the humanitarian organization.[19]

The initial days after the press release saw a significant degree of public response to the suit, especially on the Johnson & Johnson company weblog. Jordan remarked that the site was "set up for situations like this" in which information disseminates rapidly and a "strong element for carrying discussion further" is needed.[20] A message was also sent to all Johnson & Johnson employees from the Chairman to clearly state that the sole intention behind the lawsuit was to stop the licensing of the red cross symbol to Johnson & Johnson's commercial competitors.

Johnson & Johnson: Surveying Public Opinion

A main concern among the leadership at Johnson & Johnson was the degree to which the lawsuit was visible to

---

13. Telephone conference with Carrie Martin, American Red Cross. Washington DC. 4 October 2007.

14. Ibid.

15. "Johnson & Johnson Sues American Red Cross over Use of Emblem." Associated Press. 8 August 2007.
    http://www.iht.com/articles/ap/2007/08/09/america/NA-GEN-US-Red-Cross-Lawsuit.php.

16. Telephone conference with Ray Jordan, Johnson & Johnson.

17. "American Red Cross Defends Use of Emblem and Mission." 10 August 2007.
    http://www.redcross.org/pressrelease/0,1077,0_314_6907,00.html.

18. Telephone conference with Ray Jordan, Johnson & Johnson.

19. Ibid.

20. Ibid.

employees, the public, and lawmakers. Thus, the company polled employees, the general public, and opinion leaders in Washington, DC, three days after the filing of the suit was publicized by the American Red Cross.

The polls provided two key results, specifically that the issue had remarkably little visibility and, secondly, that the American Red Cross suffered a larger drop in public favorability than Johnson & Johnson experienced.[21] With respect to the issue of visibility, the company found that approximately ten percent of the people polled were aware of the legal battle with the American Red Cross, with less than five percent exhibiting unaided recall of the subject. Only three percent of employees knew about the lawsuit prior to the distribution of the Chairman's letter explaining proceedings with the American Red Cross.

With respect to measuring public favorability following media coverage of the lawsuit, the American Red Cross dropped nineteen points in favorability, while Johnson & Johnson fell by only six points. Jordan noted that he was surprised by the fact that the public ironically viewed the humanitarian organization in a manner even less favorable than it viewed Johnson & Johnson. Likewise, he was proven correct in his prediction that neither party stood to benefit from the decision made by the American Red Cross to publicize the filing of the lawsuit. The non-profit was made aware of this reality once Johnson & Johnson shared the results of the survey with them. The company found that the delivery of the survey results tempered any residual desire the non-profit had to further publicize the lawsuit, for later press releases made by the American Red Cross were not broadcast on the public newswires.

Discussion Questions

Faced with the challenge of withstanding media coverage of the lawsuit against the American Red Cross, Johnson & Johnson must remain prepared to manage the following issues:

1. What is the business problem in this case? In what manner does it stem from the proper handling of corporate communications?

2. How will the company rebuild its longstanding relationship with the American Red Cross?

3. How will the company improve its corporate image if, as the lawsuit progresses, its public favorability begins to wane? What channels of communication should be addressed?

21. Ibid.

Part 2
Tactics of Business Communication

Part 1 of the text has covered the steps in the strategic process of message formulation in a business and organizational setting. Part 2 of the text discusses the tactics to be implemented in differing communication contexts: writing, presentations, group and teamwork, employment, and organizational communication.

In many business communication texts, the focus of discussion is on tactics, presenting them as the "rules" of message formulation. However, once you have mastered a strategic approach to business communication, the tactics can be deduced logically from such a contextual analysis. From this perspective, the tactics presented here are "more like guidelines," in the words of Disney pirate Jack Sparrow. That is, the strategic elements should drive tactical decisions and not vice versa.

Unlike many business texts that present tactical issues as rules to never be broken then, this text sees communication as more of an art that depends upon analysis of the contextual elements of any communication situation. It is an art that requires foundational knowledge, observational skills, critical thinking and assessment, and a willingness to "work without a net." This latter idea simply means that no one right answer generally exists in many communication situations (unlike other business disciplines) and thus one must build the needed skill base and subsequent level of confidence to master a strategic approach to messaging.

Without this knowledge and ability, though, one can use the tactical rules as a general guide for coping with different communication contexts. Without the meta-skill of strategic thinking and analysis, however, communication becomes more rule-bound and focused on the details, much like a copy editor approaches his or her work. This approach thus risks losing sight of the strategic, "big picture" perspective needed to be an inspirational and visionary leader.

Chapter 6

Communicating in Writing

After reading this chapter, you will be able to

- *Plan and develop content for informative and persuasive messages as well as longer documents: reports and proposals.*

- *Consider and incorporate the elements of visual impression into a written message, as appropriate.*

- *Revise written messages for coherence and logical flow.*

- *Revise written messages for style and tone.*

- *Proofread for mechanical correctness.*

Case Questions

1. What was wrong with the e-mail message sent by Alex?
2. What are the specific changes that should be made to improve it? How will each change improve the message?
3. What is the appropriate response that Kevin should make to Alex's request? Why?
4. What tips can you provide to writers to avoid creating messages such as the one sent by Alex?

The Case of the Consultants

"Hey, Josh." At the sound of his name, Joshua Suchin turned to identify the caller. Kevin Lee stood motioning him to come into his office.

"What's up?" Josh asked upon entering.

"Look at this e-mail message. Can you believe this?" Kevin said, as he stared at the computer screen in front of him.

Josh moved to Kevin's side to read the message, but his colleague couldn't wait. "I was very put off by your comments during our meeting this morning," Kevin read out loud. "You said that employees who do not report at least twenty billable hours spent with clients a week will be penalized with lower quarterly bonuses. That is patently unfair and ridiculous! How can you expect me to put in twenty hours with clients when I have been on workers' comp because of my back injury for the past six months? I just get back in the office and you think I will immediately go back to my prior level of productivity? You need to rethink this policy change. I await your response. Alex."

"Wow! It sounds like Alex is all fired up," Josh said.

"Do ya think?" Kevin replied, then laughed. "I think I'll print this message out and hang it by the water cooler. It's a prime example of how 'not to make friends and influence people.'"

Josh chuckled. "That's what he probably deserves, but how are you really going to deal with this?" he asked.

Good writing skills are critical to your success in the workplace. According to a survey of human resource directors, "people who cannot write and communicate clearly will not be hired and are unlikely to last long enough to be considered for promotion."[1] Unfortunately, the *Wall Street Journal* reports that 80 percent of businesses surveyed believed that their employees' biggest weakness was written communication.[2] This finding presents an opportunity, however, for those who can communicate well in writing. They can positively distinguish themselves from their peers through their written communication skills.

When writing, as with all messages, you should first identify your purposes for communicating; analyze your audience to identify its values, beliefs, interests, concerns, and objections; consider the context of the communication; and choose a medium. After considering these strategic issues, you should then select the appropriate tactics to help you achieve your broader communication goals.

This chapter addresses the tactical elements that can be deployed for messages using the written channel of communication. These tactical elements, or what are often referred to as the common steps in the writing process, can be broadly categorized as follows:

1. Planning and developing the message: routine, persuasive, and more formal types such as reports and proposals
2. Selecting and incorporating visual elements
3. Revising for organization, coherence, and flow
4. Revising for style and tone
5. Proofreading for correctness

Depending on the audience, purpose, and context of the message, some of these steps may be eliminated. For many routine messages—often short responses or queries to frequent correspondents—it isn't necessary to consider every element of the writing process. For example, if you are sending a text or instant message response to a query you received ten seconds ago from a colleague using the same medium, no planning, little development, no visual aids, and little concern for coherence and flow may be needed. In contrast, an important response to a request for proposal from a government agency may require all of the steps in the writing process be followed to the letter. Likewise, messages to important or new audiences or for less routine purposes should be planned using the strategic approach and steps in the writing process. As with most communication situations, once you are accustomed to following the steps in the strategic process—identifying the purpose, analyzing the audience, considering the context, and selecting the channel—you will find it much easier to determine when all the steps in the tactical portion of the writing task are necessary. Figure 6-1 provides an illustration of applicability of the steps in the writing process for different formats.

A Word About the Genre of Business Writing

Business writing is just one of several genres of writing. Obviously, it is a different genre than fiction or poetry, but we often don't consciously recognize that it is also different from academic or compositional writing in many ways and more akin to technical writing as a genre. Therefore, learning to be a good business writer often requires unlearning some of the conventions of academic or compositional writing that you may have acquired in your past writing training.

The context of business writing is very different from academic and compositional writing, particularly the elements of audience and purpose(s). Both academic and compositional writing are intended to teach students to write formally and correctly to an audience who loves writing and who has the leisure time available to linger over it and appreciate its stylistic qualities. In an academic environment, the audience is a teacher who often loves literature and is paid to read and analyze writing for its finer qualities.

Figure 6-1 Applicability of the Steps in the Writing Process for Different Formats

Steps in the Writing Process	Message Format			
	Text Message	E-mail	Memo or Letter	Report or Proposal
STRATEGIC ELEMENTS				

Planning:
  Identify the Purposes
  Analyze the Audience
  Consider the Context
  Select the Channel and
  Media
	Generally, no; the context may drive the process as might the medium if you are responding in kind.	Depends. An immediate response to a query may require little planning, while a longer message would likely require planning.	Yes	Yes

TACTICAL ELEMENTS				
Develop the Content and Organization	No	Depends on length and importance.	Yes	Yes
Consider and Develop Visual Elements	No	Depends on length and importance.	Yes	Yes
Revise for Coherence and Flow	No	Depends on length and importance.	Yes	Yes
Revise for Style and Tone	No	Depends on length and importance.	Yes	Yes
Proofread for Mechanical Correctness	Depends. If the audience uses text abbreviations, you can, too.	Yes	Yes	Yes

This is not the case for business audiences, many of whom do not like to read or write, and if they do, they don't have the time to linger over it. Thus, most business audiences are not analyzing your writing for absolute grammatical correctness and stylistic appeal, particularly in the case of routine messages. Instead, they are reading your messages to gather information they need to move forward in their job duties. Most business audiences may not have the training to, in fact, analyze your messages for absolute grammatical correctness.

Another difference between business writing and academic or compositional writing is that because of time pressures, business audiences are reading messages quickly. That means two things: business writing should be complete yet concise and it should be easy to skim. A business reader is likely never to ask you to write a four-page report on information that might easily be covered in two or three paragraphs. It also means that you need to learn to focus on writing in such a way so as to provide sufficient "entry points" into your message so as to enable skimming. This issue will be discussed in more detail later in this chapter.

The style and tone of business writing also differs from academic or compositional writing. Because the focus of compositional writing is often on learning the rules of English as used in the conservative environment of the academy, the style is often formal with a stilted tone, which is created through the use of overly long sentences and multi-syllabic words. This makes writing more time-consuming to read—a "no-no" in a business context. In contrast, business writing tends to use less complex sentences, plain language, and a friendly, personable tone as relationship as a strategic goal is so important.

This latter issue becomes more critical in a growingly diverse, multi-cultural world in which business is global and often conducted using technological means. This means that messages are often shorter, and more instantaneous, and may not be absolutely grammatically correct as English may not be participants' first language. To address this change, researchers have developed approaches to English use to better account for how business people actually communicate in multi-cultural situations. For example, English for Specific Purposes (ESP) and Business English as

Lingua Franca (BELF) look at how users with different native languages use English to communicate in a business setting. Research on BELF has shown that

- The grammatical rules and communication norms for BELF use are heavily influenced by the reason for its use (e.g. business, travel, etc.).
- BELF communication norms are more heavily influenced by situational or functional circumstances than native-speaker norms.
- BELF users place a higher importance of using the language to achieve goals rather than being grammatically correct.
- BELF speakers will intersperse other–mutually known–languages when doing so will improve goal achievement.

In conclusion, it is important to remember that business writing is a different genre than academic writing, occurring in a different context with different audience expectations and considerations. Academic writing often ignores the rhetorical strategies used in this text and instead focuses more narrowly on tactical issues, such as correct formatting, language use, and style. These are less important today as we move to technological forms of interaction with more diverse audiences. For the purposes of this text, a focus on these latter elements of writing also undermines a strategic approach as they are rule-bound and a strategic approach is less about following rules but instead about adapting to and addressing specific situations or contexts.

Planning and Developing Informative Messages

Like much of workplace communication, business writing has changed significantly with the increased use of technology. Paradoxically, while workplace writing may have diminished significantly in terms of average message length and time spent composing, the use of writing as a key tool for communication has increased, primarily because of the predominance of e-mail use.

While many e-mail messages are often short responses to inquiries, some are lengthier, providing instructions, changes in procedures or policies, and other types of information. Similarly, in some organizations, these types of messages may be delivered on paper in the form of a memo, although this is occurring less and less today. External messages to customers, clients, and suppliers also may be printed in the form of a letter. Other types of informative messages include good and bad news messages.

Regardless of the media or format of delivery, however, the steps in formulating business messages may be applied to all of these informative messages, as shown in Figure 6-2. These are covered in the following sections.

Figure 6-2 Steps in Formulating Written Business Messages

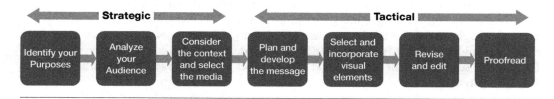

Please note that examples of different types of written business messages are provided in Appendix A, "Model Documents" while the common rules of punctuation, sentence structure, and usage are provided in Appendix B.

Parts of a Message

Good organization helps you achieve three objectives: (1) It can help your reader access critical information more quickly 2) It helps your reader understand your message and (3) it demonstrates the quality of your thinking. From a strategic perspective, the first two objectives are also aimed at meeting your audience's needs, which may help you achieve one of the purposes of communication—conveying goodwill. The second objective performs a second purpose: It reflects on your credibility or image as a professional.

For these reasons, it is important to plan the development of both longer, complex messages and those to important or unfamiliar audiences. Even for the most routine of messages, though, a little thought to organization, structure, and content can go a long way to ensure that a message is clear, considers audience knowledge and needs, maintains your credibility, and potentially enhances your relationship with your audience. These considerations may be even more important with the advent of e-mail and instant and text messaging because of their spontaneous nature.

All informal business messages—e-mails, memos, letters, informal reports—typically contain three parts, however brief: the introduction, the body, and the close. The only exception to this rule might be text messages and brief, routine e-mails. More and more, electronic communications are like a conversation, particularly those that are immediate responses to a query such as instant or text messages. For these, the response may be the only content, particularly if it is part of an immediate conversation where contextual or background information isn't necessary for the reader's understanding.

The Introduction

There are two types of message approaches, depending on the purpose of a message. These are the *direct* and *indirect approaches*. The direct approach is used for most messages in the United States, while the indirect approach is used for bad news messages and some persuasive messages when you expect the audience may be resistant to your proposal.

Direct Approach In longer routine messages and those where a more formal approach is appropriate, depending on the audience, you should develop a brief introduction that states the purpose of the message and provides an overview of those subtopics. In a good news message, the "good news" or purpose would also be stated immediately. For example, an introduction to a good news message written to a colleague who recently has been promoted might read: "Congratulations, Amy, on your promotion to director of communications. All of your excellent work on the recent corporate responsibility campaign appears to have paid off in a well-deserved promotion."

Stating the purpose of the message and providing a road map of its contents is important in professional messages because businesspeople are typically pressed for time and bombarded with information, as was discussed in Chapter 4. Given these pressures, they often try to find ways to process information more rapidly or to cull messages that are not of high importance. In fact, you have only one to seven seconds to convince a reader that the information is relevant and only 90 seconds to confirm and keep the reader's interest.[3]

An introduction should indicate to your audience why it is important for it to read your message. It should also provide your audience with a road map of what the message contains to either help it skim a written document or better follow the logic or contents of your message.

In addition, the beginning and the end of a message are considered its most important parts because they are the most read and therefore often the most remembered. For that reason, you should make it clear in the introduction why your message is important to your audience.

Examples of a direct introduction to an informative message include the following:

You will find the agenda for next Monday's meeting below. As the agenda shows, we will discuss new product lines, product manager assignments, and initiate beginning discussions on scheduling.

Congratulations on selecting Lifelong as your insurance carrier! We would like to introduce you to all the benefits you will receive, provide you information on additional products you may wish to learn more about, and give you information about contacting customer service if you have any questions or wish to change or upgrade your insurance package.

Indirect Approach The *indirect approach* is sometimes used for bad news messages as well as some persuasive messages. In the case of a bad news message, you might need to tell a client that you cannot grant a request, you may need to inform a job applicant that he or she was not selected for a position, or you may need to tell employees that they will not be receiving raises this year.

With the indirect approach, the purpose of a bad news message is not stated immediately. Instead, the message opens with what is called a *neutral buffer*, which is intended to maintain goodwill with the recipient. In addition, the buffer should logically lead the reader to the bad news, which is delivered and explained in the body of the message.

Thank you for choosing Primo, Ltd. for your credit needs. Primo specializes in services to small businesses just like yours who need ready access to credit for day-to-day operations and rapidly changing financial situations.

In this example, the bad news is cushioned by expressing gratitude to the reader for considering the company to do business with as well as recognizing the reader's specific needs. The "bad news" of the credit rejection is not delivered until the second paragraph, as shown in Figure 6-3.

? Critical Thinking

Do you always immediately state the purpose of longer messages in such a way that it is clear to your readers or listeners why your message is important to them? Do you also provide a brief yet clear overview of the topics your message will address?

The Body

The body of an informative message may differ in content depending on the approach.

Direct Approach The body of a message that uses the direct approach provides the necessary supporting details for the purpose of the message and the audience's needs. These might include the reason for the decision, procedures for the reader to follow, background information, a description of the situation, or evidence to support the claims that are made in the case of a persuasive message. In other words, the strategic steps to message formulation should help you to determine the appropriate content and organization of the message.

Indirect Approach For bad news messages using the indirect approach, the body of the message might provide the details that led to the bad news being communicated. After the reason for the bad news has been conveyed, the bad news would be delivered tactfully. Alternatively, the body might discuss ways to avoid similar bad news or explain what is being done to avoid such situations in the future. An example of a bad news message is provided in Figure 6-3.

The Close

As stated earlier, the conclusion is one of the most important parts of a message because your audience will be more likely to remember it because of the *recency effect*, or the principle that the most recently presented items or experiences will most likely be remembered best. Consequently, you should take care to ensure that the conclusion is, in fact, memorable and focuses on the final message that you want your audience to take away.

Figure 6-3 Example of a Bad News Message Refusing a Credit Card Application

Ultra Max, Ltd.
1800 Speedway Avenue
Tucson, AZ91240
215-555-7800

April 8, 2018

Howie Leonard
2407 Kearney St.
San Francisco, CA 98807

Dear Mr. Leonard:

Thank you for choosing Ultra Max, Ltd. for your credit needs. Primo specializes in services to small businesses just like yours who need ready access to credit for day-to-day operations and rapidly changing financial situations.

After checking your credit rating with the three national credit-reporting firms, we are unable to fulfill your request for a Ultra Max Credit Card at this time.

We are eager to fulfill your credit needs and encourage you to obtain your credit report so that you can discover whether errors regarding your credit history are affecting your credit status. You can obtain your credit report via the Internet at creditrating.com.

Once your credit rating has improved, please reapply for your Ultra Max Credit Card. Ultra Max, Ltd. provides many benefits to its clients, including a competitive interest rate and signature loans for quick access to needed operational funds.

Sincerely,

Leili Wang
Customer Service Manager

There are three basic types of conclusions: goodwill, summary, and sales. Goodwill conclusions are used for short, routine messages in which another type of conclusion might be inappropriate or for messages sent simply for goodwill purposes. They are also used for bad news messages. Summary conclusions are typically used for more complex, informative messages, and sales conclusions are used for persuasive messages. Each type is discussed below.

Goodwill Conclusions If you are sending a goodwill message or even if you are conveying a short routine message such as an e-mail, then you will probably want to close with a few simple sentences or statements aimed at maintaining your relationship with your reader. This type of conclusion is called a *goodwill close* and might sound something like this: "I look forward to meeting you Tuesday to further discuss the proposed flex-time plan." A goodwill close should avoid sounding generic because your purpose is to maintain your relationship with your audience. Therefore, your close should be as specific as possible to the situation and the person with whom you are communicating, as in the example above. A goodwill close provides you an opportunity to distinguish yourself as a person who truly recognizes and appreciates others. Because we often feel like little more than numbers in our busy, impersonal society, the ability to make others feel like special individuals can be a welcome, appreciated talent.

A goodwill close is also appropriate for bad news messages. A goodwill close in this situation might suggest an alternative course for the reader or point to a brighter future or a continued relationship. (See Figure 6-3 for an example.)

Summary Conclusions If you are conveying a longer, more complex, informative message, such as procedural or policy changes or an informal report, you should create a summary conclusion in which you restate the subtopics of your message in a slightly different manner. You have probably heard the old saw: "Tell 'em what you're going to tell 'em, then tell 'em, then tell 'em what you just told 'em." This is the organizational formula for an informative message and is intended to ensure that readers who skim or who are not listening well get your message through repetition. Repetition is not the same as redundancy, however; when you repeat information, you should do so in a slightly different manner. Sometimes stating information differently can also help your reader or listener with comprehension. The first time we hear or read something, its meaning may not be completely clear. But if additional explanation is provided or if the message is stated again in a slightly different way, then the chances improve that the meaning will be understood.

Sales Conclusions If you are conveying a persuasive message, your conclusion should focus on restating the benefits your reader will receive from adopting your proposal. This type of conclusion is considered a sales conclusion. In some persuasive situations, it may also be appropriate to conclude with a **call to action.** You use a call to action when you want your audience to take the next step in your proposal. A call to action might be "Let's meet later this week to discuss the details of my proposal. I will call you tomorrow to discuss a day and time that is convenient for you." In this example, you are attempting to get the reader to fully consider your proposal and, ideally, to commit to a decision.

call to action

A conclusion to a persuasive message that is intended to convince the reader to fully consider the writer's or speaker's proposal and, ideally, commit to a decision or take the next step.

Calls to action are generally not as effective, however, if you as the communicator are not the person charged with following through. For instance, in the example above, you might write, "Let's meet later this week to discuss the details of my proposal. Please call me to let me know a convenient time for you." In this case, you have provided the reader an opportunity to "drop the ball" or not follow up. If he or she does not call to set up an appointment, then your proposal is dead unless, after a week passes without a call, you follow up instead to schedule the meeting.

Planning and Developing Persuasive Messages

In business situations, we are almost always persuading or attempting to influence others. We are almost always attempting to sell ourselves, our ideas, our company's products or services, or our company and its reputation to others. Included in these types of messages are sales messages, job-application letters and résumés, persuasive requests, proposals, and so on. Even if we believe that we simply are informing our audience, it is important to recognize that there may be some elements of persuasion to which we should attend, that is, we may also be attempting to persuade our audience that we are credible and knowledgeable and that we value our relationship with it. As this latter sentence implies, to be more successful at persuasion, you should pay attention to the third and fourth purposes of communication: establishing and maintaining goodwill and credibility. If we do not have a credible, likable persona or image, then it will be more difficult for us to persuade an audience to accept our ideas.

The information you provide in persuasive situations is almost totally dependent on your audience's perspective or view of your proposal. For example, if you believe that your audience is very receptive to your idea, you might simply ask it to accept your proposal with minimal information provided. This approach is sometimes called a *direct request*. However, the less receptive your audience is to your proposal, the more time you may need to take to formulate a strategy for its presentation and the more information you may need to provide to be persuasive. To determine the strategy and information you will need to provide in a persuasive message, you should ask and answer the following questions:

1. **How will my audience initially react to my proposal?**
   A second question that may help to clarify the issues involved in the first is "What feelings or fears might my proposal elicit in my audience?" The answers to this question may help you to determine whether using the direct or indirect approach, as discussed earlier, would be most effective. If your audience might have a negative reaction to your proposal, you

might be more indirect. For example, you would likely not open a sales message with the statement: "You are going to need a funeral sooner or later, so please consider Thompson's Funeral Services." Instead, a better approach might be: "No one likes to think of their own passing, but doing the necessary planning can make a difficult time much easier for one's family and friends." The key message in both examples is the same, but in the latter case, it would come later in the message.

2. **How does my audience feel about me, my company, or my product or service?**

You or other representatives of your organization may have had past encounters with your audience that did not go well. These events may have left your audience feeling reluctant to communicate with you or your organization's representatives. If this is the case, it would be helpful to consider what you might say to help overcome or eliminate this reluctance. One way might be to approach the situation directly with some recognition of what you have learned. In this case, an indirect introduction to the situation might be used:

Although our last meeting did not result in a contract between our companies, the information that you provided us has helped us to develop a product that is much more effective in addressing the needs of small businesses like yours. Our new product, AccountAble, can be scaled to meet the specific needs of small companies like yours, and as they grow, affordable add-ons can be easily installed with no downtime.

3. **What are your audience's needs? In what ways does your idea or proposal fulfill those needs?**

If you can identify your audience's needs, you then can tailor the content of your message to explain how your proposed idea—or, in the case of customers, your product or service—meets those needs. In other words, answering Question 3 might provide most of the content you need for the entire message. This step can thus make the message much easier to draft and organize. A second advantage is that your audience will likely be more interested in the information you present if it is narrowly focused on explaining how your proposal meets its needs or will benefit it. Thirdly, this strategy shows that you are interested in your audience, which helps you to convey goodwill.

4. **What benefits does your proposal provide to your audience?**

The answer to this question may be similar to that of the previous one. However, you may find in asking this question that you may be placed in the role of educating your audience about your proposal. For example, your audience may have voiced its needs, but it may not have identified all the potential benefits your idea will provide. By giving some thought to all the benefits that your proposal might deliver to your audience, you have the potential to make your idea more persuasive. In fact, as mentioned earlier, the bulk of the content of your message might focus almost solely on the benefits your audience will derive from your proposal.

Generally, the type of benefit that is most persuasive to a business audience has to do with money: making it or saving it in some way. That does not mean that you ignore the other types of benefits that might accrue, such as the satisfaction one might feel from a job well done. Such a benefit is called an *intrinsic motivation*. However, this type of benefit is generally less persuasive than more *extrinsic motivations* such as those that save or make money in some way. Typically, you would use intrinsic motivators such as satisfaction, pleasure, and so on as additional information to make your proposal more persuasive. As always, let your audience be the guide. For example, a nonprofit organization may be more influenced by calling on intrinsic motivations that fall within their mission than extrinsic motivations such as making money.

5. **What obstacles or objections must you overcome?**

Answering this question might help you to determine whether the direct or the indirect approach would be most effective. It may also help you to identify what information you need to provide in your message as well as how much. For example, if your audience is resistant to your proposal, then you will probably need to provide more information in the form of benefits or good reasons to persuade it than you might for an audience to which you know you can simply make a direct request and it will be acted upon. If your audience holds another position, you may need to provide information that shows that view is not the best and explain why. How you accomplish this goal has to do with the tone as well as the content of your message. That is, a tactful approach would be required to show that a desired solution is not the best. (Tone is discussed later in this chapter.)

Often you must eliminate your audience's objections in order to set the stage for it to be open to hearing your proposal. If you do not eliminate your audience's objections or weaken the strength of its position through the quality of the information you provide in a tactful manner, then you will probably be faced with addressing those objections once you deliver your proposal, and you may ultimately find yourself back at step one in the process of persuasion.

If your audience is resistant, another tactic that may make your message more persuasive might be to supply information that shows that your proposal is easy to accept. For example, if you are attempting to persuade your department manager to change a procedure, you should also explain how to implement that procedure; maybe even volunteer to do so. Doing so makes the change easier for your manager to accept and implement and thus makes your message potentially more persuasive. A secondary benefit is that such an approach may lend you credibility as a person with initiative and good problem-solving skills. However, in some politically charged environments, be wary of such proposals. An insecure boss may read such a proposal as a threat and your credibility will instead be damaged. Again, let the context, in the form of the corporate culture and your audience, be your guide.

6. **Is this a sales proposal or competitive message? If so, what do my competitors offer? How might I distinguish myself or my ideas favorably from my competitors?**

Whenever you are competing with others for scarce resources—a job, a contract, a raise, a promotion, or a sale—you must consider how you compare to your competitors for those resources and how you can favorably distinguish yourself from them. You must therefore have some idea of what your competitors offer. This entails an additional step in the strategic process in which you not only must analyze your audience to identify its needs, concerns, and expectations but also your competitors to identify what they offer and how they differ from your or your organization's offerings, not only in terms of additional benefits but in terms of weaknesses. This knowledge should enable you to showcase the advantages of going with you or your organization and help you to anticipate how to respond to questions about your or your organization's shortcomings, if these exist.

When you apply for a job, for example, you are competing with dozens, perhaps hundreds, of others. You should give some thought to the qualifications those competitors might bring to the situation and then attempt to show that you are at least as well qualified as they are and ideally, more so. Reaching this objective depends on the quality of the content or information about yourself that you are able to provide and whether that information speaks to your audience's needs as well or better than your competitors—other job applicants—might.

Once you have answered these questions, you should have a good idea about the amount and type of information you need to provide to successfully persuade your audience to accept your proposal. These questions may also help you determine the most effective organizational approach to your message.

? **Critical** Thinking

Identify a time that you were unsuccessful at persuasion. Why were you unsuccessful? In retrospect, what could you have done to have improved your chances of success?

Basic Components of a Persuasive Message

claim

Often a general or abstract idea presented as fact.

evidence

More specific statement of fact that supports a statement.

Entire courses are devoted to the teaching and learning of persuasion. In fact, persuasion, or *argumentation* as it is called in the academy, is its own field of study. Subsequently, the study of persuasion involves a detailed history, content, and discussion that will not be reproduced here. However, it is helpful to know the basic components of a persuasive message. At the most foundational level, persuasion consists of two parts: a **claim** and the information or **evidence** that supports it. Another way to think about these two components is that a claim is often general or more abstract, while evidence is more specific. This way of thinking about evidence also helps us understand why evidence is often necessary for the clarity of our message in addition to persuasiveness. Below are examples of claims and supporting evidence.

> *Claim:* Effective writing will save your business money.

> *Evidence:* Studies indicate that employees waste one hour a day attempting to interpret or follow up on poorly written messages. This means that a company loses one hour of pay a day for each employee because of poorly written messages. This hour could be used more productively for other activities, or the money that goes to pay that wasted wage could be invested in other resources.

> *Claim:* You should buy our hybrid automobile, the Solare, because it will provide you with several benefits.

> *Evidence:* The largest benefit you will receive from purchasing our hybrid automobile, the Solare, is the savings you will receive from lower gasoline use and its purchase. The Solare is primarily fueled by hydrogen and requires gasoline only for sudden acceleration or unusual engine loads such as driving up steep inclines. If most of your vehicle use is confined to city streets and you avoid rapid acceleration, then you may rarely, if ever, require a stop at the gas station!

Types of evidence include facts, statistics, examples, analogies, and expert testimony, and almost all of these help us to show our logic and reasoning abilities (the quality of our thinking) as well as our knowledge of the topic (our credibility). Other types of evidence such as anecdotes and stories may help us to pique our audience's emotional interest. These three types of classic appeals are discussed in the next section.

Types of Persuasive Appeals

logos

Consists of information such as facts or statistics; also known as *logical appeal*.

More than 2,000 years ago, Greek philosopher Aristotle (384–322 B.C.E.) proposed that evidence or the information provided in a persuasive message could be divided into three broad categories: logical, ethical, and emotional. Although this schema is centuries old, it is still useful to us today.

A logical appeal, or **logos**, consists of such information as facts and statistics. It is a fact, for example, that mammals breathe oxygen. A fact is any information that is broadly accepted as true. Business audiences tend to be persuaded by logical evidence, particularly numbers, dollar or other currency amounts, and statistics. They also often prefer that this information be presented in the form of graphs. (Choosing and integrating graphs into text is discussed later in this chapter.) Both of the examples of claims and evidence previously provided largely rely on logical appeal for their persuasiveness.

An ethical appeal, or **ethos**, does not refer to ethics as we normally think of the concept but rather to information that provides credibility for ourselves or to our position. One of the easiest ways to make an ethical argument is to cite authorities in the subject of discussion. Most of us have used this method when we have been asked to write a research paper in school. In the first example of a claim and its evidence in the previous section, the reference to "studies" is an ethical appeal because it implies that experts were involved in the gathering of this information. This appeal might be stronger if the names of the experts involved in the studies were known to the audience. In this case, this information might carry greater weight or persuasiveness.

ethos

An ethical appeal that refers to information that provides credibility to ourselves or our position.

Another way to build credibility is to consider both sides of an issue. If you discuss both the pros and the cons, you will probably be considered fair-minded and thus more credible (i.e., you are not biased and therefore one-sided in your argument). You can also establish your credibility by showing that you are experienced and knowledgeable in a particular relevant area. For example, if you are selling photocopiers, you might tell your audience that you have been in the photocopier business for ten years. Such a statement indicates that you are knowledgeable about that industry, your product line, and most likely your competition.

The final type of evidence is the emotional appeal, or **pathos**. An emotional appeal does not work by simply writing or stating emotional words. An emotional appeal often depends on telling a story or evoking a picture or experience that your audience can identify with or feel empathy toward. For example, commercials that show pictures of starving children are intended to make us empathize with them so that we will contribute money to help lessen their plight. Similarly, advertisements that show young people at the beach in an SUV are intended to make us identify with them. Advertisers want us to identify with the youthful fun we see and then associate that fun with the SUV. These feelings are expected to make us want to buy the SUV so that we can have the same experience. Most of this emotional work goes on at the subconscious level, making it very effective at influencing our feelings and behaviors.

pathos

An emotional appeal; an attempt to win over the audience by appealing to its emotions, often by telling a story or evoking a picture with which the audience can empathize.

An emotional appeal might be used in a professional setting to motivate employees or colleagues. For example, if you want your staff to increase its quarterly sales, then you might hold a meeting at a lush resort that also involves group activities aimed at increasing camaraderie and overall good feelings toward the company and among sales staff members. Such an event might include an awards ceremony and closing speech intended to motivate employees to feel valued and to do their best to reach company goals. Such an event is intended to play on the emotions and identities of the participants in such a way as to make them feel special, recognized for their efforts, and part of a team—all effective at the emotive level in persuading them indirectly to put in the necessary effort to achieve the company's objectives.

Different types of audiences are convinced by different types of evidence and by varying amounts. Generally, the more resistant an audience is to your idea, the more evidence you will need to present. More resistant audiences may also require the use of all three types of evidence in varying amounts. Sometimes the situation dictates, to some degree, the type of evidence required. For example, when we are at home in front of the television or computer, we may want to relax and be entertained. That's why so many commercials rely on the emotional appeal; they work subtly on our feelings rather than requiring a lot of mental work. After a long day at work, we may be less receptive to a half hour long, fact-filled discussion of the benefits and disadvantages of buying a particular product, although that sort of discussion is generally expected in the workplace.

? Critical Thinking

What are the key elements of persuasion as a strategy? Should you state the opposing view when you write a persuasive message?

Quality of Evidence

Not all evidence is relevant or of high quality. Evidence can be used to mislead an audience intentionally or unintentionally. However, evidence can also be tested for its validity. The three primary tests of evidence and its quality are provided in the box Tests of Evidence.

The misuse of statistics is common when one instance is used to represent all cases. For example, the statement "Intel saved $10 million by outsourcing the production of its microprocessors to India" would be misused if it were used to support the claim "All companies will save millions of dollars by outsourcing their manufacturing and services to foreign countries." One company's experience does not represent the experiences of all companies, because organizations have varying resources, produce different products with differing requirements, provide various services, have differing resources and needs, and so on.

Similarly, testimonial evidence can be used to present a biased opinion. For example, if the testimony of a U.S. Department of Commerce official is used to support outsourcing, then the testimony might be considered biased because such a person would presumably lean toward supporting pro-business interests and positions and would thus ignore or downplay social or ethical considerations.

Finally, analogies can be faulty. For example, the analogy "Outsourcing is like farming because most farm labor in the United States is now provided by migrant workers from Mexico" is faulty. Not all outsourced jobs can be performed by relatively unskilled workers, for example, so there may be other costs of outsourcing that do not occur in the farm-labor situation. Furthermore, the pay scales of U.S. farmworkers may not match those of workers in another country in relation to the costs of living of both countries. Finally, it might be argued that many migrant workers from Mexico provide U.S. farm labor because U.S. citizens are unwilling to do that work. However, U.S. jobs might be outsourced even though a workforce exists that is willing to perform those particular jobs. In summary, the conditions and details of the two situations may not match in ways that then make the comparison dissimilar.

Tests of Evidence

- **Statistics.** Tests for quality of statistical evidence include the following:
    1. Is the sample from which the statistics are drawn a representative one?
    2. Is a single instance used as an example of all instances?

- **Testimony.** Tests for quality of testimonial evidence include these:
    1. Is the person an authority on the subject? If so, how reliable is he or she?
    2. Was the person giving the testimonial close enough to witness the event?
    3. Is it possible that the person giving the testimony is biased?

- **Comparison and analogies (the fallacy of faulty comparison or faulty analogy).** Tests for the quality of a comparison or analogy include the following:
    1. Do both items or activities have the same resources or authority?
    2. Are both items or activities governed by the same rules?
    3. Do both activities occur during the same time period?
    4. Are both items or activities measured in the same way?

Organizing Persuasive Messages

Various models are available for organizing persuasive messages, because persuasion can be a more difficult communication purpose to achieve and thus may require more preparation, strategy formulation, and time.

Broadly speaking, two persuasive situations exist: one in which you believe your audience is more or less receptive to your ideas or proposal and one in which you believe your audience is resistant or even hostile to you, your organization, or your ideas. In the former case, your audience may be so receptive that you simply need to request its agreement and you will receive it, as mentioned earlier in the case of a direct request. In other cases, it might be useful to consider the use of one of the models for persuasive messages.

One popular model for organizing persuasive messages is called the **AIDA approach**. AIDA is an acronym that stands for *attention, interest, desire,* and *action*. The AIDA approach can be adjusted to meet the needs of both types of audiences in persuasive situations: those who are more or less receptive and those who are resistant or even hostile. However, it is more difficult to use for resistant or hostile audiences if you are a less experienced persuader. For that reason, a more detailed discussion of an indirect organizational strategy for dealing with resistant and hostile audiences is also provided in this section.

AIDA approach

A popular model for organizing persuasive messages; AIDA is the acronym for *attention, interest, desire,* and *action*.

Using the AIDA Approach

Each step in the AIDA approach is discussed below. An example of a persuasive message created using the AIDA approach can be found in Figure 6-4.

1. **Attention.** The first step is to gain the audience's attention and interest, so you should begin every persuasive message with a brief statement that is personalized, audience-centered, and relevant to the situation and the audience. Your audience probably wants to know "What's in this message for me?" so you might call attention to the benefits it will receive.

2. **Interest.** In the second step, you should attempt to heighten the audience's interest in your topic or proposal. You can do this by explaining in more detail why your message is relevant to your audience. In this section, you might explain why current practices are not the best, if appropriate. In other situations, you might provide examples, data, testimony, or other kinds of evidence to show your audience what life would be like if it adopts your proposal.

3. **Desire.** In the third step, you should provide evidence to prove the claims made earlier in your message. In product-related persuasion, you might provide evidence of the benefits your audience will receive.

4. **Action.** In the fourth step, you should suggest a specific step the audience can take and make that action easy. You might also restate how the audience will benefit by acting as you wish. This last stage is similar to the issues discussed earlier in the section "Sales Conclusions."

Figure 6-4 Example of a Persuasive Message Using the AIDA Approach

To: Juan Garcia <jgarcia@hotmail.com>

From: Peggy Newman <pnewman@motorsports.com>

Hi, Juan,

Renowned racing legend Mike Nichols is coming to town! Jackson Motorsports is happy to host the 20-time winner at its May 20 event to recognize its gratitude to loyal customers like you on our annual Customer Appreciation Day.

Nichols will be representing CustomRods, Inc., which will be rolling out its new line of chrome accessories designed especially for "rods" like yours. Car enthusiasts have voted CustomRods' line of classic car accessories "Best in the Business" for the past five years in *HotRod* magazine.

This year's Customer Appreciation Day promises to be the best yet. Nichols will be signing autographs, the rock band Haywire will play, free tacos will be served, and special sales will occur every half hour during the day.

We hope to see you at this year's event. Please accept the included special 40 percent off coupon sent only to our most loyal customers. The coupon can be used toward any purchase on your special day!

Best regards,

Peggy Newman
Marketing Manager

Using the Indirect Approach for Resistant Audiences

As discussed earlier in this chapter, attempting to persuade a resistant or hostile audience requires a somewhat less direct approach. This is because such an audience may have already made up its mind about you, your organization, or your ideas. Even though you, your organization, and your ideas are separate from one another, they are associated, and some audiences will make this association. In this situation, you need to use a communication that will best help to ensure that your audience is open to hear or read and consider your persuasive message. For this reason, you may not want to announce your specific solution or proposal at the beginning of the message because your audience already has an opinion about it and will stop listening to your message. That is why the ordering of a message delivered to a resistant or hostile audience is important if you are to get the opportunity to persuade it.

The steps in persuading a resistant or hostile audience are explained below.

1. You should open your message with a statement of common ground to defuse any differences that may exist between you and your audience. This statement should be followed with an indirect statement of purpose that generally explains your idea. You should also provide an overview of the contents of the body of your message but generally should not include your specific recommendation.

2. The body of your message should begin by explaining the need for your proposed idea. Your goal is to show in a persuasive manner that there is a need for change of the type you are proposing.

3. After demonstrating the need for change, you must eliminate your audience's objections to your proposal. Your audience's objections might focus on several issues. In fact, you may have already addressed one objection: your belief in the need for change. Another objection your audience might have is that it favors another approach or solution. In this case, you must consider all the alternatives, discussing their benefits and disadvantages. In this section of your argument, you are working toward showing that your proposed solution is clearly best of all the alternatives. You must do so in an objective, tactful way, however, to reduce the potential for judgments of bias. Your intent is to show that you are a reasonable, knowledgeable, and objective person who is systematically yet thoroughly exploring the various options and the relevant issues.

4. After you tactfully eliminate your audience's objections through your careful analysis, you announce your specific solution or recommendation and emphasize why it is the best of all possible choices. The strategy in this situation is to eliminate your audience's objections before announcing your idea; announcing it earlier might affect the audience's receptivity to your idea. In other words, you are attempting to keep the audience open to your message so that you have an opportunity to be persuasive.

5. If appropriate, an additional step might include a plan for implementing your proposed solution. The easier the change is to make, the more attractive it may be to your audience.

When using this approach to persuasion, however, it is important to avoid deception or misleading statements so as to maintain your credibility as an ethical leader.

Planning and Developing Reports and Proposals

Depending on your position and the industry in which you work, you might be called on to write longer messages, reports, or proposals. Common types of reports include feasibility reports, research reports, progress reports, incident reports, and proposals. This section discusses not only how to prepare to write a report but also how to select the appropriate report type. It also explains the different sections that are commonly included in reports and proposals.

Preparing to Write the Report

The report-writing process is much like that for any message that requires some thought and preparation. For most reports, this process includes the following steps.

1. Define the problem that will be addressed in the report.

2. Gather information and data. Before developing recommendations, it is a good idea to gather information about the problem. Generally, research for reports consists of primary evidence, which is gathered by conducting interviews, surveys, experiments, and observation. Secondary research—that which has already been published—might also be helpful in determining appropriate recommendations to solve the problem that is the focus of the report.

3. Develop recommendations. Data and evidence gathered during step two should be selected to support the report recommendations.

Selecting the Report Type and Organizational Pattern

Reports and proposals can be either informal or formal in design, style, and content. Informal reports and proposals typically use memo formats. A formal report format should be used when the preparation time is longer, the findings and recommendations are more significant, a formal report format has been used in the past, and the importance of the audience demands it.

There are many patterns a writer can use to organize his/her ideas in formal or informal reports. The specific pattern (or combination of patterns) chosen depends upon the particular topic and the objectives the writer has identified for the document. There is no rule to follow in choosing a pattern of organization; one must simply think carefully about which pattern makes the most sense in helping the reader to better understand and remember the information. There are many different ways of organizing the same information, and often two or more different organizational patterns are combined to create a final outline of information.

- **Problem-Solution.** A problem-solution pattern is one of the most common used in an organizational context. It typically consists to two main sections, one that describes a problem and one that describes a solution. This pattern is typically used in persuasive writing, where the writer's general purpose is to convince the reader to support a certain course of action. The pattern is designed to compel the reader to make some kind of change in opinion or behavior by establishing that a problem exists, then providing a solution. In the problem section, the writer identifies different aspects of the problem being discussed and offers evidence of these problems. In the solution section, the writer identifies a potential solution and supports the effectiveness of this solution over others.

- **Chronological.** A chronological pattern of organization arranges information according to a progression of time, either forward or backward. When a topic is best understood in terms of different segments of time, a chronological format works well. For example, topics of an historical nature are best organized using this pattern. When using a chronological pattern, each main section of information represents a particular period of time, and the sub-points contained within each main section refer to significant events that occurred within that time frame.

- **Sequential.** A sequential pattern of organization is similar to a chronological pattern, but arranges information according to a step-by-step sequence that describes a particular process. Using a sequential pattern, each main section of information represents a main step that the reader would follow in the actual process.

- **Spatial.** A spatial pattern of organization arranges information according to how things fit together in physical space; i.e., where one thing exists in relation to another. This pattern works well when a writer wishes to create a mental picture of something which has various parts distinguished by physical location.

- **Compare-Contrast.** A compare-and-contrast pattern arranges information according to how two or more things are similar to or different from one another (or both). This is an effective pattern to use when the reader can better understand one subject when it is described in relation to another. If the reader is familiar with one topic, the writer can compare or contrast it with another topic to shed insight on it.

- **Advantages-Disadvantages.** This pattern organizes information about a topic by dividing it up into its pros and cons. It is effective to use when a writer wishes to objectively discuss or analyze both sides of an issue without taking a persuasive stance.

- **Cause-Effect.** This pattern is used to show the different causes and effects of various conditions. This pattern is particularly effective when writing a persuasive document in which the writer advocates some action to solve a problem, because it demonstrates important relationships between variables. There are two major variations to this pattern: (a) dividing the outline into two major sections comprised of causes and effects; or (b) dividing the outline according to the different causes, with the effects of each cause contained within the larger "causes" section.

- **Topical.** A topical pattern arranges information according to different sub-topics within a larger topic, or the "types" of things that fall within a larger category. Using this pattern, each "type" represents a main section of discussion.

Report Format

An informal report contains the same parts as a typical memo: an introduction, a body, and a close. As with a regular memo, the body of an informal report may be divided into a number of sections set off by headings. These sections may correspond to the contents of the body of a formal report (see the following).

The format of a formal report is more complex than an informal report in that it generally includes front and back matter in addition to the body. The front matter of a formal report may include the following:

- **Title page.** This page tells the reader the name of the report, the names of the writers and company submitting the report, and the date it was completed.

- **Transmittal document or cover letter.** The cover letter tells the reader the subject of the report, what is of most importance in it, the action that should be taken, and what follow-up will occur or is needed.

- **Table of contents.** The table of contents should be a complete listing of the major and minor topics addressed in the report. Typically, it is a listing of the headings contained in the report along with the number of the page on which each section begins.

- **List of illustrations.** If the report contains tables or figures, they should be listed on this page.

- **Executive summary.** The executive summary summarizes the major topics covered in the report. These topics include a purpose statement for the report, an overview of the key ideas, identification of key problems that will affect the outcome of the report, solutions to the problems, and a recommended course of action.

The report proper or body of the report typically includes the following sections:

- **Introduction.** An introduction should include the purpose of the report, an overview of the report, and background information if appropriate, or an identification of the problem addressed in the report.

- **Discussion or body.** This section consists of the analysis of relevant information or a discussion of the details relevant to the problem solution.
- **Conclusions.** This section is typically a summary of the discussion that focuses on the important implications of the analysis provided in the body or discussion, and it provides the solutions and their benefits.
- **Recommendations.** This section provides the suggested course of action.

The back matter may include references, a bibliography, or appendices. An appendix typically includes additional related information that is not of primary importance such as letters, tables, figures, survey results, or previous report findings. An example of an informal report can be found in Appendix A, "Model Documents."

Proposal Format

Proposals are sales documents that are intended to recommend changes or purchases within a company—or show how your organization can meet the needs of another if the proposal is intended for an external audience. Some external proposals are responses to a request for proposal (RFP) that is submitted by outside entities, such as government agencies and other contracting entities. Like reports, proposals may be informal or formal. Like informal reports, informal proposals typically use a memo format. A formal proposal may include the following components:

- Proposed idea and purpose, or what is often called the "project description"
- Scope, or what you propose to do
- Methods or procedures to be used
- Materials and equipment needed
- Qualifications of personnel who will be working on the project
- Follow-up or evaluation of the project
- Budget or costs of the project
- Summary of proposal
- Appendices, if appropriate

An example of an informal proposal can be found in Appendix A, "Model Documents."

Visual Impression in Written Messages

More and more messages these days are sent electronically. With this development, the need to understand the various formatting conventions for business messages has declined. However, it is useful to understand when the use of conventional business formats is appropriate. Memos are typically used for more formal occasions to send messages to internal audiences. Likewise, letters are also used for more formal occasions but for external audiences. Templates for creating different types of written business messages and examples of different types of business messages are provided in Appendix A, "Model Documents." Most word processors also provide templates for common business documents, making formatting of these more formal documents much easier.

One important formatting feature for e-mail messages is the subject line. As with any message, because of time pressures and the deluge of information that most businesspeople must deal with every day, it is important to get your audience's attention by providing an informative subject line. The best way to do this is to signal that this message is relevant and needed by the reader. For example, the subject line "Meeting Dates for Project Development Team" is much more informative than a single-word subject line such as "Meeting." "Please Call Me Regarding Insurance Report" is better than "Call me."

In addition to format, a number of other visual elements can be incorporated into written business messages. These include white space, headings, lists, and graphics. All of these elements help to improve the "skimmability" of a message. As business readers are often pressed for time, just like students, they often skim messages to identify the critical information they need to move forward with their job duties. A good writer will anticipate this need and will provide multiple entry points to a document to aid in skimming, thus, enhancing his or her goodwill and credibility with the reader. This is a strategic issue as the writer is selecting organizational cues to emphasize or lead the reader to the key points.

For example, an introduction might include a list that announces the key points to be addressed in the message. These points might then be repeated or emphasized in headings and topic sentences. This "cueing" approach, provides cues as to the content of a message and thus leads the reader through that critical information in an accessible way.

White Space

One difference in academic writing and business writing is a concern with *white space*. The inclusion of sufficient white space is also of concern when writing content for Web messages, since as with other business writing, most readers skim to find the information they are looking for.

Because of time pressures felt by most business professionals, it is important for writers to ensure that their writing looks easy to read and accessible. This goal is partially accomplished by *chunking* information in short, well-focused paragraphs. Paragraphs should be kept short—no more than eight or nine lines in length—to provide more white space between paragraphs. Chunking makes a message appear easier to read because it divides it into easily digestible chunks. The increased white space also makes the message look less dense.

To enhance "skimmability," paragraphs would also begin with a clear, concise topic sentence. Developing coherent paragraphs is discussed later in "Revising for Organization, Coherence, and Flow."

In addition to chunking, writers should ensure that sufficient white space is provided for margins. Additional white space can be provided through the use of visual aids or graphic elements as well (also discussed later in this chapter).

Use of Headings

The use of design features such as *headings* and lists is both a graphic technique and a tactical issue because you, as the writer, decide whether and how to use them and what form they will take. The use of headings is considered a graphic technique; it is one way to incorporate additional white space into a document and thus add visual interest. Headings also are cueing devices that let your audience know what to expect in terms of content and organization. They are therefore very useful as a skimming device. Headings should not, however, take the place of accurate topic sentences, because people read differently: Some people read headings, and some people skip them and read the first sentence of each paragraph.

Headings also indicate the relationship between ideas. For less complex documents such as memos and longer e-mails, most headings indicate an equal or parallel relationship between ideas. However, for more complex documents such as reports and proposals, information can be arranged in a hierarchy. In other words, some elements of the information provided in the document are more important than others, encompass others, and come before or after others. An outline is an example of a hierarchy of information. Figure 6-5 illustrates the hierarchical arrangement of heading levels.

What this means in terms of heading use is that more complex documents need headings that show your reader the hierarchical ordering of information. Typically, ideas of a higher order in the hierarchy are indicated by a heading that is of larger size than headings that indicate information lower in order.

The most important considerations for headings are that you use a consistent style and format and that you place them strategically to position your points to their best advantage and for your audience's benefit. When choosing a heading design, you can consider the use of three characteristics: font appearance, font size, and placement.

- **Font appearance.** Font appearance refers to whether the font is italicized, bolded, underlined, or capitalized. As with font type, the appearance of the font you choose to use can affect the impression of your document. For example, the use of italicized or all-capital-letter headings tends to make a document feel more traditional or conservative, whereas the use of upper and lowercase letters makes a document appear more modern.

- **Font size.** A common way to distinguish heading levels is to use a different font size. As explained earlier, higher-order headings typically use a larger font size; those of a lower order use a smaller font.

- **Placement.** Placement refers to where the heading is placed on the page. Typically, headings are left justified, centered, or indented, depending on the feel you wish to create and the order of the heading. Centered headings, like the use of serif type, tend to give a document a more conservative feel than those that are left justified.

Figure 6-5 The Hierarchical Arrangement of Heading Levels

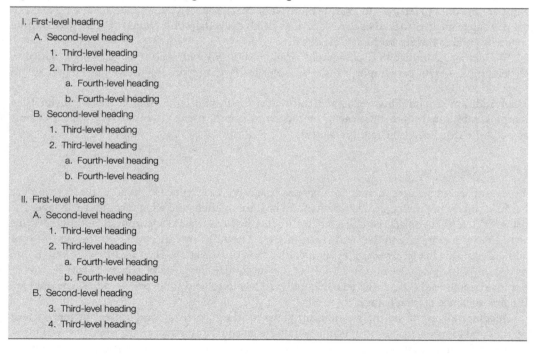

I. First-level heading
   A. Second-level heading
      1. Third-level heading
      2. Third-level heading
         a. Fourth-level heading
         b. Fourth-level heading
   B. Second-level heading
      1. Third-level heading
      2. Third-level heading
         a. Fourth-level heading
         b. Fourth-level heading

II. First-level heading
   A. Second-level heading
      1. Third-level heading
      2. Third-level heading
         a. Fourth-level heading
         b. Fourth-level heading
   B. Second-level heading
      3. Third-level heading
      4. Third-level heading

When deciding on a heading design, you should limit the number of devices you use to no more than three. More than three may detract from the professional image you wish to convey by making your design look amateurish and chaotic. A common practice for creating business headings is to use the same font type and placement and to distinguish different heading levels by size only. This creates a simpler, more contemporary look to a message.

In addition, headings should be informative: They should contain sufficient information to be meaningful. One-word headings are called *labels* and tend to be less informative than short phrases used as headings. On the other hand, you should avoid overly long headings that begin to read like a topic sentence. In that case, you may have inadvertently provided two topic sentences for the section you are referencing—one your actual topic sentence and the other your heading—creating a redundancy problem.

Use of Lists

Lists are useful devices for providing more white space in a document and making it easier to skim. Two types of lists exist—numbered and bulleted—and they have differing purposes. *Number lists* are used for information that is to be used sequentially, as in a series of steps for instructions. *Bullet lists* are used to identify separate items that are equal and related or parallel in importance. Bullet lists are often useful devices for forecasting the contents of a message, as in the case below.

Example of a bullet list for forecasting:

This memo will show you the advantages of adopting a flex-time policy for employees. More specifically, it will explain

- Why a policy change is needed.
- How the policy change will benefit employees and the company.
- How to implement the policy change.

You should resist the temptation to overuse or misuse bullet lists. Inexperienced business writers often make the mistake of believing that they can use bullet lists to provide all the information in a message. This belief arises from an understanding that business messages should be concise; however, it ignores the corresponding importance of clarity. If your entire message is made up of bulleted phrases, for example, those phrases may not convey complete meaning but merely fragments of information that your reader must attempt to interpret, elaborate on, and connect. Such messages often take on the appearance and content of an outline rather than a well-written and well-reasoned message. The overuse of bullet lists is particularly problematic in persuasive messages that generally require solid reasoning and quality evidence to support major claims.

Whenever you place the burden of interpretation on your reader, you risk two outcomes: (1) Your reader will not wish to take on that burden, so he or she will stop reading in frustration and (2) your reader will interpret your meaning incorrectly. Furthermore, if you are attempting to persuade, a list format typically will not help you achieve that goal because it will probably not contain the necessary evidence.

To reiterate, lists are typically used as forecasting devices, not to deliver the main content of your message.

Lists should be grammatically parallel in structure, which means that each item in the list should begin with the same kind of word. For example, in the sample list just presented, each list item begins with an adverb. In business writing, it is useful to consider using a verb as the beginning word of a list because it implies action.

Use of Graphics

Using graphics appropriately provides three main benefits:

1. Information is more easily understood than the use of words alone.
2. Visuals help to make the information conveyed more memorable.
3. Visuals enhance your professionalism and credibility.

However, as with all forms of information, graphic information can be misused. When using graphics to convey information, be sure your data is valid, reliable, and drawn from a representative sample if appropriate.

The most common forms of visual aids used in both written and oral presentations are the graph, table, and diagram or drawing. Many of these elements can easily be developed with the use of word processing, spreadsheet and presentation programs, and other graphic tools.

Graphs

Graphs, sometimes called *charts*, are used to compare the value of several items: the amount of advertising money spent on different media, the annual profit of a company over time, and so on. Two common types of graphs are the bar graph and the pie graph. Examples of each are provided in Figure 6-6 and Figure 6-7.

graph

A visual element used to compare the values of several items.

Figure 6-6 Example of a Bar Graph

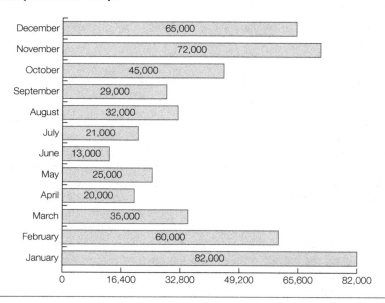

Figure 6-7 Example of a Pie Graph

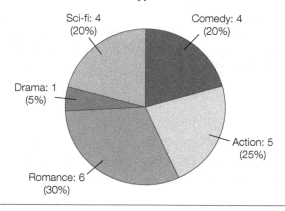

Source: U.S. Department of Labor.

The bar graph is typically used to emphasize comparisons or contrasts between two or more items. A pie graph is often used to indicate the distribution of something or the relative size of the parts of a whole.

Tables

table

A visual element used to present data in words, numbers, or both, in columns and rows.

Tables are useful for emphasizing key facts and figures. They are especially effective for listing steps, highlighting features, or comparing related facts. A **table** presents data in words, numbers, or both in columns and rows. An example of a table comparing the benefits of large and small companies is shown in Figure 6-8.

Figure 6-8 Example of a Table

Comparison of Company Benefits by Size		
Type of Benefit	Companies with Fewer than 100 Employees	Companies with 100 or More Employees
Paid vacation	88%	96%
Paid holidays	82	92
Medical insurance	71	83
Life insurance	64	94
Paid sick leave	53	67
Dental care	33	60

Source: U.S. Bureau of Labor Statistics.

Tables easily convey large amounts of numerical data and often are the only way to show several variables for a number of items.

Diagrams and Drawings

diagram

A two-dimensional drawing that shows the important parts of objects.

Diagrams are two-dimensional drawings that show the important parts of objects. They are useful for conveying information about size, shape, and structure. Types of diagrams include drawings, maps, and floor plans. An example of a diagram is shown in Figure 6-9.

Figure 6-9 Example of a Diagram: Organizational Chart

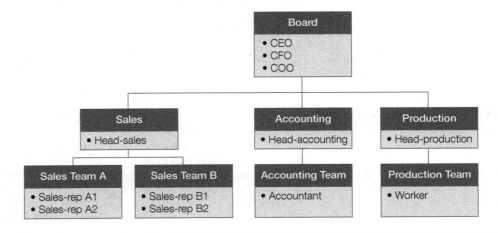

An organizational chart is a form of block diagram that indicates lines of authority and responsibility in an organization.

The following box insert offers a guide for selecting appropriate graphics.

Selecting the Right Graphic

- To present detailed, exact values, use a table.
- To illustrate trends over time, use a line graph or a bar graph.
- To show frequency or distribution, use a pie graph or segmented bar graph.
- To compare one item with another, use a bar graph.
- To compare one part with the whole, use a pie graph.
- To show correlations, use a bar graph, a line graph, or a scatter graph.
- To show geographic relationships, use a map.
- To illustrate a process or a procedure, use a flowchart or a diagram.

Responsible Communication

Statistics can be misused in a myriad of ways. Some misuses are intentional, but others are not. Even some scientists have been known to fool themselves accidentally with statistics because of a lack of knowledge of probability and a lack of standardization in their tests. Common methods of misusing statistics follow.

Misuse of Statistics by Being Selective or Discarding Data

In marketing terms, all you have to do to promote a product is to find one study with a certainty level of 95 percent that is favorable to the product. There may be nineteen other studies with unfavorable results, but these studies are simply ignored. Similarly, a study might indicate that a product is inferior in all aspects except for one very narrow range in which it is considered superior. When the statistics are used from the narrow range and the rest is not used, this is known as *discarding data* and is lying by omission.

Choosing the Question to Get a Certain Answer

You can easily influence the answer to a survey question by asking it in a different way. You can also precede the question by ten others that make the respondent aware of ten issues that seem unfavorable to your cause or candidate. Or you can omit the third-party view from the questionnaire; this will make many would-be third-position supporters take the side you favor.

Biased Samples

If you conduct a survey of homelessness by calling participants' home phone numbers, you will find a homeless rate near zero. That's because homeless people don't have home phones! For samples to be unbiased, they must be representative of the general population. For that reason, studies that are conducted using college students are not representative of the general population; they are only representative of college students.

The Truncated Graph or One-Dimensional Drawing

Sometimes graphs can be misleading. This can occur when the bottom portion of a graph is cut off, which can make a trend look more significant than it is because of the change in proportion. Likewise, you might use a drawing to indicate double the proportion of a comparable object; however, the drawing might be twice as tall but four times as large in total volume. Therefore, the drawing looks twice as large as you intended.

The Well-Chosen Average

Most measures follow a normal bell-curve distribution. However, not all things follow this distribution, one of them being income. For example, most incomes may fall below $35,000, but if you add in the comparatively small number of people with incomes above $1 million, the average will raise disproportionately. Therefore, when an income average is given in the form of a mean, nearly everybody makes less than that.[4]

Statistical Error

Many measures are useful within a certain range of statistical error. For example, the revised Stanford-Binet IQ test has a statistical error range of 3 percent. What that means is that a child who measures 97 may not be less intelligent than one who measures 100 on the test because the precision of the test may vary by as much as 3 percent. Ignoring this range of reliability can significantly affect the intelligibility of the results of some surveys with outcomes of little variability.

False Causality

The interrelation of cause and effect can also be obscured by statistics. Throughout the ages, many erroneous assumptions of cause and effect have occurred. For example, leeches were believed to cure sick people when it was often unknown what actually caused the recovery. Similarly, the people of the Hebrides once believed that body lice produced good health. It didn't occur to them that the inverse might be true: Body lice preferred healthy people.[5]

Questions for Discussion

1. Have you heard of incidents in which statistics were misused to make a false or misleading argument? Can you identify advertisements that misuse statistics?

2. What are some steps you might take to avoid the misuse of statistical information?

?   Critical Thinking

What type of information would best be illustrated through the use of a bar graph? A pie graph? A table? A diagram or drawing? Why?

Integrating Graphics into Text

Once you have identified the need for a graphic and then selected the appropriate type and created it, you need to consider how best to integrate it into your text if you are using a written message. Those considerations include the following:

- **Place the graphic in an appropriate location.** For ease of use by your reader, a graphic should be placed directly after the related point in the text.
- **Label the graphic.** Every graphic should have a brief, clear, and informative label.
- **Introduce the graphic in the text.** You should refer to the graphic in the text before it appears.
- **Explain the graphic in the text.** You should explain in the text what your readers should learn from the graphic.

Revising for Organization, Coherence, and Flow

Writing is a reflection of the quality of our thinking—or at least it should be. Some readers will certainly read it as such. Therefore, it is important to take the time after drafting the message to revise for logical flow and coherence. There are three steps to this process:

1. Check for accurate topic sentences.
2. Check for paragraph coherence.
3. Include transitions and forecasting where appropriate.

Check Topic Sentences

A crucial element in making written messages easy to skim is the inclusion of an accurate topic sentence for each and every paragraph. Ideally, in business messages, each paragraph should *begin* with an accurate topic sentence or transitional phrase that mentions one of the subtopics referred to in the introduction if the direct approach was used. This strategy makes your messages more coherent because you are providing the connections between your ideas, announcing the progression of your ideas, and reminding your audience of your topic and its subtopics. This strategy also makes written messages easier to skim. If you have announced the subtopics in your introduction, your reader may decide that he or she only wants to read information about one of them. In that case, your reader will attempt to skim the paragraphs of your message to locate that information.

In written messages that your reader may skim, you should focus the content of each paragraph narrowly on the subtopic announced in the topic sentence. Otherwise, if paragraphs cover more than one topic, your reader may be unable to quickly locate the information that he or she is looking for—or your reader may become confused about the relationship of the ideas covered in a paragraph. In either case, you have created a written message that is not audience-centered and that may not reflect well on the quality of your thinking.

Ensure Paragraph Coherence

Another issue to consider at the paragraph level is **coherence**, or the logical flow of ideas throughout and within a paragraph. In other words, each sentence should clearly lead to the next, and clear connections should be provided between each point or each sentence. An easy way to establish coherence is to consistently end each sentence with the topic that will be discussed in the sentence that will follow. The example below indicates how sentences can be constructed to provide coherence within a paragraph.

> *John is an avid golfer. He loves golf so much that he has purchased a miniature golf game that he has set up in his office. As I entered his office last week, he almost put my eye out with a wild, flying golf ball!*

In the example, the first sentence ends and the second begins with a reference to golfing, while the second sentence ends and the third begins with a reference to "office." The final sentence also ends with the topic stated in the first and second sentences, golf. This repetition provides coherence between each sentence, carrying the topic over from one sentence to the next and clearly focusing the entire passage on a single, primary topic—golf. In contrast, writing that is not coherent is often described as "choppy" or as lacking "flow."

coherence

The logical flow of ideas throughout a paragraph.

Provide Transitions and Forecasting

Transitions assist your audience in moving from one topic to another through words and phrases that link the ideas you are developing. It is important to recognize that a little repetition is not a bad thing in business messages. Again, because businesspeople are often faced with time pressures and we are poor listeners in oral situations, it is often necessary to restate information briefly yet in a slightly different manner to ensure that our audience receives our message successfully. Repetition is also helpful because it aids retention for many types of information. In other words, to move information from our short-term memory to long-term recall, it may need to be repeated. Repetition is not the same as redundancy, however. Redundancy is saying the same thing in the same way without adding anything new or moving the message forward through the progression of its ideas or toward its intent.

Forecasting, like transitions, tells your audience what you will cover next. Bulleted lists, summaries, and preview statements or overviews are also effective forecasting devices.

transitions

Elements that assist the audience in moving from one topic to another through words and phrases that link the ideas being developed by the writer or speaker.

forecasting

Elements that tell the audience what the writer or speaker will cover next.

Revising for Style and Tone

A communicator selects the style and tone, or verbal expression of a message, depending on the purposes of that message, the audience's needs and expectations, the communicator's relationship with the audience, and an organization's culture.

Style is the level of formality of your written communication. Business communication typically should use business style, which is less formal than traditional academic writing but more formal than a conversation. Business style is friendly and personal (you may refer to your audience by name and to its specific circumstances) yet typically correct, although this is changing with the use of instant and text messaging where emoticons, slang phrases, and abbreviations are commonly used and writers may have a first language other than English.

This means that written business messages should use the following:

- Short, simple, precise words, and yet avoid slang
- Short yet complete sentences and short paragraphs
- Standard English
- First- and second-person pronouns

style

The level of formality in written communications.

Using first- and second-person pronouns such as *I*, *we*, and *you* helps you achieve a friendly and personal style that can help you convey goodwill. Using *you* as the predominant pronoun in your writing also subtly sends the message that you are interested in your audience and in meeting its needs, concerns, and interests. Some examples of the *you* focus follow.

Examples of you focus:

> *The benefits you will receive from the Solare hybrid-fuel vehicle include lower fuel bills, a quieter ride, and the satisfaction that you are doing your part to protect the environment.*

> *In this package, you will find the information you requested to put you on the path to a more secure financial future.*

However, there are instances when you should not use *you* as the predominant pronoun in your writing: in cases where it might sound as if you are blaming your audience. In these cases, you should communicate as impersonally as possible, focusing on the solution rather than the problem and its cause. Not only does this approach avoid blame and the subsequent potential for alienating your audience and blocking effective communication, but it also sends the positive message that you are a solution-oriented person. Examples of the improper use of the *you* focus follow.

Examples of improper use of you focus:

> *How can you justify these departmental expenditures?*

> *You improperly filled out the form for supplies, and now our department will have no copier paper for another week.*

If these statements were aimed at you, how would you feel? You might become defensive. That is because the problem has become personal; in effect, you are the problem, and the intent of such a message is to find fault rather than solutions.

tone

The implied attitude of the communicator toward his or her audience.

Tone is the implied attitude of the communicator toward his or her audience. Just as tone of voice can convey the speaker's attitude about his or her audience or a situation, attitude can also be conveyed in writing. When considering tone, you should think about language choices, level of formality or familiarity, the power relationship between you and your audience, and your use of humor or sarcasm. In other words, appropriate tone depends on who you are, who your audience is, your relationship, and the situation. Consideration of the corporate culture and the context of the situation may also be helpful in determining the appropriate tone of a message.

This assessment leads to another general principle of business communication: Focus on the positive whenever possible. In the preceding examples of the improper use of *you*, how might you rephrase or reframe the statements to have a more positive tone, one that avoids blaming?

Generally, such statements can be rephrased by removing the personal pronouns, writing the sentence in passive voice, or taking responsibility for the situation yourself. Sometimes the situation can be reframed as an opportunity to implement better procedures to avoid such problems in the future, or what might be considered a "problem-solving orientation." The following two examples have rephrased the preceding examples to create a more positive communication situation.

Examples of neutral tone and problem-solving orientation:

> *I am concerned that some of the money that was spent in the department might have gone to more productive uses. We need to review the department expenditures, identify ways to better spend our funds, and perhaps implement policies to ensure that this objective is consistently reached in the future.*

> *Because of a mistake that was made in the ordering of supplies last week, we will not have copier paper for another five days. To ensure that this situation does not recur, I have attached instructions for properly ordering supplies to this e-mail message.*

As mentioned above, effective business communication should be positive in tone whenever possible. In the worst-case scenario, it should be neutral. Business messages should *never* be negative in tone because that will likely have adverse effects on your relationship with your audience—and potentially your credibility.

Some people confuse a negative tone, however, with the ability to analyze and identify problems and to promote positive change. What this means is that being able to identify areas for improvement in an organization and to communicate steps to achieve that improvement—being a critical thinker and problem solver—is not the same as being negative. However, some people are extremely sensitive to any communication that might be considered critical—this is because we often have a tendency to take such criticism personally—so it is generally useful to phrase such suggestions as positively as possible and to downplay any critical aspects. In some cases, depending on your audience and its attitude and personality, you may want to avoid any mention of the problems that are being experienced and focus your message solely on your ideas for improvement and their benefits. However, you may run the risk that some individuals will still interpret such messages as personal criticism, even though the intended message is not about them at all. In such cases, working to establishing a trusting relationship with these individuals may lessen their defensiveness.

More generally, it is critically important to avoid communicating negative emotions in a business situation. In other words, you should not send messages that sound angry, frustrated, or hostile, because they have the potential to diminish your credibility as well as negatively affect your relationship with your audience. This is because businesspeople are generally expected to be reasonable persons who make objective decisions based on good information. Consequently, expressing excess negative emotion can make you appear irrational, unreasonable, and lacking in judgment and self-control.

Anger can also be communicated in our written communication. We should never write a message when we are feeling a negative emotion. Instead we should wait until we have calmed down to express ourselves. Although it can feel good to vent negative feelings, we should immediately delete or erase messages written in anger. Unfortunately, with the popularity and proliferation of e-mail, it is easy to pound out our frustrations in an electronic message. "Then we click 'send.' In a frenzied span of 15 minutes we have managed to do some real psychological damage, usually more to ourselves than to anyone else."[6] That damage may come in the form of a loss of credibility and damaged relationships.

? Critical Thinking

Have you read e-mail or other written messages that conveyed a negative tone? What was your reaction? Did the tone of the message affect the writer's credibility? Did the tone affect your relationship with the writer?

Proofreading for Mechanical Correctness

The last step in the message-formulation process is to proofread for mechanical correctness. Mechanical correctness includes the use of proper formatting conventions as well as correct spelling, grammar, sentence structure, and word choice. Most word processors provide templates for most common business messages, which makes formatting much easier. (Examples of common business formats can be found in Appendix A.)

Proofreading for mechanical correctness has become a bit simpler as well through the use of spelling and grammar checkers provided in most word processing applications. Many e-mail applications also provide spell checking tools. These resources should be turned on at all times to help eliminate spelling errors in messages that may negatively affect your credibility as a professional.

If you have trouble with grammar and punctuation, you might consider drafting e-mail messages using a word processor that provides a grammar checking tool and then copying and pasting the revised message to your e-mail program for sending.

Not all errors in writing are created equal, however. Unlike academic writing in which a great deal of focus is aimed at correct grammar, sentence structure, and punctuation—"word smithing" as it is sometimes referred to—business readers are often more interested in clarity and conciseness because of time pressures. In the box below, writing errors are categorized from the most severe to the least in terms of their effects on message clarity and writer credibility. As you will notice, those that affect the clarity of the message such as wrong word choice or unintelligible sentences are much more damaging, while errors that are commonly seen in the writing of some nonnative English speakers, what are called *accent errors*, are much less disruptive. These include missing articles and pronouns.

For more on common mechanical errors and instructions on how to fix them, please see Appendix B, "Punctuation, Sentence Structure, and Usage."

The Varying Severity of Mechanical Errors in Communication

Mechanics and Error Interference

Assess whether errors interfere with a writer's clarity and credibility. A writer's communication may be judged partly on how closely the language follows conventions in sentence structure, grammar, usage, mechanics, spelling, and so on. Severe and frequent errors (and, in some circumstances, even milder forms and degrees of error) can negatively affect both clarity and credibility. All errors are not equally intrusive or offensive to all readers, however. Below, errors are categorized by severity, beginning with the most severe and ending with the least.

- **Disruptive errors** may interfere with communication, preventing the reader from comprehending what the writer means. These include unintelligible sentences, unclear pronoun references, incorrect verbs, run-on sentences, fragments, and the use of wrong words.

- **Credibility errors** don't usually disrupt communication, but they do tend to reflect negatively on the writer's credibility, reducing the reader's confidence in what a writer has to say. These include faulty subject–verb agreement, passive voice, and punctuation and spelling errors.

- **Etiquette errors** are errors that many readers—but not all—hardly notice, especially if reading quickly for meaning. However, etiquette errors can reduce a writer's credibility, especially with those readers who are concerned about professional image or those who believe that critical thinking is reflected in the observance of grammar rules. These include pronoun usage, false subjects, and misplaced apostrophes.

- **Accent errors** commonly characterize the writing of nonnative speakers or the use of local idioms and dialects. Accent errors, which are nearly impossible for nonnative speakers to correct in the short term, may be ignored by readers. These errors rarely interfere with communication and usually do not damage the writer's credibility. These generally entail missing or wrong articles or prepositions.

Source: Adapted from Rogers, P. S., & Rymer, J. (1996). *Analytical Writing Assessment Diagnostic Program* (McLean, VA: Graduate Management Admission Council): 41.

Submitting the Message

Now that all of the needed steps in the writing process have been completed, the message or document is ready to be sent to its audience. In the past this last step was fairly minimal, involving only the application of proper postage or routing to the proper audience through the mailroom. But with the use of e-mail and other technological tools, this step has gained increased importance. The final considerations below can help to reduce some of the problems associated with e-mail use in organizations discussed in Chapter 5.

- Consider the formality of the salutation. Typically, "Hi," or "Hello," are used for those in your organization. But a greater level of formality may be appropriate for those outside your organization or circle, particularly if they are not known by you. When requesting a favor of someone you don't know, it may be more appropriate to use the more formal "Dear Mr. Johns" on the first contact. A response will typically provide a clue as to the level of formality the person prefers in the signature line.

■ Only send copies to those who *need* the information. If you do copy the message, make the appropriate adjustments to the content for these audiences.

■ Avoid the use of "BCC" (blind carbon copy). Using BCC may be perceived as sneaky and may involve ethical concerns or result in more serious consequences. It is better to be open about information in a healthy organizational culture.

■ Include a signature line. E-mail programs provide the option of creating a signature line that includes your full name, title, company, and possibly your phone number. Once created, your signature line will appear automatically in every e-mail that is sent and create a greater air of professionalism.

Summary

Following the steps in the strategic process of developing a message should help you to identify the purpose of the message, your approach, and the content of the message through audience analysis. After the strategic analysis is completed, the tactical steps of writing, or what is commonly referred to as the writing process, should be followed. These include planning, drafting, revising, and proofreading.

- Plan and develop content for routine messages. Identify the type of message. These correspond to the purposes of communication: informative, persuasive, and goodwill messages. Informative messages also include good news and bad news messages. After identifying the type of message, the parts of the message—the introduction, body, and close—should be planned and drafted. Two organizational approaches—direct and indirect—may be used. The direct approach in which the purpose of the message is immediately stated is most commonly used. However, the indirect approach may be chosen for some bad news and persuasive messages. When using the indirect approach, the message begins with a neutral buffer that enables the writer to introduce the topic broadly before stating the bad news—or, in the case of a persuasive message, presenting good reasons why the proposed idea should be accepted before announcing that recommendation.

- Persuasive messages often consist of two basic components: a claim and evidence to support that claim. Common types of evidence include facts, statistics, examples, and analogies. In addition to considering the claims and evidence to be used in a persuasive message, writers should also consider the types of persuasive appeal that might be most appropriate for the audience. *Logos*, or the logical appeal, depends on facts; *ethos*, or the ethical appeal, is a call to the credibility of the writer or to other experts. *Pathos*, or an emotional appeal, often uses images to evoke an emotional response in the reader. When selecting evidence, it is important to test for quality. Tests of quality of evidence focus on the quality of statistics, testimony, and comparisons and analogies.

- In addition to routine and persuasive messages, longer documents such as reports and proposals are commonly written in professional environments. Both reports and proposals may be informal or formal, depending on their length, the intended audience, and the significance of the information they contain. Informal reports and proposals typically use a memo format, whereas formal reports and proposals may include front and back matter in addition to the body of the message.

- In addition to selecting the proper format for a message, most messages regardless of format may use a number of visual elements to make them easier to read and to convey information more quickly. These visual elements include the use of headings, bullet and step lists, and graphic elements such as charts, tables, diagrams, and drawings.

- After drafting the contents of a message, the writer should revise for organization, coherence and logical flow. To improve the logical flow and readability of a message, accurate topic sentences should be provided at the beginning of each paragraph, and the writer should ensure that the content of the paragraph is narrowly focused on that topic. Writers can also use forecasting and transitions to improve the logical flow and coherence of a message.

- Business writing should also be professional yet friendly in style and tone. This can often be accomplished by using a "you attitude," although this device should be avoided in bad news messages because it can create a negative, blaming tone. Written messages should never be negative in tone; at worst, they should be neutral. This can be accomplished by using passive voice when constructing sentences.

- The last step in the writing process is to proofread for mechanical correctness, which includes checking that formatting follows conventions and that spelling, grammar, word choice, and sentence structure are correct.

Key Terms

call to action **130**	pathos **134**	coherence **148**
claim **133**	AIDA approach **136**	transitions **148**
evidence **133**	graph **144**	forecasting **148**
logos **133**	table **145**	style **148**
ethos **134**	diagram **145**	tone **149**

Discussion Questions

1. How do the reading practices of academic audiences, such as instructors, differ from those of business-people? What are the factors that lead to these differences?
2. What tactics have you used to ensure that your messages are logically organized? What new tactics might you incorporate into your message-creation process to ensure well-organized messages?
3. Do you think that using the indirect approach to organizing a message is manipulative or unethical?
4. What are some of the challenges you have encountered while attempting to persuade? How might the AIDA approach be used to better deal with these situations?
5. Which types of evidence would be most persuasive to a business audience? Give examples.

Applications

1. Revise the following message so that it is more logically ordered. You may also discover that some of the content is irrelevant and thus can be eliminated and that the message also is missing some critical information needed to fulfill the customer's request. Be sure to check the subject line of the message for clarity.

To: Martha Reeves <mreeves@prooffice.com>
From: Stan Liu

Subject: Accounting Software

Dear Ms. Reeves:

I recently purchased your new accounting software at Professional Office Products. When I got the product home, I was unable to install the product on my Apple brand computer. I am a small business owner and think that your product will be very helpful to me in improving my productivity and potentially my company's profits.

I returned the product to your store to receive a refund or to exchange the product for one that might work on my computer. The manager told me that he could not make the exchange but that I should contact you, the maker, with my request.

Can you help me? I have overnighted the product to your office.

Regards,

Stan Liu
902 Oak Street
Portland, OR 90042

---

2. You are a customer service representative for RichRUs, a company that organizes and holds seminars across the United States. These seminars are intended to help educate "regular" people on how to become financially independent through the purchase, resale, and rental of foreclosed properties. In addition to the seminars, the company sells DVD recordings of its founder, Leonard Samson, espousing his sales methods and techniques. Leonard's seminars and DVDs have become so popular that your production has not kept up with demand. To make matters worse, you advertise "same-day" shipping in your promotional materials. You have just received approximately 50 orders for the two-volume DVD set that sells for $95. Write a bad news letter that you can send to these customers in which you explain the situation.
3. Using the AIDA approach, create a message to persuade your boss to approve your plan to hire two new people. You must show that the benefits will outweigh the costs of hiring and additional salaries and benefits.
4. Using the steps to formulate a message to a reluctant or hostile audience, create a message to persuade a customer to consider the purchase of a new service or product your company is offering. Assume that the customer has previously had a bad experience with your company that involved the late delivery of your product or service, which resulted in a small financial loss for the customer. Also assume that the customer is currently pleased with the services he or she is receiving from one of your competitors.

5. You work in the information services department of SynSystems, Inc., a maker of computer connectivity products. Your job, along with the other members of your department, is to provide computer support to the employees of SynSystems. Several years ago, SynSystems was purchased by computer products giant World Connectivity Solutions (WCS). Because your company had an excellent reputation for its customer service and extensive and positive brand recognition, WCS chose to leave your division with its well-respected name.

Coincidentally, perhaps, SynSystems uses the same product—GroupPRO—as its parent company for electronic collaboration among project development teams. GroupPRO was created by another company that WCS now owns, but it is not the only product of its kind on the market. Because of lingering bitter feelings about the company takeover, there is a move among the employees of your department to switch to a newer collaboration product, TeamMAX. Write a persuasive letter to your supervisor, Jonathan Reeves, to persuade him to stay with the GroupPRO product. Include a visual element to compare the values of several items.

Endnotes

1. Casner-Lotto, J., Rosenblum, E., & Wright, M. (2009). The ill-prepared U.S. workforce: Exploring the challenges of employer-provided workforce readiness training. New York: The Conference Training Board, Inc. Retrieved from *http://www.conference board. org/publications/publicationdetail.cfm?publicationid=1676*.

2. Price, H. T. (2004). Writing well in business. *Business & Economic Review*, 50 (3), 13.

3. Watson, J. (n.d.). Writing: Expanding your sphere of influence through better business communications. Retrieved April 27, 2004, from *http://jwatsonassociates.com/Articles*, p.2.

4. Huff, D. (2005). How to lie with statistics. In K. J. Harty (Ed.), *Strategies for Business and Technical Writing*, pp. 347–354. New York: Pearson Education.

5. Huff, D. 2005.

6. Manley, W. (2001). Mightier than the pen, *American Libraries*, 32 (9), 124.

Cerner Corporation: *A Stinging Office Memo Boomerangs*

"We are getting less than 40 hours of work from a large number of our KC-based EMPLOYEES. The parking lot is sparsely used at 8 a.m.; likewise at 5 p.m. As managers – you either do not know what your EMPLOYEES are doing; or YOU do not CARE.

I will hold you accountable. You have allowed this to get to this state. You have two weeks. Tick, tock."

Neal L. Patterson, CEO Cerner Corporation

April 5, 2001: *The New York Times* by Edward Wong. The only things missing from the office memo were expletives. It had everything else. There were lines berating employees for not caring about the company. There were words in all capital letters like "SICK" and "NO LONGER." There were threats of layoffs and hiring freezes and a shutdown of the employee gym.

The memo was sent by e-mail on March 13 by the chief executive of the Cerner Corporation, a health care software development company based in Kansas City, Missouri, with 3,100 employees worldwide. Originally intended only for 400 or so company managers, it quickly took on a life of its own.

The e-mail message was leaked and posted on Yahoo. Its belligerent tone surprised thousands of readers, including analysts and investors. In the stock market, the valuation of the company, which was $1.5 billion on March 20th, plummeted 22 percent in three days. Now, Neal L. Patterson, the 51-year-old chief executive, a man variously described by people who know him as "arrogant," "candid," "passionate," says he wishes he had never hit the send button. "I was trying to start a fire," he said. "I lit a match, and I started a firestorm."

That is not hard to do in the Internet age, when all kinds of messages in cyberspace are capable of stirring reactions and moving markets. In the autumn of 2000, for example, a young California investor pleaded guilty to criminal charges that he made $240,000 by sending out a fake news release that resulted in a sharp drop in the stock of Emulex, a communications equipment manufacturer.

In Mr. Patterson's case, this is what the world saw: "We are getting less than 40 hours of work from a large number of our K.C.-based EMPLOYEES. The parking lot is sparsely used at 8:00 a.m.; likewise at 5:00 p.m. As managers – either you do not know what your EMPLOYEES are doing; or YOU do not CARE. You have created expectations on the work effort which allowed this to happen inside Cerner, creating a very unhealthy environment. In either case, you have a problem and you will fix it or I will replace you. NEVER in my career have I allowed a team which worked for me to think they had a 40-hour job. I have allowed YOU to create a culture which is permitting this. NO LONGER."

Mr. Patterson went on to list six potential punishments, including laying off five percent of the staff in Kansas City. "Hell will freeze over," he vowed, before he would dole out more employee benefits. The parking lot would be his yardstick of success, he said; it should be "substantially full" at 7:30 a.m. and 6:30 p.m. on weekdays and half full on Saturdays.

"You have two weeks," he said. "Tick, tock."

For Cerner Corporation, the message apparently promoted a market upheaval. On March 22nd, the day after the memo was posted on the Cerner message board on Yahoo, trading in Cerner's shares, which typically runs at about 650,000 a day, shot up to 1.2 million shares. The following day, volume surged to four million. In three days, the stock price fell to $34 from almost $44. It closed at $30.94 on April 4, 2001.

"While the memo provided some much-needed laughter on Wall Street after a tough week, it probably got overblown as an issue," said Stephen D. Savas, an analyst with Goldman, Sachs who rates the stock a market performer, which is relatively low. "But it did raise two real questions for investors. One: Has anything potentially changed at Cerner to cause such a seemingly violent reaction? And two: Is this a CEO that investors are comfortable with?"

Mr. Patterson said that the memo was taken out of context and that most employees at Cerner understood that he was exaggerating to make a point. He said he was not carrying out any of the punishments he listed. Instead, he said, he wanted to promote discussion. He apparently succeeded, receiving more than 300 e-mail responses from employees.

Glenn Tobin, chief operating officer at Cerner, said he had read several. "Some people said, 'The tone's too harsh, you've really fouled this one up,'" he said. "Some people said, 'I agree with your point.'" Mr. Patterson, who holds an MBA from Oklahoma State University and worked as a consultant at Arthur Andersen before starting Cerner with two partners in 1979, attributes his management style to his upbringing on a 4,000-acre family wheat farm in northern Oklahoma. He spent day after day riding a tractor in the limitless expanse of the fields with only his thoughts for company, he said, and came to the conclusion that life was about building things in your head, then going out and acting on them. "You can take the boy off the farm," he said, "but you can't take the farm out of the boy."

And his directness with subordinates is not necessarily a management liability. Cerner is a fast-growing company that had $404.5 million in revenue in 2000 and met earnings projections for the first three quarters of 2001. The company made *Fortune* magazine's lists in 1998 and 2000 of the "100 Best Companies to Work for in America."

"He has opinions," Mr. Tobin, Cerner's No. 2 executive, said. "He gives his opinions. He can have a blunt style with people who he thinks don't get it, don't understand the challenges they're facing."

March 13th began like any other day. Mr. Patterson said he woke up at 5:00 a.m. and did some work at home. Then he drove the 30 miles to Cerner's corporate campus, seven brick-and-glass buildings, surrounded by 1,900 parking spaces atop a hill in northern Kansas City. In the elevator, he spoke with the receptionist, a woman who had been with the company for 18 years. She remarked that the work ethic had been declining at the company, he said, reinforcing his own fears.

At 7:45 a.m., he walked into his sixth-floor office and typed up a draft of the memo. He met with a client downstairs, then had two managers and his assistant read over the memo. At 11:48, he sent it. The memo went up on the Yahoo message board a week later. Analysts began getting calls from investors. They, in turn, called Cerner to verify the authenticity of the memo, then exchanged a flurry of phone calls and e-mail messages, trying to divine the tea leaves of Mr. Patterson's writings.

"The perception was that they have to work overtime to meet their quarter," said Stacey Gibson, an analyst with Fahnestock & Company, who rated the company's stock a "buy" and was among the first to post a warning on Thomson Financial/First Call about the memo. "Whether that's true or not, I don't know," she said. "This is how it was taken on the Street."

Some analysts say that other factors could have contributed to the drop in stock price. The overall market was shaky. There were investors who wanted to sell the stock short, betting that it was ready for a fall. One analyst was especially bearish about the company. But even Mr. Patterson acknowledged that his memo "added noise" to what was already out there.

At the end of the week, as the stock fell, Mr. Patterson sent out another e-mail message to his troops. Unlike the first memo, it was not called a Management Directive, but rather a Neal Note. It began this way: "Please treat this memo with the utmost confidentiality. It is for internal dissemination only. Do not copy or e-mail to anyone else."

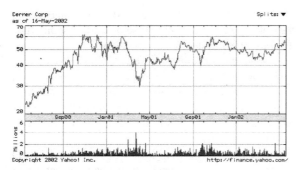

Table 1.1: Cerner Corporation Stock Performance. June 2000 to May 2002.
Source: Yahoo Finance. Used by permission.

Discussion Questions

1. What's the principal business problem here?

2. From the company's perspective, what would an optimal outcome look like?

3. Who are the key stakeholders in this case?

4. If Mr. Patterson were to ask for your counsel on this matter, what would you advise?

5. Which actions would you encourage him to take first? What measure would you use to determine success in resolving the business problem identified in question number one?

6. What sort of problems did Mr. Patterson create for himself when he chose e-mail as his communication medium?

7. How should discussions of this sort be conducted?

Sources

"Boss's e-Mail Bites Back," BBC News Online. *http://www.news.bbc.co.uk/hi/english/world/americas/newsid_1263000/1263917.stm. British Broadcasting Corporation.* 5/17/2002. 2:38 p.m.

Burton, T.M. "Irate CEO's E-Mail Puts Him in Hot Water," *WSJ.com*: Career Journal. *ttp://www.careerjournal.com/myc/killers/20010427-burton.htm. The Wall Street Journal.* 5/17/2002. 2:44 p.m.

Clancy, J. "Weekend Work Piles Up for Execs," *cnn.com. wysiwyg://17http://www.cnn.com/2001/world/europe//04/06/executive.stress. The Cable News Network.* 5/17/2002. 2:47 p.m.

From Cerner Corp to Employees. *http://www.clas.ufl.edu/users/creed/Business/Professional/Communication/Assignments3.*

Gillis, W.C. "Think Twice Before Hitting Send," Small Business Computing. *http://www.smallbusinesscomputing.com/biztools/.* 5/17/2002. 3:04 p.m.

Korzeniowski, P. "Firms Try to Stamp Out 'Bad' E-mail Disclosures," Omniva Policy Systems. *http://www.disappearing.com/ann/investorsbusinessdaily_inthenews.htm. Investors Business Daily.* 5/17/2002. 2:43 p.m.

Wendland, M. "Masses of Sloppy e-Mail Are Holding Workers Back," Freep.com. May 3, 2001. *http://www.freep.com/money/tech/mwend3_20010503.htm. The Detroit Free Press.* 5/17/2002. 2:42 p.m.

Wong, E. "A Stinging Office Memo Boomerangs: Chief Executive Is Criticized After Upbraiding Workers by E-Mail," *The New York Times*, Thursday, April 5, 2001, pp. C1, C13. Reprinted with permission.

Writing Assignment

Please respond in writing to the issues presented in this case by preparing two documents: a communication strategy memo and a professional business letter.

In preparing these documents, you may assume one of two roles: you may identify yourself as a Cerner Corporation senior manager who has been asked to provide advice to Mr. Neal Patterson regarding the issues he and his company are facing. Or, you may identify yourself as an external management consultant who has been asked by the company to provide advice to Mr. Patterson.

Either way, you must prepare a strategy memo addressed to Neal Patterson, Chairman and Chief Executive Officer of the company, that summarizes the details of the case, rank orders the critical issues, discusses their implications (what they mean and why they matter), offers specific recommendations for action (assigning ownership and suspense dates for each), and shows how to communicate the solution to all who are affected by the recommendations.

You must also prepare a professional business letter for Mr. Patterson's signature. That document should be addressed to all Cerner Corporation employees. If you have questions about either of these documents, please consult your instructor.

----- **Original Message** -----

From: Patterson, Neal. To: DL_ALL_Managers.

Subject: MANAGEMENT DIRECTIVE: Week #10_01: Fix it or changes will be made. Importance: High.

To the KC-based managers:

I have gone over the top. I have been making this point for over one year. We are getting less than 40 hours of work from a large number of our KC-based EMPLOYEES. The parking lot is sparsely used at 8 AM; likewise at 5PM. As managers – you either do not know what your EMPLOYEES are doing; or YOU do not CARE. You have created expectations on the work effort which allowed this to happen inside Cerner, creating a very unhealthy environment. In either case, you have a problem and you will fix it or I will replace you.

NEVER in my career have I allowed a team which worked for me to think they had a 40-hour job. I have allowed YOU to create a culture which is permitting this. NO LONGER. At the end of next week, I am planning to implement the following:

1. Closing of Associate Center to EMPLOYEES from 7:30 AM to 6:30 PM.

2. Implementing a hiring freeze for all KC-based positions. It will required Cabinet approval to hire someone into a KC-based team. I chair our Cabinet.

3. Implementing a time clock system, requiring EMPLOYEES to "punch in" and "punch out" to work. Any unapproved absences will be charged to the EMPLOYEES vacation.

4. We passed a Stock Purchase Program, allowing for the EMPLOYEE to purchase Cerner stock at a 15% discount, at Friday's BOD meeting. Hell will freeze over before this CEO implements ANOTHER EMPLOYEE benefit in this Culture.

5. Implement a 5% reduction of staff in KC.

6. I am tabling the promotions until I am convinced that the ones being promoted are the solution, not the problem. If you are the problem, pack your bags.

I think this parental-type action SUCKS. However, what you are doing, as managers, with this company makes me SICK. It makes me sick to have to write this directive. I know I am painting with a broad brush and the majority of the KC-based associates are hard-working, committed to Cerner success and committed to transforming health care. I know the parking lot is not a great measurement for "effort." I know that "results" is what counts, not "effort." But I am through with the debate.

We have a big vision. It will require a big effort. Too many in KC are not making the effort.

I want to hear from you. If you think I am wrong with any of this, please state your case. If you have some ideas on how to fix this problem, let me hear those. I am very curious how you think we got here. If you know team members who are the problem, let me know. Please include (copy) Kynda in all of your replies.

I STRONGLY suggest that you call some 7AM, 6PM and Saturday AM team meetings with the EMPLOYEES who work directly for you. Discuss this serious issue with your team. I suggest that you call your first meeting – tonight. Something is going to change.

I am giving you two weeks to fix this. My measurement will be the parking lot. It should be substantially full at 7:30 AM and 6:30 PM. The pizza man should show up at 7:30 p.m. to feed the starving teams working late. The lot should be half full on Saturday mornings. We have a lot of work to do. If you do not have enough to keep your teams busy, let me know immediately.

Folks this is a management problem, not an EMPLOYEE problem. Congratulations, you are management. You have the responsibility for our EMPLOYEES. I will hold you accountable. You have allowed this to get to this state. You have two weeks. Tick, tock.

Neal

Chairman & Chief Executive Officer
Cerner Corporation *www.cerner.com*
2800 Rockcreek Parkway, Kansas City, Missouri 64117
"We Make Health Care Smarter"

----- **End of Original Message** -----

Communicating in Oral Presentations

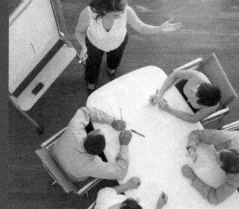

The Case of the Novice Presenter

"Good morning, everyone," Lara Bright, head of marketing, announced with a smile from the front of the conference room. "I am excited to welcome Georgia Egans, president of Interactive Learning, and Tom Hayes, her marketing director, to LearningFun. We are eager to show you our new line of interactive computer learning programs aimed at elementary school children. We believe they are the best programs available in terms of the graphic elements and game-based learning tools. Now let me turn the time over to our marketing person for this product line, Ben Williams, and he will walk you through the Play&Learn series. Ben?"

Ben rose abruptly from his chair, bumping the table and spilling everyone's coffee. "Oops, sorry, everyone. Let me get some more napkins." He quickly turned to the side table and grabbed a stack that he then placed randomly around the table as he made his way to the computer located at the front of the room.

"Well, that was a bad start," he said, followed by an awkward laugh. "I wish I was better at making jokes—this would be a prime place to insert one." Another awkward chuckle bubbled out as he turned his attention to the computer screen.

Clearing his voice loudly then taking a few audible breaths, he clicked to the next presentation slide. He began, looking up at his audience. "This morning, we will begin by discussing the company background of LearningFun. Then we will move on to a brief overview of our complete product line, then I will get to the stuff you are probably here to learn more about, the new Play&Learn system."

He jammed his pointer finger down loudly on the Enter key once again as if to punctuate that segment of the presentation, then went on, "As you probably know, LearningFun was created ten years ago by Georgia Egans…"

After reading this chapter, you will be able to

- Understand when and how to use the oral channel for presentations.
- Plan the message and select a proper organizational structure for a presentation.
- Develop the presentation.
- Design visual aids to support an oral presentation.
- Achieve the appropriate vocal delivery and become more aware of your nonverbal communication to better align it with the oral message you wish to express.
- Prepare for an oral presentation and reduce speech apprehension.
- Handle question-and-answer sessions.
- Plan and manage presentations for alternate situations, such as those involving multi-cultural audiences, team delivery, distance discussions, and crisis communication situations.

Case Questions

1. From a strategic perspective, how would you rate Ben's presentation thus far? Has he clearly identified the communication purpose(s) of his presentation during the planning stage and executed them well? What are they? How well has he focused on addressing his audience's needs, interests, and concerns?

2. If his presentation could be improved from a strategic perspective, what changes would you make? Why?

3. What nonverbal communication messages has he been implicitly sending? How might these be interpreted by his audience in terms of his ability to meet his strategic goals? How should these nonverbal communication messages be changed? Why?

As with all messages, when planning an oral presentation, you should first identify your purposes for communicating; analyze your audience to identify its values, beliefs, interests, concerns, and objections; consider the context of the communication; and choose a channel—in this case, an oral one. This process will help you to determine the approach and content of your message.

This chapter explores tactics that can be deployed in oral presentations and meetings to more effectively reach your strategic-communication goals. The tactical elements to be applied in oral presentations can be broadly categorized as follows:

1. Planning and organizing the content

2. Designing the visual aids

3. Practicing the delivery, including the reduction of presentation anxiety

4. Giving the presentation, including handling the question-and-answer session (please see Figure 7-1 below).

But before moving on to a discussion of the steps in the tactical process, let's review one of the steps in the strategic process of message formulation, how and when presentations should be used as a communication medium.

Figure 7-1 Steps in Preparing an Oral Presentation

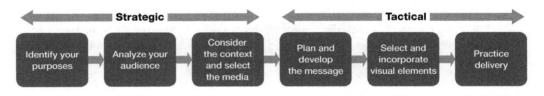

Channel Considerations

Probably one of the most misused media of communication is the oral presentation. For this reason, it is important to emphasize when to choose an oral presentation as the method of message delivery. Presentations are good for the following situations:

- **Inspiring and motivating others.** If the presenter is able to bring enthusiasm and energy and an inspirational message to the situation, then oral message delivery is highly appropriate.

- **Demonstrations of products and services or for training purposes.** Oral presentations work well when audience members are able to view how a product or service works and better understand its functions. They are also useful for training purposes, particularly if the audience is able to apply the presented material through practice or use as part of the presentation.

- **To introduce a complex persuasive written message (generally a report or a proposal).** This helps increase audience interest by emphasizing the key benefits of the proposal in an engaging manner and allows the presenter to answer audience questions. As an introduction only, the presentation focuses on key issues and uses the written channel to elaborate on the details.

- **As a follow-up to a complex persuasive written message (generally a report or a proposal).** The personal presence of an advocate can help establish goodwill and credibility and move the persuasive process forward. In these cases, the oral message should generally emphasize the benefits of the proposal and answer audience questions.

- **To deliver bad news to a large audience.** In some circumstances, the personal presence of an organizational representative helps to establish or maintain goodwill and credibility and, by extension, the image and reputation of the firm.

Presentations are often not good for delivering a large amount of complex information, simply because (1) audience members won't remember it all and (2) they will likely become bored and tune out. This last occurrence can also damage the presenter's credibility because a boring presentation often reflects poorly on the reputation of the presenter as a communicator. Instead, details should typically be delivered using the written channel.

The biggest mistake that presenters make is not clearly understanding that oral presentations as a medium of communication are quite different from written messages in terms of the kind of information they are useful for conveying. In other words, the biggest mistake that presenters make is treating a presentation as if it were a written document or formal report. The written channel and the oral channel are generally good for communicating different kinds of information and for achieving quite different goals. Even if a presentation is based on written material, the presenter should start planning as if he or she was developing an entirely new message because of this fact. If this isn't understood from the beginning, an oral presentation is likely to fall flat—and the presenter with it in terms of enhancing credibility and goodwill.

Another risk of selecting a presentation as the channel for communication is that most are designed to be monologic rather than dialogic, one way rather than two way. This drawback can have a negative impact on listener engagement and cannot be overstated in terms of the risk involved. For this reason, it is critically important to consider whether you have the time needed to adequately prepare for a presentation and the skills to deliver it professionally and memorably.

Planning and Developing the Presentation

As stated in the previous section, the oral channel of communication should be used differently from the written channel. The main reason for giving a presentation is to benefit from the nonverbal cues that a person brings to the message and to illustrate information that is best conveyed visually. To put it another way, the skill of the presenter should be the primary consideration when choosing an oral presentation as the mode of communication. Steve Jobs of Apple Computer was often noted for his skill at presenting. One reason his presentations were so successful is that he understood the channel and treated a presentation as an event. In other words, a good presentation should engage the audience as only a skilled presenter can. If you cannot engage the audience, then it might be worth considering another medium of communication for message delivery, such as the written channel or a more interactive discussion.

Planning the Presentation

To make presentations more engaging, time should be spent identifying the key message or theme and considering other aspects of a strong oral message. These are simplicity, interest, stories, and vividness.

- **Simplicity.** In presentations, you should aim to achieve or communicate one idea. The first question to ask is, what is the idea or theme of my presentation? This step can be the most time-consuming and may require some creative thinking. An example of the use of an excellent theme is the presentation by epidemiologist Elisabeth Pisani entitled "Sex, Drugs and HIV—Let's Get Rational" found on TED Talks (*www.ted.com*).

    The purpose of that presentation is to ask the audience to support HIV and AIDS programs. However, the presenter apparently knows that HIV is not a burning issue for much of the audience, which is largely made up of well-educated, upper middle-class people, most of whom don't have to cope with the challenges of the disease. Therefore, Pisani is faced with the challenge of engaging the audience with this topic, and she does so by making it real to them. She begins her talk with the statement, "People do stupid things—that's what spreads HIV," and follows with the explanation, "Yes, people do stupid things for perfectly rational reasons." In this way, she gets the audience's attention by making a dramatic statement and introduces her theme of "rationality." She then proceeds to tell the story of AIDS from the perspective of those most likely to have the disease by explaining what "rationality" means from each one's perspective. By the end of her story, she has succeeded in educating her audience about the predicament of HIV and AIDS sufferers, making the audience more likely to care about it and them.

- **Interest.** As indicated in the previous example, you need to engage your audience and keep them engaged. One way is to raise questions that your audience wants answered and then answer them as you proceed through the presentation. What are the questions that your audience may have? How might you use these to organize your message? Can you tie them to your theme? Another way to raise interest is to tell a story that your audience may find engaging.

- **Stories.** As the previous example illustrates, the use of stories is a way to humanize your message and draw in your audience through the use of emotional appeal or *pathos*. Stories help engage your audience if its members can relate to them. Stories also make your presentation easier to follow and your message often more concrete and vivid and thus more impactful.

- **Vividness.** Generalities are boring and, in some cases, unclear. To avoid this problem, use concrete and vivid language and descriptions that bring your presentation to life and make them memorable.

Above all else, when planning a presentation, keep the message simple. Most experts say that a presentation can only cover one topic effectively. Using a theme can help you to accomplish this goal by hanging all of your points on that theme or organizing principle.

In addition, in the workplace, you generally present information about which you are a recognized expert. When planning a presentation, it is important to recognize this fact because it can make you much more confident in your ability to deliver your message and eliminate any presentation anxiety. If you find yourself in a situation, though, in which you are presenting material about which you do not feel like an expert, then it can be helpful to consider how you might frame your topic in such a way so as to connect it to a relevant issue about which you are an expert. This step may be the key to unlocking the theme of your presentation, in fact.

For example, you may be asked to present a motivational speech to a group of inner-city youth. If you came from a different socioeconomic background, are of a different race or ethnic group, have a different educational level, and are in a different age group, you may feel as if you have little in common with your audience or it with you. In this case, rather than pretending to be of this group, you might call upon your own youthful experiences to create a story that links with some of their concerns. In this way, you will likely sound, feel, and appear more confident and sound, feel, and appear more authentic while at the same time, hopefully, telling an engaging story that addresses some of their own concerns in an enlightening way. This approach should then help you to establish your credibility and convey goodwill, while at the same time appealing to your audience's interests and concerns. It can heighten your credibility as well because you will likely feel and look more confident. At the same time, though, you must be careful not to diminish critical differences of which your audience will likely be aware. Doing so, can severely damage the credibility of your message.

As this discussion implies, some messages require considerable time spent in the planning stage. In addition to identifying the topics you will cover and the theme, you may need to spend time creating a logical structure through the process of outlining and gathering additional information, perhaps by conducting research, to enhance your presentation's informative and persuasive appeal.

Doing research to provide relevant, concrete details can make the presentation more interesting because details such as examples and anecdotes make points more vivid and clear than generalizations and abstractions. Just remember, the point of the presentation is not to deliver details—it is to use carefully selected details to bring your important points to life. The time spent in planning, though, can make the remainder of the process much easier and much quicker to complete and the final product much more successful.

Selecting the Appropriate Structure

Depending on the purposes, the audience, the situation, or the information you are providing, the ordering of your message may affect its success. Several strategies are available to make your messages more logical and understandable for your audience. You can choose to put information in different types of order, including these:

- Old information before new
- By chronology
- Spatially
- From general to particular
- By problem and solution
- By cause and effect
- By comparison and contrast.

These common organizing patterns were discussed in Chapter 6 and are illustrated in Figure 7-2.

Figure 7-2 Common Organizing Patterns for Presentations

Old Information before New	Present information that is known to your reader or listener before you present new information.
Organize Information Chronologically	Presents ideas in the order of their occurrence.
Geographical/Spatial	Organizes ideas conceptually, according to an actual spatial arrangement or a physical metaphor or analogy.
General to Particular	Arrange ideas from the general to the particular.
Problem/Solution	Explain the problem then present the solution.
Cause/Effect	Explain the cause then present its effect(s).
Comparison/Contrast	Compare and contrast one topic with another.

Present old information before new. One organizational strategy is to present information that is known to your reader or listener before you present new information. This strategy makes the new information easier to understand because your reader or listener has a basis of understanding—the old information—on which to draw to comprehend the less familiar material.

Organize information chronologically. Chronological ordering presents ideas in the order of their occurrence. Such a pattern might also be used to explain the steps for a procedure. In this case, each step must be performed in a particular order to achieve the desired result. Chronological ordering is easy to achieve, easy to recognize, and easy to follow, partly because it is similar to the narrative pattern used in storytelling of all kinds—movies, novels, and television sitcoms. Because of our exposure to such media, we are all familiar with chronological ordering.

Use a geographic or spatial pattern. The spatial pattern organizes ideas conceptually, according to an actual spatial arrangement or a physical metaphor or analogy. For example, you might give a presentation about your company's worldwide distribution network and how that provides a competitive advantage. The talk would then discuss each of the distribution centers located in different areas of the globe.

This pattern can also be used to arrange topics in a spatial pattern such as a pyramid or concentric circles. The pyramid, for example, might be used to represent the five platforms of your product that distinguish it from others.

Use a general-to-particular pattern. Another common organizational strategy is to arrange ideas from the general to the particular. General to particular is a common organizational arrangement in persuasive messages. The general statement is considered your claim. For example, you might state, "Our company has made a number of changes to benefit our employees." The particular information would then include the specifics of those changes as well as the benefits. Another way to think about the general-to-particular strategy is in terms of levels of abstraction. In other words, the general statement is more abstract than the particular information, which is more concrete.

Use a problem–solution pattern. The problem–solution pattern is common in business because it is highly persuasive and can include other patterns of reasoning such as question and answer. When using this pattern, the communicator begins with a shared, recognizable problem, situation, or question and progressively moves to a solution supported by information or evidence. Such a pattern typically begins with a definition of the problem that proceeds to an analysis of the problem or an evaluation of the solutions, and then concludes with a redefinition of the problem or a suggestion for action. In business, this pattern might also be tweaked to discuss issues and actions, which are quite similar to problems and solutions, or to propose opportunities and discuss how your organization is best suited to leverage those opportunities.

Use a cause-and-effect pattern. The key to using the cause-and-effect pattern successfully is to build a case that supports your claim of cause and effect. In other words, this pattern forces you to make and support an inference that one event caused or will cause another. The fact that one event followed another (the chronological ordering discussed earlier) does not prove that one event caused the other.

Use a comparison-and-contrast pattern. In a business presentation, this type of pattern might be used to compare an organization with its competitors to illustrate where it stands in the industry. This pattern should be used strategically to show that your company clearly is the best in all regards to the competition. If the pattern is not used wisely, however, it might backfire.

Developing the Presentation

Once the theme of the message has been determined, thought has been given to how to engage the audience related to the theme, and an appropriate structure has been determined, it is time to develop the presentation in more detail. This generally involves developing the three parts of the presentation: the beginning or introduction, the middle or body of the message, and the end or conclusion. See the template for planning oral presentations.

Presentation Planner

I. Introduction:

    a. Attention-getting material:

    b. Purpose statement:

        1. Subpoint:

        2. Subpoint:

        3. Subpoint

    c. Transition to body of presentation:

II. Body

    a. Main Point 1:

    b. Transition to main point 2:

    c. Main Point 2:

    d. Transition to main point 3:

    e. Main Point 3:

    f. Transition to conclusion:

III. Conclusion:

    a. Summary:

    b. Concluding remarks:

Each of the main parts included in the presentation planner is discussed in more detail in the sections that follow.

The Beginning

After identifying the main topic of your message and its subtopics, you should develop an introduction that provides an attention-getting statement, gives the purpose of the message, and provides an overview of those subtopics.

An introduction should get the audience's attention and indicate why it is important to listen to your message. It should also provide your audience with a road map of what the message contains to help it better follow the logic or contents of your message.

In oral presentations, many techniques exist for gaining your audience's attention at the start. (Examples of attention getters are provided in Figure 7-3.) These include

- **Showing the product or the object.** If you are going to be speaking about a product, show it and perhaps demonstrate its use.

- **Highlighting the benefits.** Briefly state the benefits your audience will receive from your proposal.

- **Asking a question.** Invite your audience to participate by asking relevant questions about the audience itself or your topic. Be careful about the use of rhetorical questions, though, because they can sound unplanned from a strategic perspective and they open up the possibility that your audience might respond negatively (at least in their heads) to the query.

- **Opening with a relevant video or sound clip.** These might include slides containing pictures or other images, a short film or video, and music or a sound clip. This technique should be used with care; you don't want the film or video to become your presentation, only to introduce and highlight your message.

- **Telling a relevant story or personal anecdote.** Arouse audience curiosity by telling an engaging yet related story, perhaps about the history of the company or an experience you had recently that illustrates the theme of the presentation.
- **Stating a striking fact or statistic.** A startling fact or statistic can be used to alert your audience to a problem or opportunity that needs to be addressed.
- **Delivering a relevant quotation.** A well-known or apt quotation can often sum up the theme of a presentation and set the stage for its elaboration.

As stated earlier, identifying the theme of your presentation and its key message can help you determine the appropriate attention getter for an oral presentation.

Figure 7-3 Attention Getters in Business Situations

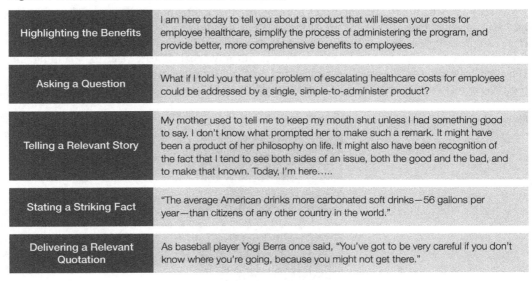

Highlighting the Benefits	I am here today to tell you about a product that will lessen your costs for employee healthcare, simplify the process of administering the program, and provide better, more comprehensive benefits to employees.
Asking a Question	What if I told you that your problem of escalating healthcare costs for employees could be addressed by a single, simple-to-administer product?
Telling a Relevant Story	My mother used to tell me to keep my mouth shut unless I had something good to say. I don't know what prompted her to make such a remark. It might have been a product of her philosophy on life. It might also have been recognition of the fact that I tend to see both sides of an issue, both the good and the bad, and to make that known. Today, I'm here…..
Stating a Striking Fact	"The average American drinks more carbonated soft drinks—56 gallons per year—than citizens of any other country in the world."
Delivering a Relevant Quotation	As baseball player Yogi Berra once said, "You've got to be very careful if you don't know where you're going, because you might not get there."

One last note: Some speakers think that every presentation should begin with a joke, but if a joke is inappropriate or irrelevant, or you are poor at telling jokes, then it's much better to skip it. Only tell a joke if it is relevant to the topic of your presentation and you know that your audience will appreciate it.

The Middle

As stated in Chapter 6, a skilled business communicator will not place the burden of interpreting a message on the receiver. Therefore, you should make sure that you use all available means to "connect the dots" or provide a road map for your audience. Two of those elements that can be used in an oral presentation are forecasting and transitions.

Forecasting tells your audience what you will cover next. Summaries and preview statements or overviews are effective forecasting devices.

Transitions assist your audience in moving from one topic to another through your use of words and phrases that link the ideas you are developing. In oral presentations, a transition should clearly and thoroughly link the topic you are moving from to the one you are moving to. An example of a complete transition is the following: "Now that I have explained why we should adopt a policy allowing flex-time scheduling, I will tell you about some of the benefits such a change would provide to the company and its employees." This type of transition can begin to sound mechanical, though, so it can be worthwhile to spend some time creating more elegant transitions that show the logical

forecasting

Elements of a text or oral presentation that tell the audience what the reader or speaker will cover next.

transitions

Elements that assist the audience in moving from one topic to another through words and phrases that link the ideas the writer or speaker is developing.

connections between the topics. An example might be "Not only would a flex-time policy address some current challenges we face, it will provide the company additional benefits. Let me illustrate a few of them for you."

In oral presentations, it is particularly important to fully link the topic you have just discussed to the one you are about to discuss. Remember, we tend to be poor listeners; in fact, research indicates we only remember 10 percent of what we hear. Your intention in restating the topic you have just covered is to remind those listeners who may tune out for a moment what you are covering and to indicate where you are in the overall structure of your presentation. Generally, the transitions commonly used in written messages—"first," "second," "third," "next," and so on—are not sufficient for a presentation. None makes the logical connection between the previous point and the one that follows, and they can pass so quickly that the listener's ear may not catch them. These transitional statements thus provide the coherence needed to smooth understanding and reception.

As stated in Chapter 6, it is important to recognize that a little repetition is not a bad thing in business messages because of time pressures and poor listening habits. In addition to providing a clear road map of your message, it is important to determine the types of information and evidence that would best enable you to achieve your communicative goals. Please refer to "Planning and Developing Persuasive Messages" (page 130) in Chapter 6 for more on the content of a persuasive message. Figure 7-4 illustrates these concerns in abbreviated form.

Figure 7-4 Elements of a Persuasive Message

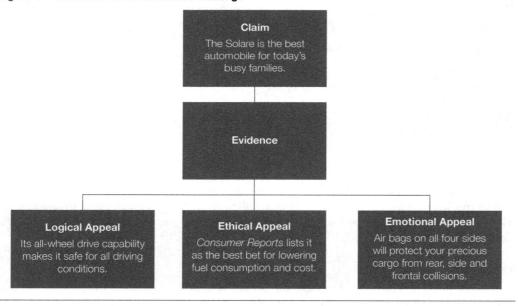

The End

As stated in Chapter 6, the conclusion is one of the most important parts of a message. Your audience will be more likely to remember it because of the *recency effect* (the principle that the most recently presented items or experiences will most likely be remembered best). Consequently, make sure that the conclusion is, in fact, memorable and focuses on the final message that you want your audience to take away.

As discussed in Chapter 6, there are three basic types of conclusions: goodwill, summary, and sales. Goodwill conclusions are generally not appropriate for a presentation as, hopefully, the purpose is more substantive in a business context, so they will not be discussed here. (This is because attending presentations can be seen as time-consuming and as an inconvenience for busy people so it is important to make them count.) Summary conclusions are typically used for informative messages, and sales conclusions are used for persuasive messages.

Summary Conclusions for Informative Messages. If you are conveying an informative message, you should create a summary conclusion in which you restate the subtopics of your message in a slightly different manner. Sometimes stating information differently can also help your listener with comprehension. The first time people hear something, its meaning may not be completely clear. But if additional explanation is provided or if the message is stated again in a slightly different way, then the chances improve that the meaning will be understood.

Sales Conclusions for Persuasive Messages. If you are conveying a persuasive message, your conclusion should focus on restating the benefits your listeners will receive from adopting your proposal. In some persuasive situations, it may also be appropriate to conclude with a **call to action**. Use a call to action such as "Visit our website today to sign up for a 10 percent discount on our call-package rates" when you want your audience to take the next step in your proposal. In this way you can encourage your audience to commit to your proposal.

call to action

A conclusion to a persuasive message that is intended to convince the reader to fully consider the writer's or speaker's proposal and, ideally, commit to a decision or take the next step.

? Critical Thinking

Do you generally provide clear beginnings, middles, and ends in your messages? If so, what are the results? If not, what strategies might you use to produce these three parts of a message consistently?

Designing Visual Aids

The power of conveying information visually has been recognized for hundreds of years. In 1801, William Playfair, the father of modern graphics, claimed, "As much information may be obtained in five minutes [from a graph] as would require whole days to imprint on the memory" if it were communicated in a series of figures. Playfair's quotation clearly communicates the purpose of a visual aid. Using graphics appropriately provides three main benefits:

- Information is more easily understood than with the use of words alone.
- The use of visuals helps make the information conveyed more memorable.
- The use of visuals enhances your professionalism and credibility.

Delivering the content of your message in text form is not an appropriate use of visual aids. The content of the message should be delivered orally by the presenter. Visual aids are intended to be just that—an aid to the presentation—not a way to deliver content. In other words, the script of your presentation should not be provided on presentation slides. If you believe this is the best way to deliver the information to your audience, you might consider e-mail, memo, or informal report instead. You don't want your audience to respond to a text-based presentation aid that asks it to read along while you recite the script of the presentation. Some audience members may react with frustration by questioning why they were asked to waste their time in a presentation when they could have read the message from their own computer screen at their convenience.

Other types of visual aids exist, including whiteboards, transparencies, flip charts, and handouts, but the most commonly used in the workplace is slide presentation software such as Microsoft PowerPoint. It is not the only slide presentation software used, however. Some Apple users prefer Keynote, while Prezi, a web-based program, provides a more interactive approach to transitioning between topic illustrations and visual elements. Much has been written about the uses and misuses of slide-presentation software. As stated above, the biggest mistake that presenters make is believing that all of their information should be delivered in text form on their slides. Instead, presentation software, like other visual aids, should be used for two primary purposes: (1) to indicate the main ideas you will cover or the structure of your presentation and (2) to convey information that is more easily understood visually.

Designing PowerPoint Presentations

When designing presentation aids, make sure all their elements are *visible* from anywhere in the room. Presentation aids should *emphasize* the main points of your speech. Visuals should therefore be simple, and each one should make only one point.

The basic rules for creating PowerPoint slide presentations follow:

- The colors for the slide background and the text should have high contrast: light on dark or dark on light.
- The type size should be large enough to be read from the back of the room (generally 28 points or larger).
- Consider altering the background colors on PowerPoint design templates to create a fresher look or create your own master slides. Potentially, the best design element you might use on your PowerPoint master slide is your company logo and colors to add name recognition and a more custom look.
- Use the "SmartArt" feature in PowerPoint to incorporate more graphic elements onto your slides. Even a simple bullet list can become a graphic element through the use of the SmartArt features.
- If you must use text, limit it to informative phrases presented using a bullet-list format. Avoid presenting text in sentence or paragraph form.
- As a rule of thumb, try to limit text-based slides to "Agenda" or "Overview" and "Conclusion" slides, if possible. Remember, the SmartArt feature can help you to convert text-based slides to visual aids.
- If used, bullet lists should be grammatically parallel in structure and, whenever possible, begin with or contain a verb so that list items are more informative. In other words, you should avoid list items that contain only one word, because one word often does not convey much information and is more like a placeholder.
- Each slide should contain no more than five to six bullet points.
- Consider the use of clip art. Make sure that it clearly relates to your topic, and avoid pictures that might appear too cartoonish for the occasion.

Remember that a PowerPoint presentation should not deliver all of the details of your oral presentation. It is a *visual aid*. Therefore, it is best used to remind your audience of the main points you will cover (like a map) and illustrate information best conveyed in visual form such as charts, tables, and diagrams. These are discussed more below.

? **Critical** Thinking

Whether you are a traditional student or a workplace professional, you have probably viewed many PowerPoint presentations. What is the most common mistake you observe in the presentations you've seen? Do you believe that PowerPoint is often misused or overused? Why?

Organizing PowerPoint Presentations

Just as in a written message, your PowerPoint presentation should include slides for each of the three main parts of a message: introduction, body, and conclusion.

The Introduction

The introduction should include two slides:

- **Opening title slide.** This slide contains the title of your presentation, the name of the presenter, and the organization he or she represents.
- **Overview slide.** This slide lists the main topics covered in the presentation.

Examples of a title and overview slide are provided in Figures 7-5 and 7-6.

Figure 7-5 Example of a Title Slide

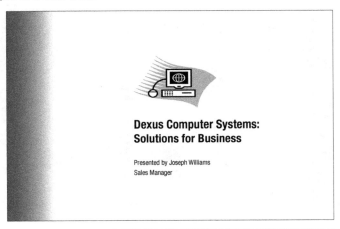

Figure 7-6 Example of an Overview or Agenda Slide

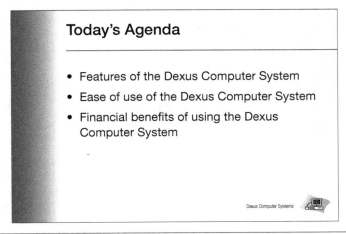

The Body

For the body of your presentation, you should include at least one slide for each of the main points of your presentation. In addition, you should include slides that convey the information that is best communicated visually in the form of tables, charts, graphs, and diagrams (see also Chapter 6) or use the SmartArt feature included in PowerPoint to add visual interest to text-based slides.

The most common forms of visual aids used in both written and oral presentations are the graph, table, and diagram or drawing. All of these elements are easily created using the tools provided in most presentation programs, including PowerPoint.

Graphs Sometimes called charts, **graphs** are used to compare the value of several items: the amount of advertising money spent on different media, the annual profit of a company over time, and so on. The bar graph is typically used to emphasize comparisons or contrasts between two or more items. A pie graph is often used to indicate the distribution of something or the relative size of the parts of a whole. Examples of bar and pie graphs as used in PowerPoint slides are provided in Figures 7-7 and 7-8.

graphs

A visual element used to compare the values of several items; sometimes called *charts*.

Figure 7-7 Example of a Bar Graph Presented on a PowerPoint Slide

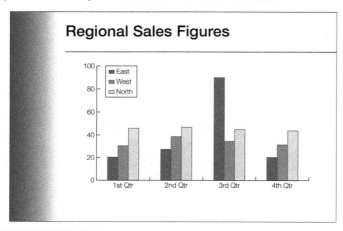

Figure 7-8 Example of a Pie Graph Presented on a PowerPoint Slide

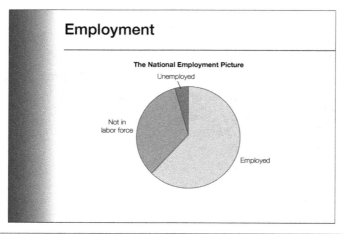

Tables Tables are useful for emphasizing key facts and figures. They are especially effective for listing steps, highlighting features, or comparing related facts. A **table** presents data in words, numbers, or both, in columns and rows. An example of a PowerPoint slide containing a table is shown in Figure 7-9.

table

A visual element used to present data in words, numbers, or both, in columns and rows.

Figure 7-9 Example of a Table Presented on a PowerPoint Slide

Company Benefits

Comparison of Company Benefits by Size

Type of Benefit	Companies with Fewer than 100 Employees	100 or More Employees
Paid vacation	88%	96%
Paid holidays	82	92
Medical insurance	71	83
Life insurance	64	94
Paid sick leave	53	67
Dental care	33	60

Source: U.S. Bureau of Labor Statistics

Tables easily convey large amounts of numerical data and often are the only way to show several variables for a number of items.

diagram

A two-dimensional drawing that shows the important parts of objects.

Diagrams and Drawings Diagrams are two-dimensional drawings that show the important parts of objects. They are useful for conveying information about size, shape, and structure. Types of diagrams include drawings, maps, and floor plans. An organizational chart is a form of block diagram that indicates lines of authority and responsibility in an organization. Figure 7-10 provides an example of a diagram presented on a PowerPoint slide.

Figure 7-10 Example of a Diagram (Organizational Chart) Presented on a PowerPoint Slide

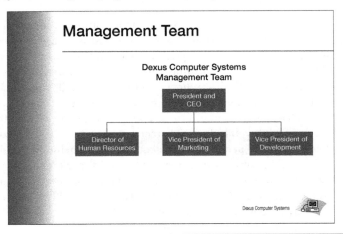

Management Team

Dexus Computer Systems
Management Team

President and CEO

Director of Human Resources — Vice President of Marketing — Vice President of Development

Dexus Computer Systems

The Conclusion

The conclusion of your presentation should include two slides.

- **The conclusion slide.** This slide should summarize your main points or, in the case of a persuasive presentation, highlight the benefits of your proposal to your audience.

- **Ending title slide.** Ending with the slide you began with provides closure for your audience because it indicates you have come full circle. In addition, this slide acts as a subtle sales message, much like giving your audience your business card, which contains your name and the name of your company. It is a better backdrop for a question-and-answer session than a slide that contains the single word "Questions" or the phrase "Thank you" because it enhances name recognition.

Using PowerPoint Slides

Presentation aids should be skillfully *integrated* into the presentation. That means that a visual should not be displayed until you are ready for it and it should be removed after discussing it. The use of visual aids should be *practiced* so that their use does not distract from your presentation or adversely affect your credibility by making you look unprepared.

Remember, your presentation slides are intended to engage and guide your audience and to emphasize key points. Although many presenters often use them as note cards, you should avoid reading from them or using them in such a way that your attention is drawn away from your audience.

Delivery in Oral Presentations

Nonverbal communication is critically important in oral presentations. It is the primary reason to give a presentation over other channels or media of communication, because nonverbal communication enables us to make that personal connection and establish our credibility by demonstrating confidence and composure. If you are not able to do so, you should avoid oral presentations. Nonverbal communication includes the qualities of the voice and spoken patterns as well as body language, dress, and general appearance.

Vocal Delivery

Your voice plays an important role in the meanings listeners find in your words. By varying the volume, rate of delivery, pitch, or inflection of your voice and message delivery, you can easily change the meaning of your message. In oral presentations, your vocal delivery can also enhance your message by making it more lively, interesting, and convincing to your audience. Vocal delivery can also affect your relationship with the audience and your credibility. As discussed in Chapter 3, you are better able to establish a relationship with your audience if you are considered likable. Your vocal delivery, as well as the content of your speech, will help you achieve this goal. It is also important to appear confident; if you lack this characteristic, your credibility may also be undermined. We are less likely to believe people who lack confidence in themselves and their ideas.

Norms of vocal delivery differ by culture. For example, Arabs speak loudly because they believe doing so is a sign of strength. In contrast, people from the Philippines tend to speak softly, believing this is a sign of good breeding and education. Rate of delivery also differs among cultures: Arabs and Italians speak faster than do most people in the United States.

The elements of vocal delivery are described below.

- **Volume.** The **volume** of your speech must be loud enough to be heard but not so loud as to be overwhelming. When speaking before a group, you generally need to speak louder than you do in general conversation.

volume

The relative sound level of speech; it must be loud enough to be heard, but not so loud as to be overwhelming.

- **Rate of delivery.** The **rate of delivery** refers to the speed at which you speak. For a speech to be effective, vary the rate of delivery to reflect changes in the content of the material being presented or its desired effect. Serious material calls for a slower, more deliberate rate, while lighter topics need a faster pace. Beginning speakers, because of their anxiety, have a tendency to speed up their presentations and run their words together, making it difficult to understand

rate of delivery

The speed at which one speaks.

their message. An audience will thus interpret rapid delivery as a sign of anxiousness or lack of confidence. Be sure to focus your efforts on slowing your delivery so that your credibility is not undermined, even if you are struggling with speech apprehension.

pitch

The sound quality of the speaker's voice, ranging from low and deep to high and squeaky.

- **Pitch. Pitch** ranges from low and deep to high and squeaky. Optimal pitch is the level at which you can produce your strongest voice with minimal effort and also allow variation up and down the scale. Pitch is an issue that deserves some attention; those with high, squeaky voices or breathy ones may be judged as being less competent, serious, and credible. Through practice and training, you can lower the pitch of your voice.

vocal variety

The varying use of the vocal aspects of volume, rate, and pitch.

- **Vocal variety. Vocal variety** refers to the varying use of the vocal aspects of volume, rate, and pitch. Speaking in a monotone without such variations sends the message that the speaker is not interested in his or her topic, is nervous, or lacks confidence. Making any of these impressions can undermine your credibility as well as make your message less engaging.

articulate

To pronounce all words clearly and fluently.

- **Articulation.** Speakers should **articulate** words clearly. Clear articulation is important for two reasons: (1) so you are easy to understand and (2) to avoid negatively affecting your credibility with your audience.

pauses

Temporary breaks in speech used to emphasize important points and enhance the meanings of words and phrases.

- **Pauses. Pauses** should be used to emphasize important points and enhance the meanings of words and phrases. Beginning speakers often do not use pauses effectively because they feel uncomfortable with silence. This lack of comfort with silence also can lead to the problem discussed below: vocal distractions or disfluencies.

vocal distractions or disfluencies

Speaking "errors" such as stammers, stutters, double starts, and excessive use of filler words such as *um* and *uh*.

- **Fluency.** Avoid **vocal distractions or disfluencies.** These include stammers, stutters, double starts, and the excessive use of empty filler words such as *uh* and *um*. Too many vocal distractions make a speaker sound disorganized, nervous, and uncertain, leading to a potential loss in credibility. You can reduce vocal distractions in your delivery by focusing on them and practicing to eliminate them during day-to-day conversations.

Many of these aspects of vocal delivery can positively or negatively affect your credibility, so it is important to sensitize yourself to each one and to identify those that you might work to improve. Mastering these aspects of vocal delivery can also help make your speaking more engaging and even charismatic. However, vocal delivery is just one aspect of successful oral presentations. The next section discusses another element—nonverbal expression or body movement.

? **Critical** Thinking

How important is the quality of vocal delivery in a presentation? Have you witnessed presenters whose vocal delivery was lacking in one of the elements mentioned above? What was your reaction? Do you struggle with any of the elements of vocal delivery in your oral presentations?

Body Movement

Nonverbal communication is critical in making an oral presentation effective. Your nonverbal communication in an oral presentation situation can help you engage your audience and convey goodwill. It can also help reinforce your message.

For beginning speakers, it is important to pay attention to and identify the types of nonverbal signals you give your audience, because they can have an immediate and immense impact on your credibility and perceived professionalism. To develop a professional, credible persona, you must identify the particular nonverbal signals you may be sending that indicate you lack confidence or are anxious. (See "Reducing Presentation Anxiety" later in this chapter.)

Nonverbal Signals That Indicate Anxiety. Common indicators of a lack of confidence include these:

- Poor eye contact
- Rigidity or stiffness of the body and its movements
- Crossed arms or hands jammed into pockets
- Unintentional body movements

Some nervous speakers look at the floor, for example. Another common cause of poor eye contact is the overuse or inappropriate use of notes. You should *not* use notes if you have a tendency to read them once you become nervous.

Standing stiffly with your arms locked (behind your back, for example) also is often interpreted as a sign of fear by audiences. Ideally, you should stand with your hands hanging loosely at your sides so that you can more easily, naturally, and spontaneously gesture. Letting your hands hang loosely at your sides sends a second message to the audience: You are open to it and its ideas. Placing your hands or arms across the front of the body may be interpreted as a sign of defensiveness or anxiety or as a cue that you are not open to your audience and its perspectives.

Unintentional body movements include playing with or tossing your hair or an article of clothing, twisting your body, swaying, pacing, and fidgeting with your feet. All these actions may be signs of anxiety. Ideally, speakers stand solidly on the floor with their feet apart and only move their body to lean forward or to gesture naturally to emphasize their message. Moving intentionally around the room can help you engage your audience, but beginning speakers should first master the ability to stand in one place without displaying other unintentional body movements before they move on to this step. If you begin moving around the room before you have learned to control your anxiety, then your nervousness may be exhibited through pacing.

Each person typically displays anxiety in a way unique to him or herself. It is helpful if you can enlist the help of others to observe you presenting and to provide you feedback on the body movements you might be making that indicate your nervousness. Once you identify how you display your anxiety, you can focus your attention on eliminating that behavior.

Nonverbal Signals That Indicate Confidence. An important goal of a business presentation is to make an immediate, positive, and confident impression of yourself with your audience. (This objective is true for all business communication situations.) To do so, smile confidently at your audience when your presentation begins and greet it warmly and sincerely, if appropriate for the message you are about to deliver. As the presentation continues, be sure your body language is not telling your audience that you are unduly fearful, anxious, or nervous, because this knowledge can undermine your credibility. In professional presentation situations, you never want to "let them see you sweat."

A list of the specific nonverbal behaviors that generally enhance a professional presentation follows:

- A speaker should establish and maintain *direct eye contact* with the audience. Talking directly to the audience is seen as more sincere and more engaging with the audience.

- An effective speaker should *stand up straight and use good posture* without becoming stiff. Good posture projects a confident yet relaxed image. For smaller people, good posture can also help you to take up more space. For those in a leadership position or who aspire to be perceived as leaders, this is important because studies show that confident, charismatic leaders generally take up more space; they don't make themselves small by slouching or crossing their arms or legs.

- Speakers should use *natural gestures* to animate the presentation. Gestures should grow out of a response to your material and appear natural and spontaneous, prompted by your feelings. If you are speaking to a large group that may have trouble seeing your gestures, then make the gestures larger than in normal conversation.

- Speakers should *move* around the presentation area or room *intentionally* to engage the audience and keep its attention. Again, for smaller persons, moving around the room with intention can help you to take up more space and appear more like our stereotype of a confident leader. Moving around a room, though, always should be purposeful. Nervous pacing distracts the audience from your message and makes you appear less confident.

- Speakers should use *facial expressions* to communicate and build rapport with the audience. Your face should reflect and reinforce the meanings of your words. An expressionless face suggests that the speaker is afraid or indifferent.

Establishing a relationship with your audience, maintaining its interest in your topic, and developing your credibility are important objectives for a successful professional presentation. To accomplish these goals, you must be well prepared and control your anxiety about speaking. Hopefully, preparation can help you reduce speech apprehension. These two issues are discussed later in this section.

? Critical Thinking

What nonverbal behaviors do you exhibit during oral presentations that may indicate to your audience that you are nervous? What can you do to eliminate or control these behaviors?

Dress and Appearance

Clothing, jewelry, hairstyle, and general appearance create an immediate impression of who you are. These aspects can also affect your credibility, your image as a professional, and whether you belong to the group. For these reasons, it is important to select clothing and other aspects of appearance that are appropriate for each presentation situation. If you are uncertain about what is appropriate for a particular situation, such as an employment interview, err on the side of formality and conservatism.

Preparing for Your Presentation

Preparing for your presentation involves three basic steps: (1) planning your presentation, (2) gathering and organizing your material, and (3) practicing your delivery.

As stated earlier, planning the presentation can help make preparation easier by focusing the message on a single theme or key point. Many presentations are too ambitious in terms of the amount of information intended for delivery. A better approach is to simplify the message to one key point that is illustrated in various ways to increase impact. Simplifying the message in this way also makes preparation easier because complexity is reduced.

A second way to reduce anxiety and enhance your credibility is to increase your confidence by being or becoming an expert in the subject you will be discussing. Consequently, it is very important that you thoroughly research your topic and look at it from all angles. This latter point is important because your audience may detect that you have a one-sided or superficial understanding of the topic, which would undermine your credibility. Another way to confront this issue is to find a way to approach the topic by attaching it or relating it to something you already know or care about. This can help you to connect more personally with the topic, potentially increasing your passion or conviction.

You may also be faced with questions from your audience, some of which may be objections to your idea, and you must be able to answer these questions with reasonable, quality information in order to maintain your credibility and persuasiveness, so it is important to plan for those questions and be prepared to answer with confidence All of these steps can help you to actually feel confident when it comes time for your presentation.

After you have simplified the message and gathered needed information, practice delivering your presentation. Typically, business presentations are expected to be delivered **extemporane-ously**. That means that you should be well prepared for your presentation but be able to deliver your material spontaneously. In other words, you should not read your material or memorize it, although you may want to memorize important parts of your speech such as quotations, figures, or examples. If you read your presentation, you will lose your audience's interest because you will probably have difficulty maintaining eye contact with people, and your voice will tend to be monotone in delivery.

In addition, if you memorize your speech, you increase the risk of heightening your anxiety and losing credibility; if you forget a passage, you probably will need to stop and repeat your presentation quietly to yourself to find the place in your memorized script at which you can resume speaking. These long pauses can be distracting to your audience and increase your own discomfort, affecting the overall quality and credibility of your speech. Memorized speeches also tend to lack spontaneity, which decreases audience interest. Your goal should be to appear and sound like an expert in your subject, one who can speak about it in an informative, well-organized yet spontaneous manner. To eliminate these problems, it is helpful to avoid writing a script for the presentation. Instead, identify the key points and parts of the presentation, develop examples to illustrate these points, and then design the needed visual aids. This process will help you to refine and internalize your message. Practice delivering this information from memory until you feel confident that you can remember and deliver it in a spontaneous way.

To enhance the spontaneity of your presentation, use notes sparingly and judiciously. If you can deliver your presentation without notes, your credibility and ability to relate to the audience will be enhanced. However, if you need to use notes, the following guidelines will help you use them properly.

- **Use only 3" × 5" note cards.** Small note cards are less obtrusive and distracting for your audience. If you use 8½" × 11" sheets of paper, as when you print your presentation from PowerPoint, you may become nervous and unintentionally wave them as you gesture. You don't want to look like a sailor on a flight deck, guiding a plane through its landing, signal flags waving.
- **Put only an outline or keywords on your notes.** If you write out your entire presentation on the cards, you are more likely to read from them.
- **When you look at your notes, stop speaking.** The proper way to reference your notes is to stop speaking, glance down at your cards, and then look up and resume speaking. In most cases, you should not speak unless you are looking at your audience.

Many people use the slides as they appear on the computer as notes. This is permissible if you are able to glance at them quickly as a reminder and then refocus your attention on your audience. If you are anxious, though, there is a risk that you will find yourself reading from them rather than engaging with the audience through direct eye contact. You must know your weaknesses and find ways to avoid them.

You might find it helpful to practice your presentation in front of a mirror or before a small audience of family members or friends. Either way, you can receive feedback about how you look and sound, and you can adjust your delivery and nonverbal communication to better support the message you wish to send. Practice can also help you reduce your anxiety about speaking because it may help you feel more confident. Techniques to reduce speech apprehension are discussed in the following section.

Lastly, as part of preparation, it is also advisable to consider the setting in which the presentation will take place. How large is the room? How many people will be in attendance? What type of equipment is available? Are there distractions that you need to consider or try to eliminate? How should you transport your presentation software? Is the software that is available compatible with

extemporaneous speaking

Public speaking that is delivered spontaneously rather than being read or memorized in advance.

what you are using? These considerations can help eliminate problems and ensure that you will be confident and well prepared for the event.

Reducing Presentation Anxiety

As mentioned earlier, preparing properly for a presentation can go a long way in eliminating presentation anxiety. Simplifying the message, selecting a topic about which you feel confident, and practicing sufficiently should enable you to feel more confident about the material.

However, feeling some anxiety when faced with an oral presentation situation is not unusual or necessarily bad. Generally, we perform better if we feel a small amount of anxiety. However, it is best to keep your anxiety at a manageable level, one that does not affect your ability to perform.

If you still feel some anxiety after following the appropriate planning and preparation steps, it may be reduced through visualization and breathing techniques. Visualizing yourself giving a successful presentation can sometimes help you achieve those results. Taking deep, slow, regular breaths—during which you visualize yourself drawing your breath down into and expanding your stomach rather than your chest—can also help calm you. This technique triggers a natural relaxation response. You might try both these techniques to find which one works better for you.

Another technique is to ask yourself whether your fears are reasonable. For example, we may believe that if we make one mistake, our audience will judge us harshly. But this is typically not the case; most audiences want us to succeed. By realizing that your audience is probably on your side, you may be able to reduce some of your fears and perform more confidently. It can be helpful to ask yourself whether some irrational belief is fueling your anxiety. If so, identify it and eliminate it by changing it to a more realistic, positive belief.

Handling Question-and-Answer Sessions

Question-and-answer (Q&A) sessions are a common part of business presentations and typically take place at the end of a presentation. How you handle Q&A sessions can affect your ability to maintain credibility and goodwill as well as achieve your larger communication purposes. Because of their importance in achieving your communication goals, these sessions also deserve adequate preparation and strategy formulation. These issues are addressed in the following sections.

Preparing for Q&A

The steps for preparing for an important question-and-answer session follow. Prepare for questions by listing every fact or opinion you can think of that challenges your position.

1. Divide potential questions into three categories: the known, the knowable, and the notable.
   - The known list contains questions to which you know the answers. Depending on how well you know the particulars, you may want to write down the answers and practice them out loud.
   - The knowable list contains questions to which you may not know the answers. Do the research, find the answers, and practice them.
   - The notable list contains the questions that require a strategy. These are the broad questions that do not have simple answers or which may jeopardize the success of the presentation without planning. Your strategy for answering these questions should validate the overall purpose and message of your presentation.

2. Treat each objection seriously and try to think of a way to deal with it.

3. If you are talking about a controversial issue, then you may want to save one point for the question period rather than make it during the presentation.

4. Speakers who have visuals prepared to answer questions seem especially well prepared and thus enhance their credibility and professionalism.

During the Q&A

During the Q&A session, follow some basic rules. Remember, you are in control of the Q&A period, so you should state the rules for the process, if appropriate. For example, near the beginning of your presentation, you might ask the audience to hold its questions until the end of the presentation. At the beginning of the Q&A session, you might state a time limit, limit the number of questions per person, and identify who will answer the audience's questions (if this has been a team presentation).

During the Q&A, keep the discussion focused on the topic or issue at hand. Most important, you do not want to lose your temper, appear confused, or become emotional. Your objective is to appear well prepared, confident, objective, reasonable, and calm. If you become agitated or confused, or if the session becomes a free-for-all, then you have lost control of the situation and probably damaged your credibility and perhaps jeopardized your ability to achieve your other communication purposes. The basic rules for question-and-answer sessions follow:

- Don't nod your head to indicate that you understand a question as it is being asked; it may be misinterpreted as a sign of agreement.
- Look directly at the questioner.
- When you answer the question, expand your focus to take in the entire group.
- If the entire audience may not have heard the question or if you want more time to think, repeat the question before you answer it.
- Ask for clarification if you don't understand the question.
- If a question starts to take your talk into a new direction, offer to discuss that issue at a later date.
- Link your answers to the points you made in your presentation.
- Keep the purpose of your presentation in mind and select information that advances your goals.
- Sometimes someone will ask a question that is designed to state his or her opinion. Respond to the question if you want or say, "I'm not sure what you are asking" or "That's a clear statement of your position. Any other questions?"
- If someone asks a question that you have explained in your presentation, answer it rather than embarrass him or her.
- Look for a point of agreement in your answers. An example is provided below.

Audience member: Your ideas about this new business proposal sound farfetched to me. I think that we need to solidify our regional market before we try to expand abroad.

Speaker: You have a good point—our regional sales have traditionally been the backbone of this company. But we need to expand so that we can avoid slumps if the regional economy takes a downturn.

If you don't know the answer to a question, say so. You can tell the questioner that you will get back to him or her with the answer. You might also ask if someone else in the room knows the answer; if they don't, then your "ignorance" is vindicated. This strategy can also present a risk: Don't do it if you think you will lose control of the questioning period. You can also ask your group members if one of them knows the answer and you are presenting as a team.

At the end of the Q&A, take the opportunity to summarize your position one more time. Take advantage of having the floor to repeat your message briefly and forcefully.

Dealing with Hostile Questions

On some occasions, you may be faced with audience members who do not like you, your company, your product or service, or your proposed idea. Sometimes, these audience members may have such strong feelings that they are unable or unwilling to control them. Do not stoop to their level. Your goal in these situations is to enhance yourself and your position by remaining confident, objective, reasonable, and calm. In these cases, the hostile audience members may undermine their own credibility without your help or comment. However, if you are faced with hostile questions, the following are strategies for dealing with them.

- If a question is hostile or biased, rephrase it before you answer it. "You're asking whether…," or suggest an alternative question: "I think there are problems with both positions you describe. It seems to me that a third solution …" By rephrasing or reframing the question, you are attempting to remove the hostile or biased perspective from the situation.

- Be fair to a hostile questioner, perhaps by indicating the need to disagree, and then agree on a statement of that disagreement.

- Most important, if someone asks a hostile question, do not respond in kind. You might even try to respond with a compliment as long as it isn't insincere. "That's a very important question. Thank you for asking it."

To handle Q&A sessions effectively, you must anticipate your audience's questions and prepare answers that advance the overall purposes of your message. You must strategize ways to maintain control of the session and to remain calm, confident, and reasonable.

Adapting to Alternate Delivery Situations

As you've learned, presenting a dynamic presentation that focuses on the audience's needs and expectations is the fundamental principle in presenting effectively. Along with the solid foundation you've set for spoken communication, you'll also need to adapt your presentation style to the ever-changing business environment and the special needs of culturally diverse audiences. Delivering team presentations, presenting using distance formats, and managing crisis situations are other common circumstances you may need to master.

Culturally Diverse Audiences

When speaking to a culturally diverse audience, you will want to be as natural as possible, while adjusting your message for important cultural variations. Using empathy, you can effectively focus on the listener as an individual rather than a stereotype of a specific culture. Be open and willing to learn, and you will reap the benefits of communicating effectively with people who possess a variety of strengths and creative abilities. Additionally, follow these suggestions for presenting to people from outside your own culture:

- Speak simply. Use simple English and short sentences.

- Avoid acronyms and expressions that can be confusing to nonnative English speakers—namely slang, jargon, figurative expressions, and sports analogies.

- Avoid words that trigger negative emotional responses such as anger, fear, or suspicion. Such "red flag" words vary among cultures; thus, try to anticipate audience reaction and choose your words carefully.

- Enunciate each word precisely and speak somewhat slowly. Clear, articulate speech is especially important when the audience is not familiar with various dialects and vocabulary. Avoid the temptation to speak in a loud voice, a habit considered rude in any culture and especially annoying to the Japanese, who perceive the normal tone of North Americans as too loud.

- Be extremely cautious in the use of humor and jokes. Cultures that prefer more formality might think you are not serious about your purpose or find your humor and jokes inappropriate. Asians, for instance, do not appreciate jokes about family members and the elderly.

- Learn the culture's preferences for a direct or indirect presentation. While North Americans tend to prefer directness, with the main idea presented first, people from many cultures, such as Japanese, Latin American, and Arabic, consider a straightforward approach tactless and rude.

- Adapt to subtle differences in nonverbal communication. The direct eye contact expected by most North Americans is not typical of Asian listeners who often keep their eyes lowered and avoid eye contact to show respect. Arab audiences might stare into your eyes in an attempt to "see into the window of the soul." Cultures also vary on personal space and degree of physical contact (slap on the back or arm around the other as signs of friendship).

- Adapt your dress and presentation style to fit the formality of the culture. Some cultures prefer a higher degree of formality than the casual style of North Americans. To accommodate, dress conservatively; strive to connect with the audience in a formal, reserved manner; and use highly professional visuals rather than jotting ideas on a flip chart.

- Seek feedback to determine whether the audience is understanding your message. Observe listeners carefully for signs of misunderstanding, restating ideas as necessary. Consider allowing time for questions after short segments of your presentation. Avoid asking "Is that clear?" or "Do you understand?" as these statements might elicit a "Yes" answer if the person perceives saying "No" to be a sign of incompetence.

Potential frustrations can also occur when presentations or meetings bring together North Americans, who see "time as money," with people of cultures who are not time conscious and who believe that personal relationships are the basis of business dealings (e.g., Asian, Latin American). When communicating with cultures that are not time driven, be patient with what you might consider time-consuming formalities and courtesies and lengthy decision-making styles when you would rather get right down to business or move to the next point. Recognize that the presentation might not begin on time or stay on a precise schedule. Allow additional time at the beginning of the presentation to establish rapport and credibility with the audience, and perhaps provide brief discussion periods devoted to building relationships during the presentation. Be patient and attentive during long periods of silence; in many cultures people are inclined to stay silent unless they have something significant to say or if they are considering (not necessarily rejecting) an idea. In fact, some Japanese have asked how North Americans can think and talk at the same time. Understanding patterns of silence can help you feel more comfortable during these seemingly endless moments and less compelled to fill the gaps with unnecessary words or to make concessions before the other side has a chance to reply.

Other significant points of difference between cultures are the varying rules of business etiquette. Should you use the traditional American handshake or some other symbol of greeting? Is using the person's given name acceptable? What formal titles should be used with a surname? Can you introduce yourself, or must you have someone else who knows the other person introduce you? Are business cards critical, and what rules should you follow when presenting a business card? Should you have business cards that are printed in two languages?

Gift giving can be another confusing issue. When you believe a gift should be presented to your event host, investigate the appropriateness of gift giving, types of gifts considered appropriate or absolutely inappropriate, and colors of wrapping to be avoided in the speaker's culture. Liquor, for example, is an inappropriate gift in Arab countries.

Gaining competence in matters of etiquette will enable you to make a positive initial impression and concentrate on the presentation rather than agonizing over an awkward, embarrassing slip in protocol. Your audience will appreciate your willingness to learn and value their customs. Being sensitive to cultural issues and persistent in learning specific differences in customs and practices can minimize confusion and unnecessary embarrassment.

Group Presentations

Because much of the work in business today is done in groups and teams, many presentations are planned and delivered by small groups of presenters. Well-conducted group presentations give an organization an opportunity to showcase its brightest talent while capitalizing on each person's unique presentation skills. E-mail, collaborative software, and other technologies make it easy to develop, edit, review, and deliver impressive group presentations.

The potential payoff of many group presentations is quite high—perhaps a $200,000 contract or a million-dollar account. Yet, according to experts, team presentations fail primarily because presenters don't devote enough time and resources to develop and rehearse them. Resist the sure-to-fail strategy of "winging" a team presentation rather than taking the time to do it correctly. Instead, adapt the skills you already possess in planning and delivering an individual presentation to ensure a successful team presentation. Follow these guidelines as you plan and prepare your group presentation:

- *Select a winning team.* Begin by choosing a leader who is well liked and respected by the team, is knowledgeable of the project, is well organized, and will follow through. Likewise, the leader should be committed to leading the team in the development of a cohesive strategy for the presentation as well as the delegation of specific responsibilities to individual members. A member of a winning team will have:
  - Complementary strengths/style
  - Ability to meet expectations
  - Willingness to support team strategy
  - Willingness to commit to schedule

- *Carefully select presenters.* The core team members, along with management, should choose a balanced mix of individuals who each has something important to contribute to the team. Use these questions to guide team selection:
  - What are this member's complementary strengths and style (e.g., technical expertise, personality traits, and presentation skills)?
  - Can this member meet the expectations of the audience (e.g., a numbers person, technical person, person with an existing relationship with the audience)?
  - Is this member willing to support the team strategy and commit to the schedule?

- *Agree on the purpose and schedule and develop a plan.* The team as a whole should plan the presentation using the same process used for an individual presentation. Agreeing on the purpose to be achieved and selecting content that focuses on a specific audience will prevent the challenges caused by an individual's submitting off-target material. The quality of the presentation deteriorates when material must be redone hurriedly in the final days before the deadline or when unacceptable material is included just because the team worked so hard on it. Mapping out a complete presentation strategy can also minimize bickering among team members because of uneven workloads or unfavorable work assignments.

  The team will also need to agree on a standard design for presentation visuals to ensure consistency in the visuals prepared by individual presenters. Assign a person to merge the various files, to edit for consistency in design elements and the use of jargon and specialized terminology, and to proofread carefully for grammatical accuracy.

  Developing a rehearsal schedule ensures adequate time for preparation and practice. Many experts recommend five practice sessions to produce team presentations that are delivered with a unified look. Planning time in the schedule to present before a review team is especially useful for obtaining feedback on team continuity and adjustments needed to balance major discrepancies in the delivery styles of individual presenters.

- *Practice ahead of time.* The team must be well prepared, which will require several rehearsals. Each member must know what others will say to avoid repetition and to fit the time slot. The team must also work out logistical details such as where people will stand, who will run the slides, and when handouts will be distributed. A great deal of the rehearsal time for a team presentation should be spent planning and rehearsing appropriate verbal and physical transitions between team members. The transitions serve to introduce each part of the presentation and make the whole presentation cohesive. This continuity makes the team look polished and conveys team commitment.

Follow these suggestions for delivering seamless, impressive team presentations:

- *Decide who will open and conclude the presentation.* The team member who knows the audience and has established rapport is a logical choice for these two critical sections of a presentation. If no one knows the audience, select the member with the strongest presentation skills and personality traits for connecting well with strangers. This person will introduce all team members and give a brief description of the roles they will play in the presentation.

- *Build natural bridges between segments of the presentation and presenters.* A lead presenter must build a bridge from the points that have been made that will launch the following presenter smoothly into what he or she will discuss. If a lead presenter forgets to make the connection to the next section clear, the next person must summarize what's been said and then preview his or her section. These transitions might seem repetitive to a team that has been working extensively with the material; however, audiences require clear guideposts through longer team presentations. Also, courtesies such as maintaining eye contact, thanking the previous speaker, and clearing the presentation area for the next speaker communicate an important message: that the presenters are in sync and work well together.

- *Deliver as a team.* You must present a unified look and communicate to the audience that you care about the team. Spend your time on the "sideline" paying close attention to the current presenter, monitoring the audience for feedback, and being ready to assist the presenter with equipment malfunctions, handouts, and so on. Avoid side conversations and reading notes, yawning, or coughing. To keep an audience engaged in a team presentation, team members not presenting should focus on the presenter at least two-thirds of the time.

- *Field questions as a team.* Decide in advance who will field questions to avoid awkward stares and silence that may erode the audience's confidence in your team. Normally, the person presenting a section is the logical person to field questions about that section.

You can refer questions to team members who are more knowledgeable, but avoid pleading looks for someone else to rescue you. Rather, check visually to see if the person wants to respond and ask if he or she would like to add information. Tactfully contradict other presenters *only* when the presenter makes a mistake that will cause misunderstanding or confusion. While you should be ready to help presenters having difficulty, resist the urge to tack on your response to a presenter's response when the question has already been answered adequately.

Distance Presentations

Videoconferencing has been used for some time for large, high-exposure activities, such as quarterly executive staff presentations, company-wide addresses, new product launches, and crisis management. The technology's lower cost, improved quality, and increased ease of use have opened videoconferencing to many settings.

Substantial cost savings from reduced travel is a compelling reason for companies to use video-conferencing. Threats of terrorism and contagious disease provide more reasons for companies to restrict business travel and look for alternative delivery methods. In addition, important communication benefits, such as the following, can be achieved with videoconferencing:

- improving employee productivity by calling impromptu videoconferences to clear up issues
- involving more people in key decisions rather than limiting important discussions to those who are allowed to travel
- involving expertise critical to the mission, regardless of geographic boundaries
- creating a consistent corporate culture rather than depending on memos to describe company policy
- improving employees' quality of life by reducing travel time that often cuts into personal time (e.g., Saturday night layovers for a reasonable airfare)

Internet conferencing

Sometimes known as *webcasting*, allows one a group to conduct a presentation in real time over the Internet simultaneously with VOIP or a conference telephone call.

Internet conferencing, or *webcasting*, allows a company to conduct a presentation in real time over the Internet simultaneously with VOIP (voice over internet protocol), or a conference telephone call. Because it runs on each participant's Internet browser, a presentation can reach hundreds of locations at once. While listening to the call, participants can go to a designated website and view slides or a PowerPoint presentation that is displayed in sync with the speaker's statements being heard on the phone. Participants key comments and questions in chat boxes or press a keypad system to respond to an audience *Internet conferencing poll,* thus giving valuable feedback without interrupting the speaker.

Follow these guidelines for adapting your presentation skills to videoconferences and web presentations:

- Determine whether a distance delivery method is appropriate for the presentation. Is the presentation purpose suited to the technology? Can costs in time, money, and human energy be justified? Are key people willing and able to participate? For example, a videoconference for a formal presentation such as an important speech by the CEO to a number of locations justifies the major expense and brings attention to the importance of the message.

- Distance delivery formats are inappropriate for presentations that cover highly sensitive or confidential issues, for persuasive or problem-solving meetings where no relationship has been established among the participants, and whenever participants are unfamiliar with and perhaps unsupportive of the technology.

- Establish rapport with the participants prior to the distance presentation. If possible, meet with participants beforehand to get to know them and gain insights about their attitudes. This rapport will enhance your ability to interpret subtle nonverbal cues and to cultivate the relationship further through the distance format. E-mailing or faxing a short questionnaire or posting presentation slides with a request for questions is an excellent way to establish a connection with participants and to ensure that the presentation is tailored to audience needs. Some enterprising distance presenters engage participants in e-mail discussions before the presentation and then use this dialogue to develop positive interaction during the presentation.

- Become proficient in delivering and participating through distance technology. Begin by becoming familiar with the equipment and the surroundings. Although technical support staff might be available to manage equipment and transmission tasks, your goal is to concentrate on the contribution you are to make and not your intimidation with the delivery method.

■ Concentrate on projecting positive nonverbal messages. Keep a natural, friendly expression; relax and smile. Avoid the tendency to stare into the camera. Instead, look naturally at the entire audience as you would in a live presentation. Speak clearly with as much energy as you can. If a lag occurs between the video and audio transmission, adjust your timing to avoid interrupting other speakers. Use gestures to reinforce points, but avoid fast or excessive motion that will appear blurry. Avoid side conversations, coughing, and clearing your throat, which could trigger voice-activated microphones. Pay close attention to other presenters to guard against easy distraction in a distance environment and to capture subtle nonverbal cues. You will need to judge the vocal tone of the person asking a question because you might not see faces.

■ Adjust camera settings to enhance communication. Generally, adjust the camera so that all participants can be seen, but zoom in more closely on participants when you wish to clearly observe nonverbal language. Project a wide-angle shot of yourself during rapport-building comments at the presentation's beginning and zoom in to signal the start of the agenda or to emphasize an important point during the presentation. Some systems accommodate a split screen, but others allow participants to view either you or your presentation visuals only. You will want to switch the camera between a view of you and your visuals, depending on what is needed at the time.

■ Develop high-quality graphics appropriate for the particular distance format. Even more than in a live presentation, you will need graphics to engage and maintain participants' attention. Graphics are a welcome variation to the "talking head"—you—displayed on the screen for long periods. Some companies provide assistance from a webmaster or graphics support staff in preparing slide shows specifically for distance presentations. Also, e-conferencing companies will develop and post presentation slides and host live web presentations including managing e-mail messages and audience polling. Regardless of the support you receive, you should understand basic guidelines for preparing effective visuals for videoconferencing and web presentations.

■ Readability of text will be a critical issue when displaying visuals during a videoconference because text becomes fuzzy when transmitted through compressed video. Select large, sturdy fonts and choose a color scheme that provides high contrast between the background and the text. Stay with a tested color scheme such as dark blue background, yellow title text, and white bulleted list text to ensure readability. Projecting your visuals ahead of time so you can adjust the color scheme, font selections, and other design elements is an especially good idea.

■ Load time and compatibility. In addition to considering overall appeal, clarity, and readability, web presentations must be designed for minimal load time and compatibility with various computers. For your first presentation, consider using a web template in your electronic presentations software and experiment with the appropriateness of other designs as you gain experience. Stand-alone presentations designed specifically for web delivery require unique design strategies to compensate for the absence of a speaker.

  ▪ Consider posting text-based explanations in the notes view area or adding vocal narration.
  ▪ Develop interactive slide formats that allow viewers to navigate to the most useful information in your presentation. For example, design an agenda slide that includes hyperlinks to the first slide in each section of the presentation.
  ▪ Select simple, high-quality graphics that convey ideas effectively.
  ▪ Plan limited animation that focuses audience attention on specific ideas on the slide.
  ▪ Consider adding video if bandwidth is not an issue.

Crisis Communication

Crisis communication requires management in situations that affect an organization's relationships with its stakeholders, particularly those that draw media attention. Discussions of crisis management typically focus on three issues: (1) planning and preparing for crisis events, (2) behavior of the organization during a crisis, and (3) communicating with important publics during the crisis.

The types of disasters that an organization might face can be divided into three categories: natural disasters, normal accidents, and abnormal or intentional accidents.

Natural disasters include fires, earthquakes, or hurricanes. Normal accident is a term to describe industrial disasters such as those that occurred at Three Mile Island, Chernobyl, Bhopal, Alaska due to the Exxon Valdez spill, and Louisiana because of the BP oil spill. Abnormal accidents occur because of deliberate action, such as bombings, kidnappings, cyber attacks, and other types of sabotage.

The communication objective in any crisis management strategy should depend upon the stage of the crisis. In cases when communication programs can begin before a crisis occurs, messages should provide internalizing information to build a positive public opinion toward the organization. When it appears a crisis is imminent, the strategy should shift from internalizing messages to instructing messages that tell the public how to respond to the crisis; instructing communication should intensify so that the affected publics know what to do. As the crisis subsides, communication may shift to adjusting messages intended to help people cope with the effects of the crisis. When the crisis is over, the organization can shift back to an internalizing message strategy.

Any crisis communication plan should provide training for dealing with the media regarding crisis management; identify communication lines with local communities and intervening agencies, such as the police; and provide a strategy for communicating with employees.

During a crisis, an organization should follow the steps outlined below:

1. *Get control of the situation.* This involves defining the problem and setting measurable communication objectives. In addition, it is important to communicate to employees how and where to get information.

2. *Gather information about the situation.* It is important that an organization has a means to stay up-to-date with the situation as it is happening so that it can respond quickly and appropriately. One way to accomplish this task is to create a crisis center that creates crisis response plans, monitors potential crises, and develops crisis response capabilities.

3. *Communicate early and often.* It will benefit the organization's credibility to be prepared and to explain what is happening, what the company is doing about it, and providing information about resources available to affected parties to deal with the situation.

4. *Communicate directly with affected parties.* It is important to be prepared to communicate with the media and to do so promptly. It is also important to communicate directly with others who are affected, such as employees, customers, shareholders, and communities.

An organization should not wait for a crisis to develop relationships with members of the media if it wants to take advantage of the media's image-building capabilities. It is important that someone in the organization takes time to cultivate these relationships. Building relationships with the media is a generally considered a better method than sending out mass-produced public releases, that may average a response rate of only 2%.

Preparing to deliver a crisis briefing requires special attention to maintaining credibility, particularly composure. At the time of the briefing, make sure that you arrive on time and look professional. It might be helpful to take a page from presidential candidates and consider whether loosening your tie or taking off your jacket will help you to better establish common ground with an audience who doesn't wear a suit to work.

During the briefing, practice the following points:

- *Anticipate questions and determine who will answer them.* Ideally, question-and-answer sheets should be prepared for management personnel who may be asked questions by the news media.

- *Prepare and deliver a brief statement.* After introducing yourself and others representing your company, deliver a brief statement (less than two minutes in length) that focuses only on the facts that can be confirmed at that time.

- *Outline your organization's current response effort and action plan.*

- *Express your key points from the public's point of view.* Telling the audience how the company's actions will contribute to better health or preserve jobs in the community may help it to better appreciate your points.

- *Use plain language.* Avoid language with which only those in your industry, company or professional specialization are familiar.

- *Maintain control.* Focus on your goals for the interview and offer responses aimed at achieving those goals.

- *Be honest.* Unless the corporate attorney has advised you against it, tell the truth. If there is a problem, then focus the bulk of your discussion on the steps you are taking to avoid the problem in the future. Don't guess at the answer. If you don't know something, say so.

- *Take responsibility.* Again, unless the corporate attorney has advised otherwise, take responsibility for problems rather than blaming others.

- *Remain calm and avoid arguments.* Becoming emotional can undermine your credibility and make you look as if you have lost control and composure.

- *Rephrase the question.* You don't need to accept a questioner's premise. If a reporter uses words you wouldn't, don't repeat them. Correct them if necessary.

- *Try to be friendly, helpful and patient.* Shake hands with attendees and call them by name. Be enthusiastic about your company and your job, if appropriate for the occasion. Avoid becoming impatient with attendees or acting as if they or their questions are stupid.

- *Limit the question-and-answer session to no more than 10 minutes.*

- *Don't speculate or make predictions.*

- *Don't make any remarks "off the record."* Such comments might lead reporters to believe there is more to the story that they can pursue.

As with many other types of professional communication situations, adequate preparation is often the key to a successful crisis briefing.

Summary

- Oral presentations are probably the most misused of all communication media. They are best used to excite and motivate an audience or to deliver a simple message. Unless you are training personnel, detailed and complex information should be left to the written channel because it is too difficult to remember when presented orally and will likely bore the audience.

- When planning a presentation, try to simplify the message and identify a theme or central idea that will interest your audience. Stories and vivid language that will evoke an emotional response should be used to make your presentation more interesting and memorable.

- A variety of patterns are available for organizing a presentation. Select the one that best fits the purpose of your message or that would best enable you to communicate the key aspects of your message. Just as in written messages, presentations should include an introduction, a body, and a close. Introductions of presentations include an additional element, the attention getter, to gain audience interest in your presentation. Design the remainder of the presentation to keep the audience's attention and achieve your strategic purposes.

- Visual aids can make information easier to understand than words alone. Using visuals also helps make the conveyed information more memorable and can enhance your professionalism and credibility. PowerPoint is commonly used as a visual aid in business presentations. The design of a PowerPoint slide show should ensure that the information can be clearly seen by the audience and readily grasped.

- Vocal delivery and other aspects of nonverbal communication are important for achieving goodwill and demonstrating credibility. Presenters should ensure that they maintain eye contact, speak loudly enough to be heard, and convey enthusiasm about their topic. They should use purposeful movement to convey a confident demeanor and consider dress and other aspects of appearance to suit the occasion and demonstrate belongingness to the group.

- Preparation is one of the most important aspects of delivery in a presentation. Adequate preparation can do much to enhance our credibility as well as reduce our speech apprehension. Other methods of reducing speech anxiety are to use visualization and breathing techniques.

- Not enough time is generally spent anticipating and preparing for question-and-answer sessions after presentations. A well-planned and rehearsed presentation can easily be derailed by a bumpy session, so presenters should try to anticipate their audience's questions and prepare answers and perhaps visual aids to respond to them. They should also be prepared for hostile or quirky audience members who might try to derail the presentation, and should have tactics available to maintain control of the session.

- Additional considerations may need to be taken to deal with specific presentation situations, such as presenting to a culturally diverse audience, presenting as a group, using distance technology, or delivering a crisis communication briefing.

Key Terms

forecasting **167**	diagram **173**	articulate **175**
transitions **167**	volume **174**	pauses **175**
call to action **169**	rate of delivery **174**	vocal distractions or disfluencies **175**
graph **172**	pitch **175**	extemporaneous speaking **178**
table **172**	vocal variety **175**	internet conferencing **185**

Discussion Questions

1. When should a presentation be used to communicate a business message? For what types of information are other media of communication better choices?
2. What are the critical elements that should be incorporated into an oral presentation to better ensure that an audience understands and can follow the logical progression of the message?
3. What is the purpose of visual aids that accompany an oral presentation? What sorts of information should not be provided on visual aids such as PowerPoint slides?
4. What is the worst possible thing that could happen to you during a speech? What strategies might you use to reduce this fear?

Applications

1. Using the presentation planner on page 166, create an outline for a presentation to your class that communicates the trends that will affect your industry in the next five to ten years. Make sure to create a complete, relevant, and effective attention-getter; include complete transitions between the main points; and wrap up with a memorable conclusion.
2. Find and observe a speaker. Analyze his or her vocal delivery and nonverbal communication. How did these elements contribute to or detract from the speaker's credibility and goodwill? Use this information to create a list of concrete actions you might take to improve your own presentation skills.
3. You work in the information services department of SynSystems, Inc., a maker of computer connectivity products. Your job, along with the other members of your department, is to provide computer support to the employees of SynSystems. Several years ago, SynSystems was purchased by computer products giant World Connectivity Solutions (WCS). Because your company had an excellent reputation for its customer service and extensive and positive brand recognition, WCS chose to leave your division with its well-respected name.

   Coincidentally, perhaps, SynSystems uses the same product as its parent company—GroupPRO—for electronic collaboration among project development teams. GroupPRO was created by another company that WCS now owns, but it is not the only product of its kind on the market. Because of lingering bitter feelings about the company takeover, there is a move among the employees of your department to switch to a newer collaboration product, TeamMAX.

   Create a persuasive presentation for your boss and the management team of SynSystems. In selecting the content of your presentation, focus on the benefits that you must communicate to the management team and how you can convey those benefits in a clear, vivid, and memorable way.

Airbnb: *Scaling Safety with Rapid Growth*

The Lopez Incident

When 19 year-old Jacob Lopez traveled overseas to Madrid in July 2015, he anticipated an enjoyable trip and planned to stay at an Airbnb property. His decision to book an Airbnb in Madrid stemmed mainly from his great experience at an Airbnb property in Brazil just a year prior.[1,2]

Lopez arrived in Madrid on July 4th and met his host, who turned out to be transsexual, at the subway near the property. The male-transformed-to-female walked with Lopez to the apartment and, upon arrival, locked the main door to the unit. Then, according to Lopez, the woman ordered him to perform a series of sexual acts. Lopez initially refused to obey. He was scared for his life after the host began to hint that she would harm him if he did not comply. She also severed the Internet lines to hinder his ability to reach out for assistance.

Lopez texted his mother, Micaela Giles, in the United States. Giles immediately phoned Airbnb from the family's Massachusetts home for help. However, Airbnb personnel indicated that an address to the property could not be provided as she was not the registered guest. They went on to say that Giles would need to ask the Madrid police to call Airbnb directly for the address to be released. She hung up the phone and repeatedly attempted to call the Madrid police. Each time she rang authorities, she was led through a series of prompts in Spanish only to have her calls continuously dropped. After several attempts, Giles tried to call Airbnb again, but was unable to connect to the company's emergency hotline.

Eventually, Lopez was able to escape by telling the host that he had to meet friends who knew where he was and who would call the police if he did not show up to join them. According to Lopez, the host sexually assaulted him prior to his escape. When questioned, the host maintained that the sexual actions were consensual. Lopez has undergone extensive counseling to overcome the trauma resulting from the situation.[3]

Airbnb Company Overview

In 2007, two twenty-something entrepreneurs, Brian Chesky and Joe Gebbia, saw a need in a century-old industry. These two recognized that the lodging and hospitality business had not tapped into the sharing economy. Doing so could provide convenient and economical options for consumers. So, with a website called airbedandbreakfast.com, the duo launched their idea.[4] Chesky and Gebbia decided to pair the debut of their start-up with a local San Francisco design conference in hopes of garnering more attention. For $80 a night, the friends rented air mattresses in their shared apartment and reached out to members of the city's designer population to do the same. Gaining the interest of only three guests and three hosts, the first attempt was an overall failure.[5]

This case was prepared by research assistants Matthew Beck, William Foster and Claire Kenney under the direction of James O'Rourke, Teaching Professor of Management, as the basis for class discussion rather than to illustrate either effective or ineffective handling of an administrative situation. Information was gathered from corporate as well as public sources. Editorial assistance: Judy Bradford.

1. Stump, Scott. "Airbnb Horror Story Reveals Safety Issues for Lodging Site," *Today Money.* August 17, 2015. <*http://www.today.com/money/airbnb-horror-story-reveals-safety-issues-lodging-site-t39091*>

2. Gander, Kashmira. "Airbnb safety: Sexual assault allegations against host in Madrid raise questions about website's responsibilities," *Independent.* August 16, 2015. Accessed February 2016. <*http://www.independent.co.uk/travel/news-and-advice/airbnb-safety-sexual-assault-allegations-against-host-in-madrid-raise-questions-about-websites-10457992.html*>

3. Lieber, Ron. "Airbnb Horror Story Points to Need for Precautions," *The New York Times.* August 14, 2015. Accessed February 2016. <*http://www.nytimes.com/2015/08/15/your-money/airbnb-horror-story-points-to-need-for-precautions.html*>

4. Helm, Burt. "Airbnb is Inc.'s 2014 Company of the Year," *Inc.* <*http://www.inc.com/magazine/201412/burt-helm/airbnb-company-of-the-year-2014.html*>

5. Ibid.

But Chesky and Gebbia did not stop there. Instead, they paralleled their second attempt with an even bigger event, the 2008 Democratic National Convention in Denver, Colorado. At this time, Nathan Blecharczyk, Gebbia's former and technologically savvy roommate, joined the team. The three were able to secure a steady revenue. However, when elections came to an end, revenue dropped significantly.[6]

On the advice of an established entrepreneur, the three took their gig to New York City, an area overpopulated with tourists and desperate for economical lodging options. This environment, paired with an increasingly "open" society in which members were quickly becoming more willing to share due to social media expansion, proved to be the perfect springboard for the startup.[7]

Not long after its debut, Air Bed and Breakfast, or more commonly referred to as Airbnb, transformed into a global billion-dollar company. The entity's transactional process is fairly straightforward. Airbnb hosts post pictures of their property on the company's website and online community members can search the site to find lodging. Property prices range from less than $50 to more than $1,000 a night and guests can choose between renting an entire home or apartment, a private room, or a shared room.[8]

Airbnb prides itself in fostering a community feel amongst guests and hosts. Chesky sums it up as follows, "Airbnb is about so much more than just renting space. It's about people and experiences. At the end of the day, what we're trying to do is bring the world together. You're not getting a room, you're getting a sense of belonging."[9] Airbnb's business model provides assets to both hosts and guests. Hosts are able to earn supplemental income, sometimes enough to cover the cost of their own rent or other property-related expenses, and guests have access to rela-tively low-cost accommodations that they can book efficiently.

Today, a small team of Airbnb executives manages the company. These key staff members include the Chief Executive Officer, Chief Technology Officer, Chief Product Officer, Chief Financial Officer, Head of Global Hospitality, Head of Global Policy and Government Affairs, and Chief Business Affairs and Legal Officer.[10]

Airbnb's Business Model

Airbnb is among the fastest growing accommodation companies in the world. In December 2014, Chesky shared some news via *Twitter*: "Airbnb now has 1 million homes on its platform, and is adding more than 20,000 new ones each week."[11] Equally impressive, the company's growth stemmed from a small workforce of approximately 1,600 employees globally.[12] Airbnb deliberately runs a lean operation, but what is most compelling about the company is that it does not own real estate. Unlike traditional hotel companies, which own and profit from physical real estate, Airbnb is purely in the business of connecting people with other people and, by doing so, people with places.

The company's core focus is connecting cost-focused travelers to homeowners that provide lodging solutions in desirable sections of cities that hotels traditionally underserve. Many users are repeat customers highlighting the fact that the service enables travelers to live like the locals. In essence, Airbnb provides unique travel experiences as well as quick, affordable, and safe accommodation for travelers.

Airbnb's business model is straightforward. Users fall into one of two classifications: hosts or guests. Hosts represent the asset owners who list their homes and apartments on the platform. In effect, hosts provide the listings that

6. Ibid

7. Ibid.

8. Airbnb website. "About Us," Accessed February 2016. Web. <*https://www.airbnb.com/about/about-us*>

9. Helm, Burt. "Airbnb is Inc.'s 2014 Company of the Year," *Inc.*
   <*http://www.inc.com/magazine/201412/burt-helm/airbnb-company-of-the-year-2014.html*>

10. *Bloomberg.* Company Overview of Airbnb, Inc. Accessed February 2016. Web.
    <*http://www.bloomberg.com/research/stocks/private/people.asp?privcapId=115705393*>

11. Griswold, Alison. "Airbnb's Latest Milestone: 1 Million Homes, and Hardly Anyone Noticed," *Slate.com.* December 8, 2014. Accessed April 2016. <*http://www.slate.com/blogs/moneybox/2014/12/08/airbnb_has_1_million_homes_brian_chesky_announces_ milest one_and_almost_no.html*>

12. Poletti, Therese. "What really keeps Airbnb CEO up at night," February 13, 2015. *Marketwatch.*
    <*http://www.marketwatch.com/story/what-really-keeps-airbnbs-ceo-up-at-night-2015-02-13* >

are available to customers on the Airbnb digital platform. Guests reflect the demand on the platform, representing customers that are seeking to rent listings in cities around the world.

Airbnb's two main customer segments are personal travelers and business travelers, with personal travelers comprising the majority of its users.[13] Airbnb approaches customer acquisition through two core sales channels – online advertising and word-of-mouth.[14]

According to Kenontech.com, a blog that highlights startups, "Airbnb is very aggressive with its online marketing and ads can be found through an extensive network of affiliate sites and as part of search results on major search engines."[15] Kenontech.com goes on to say that the second sales channel, which emphasizes a word-of-mouth approach, stems from the founders' belief that "if they provided their users with a great experience there would be a high probability that their users would spread the word."[16]

Furthermore, the company generates revenue from two main sources, commission from renters and commission from homeowners. Commission rates are maintained at a minimum to keep users from moving the transaction offline. Airbnb charges hosts a 3% host service fee for each booking completed on its platform. Withdrawn from the host payout, this fee covers the cost of processing guest payments.[17] Airbnb also charges a guest service fee when a customer's reservation is confirmed. The current guest service fee is a variable fee that ranges between 6-12% of the reservation subtotal (before fees and taxes). The higher the subtotal, the lower the percentage, allowing users to save

money when booking large reservations.[18] Figure 1, below, illustrates a sample calculation that the company provides on its website to explain the host service fee structure.

Figure 1 Sample Nightly Fee Rates

Example: 4-night reservation at a listing with a nightly rate of $100 and $50 cleaning fee

Subtotal: (4 nights × $100) + $50 cleaning fee = $450

- Host Payout: $450 − (3% × $450) = $436.50
- $450 − $436.50 = $14
- Host Service Fee to Airbnb = $14 (*rounded up to nearest dollar amount*)[19]

The Nature of the Sharing Economy

The sharing economy offers the ability for anyone with an asset, whether a car, home, or extra space in his or her driveway, to capitalize monetarily on that asset simply by renting it.[20] The nature of the sharing economy facilitates peer-to-peer business transactions. By way of a digital clearinghouse, companies such as Parking Panda allow consumers to find a parking space before they even enter a garage. Via Uber or Lyft's electronic platform, a consumer can summon a personal driver with just a couple of clicks.[21] As for finding a deal on overnight accommodations in an instant, Airbnb allows travelers to forego a call to the Holiday Inn by renting another consumer's bedroom for $50 a night or, if one prefers a more glamorous option, renting a beachside mansion for a $1,000 a night by simply perusing the company's website.[22]

---

13. On, Ken. "Dissecting Airbnb's Business Model Canvas," *Kenontek*. February 9, 2014. Web. <*http://www.kenontek.com/2014/02/09/dissecting-airbnbs-business-model-canvas/*>

14. Ibid.

15. Ibid.

16. Ibid.

17. Airbnb website. "What Are Host Service Fees," Accessed February 2016. Web. <*https://www.airbnb.com/help/article/63/what-are-host-service-fees*>

18. Airbnb website. "What Are Guest Service Fees," Accessed February 2016. Web. <*https://www.airbnb.com/help/article/104/what-are-guest-service-fees*>

19. Airbnb website. "What Are Host Service Fees," Accessed February 2016. Web. <*https://www.airbnb.com/help/article/63/what-are-host-service-fees*>

20. Kokalitcheva, Kia. "Who's Liable When an Airbnb Stay or Uber Ride Ends Badly?" *Fortune.* November 10, 2015. Accessed February 2016. <*http://fortune.com/2015/11/10/sharing-economy-safety-liability/*>

21. Geron, Tomio. "Airbnb and the Unstoppable Rise of the Share Economy," *Forbes/Tech.* February 11, 2013. Accessed February 2016. <*http://www.forbes.com/sites/tomiogeron/2013/01/23/airbnb-and-the-unstoppable-rise-of-the-share-economy#73ff0df56*>

22. Ibid.

All members of the sharing economy share three main attributes:

1. They rely on recent technological advances to satisfy established consumer demands in innovative ways;
2. They enter a space with well-established companies and disrupt the current competitive landscape; and
3. They function in interstitial areas of the law due to the timing of emergence.[23]

Rapid Growth of Airbnb

Since 2008, Airbnb has enjoyed unmatched growth in the accommodations industry compared to its peers. According to the *Wall Street Journal*, which reported Airbnb's most recent valuation in June of 2015, the company has a valuation of $25 billion and 2015 revenues were projected to reach $900 million.[24] By comparison, Marriott, which manages more than 4,000 hotels, is valued at $21 billion and last year reached $13.8 billion in revenue.[25] In only a few years, Airbnb grew from a small start-up to an established company with a market value larger than many of its traditional hotel competitors. Furthermore, Airbnb's valuation is approximately twice the size of rival travel site Expedia and more than five times the size of HomeAway, Airbnb's closest online competitor (see Figure 2).

Analysts contend Airbnb commands a premium valuation given the company's accelerated growth rate over the last few years. Airbnb's $900 million in projected revenue for 2015 was 360% of the company's revenue in 2013, which totaled $250 million. From 2014 to 2015, the company had an estimated revenue growth of 113% year-over-year.[26] Airbnb's next closest competitor for year-over-year growth was HomeAway at 24% and Expedia at 20%. Traditional hotels like Marriott continue to grow at more conservative rates hovering between 5% and 10% (See Figure 3).

Beyond revenue and valuation, Airbnb is quickly becoming a mainstream lodging brand recognized among travelers. According to equity research firm CB Insights, the term "Airbnb" recently surpassed "Marriott" in Google search popularity for the first year ever in 2015.[27] Analysts remain bullish that Airbnb's online dominance will likely continue to grow, further enhancing its competitive position among its primary rivals in the lodging industry (See Figure 4).

With many promising growth metrics, institutional investors continue to flock to Airbnb as a seemingly secure investment opportunity with a bright future. The Dow Jones Venture Source, an online database that tracks company performance of privately held ventured-backed companies, currently ranks Airbnb as the third most valuable private start-up in the world, trailing only Uber and Xiaomi.[28] Airbnb maintains a stable roster of prominent investors. Notable companies include Sequoia Capital, Andreessen Horowitz, Tiger Global Management, TPG Growth, T. Rowe Price, and Fidelity Investments.[29] What is clear is that the company is well capitalized and positioned to grow. What remains uncertain to some is the company's ability to sustainably manage this rate of growth.

Political and Regulatory Environment

On September 2, 2014, an independent city-wide poll from Quinnipiac University asked, "Do you think New York City residents should be permitted to rent rooms in their homes for a few days at a time to strangers, similar to a hotel, or should this practice be banned?"[30] The results of this

23. Nadler, Michael and Kaplan, Roberta. "Airbnb: A Case Study in Occupancy Regulation and Taxation," *The University of Chicago Law Review*. 2016. <https://lawreview.uchicago.edu/page/airbnb-case-study-occupancy-regulation-and-taxation>

24. Winkler, Rolfe, and Douglas Macmillan. "The Secret Math of Airbnb's 24 Billion Valuation," *Wall Street Journal*. June 17, 2015. Accessed February 2016. <http://www.wsj.com/articles/the-secret-math-of-airbnbs-24-billion-valuation-1434568517>

25. Ibid.

26. Krishnan, Nikhil. "Why That Crazy-High Airbnb Valuation Is Fair," *LinkedIn*. June 24, 2015. Accessed February 2016. <https://www.linkedin.com/pulse/why-crazy-high-airbnb-valuation-fair-nikhil-krishnan>

27. Ibid.

28. Austin, Scott; Canipe, Chris; and Slobin, Sarah. "The Billion Dollar Start Up Club," *Wall Street Journal*. February 18, 2015. Accessed February 2016. <http://graphics.wsj.com/billion-dollar-club/>

29. Ibid.

30. News Release, PDF. "New Yorkers Welcome Democratic Convention 3-1; Quinnipiac University Poll Finds; Voters Want Right To Rent Rooms Like A Hotel," Quinnipiac University, September 2, 2014. <https://www.qu.edu/news-and-events/quinnipiac-university-poll/new-york-city/release-detail?ReleaseID=2076> as cited in Fischer, Ben. "Q-Poll Doesn't Quite Say What Airbnb Wants It To Say," *Biz Journals*. September 2, 2014. Accessed February 2016. <http://www.bizjournals.com/newyork/blog/techflash/2014/09/q-poll-doesnt-quite-say-what-airbnb-wants-it-to.html>

poll showed a sound majority of voters, 56%, in favor of allowing short-term rentals to strangers. Only 36% of New York voters wanted to ban the use of short-term rentals.[31]

Approximately one year later, in November 2015, Airbnb commissioned a survey to gauge whether New York residents perceived the company and their rental service in a favorable or unfavorable way. David Binder Research polled more than 400 respondents over an 11-day period and found the following:

- 65% believed Airbnb should be legal in New York
- 22% believed Airbnb should be illegal in New York
- 05% answered they view Airbnb "very unfavorable"
- 10% answered they view Airbnb "somewhat unfavorable"
- 25% answered they view Airbnb "somewhat favorable"
- 12% answered they view Airbnb "very favorable"
- 48% of voters had "No Opinion" of Airbnb[32]

While Airbnb maintains sound consumer support in many of the cities where it operates, the company is no stranger to political and regulatory controversy. Over the last two years, the company has been embroiled in high-profile political battles with regulators in some of its most lucrative markets, including San Francisco and New York City. In November of 2015, San Francisco voters headed to the polls to vote on Proposition F, which was commonly known as the "Airbnb Initiative."

Proposition F was a ballot initiative drafted by city officials in an effort to toughen regulations on short-term rental apartments and homes in the city of San Francisco.[33] A political initiative capable of reducing short-term listings and revenue for Airbnb, Proposition F presented the first significant instance in which Airbnb faced an organized political effort to regulate the company's business model

in its own backyard – San Francisco. Numerous Airbnb opponents, including hotel industry backed opposition, affirmed Airbnb was operating under interstitial areas of law and urged regulators to codify clear rules that would regulate online rental platforms to a similar standard that traditional hotels must comply with under the law.

Proposition F attempted to enact the following key rules for Airbnb and other short-term rental platforms. If the proposition passed by a majority vote, each company, and their rental hosts, would be required to comply with the following rules:

1. A 75-day imposed limit over the course of a year on all forms of short-term rentals where the host is not present during the stay. Hosts prohibited from listing a unit if it exceeded the 75-day limit.
2. Require hosts and rental platforms to submit quarterly reports to the San Francisco Planning Department detailing which nights the unit was rented out and which nights the host occupied the unit.
3. Insert Legal Standing provisions enabling permanent residents and nonprofit housing groups the right to sue hosts and rental platforms for violating the rules.

On November 4, 2015, Airbnb scored a victory as voters favored letting city residents rent out their homes.[34] Proposition F lost by a vote of 55 percent to 45 percent. Airbnb outspent its opposition by a factor of 16 to 1, spending $8 million dollars to defeat the measure. In comparison, Unite Here, a hotel workers' union, raised only $482,000 in support of the measure. In the wake of Airbnb's victory, Christopher Nulty, a spokesman for the company, released the following statement: "Voters stood up for working families' right to share their homes and opposed an extreme, hotel-industry-backed measure."[35]

31. Ibid.
32. Noto, Anthony. "Poll: Majority of New Yorkers view Airbnb in positive light," *Biz Journals*. November 5, 2015. Accessed February 2016. <http://www.bizjournals.com/newyork/news/2015/11/05/majority-of-new-yorkers-view-airbnb-in.html>
33. Lien, Tracey. "Everything you need to know about San Francisco's Airbnb ballot measure," *Los Angeles Times*. October 30, 2015. Accessed February 2016. <http://www.latimes.com/business/technology/la-fi-tn-airbnb-prop-f-san-francisco-20151029-htmlstory.html>
34. Said, Carolyn. "Prop F: S.F. voters reject measure to restrict Airbnb rentals," *SF Gate*. November 4, 2015. Accessed February 2016. <http://www.sfgate.com/bayarea/article/Prop-F-Measure-to-restrict-Airbnb-rentals-6609176.php>
35. Ibid.

Terms of Service and User Liability

As opposition groups across the country remain committed to portraying Airbnb as unsafe and preoccupied with evading sensible regulations, Brian Chesky, CEO and Co-Founder of Airbnb, provides his viewpoint as it relates to the sharing economy. Chesky asserts, "There were laws created for businesses, and there were laws for people. What the sharing economy did was create a third category: people as businesses."[36] Regulators in cities across the world, in particular where Airbnb operates, continue to grapple with the new business model that has risen from the sharing economy. While consumers continue to lend support to Airbnb and similar sharing economy services, questions still remain on where liabilities rest in this new way of doing business. Do liabilities rest with the users of the service or the company facilitating the service?

Airbnb's Terms of Service agreement clearly defines which party assumes liability and how Airbnb approaches risk management and legal strategy. Airbnb operates in hundreds of countries, territories, and cities across the world. Naturally, this diverse geographical presence makes it inherently difficult to inform users of all the applicable public safety, housing, and zoning laws that might apply to them as hosts or guests. Instead of opting to educate all users of the relevant housing and safety laws that apply to them in their respective territories, Airbnb chooses to place all legal responsibility on the user through their terms of service agreement.

Airbnb's Terms of Service state, "Please read these terms of service carefully as they contain important information regarding your legal rights, remedies, and obligation." Airbnb's Terms of Service are over 16,000 words in length.[37] In comparison, Marriott's Terms of Use for the United States and Canada are just under 2,500 words.[38] Uber's Terms are under 5,000 words,[39] and HomeAway, an Airbnb competitor which owns more than five other rental companies, has a Terms page on their website that totals just under 13,500 words.[40] As of February 14, 2016, Airbnb's Terms of Service were last edited on July 6, 2015, two days after the Lopez incident.

Airbnb says that it has no control over the conduct of its hosts, guests, or any other user of the site. The company disclaims all liability in this regard to the maximum extent permitted by the law. Airbnb states that it does not control the content contained in any of its listings and the condition, legality, or suitability of any accommodations. Moreover, Airbnb states that all bookings are made and accepted at the member's own risk. The Terms of Service agreement also states that Airbnb does not act as an insurer.

However, as of May 2012, Airbnb began offering a Host Protection program or Host Guarantee, in which hosts are covered up to $1 million for damage and injuries. Airbnb's website states that the Host Guarantee does not cover cash and securities, pets, personal liability, or common areas.[41] Furthermore, the insurance is "secondary," meaning the Airbnb policy takes effect only after a host exhausts his or her personal insurance coverage.[42]

Members of Airbnb are sometimes listed as "verified" or "connected" which simply indicates that they went through the verification process. Per the Terms of Service, this is not a guarantee of the member's identity or whether they are trustworthy, safe, or suitable. Members are encouraged to use their own judgment when accepting and selecting hosts and guests.

Airbnb's preferred strategy of informing users of their legal responsibilities through the Terms of Service agree-

36. Kessler, Andy. "Brian Chesky: The 'Sharing Economy' and Its Enemies," *Wall Street Journal*, Jan. 17, 2014. <*http://www.wsj.com/articles/SB10001424052702304049704579321001856708992*>

37. Airbnb website. "Airbnb Terms of Service." Accessed February 2016. Web. <*https://www.airbnb.com/terms*>

38. Marriott.com "Marriott Terms of Use for United States & Canada." Accessed February 2016. Web. <*http://www.marriott.com/about/terms-of-use.mi*>

39. Uber website. "Uber Terms and Conditions." Accessed February 2016. Web. <*https://www.uber.com/legal/usa/terms*>

40. Homeaway.com "Homeaway Terms and Conditions." Accessed February 2016. Web. <*https://www.homeaway.com/info/about-us/legal/terms-conditions*>

41. Airbnb website. "Airbnb Host Guarantee Terms and Conditions." Accessed February 2016. Web. <*https://www.airbnb.com/terms/host_guarantee*>

42. Lieber, Ron. "A Liability Risk for Airbnb Hosts," *The New York Times*. December 5, 2014. Accessed February 2016. <*http://www.nytimes.com/2014/12/06/your-money/airbnb-offers-homeowner-liability-coverage-but-hosts-still-have-risks.html*>

ment does not come without contention between users and the company. Many users confirm they do not read the Terms of Service agreement and the company is aware of this significant caveat.

In September 2012, Nigel Warren, a New York City resident, illegally rented out his bedroom for $100 a night while he was away in Colorado for a three-night trip. Upon his return from Colorado, Nigel was contacted by his landlord who had been cited for five violations for operating as an "illegal transient hotel."[43] The fines, if enforced, would have amounted to $40,000 in punitive damages. Fortunately for Mr. Warren and his landlord, the city dropped the sizable fines due to an administrative error of the city's buildings department.

Due to his experience, Mr. Warren posed a pressing question that many stakeholders wish the company would more thoroughly address. Acknowledging that Airbnb knows within reason that many of its hosts who live in large cities are violating rules, he wondered why Airbnb doesn't warn people about the potential for legal hassles. "By ignoring local laws, you (Airbnb) are making casualties of the very people you need to make your site a success," Warren said.[44]

Airbnb's Safety Tips

Tips for Guests

Clicking on the link "Trust and Safety" at the bottom of Airbnb's homepage directs viewers to another page with a link entitled "I'm a guest. What are some safety tips I can follow?" Airbnb suggests reading the reviews of other guests to ensure the host is reputable. If guests are skeptical about the host after reading the review, they are encouraged to use their intuition and not book their stay with that host. Guests can also ask hosts to complete "profile verifications" before booking with them. Airbnb suggests that guests talk to the host and start a conversation about the upcoming stay. It also recommends traveler's insurance and reminds guests to call the local police or emergency services immediately if personal safety is threatened.[45]

Tips for Hosts

Above the link for guest safety tips, customers can learn about how to stay safe as a host. Airbnb encourages hosts to read reviews of the guests and to use common sense when accepting a guest's request to stay at their listing. Hosts can require guests to complete verifications before they book, such as Verified ID. With Verified ID, guests might be asked to upload their government-issued ID, link their Airbnb account with their page on another social media site (i.e. Facebook), or upload an Airbnb profile photo. Airbnb also asks hosts to call the local police or emergency services if their personal safety is threatened. Airbnb suggests that hosts designate a safe location in case of an emergency. Hosts can also notify their neighbors that they are hosting an Airbnb guest as a precautionary measure.[46]

Other Incidents Leading Up to July 2015

Incident 1

In June of 2011, an Airbnb host who identified herself as "EJ" reported that the person who rented her apartment trashed it and stole jewelry, cash, and electronics. EJ wrote about this incident on her personal blog. Airbnb initially responded by trying to persuade EJ to remove her blog post and declined to help her recover from the damages. Following the incident, Chesky stated in a blog on Airbnb's website on August 1, 2011 that he hopes "this can be a valuable lesson to other businesses about what not to do in a time of crisis. With regards to EJ, we let her down, and for that we are very sorry. We should have responded faster, communicated more sensitively, and taken more decisive action to make sure she felt safe and secure. But we weren't prepared for the crisis and we dropped the ball. Now we're dealing with the consequences."

43. Lieber, Ron. "A Warning for Hosts of Airbnb Travelers," *The New York Times*. November 30, 2012. Accessed February 2016.
    <*http://www.nytimes.com/2012/12/01/your-money/a-warning-for-airbnb-hosts-who-may-be-breaking-the-law.html?_r=1*>

44. Ibid.

45. Airbnb website. "Airbnb Trust and Safety." Accessed February 2016.
    Web. <*https://www.airbnb.com/help/article/241/i-m-a-guest--what-are-some-safety-tips-i-can-follow*>

46. Airbnb website. "Airbnb Trust and Safety." Accessed February 2016.
    Web. <*https://www.airbnb.com/help/article/231/i-m-a-host--what-are-some-safety-tips-i-can-follow*>

Following the response Airbnb said they would provide a $50,000 insurance guarantee for any loss or damages at the property of an Airbnb host. Since the incident, the policy has increased to $1 million but is secondary to the host's personal insurance. Also, Airbnb planned to launch a 24/7 hotline for its users to report problems. Finally, Chesky offered his own e-mail address in case customers had trouble getting in contact with an Airbnb representative.[47]

Incident 2

A couple rented an Airbnb property in the Hamptons (New York) in June 2014. Following Airbnb's safety tips, the couple read the reviews of the host and, because of the positive nature of the reviews, decided to book the stay. Before arriving at the home and meeting with the host, the couple texted the host to let him know the timing of their arrival and asked a few questions about items in the house and where to pick up the keys. The host was reportedly friendly and responsive.

Later that night at 2:45 a.m., the male guest received a text from the host that read, "Do you want to try." Shortly after, the host let himself into the locked house with another set of keys and appeared to be inebriated. The host then asked the male guest, "The girlfriend, she's cool, right?" The male guest calmly asked the host to leave, but not before the host picked up the guest's keys and wallet. The male guest asked the host to put the items down and the host did so before departing.

Shortly afterward, the terrified couple left the home. The female guest tried to call the 24-hour emergency line, but could not reach an Airbnb representative after waiting on the line for 45 minutes. The couple then filed a complaint and received a response that Airbnb would be forwarding the case to their Trip Experience Team. The couple drove back to Manhattan where they found a hotel priced at $350 per night. That Monday, the couple called Airbnb twice by phone, but no one returned their calls.

Only after *Business Insider* reached out to Airbnb for comment on the incident did Airbnb take down the host's listing and ban him from the site permanently. They reimbursed the couple for their stay, apologized for the delay, and gave them a $500 credit to try Airbnb again. A spokesperson for Airbnb commented about the incident in a *Business Insider* article, "We deeply regret that this matter was not handled properly and our response fell well short of the standards we set for ourselves. This behavior is totally unacceptable and the host has been permanently removed from Airbnb."[48]

In September 2015, the couple ventured back onto Airbnb's site and found that the same property where the incident occurred was relisted on the site under a different name. As a result, Airbnb banned the property again.

Nick Papas, an Airbnb spokesman, commented in another *Business Insider* article, "We have technological tools and procedures that help ensure bad actors don't try to come back to our community. In this case, one investigator didn't properly employ these tools. We've since addressed this issue and we are implementing procedures to ensure it doesn't happen again. We will also make it clear to the host that he is not welcome and has no place in the Airbnb community."[49]

Response to Lopez Incident

The onus was left on Jacob Lopez's mother to rescue her son in Spain. At the time of the incident, Airbnb's policy was to withhold the location of the guest if anyone other than the guest were to ask and would not report a crime unless contacted by the guest. Lopez's mother called the Madrid police department, but was unsuccessful in her attempts. Even if she had been able to reach someone in Madrid, the inefficiency of Airbnb's protocol would likely not have allowed for police to reach her son in time.

Nick Papas commented in a *New York Times* article, "We realize we can learn a lot from this incident and we can do better. We are clarifying our policies so that our team

47. Olivarez-Giles, Nathan. "Airbnb offers $50,000 insurance policy after user's 'nightmare.'" *Los Angeles Times.* August 1, 2011. Accessed February 2016. <http://latimesblogs.latimes.com/technology/2011/08/airbnb-insurance-guarantee.html>

48. Bort, Julie. "An Airbnb Host Got Drunk And Let Himself Into The House While A Business Insider Employee Was Sleeping." *Business Insider.* June 24, 2014. Accessed February 2016. <http://www.businessinsider.com/bi-employee-has-airbnb-horror-story-2014-6>

49. Bort, Julie. "Banned Airbnb Host Who Entered The House While His Guests Were Sleeping Was Back On Airbnb." *Business Insider.* October 6, 2014. Accessed February 2016. <http://www.businessinsider.com/banned-airbnb-host-was-back-on-the-site-2014-10>

will always contact law enforcement if we are made aware of an emergency situation in progress. Safety is our number one priority, and we want to get our hosts and guests as much help as possible."[50]

As reported on July 13, 2015, Belinda Johnson was promoted to Airbnb's Chief Business Affairs and Legal Officer. In this role, she is responsible for legal matters, civic partnerships, public policy, social and philanthropic initiatives, and communication. According to Airbnb CEO Brian Chesky, she'll "become more of the face and the voice of the company."[51]

Discussion Questions

1. If the press posed the following question to you as an Airbnb executive, how would you respond? "You claim that safety is your first priority, yet a teenager was sexually assaulted in one of your properties. How do you explain this?"
2. Is it Airbnb's responsibility to protect its guests? Should the company implement an automaticity plan?
3. Should Airbnb communicate all safety and policy changes to customers? How should it communicate changes?
4. Is Airbnb being proactive enough in its safety efforts? Is the business growing too fast to properly protect guests?
5. Although it would slow growth, is a more thorough vetting process for hosts and guests needed?

Writing Assignment

Please respond in writing to the issues presented in this case by preparing two documents: a communication strategy memo and a professional business letter.

In preparing these documents, you may assume one of two roles: you may identify yourself as an Airbnb senior manager who has been asked to provide advice to Chip Conley, Strategic Advisor for Hospitality and Leadership, regarding the issues he and the company are facing. Or, you may identify yourself as an external management consultant who has been asked by the company to provide advice to Mr. Conley.

Either way, you must prepare a strategy memo addressed to Chip Conley, that summarizes the details of the case, identifies critical issues, discusses their implications (what they mean and why they matter), offers specific recommendations for action (assigning ownership and suspense dates for each), and shows how to communicate the solution to all who are affected by the recommendations.

You must also prepare a professional business letter for the signature of Mr. Brian Cheskey, Airbnb Chief Executive Officer. That document should be addressed to all Airbnb customers and prospective customers, explaining the actions the company is taking. That letter, which would contain no inside address or by-name salutation, would be posted to the company's website. If you have questions about either of these documents, please consult your instructor.

50. Lieber, Ron. "Airbnb Horror Story Points to Need for Precautions." *New York Times*. August 14, 2015. Accessed February 2016. <*http://www.nytimes.com/2015/08/15/your-money/airbnb-horror-story-points-to-need-for-precautions.html*>
51. Bellstrom, Kristen. "Exclusive: Meet Airbnb's highest ranking female exec ever." *Fortune*. July 13, 2015. Accessed February 2016. <*http://fortune.com/2015/07/13/airbnb-belinda-johnson-promotion/*>

Figure 2

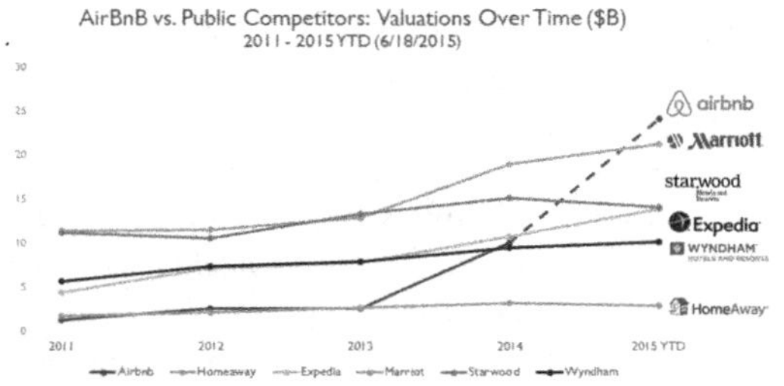

AirBnB vs. Public Competitors: Valuations Over Time ($B)
2011 - 2015 YTD (6/18/2015)

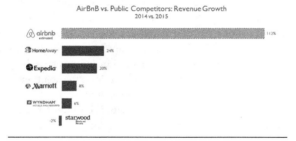

Figure 4 Google Search Popularity (2015)

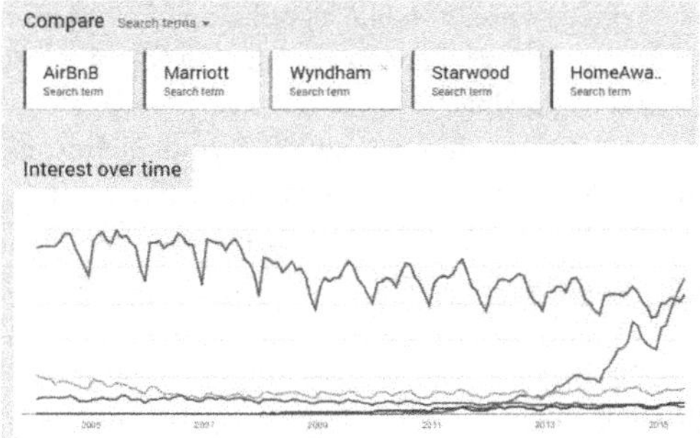

Compare Search terms ▾

| AirBnB | Marriott | Wyndham | Starwood | HomeAwa.. |
| Search term | Search term | Search term | Search term | Search term |

Interest over time

Figure 3

AirBnB vs. Public Competitors: Revenue Growth
2014 vs. 2015

airbnb estimated — 112%
HomeAway — 24%
Expedia — 20%
Marriott — 8%
WYNDHAM — 6%
starwood — -2%

Chapter 8

Preparing Employment Messages

© endomotion / bigstockphoto.com

- *Perform research needed to conduct a job search and complete the application process.*

- *Write employment messages, including résumés, application letters, and thank-you notes.*

- *Understand the steps in the job interview process and be more confident in both performing and conducting them.*

- *Implement an effective performance appraisal process and become more confident in both receiving and giving performance feedback.*

Case Questions

1. How important is it for employers to create a working environment that is attractive to potential employees? What would be the characteristics of such an environment?

2. From an employee perspective, how important is it to target positions in which one would be a good fit? What are the advantages to the employee and the employer?

3. What steps are needed to identify organizations in which an applicant will potentially fit well with the culture? Does taking these steps provide a potential persuasive opportunity for the applicant? If so, how?

The Case of the Gen-Y Workforce

"I have called today's meeting to discuss our recent numbers on job turnover rates here at DataTel," Jennifer Fielding announced from the head of the table. Jennifer, head of human resources, scanned the twelve first-line supervisors and managers attending the meeting to see if she had gotten their attention before going on. "In the past twelve months, 19 percent of our employees in the Gen-Y age group have left the company. That may sound surprising given today's sluggish job market, but it is in line with industry forecasts. I would like to get your ideas about how we might better keep these employees, since hiring costs continue to increase while our budget for hiring remains static.

"Before we get into the discussion phase of the meeting, however, I would like to provide you with some information about this age group. Because they have grown up with technology and understand the flexibility it can bring to the workplace, they expect companies to capitalize on that flexibility. Gen-Yers don't mind long hours as long as they have the flexibility to choose when and where they work.

"Some companies have moved in this direction, but they are the exception. For example, Google designated 20 percent of employees' paid time as time to work on creative personal projects. The company also offers unlimited fruit, Luna Bars, and Vitamin Water, a gym, and a playroom to keep people energized and let them take breaks when needed.

"We don't need to copy Google's program, but I would like us to take this opportunity to consider what we could do regarding our HR policies to be more attractive to Gen-Yers, who are expected to make up 77 percent of the workplace within the next ten to twelve years," Fielding said. "So what is your response? What can we do to become a company that will attract and hold the Millennial generation?"

As was discussed in Chapter 6, employment messages are persuasive messages. Furthermore, they are persuasive messages that require that two additional business communication purposes are achieved: credibility by demonstrating that the applicant is knowledgeable and experienced, and goodwill by showing that he or she is a likeable, responsive person with which to work. Therefore, the same steps provided in Chapter 6 for analyzing the audience and the competitors should be followed when preparing résumés, application letters, and thank-you notes as well as for interviews.

In less competitive job markets, the goal of establishing credibility and goodwill also is important for the employer who is hiring. The employer also may be competing with others for the best job applicants and thus should consider how knowledgeable, well prepared, and pleasant to work with he or she appears. This concern should expand to include the type of workplace environment and culture that the employer offers.

In addition to these strategic issues, this chapter will explore the tactical elements involved in applying for jobs as well as hiring. The final section will discuss another important element related to employment: Conducting performance appraisals and receiving performance feedback.

Steps in the Application Process

If you have not been involved in the hiring process, it can be challenging to take on the perspective of your audience, the employer. The employer will likely receive many applications for one position, depending on the economic climate and the available job pool. The employer will likely have many applicants to choose from. His or her job may thus involve several steps to winnow down the pool to a number that could reasonably be interviewed. These steps might involve

- Quickly eliminating candidates who on the surface do not appear to be qualified. This task might be done by a computer program that is searching for keywords found in the job advertisement or description. It might also be done by an assistant who has little knowledge of the job but, like the computer program, has been asked to look for particular keywords or skills. Additional considerations in this process might include eliminating applications that are

  - Improperly submitted
  - Improperly formatted
  - Incomplete
  - Poorly written and that include grammatical, punctuation, or spelling errors.

  In this step, most of the applications are generally eliminated for one of these reasons.

- Reviewing the remaining application packages more carefully. This step involves comparing the remaining applicants' materials to identify who appears to be the best qualified. It is this step that many first-time job applicants may miss. In other words, if you have followed all of the instructions provided in most classes on creating job application messages, you still may not get an interview if you don't recognize that you are competing with others for a scarce resource, that is, a job. Therefore, in addition to addressing the qualifications listed in the job description and creating a well-written and professionally formatted employment package, you should also attend to how you might distinguish yourself positively from other applicants.

This step can be a bit daunting not only for first-time applicants but for more seasoned professionals as well. But it might be easier than it appears on the surface by following the strategic and tactical steps discussed in this section.

1. Perform a self-inventory: List your skills, abilities, and experiences.
2. Identify your purposes: To inform, persuade, establish your credibility, and convey goodwill.

3. Analyze your audience by conducting research to learn more about its needs, concerns, and objectives.

4. Match the audience's expectations with your abilities and skills.

5. Consider your competition and how you might distinguish yourself from it.

6. Prepare the employment messages that are requested or required.

7. Review and revise your social media content.

Performing the Self-Inventory

In order to be persuasive and to increase self-confidence in the job application process, it is generally necessary to do a thorough self-inventory. A self-inventory involves listing all of the skills, experiences, and abilities you have that may be transferable or applicable in a workplace situation. For those who have held relevant jobs, this process can be relatively simple, since they should have many of the skills that are needed if they are applying for a similar position. However, for those entering the professional workplace or changing jobs, this task can be more challenging. It is not uncommon for first-time applicants to believe they have little to offer beyond some attractive personal characteristics and the proper college degree. However, performing a thoughtful self-inventory can often illuminate other needed skills and abilities.

To get started, it is generally helpful to identify the skills and abilities that employers are looking for. Start by finding job descriptions for positions to which you would like to apply. Read them carefully, and list all of the skills, abilities, and personal characteristics for which they are looking. Then match those skills and abilities with your own personal experiences. These do not have to be demonstrated on the job but can also be skills and abilities that you have demonstrated in classes, college organizations, volunteer organizations, and your personal life.

Below is a list of questions to help get you started on a self-inventory:

1. What jobs have you held?

2. What organizations have you belonged to?

3. What training or education do you have?

4. In all of the above categories, what skills have you used or exhibited?

5. What have been your concrete achievements in all of these categories?

6. Based on this analysis, what personal characteristics, abilities, and skills might you address during the job application process?

For example, if you are a student, it is likely that you have been involved in a number of group projects during your academic career. Many organizations nowadays expect employees to have excellent group communication skills. If this is the case, what experiences have you had in your group work that would highlight and communicate your skills in this area? These examples can be used when writing a résumé, application letter or during job interviews.

Analyze Your Audience, the Industry, and the Overall Job Climate

The next step in the process is to do a careful analysis of your potential audience, the industry in which you hope to work, and the overall job climate. It is important to understand the overall job climate for a variety of reasons. If the job market is tight, it is likely that the applicant will have much less leverage in negotiating salary, work location, and benefits. However, this depends on the industry. For example, you may be looking for work in a tight job market generally speaking, but there may be industries or fields that are begging for applicants. This is why it is helpful to get a sense of the broader context of the job market, so that you will have a better understanding of your overall value in that market.

It is also important to determine the specific skills for which your audience is looking, so that you can show that you are well qualified for a particular position. This is the first goal of any job applicant: to demonstrate that he or she is qualified for the job, so that his or her application will not be eliminated from further consideration. Figure 8-1 provides an example of a typical job description, this one for an office manager. It is important to recognize that most job descriptions contain two parts: a description of the overall job and a list of requirements. When analyzing job descriptions, be sure to carefully read the entire job description and list all of the skills that are listed. For example in the job description shown in Figure 8-1, interaction with other departments, customers, and management is required. Carefully reading this job description would provide the applicant with an opportunity to highlight his or her communication skills and experience interacting with varied audiences successfully.

The final consideration is the competition. If it is a tight job market, the employment process may be extremely competitive. If so, the question is, "What can you provide an employer that will make you as attractive, or even more so than your competition?" A thorough self-analysis as well as an analysis of the industry, job market, and competition should provide you some ideas about how to answer this question. Sometimes the answer to this question may be a collection of small actions, such as better addressing the employer's needs in your application package, writing a follow-up thank-you note after the interview, and conveying the right attitude during the job interview.

Figure 8-1 Job Description for an Office Manager Position

Regional environmental laboratory is seeking a motivated individual for Office Manager. Responsible for three departments central to the operations of Energy Laboratories:

> Sample Receiving and Sample Preparation/Login
>
> Report Preparation/Customer Service
>
> Shipping and Receiving

Requires professional interaction with all aspects of the laboratory, including all analytical departments, upper management, project management, accounting, sales, and customer service.

Office Manager is responsible for database management and related problem solving. Must have ability to gather necessary information and resources to make effective decisions that impact laboratory operations.

Requirements:

- Proven and demonstrated leadership experience
- Goal-oriented management style
- Independent problem solver
- Decision making
- Microsoft Office suite programs
- Customer service focus
- Experience in the environmental services industry or laboratory setting

Drafting and Developing a Résumé

When applying for a position, there are two common documents that the employer might request: the application letter and a résumé. With most positions now applied for online, you will find that some only request a résumé. There are two key differences between a résumé and an application letter: (1) the format and (2) the content. A résumé is little more than a bullet list, while a letter is a persuasive message. A résumé can be a bit more general in terms of its content because it is aimed at a position. For example, if you are applying for an entry-level accounting position at a number of organizations, the content may need little change, since most entry-level accounting positions are similar in the types of skills that are required. The content of a letter, on the other hand, should be more focused on a particular employer and its needs. Therefore, the content of a letter might change more depending on the particular employer to whom it is aimed.

The steps in drafting and developing a résumé are listed below:

1. Choose or create a template.

   Most résumés are one page in length in the United States, particularly for those just entering the workforce, and most other countries, such as Canada and France. There are exceptions, though, such as in Germany, where a complete dossier of perhaps twenty pages is not unusual. In the United States, if you have been working in a profession for several years, your résumé may be longer than a page.

   The simplest way to develop a résumé is to start with the templates that are provided in Microsoft Word or another program and then customize the template. A typical résumé format is provided in Figure 8-2.

Figure 8-2 Sample Résumé

Jennifer Isaacs
141 Rowman Street, Apartment 1
Torrance, CA 90081
(213) 556-2323, *jisaacs@gmail.com*

Education	California State University, Los Angeles, CA
	▪ Bachelor's Degree in Business Administration, 3.7 GPA, Expected Graduation 2019
	▪ Dean's List All Semesters
	▪ Coursework: Business Communication, Introduction to Marketing, Micro and Macro Economics, Fundamentals of Accounting, Fundamentals of Management, Introduction to Public Relations, Sales.
Employment	Kaiser Public Relations, Los Angeles, CA
	Public Relations Intern, 2017–Present
	▪ Met with clients to determine their public relations needs
	▪ Wrote public relations materials, such as press releases, company backgrounders, brochure content, and information sheets
	▪ Contacted media outlets to inform them about newsworthy events involving clients
	Torrance Parks Department, Torrance, CA
	Lifeguard, Torrance City Beach, 2014–2016
	▪ Responsible for safeguarding the lives of swimmers at Torrance City Beach
	▪ Interacted with the public, coworkers, and supervisors to ensure the safety and well-being of the public
	▪ Received the Torrance City Beach "Best Lifeguard" Award in 2015 and 2016

Organizations and Leadership

▪ Vice President, Alpha Kappa Psi Sorority, 2015–Present

▪ Volunteer, Habitat for Humanity, 2016–2017

▪ Member, CSU Marketing Association, 2015–Present

2. Generally, provide three categories of information with an eye toward audience expectations and interests. These categories are typically

   - Education
   - Work experience
   - Organizations, awards, and leadership.

   However, there are additional categories you may want to include, such as "Career Objective," which would appear at the top of the résumé before "Education." Categories included in a résumé also may differ depending on the country. For example, in China personal information is included while in Germany and Spain information about one's family may also be included.

Depending on your career situation, there are other résumé formats that may be used. For example, if you have worked in several different professional positions and are wishing to change careers, a functional résumé may be more suitable than the chronological résumé described earlier. A functional résumé organizes information by skills or accomplishments that best address future career goals.

The organization of the main headings in a chronological résumé may also change depending on the place you are at in your career. For example, if your most recent and most notable accomplishment is attaining a bachelor's degree in your desired field, the category "Education" will likely appear first on your résumé. However, if you have been working in your chosen field for several years, the category "Work Experience" may appear first and "Education" may drop to the bottom. This is because work experience is generally more desirable to employers than a college degree without relevant work experience.

When deciding which information to provide, remember to consider your audience. Are there certain phrases or words that are commonly used in your desired profession to describe certain skills or abilities? If you don't know, you can find out by reading job descriptions and other information related to your chosen profession. Then use these words and phrases as appropriate to describe the skills and abilities you offer.

In addition, avoid "padding" your résumé with unnecessary information. Based on your previous research, you should have a very clear understanding of the types of skills and abilities for which employers are looking. Provide only information that relates to these skills and abilities. Finally, if you are in college, you should avoid listing accomplishments from high school unless they are relevant to the job because it may make you look as if you have not achieved much in college if you need to rely on past honors.

3. Use a bullet list format.
    - Begin with an action word.
    - Use parallel structure.
    - Ideally, include concrete achievements.

A list of common action words used at the beginning of lists in résumés is provided in the box below.

List of Action Words for Use in Résumés and Lists

accomplished	demonstrated	handled	performed	repaired
achieved	determined	hired	planned	reported
administered	developed	improved	predicted	researched
advised	devised	increased	prepared	retrieved
aided	diagnosed	initiated	presented	reviewed
allocated	directed	interviewed	prioritized	revised
analyzed	distributed	inventoried	processed	scheduled
balanced	earned	led	produced	screened
budgeted	enlisted	maintained	programmed	selected
calculated	established	managed	promoted	served
coached	estimated	mediated	provided	sold
communicated	expedited	monitored	purchased	started
compared	facilitated	motivated	recommended	supervised
compiled	formed	negotiated	recorded	taught
coordinated	formulated	operated	recruited	trained
created	generated	organized	reduced	verified
decided	guided	oversaw	reorganized	

When creating bullet lists of skills and abilities, refer back to your self-inventory for evidence of accomplishments. Including these in your résumé is another way that you can distinguish yourself from the competition.

Examples of a bulleted item without specific evidence or a relevant accomplishment:

- Managed the budget of the Kappa Kappa Pi Fraternity
- Won the "Best Salesperson of the Year" Award

Examples of a bulleted item with specific evidence or a relevant accomplishment:

- Managed the $250,000 annual budget of the Kappa Kappa Pi Fraternity
- Won the "Best Salesperson of the Year" Award for sales of more than $300,000 in clothing and accessories

Hopefully, as these latter examples show, a few additional words that provide specific evidence and results is more vivid, clear, and impressive than the general information provided in the first examples.

4. Ensure that you have included keywords from the job description.

   Since most job applications are done electronically, it is important to check that you have included important words from the job description in your résumé. That's because most companies use software programs called application tracking systems to scan electronically submitted résumés and search for such keywords to identify applicants who are potentially qualified for a position. These systems typically look for nouns that are related to the industry, so your earlier research should serve you well in accomplishing this step. Place the keywords in the proper context within your listing of accomplishments.

Drafting and Developing the Application Letter

The first objective of an application letter is to show you are well qualified for the position for which you are applying. Reaching this objective depends on the quality of the content or information about yourself that you are able to provide and whether that information speaks to your audience's needs as well or better than your competitors—other job applicants—might. In other words, much of your ability to accomplish this goal depends on your knowledge of the audience and your ability to write in such a way to show that you have that knowledge. Earlier steps in the job application process should have prepared you well to draft and develop the application letter. The steps in drafting the application letter are

Step 1:   Analysis of your strengths, abilities, knowledge, experience, and weaknesses.

Step 2:   Research the organization and its needs beginning with the job description and other resources about the company.

Step 3:   Analysis of the organization's needs and culture. Analyze each job description carefully. Identify the abilities and skills for which the organization is looking. Don't limit your analysis to the listed qualifications. Also analyze the job description portion to identify more specific descriptions of those qualifications written in the context of the organizational or job task.

Step 4:   Match the most valued or important needs of the organization with your abilities and experience.

Step 5:   Draft a statement for each that:

- Clearly identifies the skill or ability.
- Provides a concrete example of a time you have demonstrated that ability or skill.

Figure 8-3 Sample Job Application Letter

Clara Robards
1312 Apple Avenue, Boise, ID 87402
(208) 324-6779, *crobards@gmail.com*

January 4, 2019

Linda Edwards, Public Relations Manager
Idaho Forestry Products, Inc.
2330 Fairview Avenue
Boise, ID 87421

Dear Ms. Edwards:

I am writing to apply for the Public Relations position that was posted on your Web site. I believe I am well qualified for this position because I have a degree in communication with a public relations emphasis, experience working in the public relations field, and am self-motivated and hard working.

While a student at Boise State University, I had several public relations internships, where I had the opportunity to practice many of the skills for which you are looking. I have written press releases, compiled press kits, pitched stories to the media, tagged editorial coverage, and worked with editors to provide contacts and other information. While interning at Micron, Inc., I acted as head PR person for the release of its X10 processor and successfully obtained coverage in major trade magazines, including LAN Times, Computer World, and Software News.

I am able to multitask, manage time well, and maintain a high level of performance. At BSU, I maintained a 3.8 GPA, while working part time, interning, and serving as scholarship chair for my sorority.

I would like to schedule an interview with you to discuss my qualifications further. I will call next week to set up an appointment with you at your earliest convenience.

Sincerely,

Clara Robards

- Ideally, mentions an achievement or concrete outcome of that skill or ability demonstration.
- Ends with a statement of how that skill or ability might contribute to the organization's specific needs or goals.

Sample body paragraph:

I have had several public relations internships, where I had the opportunity to practice many of the skills for which you are looking. I have written press releases, compiled press kits, pitched stories to the media, tagged editorial coverage, and worked with editors to provide contacts and other information. While interning at Micron, Inc., I acted as head PR person for the release of its X10 processor and successfully obtained coverage in major trade magazines, including *LAN Times, Computer World*, and *Software News*.

Step 6: Write an introduction that

- States the position you are looking for and where you learned about the opening.
- Provides a confident statement that introduces the skills and abilities you will address in your application letter.

Sample introduction:

I am writing to apply for the Public Relations position that was posted on your Web site. I believe I am well qualified for this position because I have a degree in communication with a public relations emphasis, experience working in the public relations field, and am self-motivated and hard working.

Step 7:   Write a conclusion that

- Confidently restates how you might contribute to the organization's needs or goals.

- Closes with a positive forward-looking statement.

Sample conclusion:
I would like to schedule an interview with you to discuss my qualifications further. I will call next week to set up an appointment with you at your earliest convenience.

Reviewing Your Social Media Content

If you have a Facebook page or Twitter feed, remember that your résumé isn't the only thing job recruiters will have an eye on. They'll be looking at your social media sites as well to determine whether you are the type of person they want to hire. What this means is that before starting the job application process, you should review the content of the social media in which you are involved. Here are a few tips:

Know the red flags. Certain issues are likely to create a question in an employer's mind about you as an employee. These include provocative photographs, inappropriate remarks, illegal activities, discriminatory or insensitive language, and negative comments. Remember to dig deep: With Facebook's recent switch to timeline profiles, users can quickly search a few years back with the click of a button.

Change your settings. If your accounts aren't set up to be private, now's the time to make that switch.

Use Facebook as a mini résumé. Consider using your Facebook as a way to highlight your skills and abilities, particularly those that are attractive to potential employers. Likewise, eliminate anything that reflects poorly on you—even complaints about homework.

Get rid of "text speak." Consider eliminating the use of numbers instead of words and extra letters and check for proper punctuation. Employers may use your posts as an indicator of your writing ability or the care that is taken when writing and doing other tasks.

Job Interviews

A successful interview depends on the quality of research you have done on the employer and the industry or field, your preparation, and good interpersonal skills. During an employment interview, the interviewer is typically attempting to discover whether the interviewee is a good match with the company culture in terms of attitude, values, and motivation as well as attempting to ensure that the interviewee has the skills, knowledge, and experience needed for the position. Like the initial steps in the application process, an interview is a competitive situation in which the interviewee must show that he or she is a better match and has the best skills compared to other applicants. During this process, both parties—the interviewee and the interviewer—can learn much about the other participant by demonstrating good listening skills and paying close attention to nonverbal cues. Because of this, both parties should ensure that their nonverbal cues are in alignment with the verbal message that they are attempting to send.

This section will discuss interviews from both perspectives: what an applicant should do to prepare for, perform, and follow up on an employment interview and what the interviewer should do to prepare and perform an effective interview.

Preparing for an Employment Interview from the Applicant's Perspective

Many of the issues of concern for effectively handling presentations and question-and-answer periods—as well as the techniques for preparing for and handling both those situations—are similar to those for employment interviews. In both, you have a communication purpose or purposes to achieve; often these are to persuade, to convey goodwill, and to establish your credibility. In the case of an employment interview, the purpose is to persuade your audience that you are the best person for the job by informing the interviewer that you have the skills, experience, knowledge, and personal characteristics for which the organization is looking. You are also attempting to convey goodwill by establishing the beginnings of a relationship with the interviewer and to show that you are a professional, honest, likeable, competent, motivated, and responsible person and potential employee.

In addition, in both presentations and question-and-answer sessions, as well as in job interviews, you must prepare by conducting research, strategizing, and practicing your message or answers to help ensure your ability to achieve your communication purposes and to meet your audience's needs. To prepare for a job interview, you should follow the same steps as those for writing a résumé and application letter. These are

1. *Research the organization.* The most important information you must gather is related to the job for which you are applying. What skills, experience, and knowledge is the organization looking for? What personal characteristics does the job require or does the company seek in applicants? This information is critical because it will help you to identify the key messages you must successfully convey to the interviewer. The best resource for this information can often be the advertisement for the job itself. Typically, the job posting includes all the qualifications and skills for which the company is looking.

    Of course, you should also gather other information about the company, such as the industry in which the organization is involved, the company's history, its products and services, its financial situation, its future directions and growth potential, and its corporate culture. You will need this information to show how your skills, experience, knowledge, and personal characteristics are useful to the organization. Your secondary purpose is to show the interviewer that you want the job enough to spend time learning more about the organization. Showing that you are knowledgeable about the company can also indicate that you possess other personal characteristics, such as thoroughness, preparedness, initiative, and professionalism. Demonstrating these characteristics can help set you apart from other applicants who may be less well prepared.

    Gathering this information can also help you to determine whether you are a good fit for the organization and its culture. The theory of person–organization fit essentially says that people leave jobs that are not compatible with their personalities.[1] So it is important to know yourself and your preferences regarding the kind of environment in which you will work, and to find out whether prospective employers offer that type of environment.

    In addition to the organizational culture, you should also ask questions about your direct supervisor and perhaps the company's general management philosophy. According to employment consultant Gary Moore, "It's easy to underestimate the influence individuals you'll interact with on a daily basis will have on your accomplishment or failure".[2] Moore recommends that you ask the following questions to determine the organizational culture and management philosophy of a company:

    - How does the manager deal with problems in the workplace?

    - Does the employee group work well together as a team?

    - Are there internal candidates for the position? (If not, it may be indicative that the job, or the boss, really isn't a desirable one, according to Moore.)

- Why do the employees like to work for the company?
- What is the average length of employment for employees? (If the average is less than one year or more than five years, this may be a clue to the attractiveness of working at this organization.)

2. *Identify your skills, experience, knowledge, and personal characteristics that match those for which the company is looking.* For example, if you are applying for a position that has a lot of customer contact, the hiring organization is probably interested in your people skills. These might include patience, desire to help others, and the ability to put others at ease. If you are applying for a job in which you produce data that others use, the organization might be interested in your analytical skills. In this case, you might talk about your accuracy, attention to detail, and systematic or organized approach to completing tasks.

3. *Obtain lists of the various types of questions an interviewer might ask you.* (Refer to Table 8-1 for a list of behavioral interview questions.)

Table 8-1 Behavioral Interview Questions by Skill

To answer behavioral interview questions effectively, you should first identify the skill the interviewer is asking you about; provide a brief yet relevant example in which you exercised that skill; describe your actions in the situation; and end by stating the results of that action. The following are some typical behavioral interview questions by skill.

Adaptability
- Tell me about a situation when you had to be tolerant of an opinion that was different from your own.
- Tell me about a time when you had to adjust to changes over which you had no control.

Communication
- Tell me about a time when you were able to use persuasion to convince someone to see things your way.
- Tell me about a time when you dealt with an irate customer.

Goal Setting
- Describe a goal you set for yourself and how you reached it.
- Tell me about a goal that you set and did not reach.

Problem Solving
- Tell me about a situation where you had to solve a difficult problem.
- Tell me about a time when you had to analyze information and provide a recommendation.

Teamwork
- Tell me about a time when you worked on a team and a member was not doing his or her share.
- Tell me about a time when you were working in a team in which the members did not get along.

Time Management
- Describe a situation in which you had to do a number of things at the same time.
- Tell me about a time when you were unable to complete a project on time.

4. *Practice answering the interview questions you have gathered.* Your answers should, whenever possible, highlight the skills, experience, knowledge, and/or personal characteristics that you know the company is seeking (see the previous step 2). Your goal is to show that you are a perfect fit for the job and the organization.

   If you know who will be interviewing you, you can also learn more about him or her by doing some research using the Internet and social media sites such as Facebook and LinkedIn. Stalk your interviewer on LinkedIn. What school did he or she go to? What were his or her past jobs? Do you have any similar interests in common? You never know, you may find a great point of connection. Most people won't mind if you bring up this Internet-sleuthing directly—in fact, they may appreciate that you took the time to learn more about them.

   Because hiring can be a costly undertaking for organizations, some have begun to practice interview techniques designed to better identify how an individual will actually perform on the job. One such technique is called a *behavioral interview*, which is intended to identify an individual's attitude toward and abilities in planning, communicating, problem solving, leadership, teamwork, goal setting, and decision making, among others. (See Table 8-1 for a list of sample behavioral interview questions.) One technique for formulating responses to behavioral interview questions is called the STAR, an acronym for situation, task, action, and result. To use the STAR approach, briefly describe the situation you want to use as an example, the task you or your team were to complete, the action you took to complete the task, and the result of your actions.

Example:

Question: Tell me about a time when a team member was not doing his or her share.

Response: I was working in a team for a marketing class project and one of our team members came to meetings unprepared. I decided that I would call this person every day to see whether he needed help and to see where he was on the project. I think my daily contact with him made it more difficult for him to blow off our meetings, and he realized that I valued him as a team member. The result was that he no longer came to meetings unprepared.

5. *Prepare questions to ask the interviewer about the job and the company.* (Some of these questions were addressed in step 2, but Table 8-2 provides additional questions to ask interviewers.)

- What challenges might I anticipate in this position?
- What are the expectations for the person who will fill this position?
- How would you describe the culture around the office?
- What do you like about your job?
- What do you like about working for this organization?
- What don't you like about your job?
- If given the opportunity, what suggestions would you provide if asked the question: how might this organization be improved?
- What is the average length of employment for most of the organization's employees?
- (Question to immediate prospective supervisor) How would you describe your management style?
- Can you provide me some feedback based upon our interview and my employment materials on my fit for this position?
- What is a typical day like in this job?
- What types of people would I be working with, both peers and supervisors?
- Would you describe the initial training program for this position?
- When do you expect to make a decision about this position?
- What initial advice do you wish you had been given when starting this career?

Performing the Employment Interview

As in other business communication situations, your primary purposes in a job interview are to (1) convey goodwill by showing your enthusiasm and general likeability; (2) establish credibility as a professional; and (3) persuade the interviewer that you are the best person for the job by providing quality evidence of your skills, experience, knowledge, and personal characteristics.

Table 8-2 Questions to Ask Interviewers

1. Why is this position open?
   (The response to this question may provide the interviewee insight into why the previous job holder left.)

2. What challenges might I anticipate in this position?

3. What are the expectations for the person who will fill this position?

4. How would you describe the culture around the office?

5. What do you like about your job?

6. What do you like about the company?

7. What don't you like about your job?

8. If given the opportunity, what suggestions would you provide if asked the following question: How might this organization be improved?

9. What is the average length of employment for most of the organization's employees?

10. *(Question to ask immediate supervisor)* How would you describe your management style?

11. Can you provide me some feedback based upon our interview and my employment materials regarding my fit for this position?

In other words, you must immediately make a good impression on the interviewer and then show that you are a doer—an action-oriented individual—who knows how to be a valuable contributor to the organization. Making a good first impression is critical, because research shows that most interviewers make up their minds about an applicant in the initial thirty seconds of an interview.

To achieve these purposes, you should do the following during the interview:

1. Dress professionally to help you establish your credibility. This means that, in most cases, you should dress conservatively: Wear a suit; avoid excessive jewelry, makeup, perfume, or cologne; and wear conservative shoes and a conservative hairstyle.

2. Arrive on time; be friendly to the receptionist; and bring a notepad, pen, and extra copies of your résumé.

3. Greet the interviewer with a smile and a firm handshake.

4. Sit forward in your chair to indicate interest, show enthusiasm for the interview and job, maintain eye contact, and be clear and specific in your answers and questions.

5. At the close of the interview, you should bring up any positive points about yourself that you may not have been able to address during the interview. Depending upon the situation, you might ask for feedback from the interviewer regarding your suitability for the position. If the interviewer has not provided this information, you should ask what the next steps in the hiring process are, when you might receive a response, or what you need to do to follow up. If you are really interested in the job, you might ask for it.

These same steps apply if the interview is conducted using videoconferencing. In a phone interview, your voice will be a critical tool in communicating your enthusiasm and confidence. Some tips for performing well in a phone interview are

1. **Find a good location.** Make sure you are in an area with good cellphone reception (or, ideally, use a landline), where it's quiet enough to hear and calm enough to give the interview your full attention.

2. **Prepare notes (and keep them handy).** One advantage of a phone interview is that you can create a cheat sheet for yourself. Go ahead and jot down questions, and outline answers to common questions or other information you want to make sure you mention.

3. **Practice your answers.** In many ways you'll want to treat the phone interview as you would an in-person interview. Consider your answers to common interview questions beforehand

(your best/worst traits, occasions in which you faced a challenge, where you see yourself in five years, etc.)

4. **Dress the part.** The image we project of ourselves doesn't just communicate through appearance—it shows in our mannerisms, speech, and other subtle cues. Dressing up for a phone interview may sound silly, but the right clothing will put you in the right mindset.

5. **Keep your resume, cover letter, and the job description handy**, whether in paper form on your desk or a few clicks away on your computer.

6. **Smile**. Your interviewer will pick up on your emotional state. In fact, she will be paying even more attention to it, since she or he doesn't get to see you. People can *hear* your smile, which makes them smile and think positive thoughts about you on the other end of the line.

7. **Keep it conversational.** Remember, interviewers aren't just looking for the perfect candidate—they want to find an employee they will enjoy working with, too.

8. **Speak clearly.** Speak clearly so your interviewer can hear you well, and keep water handy in case your mouth gets dry.

9. **Ask about different aspects of the job and express genuine interest and excitement about the opportunity.** Don't be afraid to dig for more details about the position. You need to get a *real* sense of the job to know if it's a good fit for you.[3]

After the interview, if you are interested in the position, you should write the interviewer a thank-you note, reiterating your interest in the position and covering any points you were unable to make in the interview. This is one last opportunity for you to distinguish yourself from other applicants, who often do not follow through with this last step. Handwritten notes often make the best impression, because they are personal. However, if you have been communicating with the interviewee via e-mail, this channel has become more acceptable as a means of expressing appreciation.

? Critical Thinking

Based on your past interviewing experiences, with which steps in the interviewing process do you feel most confident? Which steps might you improve? What can you do immediately to improve your interviewing skills?

 ## Responsible Communication

Those little lies on people's résumés tend to grow during important job interviews, say researchers at the University of Massachusetts at Amherst. "Basically, the more stringent the job requirements, the more candidates lie about their qualifications," says Brent Weiss, a psychology graduate student and coauthor of a study presented at a meeting of the Society for Personality and Social Psychology.[4]

Weiss's study examined how often people lied in job interviews and how personality influences the propensity to fib. Thirty-eight college students applied for and were granted interviews for tutorial jobs that didn't exist.[5] The interview focused on their math or verbal skills. After researchers came clean about the study, they asked students to review their videotaped interviews and identify what they had lied about. Overall, 84 percent admitted to lying at some point. People told straight-out lies, such as, "I'm very good at math," when they had no facility with arithmetic whatsoever.[6]

Other studies indicate the rate of lying on résumés or in job interviews at 20 to 44 percent.[7] That includes lies about degrees, past jobs, and responsibilities.

"A lot of HR managers are recognizing that lying is pervasive," said Westaff vice president and director of human resources Joe Coute. "For too many candidates, the desire to get ahead at all costs is more important than honesty. Because of that, interviewers can find themselves focusing on what might be wrong with what someone's saying rather than what might be right. They figure that if a candidate will lie during the interview, then they are going to lie once they're in the door."[8]

Questions for Discussion

1. What are the dangers of lying during a job interview?

2. Is omitting information during an interview a form of lying?

Writing the Thank-You or Follow-Up Message

Another simple way to distinguish yourself from the competition is to write a thank-you e-mail immediately after the interview. According to a study by Accountemps, only half of job applicants send thank-you messages, while 88 percent of executives say that a thank-you note influences their hiring decisions. A thank-you message should

1. Sincerely state the main idea of appreciation for the interview and the information gained.
2. Include unique points discussed during the interview and relate them to the position, which ideally increases goodwill.
3. Assure the employer of continued interest in the position.
4. Close on a confident, forward-looking note.

Figure 8-4 provides a sample thank-you e-mail.

Figure 8-4 Sample Thank-You E-mail

To: Daniel Rosko

From: Terri Edwards

Subject: Thank You for the Interview

Dear Mr. Rosko:

Thank you for the opportunity to visit Global Aerospace for an on-site interview yesterday. I enjoyed meeting you and appreciated the tour of your operation and the opportunity to learn about the exciting technological developments being made at Global Aerospace.

I was impressed with the many friendly and knowledgeable employees and their willingness to speak with me about their work and loyalty to Global Aerospace.

My visit reinforced my interest and assured me that my internship with Stark Technologies would enable me to contribute immediately to your design efforts. My work at Shelland University on the drone project is particularly applicable to some of the projects being developed in your labs.

Mr. Rosko, I am eager to receive an offer from Global Aerospace for the entry-level engineering position. If you need additional information in the meantime, please contact me.

Thanks again,

Terri Edwards

Conducting Employment Interviews

Conducting employment interviews is a critical task because of the potential costs to the organization. One survey shows that the direct cost to fill a $60,000 position ranges from $9,777 to $49,000: costs of advertising, interviewing, testing and conducting background and reference checks, relocation fees, and training costs.[9] However, indirect costs can be even higher. These include opportunity costs or lost revenue; ramp-up time, which is about three months in length; and consulting fees, among other things. If an appropriate candidate isn't selected, then costs go even higher as a replacement must be sought.

The Pre-Interview Process

A number of steps are involved in the pre-interview process. Depending upon the company's policies and procedures, managers may be involved in different aspects of this process.

The interview process typically begins by communicating that an employee is being sought. A variety of media is used to advertise open positions, including word of mouth, electronic job boards, company Web sites, and print media, such as magazines and newspapers. These postings should identify the qualifications that are being sought for the position; these can help to weed out applicants who are not qualified.

Applications can be received in a variety of ways as well. More and more, applications are being received via electronic methods, although some organizations still solicit and accept paper submissions.

Once the application packages start rolling in, the interviewer's work generally begins. The first step might be to screen the application packages to identify potentially well-qualified applicants. If the job posting contained a list of qualifications, skills, and experiences for the position, this list can be used to identify the potentially well-qualified candidates as well as those who may not be qualified or not as well qualified. The appearance and completeness of the application package might also be used as an indicator of applicants' care and attention to detail.

Once potentially qualified candidates are identified, a telephone interview might be considered as a low-cost, efficient way of determining whether a candidate's qualifications, experience, workplace preferences, and salary needs are congruent with the position and organization.

Once the best candidates have been identified, the interviewer must develop a list of questions for the interview itself. An interviewee's list of qualities, skills, knowledge, and experience developed for the résumé-screening process should be used to create or select the questions. Because hiring can be such a costly undertaking, you might consider using behavioral interviewing to determine how an individual will actually perform on the job. As discussed previously, behavioral interviewing is intended to identify an individual's attitude toward and abilities in planning, communicating, problem solving, leadership, teamwork, goal setting, and decision making, among others. (See lists of sample behavioral interviewing questions in Table 8-1.)

When developing the list of interview questions, it is important to avoid those that might make your company the target of a lawsuit from the U.S. Equal Employment Opportunity Commission (EEOC). Avoid questions that have to do with a person's marital status, age, weight, race, sexual orientation, religion, or ethnicity, and whether they have children, a disability, or an arrest record.

The following are examples of questions to avoid in interviews because they may be alleged to show illegal bias:

- Are you a U.S. citizen? (national origin)
- Do you have a visual, speech, or hearing disability?
- Are you planning to have a family? When?
- Have you ever filed a workers' compensation claim?
- How many days of work did you miss last year due to illness?
- What off-the-job activities do you participate in?
- Would you have a problem working with a female partner?
- Where did you grow up?
- Do you have children? How old are they?
- What year did you graduate from high school? (age)

In addition to preparing a list of questions, the interviewer should consider how to open the interview, the order of the questions, and how to close the interview. The opening for an interview establishes the climate of the exchange. Nonverbal communication plays a critical role. A friendly greeting, firm handshake, and smile should help to put interviewees at ease. Some time might also be spent on small talk to help establish rapport and a friendly, positive climate for the exchange.

This climate can be extended into the interview itself by positioning more general, less pointed questions at the beginning and then working toward more specific questions or those that are more difficult or pointed.

The close of the interview should reinforce the initial climate of the interview. The interviewer might summarize the next steps in the process, offer to answer questions, and provide a statement of appreciation and a handshake. Any promises of employment should be avoided.

Holding the Interview

One of the challenges of an employment interview is the fact that the interviewer and the interviewee have differing interests. That is, the interviewer wants to know what the prospective employee's strengths *and* weaknesses are, whereas the interviewee generally wishes to focus on strengths. There are also the problems associated with inaccurate perceptional inferences, such as stereotyping, attribution, and impression formation, which were discussed in Chapter 2.

During the job interview, the interviewer should be aware of these challenges and try to compensate for them. The interviewer should try to make the candidate feel comfortable so as to better enable him or her to demonstrate knowledge, skills, and experience.

As an interviewer, you might consider taking brief notes during the conversation so that you can provide a more complete report at the end. However, note-taking should not detract from your ability to listen to the candidate or to maintain eye contact and provide other nonverbal behaviors that signal interest. Remember, you are there to gather information, so let the interviewee do the bulk of the talking.

After the interview, you should immediately flesh out your notes, because we don't retain much of what we hear. You might consider creating a form to streamline the evaluation and note-taking process.

Performance Appraisals

performance appraisal

A structured formal interaction between a subordinate and supervisor that usually takes the form of a periodic interview in which the work performance of the subordinate is examined and discussed, with a view to identifying weaknesses and strengths as well as opportunities for improvement and skills development.

Second only to firing an employee, managers cite performance appraisal as the task they dislike the most.[10] This is understandable given that the process of performance appraisal, as traditionally practiced, is often not well planned or carried out. **Performance appraisal** may be defined as a structured formal interaction between a subordinate and supervisor that usually takes the form of a periodic interview in which the work performance of the subordinate is examined and discussed, with a view to identifying weaknesses and strengths as well as opportunities for improvement and skills development.

Performance appraisal systems began as a simple method to determine whether the salary or wage of an individual employee was justified. Little consideration, if any, was given to the developmental possibilities of appraisal. It was felt that a cut or rise in pay should provide the only required impetus for an employee to either improve or continue to perform well. However, studies found that extrinsic motivators were not the only issues that mattered to employees. In addition to pay rates, it was found that other issues, such as morale and self-esteem, could also have a major influence on performance.

In many—but not all—organizations, appraisal results are used, either directly or indirectly, to help determine reward outcomes. That is, the appraisal results are used to identify the better-performing employees who should get the majority of available merit pay increases, bonuses, and promotions.

Appraisal results are also used to identify the poorer performers who may require some form of counseling or, in extreme cases, demotion, dismissal, or decreases in pay. (Organizations need to be aware of laws in their country that might restrict their capacity to dismiss employees or decrease pay.) Whether the assignment and justification of rewards and penalties are an appropriate use of performance appraisal is a very uncertain and contentious matter.

Many reputable sources have expressed doubts about the validity and reliability of the performance appraisal process. Some have even suggested that the process is so inherently flawed that it may be impossible to perfect it.[11]

At the other extreme, there are many strong advocates of performance appraisal. Some view it as potentially "… the most crucial aspect of organizational life."[12]

Clearly, there are many different opinions on how and when to apply the performance appraisal process. For instance, some believe that performance appraisal has many important employee development uses, but scorn any attempt to link the process to reward outcomes, such as pay raises and promotions.

This group believes that the linkage to reward outcomes reduces or eliminates the developmental value of appraisals. Rather than an opportunity for constructive review and encouragement, the reward-linked process is perceived as judgmental, punitive, and uncomfortable. In addition, employees under review may feel compelled to distort or deny the truth. They may become defensive. Whenever the employee's performance is rated as less than the best, or less than the level at which he or she perceives, the appraiser may be viewed as punitive. This can affect the manager's credibility and negatively impact the relationship with the employee. Even worse, the result can be resentment and serious morale damage, leading to workplace disruption and productivity declines.

Many appraisers feel uncomfortable with the combined role of judge and jury. The task also requires good record-keeping and interpersonal skills. The manager should justify the evaluation with specific examples. No one likes receiving criticism, so the manager must be skilled at avoiding a defensive response from the employee and dealing with conflict productively if it occurs. Because of a lack of comfort with these potential outcomes, managers may avoid giving honest feedback.

It is important, however, that when appraisals are conducted, the results are clearly linked to the rewards. This can help avoid situations in which employees perceive that merit raises and bonuses are decided arbitrarily and sometimes in secret by managers and supervisors.

Most of these problems can be avoided with the proper process in place and effective communication skills. Creating an effective performance management system starts with how a position is defined and ends when it has been determined why an excellent employee left the organization for another opportunity.

Within such a system, feedback to employees occurs regularly. Individual performance objectives are measurable and based on prioritized goals that support the accomplishment of the overall goals of the total organization. The vibrancy and performance of the organization can better be ensured because the focus is on development and providing appropriate opportunities for each employee.

Providing Performance Feedback

In a performance management system, feedback remains integral to successful practice. Ideally, however, the feedback is a discussion. Both the staff member and the manager have an equivalent opportunity to bring information to the dialogue. Feedback is often obtained from peers, direct-reporting staff, and customers to enhance mutual understanding of an individual's contribution and developmental needs. (This is commonly known as 360-degree feedback.) The developmental plan establishes the organization's commitment to help each person continue to expand his or her knowledge and skills. This is the foundation upon which a continuously improving organization builds.

When providing performance feedback, consider the following:

- **Encourage discussion.** Research studies show that employees are likely to feel more satisfied with their appraisal result if they have the chance to talk freely and discuss their performance. It is also more likely that such employees will be better able to meet future performance goals.[13]

  Employees are also more likely to feel that the appraisal process is fair if they are given a chance to talk about their performance. This is especially so when employees are permitted to challenge and appeal their evaluation.[14]

- **Be constructive.** It is very important that employees recognize that negative appraisal feedback is provided with a constructive intention, that is, to help them overcome present difficulties and to improve their future performance. Employees will be less anxious about criticism and more likely to find it useful when they believe that the appraiser's intentions are helpful and constructive.[15]

  In contrast, other studies have reported that "destructive criticism"—which is vague, ill-informed, unfair, or harshly presented—will lead to such problems as anger, resentment, tension, and workplace conflict, as well as increased resistance to improvement, denial of problems, and poorer performance.[16]

- **Set performance goals.** It has been shown in numerous studies that setting goals is an important element in employee motivation. Goals can stimulate employee effort, focus attention, increase persistence, and encourage employees to find new and better ways to work.[17]

  The usefulness of goals as a stimulus to human motivation is one of the best-supported theories in management. It is also quite clear that goals that are "specific, difficult and accepted by employees will lead to higher levels of performance than easy, vague goals (such as do your best) or no goals at all."[18]

- **Maintain credibility.** It is important that the appraiser be well informed and credible. Appraisers should feel comfortable with the techniques of appraisal and should be knowledgeable about the employee's job and performance. When these conditions exist, employees are more likely to view the appraisal process as accurate and fair. They also express more acceptance of the appraiser's feedback and a greater willingness to change.[19]

Dealing with Conflict

Invariably, when conducting performance appraisals, the need arises to provide an employee with less than flattering feedback. The skill and sensitivity used to handle these often difficult sessions is critical. If the appraisee accepts the negative feedback and resolves to improve, all is well. However, if the result is an angry or hurt employee, then the process of correction has failed. The performance of an employee in such cases is unlikely to improve and may deteriorate even further.

When providing criticism to an employee, consider the following techniques:

- **Self-auditing.** Appraisers should not confront employees directly with criticism. Rather, they should aim to let the evidence of poor performance emerge "naturally" during the course of the appraisal interview. This is done by way of open-ended questioning techniques that encourage employees to identify their own performance problems.[20]

  Instead of blunt statements or accusations, an appraiser should encourage an employee to talk freely about impressions of his or her performance. For example, consider the case of an employee who has had too many absent days. The appraiser, in accusatory mode, might say:

  "Your attendance record is unacceptable. You'll have to improve it."

  A better way to handle this might be to say:

  "Your attendance record shows that you had seven days off work in six months. What can you tell me about this?"

  Using this technique allows an appraiser to calmly present the evidence (resisting the temptation to label it as good or bad) and then invite the employee to comment. In many cases, an employee with problems will admit that weaknesses do exist. This is more likely to occur when an employee does not feel accused of anything, nor forced to make admissions that he or she does not wish to make. This technique described by Krein is a type of self-auditing, because it encourages underperforming employees to confront themselves with their own work and performance issues.

■ **Ownership of problems.** Perhaps the most powerful aspect of the self-auditing process is that employees are generally more willing to accept personal "ownership" of problems that have been self-identified. This sense of ownership provides an effective basis for stimulating change and development.

Nevertheless, some individuals will not admit to anything that appears to reflect poorly on them. With ego defenses on full alert, they will resist the process of self-auditing very strongly. In such cases, appraisers may have no choice but to confront the poor performer directly and firmly with the evidence they have.

Sometimes the shock of direct confrontation will result in the employee admitting that he or she does need to make improvements. Sometimes it will just make his or her denial of the problem worse.

In providing any feedback—especially negative feedback—appraisers should be willing and able to support their opinions with specific and clear examples. Vague generalizations should be avoided. The focus should be on job-related behaviors and attitudes. If a specific observation cannot be supported by clear evidence, or touches on issues that are not job-related, it may be best to exclude all mention of it.

Receiving Performance Feedback

As uncomfortable as giving performance feedback might be without the proper skills and preparation, receiving feedback might be worse, particularly if we aren't prepared. Probably the biggest danger of receiving feedback is becoming defensive. It is natural to want to defend ourselves if we feel we are being attacked. However, becoming defensive isn't helpful because it might damage our credibility and it inhibits our ability to listen. It can be helpful to remember that the comments from a trusted supervisor or manager are not meant to hurt you but to help you to perform better. Therefore, your purpose is to listen and to gather important information during the feedback process.

If you do have a tendency to become anxious or defensive in performance appraisal situations, you might find the tactics for dealing with presentation anxiety that were described in Chapter 7 to be helpful. Tactics for receiving feedback include the following:

■ Listen carefully and avoid interrupting the appraiser.

■ Ask questions for clarification.

■ Acknowledge the feedback. Use the active listening techniques described in Chapter 9, such as paraphrasing, to let the appraiser know you understood what was said.

■ Agree with what is true and possible, and acknowledge the appraiser's point of view (for example, "I can see how you got that impression."). Agreeing with what's true or possible does not mean that you agree to change your behavior or that you agree with a value judgment about you.

■ Try to understand the appraiser's perspective. Doing so may enable you to gain a greater understanding of the issues.

■ Ask for time to reflect, if needed. It is reasonable to ask for time to think about what was said, but don't use this time to avoid the issue. Make an appointment to get back to the appraiser.

Summary

When preparing for the job application process, researching potential employers, your chosen field or industry, and the overall job market will provide you the information you need to develop most of the content of your employment message. The other information you will need are the skills, abilities, experience, and personal characteristics that might appeal to a potential employer. With this information, you are prepared to draft and develop a résumé and an application letter as well as prepare for the job interview process.

A résumé is a list of the skills, abilities, and experience that you bring to an employer and is aimed at getting you a job interview. Templates for creating résumés are available in Microsoft Word and other software programs. A résumé must show that you are qualified for the position for which you are applying and should be carefully prepared to eliminate any errors.

An application letter is generally targeted to a specific employer and is a persuasive message that is intended to highlight your accomplishments and relate them to the specific contributions you can make to an organization. Your research should provide the information you need to identify the organization's needs and match your own abilities and skills to those needs.

During the job interview process, the interviewer and the interviewee are attempting to convey and obtain information verbally, a process that requires good listening skills on both their parts. Much information that is passed may be in the form of nonverbal communication. As with many communication situations, proper preparation and planning can help ensure a successful interview, both on the part of the interviewee as well as the interviewer. After each interview, it is important to immediately send a thank-you e-mail to help distinguish yourself from the competition.

During the performance appraisal process, preparation on the part of the appraiser as well as the appraisee can help to ensure that the appraisal is useful to both parties. To ensure success, an effective performance appraisal process needs to be in place, one that ensures that both parties know the specific requirements of the job so that specific issues related to its performance can be addressed clearly.

Key Term

performance appraisal **217**

Discussion Questions

1. What is the purpose of researching employers, your chosen field or industry, and the job market before beginning the application process? How can doing so benefit the applicant?
2. What are the differences between a résumé and an application letter?
3. What is behavioral interviewing? Describe the STAR approach for formulating responses to behavioral interview questions.
4. Why is it important to send a thank-you e-mail after an interview?
5. What is the appropriate stance to take during a performance appraisal? What are some of the phrases or statements that might be used to help create this stance?

Applications

1. Find and print a job description for a position for which you might apply. Working alone, write down the skills and abilities that are described in the job description.
   - Identify situations in which you have demonstrated these skills.
   - Write down an example of a time you exhibited that skill.
   - Consider whether you can add a specific result.
   - Pair up with another student and share your list.
     - Could the wording be improved?
     - Brainstorm additional skills you might address and their wording.

   How would this exercise change the content or approach to your résumé? Application letter? Job interview?

2. Review your Facebook page, Twitter feed, or other social networking site. Identify the changes that need to be made and write a plan for revising your content so that it showcases the abilities and skills that employers may find attractive.

3. Prepare written answers to all the behavioral interview questions listed in Table 8-1, which can be found on page 211 of this chapter.

4. Identify a job for which you might be interviewing applicants in the future. Prepare a list of questions that you might use to conduct an employment interview for the position.

5. Prepare for a performance appraisal by listing your accomplishments over the past year and your goals for improvement and growth for the coming year. Be sure to provide specific evidence of your accomplishments and identify the concrete ways that your goals will benefit your employer and you as an employee in terms of your contribution.

Endnotes

1. Robbins, S. P. (2001) *Organizational Behavior* (9th ed.). Upper Saddle River, NJ: Prentice Hall, p. 103.

2. Moore, G. (2004, August 29). Investigation during job search allows you to select wisely. *The Daily Breeze*, E1.

3. Kim., L. (n.d.). Seventeen phone interview tips to guarantee a follow-up. *Inc.* Retrieved August 18, 2017 from *https://www.inc.com/larry-kim/17-phone-interview-tips-to-guarantee-a-follow-up.html*

4. Pirisi, A. (2003). Lying in job interviews. *Psychology Today* (May–June). Retrieved March 25, 2005, from *http://www.psychologytoday.com/articles/pto-20030711-000001.html*.

5. Ibid.

6. Ibid.

7. Lying: How can you protect your company? (n.d.) *Your Workplace*, Monthly Newsletter of Westaff XXXVI. Retrieved March 25, 2005, from *http://www.westaff.com/yourworkplace/ywissue37_full.html*.

8. Lying: How can you protect your company? (n.d.) *Your Workplace*, Monthly Newsletter of Westaff XXXVI. Retrieved March 25, 2005, from *http://www.westaff.com/yourworkplace/ywissue37_full.html*.

9. Del Monte, J. (2009). IT employer information – Cost of hiring/turnover. JDA Professional Services, Inc. Retrieved October 16, 2009, from *http://www.jdapsi.com/Client/articles/Default.php?Article=coh*.

10. Heathfield, S. M. (2009). Performance appraisals don't work: The traditional performance appraisal process. Retrieved October 16, 2009, from *http://humanresources.about.com/od/performanceevals/a/perf_appraisal.htm*.

11. Derven, M. G. (1990). The paradox of performance appraisals. *Personnel Journal*, 69 (February), 107–111.

12. Lawrie, J. (1990). Prepare for a performance appraisal. *Personnel Journal*, 69 (April), 132–136.

13. Nemoroff, W. F., & Wexley, K. N. (1979). An exploration of the relationships between the performance feedback interview characteristics and interview outcomes as perceived by managers and subordinates. *Journal of Occupational Psychology*, 52, 25–34.

14. Greenberg, J. (1986). Determinants of perceived fairness of performance evaluation. *Journal of Applied Psychology*, 71, 340–342.

15. Fedor, D. B., Eder, R. W., & Buckley, M. R. (1989). The contributory effects of supervisor intentions on subordinate feedback responses. *Organizational Behavior and Human Decision Processes*, 44, 396–414.

16. Baron, R. A. (1988). Negative effects of destructive criticism: impact on conflict, self-efficacy, and task performance. *Journal of Applied Psychology*, 73, 199–207.

17. Locke, E. A., Shaw, K. N., Saari, L. M., & Latham, G. P. (1981). Goal setting and task performance: 1969–1980. *Psychological Bulletin*, 90, 125–152.

18. Harris, D. M., & DeSimone, R. L. (1994). *Human Resource Development*. Fort Worth, TX: Dryden Press.

19. Bannister, B. D. (1986). Performance outcome feedback and attributional feedback: Interactive effects on recipient responses. *Journal of Applied Psychology*, 71, 203–210.

20. Krein, T. J. (1990). Performance reviews that rate an "A." *Personnel Journal*, 67 (May), 38–40.

RadioShack: *You've Got Mail!*

Julian Day was brought on as CEO of RadioShack to turn the company around following years of financial decay and instability in upper management. The British executive had been part of the turnaround of other U.S. corporations including K-Mart, now owned by Sears, and Safeway, Inc.[1] Day wanted to waste no time implementing the turnaround plan that the executives and Board had agreed upon prior to his arrival.

RadioShack Corporation

RadioShack is a consumer electronics goods and services retailer that operates more than 4,460 retail stores in the U.S., Puerto Rico, and the Virgin Islands. In addition to the RadioShack retail store chain, the company also operates nearly 800 non-branded kiosks, offering wireless handsets and accessories. They also manage direct-to-home satellite services through 1,500 dealer outlets offering both RadioShack and third party products and services to consumers who live in smaller markets, and an e-commerce web site, *www.RadioShack.com*. The electronics goods industry is highly competitive and RadioShack is currently third in the U.S. market behind big box stores Best Buy and Circuit City. The company is headquartered in Fort Worth, Texas and had approximately 40,000 employees at the end of 2006.[2]

Instability in Upper Management

Over the past several years, RadioShack has undergone a series of executive management changes including ten new appointments to vice presidential and c-suite level positions since 2004. The most significant change in the executive-level shuffle of employees is the instability in the CEO position: Leonard Roberts, David Edmondson, and Julian Day have all reported for the position in the last two years. Roberts retired from his chief executive position in favor of a seat on RadioShack's Board of Directors.[3] Edmondson, however, left his position after making the scandalous revelation that he had falsified his resume by claiming to hold two academic degrees he had never earned.[4] Day was brought in at the beginning of July 2006 to help turn RadioShack around because of his positive record in reviving financially unstable retail companies.

Financial Troubles and Turnaround Plan

The change in management and the intense competition in the marketplace have not gone unnoticed in the company's financials. RadioShack's stock price had been underperforming and both its 2005 and 2006 Annual Reports contain letters to shareholders that are apologetic in nature. As the following tables show, stock prices were down from 2004 and RadioShack lagged its major competitors in revenues and earnings.

Competitor Financials, RadioShack
Prepared by Mergent Online, obtained May 3, 2007

	Revenues	Net Income	EBITDA
Best Buy Inc	30848000000	1140000000	2100000000
Circuit City Stores, Inc.	11597686000	139746000	402921000
RadioShack Corp.	*4777500000*	*73400000*	*286400000*

This case was prepared by Research Assistant Ashley Frankart under the direction of James S. O'Rourke, Concurrent Professor of Management, as the basis for class discussion rather than to illustrate either effective or ineffective handling of an administrative situation. Information was gathered from corporate as well as public sources.

1. RadioShack Corporation. RadioShack Corporation Elects Julian Day Chairman and Chief Executive Officer: Retail Veteran Brings Strong Track Record to RadioShack. 7 July 2006. 1 May 2007 <*http://www.radioshackcorporation.com/ir/release_details_main. php?id=570*>.

2. Mergent Online. *RadioShack Corporation*. 2007. 2 May 2007 <*http://www.mergentonline.com.lib-proxy.nd.edu/ compdetail.asp?company=-1&company_mer=8097&fvtype=a&Page=business*>.

3. Norris, Floyd. RadioShack Chief Resigns After Lying. 21. Feb. 2006. 2 May 2007 <*http://www.nytimes.com/2006/02/21/ business/21radio.html?ex=1298178000&en=e17273c6993a9393&ei=5090&p artner=rssuserland&emc=rss*>.

4. RadioShack Corporation 2005 Annual Report, *RadioShackCorporation.com*.

Common Stock Information
Trading Price Range for RadioShack Corporation

Per Share	Quarter End (March 31)			Quarter End (June 30)		
	2006	*2005*	*2004*	**2006**	*2005*	*2004*
High	$ 22.90	$ 34.48	$ 36.24	$ 18.83	$ 26.43	$ 33.73
Low	$ 18.74	$ 23.75	$ 28.86	$ 14.00	$ 23.11	$ 28.28
Close	$ 19.23	$ 24.50	$ 33.16	$ 14.00	$ 23.17	$ 28.63

Per Share	Quarter End (Sept. 30)			Quarter End (Dec. 30)		
	2006	*2005*	*2004*	**2006**	*2005*	*2004*
High	$ 19.71	$ 27.24	$ 31.27	$ 20.40	$ 25.00	$ 34.06
Low	$ 13.76	$ 22.81	$ 26.04	$ 16.49	$ 20.55	$ 28.09
Close	$ 19.30	$ 24.80	$ 28.64	$ 16.78	$ 21.03	$ 32.88

Created using information obtained from 2005 and 2006 Annual 10-K Report

Additionally, total stockholder equity had deteriorated from 922,100,000 in 2004 to 653,800,000 in 2006.[5] Management has realized its obligation to increase the firm's financial performance and has laid out a turnaround plan with the following three objectives: increase average unit sales volume, rationalize the firm's cost structure, and grow profitable square footage of retail space. In describing how the goals would be attained, management addressed the consolidation of distribution centers, reallocation of resources among RadioShack stores to reflect profitability, updating the inventory and product line offerings, and reducing overhead costs.[6]

Overhead Costs = Hundreds of Jobs

The public's initial response to Day's appointment as CEO and the turnaround plan was positive and RadioShack was given the confidence to move forward with the plan. One month after assuming the chief executive's position, Day issued the following press release:

August 10, 2006:

RadioShack Corporation (NYSE: RSH) announced today that the company plans to reduce its workforce by approximately 400 to 450 positions across its various support functions. This move will reduce the company's overhead expense and improve its long-term competitive position in the marketplace.

Most of RadioShack's planned reductions will affect positions at its headquarters operation. The exact number of employees affected has yet to be determined; however, the reduction will include employees at all levels. RadioShack will notify affected employees by early September.

Earlier this year, RadioShack announced a turnaround plan designed to increase average unit volume, lower overhead costs and grow profitable square footage. Since the plan's announcement in February, the company has closed 480 underperforming stores, consolidated its distribution centers, embarked on a cost restructuring program, and liquidated end-of-life merchandise to make room for a new product assortment in its more than 6,000 stores nationwide.

---

5. RadioShack Corporation. *Official Press Release Announcing Impending Layoffs: RadioShack Corporation Announces Planned Reduction in Its Workforce*. 10 Aug. 2006.2 Apr. 2007 <*http://www.radioshack.com/ir/release_details_main.php?id=576*>.

6. USA Today. RadioShack Lays off Employees via Email. 30 Aug. 2006. 12 Apr. 2007 <*http://www.usatoday.com/tech/news/2006-08-30-radioshack-email-layoffs_x.htm*>.

Employee Perceptions

RadioShack corporate headquarters employees were unprepared for the sudden announcement as recent communications had praised their talents as RadioShack's principal enabling factor in turning the company around. Managers approached their teams soon after the press release to inform them that the workforce reduction would be a swift process enabled by the company's intranet. Employees soon began losing confidence in many of the company's public claims, however, including the following, used on the corporate careers website: "It begins by celebrating diversity and passion in every department and at every level. Our professional development programs, workflow and communication processes make great thinking possible. Our people make great things happen."

You've Got Mail!

Employees and investors awaited the impending layoffs in September of 2006 and, on an otherwise uneventful autumn day, nearly 400 employees were given their termination notice with the following words:

> "The workforce reduction notification is currently in progress. Unfortunately your position is one that has been eliminated."

If these words seem stark, then consider their method of delivery: *this message was sent out to the affected employees via their company e-mail account.*

The press and professional organizations of communications and human resources professionals balked at the communication method used in the layoffs. A *Fort Worth Star-Tribune* reporter wrote the original story which made AP news and appeared in national publications such as *USA Today* and *The New York Times* and web logs popped up as seemingly everyone on the Internet was talking about the e-mailed termination notices.

Discussion Questions

1. Additional layoffs, distribution center and retail location closings, and the redistribution of resources throughout the organization continue to loom on the horizon as Day puts RadioShack's turnaround plan into action. What can be done by RadioShack to ensure future communications are handled appropriately?
2. Who is responsible for the communications decision and should there be action taken against the individual(s)?
3. What should RadioShack have done in response to the negative publicity?
4. Can you identify the stakeholders in this case and specify what's at stake for each of them?
5. Which issues are most critical for RadioShack corporate management at this point? Can you rank-order those issues according to urgency?
6. Does the company have sufficient internal expertise and staff to manage this issue on their own, or will they require the assistance of a communications consultant?

Writing Assignment

Please respond in writing to the issues presented in this case by preparing two documents: a communications strategy memo and a professional business letter. You should assume the role of a senior level task force member from either human resources or corporate communications. The task force has been put together to address the issues presented by the case. The strategy memo addressed to Julian Day, CEO of RadioShack Corporation, should communicate the details of the case, discuss critical issues and their implications, offer recommendations for action and show how to communicate the solution to those who are affected.

Chapter 9

Communicating with Employees

The Case of Resisted Change Efforts

"What's wrong?" Rita asked her friend Lucy as the waiter placed their coffee on the table. Both women said "thanks" simultaneously to the young man and then Rita resumed. "You sounded so demoralized on the phone. I hope it isn't your new job."

"Well, unfortunately, it is," Lucy replied, taking a sip of coffee. "I feel like I've been bushwhacked."

"How so?" Rita asked.

"You know that I've been appointed team leader for the COMPLEXion line. My supervisor told me that she was appointing me because she wanted to see some changes. When I got hired, I heard so many positive things about my colleagues, but now I'm wondering if any of them are true." Lucy paused and picked up a menu. "You know, I haven't had any lunch. Do you want to get something to nibble on?"

"Unfortunately, I've had my lunch and I'm afraid I overate," Rita giggled, then added, "As usual. But please, go ahead and get something. I don't mind if you eat. Just don't order anything too yummy. I may be tempted to eat more."

Lucy signaled to the waiter.

"So what's going on?" Rita prodded. "What's the deal with your colleagues?"

"Well, to sum it up, they don't want to change. They have been working on this product line, some for ten years or more, and they don't see any need for it. You know the old saw, 'If it ain't broke, why fix it?' And, of course, they wonder who am I—a newcomer—to tell them any different. You would have thought that my supervisor would have expected this and would have warned me. After all, she's worked there a decade, too." Lucy stopped and took another drink from her cup, then added, "Maybe I'm not the right person for the job."

She turned to the waiter who had approached the table. "Yes, miss," he said. "What can I get you?"

After reading this chapter, you will be able to

- *Identify different interpersonal styles of communication and recognize the importance of being assertive and creating a genuine dialogue in the workplace.*

- *Understand the different elements of nonverbal communication.*

- *Identify whether you are an effective listener and put into practice the steps to become a more effective listener.*

- *Plan and facilitate effective meetings.*

- *Understand how to motivate employees through communication practices.*

- *Communicate change to employees.*

Case Questions

1. As a newcomer to the organization, what does Lucy need to do to successfully make change within her team? What obstacles must she overcome and how might she do so?

2. Did Lucy's supervisor make the right call in appointing Lucy team leader? Are there advantages to her being a newcomer to the organization? What might her supervisor have done, if anything, to make Lucy's transition to team leader easier?

3. How difficult is it to make change within an organization? What factors may affect the success of organizational change efforts?

Interpersonal Communication in the Workplace

From an organizational perspective, relationships can play an important role in producing effective supervision, promoting social support among employees, building personal influence, and ensuring productivity through smooth work flow. **Interpersonal communication** involves mutual influence, usually for the purpose of managing relationships.[1]

The recent flattening of organizational hierarchies and resulting interdependency of work tasks among employees, as well as the increasing diversity of the workplace, creates a need for corporate cultures of trust built on respect for differences and mutual cooperation. Informal interpersonal relationships and communication networks are the most dynamic sources of power in organizations today. (Communication networks are discussed later in this chapter.) This change provides an opportunity for leaders and aspiring leaders whose task is to motivate and inspire others through their communication skills and knowledge. Compared to these dynamic sources of power, more formal relationships are slower and less trustworthy sources of information. Knowing this, most decision makers rely heavily on verbal information from people they trust.

The need for excellent interpersonal skills is echoed in a *Wall Street Journal* survey, in which recruiters said that such skills and the ability to work well in a team were the top two characteristics they found most attractive in prospective employees. Interpersonal skills and the ability to work well in a team are founded upon trust. **Trust** can be understood as the confidence that our peers' intentions are good.[2] In other words, we must believe that those with whom we work will not act opportunistically or take advantage of us and others to narrowly pursue their own self-interests.

Recent studies indicate that trust has five components: integrity, competence, consistency, loyalty, and openness.[3] *Integrity* refers to a person's ethical character and basic honesty. To feel that our peers are *competent*, we must be convinced that they have the technical knowledge and interpersonal skills to perform their jobs. If we don't believe coworkers are competent, we are unlikely to depend upon them or respect their opinions on work-related matters. We are more able to trust those who appear *consistent* in their behavior or who are reliable, predictable, and demonstrate good judgment. We tend to trust others who are *loyal* and willing to protect and help others to save face. Finally, we tend to trust those who are *open* and, conversely, find it difficult to trust those who appear evasive, deceptive, or secretive.

Additional factors affect our ability to forge the relationships businesspeople depend upon so much: valuing relationships, assertiveness, and active listening.[4] The first step in building interpersonal relationships at work is learning to *recognize the importance of relationships* in business—if you haven't already. This issue was discussed in much detail in Chapter 3 in the examination of the purposes of communication, in which establishing goodwill was seen as critical in the workplace. For many individuals, interpersonal communication is the work, particularly for managers.

interpersonal communication

Communication involving mutual influence, usually for the purpose of managing relationships.

trust

The confidence that our peers' intentions are good.

? Critical Thinking

Of the five elements of trust, which do you most consistently demonstrate in your relationships? To which element might you devote more attention to develop more trusting relationships, not only with friends but also with colleagues and peers?

This chapter begins with a discussion of the critical elements of interpersonal communication: different styles of interpersonal interaction, nonverbal communication, and techniques of effective listening.

After discussing the "basics" of interpersonal communication, this chapter will examine their use in specific contexts: planning and managing meetings, motivating others, and engaging in change efforts, all common interpersonal activities of effective organizational leaders. (Other common activities, interviewing job applicants and providing performance feedback, were discussed in Chapter 8).

Interpersonal Style

Broadly, there are three interpersonal styles: assertiveness, avoidance, and aggressiveness. Of these, assertiveness is generally considered the most effective. This becomes clearer when you consider the alternatives.

Avoiding, passive-aggressive individuals tend to whine, complain, and fret about problems at work, but when asked directly what is wrong, they say nothing.[5] This strategy, known as **avoidance**, is defined as a conscious attempt to avoid engaging with people in the dominant group.[6] Avoidance, which is an attempt to separate by having as little to do as possible with the dominant group, is also considered *passive*. The result of an avoiding, passive approach is a consistent inability to raise and resolve problems, needs, issues, and concerns.

At the other extreme, **aggressiveness** in individuals sabotages their ability to meet their needs and to establish supportive relationships by creating defensiveness and alienating others.[7] Aggressive behaviors include those perceived as hurtfully expressive, self-promoting, and assuming control over the choices of others.[8] Aggressive individuals are also described as argumentative. Not only are such individuals more aggressive, they are more insecure and less likely to be well regarded or happy at work.[9]

In contrast to avoidance and aggression, **assertiveness** is defined as "self-enhancing, expressive communication that takes into account both the communicator's and others' needs."[10] Assertiveness involves clearly articulating what you want from others in terms of behavior. It is direct, yet not attacking or blaming. Assertiveness is associated with positive impressions and overall quality of work experience.

It is common to withdraw in conflict situations, but you can be more assertive by following these four steps:

1. Describe how you view the situation.
   Example: *I noticed that you didn't clock in on time three days this week.*

2. Disclose your feelings.
   Example: *I'm concerned that this may become a pattern.*

3. Identify the effects.
   Example: *When you are late, it disrupts the work flow in assembly.*

4. Be silent and wait for a response. Make sure that your nonverbal cues are in alignment with your message.

Assertiveness, however, should not be confused with aggression, because it not only involves stating our own needs clearly but also being sensitive to the needs of others. The goal of conversations should be to establish a genuine dialogue rather than to debate or win an argument.[11] As was discussed in Chapter 2, dialogue involves establishing a climate of equality, listening with empathy, and trying to bring assumptions out into the open. Table 9-1 illustrates the difference between an argumentative style of communication and a dialogue.

avoidance

A conscious attempt to avoid engaging with people in the dominant group.

aggressiveness

Behavior in which individuals sabotage their ability to meet their needs and to establish supportive relationships by creating defensiveness and alienating others.

assertiveness

Self-enhancing, expressive communication that takes into account both the communicator's and others' needs.

Table 9-1 Comparison of Debate versus Dialogic Style of Communication

Debate	Dialogue
■ There is one right answer and you assume that you have it.	■ Many people may have part of the answer; together we can find the best solution.
■ The goal is to win.	■ The goal is to seek common ground and agreement.
■ The focus is on winning; to do so, you must prove the other person wrong.	■ You search for the strengths in what others say and value those aspects.
■ You defend your views.	■ You use the contributions of others to improve your own thinking.

Source: Adapted from Yankelovich, D. (1999). *The Magic of Dialogue: Transforming Conflict into Cooperation* (New York: Simon & Schuster).

As was discussed in Chapter 5, organizations may have supportive or defensive climates of communication. As a leader, you can do much to create a supportive communication climate by adhering to the following steps:

1. **Describe your own feelings rather than evaluate the behavior of others.** One way to avoid evaluating others is to use a passive sentence structure and eliminate the use of the word *you*. Instead, use the word *I* to describe your own thoughts or feelings about the situation. Example: *I am concerned that we won't meet the deadline if we all aren't here every day performing our part of the project.*

2. **Solve problems rather than try to control others.** In reality, we have little control over others. Consequently, it is generally better to get people involved in providing solutions to problems that exist.
    Example: *What are your thoughts on dealing with this issue?*

3. **Empathize with others.** Empathy is the ability to understand the feelings of others and to predict the emotional responses they may have to situations. (Recall the discussion of emotional intelligence in Chapter 2.)
    Example: *I can see that you are very frustrated by this situation.*

4. **Be genuine rather than manipulative.** A manipulative person has hidden agendas. A genuine person discusses issues and problems openly and honestly.

5. **Be flexible rather than rigid.** A "you're wrong, I'm right" attitude creates a defensive climate. Instead of making rigid pronouncements, you can qualify your statements.
    Example: *I may be wrong, but it seems to me that …*

6. **Present yourself as equal rather than superior to others.** Although you may have authority over others, "pulling rank" does not create a cooperative communication climate.
    Example: *Let's work on this together.*

Like assertiveness and dialogue, *listening* is a learned skill and one that very few individuals ever master. Talking to someone who really knows how to listen actively makes you feel valued, important, and free to speak your mind.[12] (Active listening is discussed in more detail later in this chapter.) In an ideal communication situation, assertiveness and active listening go hand in hand as people are able to express their own perceptions and desires and simultaneously attend to the perceptions and desires of others. As you may recognize, these two skills are the foundation of the dialogic model of communication introduced in Chapter 2.

Nonverbal Communication

strategic alignment
The degree in which your oral messages match your nonverbal ones.

nonverbal communication
The "attributes or actions of humans, other than the use of words themselves, which have socially shared meaning, are intentionally sent or interpreted as intentional, are consciously sent or consciously received, and have the potential for feedback from the receiver."

Developing an awareness of nonverbal communication is important, because during face-to-face communication, most of the information that is provided comes in the form of nonverbal cues. In fact, some say that nonverbal cues provide 93 percent of the meaning exchanged in face-to-face communication situations, including oral presentations and meetings. Of that percentage, 35 percent of the meaning comes from tone of voice, whereas 58 percent comes from gestures, facial expressions, and other physical cues.

These statistics mean that the way business communicators think and talk about themselves and others must be consistent with the way they act in that regard to be believable and credible. This notion is reflected in the adage "actions speak louder than words." Because of this belief, it is important to ensure **strategic alignment** between your oral messages and your nonverbal ones.

Nonverbal communication is defined as the "attributes or actions of humans, other than the use of words themselves, which have socially shared meaning, are intentionally sent or interpreted as intentional, are consciously sent or consciously received, and have the potential for feedback from the receiver."[13]

In nonverbal communication, communication signals are multiple and simultaneous. These signals include information that we receive from another person's facial expressions and eyes; body posture, movement, and appearance; the use of space; the use of time; touching; vocal cues; and clothing and other artifacts.

Paralanguage

Paralanguage refers to the rate, pitch, and volume qualities of the voice that interrupt or temporarily take the place of speech and affect the meaning of a message.[14] Paralanguage includes such vocal qualifiers as pitch (high or low); intensity (loud or soft); extent (drawls and accents); emotional characterizers, such as laughing or crying; and segregates, such as saying, "uh," "um," or "uh-huh." In the United States, some vocal qualifiers may communicate emotion; increased volume or rate may indicate anger, for example.

Cultural differences also exist. Arabs speak loudly to indicate strength and sincerity, while Filipinos speak softly to indicate good breeding and education. Italians and Arabs speak more rapidly than Americans.

The lack of vocalization, or silence, also communicates differing meanings depending on culture. People in the United States, Germany, France, and Southern Europe are uncomfortable with silence. People in East Asia consider silence an important part of business and social discourse and not a failure to communicate. Silence in Finland and East Asia is associated with listening and learning; silence protects privacy and individualism and shows respect for the privacy and individualism of others.[15]

Bodily Movement and Facial Expression

The study of posture, movement, gestures, and facial expression is called **kinesics**. Like many aspects of communication, the meaning of body movements and facial expressions can differ by culture. Although many people in the United States may sprawl when they are seated and slouch when they stand, such postures would be considered rude in Germany. Crossing the legs or feet is common in the United States, but doing so in the Middle East is inappropriate, because showing the sole of your shoe or bottom of your foot to someone is considered rude.

Gestures have different meanings depending on the culture, too. In the United States, people generally gesture moderately, whereas Italians, Greeks, and some Latin Americans use more dramatic gestures when speaking. The Chinese and Japanese, in contrast, tend to keep their hands and arms close to their bodies when speaking.

Even the use of facial expressions differs by culture. In China, people rarely express emotion, whereas the Japanese may smile to show a variety of emotions, such as happiness, sadness, or even anger.

Gaze and eye contact also differ by culture. People of the United States, Canada, Great Britain, and Eastern Europe favor direct eye contact. In these cultures, eye contact is considered a sign of respect and attentiveness. People who avoid contact may be considered untrustworthy, unfriendly, insecure, or inattentive.[16] People from Germany and the Middle East favor direct eye contact but the gaze is so intense it may make people otherwise accustomed to direct eye contact uncomfortable. In other countries, respect is shown by avoiding direct eye contact. These places include Japan, China, Indonesia, Latin America, the Caribbean, and parts of Africa. In Egypt, there is no eye contact between men and women who do not know each other and in India, eye contact is avoided between people of different socioeconomic levels.[17]

kinesics

The study of posture, movement, gestures, and facial expression as channels of communication.

In the United States, Albert Mehrabian studied nonverbal communication by examining the concepts of liking, status, and responsiveness of people in communication situations. He found the following:

■ Liking was often expressed by leaning forward, standing face-to-face and in close proximity, increased touching, relaxed posture, open arms and body, positive facial expression, and eye contact.

■ High status or power is communicated nonverbally by taking up more space through bigger gestures and a relaxed posture, including when sitting, and less eye contact. This is an important issue for women and some people from cultures other than the United States to consider since they may have been socialized to appear small by taking up less space.

■ Responsiveness is exhibited nonverbally by moving toward the other person, using spontaneous gestures, shifting posture and position, and facial expressiveness. The face and body should provide positive feedback to those with whom you are communicating.

In other words, body language is a strong indicator of the extent to which communicators like one another and are interested in each other's views. In addition, it indicates the perceived status, or power relationship, between the communicators. Understanding the use and meaning of body language is helpful in all types of face-to-face communication situations, including job interviews. During a job interview, you can indicate your interest in the position by leaning forward in your chair, maintaining eye contact with the interviewer, using animated facial expressions, and varying the volume, rate, and pitch of your voice.

All these nonverbal communication behaviors can be used when appropriate to increase your ability to establish credibility and a positive relationship with your audience in speaking situations.

Bodily Appearance

Our body type and physical attractiveness also affect our ability to communicate with others because of their perceptions about these issues.

somatotype

Body type comprised of a combination of height, weight, and muscularity

Body type, or **somatotype**, is comprised of a combination of height, weight, and muscularity. Tall people are generally more successful and are viewed more positively by others. Taller people are more likely to be hired in employment interviews, and they tend to have higher incomes.[18] Regarding attractiveness, women generally find tall men more attractive than short ones; however, they view men of medium height as the most attractive and likeable. Those who are short, soft, and round are often judged negatively in terms of their personalities and their concern about self-presentation.

Particular physical characteristics are considered as universal aspects of attractiveness: bright eyes, symmetrical facial features, and a thin or medium build.[19] Physical attractiveness generally leads to more social success in adulthood; attractive people receive higher initial credibility ratings than do those who are viewed as unattractive.[20] Physically attractive people are more likely to be hired and to receive higher salaries.[21] However, these views may not hold for gender. Studies have shown that attractive females are sometimes judged as less competent than less attractive females.[22]

proxemics

The study of human space that revolves around two concepts: territoriality and personal space.

Even though there is little that we can do to change our height, we can control to some degree our body type and our attractiveness, the latter through attention to good grooming and by conveying a positive attitude.

territoriality

Your need to establish and maintain certain spaces as your own.

Space

The study of human space, or **proxemics**, revolves around two concepts: territoriality and personal space. **Territoriality** refers to your need to establish and maintain certain spaces as your own. In a workplace environment, the walls of your cubicle or office often establish your territory. **Personal space** is the distance between you and others with which you feel comfortable. When someone

personal space

The physical distance between you and others with which you feel comfortable.

invades your personal space, you often automatically move away from that person. However, personal space preferences can differ among people. For example, large people also usually prefer more space, as do men.

Similarly, personal space preferences differ by culture. People of the United States tend to need more space than those from Greece, Latin America, or the Middle East. The Japanese tend to prefer a greater distance in social situations than do people of the United States.

Anthropologist Edward T. Hall defined four distances people use when they communicate. **Intimate distance** is used more in private than in public and extends to about 18 inches. This distance is used to communicate affection, give comfort, and to protect. **Personal distance** ranges from 18 inches to 4 feet and is the distance used by those in the United States for conversation and non-intimate exchanges. **Social distance** ranges from 4 to 8 feet and is used for professional communication. The higher the status of the person, generally the greater the social distance he or she maintains. **Public distance** exceeds 12 feet and is used most often for public speaking.

Your relationship to other people is related to your use of space. You stand closer to friends and farther from enemies, strangers, authority figures, high-status people, physically challenged people, and people from different racial groups than your own. The effectiveness of communication, or the way you respond to others, can be affected by personal space violations.

What this knowledge means for those who are leaders or who aspire to be leaders is that they need to become attentive to their use of space. As mentioned earlier, this is particularly true for women since studies have shown that they tend to take up less space than men and thus may sabotage their efforts to be seen as a person of power. Even though many women may be of smaller stature than some men, they can better claim their space by squaring their shoulders, pulling themselves up to their full height, using larger gestures, and when appropriate, such as in presentation situations, using the entire room. They can also work to create an authoritative voice that commands respect. This is also true culturally, since some cultures socialize people to take up less bodily space.

Cultural differences also extend to how people communicate through space in seating arrangements and the layout of offices. People in the United States, for example, prefer to converse face-to-face, while people in China prefer to sit side by side. This preference may allow them to avoid direct eye contact, which is the custom in that culture. In terms of the office environment, private offices have more status in the United States, while in Japan, only executives of the highest rank may have a private office, although it is just as likely that they have desks in large work areas.[23] In the United States and Germany, the top floor of office buildings is generally occupied by top-level executives, while in France, high-ranking executives occupy the middle of an office area with subordinates located around them.[24]

Time

Chronemics, or values related to time, refers to the way that people organize and use time and the messages that are created because of our organization and use of time. Our use of time communicates several messages. Our urgency or casualness with the starting time of an event could be an indication of our personality, our status, or our culture. Highly structured, task-oriented people may arrive and leave on time, whereas relaxed, relation-oriented people may arrive and leave late. People with low status are expected to be on time, whereas those with higher status are granted more leeway in their arrival time. Being on time is more important in some cultures than others; for example, being on time is more important in North America than in South America, whereas people of Germany and Switzerland are even more time-conscious than people from the United States.

Another cultural issue to recognize is whether a country follows **polychronic time (P-time)** or **monochronic time (M-time)**. Countries that follow polychronic time work on several activities simultaneously. In these cultures people are more important than schedules so they don't mind interruptions and are accustomed to doing several things at once. People in polychronic cultures

intimate distance

This distance is used to communicate affection, give comfort, and to protect. It is used more in private than in public and extends to about 18 inches.

personal distance

The distance ranging from 18 inches to 4 feet used by those in the United States for conversation and non-intimate exchanges.

social distance

The distance ranges from 4 to 8 feet and is used for professional communication.

public distance

The distance exceeds 12 feet and is used most often for public speaking.

chronemics

Values related to time, refers to the way that people organize and use time and the messages that are created because of our organization and use of time.

polychronic time (P-time)

A cultural orientation to time in which people are well adapted to working on several activities simultaneously.

monochronic time (M-time)

A cultural orientation to time in which people do one thing at a time and are more task oriented than relationship-oriented.

borrow and lend things and tend to build lifelong relationships. People from high-context cultures tend to be polychronic, including Latin America, the Middle East, and Southern Europe.[25]

Countries that are monochronic in their time orientation include the United States, Germany, Switzerland, and England. In monochronic cultures, time is considered as something tangible, as is reflected in such sayings as "wasting time" and "time is money." Time is seen as linear and manageable in such cultures. It is considered rude to do two things at once, such as answering the phone while someone is in your office or stopping to text someone while in a conversation. However, with the prevalence of cell phones, this consideration is rapidly changing. Monochronic people tend to respect private property and rarely borrow or lend and are accustomed to short-term relationships.[26]

Touching

haptics

Communicating through the use of bodily contact or touch.

Haptics, or touch, communicates a great deal. What is appropriate and people's tendency to touch differs by gender and culture. Studies indicate that women in the United States value touch more than men, women are touched more than men, men touch others more than women do, and men may use touch to indicate power or dominance.[27]

People from different countries also handle touch differently. Sidney Jourard determined the rates of touch per hour among adults of various cultures. Adults in Puerto Rico touched 180 times per hour; those in Paris touched about 110 times an hour; those in Gainesville, Florida, touched 2 times per hour; and those in London touched once per hour.

In touch-oriented cultures, such as those of Italy, Spain, Portugal, and Greece, both males and females may walk arm in arm or hold hands. In Mexico, Eastern Europe, and the Arab world, embracing and kissing are common. However, in Hong Kong, initiating any physical contact should be avoided.[28]

Some cultures also restrict where touching may occur on the body. In India and Thailand, it is offensive to touch the head because it is considered sacred. In Korea, young people do not touch the shoulders of elders.[29]

Clothing and Other Artifacts

Your clothing and other adornments, such as jewelry, hairstyle, cosmetics, shoes, glasses, tattoos, and body piercings, communicate to others your age, gender, status, role, socioeconomic class, group memberships, personality, and relation to the opposite sex. Such cues also indicate the historical period, the time of day, and the climate. Clothing and other artifacts also communicate your self-concept or the type of person you believe you are.[30] Conforming to current styles has been correlated to a person's desire to be accepted and liked by others.[31]

Individuals believe that clothing is important in forming first impressions.[32] Clothing has been shown to affect others' impressions of our status and personality traits.[33] For this reason, most advise that you should pay attention to dressing professionally in business situations because it can affect your credibility, attractiveness, and perceived ability to fit within a professional culture. This rule can be particularly important when dealing with international audiences because they tend to make assumptions about another person's education level, status, and income based upon dress alone.[34] Therefore, those who are interested in careers in international business should follow Molloy's rules for business dress: Clothing should be conservative, upper class, and traditional.[35]

? Critical Thinking

How important is another person's dress to you? Does it affect your response to that person or your judgment about him or her? Do you clearly understand the expectations regarding professional dress in the workplace?

Effective Listening

Although you may be asked to communicate orally in a professional workplace setting, you will more likely be on the receiving end of such messages. In fact, in the business world, people, both those with and without management responsibilities, spend most of their time listening. Business people, in general, spend nearly 33 percent of their time listening, about 26 percent of their time speaking, and nearly 19 percent of their time reading.[36] Executives may spend more time listening— as much as 80 percent of their day.[37]

Although we spend most of our time in communication situations involved in listening, the skill often receives little attention. A survey conducted by a corporate training and development firm indicated that 80 percent of the corporate executives who responded rated listening as the most important skill in the workforce. However, nearly 30 percent of those same executives said that listening was the communication skill most lacking in their employees.[38] Only 35 percent of us are efficient listeners.[39] The lack of effective listening can often lead to missed opportunities, misunderstanding, conflict, or poor decision making.

Conversely, the ability to listen effectively can have a big impact on our ability to communicate well with others. Effective listening can help us build relationships, be more productive, and determine whether others are being deceptive.

Listening does not mean the same thing as hearing. Hearing is the sensory ability to receive sound. Hearing takes no effort or energy on your part. You receive and hear sounds constantly. However, listening is a more active, engaged process. According to the International Listening Association, listening is "the active process of receiving, constructing meaning from, and responding to spoken and/or nonverbal messages. It involves the ability to retain information, as well as to react empathically and/or appreciatively to spoken and/or nonverbal messages." Listening requires energy and effort, whereas hearing is automatic and passive.

We tend to be poor listeners for a number of reasons. We may be distracted by the external environment or by internal factors: We may be ill or tired, or we may have other tasks that need our attention. A speaker may say something that triggers a negative emotion in us and we may tune out or turn our attention to formulating our rebuttal. Another big problem is that we think much faster than a person can speak. Because of these distractions or barriers, listeners need training to slow down the mental processes and focus on what others are saying.

Listening Styles

There are three levels of listening, and it is beneficial to distinguish between them and identify which type of listener you are.

Level one is referred to as a good listener. A level-one listener exhibits all the qualities of being involved in conversations, including taking the other person's interests into consideration and staying focused on the speaker.[40] A level-one listener keeps an open mind and is always eager to hear what the other person has to say. A level-one listener is respectful of the other person's feelings and is not quick to pass judgment.

Level-two listeners hear the words being spoken but do not have full understanding of what the words mean.[41] Many times, listening involves recognizing nonverbal forms of communication. Level-two listeners focus on the words being said, but might not pay attention to the facial expressions, hand gestures, or tone of voice. They do not give much effort to understanding the speaker's intent, and this oversight can lead to conflicts and misunderstandings.

Level-three listeners do not acknowledge the speaker at all. While another person is speaking level-three listeners spend time thinking about something else.[42] Level-three listeners' thoughts are centered on themselves, and they may only appear to be listening. The problem that arises with this level of listening is the amount of confusion it can create. While the speaker is talking, these listeners are daydreaming about something else and may have possibly missed an important piece of information. This can lead to making unhealthy life decisions and to poor judgment, and can create barriers to effective communication.

Only about 20 percent of people in the workforce listen at level one. The rest (80 percent) go back and forth between levels two and three, and only sometimes are at level one.[43]

Listening Types

Listening is classified into four main types: active, empathic, critical, and listening for enjoyment. Listening for enjoyment is typically not an activity in which we engage in the workplace, so it will not be discussed here.

However, the other three types of listening are relevant to and useful in the workplace. **Active listening** is "listening with a purpose."[44] Active listening is a key part of successful interpersonal or face-to-face communication. It involves the following four steps:

1. Listen carefully by using all available senses, including observation.

2. Paraphrase what is heard both mentally and verbally. This step is intended to help you remember the information and to accomplish step 3. Paraphrasing involves such statements as "If I hear you correctly, you are saying…"

3. Check your understanding to ensure accuracy. To check understanding, you might follow your paraphrased statement by asking, "Is that right?"

4. Provide feedback.

Table 9-2 provides a short quiz you can take to get some insight into your listening skill level.

active listening

"Listening with a purpose" which involves paraphrasing, asking questions for clarification, and providing feedback.

Table 9-2 **Are You a Good Listener?**

Take this short quiz, using the following rating scale: A "3" means you are very strong in this area; a "2" means you try to perform the stated behavior; and a "1" means you are not sure how often you perform the behavior.

1. I am aware that I must listen with a purpose to listen effectively.
2. I have trained myself to listen at least twice as much as I speak.
3. I listen for understanding rather than evaluation.
4. I recognize the importance of my nonverbal signals to the speaker.
5. I am aware of the words, phrases, or behaviors that are likely to make me defensive.
6. I wait until the speaker has finished before responding.
7. I have often heard a person say to me, "Thank you for listening."
8. I concentrate on what the speaker is saying, even though other things could distract me.
9. I am able to exercise emotional control when listening, even if I disagree with the message.
10. I realize that listening powerfully may be the key to my success.

If you scored 12 or less, you probably need a listening program. If you scored 13 to 20, you are an average listener. If you rated higher than 20, you are an excellent listener.

Source: Adapted from "Effective Listening Skills." (1994). *Women in Business*, 46 (2), 28–32, March/April.

feedback

The listener's verbal and nonverbal responses to the speaker and his or her message.

Feedback consists of the listener's verbal and nonverbal responses to the speaker and his or her message. Feedback can be either positive or negative. Positive feedback consists of the listener's verbal and nonverbal responses that are intended to affirm the speaker and his or her message. Negative feedback consists of a listener's verbal and nonverbal responses that are intended to disaffirm the speaker and his or her message. In productive communication situations, negative feedback should not be used to disaffirm the speaker or typically to discredit the message, because this may negatively affect your relationship and your ability to communicate effectively in the future. However, you should feel free to say "no" to the speaker or to disagree with the message. Disagreement is generally more effective if you can provide good reasons for doing so.

Empathic listening is a form of active listening with the goal of understanding the other person. To listen empathetically, you must be fully engaged in the conversation at the moment and empathize with the person who is speaking. Empathic listening is useful in the workplace if you find yourself in a situation in which it is appropriate to be supportive of colleagues and team members or if you are a supervisor dealing with an employee with a problem. Empathic listening is useful in establishing and maintaining relationships with others by showing that you care about them and their concerns. Empathetic messages include such statements as "I understand why you feel that way" and "I can see how you might interpret my actions as you did."

empathic listening

A form of active listening with the goal of understanding the other person.

Critical listening is used to evaluate the accuracy, meaningfulness, and usefulness of a message. In the workplace, critical listening is particularly important in any decision-making process. Critical listening can help you to determine whether information is sound, relevant to the issue, and adequate. It can also help you to determine whether the speaker is pursuing a hidden or personal agenda or the objectives of the group, and whether the person is objective and forthright. All this information is necessary and may affect your ability to reach a sound business decision.

critical listening

Listening used to evaluate the accuracy, meaningfulness, and usefulness of a message.

Your skills as a critical listener are dependent upon your abilities as a critical thinker. *Critical thinking* is necessary to analyze a communication situation—your purposes, your audiences, and the situational factors that affect the way you communicate—and based upon that analysis, to create an effective communication strategy for that situation. Conversely, critical thinking is also used to analyze a speaker, the situation, and the speaker's ideas to make critical judgments about the message being presented. This last issue, message analysis, requires two steps: (1) evaluating the process by which information or knowledge was discovered and (2) evaluating specific elements of message content. In other words, you should evaluate whether the information contained in the message is accurate and unbiased to ensure that the speaker has drawn logical conclusions from the information.

? Critical Thinking

Are you skilled at practicing active listening? Empathic listening? Critical listening? If not, what steps might you take to become a more effective listener? How might improving your listening skills provide you opportunities in the workplace?

Verbal Tactics for Effective Listening

One way to indicate to the person with whom you are communicating that you are actively engaged in the listening process is to use effective verbal communication techniques, such as the following:

- **Ask questions.** Asking questions shows that you are interested in what the speaker has to say and enables you to gather more information, which is necessary for clear understanding.

- **Show interest and support.** You can do this by encouraging the speaker to continue or by encouraging him or her to share ideas.

- **Use descriptive, non-evaluative responses when paraphrasing or responding.** An example of such a statement would be: "Your information comes from a think tank that has openly expressed its partisan affinities. I am not sure that the data gives us a complete picture of the situation." Compare that to the following response: "You give us biased and therefore one-sided information, because its source clearly has a political agenda." The second response contains language that has negative connotations—"biased," "one-sided," "political"—which can put the speaker on the defensive or make him or her feel attacked. Use of such language can also be interpreted as a subtle form of name-calling because it implies that the speaker is biased, one-sided, and political in his or her intentions.

■ **Identify areas of agreement or common interests.** An example of such a statement is: "I believe we both are interested in pursuing decisions that will enable the department to meet its objectives." Such statements are intended to reduce the perception that you and the speaker are far apart in your bigger concerns or experiences.

■ **Respond with affirming statements.** Making such statements as "I understand," "I know," and "yes," indicates support for the speaker and his or her ideas or feelings, as well as empathy.

■ **Avoid silence.** Silence can be interpreted in a variety of negative ways, such as a sign of a lack of interest, inattentiveness, or disapproval. However, the use of silence has cultural dimensions. Some cultures have a greater tolerance and appreciation for silence, so in cases in which you are dealing with persons from such cultures, silence might be appropriate.

■ **Don't dominate a conversation or cut off the other person.** If you wish to indicate that you are interested in a speaker's ideas or feelings, you should allow that person to express himself or herself fully. If you are perceived as someone who dominates a conversation or cuts off people, others will typically begin to avoid conversing with you.

■ **Restate and paraphrase the speaker's message as well as the intent**. This activity shows that you are listening and are concerned about interpreting the speaker's message accurately. It may be appropriate in certain situations to openly express your interpretation of the speaker's intentions. An example might be, "As I understand it, you are telling me this information so that it can be used to make a decision about the pending policy change. Is that correct?"

In Table 9-3, active listening responses are compared to those that block communication.

Table 9-3 Active Listening versus Blocking Responses

■ **Active response: Paraphrasing content**
  "You're saying that you don't have time to finish the report by Friday."
  Blocking response: Ordering, threatening
  "I don't care how you do it. Just get the report on my desk by Friday."

■ **Active response: Mirroring feelings**
  "It sounds like the department's problems really bother you."
  Blocking response: Preaching, criticizing
  "You should know better than to air the department's problems in a general meeting."

■ **Active response: Stating one's feelings**
  "I'm frustrated that the job isn't completed yet, and I'm worried about getting it done on time."
  Blocking response: Interrogating
  "Why didn't you tell me that you didn't understand the instructions?"

■ **Active response: Asking for information or clarification**
  "What parts of the problem seem most difficult to solve?"
  Blocking response: Minimizing the problem
  "You think that's bad? You should see what I have to do this week."

■ **Active response: Offering to help solve the problem together**
  "Is there anything I could do that would help?"
  Blocking response: Advising
  "Why don't you try listing everything you have to do and seeing which items are most important?"

Source: The five responses that block communication are based on a list of twelve in Thomas Gordon's and Judith Gordon Sands's *P.E.T. in Action* (New York: Wyden): 117–118.

Nonverbal Tactics for Effective Listening

As has been expressed earlier, your nonverbal communication is as important, if not more so, than your oral statements in interpersonal communication situations. Therefore, providing appropriate nonverbal communication is also useful in indicating that you are actively listening to others. The following are nonverbal communication behaviors that indicate active listening:

- **Use movements and gestures to show understanding and responsiveness.** You can nod your head to show approval or understanding or shake your head in disbelief.

- **Lean forward.** Leaning toward a speaker shows interest. This technique is also useful in job interview situations, because it expresses your interest in the speaker and the position for which you have applied.

- **Establish an open body position.** Crossing your arms or legs sends a subtle message that you are not completely comfortable with the speaker or that you are not receptive to the ideas. This principle is also true in oral presentations. You should maintain an open body position while delivering speeches or presentations to indicate your confidence and receptiveness to the audience.

- **Use an alert but relaxed posture.** In other words, do not look too relaxed or too stiff. Being too relaxed may indicate that you don't take the speaker or situation seriously. Being too stiff may show that you are uncomfortable or rigid in your thinking.

- **Use direct body orientation.** You should face the speaker or your audience directly rather than from an angle. An angled position may be interpreted as a sign that you are attempting to move away from the speaker. It may also inhibit your ability to observe the nonverbal communication of the speaker.

- **Use facial expressions that indicate involvement.** You can raise your eyebrows to express interest and smile to show encouragement.

- **Maintain direct eye contact.** Failing to maintain direct eye contact may be interpreted as showing deceptiveness, a lack of interest, or a lack of confidence in some cultures, particularly in the United States.

Meeting Management

Meetings may be a more effective alternative to giving an oral presentation as if appropriately planned and facilitated, they are a more dialogic form of communication than a presentation, which tends to be monologic. One risk of selecting a meeting as an alternate to a presentation is that there is greater risk of losing control of the message, depending on the topic and the audience. Following the steps in the strategic process of message formulation can help you to make these channel choice decisions more effectively.

Meetings are a common means of communication within organizations because they provide the potential for employees to ask and answer questions in an efficient manner. Probably the most effective use of meetings, however, is for problem solving and decision making as they are more likely to engage all attendees in the discussion. If the discussion is managed appropriately, participants are more likely to accept and commit to the decisions that are reached.

Meetings also provide communicators access to nonverbal cues, which enable those who have good observation skills to check and respond to messages that are not verbalized. Just as with most communication media, though, meetings present challenges, the primary one being the cost in time. There are 11 million meetings in the United States every day, according to the National Statistics Council. Furthermore, professionals attend an average of 61.8 meetings a month and say that fully half of that time is wasted.[45] With such numbers, it is imperative to consider whether a meeting is needed or the best media of communication. One rule of thumb to apply is that if the communication goal can be reached via any other medium—an informational e-mail, an informal report, or a departmental wiki, for example—then use that medium rather than plan a meeting as these methods are more time-sensitive and convenient for recipients.

However, if a meeting is the best way to achieve your purposes for communicating, there are ways to make it productive and efficient. This section discusses the common types of meetings and the steps for ensuring a successful and efficient meeting. Special considerations for electronic meetings—videoconferencing, teleconferencing, Web conferencing and mobile conferencing—are also discussed.

Types of Meetings

Defining the purpose of a meeting can help you prepare for it. There are three key reasons to hold a meeting: to inform, to discuss or evaluate decisions, and to discuss performance.

- Informative meetings focus on giving or receiving information. They may incorporate discussions, demonstrations, or lectures to aid in the exchange of information. The group size for these types of meetings can vary from as few as two people to as many as a hundred individuals.

- Discussions are held to form decisions or agree on a plan of action. These meetings are successful if participants actively brainstorm, discuss, and evaluate ideas. These meetings work best with small groups of three to nine participants.

- Performance meetings are held to accomplish a specific task or to plan an event. The key to making these meetings successful is to make sure everyone understands their particular responsibilities. Performance meetings are more effective when limited to six or fewer participants.

Steps in Meeting Management

After you have identified the primary purpose of your meeting, spend time on the three phases of meeting management to ensure that the discussion is productive and efficient. These three steps are (1) planning the meeting, (2) conducting the meeting, and (3) following up after the meeting has been held.

Planning the Meeting

When considering a meeting, you must recognize that you have an obligation to show respect for all participants and the time they spend attending this meeting. Doing so can enhance your credibility and goodwill with attendees. This is why planning is the most critical step in conducting a meeting. Before you send out notifications to initiate any type of meeting, answer the following questions:

- Which participants are essential to achieve the purpose of the meeting? What are the key roles each participant will have in the meeting? Will the setting be formal or informal? Meetings are productive only when attended by the right people. It may not be to the best advantage to invite those who are simply interested. Your team should comprise individuals who have direct experience with the issues to be discussed or decided and who have a stake in the outcome of such discussions.

- What agenda will be most effective and efficient for the purpose of the meeting? You will need to decide how to bring the participants together in terms of when and where you will meet. Will the meeting be by teleconferencing, videoconferencing, e-mail, on site of the business location, or away from its premises?

- What information, equipment, and tools are required to conduct the meeting?

- How much time will be needed for decision making or to obtain the information needed to achieve the results of your objectives? Allow enough time to have questions answered and clarity established for the meeting.

Although the arrangements may be complex and the nature of your meeting will vary, the following suggested guidelines apply in most cases in conducting a successful meeting:

- Give advance notice to all participants.

- Provide information such as the date, time (both starting and predicted ending), and location (include travel arrangements, if needed), and include the names of participants, their key roles, titles, and business affiliations.

- Design a structured agenda with the stated objectives, a list of the main topics of interest, and time allotted for each topic of discussion. Group related topics together to avoid having to backtrack on a subject in order to keep the meeting flowing in an orderly fashion. Limit the agenda to one page in length. (A generic format for an agenda is provided in Figure 9-1.)

- Provide the agenda in advance to all participants so they can be prepared. Inform all attendees what is expected from each one in preparing for the meeting. Confirm that all participants have received the notice of the meeting agenda.

Figure 9-1 Formal Generic Agenda for Meetings

**Agenda for [name of group] Meeting Prepared on
[date agenda created] by [name of author of agenda]**

Attendees: [those invited to attend, often in alphabetical order]
Date and time of meeting:
Location of meeting:
Subject: [major issues to be discussed or purpose of meeting]
Agenda items:

1. Call to order

2. Routine business [procedural or administrative matters]   (10–15 mins.)
    a. Approval of agenda for this meeting
    b. Reading and approval of minutes of last meeting
    c. Committee report

3. Old business [unfinished matters from previous meeting]   (15–20 mins.)
    a. Discussion of issue(s) carried over from previous meeting
    b. Issue(s) arising from decision(s) made at previous meeting

4. New business   (20–25 mins.)
    a. Most important issue
    b. Next most important issue
    c. Other issues in decreasing order of importance
    d. Business from the floor not included on the agenda [only as time permits; otherwise, these issues should be
        addressed in the next meeting]

5. Adjournment

Conducting the Meeting

Meetings have four major stages: (1) the introduction and vision statement, (2) the meeting kickoff, (3) the summary of accomplishments and the management presentation, and (4) an evaluation exercise and closing remarks.[46] The facilitator is responsible for making sure these steps are followed and completed. The success of the meeting largely depends on the facilitator's communication skills.

The facilitator's first goal is to set a positive, professional tone from the very beginning that is intended to make attendees say, "I'm glad to be here." Creating a welcoming atmosphere can be accomplished by encouraging open communication. Effective facilitators promote individual participation to gain the benefit of diverse points of view. To gain the most information, facilitators should ask open-ended questions to avoid getting simple "Yes" or "No" responses. Facilitators are responsible for getting attendees to participate. They can do so by asking such questions as "What do you think about the topic?" "Can you tell me what we can do to make this better?" or "What other suggestions do you have?" The best solutions are always the result of input from many people.

The facilitator needs to be aware of the time and, with that in mind, keep the conversation on topic. It has been estimated that executives spend an average of 7.8 hours a week in meetings that are unnecessary.[47] Many inefficient or unnecessary meetings can be directly tied to a late start time, poor facilitation, or a late ending time. Good facilitators keep a meeting on schedule and on topic. Everyone's time is valuable. It's very important to respect others' time; it shows that you value the presence and schedules of those who were prompt. Keeping a meeting on schedule not only establishes goodwill and your credibility as a facilitator but also has a positive effect on future meetings.

Facilitators and presenters should avoid lecturing. According to a study by the MPI Foundation, meeting attendees do not care for "speakers who have poor presentation skills."[48] Speakers who wish to catch the attention of listeners should try to involve the participants emotionally in the meeting. Speakers should be spontaneous, but that does not mean that such discussions should not be planned. Just as with other types of presentations, speakers should plan what they have to say but deliver their message as extemporaneously as possible.

Holding a difference of opinion about the same subject is typical in meeting discussions. But proving a point or being right is secondary to your team's objectives. By following the suggestions below, facilitators can demonstrate leadership and, most importantly, focus everyone's energy on a solution that will progress the group.

Try to see things from each participant's point of view.

- When someone is speaking, never say, "You're wrong."
- Avoid right or wrongs; treat different opinions as different ways of looking at the same issue.
- Remember that you and others are all working toward the same goal.

Meeting conflicts can be harder to solve than some of the toughest mathematical problems. One way to handle conflict is to turn the point of conflict into a question and get other opinions on the topic. Another strategy is to try to lighten the situation with humor. Facilitators can also show concern by asking the person who seems to have the biggest issues what is wrong. If the person is standing, then the facilitator can ask him or her to sit down. It is harder to be mad when sitting. More generally, facilitators should try to make it a win–win situation for everyone involved in the conflict. They can do so by staying neutral and avoiding taking sides. As the meeting draws to a close, facilitators should summarize the main discussion points and any decisions that are made during the meeting. This information can help pull all information together for attendees participating in the meeting.

One of the reasons that meetings are unsuccessful is because of poor meeting management. However, if you are not the official meeting manager, you can still influence the meeting process and its outcomes. The following list provides some actions that can be taken to address common meeting management shortcomings:

- **If there is no agenda:** If the meeting manager has not provided an agenda before the meeting, politely ask for one by saying something like, "To help me better prepare for the upcoming meeting, may I please see an agenda?" Or "Can you tell me what are the key issues and questions we'll be considering at our meeting?" If you are unable to get this information, you can also ask for some structure at the beginning of the meeting by saying, "What are our key goals today?" Politely asking for an agenda might spur the manager into developing one. And even if there is no agenda forthcoming, you have at least done your part by asking for one.

- **If the conversation is unstructured and disconnected**: You can try to get more clarity about the direction of discussion by making observations and asking for structural clearness. An example might be "I'm not sure where we are on the agenda. Could you provide me some direction? " or "I'm not sure how this discussion relates to the topic at hand. Could you please provide some explanation?" These comments can help make the entire group more aware of whether it is on or off task.

- **If the group is not on task or is off the agenda:** Summarize what the meeting has accomplished. By periodically summarizing what has been accomplished in a meeting you help the group be more aware of where it is on the agenda. Summarizing the progress of the meeting can also energize the group by reminding the meeting participants what has been accomplished.

- **If tangents derail progress:** Suggest a private meeting between two people who are monopolizing the conversation. Invite them tactfully to continue the conversation "offline" rather than using the meeting to hash out an issue that may not be relevant to the entire group.

- **If some participants are dominating or not participating:** Serve as a gatekeeper. You don't have to be the meeting leader to invite quieter members to participate in the meeting. If you notice that some meeting members are not participating or seem disengaged in the meeting, simply ask for their ideas and opinions by saying, "Elena, I'd like to hear your ideas."

- **If the meeting is behind schedule:** Make the group aware of the time left to talk about an issue. Sometimes groups simply aren't aware of the resource of time and by reminding them, they may spend it more wisely.

- **If no one is assigned to take notes:** Volunteer to take notes or record the minutes. Being the note taker gives you additional authority to ask questions, summarize, and make sure that the group is staying on track. The person who takes the minutes has the power to shape the meeting results. You can also influence what happens after the meeting by ensuring that the action steps are recorded and that it's clear who is supposed to do what to achieve the meeting goals.

After the Meeting

After the meeting has concluded, minutes should be posted as soon as possible—within two days at the latest. The meeting minutes should include key topics covered, any decisions or conclusions that were drawn, any projects due and their deadlines, and specific information on future meetings. Minutes are important as they serve as a record of the discussion that can be referred back to as needed for informational purposes. Remember, people only remember about 10 percent of what they hear so oral discussions that are important should be accompanied by written messages for clarity and as a source of institutional memory.

More specifically, the meeting minutes should include the following:

- Time, date, and location
- Names of attendees
- Agenda items and any other items discussed
- Decisions made
- Assignments and the persons responsible
- Length of meeting
- Time, date, and location of the next meeting.

It may also be appropriate to communicate to participants any progress being made on the implementation of decisions or plans of action arrived at during the meeting.

Additional Considerations for Electronic Meetings

As discussed in Chapter 5, the rapid development of technology has provided a number of means for holding meetings with those who are not in the immediate proximity. These include videoconferencing, teleconferencing, web conferencing and mobile conferencing apps. Even though these technologies are convenient and comparatively less expensive than air travel, they do have such potential disadvantages as lost connections or other technical problems.

To avoid some of these problems, it is important to train participants in the use of the technology and to test it for proper performance before the meeting. As with face-to-face meetings, participants should be informed of the time, date, time zone, and length of the meeting and provided any necessary dial in, log in or written materials before the meeting.

In addition, at the beginning of the meeting, all participants should introduce themselves. All questions and comments should then be directed to specific individuals. It is also important to reduce outside noise and distractions, so cell phones and pagers should be turned off during face-to-face meetings, phones should be on mute in a virtual meeting if not speaking, and all side conversations should be limited.

For videoconferences, it is also important to remember that you are on camera, so avoid distracting behaviors (such as playing with your hair or a pencil) or those that might not be perceived as professional. Because you are on camera, it is important to look at the camera as you speak and thus maintain eye contact.

Motivating Employees

This textbook opened with a discussion of the importance of leadership in today's organizations. In that discussion, the leader's task was distinguished from that of the manager. "What leaders really do is prepare organizations for change and help them cope as they struggle through it. It's the manager's job to promote stability, and only organizations that embrace both sides of the equation can succeed in tough times."[49]

Kotter maintains that many U.S. companies today are over-managed and under-led. Organizations need to recognize that leaders are responsible for setting direction, whereas managers plan and budget. Setting a direction requires developing a vision as well as strategies to achieve that vision.

A second task for leaders is to identify those who can help spread the vision and are committed to its achievement. This task is largely a communication issue. It requires active involvement, credibility, and empowering people. Empowerment promotes buy-in and communication.

To achieve the vision, leaders must motivate and inspire those in the organization. Successful motivation ensures employees will have the energy to overcome obstacles. It is useful to repeat that leaders are not necessarily given organizational power but can influence others through their strategic abilities, knowledge, and communication skills. What this means is that the information provided in this chapter not only applies to those with formal power but to those who also wish to practice the leadership skill of motivating others.

Motivation Defined

Motivation consists of three interrelated elements: needs, drives, and goals. A lack or imbalance that creates dissatisfaction in an individual is a **need**. Needs may vary in type and intensity among people and may change over time, but they significantly influence behavior. A **drive** is the state of an individual associated with a need, such as hunger or thirst. The **goal** is the outcome that the person perceives will eliminate the need. For someone who is hungry, the goal might be a meal. Although the drive arouses activity, a **motive** is the learned state that affects behavior by moving an individual toward a perceived goal. Motivation is the reason behind the behavior or action.

need
A lack or imbalance that creates dissatisfaction in an individual.

drive
The state of an individual associated with a need, such as hunger or thirst.

goal
The outcome that the person perceives will eliminate the need.

motive
The learned state that affects behavior by moving an individual toward a perceived goal.

Within an organization, symptoms of low motivation among employees may be low morale, high waste costs, absenteeism, high turnover, high training costs, and high health insurance costs. Individual symptoms of low motivation include boredom, inattention, lack of concentration, resistance, apathy, sabotage, errors, and resistance to change.

Many theories of leadership have been developed to deal with the problem of motivating employees. Some of the early work on motivation and control of employees was driven by traditional human relations values and beliefs in the linkage between communication and effective supervision. One important study in the area of organizational communication that examined supervisors' communication dispositions and drew the following five major conclusions:

- The best supervisors tend to be more "communication-minded." They enjoy talking and speaking in meetings, they are able to explain instructions and policies, and they enjoy conversing with employees.

- The best supervisors tend to be willing, empathic listeners. They respond to silly questions from employees with understanding, they are approachable, and they will listen to suggestions and complaints with an attitude of fairness and openness to take action.

- The best supervisors tend to be sensitive to the feelings of others. For example, they reprimand in private rather than in public.

- The best supervisors tend to "ask" or "persuade" rather than to "tell" or "demand."

- The best supervisors tend to more readily pass along information. They give notice of impending changes and provide reasons for the change.[50]

The conclusions of this study bear a strong resemblance to many of the prescriptions of traditional human relations theorists who claimed that management gained compliance by promoting employee morale and satisfaction. The study indicates that employee morale and satisfaction depend on effective interpersonal communication skills, namely, empathy, sensitivity, and receptivity.

It is important to recognize that employee morale and satisfaction are not entirely dependent upon the behavior of leaders and managers. For example, employee satisfaction was negatively related to role ambiguity and positively related to fatigue. As role ambiguity increased, satisfaction went down, whereas fatigue, to some extent, led to greater satisfaction.[51] In other words, good management practices at the organizational level are also important for better ensuring a motivated workforce.

In fact, some early motivational theories have also pointed to the limits of quality leader-member relationships to influence motivation. For example, Herzberg's motivator-hygiene theory found that satisfaction and dissatisfaction are not opposite conditions. That is, the opposite of satisfaction is simply the absence of satisfaction. Herzberg found that factors leading to job satisfaction and to motivation are different from those that lead to job dissatisfaction.[52]

Herzberg called the factors that lead to job satisfaction *motivators*. These include achievement, recognition, advancement, the work itself, responsibility, and potential for growth. The factors that led to dissatisfaction were identified as *hygiene factors*. These were policy and administration, technical supervision, relationship with supervisor, relationships with peers, relationships with subordinates, salary, job security, personal life, work conditions, and status. Failure to provide for employees' hygiene needs will lead to job dissatisfaction and poor performance, but merely meeting these needs does not provide motivation to improve performance.

Developing Communication Networks

Many senior managers and leaders use their personal contacts to have things done or to get information. As discussed earlier in this text, one of the more recent changes in the business world is the rise in the power of interpersonal communication and use of technology for communication purposes. These changes have created a challenge for managers because with them, more formal structures have decreased influence. The change has created an opportunity, however, for savvy managers and leaders, since these informal relationships or communication networks can be developed systematically.

There are four common role-players whose performance is critical to the productivity of any organization. These four role-players have huge influence within an organization:

central connectors

Link most people in an informal network with one another.

- **Central connectors** link most people in an informal network with one another. These central connectors are the "go-to" people for information in a group. These people do not necessarily have to be leaders of a group. Sometimes the central connectors may be bottlenecks, for example, using their roles for gains, not responding fast enough, or struggling to keep up with their own work while fulfilling the central connector role. The solution is to map informal network flow so as to identify central connectors and reassign some duties, if appropriate. (See Figure 9-2 for an example of a network map.)

boundary spanners

Connect an informal network with another information network.

- **Boundary spanners** connect an informal network with another information network, for example, other parts of the company or similar networks in other organizations. One problem that might arise with boundary spanners is that they may be networking with the wrong person in another network. In this case, senior management can step in and help shape spanners' network contacts.

information brokers

Keep the different subgroups in an informal network together.

- **Information brokers** keep the different subgroups in an informal network together. They are like boundary spanners, but they only operate within the network. They may not be the central connector, but they wield the same power. They are characterized by a wealth of indirect connections. However, heavy reliance on information brokers can have a negative impact when they leave the firm. To solve this problem, central connectors should develop more connections with subgroups so that they may take on the role of information broker if needed.

peripheral specialists

Those in informal networks that others rely on for specialized expertise.

- **Peripheral specialists** are those in informal networks that others rely on for specialized expertise. Giving them more responsibilities, such as attending more meetings or traveling, may reduce their time, which they need to stay ahead in their field.[53]

Figure 9-2 **Example of an Informal Network Analysis Map**

Finding Central Connectors and Peripheral Specialists

Even though Lisa is the head of the department, Alan is considered the go-to person for information within this informal network. He plays the role of central connector. Meanwhile, Paul operates on the perimeter of the network, offering expertise to members of the group as it's needed, but not necessarily connecting with many other colleagues frequently. Paul plays the role of peripheral specialist.

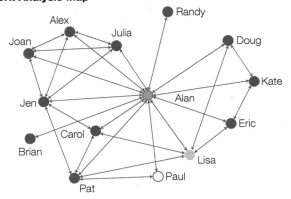

Source: Cross, R., & Prusak, L. (2002). "People Who Make Organizations Go—or Stop," *Harvard Business Review*. Retrieved June 25, 2012, from *http://hbr.org/product/the-people-who-make-organizations-go-or-stop/an/R0206G-PDF-ENG*.

Social network analysis is a technique that lets users identify and map informal networks of people. It identifies the functions or activities where connectivity is most needed to improve productivity and then maps the corresponding networks. It is a method to collect information from people that can then be used to map sets of relationships within priority areas or an organization or department. One of the most effective ways to collect information is to create and conduct a survey. The information collected from the survey can then be used to create network maps that illustrate the relationships between the members of a group.

Through social network analysis, people can identify where they need to build more or better relationships. Focusing on the four dimensions discussed here can help managers and leaders improve their connections and better manage informal communication within an organizational context.

Communicating Change

Organizations are constantly changing, but perhaps there is nothing more challenging to an organization than communicating change to employees and successfully influencing them to accept that change without enormous resistance. The success of any change program is heavily reliant on the quality of communication about that change. Successfully implementing change within an organization involves communication on all organizational levels and in all forms: group discussion, one-on-one conversations, formal meetings, and in writing.

Typically, change arises from one of two sources within an organization. The traditional source of change is management, which is assumed to be in a better position to recognize the need for change and know how to implement it. However, this approach to change may fail or meet resistance if the need for such change is not effectively communicated to employees, the benefits of such change to them is not clearly understood, and a clear system of implementing the change is not provided.

Employees are a second source of change. This approach is beneficial because participation in decision making assumedly makes the resulting change more likely to be accepted and implemented. A strategic opportunity lies in this second source of change for the aspiring leader.

In general, however, change is resisted, particularly if it is significant. People resist change for a number of reasons:

- **Disruption of social relationships.** Changes that disrupt social relationships can create discomfort and cause anxiety.

- **Threat to roles.** Changes in organizational structure and individual roles may threaten a person's position, recognition, power, and sense of self-worth. If individuals perceive the change will result in a loss of esteem or recognition, they will resist. Even increased responsibilities may result in resistance if individuals lack confidence in their ability to perform the new duties.

- **Economic loss.** Employees may resist organizational or departmental changes that may be read as a signal for lower pay, less opportunity for advancement, or job loss.[54]

Successful strategic change depends on *backing* from those who authorize change, *accessibility* in the sense that managers and leaders understand what they are working toward, *specificity* in terms of the detailed planning, and *cultural receptivity* or the receptiveness of those affected by the change.[55]

A strategic process for implementing change applies the strategic elements examined earlier in this text:

1. Performing an analysis of the context and the audience
2. Designing a communication strategy
3. Developing tactics for strategy implementation

The questions provided in Table 9-4 should be asked during each of these phases.

Table 9-4 Analysis for Communicating Change

Planning Level	Questions
Contextual Analysis	1. Have employees readily assimilated other changes? 2. Is the change congruent with the culture? 3. Is the change seen as noncomplex and manageable? 4. Is the change seen as advantageous over past practices? 5. Are the benefits readily observable? 6. Will key relationships be adversely affected?
Audience Analysis	1. Who are the major groups of employees that will be affected? 2. How will each group be affected? 3. What are the most likely points of resistance of each group? 4. What are the communication preferences of each group? 5. Who are the key opinion leaders of each group?
Strategic Design	1. What are the tentative communication goals for each audience? 2. What are the common goals for the general audience? 3. What is a unifying theme that energizes and motivates employees? 4. How should communication resources be allocated? 5. What is a general structure (phases) for achieving the goals and communicating the theme?
Tactical Analysis	1. What channels should be used? 2. What are the key messages? 3. What should be the timing of the various messages? 4. Who should communicate the messages? 5. How can employees voice their concerns? 6. How should the process be monitored?

Source: Adapted from Clampitt, P. G. (2001). *Communicating for Managerial Effectiveness*, 2nd ed. (Thousand Oaks, CA: Sage).

Chapters 4 and 5 of this text have already examined processes for analyzing the context and the audience. Many of these considerations are also applied in developing the strategic design for a program to communicate change. It is important to emphasize that persuasion is often a process, as was discussed in Chapter 3. Therefore, when developing a structure for achieving the goals of a change campaign, a number of channels and media of communication may have to be used over a period of time. The change message may have to be introduced in phases by first informing employees of the change, then persuading them of the need for the change, and finally, providing them the specifics of how the change will be implemented.

Table 9-5 identifies a number of communication practices that leaders might implement when communicating change.

The following section discusses qualities that leaders should try to communicate and practice to influence change. Following that is a discussion on delivery tactics for effectively delivering change messages. The last section on cultural adaptation identifies key areas of culture and system changes necessary to align the organization with the changes being proposed.

Leadership Qualities

In any change effort, it is critical that the organization have leaders who manage and shepherd the transformation through the organization. Current change research suggests that defining the change focus, guiding the change effort, and facilitating organizational participation are all important leader activities.[56] More specifically, the following key leadership elements in any change effort must be emphasized:

- **Articulate the plan.** What this means is that leaders must have the ability to articulate a plan for moving forward. Successful articulation means that leaders demonstrate passion for the idea, make their case in a compelling way, understand the need to focus on results, and insist on measuring outcomes.

Table 9-5 Leadership Practices for Organizational Change

Leadership Qualities	Delivery Tactics	Cultural Adaptations
Articulate the plan	**Be honest and open**	**Give them what they want**
▪ Be passionate about the change	▪ Tell the truth	▪ Tailor rewards
▪ Make a compelling case	▪ Make communication a priority	▪ Use money when feasible
▪ Focus on results	▪ Communicate face-to-face	▪ Provide public recognition
▪ Measure outcomes	▪ Talk the talk	▪ Encourage pride in work
		▪ Improve the quality of life
Work the plan	**Cut to the chase**	
▪ Drive change deeply	▪ Build a shared understanding	**Overcome resistance**
▪ Understand the work involved	▪ Be clear	▪ Replace personnel
▪ Solicit feedback	▪ Be consistent	▪ Persevere
▪ Walk the walk	▪ Repeat yourself	▪ Demonstrate the benefits
	▪ Be concrete	▪ Appeal to self-interest
Be a genuine team player	▪ Use data persuasively	▪ Encourage rule breaking
▪ Trust and support your people	▪ Be transparent	
▪ Mold consensus	▪ Be prompt	**Be resourceful**
▪ Share credit		▪ Engage leadership
▪ Be visible	**Adapt your message**	▪ Engage employees
▪ Heed communications experts	▪ Focus on internal messaging	▪ Give ownership
	▪ Communicate to all levels	▪ Work from the bottom up
Face bad news	▪ Know your audience	▪ Provide training
▪ Deal with the reality	▪ Ask, "What's in it for me?"	▪ Use outside expertise
▪ Use urgency as a motivator		
▪ Support problem solving		**Accept change as a way of life**
		▪ Be patient
		▪ Celebrate and repeat successes

Source: Adapted from King, C. L., Brooks, D., & Hartge, T. D. (2007). *Effective Communication Practices During Organizational Transformation: A Benchmarking Study of the U.S. Automobile Industry and U.S. Naval Aviation Enterprise.* Center for Defense Management Reform Sponsored Report Series. Retrieved November 7, 2009, from *http://www.defensereform.org/_files/FY2007/NPS-CDMR-GM-07-001.pdf.*

▪ **Work the plan.** Good leaders must be capable of fully executing the plan and permeating the whole organization. What this often means is that leaders must be willing to drive change throughout the organization, take the time to understand what they're asking the organization to do, solicit feedback along the way, make minor adjustments without changing course, and embody the changes in their own behaviors. Soliciting feedback might take a variety of forms, such as inviting and responding to employee e-mails, interviewing employees on a regular basis, inviting employees to short meetings with executives, and sharing lunch with employees periodically.

▪ **Be a genuine team player.** Being a team player must move beyond platitudes: Leaders need to build trust and mold consensus, share credit, become visible throughout their organization, and strongly engage with communications experts.

▪ **Face bad news.** Part of being a leader is the willingness to deal with bad news, understand the urgencies that result, use those urgencies to motivate the organization, and commit to solving problems as they come up.

Delivery Tactics

At the heart of any change effort is the effectiveness of the message. A variety of message delivery tactics can be used to support organizational change efforts:

▪ **Be honest and open.** In communicating change efforts, it's important for organizations to tell the truth, even the bad news, about the current situation. However, there are good and bad ways to be honest. To have the best impact on people, it's important to pay attention to how you communicate, to recognize the importance of face-to-face interactions, and to make sure what is communicated has integrity. The benefits of face-to-face communication include the potential for more in-depth discussion, being more informative, grabbing the listener's attention, being more persuasive, being clearer, getting feedback, and establishing a better personal connection.

- **Cut to the chase.** Messages need to be highly accessible to audiences, particularly when communicating changes. It is critical to build understanding and persuade others by providing and repeating simple, concise, and consistent messages that use concrete, transparent data. Additionally, messages need to be delivered promptly.

- **Adapt your message.** Knowing whom to target and how to target them is a constant challenge in communicating change messages. Leaders have to pay close attention to internal audiences, communicate through all levels, know the specific needs of particular audiences, listen to feedback, and understand the impact the changes will have on their audiences.[57]

Cultural Adaptations

When priorities change, the culture needs to change with it. That means that systems and norms need to reflect the new goals of the organization. There are several key requirements in creating a change culture:

- **Give them what they want.** Causes and effects drive people, and it's important that a reward system be aligned with what the organization is trying to accomplish. There are numerous ways to creative incentives for employees; among them are money, public recognition, pride in work, and quality of life issues.

- **Overcome resistance.** Change and resistance go hand in hand, and leaders may need to draw on all their resources at some point to overcome them. At times, leaders may need to fire people. However, they often need to stick to the plan, demonstrate the benefits to employees, appeal to their self-interests, and sometimes encourage people to break the rules.

- **Be resourceful.** There are numerous resources within an organization, and a robust change culture avails itself of all of them. Those that are most critical include fully engaging leadership and employees, encouraging employee ownership of their areas of responsibility, recognizing the power of bottom-up inspiration, providing necessary training, and using outside expertise when necessary.

- **Accept change as a way of life.** The ultimate lesson in change management is in understanding that change never ends. This requires leaders to be patient, celebrate and repeat successes, and to learn from success and failure.[58]

Summary

Interpersonal communication involves mutual influence, usually for the purpose of managing relationships. As such, it is an important aspect of communication within an organization. Broadly speaking, there are three aspects of interpersonal communication: verbal communication, nonverbal communication, and listening.

Verbal communication can be characterized as one of three types of interpersonal style: assertive, avoiding, or aggressive. Aggressive communication is characterized by a focus on one's own needs with little to no regard for the other. Assertiveness, on the other hand, involves both—taking care of one's own needs as well as those of the other. Ideally, conversations in the workplace would involve genuine dialogue rather than debating with others to prove who is right and who is wrong.

Nonverbal communication comprises most of the information that is exchanged in a face-to-face communication situation. In nonverbal communication, communication channels are multiple and simultaneous. These channels include information that we receive from another person's facial expressions and eyes; body posture, movement, and appearance; the use of space; the use of time; touching; vocal cues; and clothing and other artifacts.

Listening is a much-needed skill in the workplace—most of our time in communication situations involves listening—unfortunately, it is the skill that is most cited for improvement by managers. Listening is different from hearing. Listening requires time, energy, and focus, whereas hearing is the ability to discern sounds. There are three types of listening: active, empathic, and critical. Active listening is "listening with a purpose." Empathic listening is a form of active listening with the goal of understanding the other person. Critical listening is used to evaluate the accuracy, meaningfulness, and usefulness of a message.

Probably nothing damages a manager's credibility more than a poorly conceived or planned meeting. Meetings, like presentations, are a medium that should be used to leverage nonverbal communication. They should also be carefully planned so as not to be perceived as a waste of time, which will certainly damage the meeting caller's credibility. Meetings should also be followed up to ensure that attendees have a record of the actions that were taken.

Additional tasks for organizational leaders are to motivate and to communicate change to employees. These are related issues because motivation may involve change in employees' behaviors and attitudes in relation to their work; however, change in management typically involves organizational changes that originate at the top of the organization. The success of any change program is heavily reliant on the quality of communication about that change. Successfully implementing organizational change involves communication on all organizational levels and in all forms: group discussion, one-on-one conversations, formal meetings, and in writing.

Key Terms

interpersonal communication **227**

trust **227**

avoidance **228**

aggressiveness **228**

assertiveness **228**

strategic alignment **229**

nonverbal communication **229**

kinesics **230**

somatotype **231**

proxemics **231**

territoriality **231**

personal space **231**

intimate distance **232**

personal distance **232**

social distance **232**

public distance **232**

chronemics **232**

polychronic time (P-time) **232**

monochronic time (M-time) **232**

haptics **233**

active listening **235**

feedback **235**

empathic listening **236**

critical listening **236**

need **243**

drive **243**

goal **243**

motive **243**

central connectors **245**

boundary spanners **245**

information brokers **245**

peripheral specialists **245**

Discussion Questions

1. What is your interpersonal style of communication? How might you become more assertive and better ensure that genuine dialogue is taking place?
2. What are the seven channels of nonverbal communication? Provide some examples of how nonverbal messages might be interpreted differently by people of differing cultures.
3. What are some of the barriers to effective listening that you commonly encounter? What are some strategies for overcoming each of these barriers?
4. What are the communication dispositions Redding identified that were found in leaders able to effectively motivate employees?
5. What are some communication practices or behaviors that leaders might use to help employees adapt to and accept organizational change?
6. What are some pitfalls to avoid when planning and conducting a meeting? How might these be avoided?

Applications

1. Take the listening quiz on page 235 of this chapter, and then write a memo in which you identify listening skills that might be improved and set specific goals for their improvement.
2. Choose a country other than the one of your birth, and conduct research on common nonverbal behaviors and their meanings. Write a report that informs someone from the United States how to prepare for a visit to this country and better anticipate and interpret the meanings of nonverbal communication there.
3. Write an assessment of your interpersonal communication skills by identifying your interpersonal style, nonverbal communication, and listening style. It may be helpful to ask colleagues or peers questions about each of these interpersonal elements to get a clearer picture of how others see you. Be sure to choose people who will be honest in their answers. After assessing your interpersonal skills in each of these areas, create a plan to improve your interpersonal skills that identifies specific actions and outcomes within a specified time period.
4. Prepare an agenda for an actual meeting you plan to hold. Your agenda for this meeting should include the following introductory items:
   - The primary purpose of your meeting (to generate ideas, narrow a field of options, or to make a decision?)
   - The time, date, and place of your meeting
   - The names of those attending.
   Following this information, you should provide a list of *specific* topics you intend to discuss during your meeting that are organized in the order of their importance (the most important first). You may wish to include a time limit for the discussion of each item.
5. Hold the planned meeting, then analyze its effectiveness by discussing what you observed, including the communication behaviors and roles that each participant tended to play. In providing this assessment, you might consider the following:
   - What did we do in this meeting that worked well?
   - What happened that we would not want to repeat? Are there bad habits into which we keep falling?
   - What roles did different participants take on? Were these helpful in achieving group goals? Why or why not?
   - What type of communication behaviors did participants display? Were these helpful in achieving group goals? Why or why not?
   - Did participants feel valued and respected because others listened to them and responded to what they said in a way that fostered participation?
   - Other issues to consider include how well you
     - Were able to keep the discussion of a particular topic within a reasonable amount of time?
     - Were able to keep the discussion focused on the agenda topics?
     - Were able to deal with conflict and individualistic behaviors effectively and productively?
     - Were able to reach your goals for the meeting?
6. Create an informal communication network map of a group in which you are involved. After identifying the four network roles, assess whether changes need to be made to make the persons who play those roles more effective. Write up your assessment and your recommendations.
7. Identify a change that you would like to see happen in an organization or group of which you are a part. Create a plan to implement that change through communication strategy and practice. What risks need to be identified and accounted for? Who would you need to communicate the plan to and what messages would need to be articulated?

8. Your team should prepare an agenda for an actual meeting it plans to hold. Your agenda for this meeting should include the following introductory items:
   - The primary purpose of your meeting (to generate ideas, narrow a field of options, or to make a decision?)
   - The time, date, and place of your meeting
   - The names of those attending.

   Following this information, you should provide a list of *specific* topics you intend to discuss during your meeting that are organized in the order of their importance (the most important first). You may wish to include a time limit for the discussion of each item.

9. After your team holds a planned meeting, you may wish to analyze its effectiveness by discussing what you observed, including the communication behaviors and roles that each team member tended to play. In providing this assessment, you might consider the following:
   - What did we do in this meeting that worked well?
   - What happened that we would not want to repeat? Are there bad habits into which we keep falling?

- What roles did different team members take on? Were these helpful in achieving group goals? Why or why not?
- What type of communication behaviors did team members display? Were these helpful in achieving group goals? Why or why not?
- Other issues to consider include how well your group was able to attend to both the task and social functions of a team. More specifically, you might wish to consider the following:
- Were you able to keep the discussion of a particular topic within a reasonable amount of time?
- Were you able to keep the discussion focused on the agenda topics?
- Did participants feel valued and respected because others listened to them and responded to what they said in a way that fostered participation?
- Were you able to deal with conflict and individualistic behaviors effectively and productively?
- Were you able to reach your goals for the meeting?

Endnotes

1. Beebe, S. A., Beebe, S. J., & Redmond, M. V. (2005). *Interpersonal Communication: Relating to Others* (4th ed.). Boston: Pearson.
2. Lencioni, P. M. (2002). *The Five Dysfunctions of a Team.* San Francisco: Jossey-Bass.
3. Robbins, S. P. (2001). *Organizational Behavior* (9th ed.). Upper Saddle River, NJ: Prentice Hall.
4. Eisenberg, E. M., & Goodall, H. L., Jr. (1993). *Organizational Communication: Balancing Creativity and Constraint.* New York: St. Martin's Press, p. 252.
5. Eisenberg & Goodall, 1993, p. 252.
6. Pearson, J. C., Nelson, P. E., Titsworth, S., & Harter, L. (2003). *Human Communication.* New York: McGraw-Hill, p. 214.
7. Eisenberg & Goodall, 1993, p. 252.
8. Orbe, M. P. (1996). Laying the foundation for co-cultural communication theory: An inductive approach to studying "nondominant" communication strategies and the factors that influence them. *Communication Studies, 47,* 157–176, p. 170.
9. Infante, D., Trebling, J., Sheperd, P., & Seeds, D. (1984). The relationship of argumentativeness to verbal aggression. *Southern Speech Communication Journal, 50,* 67–77.
10. Orbe, 1996, p. 170.
11. Yankelovich, D. (1999). *The Magic of Dialogue: Transforming Conflict into Cooperation.* New York: Simon & Schuster.
12. Eisenberg & Goodall, 1993, p. 252.
13. Burgoon, J. K., & Saine, T. (1978). *The Unspoken Dialogue: An Introduction to Nonverbal Communication.* Boston: Houghton Mifflin.

14. Chaney, L. H., & Martin, J. S. (2011). *Intercultural Business Communication* (5th ed.). Boston: Prentice Hall.
15. Chaney & Martin, 2011.
16. Ibid.
17. Ibid.
18. Hensley, W. (1992). Why does the best looking person in the room always seem to be surrounded by admirers? *Psychological Reports, 70,* 457–469; Knapp, M. L., & Hall, J. A. (1992). *Nonverbal Communication in Human Interaction* (3rd ed.). Fort Worth: Harcourt Brace Jovanovich.
19. Brody, J. E. (1994, March 21). Notions of beauty transcend culture, new study suggests. *The New York Times,* A14.
20. Knapp & Hall, 1992; Widgery, R. N. (1974). Sex of receiver and physical attractiveness of source as determinants of initial credibility perception. *Western Speech, 38,* 13–17.
21. Knapp & Hall, 1992.
22. Kaplan, R. M. (1978). Is beauty talent? Sex interaction in the attractiveness halo effect. *Sex Roles, 4,* 195–204.
23. Gudykunst, W. B., & Ting-Toomey, S. (1988). *Culture and Interpersonal Communication.* Thousand Oaks, CA: Sage Publications.
24. Chaney & Martin, 2011.
25. Ibid.
26. Ibid.
27. Fisher, J. D., Rytting, M., & Heslin, R. (1976). Hands touching hands: Affective and evaluative effects of interpersonal touch. *Sociometry, 3,* 416–421; Jourard, S. M., & Rubin, J. E. (1968).

Self-disclosure and touching: A study of two modes of interpersonal encounter and their inter-relation. *Journal of Humanistic Psychology, 8*, 39–48; and Henley, N. (1973–1974). Power, sex, and nonverbal communication. *Berkeley Journal of Sociology*, 18, 10–11.

28. Chaney & Martin, 2011.

29. Axtell, R. E. (1998). *Gestures.* New York: John Wiley & Sons, Inc.

30. Fisher, P. (1975). The future's past. *New Literary History, 6*, 587–606.

31. Taylor, L. C., & Compton, N. H. (1968). Personality correlates of dress conformity. *Journal of Home Economics*, 60, 653–656.

32. Henricks, S. H., Kelley, E. A., & Eicher, J. B. (1968). Senior girls' appearance and social acceptance. *Journal of Home Economics*, 60, 167–172.

33. Douty, H. I. (1963). Influence of clothing on perception of persons. *Journal of Home Economics*, 55, 197–202.

34. Gray, J., Jr. (1993). *The Winning Image.* New York: AMACOM.

35. Molloy, J.T. (1996). *New Woman's Dress for Success.* New York: Warner.

36. Weinrauch, J., & Swanda, J. (1975). Examining the significance of listening: An exploratory study of contemporary management. *Journal of Business Communication*, 13, 25–32.

37. Nichols, R., & Stevens, L. (1983). Are you listening? *Language Arts*, 60 (2), 163–165.

38. Salopek, J. (1999). Is anyone listening? Listening skills in the corporate setting. *Training and Development*, 53, 58–59.

39. Burley-Allen, M. (2001). Listen up. *HR Magazine*, 46 (11), 115–119.

40. Burley-Allen, 2001.

41. Ibid.

42. Ibid.

43. Ibid.

44. Barker, L. L. (1971). *Listening Behavior.* Englewood Cliffs, NJ: Prentice-Hall.

45. Ethridge, M. (2004, January 12). Workplace expert offers advice on conducting meetings. *Akron Beacon Journal, via Ohio Knight Ridder/Tribune Business News*, NA.

46. Friedman, M. (1996). Facilitating productive meetings. *Training & Development*, 50 (10), 11.

47. Messmer, M. (2002). Conducting effective meetings. *National Public Accountant*, 47 (6), 15.

48. Clark, R. (1998). Meetings: Valuable but misunderstood. *Cornell Hotel & Restaurant Administration Quarterly*, 39 (4), 12.

49. Kotter, J.P. (2001). What leaders really do. *Harvard Business Review* 79 (11), 85–96.

50. Redding, W. C. (1972). *Communication Within the Organization: An Interpretive Review of Theory and Research.* New York: Industrial Communication Council.

51. Ray, E. B. & Miller, K.I. (1991). The influence of communication structure and social support on job stress and burnout. *Management Communication Quarterly*, 4 (4), 506–527.

52. Herzberg, F. (1966). *Work and the Nature of Man.* New York: Collins.

53. Cross, R. & Prusak, L. (2002, June) The people who make organizations go—or stop. *Harvard Business Review*, 80 (6), 105–112.

54. Rasberry, R. W., & Lemoine, L. F. (1986). *Effective Managerial Communication.* Boston: Kent Publishing Co.

55. Miller, S. (1997). Implementing strategic decisions: Four key success factors. *Organizational Studies*, 18, 577–602.

56. King, C. L., Brooks, D., & Hartge, T. D. (2007). Effective communication practices during organizational transformation: A benchmarking study of the U.S. automobile industry and U.S. Naval Aviation Enterprise. Center for Defense Management Reform Sponsored Report Series. Retrieved November 7, 2009, from *http://www.defensereform.org/_files/FY2007/NPS-CDMR-GM-07-001.pdf.*

57. King et al., 2007.

58. Ibid.

FedEx Corporation: *A Case Study on Employee Training and the Impact of Social Media*

FedEx Makes a Mistake

On December 19, 2011, Mike,* a FedEx delivery person, set out to do his usual rounds. Christmas was approaching, and he had delivered hundreds, if not thousands, of purchases to customers' doorsteps in time to be wrapped and nestled under a Christmas tree. But, this day was different. Mike had had a long day and there were many stops ahead of him. Naturally, he wanted to complete his deliveries as quickly as possible. As he arrived to a gated home and prepared to deliver a large computer monitor, he weighed his options and walked to the back of his truck, picked up the computer monitor, and began walking to the gate.

Not willing to go through the hassle of ringing the doorbell (located at the gate) and waiting for the home-owner to walk outside to retrieve the package, Mike decided to take a simple short-cut: he threw the computer monitor over the gate. It was in a padded box, so what would be the harm? What Mike didn't know was that this home had a security camera monitoring the gate at all times, and that the homeowner would upload the footage captured by a security camera to YouTube. In the description of the video, he writes:

"Here is a video of my monitor being 'delivered'. The sad part is that I was home at the time with the front door wide open. All he would have had to do was ring the bell on the gate. Now, I have to return my monitor since it is broken."

Source: "FedEx Guy Throwing My Computer Monitor"

In the comments section below the video, another YouTube user recalls a similar experience and claims that he "[stays] away from FedEx as much as [he] can." Other users describe FedEx as a "very inefficient company," and another user writes, "I hope you reported this. If you weren't home or he couldn't get in the gate then he should have taken it to the post office. I'm really losing confidence in FedEx."

This small slip-up by a single employee made a sizable impact on FedEx's reputation. The video garnered over 9 million views and was broadcasted by news stations throughout the country. FedEx responded with a video of its own, in which the Senior VP of U.S. Operations at the time, Matthew Thornton III, apologized to customers for the employee's actions. However, the damage had already been done.

This case examines the relationship between upper-level management and lower-level workers in FedEx Corporation, and, more specifically, how that relationship can be improved through effective communication ultimately to provide customers with the highest quality service possible.

Company Background

In 1965, while he was attending Yale University and earning a Bachelor's degree in economics, Frederick W. Smith wrote a term paper for Professor Challis A. Hall's Economics 43A class that contained a blueprint for a delivery service that would use a "hub-and-spoke" approach to handle the routing of packages. The hub-and-spoke model entails first sending parcels through a centralized sorting facility before shipping them onwards to their intended destinations. This archetype eventually became the foundation of Federal Express, a company Smith founded in 1971 upon his return from Vietnam, where he had served as a Marine Corps Officer from 1966 to 1970.

This case was originally written by Ryder White and Steven Argomaniz, as an assignment under faculty advisor Dr. RS Hubbard at the USC Marshall School of Business. Written May, 2014, used by permission of the USC Marshall School Case Study Initiative.

* Fictional name used to personify the situation and illustrate the type of issues some in this position would experience.

In a 2004 interview with *Bloomberg Magazine*, Smith claimed that the inspiration behind his paper "[came from] a very simple observation: As society automated, as people began to put computers in banks to cancel checks (rather than clerks), or people began to put sophisticated electronics in airplanes, society and the manufacturers of that automated society were going to need a completely different logistics system."

Smith identified the astounding difficulty in getting parcels and other airfreight delivered in one or two days, and he made it his company's mission to address and alleviate this problem. On April 17, 1973, with the launch of 14 small aircraft from Memphis International Airport, Federal Express officially began operations. That night, it delivered 186 packages to 25 different cities from Rochester, New York, to Miami, Florida.

In 1994, Federal Express changed its name to "FedEx," taking a hint from its customers, who often referred to the company by its shortened name. Then, in 2000, the company was renamed "FedEx Express" to reflect its position within FedEx Corporation's broader portfolio of services. This name change signified just how large Smith's company had become. No longer was FedEx strictly an overnight delivery service: it was a logistics empire.

Today, FedEx Express has a fleet of 634 aircraft that service more than 220 countries and territories, including every address in the United States. Each day, FedEx Express handles more than 3.9 million packages and over 11 million pounds of freight. In 2012, FedEx had roughly 300,000 ground level employees throughout the company, and 20,000 independently contracted workers handling their ground delivery service. For the 2013 fiscal year, the company generated over $27 billion in revenue.

Company Culture

An important part of FedEx's ethical standards is its emphasis on company culture, safety and customers, as expressed on the company's Company Overview and Facts webpage:

> *"Consistently ranked among the world's most admired and trusted employers, FedEx inspires its more than 300,000 team members to remain "absolutely, positively" focused on safety, the highest ethical and professional standards and the needs of their customers and communities."*

For a large corporation like FedEx, it is extremely difficult to realize a common company culture. However, to instill its core values, FedEx promotes a "Culture of Safety" to its 160,000 employees worldwide. FedEx invests millions of dollars in equipment and training to prevent injuries and accidents in the workplace. For FedEx Express alone, illness and injury rates have decreased by almost half over the past 35 years.

FedEx's reinforces professional standards and customer service through their Code of Business Conduct and Ethics, which states: "Throughout the world, the FedEx name is synonymous with integrity and reliability. Our reputation is an important strategic asset – it is up to all of us to protect and enhance it. In today's environment, our strong corporate reputation is invaluable."

Employee Training

FedEx strongly believes in training its ground-level workers, because it enhances employee performance and productivity, which in turn improves the service quality, reduces employee turnover, and increases profitability for the company as a whole. During its training sessions, FedEx emphasizes the slogan "P-S-P," an abbreviation for "People-Service-Profit." Thus, it is clear the company cares about its employees and understands that its profitability depends largely on their ability to provide excellent customer service.

FedEx offers on-the-job training to its employees, including mentoring programs and group discussions and interactive videos, to ensure its employees provide services to customers based on core values.

Additionally, all FedEx employees and independent contractors go through a comprehensive orientation program to equip themselves with the necessary skill sets for their respective job duties. This orientation program also teaches FedEx team members to relate to one another without discrimination. For independent contractors to be able to work with FedEx, they must participate in FedEx Culture of Safety programs, fulfill an orientation program, engage in training programs, and agree to FedEx's Code of Business Conduct and Ethics. Though numerous training and employee development resources are available to independent contractors, the contracting company is largely responsible for monitoring their own workers.

FedEx also has an employee recognition program, which gives the following awards and accolades to ground-level workers and managers:

- Five Star Award – for exemplifying excellent service and teamwork practices

- Bravo Zulu Award – for going above and beyond their job requirements to help the company's profitability
- CEO Safety Award – for promoting excellent safety standards

Perks to winning these awards include cash bonuses, trophies, movie theater tickets, etc.

FedEx Makes Another Mistake

On July 24, 2013, two FedEx workers in Manhattan made a stop at approximately 6 p.m. to pick-up and load packages into their truck. After carting around 50 medium-sized boxes (13.25" × 11.5" × 2.38") to the back of the truck, and likely wishing to take advantage of any opportunity to shorten their work day, one worker began to recklessly throw piles of 5-6 boxes into the back of the truck. Although the second worker was hesitant to join at first, the first worker gave the second worker a "thumbs up" as a sign to join in the box throwing.

The second worker took a larger and heavier brown box and sent it crashing to the back wall of the truck, hitting many other boxes on its descent. Though these two workers exchanged a warm laugh together, they had no idea that the driver of the car parked directly behind the FedEx truck was recording the entire scene on his Smartphone.

YouTube user *banstaman* uploaded the footage later that evening, and it soon reached over a million views. Days later, this video was circulating throughout national media outlets.

In the comments section, one YouTube user states, "How was she getting away with this in the first place?! Is there anyone even watching over these FedEx workers and keeping them accountable?" Another user comments, "and that is why people don't like to use FedEx."

What's Missing?

Despite its comprehensive training programs and strong efforts to promote a distinct company culture based on People-Service-Profit, FedEx has experienced the same problem of delivering inadequate customer service time and time again. Moreover, in today's media-driven world, corporate problems are magnified like never before. Anyone with a video camera or Smartphone now has the ability to impact a company's reputation with only a few clicks of a mouse.

The proliferation of social media affects all companies. More so now than ever, companies need to ensure that their ground-level workers are providing quality customer service at all times. The question is, after all of FedEx's efforts to train its employees and foster a constructive company culture, what's missing?

Discussion Question

1. What are the most pertinent questions that should be asked in order to address the critical issues, main decisions and possible solutions to this case?

© mast3r / bigstockphoto.com

Chapter 10

Communicating in and Leading Groups and Teams

After reading this chapter,
you will be able to

After reading this chapter,
you will be able to

- *Identify why groups form and understand the group formation process.*

- *Understand the roles team members take in groups and which are productive and which are not.*

- *Identify the causes of group cohesiveness and understand when high group cohesiveness might lead to low performance.*

- *Understand the types of influence exercised in groups and characteristics that lead to higher performance in a group.*

- *Understand the group decision-making process and how intercultural influences may affect it.*

- *Identify the types of conflict that arise in groups and the differing responses to conflict.*

- *Learn how to select the best brainstorming technique to enhance group creativity.*

- *Understand the elements of effective team leadership.*

- *Implement practices to effectively communicate in and lead virtual teams.*

Case Questions

1. What are some of the typical problems of working in a team or a group?

2. What additional challenges are faced by those working in a virtual team?

3. How might intercultural differences affect team functioning?

4. How might these challenges—for face-to-face groups and virtual teams—be successfully addressed?

The Case of the Virtual Marketing Team

"Hey, Jerry," Malcolm said as he entered Jerry's office. "I thought I would stop by and check in to see how the sales plan for the global rollout of the new e-reader was going."

"Seems like everything is A-OK," Jerry responded to his boss. "The team has been submitting ideas to target the product to each of our markets and it looks like there will be plenty of information to create a thorough plan."

Malcolm hesitated a moment. He knew that employees tended to tell their supervisors what they thought they wanted to hear. "Was this a case of that phenomenon?" he wondered at Jerry's response.

"Great to hear that everyone is involved and producing suggestions," Malcolm said. "But there is a downside, of course. Do you think all of this information can easily be formulated into a coherent plan by our deadline for rollout? Do you think that is even the right approach? Or do you think that we should create ad hoc committees to work on regional marketing plans?"

"Good questions," Jerry said. "But we haven't gotten that far, since we are currently in the 'gathering information' phase. That's probably the next step in the process. Trying to determine whether there are similarities by region or country in terms of the marketing approach and maybe then dividing up the marketing plan along those lines sounds like a good direction in which to go."

"Look, Jerry," Malcolm said. "This is an important product for us in terms of our revenue expectations. You're the team leader on this thing. You need to be thinking ahead to try to identify bottlenecks in the process, and then try to eliminate or streamline some the work that needs to be done. We need to be ready to go when the product is."

"I know, I know," Jerry said. "I'm not making excuses here, but leading a virtual team is a lot different than leading a typical project team. I've never met some of these people and don't know what to expect from them or how far I can push them without getting resistance or worse. I've got twenty-three salespeople scattered all over the world and I feel more like I'm trying to herd cats than run a marketing program sometimes."

During the 1980s, an explosion occurred in the use of teams in organizations. One of the goals of using teams was to do "more with less" in an era of shrinking resources and increased competition. Companies that have traditional, centralized, hierarchical structures are less efficient and responsive to rapidly changing market conditions. As the use of technology has expanded rapidly in organizations, virtual teams have become more common, bringing both benefits and new challenges to be addressed and solved.

Despite the widespread enthusiasm for teams, the definition of what constitutes a team remains ambiguous as it is commonly confused with a group. A **group** is a collection of people who share a common purpose, feel a sense of belonging to the group, and who exert influence on one another. A **team** is a coordinated group of individuals organized to work together to achieve a specific, common goal.

There are two types of teams in organizations: project teams and work teams. *Project teams* are standing groups that help coordinate the successful completion of a particular project, product, or service. One type of project team is comprised of people working to design and develop a new product. Members of such a team may include engineers, manufacturing experts, marketing specialists, and quality assessment personnel, among others. In such teams, each member is an expert in one aspect of the project necessary for its success.

Work teams are intact groups of employees who are responsible for a "whole" work process or segment that delivers a product or service to an internal or external customer. For example, an eight-member work team at a Southern California aerospace firm is responsible for metallizing all components in the company. The team is housed together, has mapped its internal work flow, and is continually improving its work process. Work teams are characterized by their degree of empowerment or ability to self-direct or self-manage their work processes. However, true self-directed work teams are rare in the United States because of our history of use of the classical, hierarchical organizational structure. In other words, such teams would require a radical reframing of the power relationships in organizations, which few members of management are genuinely prepared to examine.[1]

A third type of team that is becoming more and more common because of the global transformation of business is the *virtual team*. IBM, for example, has more than 4,500 teams worldwide who do their work in shared digital space.

The success of such digital collaboration depends not only on the technology but also on people's ability to adopt a new way of working. What is important is the process that is used to help people make the required behavior changes. (More on communicating in virtual teams can be found later in this chapter.)

Regardless of whether an organization uses teams or simply involves group coordination, group communication skills are necessary in any organization, because the group is the fundamental unit of social organization. Yet, achieving effective group communication is generally a challenge not only because of issues of empowerment and self-direction but also because of our cultural legacy. "This [increased use of groups] is perhaps the most difficult principle to adapt to Western, particularly U.S., organizations. Our romantic obsession with rugged individualism, our cultural preoccupation with individual initiative, achievement, and reward, and our philosophical and moral belief in the value of the individual all mitigate against our willing participation in groups."[2]

Christopher M. Avery, author of *Teamwork Is an Individual Skill*, agrees with this sentiment. "It's a social design problem. Teams are not unnatural, but we've made it difficult by the way we've socialized and organized ourselves [in our culture]."

However, according to Patrick M. Lencioni, author of *The Five Dysfunctions of a Team*, the challenges of creating effective groups can be overcome. The following are Lencioni's five dysfunctions of a team:

- **Absence of trust.** Without the willingness to be vulnerable to one another—to admit weaknesses, to acknowledge failures, to ask for help, to genuinely apologize from time to time—team members will suspect one another of being disingenuous and protective, Lencioni says.

group

A collection of people who share a common purpose, feel a sense of belonging to the group, and who exert influence on one another.

team

A coordinated group of individuals organized to work together to achieve a specific, common goal.

- **Fear of conflict.** Team members who don't trust one another can't engage in meaningful debate. Although some conflict is destructive, other types of conflict lead to improved processes, products, and services.

- **Lack of commitment.** Commitment, according to Lencioni, is a function of two things: clarity about the task and buy-in to goals.

- **Avoidance of accountability.** Without commitment, team members often struggle to hold one another accountable for problems and to call attention to counterproductive behavior. Communicating expectations of team members is critical at the beginning of a relationship.

- **Inattention to results.** Without accountability, team members tend to put their own needs (such as ego, career development, and recognition) before those of the team. When this occurs, achievement of the team's goals may obviously suffer.

By anticipating these dysfunctional tendencies and taking steps to avoid them, effective teams can be put into place in the workplace. In this chapter, the issues that help contribute to effective group communication will be discussed. These include group structure and development, cohesiveness, influence, performance, decision making, conflict, and brainstorming for creativity. The chapter concludes with a discussion of leadership in groups and communicating in virtual teams.

Forming Groups

Groups form for a variety of reasons, including the need to collaborate to achieve particular tasks and because of interpersonal attraction. In organizational settings, the first of these reasons is typically the reason we work in groups; however, the interpersonal attractiveness of group members can contribute to successful group formation. Similarly, cultural differences can affect our conceptions about teamwork.

Collective Endeavors

Groups are the means to achieve goals that would be beyond the reach of a single individual. In a workplace setting, individuals often form groups because they can only accomplish some goals when several individuals pool their unique talents in a coordinated effort. Other tasks can be accomplished by an individual, but a group may be more efficient.

Interpersonal Attraction

A number of factors increase attraction between individuals and can contribute to group formation. These include the following:

- **Proximity.** Proximity increases the opportunity for interaction and the likelihood a group will form. For example, students sitting in adjacent seats in a classroom often form cliques. Similarly, in a workplace situation, teams ideally would be arranged in adjacent offices or cubicles to increase communication and to help develop relationships built on trust. However, in virtual team situations, this is obviously not possible.

- **The similarity principle.** We like people who are similar to us in some way. This occurs for several reasons. First, people who adopt the same values and attitudes that we do reassure us that our beliefs are accurate.[3] Second, similarity serves as a signal to suggest that future interactions will be free of conflict.[4] Third, once we discover that we are similar to another person, we tend to immediately feel a sense of unity with that person.[5] Fourth, disliking a person who seems similar may prove to be psychologically distressing.[6] The preference for similarity may have a negative effect on intercultural teams for these reasons: dissimilarity may suggest more conflict and more difficulty because of differences in values, attitudes, and communication preferences. Similarly, many workplace teams are not founded on member similarity—although, commonalities will likely exist. Instead, workplace teams typically are formed based on how members' skills complement each other.

- **The complementary principle.** According to this principle, we are attracted to people who possess characteristics that complement our own personal characteristics.[7] For example, if you enjoy leading groups, you will tend not to be attracted to other individuals who strive for control of a group. Instead, you will probably respond more positively to those who accept your guidance. Perhaps you are an expert in marketing but also need expertise related to product manufacturing in order to create useful delivery schedules to distributors. Working in a team with experts from manufacturing can complement your skills to enable you to do your job more effectively.

- **The reciprocity principle.** Liking tends to be met with liking in return. When we discover that somebody accepts and approves of us, we usually respond by liking them in return. Negative reciprocity also occurs in groups: We dislike those who seem to reject us. In terms of the purposes of business communication, the ability to convey goodwill by establishing positive and productive relationships with others might improve the process of group formation.

- **The minimax principle.** People will join groups and remain in groups that provide them with the maximum number of valued rewards while incurring the fewest number of possible costs.[8] Rewards include acceptance by others, camaraderie, assistance in reaching personal goals, social support, exposure to new ideas, and opportunities to interact with people who are interesting and attractive. Although membership in a work team may not be voluntary, considering the minimax principle may help leaders ensure that teamwork goes more smoothly. As with the reciprocity principle, the ability to convey goodwill by establishing positive relationships with others may help in group formation.

In addition to the potential rewards of belonging to a team, people are usually attracted to groups whose members possess positively valued qualities, and they avoid groups of people with objectionable qualities. We prefer to associate with people who are generous, enthusiastic, punctual, dependable, helpful, strong, truthful, and intelligent.[9] We tend to dislike and reject people who possess socially unattractive qualities—people who seem pushy, rude, or self-centered.[10] Boring people are particularly unappealing. Such people tend to be passive, but when they do interact, they speak slowly, pause before making a point, and drag out meetings. Those perceived as boring may also sidetrack the group unnecessarily, show little enthusiasm, and seem too serious and preoccupied with themselves. Therefore, the makeup of the group in terms of personal characteristics can also affect its success and members' morale.

Still, most of us do not join just any group that promises a favorable reward (cost ratio). Our decision to join a group is based on two factors: our **comparison level** and our **comparison level for alternatives.**[11] Comparison level (CL) is the standard by which individuals evaluate the desirability of group membership; CL is strongly influenced by previous relationships. If previous group memberships have been positive, a person's CL should be high compared to someone whose previous experience with groups has been one of higher costs and lower rewards. However, comparison level only predicts when we will be satisfied with membership in a group. Therefore, team leaders may also consider member's attitudes about groups before assigning them to a team to ensure best results.

To predict when people will join and leave groups, we must also consider the value of other, alternative groups. Comparison level for alternatives (CL_{alt}) can be defined as the lowest level of outcomes a member will accept in light of available alternative opportunities. CL_{alt} largely determines whether members enter and exit groups whereas CL determines the satisfaction with membership.

comparison level (CL)

The standard by which individuals evaluate the desirability of group membership; CL is strongly influenced by previous relationships.

comparison level for alternatives (CL_{alt})

The lowest level of outcomes a member will accept in light of available alternative opportunities.

Commitment to a group is in many cases determined by the availability of alternative groups. Members who feel that they have no alternative to remaining in the group are often the most committed. Members also become more committed to a group the more they put into it. Although members in workplace situations may not voluntarily be placed on a team, seeing more productive, coherent teams may affect them negatively in the sense that members may resent being placed on a less attractive team and may affect the group dynamic negatively.

Another factor that should be considered when forming groups is cultural values. One of the most impactful of cultural values is the individualism/collectivism distinction. Table 10-1 provides a summary of member assumptions, depending on their individualism/collectivism orientation.

Table 10-1 Individualism vs. Collectivism in Small Groups

Individualistic Assumptions	Collectivistic Assumptions
■ The most effective decisions are made by individuals.	■ The most effective decisions are made by teams.
■ Planning should be centralized and done by the leaders.	■ Planning is best done by all concerned.
■ Individuals should be rewarded.	■ Groups or teams should be rewarded.
■ Individuals work primarily for themselves.	■ Individuals work primarily for the team.
■ Healthy competition between colleagues is more important than teamwork.	■ Teamwork is more important than competition.
■ Meetings are mainly for sharing information with individuals.	■ Meetings are mainly for making group or team decisions.
■ To get something accomplished, you should work with individuals.	■ To get something accomplished, you should work with the whole group or team.
■ A key objective in group meetings is to advance your own ideas.	■ A key objective in group meetings is to reach consensus or agreement.
■ Team meetings should be controlled by the leader or chair.	■ Team meetings should be a place for all team members to bring up what they want.
■ Group or team meetings are often a waste of time.	■ Group or team meetings are the best way to achieve a goal.

Source: Mole, J. (1995). *Mind Your Manners: Managing Business Cultures in Europe*. London: Nicholas Brealey.

Group Roles

Roles in groups structure behavior by dictating the "part" that members take as they interact. Once cast in a role, such as leader, outcast, or questioner, a group member tends to perform certain actions and interact with group members in a particular way. Sometimes groups deliberately create roles; this is called a formal group structure. However, even without a deliberate attempt to create a formal structure, the group will probably develop an informal group structure.

Broadly, there are three types of group roles: task roles, socioemotional or social maintenance roles, and individualistic roles. People who fulfill task roles focus on the group's goals, its task, and members' attempts to support one another as they work.

A group may need to accomplish its tasks, but it must also ensure that the interpersonal and emotional needs of the members are met. Such roles as "supporter," "clown," and even "critic" help satisfy the emotional needs of the group members. For a group to survive, it must both accomplish its tasks and maintain the relationships among its members.

A third set of roles, individualistic roles, are taken up by people who emphasize their own needs over those of the group. Members who adopt individualistic roles may do little work and demand that others take care of them. Typically, people in individualistic roles do not contribute to the proper functioning of a group. Group roles and their functions are listed in Table 10-2.

Table 10-2 Roles in Groups

Role	Function
Task Roles	
Initiator/contributor	Recommends novel ideas about the problem at hand, new ways to approach the problem, or solutions not yet considered
Information seeker	Emphasizes getting the facts by calling for background information from others
Opinion seeker	Asks for more qualitative types of data, such as attitudes, values, and feelings
Information giver	Provides opinions, values, and feelings
Elaborator	Gives additional information—examples, rephrasing, implications—about points others make
Coordinator	Shows the relevance of each idea and its relationship to the overall problem
Orienter	Refocuses discussion on the topic whenever necessary
Evaluator/critic	Appraises the quality of the group's methods, logic, and results
Energizer	Stimulates the group to continue working when discussion flags
Procedural technician	Cares for operational details, such as the materials and machinery
Recorder	Takes notes and maintains records
Socioemotional Roles	
Encourager	Rewards others through agreement, warmth, and praise
Harmonizer	Mediates conflict among group members
Compromiser	Shifts his or her position on an issue to reduce group conflict
Gatekeeper/expediter	Smoothes communication by setting up procedures and ensuring equal participation from members
Standard setter	Expresses, or calls for discussion of, standards for evaluating the quality of the group process
Group observer/ commentator	Points out the positive and negative aspects of the group's dynamics and calls for change if necessary
Follower	Accepts the ideas others offer and serves as an audience for the group
Individualistic Roles	
Aggressor	Expresses disapproval of acts, ideas, feelings of others; attacks the group
Blocker	Resists the group's influence; opposes the group unnecessarily
Dominator	Asserts authority or superiority; is manipulative
Evader/self-confessor	Expresses personal interests, feelings, or opinions unrelated to group goals
Help seeker	Expresses insecurity, confusion, or self-deprecation
Recognition seeker	Calls attention to him or herself; is self-aggrandizing
Playboy/girl	Is uninvolved in the group, cynical, and nonchalant
Special-interest pleader	Remains apart from the group by acting as a representative of another social group or category

? Critical Thinking

What group roles do you tend to play? What roles would you like to introduce into your repertoire? What roles should the competent communicator avoid?

Group Member Relations

intermember relations

The relations of the group members to one another, which are determined by patterns of status, attraction, and communication.

Intermember relations also affect group structure, or the group dynamic. Intermember relations or the relations of the group members to one another are determined by patterns of status, attraction, and communication. Those who have more status or power in the group affect its processes.

Status Hierarchies

Variations in dominance, prestige, and control among members reflect the group's status relations. Status patterns are often hierarchical and centralized. Status differences in groups violate our expectations of "equal treatment for all," but in the microsociety of a group, equality is the exception and inequality the rule. Initially, group members may start off on equal footing, but over time, status differentiation takes place. Who rises to the top of the heap and who remains on the bottom is partly determined by the individual and partly by the group. Individuals must communicate their claim to higher status, and the other group members must accept it. Individuals who deserve status are not always afforded status by their groups. Individuals who speak rapidly without hesitation, advise others what to do, and confirm others' statements are often more influential than individuals who signal submissiveness. A summary of the behaviors of high- and low-status members is provided in Table 10-3.

Table 10-3 Effects of Status Differences on Groups

High Status	Low Status
Such group members	Such group members
■ Talk more	■ Direct conversation to high-status rather than low-status members
■ Communicate more often with other high-status members	
■ Have more influence	■ Communicate more positive messages to high-status members
■ Generally abide by group norms	
■ Are less likely to be ignored	■ Are more likely to have their comments ignored
■ Are less likely to complain about their responsibilities	■ Communicate more irrelevant information
■ Talk to the entire group	■ Talk to high-status members as a substitute for climbing the social hierarchy in the group
■ Are likely to serve in leadership roles	
■ In online groups, are more likely to be instructive and use second-person pronouns	■ In online groups, are more likely than high-status members to use first-person pronouns and exclamation points

Source: Engleberg, I., & Wynn, D. R. (2012). *Working in Groups* (6th Ed.). New York, NY: Pearson.

Attraction Relations

Just as members of the group can be ranked from low to high in terms of status, so, too, can the members be ordered from least liked to most liked.[12] Popular individuals are the most liked, rejected members are the least liked, neglected members are nominated neither as most nor least liked, and average members are liked by several others in the group.[13] Cliques also form in groups; these subgroups usually display homophily. In other words, members of cliques are often more similar to one another than they are to the members of the total group.

Individuals are generally considered more attractive if they possess socially attractive qualities, such as cooperativeness and physical appeal, but social standing also depends on the degree to which the individual's attributes match the qualities the group values. This match is referred to as person-group fit.

Communication Networks

People of higher status and attraction often stay in close communication, whereas those on the bottom may be cut off from communication. The most important feature of a communication network is its degree of centralization. Networks can be centralized (one person controls the flow of information) or decentralized (all members can communicate with one another). The amount and type of information to be delivered, or what is called "information saturation," determines the best communication network for any task. If the information is simple, centralized networks work best; if the information to be transmitted is complex, decentralized networks are more efficient.[14]

A person's position in a communication network can also have effects. As discussed in Chapter 9, those who are more peripheral in a communication network are usually those who are least satisfied, whereas those in central positions are most satisfied. Because the overall number of peripheral positions in a centralized network exceeds the number of central positions, the overall satisfaction in a centralized group is lower than the level of satisfaction in a decentralized group.

Research on communication networks commonly employs five different networks, illustrated in Figure 10-1. Leavitt found that the central person in a network such as the wheel usually becomes the leader and enjoys the position more than those on the periphery, where communication is more restricted.[15] Both the chain and the Y networks have characteristics similar to the wheel. The circle and the all-channel patterns are much less centralized, on the other hand, and are sometimes leaderless or have distributed leadership.

In summary, relations among group members can be affected by three things: a member's status within the group, a member's popularity within the group, and the type of network used within the group to disseminate information and a person's position in that network.

Figure 10-1 Common Communication Networks

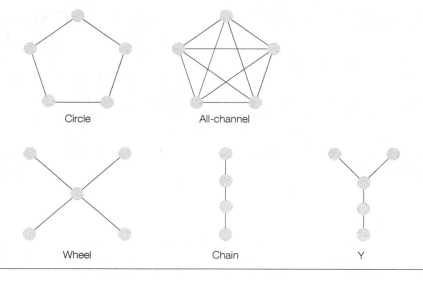

Circle All-channel

Wheel Chain Y

Power and Group Process

Members who have power influence the group process. Whether their influence will be positive or negative depends on how wisely the members use their influence. The following principles summarize the impact of power on group deliberations:

- A struggle for power among group members can result in poor group decisions and less group cohesion.
- Members who overtly seek dominance and control over a group often focus attention on themselves rather than on achieving group goals. They typically serve as aggressors, blockers, recognition seekers, dominators, or special-interest pleaders (see roles discussed earlier in this chapter).
- Group members with little power often talk less frequently in a group.

- People who talk most frequently and for the longest periods of time are assumed to be the most dominant group members. In addition, those who receive the most communication are assumed to be most powerful. While not all powerful members dominate group conversations, there is a relationship between verbal contributions to the group and influence. The exceptions to this principle are members who talk so frequently that they are ignored by the group. Cultural variations can influence this dynamic as well.

- Group members can lose power if other members think they use power for personal gain or to keep a group from achieving its goals.

- Group members usually expect individuals with greater power to have high-status privileges. However, if members believe that powerful members are having a detrimental effect on the group, their credibility and influence are likely to diminish. Too many perks and privileges given to some members sap a group's ability to do its job and can result in challenges to the influential group members.

- Too much power in one individual can lead to less group decision making and more autocratic decision making. Autocratic decision making occurs when one person with several power bases (for example, one who can reward and punish, has needed information, is well liked, and has been appointed to lead) makes a decision alone rather than with the group as a whole. Group members may not speak their minds for fear of reprisals.

- Groups with equal power distribution show higher-quality group communication than do groups with unequal power distribution.[16]

Stages of Group Development

Group cohesion, or unity, develops over time. It is the result of group development. There are five stages of group development: forming, storming, norming, performing, and adjourning.[17]

In the major processes in the *forming stage*, members become familiar with one another and the group; as well, members deal with issues of dependency and inclusion, the acceptance of a leader, and the development of group consensus. The characteristics of this stage include tentative, polite communications; concern over ambiguity and group goals; and an active leader and compliant members.

In the *storming or conflict stage*, the major processes include disagreement over procedures, expression of dissatisfaction, tension among members, and antagonism toward the leader. The characteristics of this stage include criticism of ideas, poor attendance, hostility, polarization, and coalition formation.

In the *norming stage*, major processes include the growth of cohesion; establishment of roles, standards, and relationships; and increased trust and communication. This stage is characterized by agreement on procedures, reduction in role ambiguity, and increased "we-ness."

In the *performing stage*, the major processes include goal achievement, high task achievement, and emphasis on performance and production. This stage is characterized by decision making, problem solving, and mutual cooperation.

In the *adjourning phase*, the major processes include termination of roles, completion of tasks, and reduction of dependency. This stage is characterized by disintegration and withdrawal, increased independence and emotionality, and regret.

Groups do not always develop in this order. Some groups manage to avoid particular stages, others move through the stages in a unique order, and still others develop in ways that cannot be described by this five-stage model. In addition, the demarcation between stages is often not clear-cut.

From a leadership or management perspective, it is valuable to recognize the stages of group formation and to intervene as appropriate. For example, in the norming stage, communication and other behaviors that began to appear in earlier stages is formalized into group or team norms. This process often occurs outside of members' consciousness and because of this, ineffective or undesirable norms may develop, such as an unstated norm that allows members to miss meetings or deadlines without any negative repercussions. To avoid these kinds of occurrences, team leaders can be prepared to intervene if negative norms appear within a team or can more proactively engage the team in creating norms that will help it to work effectively and efficiently.

Highly effective teams usually have at least four attributes:

1. Team goals are clear and specific.
2. Teams have well-defined team member responsibilities.
3. The rules for and expectations about how the team operates are clearly spelled out.
4. Teams usually develop a clear way of coordinating their efforts.

To better ensure that a group or team get off to a good start, it should to develop more precise rules to help accomplish its task. Group or team **ground rules** are explicit, agreed-on prescriptions for acceptable and appropriate behavior. Rules help keep order so that meaningful work can be accomplished. Rules also state what the group or organization values.

ground rules

Explicit, agreed-on prescriptions for acceptable and appropriate behavior.

To develop ground rules, the team leader should facilitate a discussion aimed at identifying and reaching consensus among group members. Groups and teams operate better if members develop their own ground rules rather than having them imposed from "on high" or from the leader as members are more likely to "buy-in" to their own ideas.

The following questions can help a group to identify its ground rules:

- How often shall we meet?
- How long should our meetings last?
- Should we have a standard meeting place and time?
- What should a member do if he or she can't attend a meeting?
- How will we communicate between meetings?
- How much time do we have to respond to telephone, e-mail, or text messages from others?
- How will we follow-up to ensure that each member is doing his or her assigned work?
- Who is going to organize the agenda for our meetings?
- How will we manage conflict?
- How will we make our decisions—by majority vote or consensus?
- What kind of communication climate do we want in our meetings?
- What other kinds of guidelines do we need to develop for completing our task?
- How do we ensure that everyone's work meets group expectations?

Even when the team is given its goal from someone outside the group—an instructor or a supervisor, for example—its members should take some time to discuss the team's ground rules so that each person clearly understands and agrees to them.

The Effects of Group Cohesion and Conformity

Members are usually more satisfied with their team when it is cohesive rather than noncohesive. A cohesive group creates a healthier workplace, at least at the psychological level. Because people in cohesive groups respond to one another in a more positive fashion than the members of noncohesive groups, people experience less anxiety and tension.[18] Members of cohesive teams more readily accept the group's goals, decisions, and norms, i.e. they tend to conform.

According to Harold Reitan and Marvin Shaw, at least five factors affect conformity to group norms.[19]

- **The individual characteristics of the group members**. Group members' past experiences and personality characteristics influence how they conform to established norms. More intelligent persons are less likely to conform than less intelligent persons; women usually conform more than men, at least on traditional tasks; there is a curvilinear relationship between age and conformity; persons who generally blame themselves for what happens to them conform more than those low on self-blame; and authoritarians conform more than nonauthoritarians.

- **The clarity of the norm and the certainty of punishment for breaking it.** The more ambiguous a group norm, the less likely it is that members will conform to it. In small groups, as soon as rules become clear and norms are established, members will usually conform.

- **The number of people who have already conformed to the norm**. Because most of us do not feel comfortable standing out in a group, we tend to conform to others' behaviors. Factors such as the size of a group, the number of people who agree with a certain policy, and the status of those who conform contribute to the pressure for conformity in a group.

- **The quality of the interpersonal relationships that have developed in the group.** A group whose members like one another and respect one another's opinions is more likely to support conformity than is a less cohesive group. Employees who like their jobs, bosses, and coworkers and take pride in their work are more likely to support group norms than those who have negative or frustrating relationships with their employers or colleagues.

- **The sense of group identification that members have developed.** If group members can readily identify with the goals of the group, they are more likely to conform to standards of behavior. For example, members of a particular political party who support its ideology are probably going to conform to the wishes of those in leadership positions. In addition, group members who feel they will be a part of a group for some time are more likely to conform to group norms.

Conforming to group norms requires participants to be aware of both *general norms* and more specific *operationalized norms*. Groups often adopt general norms very quickly. For example "We all need to communicate with one another frequently" would be a common general group norm. But while there may be clear consensus around this general norm, it may mean different things to different people. For one person, *frequently* might mean "weekly," whereas another team member may think it to mean "daily." Thus, norms tend to evolve from the general to the operational (what the norms mean in terms of actual behaviors) over time as the specifics are negotiated. As always, communication about norms is key. As discussed earlier, defining a set of rules can help to clarify group norms, particularly if they are operationalized.[20]

Although conforming to group norms can help to make a group more cohesive and thus generally more effective, cohesion can become problematic for members, if they become too dependent on the group. Furthermore, pressure to conform is also greater in cohesive groups, which also can potentially create problems. Evidence suggests that members of cohesive groups sometimes react very negatively and take harsh actions to bring dissenters into line when a group member goes against group consensus.[21] Cohesion can also increase negative group processes.[22] Cohesive groups vent their frustrations through interpersonal aggression: overt hostility, joking hostility, scapegoating, and domination of subordinate group members. In contrast, non-cohesive groups tend to form coalitions among members.

One of the biggest problems that may arise due to too much focus on conformity is **groupthink**. Groupthink occurs when group members dominate interaction, are intimidated by others, or care more about social acceptability than reaching the best solution. Groupthink occurs at the highest levels and can have serious consequences. It has been cited as causing the Bay of Pigs fiasco in the

groupthink

Conformity-seeking behavior of cohesive groups that interferes with effective decision making.

1960s, the *Challenger* disaster in the 1980s, and the lack of effective preparation and response by the U.S. government to terrorism in the twenty-first century.

To avoid groupthink, teams should consider the following suggestions:

1. The leader should encourage participants to voice objections and critically evaluate ideas.

2. Members should take an impartial stance and not get wrapped up in ego and emotions, affording a more objective view of the decision.

3. More than one group can work on a problem, which may lead to radically different recommendations.

4. Each member can be encouraged to discuss the group's deliberations with people outside the group and get their feedback.

5. The group can invite outside experts in for their input and feedback.

6. The group can appoint a member to be devil's advocate to assure that the group explores all sides of each issue.

7. The group can be divided into subgroups, each of which works the problem separately and then reports back.

8. The group can hold a "second chance" meeting after reaching preliminary consensus, to allow members to express doubts and concerns that may have come up.[21]

Generally speaking, though, groups that succeed tend to be more cohesive, and groups that fail tend to be less cohesive. The cohesion-performance relation is strongest when group cohesion is based on commitment to the task rather than attraction or group pride.[22] This finding is important for team leaders who want to ensure that a team is successful. Success is more likely if members are committed to the goals of the group or the team objectives. Cohesion also counts more when the group's task requires high levels of interaction and interdependence.[23]

These findings explain why some groups, even though they are cohesive, are not productive: The members are not committed to the group's performance goals. Surveys indicate that fairly low standards of performance can develop within highly cohesive groups. As long as group norms encourage high productivity, cohesiveness and productivity are positively related.

? Critical Thinking

Where do group norms come from? Why do we tend to conform to group norms? Is tension in a group desirable?

Sources of Influence within a Group

Three types of influence can be exercised in group situations. Through **informational influence**, the group provides members with information that can be used to make decisions and form opinions. When **normative influence** occurs, members tailor their actions to fit the group's standards and conventions. **Interpersonal influence**, in contrast, occurs when the group uses verbal and nonverbal influence tactics to induce change.

Informational influence is not immune to the effects of social influence. In other words, we may discover new information by observing others' responses. Social comparison theory assumes that group members treat other people's responses as data when formulating opinions and making decisions. In some cases, teams actively gather information about members' opinions, but generally individuals gather information about others' views through routine discussion.[24] Unfortunately, this intuitive approach tends to be biased. Members of the majority, for example, tend to underes-

informational influence
When the group provides members with information that they can use to make decisions and form opinions.

normative influence
When group members tailor their actions to fit the group's standards and conventions.

interpersonal influence
When the group uses verbal and nonverbal influence tactics to induce change.

timate the size of their group, whereas minority members tend to overestimate the degree to which others agree with them.

People who consistently violate their group's norms are often reminded of their duty and are told to change their ways. They are often disliked, assigned lower-status jobs, and are dismissed from the group in some cases.[25] Normative influence explains why certain people, such as those with a high need for social approval and those who tend to be more authoritarian, conform more than others.[26] Nonconformists tend to be more self-confident, whereas counter-conformists actively resist majority influence.

Interpersonal influence tactics include complaining, demanding, threatening, pleading, negotiating, pressuring, manipulating, and rejecting. The occurrence of rejection is more pronounced in more cohesive groups. In extreme cases, group members will eventually stop communicating with "disliked deviants," at least in cases where cohesive groups are working on relevant tasks.[27]

? Critical Thinking

How does communication influence how a team performs? Please provide examples that illustrate your point from your own work or group experiences?

Group Performance

First of all, to perform well, groups must have the resources they need. They must have the skills, talents, and energy needed to successfully complete tasks. Secondly, the group must combine its resources effectively. Even if members have the resources required for a task, the group may fail if it does not marshal these resources successfully. Performance depends on the group's resources and the methods used to combine these resources to meet the demands of the group's task.

A group's performance also depends, in part, on its members' knowledge, skills, and abilities. On the task side, groups whose members are more skilled at the work to be done outperform groups comprised of less skilled workers. On the interpersonal side, members must be able to work well with others on joint tasks. Communication skills, leadership abilities, and a talent for managing conflicts are some of the qualities possessed by members of successful work teams. Some groups fail because they simply do not include members with the qualities and characteristics needed to complete their task.

Diversity can also help a group's performance. Diverse groups have an advantage when members are all highly skilled but these skills do not overlap. Diverse groups may be better at coping with changing work conditions because their wider range of talents and traits enhances flexibility. Diversity can also help groups to seek alternative solutions to problems and enhance creativity and innovation.

Diversity can also create problems in groups, though. Diverse groups may lack cohesion because of perceived dissimilarities. In addition, diversity in skill level—some members are competent but others are incompetent—does not appear to boost productivity.[28]

Groups that bring together people with similar personalities tend to outperform groups whose members have dissimilar personalities.[29] Classroom groups performed best when they were composed of individuals whose personality characteristics were similar and focused on goal attainment.[30]

process losses

Reductions in performance effectiveness or efficiency caused by faulty group processes, including motivational and coordination problems.

Another negative effect on performance is **process losses**, or reductions in performance effectiveness or efficiency caused by faulty group processes, including motivational and coordination problems. Although a group obviously produces more than an individual, groups usually do not work at maximum efficiency. As more members are added to a group, it becomes increasingly less efficient. Secondly, people may not work as hard when they are in groups. This reduction of effort by individuals working in groups is called **social loafing**.[31] Social loafing occurs when individual input is not identifiable. When individual contributions are clearly known, evaluation apprehension sets in as we worry about how others will evaluate us. However, when we are anonymous and our contributions are unidentified, the presence of others reduces evaluation apprehension and social loafing becomes more likely.[32] Therefore, team leaders should ensure that members are assigned clearly measurable tasks that are evaluated with established outcomes.

Another cause of social loafing is the fact that group work often causes social dilemmas. Members may want to do their share to help the group reach its goals, but they are simultaneously tempted to concentrate on their own personal goals. So they engage in **free-riding**. People are most likely to free-ride when their contributions are combined in a single product and no one is monitoring the size of each person's contribution. Free-riding also increases when group members worry that their coworkers are holding back.

A third reason for social loafing is what is called the illusion of group productivity. Members of groups working on collective tasks generally think that their group is more productive than most.[33] Group members also generally do not feel that they are doing less than their fair share.

Groups can improve productivity in several ways:

1. Personal stake in the group's outcome should be increased. When individuals feel that a poor group performance will affect them personally, they do not loaf.[34]
2. Groups that set clear, attainable goals outperform groups whose members have lost sight of their objectives.[35]
3. Groups that set high goals tend to outproduce those with lower levels of aspiration.
4. Groups with realistic expectations about their chances of success also perform better. Unrealistic goals can undermine motivation, though.[36]
5. Increased unity can improve performance. However, increased cohesiveness improves performance only if group norms emphasize productivity.

Groups can take steps to discourage social loafing, such as the following:

1. **Establish a group responsibility norm.** From the beginning, group members should state the expectations for individual responsibility in the group and the importance of equal contribution by members to group tasks.
2. **Note the critical importance of each member's efforts.** The group leader should communicate the importance and essentialness of each individual's effort and contribution to completing the group task.
3. **Identify and evaluate individual contributions.** Each member should be provided specific and identifiable tasks, and the group should set aside time to evaluate each member's contribution to the project.
4. **Talk to the problem individual privately.** This step calls for the leader or a designated member to ask the member why his or her contribution is less than expected. Asking the problem individual to suggest ways that he or she might improve his or her performance may help in achieving buy-in to the group task.
5. **Confront the individual who is loafing as a group.** Group members should identify and describe the problem behavior in detail. The individual who is loafing should be asked how the problem might be solved. This step is effective only if group members avoid name-calling or personality attacks on the offender.
6. **Consult someone with more power.** When all these steps fail, the group should consult a teacher, supervisor, or someone with greater authority than the group members for advice or help. The authority figure may need to discuss the problem with the individual who is loafing.

social loafing

The reduction of effort by individuals working in groups.

free-riding

When group members do not work as hard when they believe others will compensate for this lack of effort.

7. **Fire the individual who is slacking.** This step should be taken only when all other attempts to obtain the cooperation of the individual who is loafing have failed.

8. **Sidestep the individual who is loafing.** The group may decide to reconfigure the individual responsibilities and tasks so that, even if the individual who is loafing does not contribute, the group can still accomplish its task. In the workplace, this step might result in a demotion or reassignment to another job or department.[37]

Group Decision Making

Groups can be useful in making decisions because more people potentially bring more information to the task. In addition, groups tend to process the information they have more thoroughly through discussion. For effective decision making, groups should ensure that the process they use is a productive one. Although groups can be useful for decision making, they also face some challenges.

Stages of Group Decision Making

Groups tend to make better decisions if the pattern for doing so is explicitly identified so that the group can structure its discussion. Effective group decision making includes the following steps.[38]

1. **Analyze the decision to be made by adequately assessing the present situation.** To analyze something is to break it down into its smaller components. Research suggests that how a group analyzes the information can dramatically affect the group's decision.[39] Having too little evidence—or none—is one of the reasons groups sometimes fail to analyze the present situation accurately. Even if group members do have ample evidence, it may be defective if they have not applied the proper tests of evidence discussed in Chapter 6. Whether the information a group has is good or bad, group members will tend to use the information if all members receive it, group members discuss it, and at least one group member champions the information.[40] Just having information does not mean the group will use it well. Reasoning is the process of drawing conclusions from information. Flawed reasoning, like flawed data, can contribute to a bad decision. Research suggests that groups perform better if they not only critically evaluate the information they have but also consider the impact of their final decision on solving the problem.[41]

2. **Seek input from each member.** One primary reason to work in groups and teams is the opportunity to tap the knowledge base of many people rather than just of a few individuals. Research by John Oetzel documents what makes intuitive sense: Groups make better decisions when there is more equal participation in the discussion.[42] Conversely, if several members dominate the conversation, decision quality suffers. Group members who believe they did not have an opportunity to voice their opinions and share information with others will not perceive the decision to have been reached fairly.[43]

3. **Identify and clarify the goals of the decision.** After assessing the current situation, the group should identify its objectives. A group uncertain about its task will have difficulty making a quality decision. If its goal is clear, a group can begin to identify alternatives and then weigh each as to its ability to meet that goal. A group that has not clearly spelled out what it hopes to accomplish by making a decision has no means of assessing the effectiveness of the decision.

4. **Identify multiple options.** The greater the number of alternatives a group generates, the greater the likelihood it will make a good decision. To identify good options, the group should review the information that it has gathered. Poor decision making occurs when

groups pounce on the first or second option identified and fail to consider a wide range of possible options before making a decision.

5. **Review the pros and cons of the options identified.** A group must do more than identify alternatives; it should also assess the positive and negative implications of each alternative before making a decision. The pros and cons of each option should be based on the information the group has identified. A group that is so eager to make a decision that it does not take time to consider the pros and cons of its actions is setting itself up to make a bad decision. A critical error by ineffective groups is failing to consider the consequences of their decision before they make it.[44]

6. **Select the best alternative.** The option selected should potentially have a maximum positive outcome with minimal negative consequences. A group is more likely to select the best alternative if it has carefully assessed the situation, considered group goals, identified several choices, and noted the positive and negative implications of each. Groups sometimes have a tendency to make overly risky decisions, so it is important to critically analyze each option for possible negative implications.

Methods of Group Decision Making

A variety of methods can be used to make a final decision after the alternatives have been narrowed and weighed by the group. Knowing these methods can help the group to select the best for the situation.

- **Decision by Expert in Group.** One person in a group may seem to be the best informed about the issue, and members can turn to this person to make the choice. This expert may or may not be a group's designated leader. Deferring to an expert from within a group may be an efficient way to make a decision, but if there is not adequate discussion, the group may not be satisfied with the outcome.

- **Decision by Expert Outside Group.** A group may decide that none of its members has the credibility, knowledge, or wisdom to make a particular decision, and it may feel unable or unwilling to do so. Members can turn to someone outside the group who has authority to make a decision. Although an outside expert may make a fine decision, a group that gives up its decision-making power to one person loses the advantages of the greater input and variety of approaches that come from being a group in the first place.

- **Averaging Individual Rankings or Ratings.** Group members can be asked to rank or rate possible alternatives. After the group averages the rankings or ratings, it selects the alternative with the highest average. This method of making decisions can be a useful way to start discussions and to see where the group stands on an issue. However, it is not the best way to make a final decision, because it does not take full advantage of the give-and-take of group discussion.

- **Majority Rule.** This is the most common method of group decision making because of the benefit of it being fast and efficient. But there are several drawbacks. First, it can leave an unsatisfied minority. Second, a group that makes a decision on the basis of majority rule may sacrifice decision quality and group cohesiveness for efficiency.

- **Decision by Consensus.** Consensus occurs when all group members can support a course of action. This decision-making method is time-consuming and can be frustrating, but members are usually satisfied with the decision. If group members must also implement the solution, this method works well. To reach a decision by consensus, group members must listen and respond to individual viewpoints and manage conflicts that arise. Consensus is facilitated when group members are able to remain focused on the goal, emphasize areas of agreement, and combine or eliminate alternatives identified by the group.

Table 10-4 provides a summary of the different decision-making methods.

Table 10-4 **Advantages and Disadvantages of Decision-Making Methods**

Method	Advantages	Disadvantages
Decision by Expert: Group defers to the member who has the most expertise or experience or to someone outside the group with authority to make decisions	▪ Decision is made quickly ▪ Uses the expertise of a knowledgeable source of information	▪ Group members may not be satisfied with the decision ▪ The expert could be wrong
Averaging Individual Rankings or Ratings: Group members rank or rate possible outcomes, and the alternative with the highest ranking or best rating is selected	▪ Uses a democratic process that taps all group members' thinking ▪ Useful when the group needs to assess where it stands on an issue	▪ The average ranking or rating may be an alternative that no group member supports ▪ Group loses the opportunity for give-and-take discussion
Majority Rule: Decision is made by the majority of group members	▪ Often perceived as a fair way of making decisions ▪ Can be an efficient way of making a decision	▪ Those who do not support the majority opinion may feel left out of the process ▪ Group may lose cohesiveness
Decision by Consensus: Through discussion, group members reach a decision that all members can support	▪ Group members are more likely to be satisfied with the outcome ▪ Group members are more likely to participate in implementing a decision that all members support	▪ Takes time ▪ Takes skill

The Challenges of Group Decision Making

Although group decision making can have productive outcomes, members should be aware of some of the challenges and limitations of such a process. One problem is the tendency for groups to spend too much of their discussion time examining shared information—details that two or more of the members know in common—rather than unshared information.[45] This tendency is called **oversampling**. Oversampling of shared information leads to poorer decisions when useful data might be revealed by considering the unshared information more closely. Oversampling of shared information increases when tasks have no demonstrably correct solution and when group leaders do not actively draw out unshared information.

In addition, the usefulness of group discussion is limited, in part, by members' inability to express themselves clearly and by their limited listening skills. Not all group members have the interpersonal skills a discussion demands. When researchers asked 569 full-time employees what happened during a meeting to limit its effectiveness, they received 2,500 answers, which are provided in Table 10-5.[46]

Sometimes, groups use discussion to avoid making decisions. In addition, judgment errors that cause people to overlook important information and over-utilize unimportant information are often exacerbated in groups. These errors occur more frequently when group members are cognitively busy (that is, they are trying to work on too many tasks at once).

Common sense suggests that groups are more cautious than individuals, but early studies found that group discussion generates a shift in the direction of the more risky alternative. When researchers later found evidence of cautious shifts as well as risky ones, they concluded that the responses of groups tend to be more extreme than individual members' responses (the group polarization hypothesis).[47] Polarization is sustained by the desire to evaluate one's own opinions

oversampling

The tendency for groups to spend too much of their discussion time examining shared information—details that two or more of the group members know in common—rather than unshared information.

by comparing them to others' (social comparison theory), by exposure to other members' pro-risk and pro-caution arguments (persuasive arguments theory), and by groups' implicit reliance on a "risk-supported wins" social decision scheme.[48] Groups whose members are initially more risk-prone than cautious adopt this approach. In such groups, if one person supports a risky alternative, the group will not adopt it. But if two people support it, the group often accepts the risky recommendation.[49]

Table 10-5 Group Decision Making Challenges

Problem (Frequency)	Description
Poor communication skills (10 percent)	Poor listening skills, ineffective voice, poor nonverbal skills, lack of effective visual aids, misunderstood or unclearly identified topic, repetition, use of jargon
Egocentric behavior (8 percent)	Domination of conversation and group, behaviors that are loud and overbearing, one-upmanship, show of power, manipulation, intimidation, filibustering, talking to hear self talk
Nonparticipation (7 percent)	Lack of full participation, speaking up, volunteering, active inclusion, and discussion
Sidetracked (6.5 percent)	Leaving main topic
Interruptions (6 percent)	Members interrupting speaker, talking over others, socializing, and allowing phone calls or messages from customers/clients
Negative leader behavior (6 percent)	Lack of organization, focus, preparation, control, decision making; being late, getting sidetracked
Attitudes and emotions (5 percent)	Poor attitude: defensive or evasive, argumentative, personal accusations, no courtesy or respect, complaining or griping, lack of control of emotions

Cultural differences in negotiation styles and strategies can also affect the decision-making process. For example, Russian negotiating tactics include a need for authority, a need to avoid risk, and a need to control.[50] Considering two key negotiation styles help to illustrate how cultural differences may affect decision making. The competitive approach is common in the United States; it is more individualistic and persuasion-oriented. This approach looks for a solution that is best for the negotiator's side versus the win-win style that characterizes Chinese negotiations. A second approach, problem solving, is generally considered better for intercultural situations since it identifies the need to adapt to national cultural differences as well as organizational ones. A brief comparison of the negotiation styles of different cultures is shown in Table 10-6.

Group decision making can be challenging because it requires the ability to consider and accommodate multiple interpretative frameworks—multiple versions of reality—and to emerge with a single recommendation or course of action.[51] This means that we must be willing to accept the inevitability of differences and to make a commitment to dialogue. Groups also can be more effective at decision making if they pay more attention to the procedure that they use to solve problems.[52]

Sources of Group Conflict

There are three types of group conflict: personal conflict, substantive conflict, and procedural conflict. Conflict can also be increased by other factors, such as competition within a group and the social dilemmas that groups can create for their members. Just as there are various types of conflict, group members can use several approaches to resolve it.

Personal Conflict

Personal conflict is rooted in individuals' dislike of other group members. For example, group members who treat others unfairly or impolitely create more conflict than those who are polite.[53]

Table 10-6 A Comparison of Negotiation Styles of Different Cultures

Element	U.S. Americans	Japanese	Arabs	Mexicans
Group composition	Marketing-oriented	Function-oriented	Committee of specialists	Friendship-oriented
Number involved	2–3	4–7	4–6	2–3
Space orientation	Confrontational, competitive	Display harmonious relationship	Status	Close, friendly
Establishing rapport	Short period; direct to task	Longer period, until harmony	Long period, until trusted	Longer period, discuss family
Exchange of information	Documented, step by step, multimedia	Extensive, concentrate on receiving side	Less emphasis on technology, more on relationship	Less emphasis on technology, more on relationship
Persuasion tools	Time pressure, saving/ making money	Maintain relationship, intergroup connections	Go-between, hospitality	Emphasis on family and social concerns, goodwill measured in generations
Use of language	Open/direct, sense of urgency	Indirect, appreciative, cooperative	Flattery, emotional, religious	Respectful, gracious
Decision-making process	Top management team	Collective	Team makes recommendation	Senior manager and secretary
Decision maker	Top management team	Middle line with team consensus	Senior manager	Senior manager
Risk taking	Calculated, personal responsibility	Low group responsibility	Religion-based	Personally responsible

Source: Elashmawi, F., & Harris, P. (1998). *Multicultural Management 2000*. Houston: Butterworth-Heinemann; Ruch, W. V. (1989). *International Handbook of Corporate Communication*. (Jefferson, NC: McFarland).

The relationship between dislike and conflict explains why groups with greater diversity sometimes display more conflict than homogeneous groups. Just as similarity between members increases interpersonal attraction, dissimilarity tends to increase dislike and conflict.[54] Groups whose members have dissimilar personalities (for example, differences in authoritarianism, cognitive complexity, and temperament) generally do not get along as well as groups composed of people whose personalities are similar.[55] Groups whose members vary in terms of ability, experience, opinions, values, race, personality, ethnicity, and so on can capitalize on their members' wider range of resources and viewpoints, but these groups often suffer high levels of conflict.[56]

Substantive Conflict

When people discuss their problems and plans, they sometimes disagree with one another's analyses. These substantive conflicts, however, are integrally related to the group's work. Substantive conflict does not stem from personal disagreements between individuals but from disagreements about issues that are relevant to the group's real goals and outcomes. In other words, of the three types of conflict, substantive conflict has the potential to provide the most positive outcomes, such as making plans, increasing creativity, solving problems, deciding issues, and resolving conflicts of viewpoints.[57] Substantive conflict, in fact, is one of the reasons that groups are used to complete tasks.

Even though substantive conflicts help groups reach their goals, these impersonal conflicts can turn into personal ones. Members who disagree with the group, even when their position is a reasonable one, often provoke considerable animosity within the group. The dissenter who refuses to accept others' views is less liked. Group members who slow down the process of reaching consensus are often responded to negatively. To avoid this aspect of groupthink, groups should encourage members to take on the role of devil's advocate.

Procedural Conflict

Although substantive conflicts occur when ideas, opinions, and interpretations clash, procedural conflicts occur when strategies, policies, and methods collide. Many groups can minimize procedural conflict by adopting formal rules that specify goals, decisional processes, and responsibilities.[58] Rules, however, can be overly formalized, which can hinder openness, creativity, and adaptability to change.

? Critical Thinking

Of the three types of group conflict—personal, substantive, and procedural—which is the easiest to avoid? How might you use these strategies to avoid conflict in your groups? Your workplace?

Conflict and Competition

Conflict is more likely when group members compete against each other for such resources as money, power, time, prestige, or materials, instead of working with one another to reach common goals. When people compete, they must look out for their own interests instead of the group's interests or their co-members' interests. Because competing members can succeed only when others fail, they may even sabotage others' work, criticize it, and withhold information and resources that others might need.[59]

In contrast, members of cooperative groups enhance their outcomes by helping other members achieve success. Work units with high levels of cooperation have fewer latent tensions, personality conflicts, and verbal confrontations.[60]

Few situations involve pure cooperation or pure competition; the motive to compete is often mixed with the motive to cooperate. Furthermore, as the *norm of reciprocity* suggests, cooperation begets cooperation, whereas competition begets competition.

People's personalities contribute to conflict. Some people seem to be natural competitors, whereas others are more cooperative or individualistic.[61] **Competitors** view group disagreements as win–lose situations and find satisfaction in forcing their ideas on others.

Individuals with competitive value orientations are more likely to find themselves in conflicts. Furthermore, competitors rarely modify their behavior in response to the complaints of others because they are relatively unconcerned with maintaining smooth interpersonal relations. Two other value orientations in groups are those of cooperator and individualist. **Cooperators** value accommodative interpersonal strategies, whereas **individualists** are concerned only with their own outcomes. Individualists make decisions based on what they personally will achieve, with no concern for others' outcomes. They neither interfere with nor assist others' attempts to reach their goals. It should be noted that this definition of individualist differs from the conception of individualistic roles in groups in that the individualistic inclination in a group situation can negatively affect others. In the schema discussed here, competitive behavior is more akin to the individualistic roles that can arise in groups.

Social values vary across cultures. As was discussed in Chapter 4, Western societies such as the United States tend to value competition, whereas more cooperative and peaceful societies devalue individual achievement and avoid any kind of competitive games.[62] Group-oriented cultures value reaching consensus on all decisions and individuals avoid making individual decisions. These cultures include those of Japan, China, Brazil, and Africa, as well as Polynesians and Native Americans. In individual-oriented cultures, one person will probably control the discussion and make the final decisions. The United States is probably the most individualistic culture in the world, while Latin America, Great Britain, Australia, and Canada are also individualistic.[63]

competitors

People who view group disagreements as win–lose situations and find satisfaction in forcing their views on others.

cooperators

Individuals who value accommodative interpersonal strategies in groups.

individualists

Individuals who are concerned only with their own outcomes in group situations.

Responsible Communication

A new phenomenon that is gaining attention in a hyper-competitive global economy is workplace bullying. Bullies not only stifle productivity and innovation throughout the organization, they most often target an organization's best employees, because it is precisely those employees who are the most threatening to bullies.[64]

Recent commentators have used different ways to describe bullying behavior, but they agree that a bully is only interested in maintaining his or her power and control. Because bullies are cowards and are driven by deep-seated insecurities and fears of inadequacy, they intentionally wage a covert war against an organization's best employees—those who are highly skilled, intelligent, creative, ethical, able to work well with others, and independent (who refuse to be subservient or controlled by others).[65] Bullies can act alone or in groups, and bullying behavior can

exist at any level of an organization. Bullies can be superiors, subordinates, coworkers, and colleagues.

The problem with workplace bullying is that many bullies are hard to identify because they operate surreptitiously under the guise of being civil and cooperative. Although workplace bullying is being discussed more than ever before, and there may eventually be specific legislation outlawing such behavior, organizations cannot afford to wait for new laws to eradicate the bullies in their midst. Organizations must root out workplace bullying before it squelches their employees' creativity and productivity, or even drives out their best employees, thus fatally impacting an organization's ability to compete.[66]

Eradicating bullying behavior from an organization starts at the top because it is the head of any organization that sets the tone for whether bullying behavior will be accepted, they say. An organization

reflects the values, attitudes, and actions of its leadership. Leaders who ignore, or otherwise allow, these destructive behavior patterns to occur are eroding the health of their organizations and opening the door for some of their best talent to escape from this upsetting and counterproductive environment.[67]

Questions for Discussion

1. Have you witnessed or been the victim of a bully, workplace or otherwise? Do you agree with the assertion that allowing workplace bullying to occur can fatally impact an organization's ability to be competitive?

2. Do you agree with Richardson and McCord's assertion that eradicating bullying in the workplace is the responsibility of management? Do other employees have a role?

Social Dilemmas

Groups create social dilemmas for their members. The members, as individuals, are motivated to maximize their own rewards and minimize their costs. Conflicts arise when individualistic motives trump group-oriented motives and the collective intervenes to redress the imbalance.

As mentioned earlier, one cause of conflict is the division of resources. When group members feel they are receiving too little for what they are giving, they sometimes withdraw from the group, reduce their effort, and turn in work of lower quality. Group members who feel that they are receiving too much for what they are giving sometimes increase their efforts.

As conflicts escalate, group members often become more committed to their positions instead of more understanding of the positions taken by others. Conflict is exacerbated by members' tendencies to misperceive others and to assume that the other party's behavior is caused by personal rather than situational factors. This tendency is called the **fundamental attribution error**. As conflict worsens, group members will shift from weak to strong influence tactics, such as threats, punishment, and bullying.

fundamental attribution error

Conflict that is exacerbated by members' tendencies to misperceive others and to assume that the other party's behavior is caused by personal rather than situational factors.

Conflict Resolution

In group and team work situations, the first dysfunction that occurs is a lack of trust. Trust is defined as the confidence among group members that their peers' intentions are good. In other words, we must believe that those with whom we work will not act opportunistically or take advantage of us and others to narrowly pursue their own self-interests.[68] Without trust, individuals are unable to use what is generally considered the most effective approach to conflict resolution: collaboration. Collaboration is built on trust. Collaboration is one of the five styles of conflict resolution illustrated in Figure 10-2.[69]

Figure 10-2 Styles of Conflict Resolution

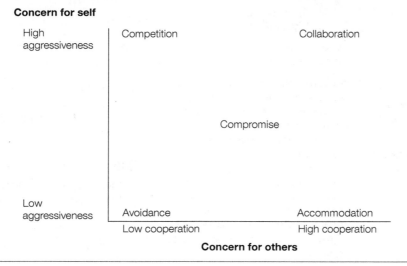

As Figure 10-2 indicates, the styles of conflict resolution can be understood by comparing how each relates in the areas of concern for others and concern for self, as well as by the level of aggressiveness and cooperation. The following is an explanation of the styles of conflict resolution:

- **Competition.** This style is characterized by high aggressiveness and low cooperation. Some people see conflict as a win–lose situation and use competitive and aggressive tactics to intimidate others. Fighting can take many forms, including authoritative mandates, challenges, arguing, insults, accusations, complaining, vengeance, and even physical violence.[70] An individual who uses a competing style exhibits a high concern for self and low concern for others.

- **Collaboration.** An individual who exhibits this style shows a high concern for others and for self. Because of this orientation, this style is characterized by assertive communication and high levels of cooperation. As such, it is considered a "win–win" approach, because a solution should be found that satisfies both parties.

- **Compromise.** This style is a middle ground. The emphasis is on achieving workable but not necessarily optimal solutions. Some consider this a "lose–lose" approach to conflict resolution.

- **Avoidance.** Individuals who practice this style show little concern for relationships or for task accomplishment. By avoiding conflict, they hope it will disappear. When students in small groups talked about their disagreements, they often said they adopted a "wait-and-see" attitude, hoping the problem would eventually go away.[71] Sometimes, however, avoiding is appropriate if you are a low-power person and the consequences of confrontation may be risky and harmful.

- **Accommodation.** This style is characterized by a high concern for relationships but a low concern for task accomplishment. Like avoiding, this can be a useful approach in groups that have shown a high degree of conflict. Accommodating others in this situation provides for an opportunity for tempers to cool and to move toward resolution. It can also be appropriate if the risk of yielding is low. For example, a group of your friends may disagree about where to eat dinner. The choice may be between two of your favorite restaurants; however, the one that most of your friends prefer is your second choice. Even so, because you like that restaurant, too, you have little to lose by yielding.

Of these five basic ways of resolving conflict, collaborating is more likely to promote group unity.

In Chapter 4, the different cultural dimensions were discussed. These distinctions can affect our attitudes and approaches to conflict. For example, Stella Ting-Toomey suggests that people in individualistic cultures are more likely to use direct, confrontational methods of managing disagreements than people who value a collective or team approach to group work.[72] She also suggests that people from collectivistic cultures, especially cultures that place considerable stock in nonverbal messages, prefer non-confrontational and indirect methods of resolving differences. She suspects this difference may be because people from individualistic cultures tend to approach problem solving from a linear, step-by-step perspective, whereas people from collectivistic cultures often use a more intuitive problem-solving process. Ting-Toomey finds that people from individualistic cultures are more likely to use facts or principles as a basis for approaching conflict, negotiation, or persuasion situations.[73] People from collectivistic cultures adopt more relationship-based messages to manage differences. It is important for people from collectivistic cultures to save face by not being perceived as having lost a confrontation.

In a low-context culture, such as that of the United States, more emphasis is placed on words and their explicit meaning than on implicit, nonverbal cues.[74] Researchers have found that people in low-context cultures give greater importance to task or instrumental issues than do people in high-context cultures.[75] In high-context cultures, the expressive or emotional aspects of managing conflict take on special importance. In expressive conflict, the goal is often to express feelings and release tension.[76] Keeping the relationship in balance, maintaining the friendship, and managing the emotional climate often take a higher priority in a high-context culture than achieving a particular outcome. Here again, saving face and avoiding embarrassment for all parties are more important in high-context cultures than in low-context cultures.

Gender is another factor that sometimes makes a difference in how people express and manage conflict in groups and teams. Research suggests that people with a feminine style of managing conflict (either men or women could have a feminine style) are more likely to be interested in issues of equity, empathy, caring, and closeness; to encourage mutual involvement; and generally to focus on relationship issues. A masculine style of conflict management emphasizes achieving specific goals and protecting self-interests, and it is concerned with equality of rights, fairness, and generally focusing on the task.[77] Research further finds sex differences (here the research notes differences between men and women—not just gender differences) in conflict-management styles: women tend to emphasize more expressive goals in conflict, whereas men emphasize instrumental or task objectives.[78]

In your group deliberations, knowing that culture and gender differences exist can help you decide which strategies will be more effective than others. It is important, though, to avoid stereotyping others by cultural, national, ethnic, or gender differences alone. Similarly, taking an egocentric view (that is, assuming your perspective is correct) or an ethnocentric view (assuming your cultural methods of managing conflict are superior to those used by others) can be detrimental to communication.

If you are in the minority in a culturally diverse group:

- Make sure that you tactfully, yet assertively, express your ideas, opinions, facts, and information to the group.

- Ask the group to consider an alternative point of view. Help the group understand that those with a different life experience or racial, ethnic, or cultural worldview may see the issue differently.

If you are in the majority in a culturally diverse group:

- Don't monopolize the conversation; be a gatekeeper by inviting those who have not spoken up to participate in the conversation.

- Encourage people to share ideas and information via e-mail. Some quieter group members may be more likely to participate in this way than by voicing their opinion in person.

- Be cautious of making sweeping generalizations about those who are from a culture different from your own. Each person's opinions and ideas are unique and may not necessarily be shared by others in the same racial or ethnic group.

- Don't expect a person from a minority group to be a spokesperson for others in that group. Don't, for example, turn to a Chinese-American student and say, "So, what do Asians think about this topic?" You can ask what an individual may think or believe, but don't ask someone to speak for a particular group.

? Critical Thinking

Describe a recent conflict you had with someone where you believe that poor communication on one or both parts was the culprit. What can be done to make sure this conflict does not occur again?

Techniques for Enhancing Group and Team Creativity

Creativity is the generation, application, combination, and extension of new ideas. Essentially, to be creative is to invent something new that wasn't in existence before you invented it. In the context of groups and teams, creativity usually refers to the invention or creation of a new idea, strategy, principle, or approach to solving a problem.

The first step in pursuing creativity in a group is to eliminate what Zig Ziglar called "stinking thinking." **Stinking thinking** consists of thoughts that limit the possibilities of an individual, group, or organization. Creativity is reduced when group or team members utter "sound bites" that discourage rather than encourage the group to think of new possibilities. Here are some examples:

- "We simply can't do this."
- "We've never done it this way before."
- "We tried that a few years ago and it didn't work."
- "They won't let us do this."
- "You can't be serious."

creativity
The generation, application, combination, and extension of new ideas.

stinking thinking
Consists of thoughts that limit the possibilities of an individual, group, or organization

A technique for overcoming negative thinking, pioneered by Prescott Lecky, is called tick-tock. The purpose is to change a negative idea into a positive comment. [79] To use the tick-tock technique, make two headings on a sheet of paper: one called "tick" and the other called "tock." Whenever there is a negative thought or idea, write it in the "tick" column. Now think of a substitute positive idea to counter the negative idea: The positive idea goes in the "tock" column. For example, you hear a group member say, "What a stupid idea. Everyone will laugh at us." That negative idea goes under the "tick" heading. Stop and think of a more positive response, such as "Who cares if people laugh if the idea works?" That positive response goes under the "tock" heading. You can use this simple "tick-tock" technique to combat stinking thinking, whether working individually or in a group or team.

To develop creative ideas, Nemiro identified parallel phases in face-to-face and virtual teams:[80]

1. Idea generation phase: Group members actively identify a range of new ideas, possibilities, and approaches to the issue at hand.

2. Development phase: Ideas are extended and additional information is gathered to support the initial nuggets of ideas.

3. Finalization and closure phase: The group agrees on the best ideas.

4. Evaluation phase: The team assesses the value and worth of the ideas selected.

Beyond understanding general principles of creativity and promoting conditions to enhance creativity, specific methods can be used to boost creativity in groups or teams. Such techniques include brainstorming, the nominal-group technique, the Delphi technique, and electronic brainstorming—each a prescriptive technique for structuring the process of generating creative ideas. Research suggests that having standard procedures and some structure can enhance group member creativity.[81]

Brainstorming

brainstorming

A creative technique designed to help a group generate several solutions to a problem.

Brainstorming is a creative technique designed to help a group generate several solutions to a problem. It was first developed by Alex Osborn, an advertising executive who felt the need for a creative technique that did not emphasize evaluating and criticizing ideas but instead would focus on developing imaginative and innovative solutions.[82] Brainstorming has been used by businesses, committees, and government agencies to improve the quality of group decision making. Although it can be used in several phases of many group discussions, it may be most useful if a group needs original ideas or has trouble coming up with any ideas at all. Research suggests that a trained facilitator can improve the execution of group brainstorming.[83]

The general assumption underlying brainstorming is that the more ideas that are generated, the more likely it is that a creative solution will be found. Research largely supports the brainstorming procedure, although some studies suggest that generating a few quality ideas is more useful to groups than merely identifying lots of bad ideas.[84] There's also research that suggests the groups who use brainstorming earlier in their deliberations perceive it to be more valuable in helping them generate quality ideas.[85] And brainstorming is helpful when the group must use evidence to help them find a specific, correct solution to a problem. Research also suggests that the most effective brainstorming groups keep at it—the more persistent group members are in generating ideas, even when idea generation slows, the better the result.[86] And there is evidence that women are more persistent than men in continuing to generate ideas during brainstorming.[87] Another factor that seems to enhance creativity when brainstorming is for group members to value group member diversity. Groups that had a higher appreciation for welcoming and even celebrating diverse approaches to solving problems had more creative approaches to finding a quality solution.[88]

Traditional brainstorming is a process that follows certain guidelines:

1. Select a specific problem that needs solving. Be sure that all group members can identify and clearly define the problem.

2. Set a clear time limit.

3. Ask group members to temporarily put aside all judgments and evaluations. The key to brainstorming is ruling out all criticism and evaluation. Osborn makes these suggestions:

   - Acquire a "try anything" attitude.
   - Avoid criticism, which can stifle creativity.
   - Remember that all ideas are thought-starters.

4. Ask group or team members to think of as many possible solutions to the problem as they can and to share the ideas with the group. Consider the following suggestions:

   - The wilder the ideas, the better.
   - It is easier to tame ideas down than to think ideas up.
   - Think out loud and mention unusual ideas.
   - Someone's wild idea may trigger a good solution from another person in the group.

5. Make sure the group understands that "piggybacking" off someone else's idea is useful. Combine ideas; add to previous ideas. Adopt the philosophy that once an idea is presented to the group, no one owns it. It belongs to the group, and anyone can modify it.

6. Have someone record all the ideas mentioned. Ideas could be recorded on a flipchart, chalkboard, whiteboard, or an overhead projector so that each group member can see them. You could also tape-record your discussions.

7. Evaluate ideas when the time allotted for brainstorming has elapsed. Consider these suggestions:

   ▪ Approach each idea positively, and give it a fair trial.

   ▪ Try to make ideas workable.

   ▪ Encourage feedback about the success of a session. If even a few of the ideas generated by a group are useful, the session has been successful.

The Nominal-Group Technique

The **nominal-group technique** is a procedure that uses some of the principles and methods of active brainstorming but has members write their ideas while being quiet and thinking before sharing them with the group.[89] Introverts will prefer using the nominal-group technique because it gives them time to think and reflect. Specifically, research has found that having group members alternate between individual, silent brainstorming with group conversation can enhance the quality of ideas generated.[90] The nominal-group technique gets its name from the principle that the group is nominal (it is a group in name only), in the sense that members work on problems individually rather than during sustained group interaction. This technique uses **silent brainstorming** to overcome some of the disadvantages researchers have discovered in oral brainstorming.

The key to making brainstorming work is that the generation of ideas is separated from the evaluation of ideas. In oral brainstorming, it's hard not to evaluate ideas. During traditional brainstorming, despite their best intentions, group members often evaluate ideas as soon as they are verbalized, so group members may be less likely to share ideas. As we discussed earlier in the chapter, criticism and evaluation diminish creativity.[91] Even if group members do not verbalize their evaluation, their nonverbal expressions often convey positive or negative evaluation of ideas. Some people are apprehensive or nervous about speaking up in a group, and traditional oral brainstorming makes it less likely that the communication-apprehensive members will participate.

Silent brainstorming overcomes that problem by encouraging even apprehensive group and team members to participate by first writing their ideas.[92] Once they have a written "script," they are more comfortable sharing their ideas. Researchers also found that people work more diligently if they have an individual assignment than if they have a group assignment.[93] In addition, researchers have found that sometimes with traditional brainstorming, the creative talents of some members seem to be restricted just by the very presence of others.[94] Group and team members may generate more ideas if members first work alone and then regroup. After they reconvene, group members can modify, elaborate on, and evaluate ideas. The generation of ideas (writing them down) has been separated from the evaluation of ideas. Silent brainstorming can be done even before a group meets for the first time; you could describe a problem and ask group members to brainstorm individually before assembling. E-mail makes this easier; communication researcher Henri Barki found that electronic brainstorming worked just as well as face-to-face brainstorming.[95]

The nominal-group technique adds structure to the brainstorming process. The following steps summarize how to use the nominal-group technique:

1. All group members should be able to define and analyze the problem under consideration.

2. Working individually, group members write down possible solutions to the problem.

3. Group members report the solutions they have identified to the entire group one at a time. Each idea should be noted on a chart, chalkboard, whiteboard, or overhead projector for all group members to see.

nominal-group technique

A procedure that uses some of the principles and methods of active brainstorming but has members write their ideas while being quiet and thinking before sharing them with the group.

silent brainstorming

Overcome some of the disadvantages in oral brainstorming by encouraging apprehensive team members to participate by first writing their ideas.

4. Group members discuss the ideas gathered, not to advocate for one idea over another but rather to make sure that all the ideas are clear.

5. After discussing all proposed solutions, each group member ranks the solutions. If the list of solutions is long, the group members can rank the five solutions they like best. The results are tabulated.

Both traditional brainstorming and the nominal-group technique can be used at any phase of the problem-solving process. For example, you could combine the nominal-group technique with force-field analysis by asking group members to silently brainstorm about the forces driving and restraining attainment of a group goal. Or, you could ask members to brainstorm possible causes or symptoms of the problem during problem analysis. Or, you could use brainstorming or the nominal-group technique to generate possible strategies for implementing a solution the group has settled on.

The Delphi Technique

Delphi technique

Method, named after the ancient oracle at Delphi, has been called "absentee brainstorming" because individuals share ideas in writing or via e-mail, without meeting face-to-face.

Whereas the nominal-group technique invites participants to contribute ideas by first writing them down and then sharing them with the group, the **Delphi technique** takes this idea one step further. This method, named after the ancient oracle at Delphi, has been called "absentee brainstorming" because individuals share ideas in writing or via e-mail, without meeting face-to-face. One person coordinates the information and shares it with the rest of the group. This approach is especially useful when conflict within the group inhibits effective group interaction, or when time and distance constraints make it difficult for group members to meet.

This method often produces many good ideas. All participants are treated equally because no one is aware of who submitted which idea. It is, however, a time-consuming process. And because there is no face-to-face interaction, some ideas that are worthy of elaboration and exploration may get lost in the shuffle. Using the Delphi technique in combination with face-to-face meetings can help eliminate some disadvantages of the procedure.[96]

Electronic Brainstorming

This technique makes it possible for a group to generate solutions or strategies by typing ideas at a computer keyboard and having them displayed to the entire group. This high-tech method resembles the nominal-group technique in that group members write ideas before sharing them with the group. Because they can see ideas in written form, group members can piggyback off the ideas of others. Electronic brainstorming can be performed with all group members in the same room or computer lab or with members at their own home or office computers.

Research suggests that groups using electronic brainstorming generate more ideas than traditional face-to-face brainstorming groups.[97] One research team found that when some members of a group meet face to face and are supported with ideas from group members not physically present but using electronic means to share information, more ideas are generated and these are of higher quality than if all members meet face to face.[98] Some researchers theorize that this happens because the ideas are generated anonymously.[99] Members feel less fear or anxiety about being criticized for unconventional ideas because no one knows who suggested them. Thus, when group members move to the phase of evaluating ideas, they are not sure whether they are evaluating an idea coming from a boss or a group leader or a new intern. All ideas are considered on their merit and quality. Another reason more ideas may be generated is because of the "piggyback effect." Group members may be stimulated to build on the ideas of other group members.

One obvious disadvantage of electronic brainstorming is the need to have access to a computer network and appropriate software. But recent evidence strongly supports the value of this variation of the brainstorming method, in which computers add structure to the process. Another disadvantage to anonymous, electronic brainstorming occurs when, because the idea sharing is supposed to be anonymous, it is difficult to publicly recognize outstanding contributions. Research has found that when someone is praised for contributing good ideas, that creativity is enhanced—both for the individual praised and for the entire group. Yet when group members privately and anonymously brainstorm ideas, it might seem like a breach of anonymity to publicly praise a good idea.[100]

Table 10-7 provides a summary of the techniques to enhance group creativity.

Table 10-7 Techniques to Enhance Group Creativity

	Advantages	Disadvantages
Brainstorming	• Easy to use • No special materials needed • Group members can piggyback on each other's ideas	• High potential for group members to evaluate ideas as they are being generated • Takes more time than highly structured methods • Quiet members less likely to participate
Nominal-group technique	• Can build on ideas of others • Provides a written record of ideas suggested • Controls more talkative, dominating group members	• Requires good leader to organize the process • Less time for free flow of ideas • Difficult to implement with a large group
Delphi technique	• Group does not have to meet face to face • Provides a written record of ideas suggested • Helps group members prepare for upcoming meeting	• No synergy created by hearing the ideas of others • Minimizes opportunities for elaborating on ideas • Group members may be suspicious that someone has manipulated the results
Electronic brainstorming	• Very efficient • Anonymity increases number of ideas generated	• Need special equipment • Need training in using computer software • It takes time to describe procedures of electronic brainstorming

Team Leadership

Leadership in work teams has become one of the most popular areas of leadership theory and research. It is critical to understand the role of leadership within teams to ensure their success. "Indeed, we would argue that effective leadership processes represent perhaps the most critical factor in the success of organizational teams."[101] By the same token, ineffective leadership is often seen as the primary reason teams fail.[102]

Team leadership may be performed by a formal team leader and/or shared by team members, a situation called **distributed leadership**.

A good leader needs to be flexible and have a broad repertoire of actions or skills to meet the team's diverse needs. The leader's role is to function in a manner that will help the group achieve effectiveness. The leader's goal is to solve team problems by analyzing the internal and external situation and selecting and implementing the appropriate behaviors to ensure team effectiveness.[103] The model of team leadership pictured in Figure 10-3 begins with the decisions that a leader must make; the next step is to take action and, hopefully, these actions will result in team effectiveness.

distributed leadership
A situation in which team members share team leadership.

Leadership Decisions

The first decision a leader must make is whether it is appropriate to continue observing the team or to intervene and take action. The second decision is to determine the general task or relational function of the intervention that is needed. The final decision is whether to intervene at the internal level, or within the team itself, or at the external level.

- **Continue to monitor or take action?** The leader must monitor both the internal and external environment of the team to determine the next step. The leader may gather information from team members, from those outside the group, or from evaluating group outcomes. After gathering and interpreting information, leaders must take the right action based upon this information.

- **Intervene to meet task or relational goals?** The two critical functions of a group, task and socioemotional or relational goals, were discussed earlier in this chapter. This decision involves determining whether the team needs help with relational or task issues.

- **Intervene internally or externally?** The third strategic decision is the level of team process that needs attention: internal task or relational goals or external environmental factors. Internal issues might be group conflict or unclear goals whereas external issues might be lack of organizational support for the team.

Figure 10-3 Hill's Model for Team Leadership

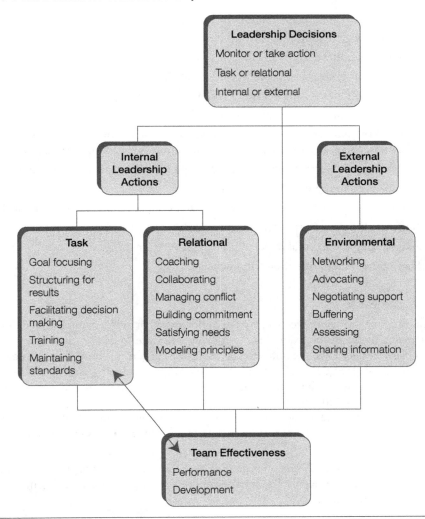

Leadership Actions

As stated in the previous section, leadership actions may be internal or external; internal actions may focus on the task or the relational goals of the team.

- **Internal task actions.** Many of the task actions a leader might take are accomplished through communication. These include the following:
  - Goal focusing (clarifying, gaining agreement)
  - Structuring for results (planning, visioning, organization, clarifying roles, delegating)
  - Facilitating decision making (informing, coordinating, mediating, synthesizing, issue focusing)
  - Training members in task skills
  - Maintaining standards of excellence (assessing performance and addressing inadequate performance)
- **Internal relational actions.** The second set of leadership actions includes those that the leader might implement to improve team relationships. Many of these also are achieved through communication. They include the following:
  - Coaching team members in interpersonal skills
  - Collaborating (including, involving)
  - Managing conflict and power issues
  - Building commitment and team spirit (socializing, rewarding, innovating, recognizing)
  - Satisfying individual member needs (trusting, supporting, advocating)
  - Modeling ethical and principled practices (fair, consistent)
- **External environmental actions.** Again, many of these actions to improve the environmental interface with the team involve communication. Such actions include the following:
  - Networking and forming alliances (gathering information, increasing influence)
  - Advocating and representing the team
  - Negotiating upward to secure needed resources, support, and recognition for the team
  - Buffering the team from external distractions
  - Assessing environmental indicators of team effectiveness
  - Sharing relevant information with the team

Team Effectiveness

Two critical functions of team effectiveness are performance or task accomplishment and development or maintenance of the team. Team performance is the "quality of decision making, the ability to implement decisions, the outcomes of team work in terms of problems solved and work completed, and finally the quality of institutional leadership provided by the team."[104] Team development is the cohesiveness of the team and the ability of group members to satisfy their own needs while working effectively with other team members.

Effective groups have a clear, engaging direction; an enabling situation that contains structure, support, and coaching; and adequate resources.[105] Successful teams consistently demonstrate eight characteristics:

- **A clear elevating goal.** Teams often fail because they are given a vague task and then are asked to work out the details. Teams also fail because they let personal agendas or power issues replace their goal.

- **Results-driven structure.** Different types of teams have different types of structures. An effective team must use the appropriate structure; members need clear roles, a good communication system, methods for assessing individual performance, and an emphasis on fact-based judgments.

- **Competent team members.** Team members need not only sufficient information, education, and training, but also interpersonal and teamwork skills, and ideally certain personal characteristics, such as openness, supportiveness, action orientation, and a positive attitude.

- **Unified commitment.** A common occurrence is to call a group a team and then treat it as a collection of individuals. Teams don't just happen; they must be developed.

- **Collaborative climate.** A collaborative climate is one in which members can stay problem-focused, listen to and understand one another, feel free to take risks, and be willing to compensate for one another. To build a collaborative climate, trusting relationships need to be developed based on openness, honesty, consistency, and respect. Effective team leaders ensure a collaborative climate by making communication safe, demanding and rewarding collaborative behavior, guiding the team's problem-solving efforts, and managing their own control needs.

- **Standards of excellence.** The organization or the team must set standards of excellence so that team members will feel pressure to perform at their highest levels. A leader can facilitate this process by requiring results, making expectations clear, reviewing results, providing feedback to resolve performance issues, and rewarding results.

- **External support.** A common mistake is to give teams challenging assignments but no organizational support to accomplish them. Organizations also often ask employees to work on difficult assignments but then do not reward them with raises or bonuses. Teams that are given the resources needed to do their jobs are recognized for their accomplishments and rewarded for team rather than individual performance and can achieve excellence.

- **Principled leadership.** Effective leaders are committed to the team's goals and give members autonomy to achieve those goals. Leaders can reduce team effectiveness by being unwilling to confront inadequate performance, having too many priorities, and overestimating the positive aspects of team performance.[106]

The model for team leadership is based on the assumption that the leader's job is to monitor the team and to take whatever action is deemed necessary to ensure team effectiveness. The model attempts to provide specific actions that leaders can perform to improve team functioning and effectiveness. In addition, team leaders need a wide repertoire of communication skills to monitor the team and take appropriate action.

Communicating in Virtual Teams

Although it is difficult to know exactly how many organizations use virtual teams, studies indicate that at least half, if not more use them and the number appears to be increasing. There are advantages to collaborating virtually, including

- Virtual communication methods work well for structured, linear tasks.

- In computer-mediated meetings, the ideas of everyone can more easily and accurately be captured and recorded.

- Virtual groups often generate more ideas when brainstorming than face-to-face groups.

Virtual teams also face many of the challenges that all teams do, but language difficulties, time-and-distance challenges, the absence of face-to-face contact, and, above all, the barriers posed by cultural differences and personal communication styles make virtual work far more complex.[107]

According to the same survey, respondents indicated that virtual teams differed from and were more challenging than face-to-face teams in the following tasks:

- Managing conflict (73%)
- Making decisions (69%)
- Expressing opinions (64%) (This issue was particularly problematic in indirect cultures.)

Some of the recommendations of the study emphasized the need for virtual teams to establish specific work rules (such as those outlining rules for respectful interaction) that are often assumed in co-located teams. It also recommended that virtual teams need to pay greater attention to team structure than co-located teams do. In addition, virtual teams must carefully monitor and adhere to the work rules they have created. Finally, they need to be aware of the influence of culture on work styles and to develop procedures to assure intercultural effectiveness.[108]

The success of digital collaboration depends largely upon team members' abilities to adopt new ways of working. The previously cited study indicated that the most important characteristics of virtual team members were

- A willingness to share information (18%)
- Being proactively engaged (17%)
- Being collaborative (17%)
- Being organized (14%)
- Having good social skills (13%)
- Providing useful feedback (11%)
- Offering assistance to teammates (10%)[109]

Although there are many similarities between face-to-face and virtual teams, some special considerations should be made when working in the latter context, particularly when developing trust, dealing with cultural differences, managing conflict, and brainstorming.

Developing Trust in Virtual Teams

Groups and teams that have limited or no face-to-face interaction develop trust differently from those where face-to-face contact is frequent. Face-to-face teams develop trust mostly through social and emotional bonds that grow as they get to know one another. In virtual teams, trust is more likely to develop through task-oriented responses, such as timely information sharing and appropriate, sound responses to electronic communications.[110] Trust will develop more rapidly in computer-mediated relationships when the participants first have an opportunity for face-to-face interaction. This is especially true when the context is competitive.[111]

Cultural Differences in Virtual Teams

Cultural differences can also affect the success of digital collaboration, particularly in terms of communication preferences and expectations. Table 10-8 provides a summary of some cultural preferences based on Hofstede's cultural dimensions. Despite cultural differences, several commonalities also exist. If you are the leader of a virtual group, four tactics will enhance team members' identification with the team: catering to the individual (asserting each team member's individuality and his or her rights to different opinions), giving positive feedback, pointing out common goals, and positively supporting team activities and face-to-face interactions.[112]

Table 10-8 Attitudes about Technology Use Based on Hofstede's Cultural Factors

Cultural Factor	Technological Considerations
Power difference	People from cultures with substantial differences in power and status may more freely use technologies that are asynchronous and allow anonymous input. These cultures sometimes use technology to indicate status differences between team members.
Uncertainty avoidance	People from cultures uncomfortable with uncertainty may be slower to adopt technology. They may also prefer technology that produces more permanent records of discussions and decisions.
Individualism–Collectivism	People from highly collectivistic cultures (those that value group and team achievement over individual success) may prefer face-to-face interactions.
Masculinity–Femininity	People from cultures with a more "feminine" orientation (concerned with nurturing, cooperation, and sharing), in contrast to a "masculine" orientation (concerned with earning visible success and possessions), may be more prone to use technology in a nurturing way, especially during team startups. They may also prefer face-to-face meetings to virtual meetings.
Context	People from cultures in which the context of a message is highly important may prefer more information-rich technologies as well as those that offer social presence (synchronous, real-time communication). They may resist using technologies with low social presence to communicate with people whom they have never met. People from cultures in which the context of a message is less important may prefer more asynchronous communications.

Source: Engleberg, I., & Wynn, D. R. (2012). *Working in Groups* (6th Ed.). New York, NY: Pearson.

Managing Conflict in Virtual Teams

Whether you're interacting in person or using e-mail or other mediated messages, the same factors that contribute to conflict in a face-to-face team or group can arise in a virtual one. The limited amount of nonverbal cues in mediated settings appears to have an effect on how mediated teams manage conflict. The challenges to managing conflict in virtual teams are that they are:

- *More likely to avoid conflict.* One study found that when groups negotiate differences in computer-mediated settings, as conflict escalates group members tend to decrease the intensity of forcefully insisting how the conflict should be resolved.[113] In addition, the researchers found that as conflict increases, negotiators generally tend to avoid conflict rather than addressing it head-on. When communicating face to face during conflict, team members are more likely to try to control the behavior of others, and there is a more reciprocal, tit-for-tat escalation of conflict than in mediated settings.[114]

- *More difficult to address conflict.* Another study found that when attempting to brainstorm and generate ideas, members of computer-mediated groups experience more negative conflict-management behaviors than those in face-to-face groups; the computer-mediated groups are less effective in managing conflict.[115] The results suggest that it may be more difficult to manage conflict in a productive way in computer-mediated groups than in face-to-face groups.

- *More difficult to manage relational conflict.* Research has also found that if a group has relational conflict, especially if the conflict is intensely personal, it may be best to sort the conflict out in person rather than using e-mail or other mediated methods. If the issue is a difference of opinion about a technical issue, then e-mail can be a useful way of clarifying and sharing information. [116]

To avoid these challenges, you should

- *Deal with conflict proactively.* Another study explored the effects of conflict management styles in virtual teams—whether team members are avoidant, competitive, or collaborative.[117] They found that it's not a good idea to suppress ideas and suggestions that are in conflict with those of other virtual team members. Avoiding conflict had a negative effect on team performance. Confronting conflict directly typically resulted in a more positive team outcome. Researchers also found that without the accompanying nonverbal cues, team members' attempts to negatively evaluate others had less impact.

- *Use a collaborative conflict-resolution style.* Research has found that collaboration is perceived as a positive conflict-management approach in both virtual teams and face-to-face teams. Attempting to reach a compromise, especially an early compromise before team members have a chance to discuss the issues, is not as productive in virtual groups as it is in face-to-face groups.
- When relational conflict erupts online, it may be time to meet face to face rather than try to manage the conflict online.

Brainstorming in Virtual Teams

As discussed previously, using electronic brainstorming has several advantages. It allows groups to generate ideas quickly and from remote locations. It may also be less expensive to invite team members to turn on their home or office computers to brainstorm ideas than to have all members travel to the same geographic location to hold a meeting. Nonetheless, there are several challenges and barriers to consider when using electronic brainstorming. In the book *Virtual Teaming*, Deborah Jude-York and Lauren D. Davis identify the following challenges in collaborating virtually:[118]

- Fear of working with technology (technophobia)
- Lack of needed technical skills
- Incompatibility of hardware and software
- Uneven writing skills due to differences in cultural background, language use, and education
- Technical difficulties (the power goes out, the computers are down)
- E-mail overload—people have too much e-mail to process

To overcome these obstacles, make sure group members understand how to use the hardware and software programs. In case there are technical problems, have a backup plan—such as a phone number to call or an alternative e-mail address to use. Have someone who is knowledgeable about technology available to help group members or, at the very least, give each group member a number to call or a Web site to use if there are technical problems.

The following steps are recommended for brainstorming in a virtual team:

1. The group leader selects a problem, issue, policy, or decision that needs to be reviewed.
2. The leader corresponds with group members in writing, informing them of the task and inviting their suggestions and input. A specific questionnaire may be developed, or the group members may be asked to individually brainstorm suggestions or reactions to the issue confronting the group.
3. The respondents complete the questionnaire or generate a list of their brainstormed responses and send it to the leader.
4. The leader then summarizes all the responses from the group and shares the summary with all group members, asking for additional ideas, suggestions, and reactions. Team members are asked to rate or rank the ideas and return their comments to the leader.
5. The leader continues the process of summarizing the group feedback and asking for more input until general consensus emerges and decisions are made. It may take several rounds of soliciting ideas and evaluating ideas before consensus is achieved.[119]

This method often produces many good ideas. All participants are treated equally because no one is aware of who submitted which idea. It is, however, a time-consuming process. And because there is no face-to-face interaction, some ideas that are worthy of elaboration and exploration may get lost in the shuffle. Using the Delphi technique in combination with face-to-face meetings can help eliminate some disadvantages of the procedure.

Proper Training for Virtual Team Success

To help virtual team members adapt to the differences of teamwork, proper training is required. IBM, for example, has developed a process that can take as long as two months and that begins with one-on-one coaching of the team leader. Then, in a two-day, face-to-face meeting, a facilitator helps the team do the following:

- Align its mission.
- Clarify each member's role.
- Understand members' differing communication and work styles.
- Decide how the team will make decisions in its virtual workspace.
- Document and agree on team norms.[120]

What IBM has found is that teams that invest in basic teamwork skills and team leadership succeed in working electronically. Teams that concentrate only on the enabling technology fail. This conclusion is supported by research that stresses the importance of building team relationships before focusing on task problems. "Virtual team leaders must be able to 'read' all the personal and contextual nuances in a world of electronic communications. They must be able to understand the possible causes of silence, misunderstanding, and slights without any of the usual signs to guide them. Leaders must be sensitive to the 'flow' of team processes, paying attention to the smallest matters to head off potential problems that could derail the team's task."[121]

The benefits of properly trained virtual teams include the following:

- When team members receive the same information at the same time and quickly, the conflict that comes from selective or secret information flow is avoided. Departmental politics are minimized.
- Accountability of team members to each other and to the work increases significantly. Participation and individual contributions by members are evident to everyone on the team.
- Even though members may be remote, decisions can be made with the knowledge and participation of the entire team.
- Because team members have the most current information, they can make high-quality decisions quickly.
- The digital space serves as a record. This has two benefits: (1) A record of any decision stays in the shared digital space, ensuring it will stick; and (2) relevant documents reside in that space and can be easily accessed. This ability also eliminates any ambiguity about which version is current.
- Important information stays with the team through changes in membership. New team members can become contributors faster because the team's history and intellectual capital reside in the shared space.[122]

As with many aspects of communication, the success of virtual teams often depends on adequate planning and preparation.

Summary

One channel of communication that has received a lot of attention in recent years in both the workplace and academic settings is group communication. Although the purposes of business communication and the importance of audience analysis apply to group communication just as they do to other channels of communication, the complex dynamics that arise from group situations require additional knowledge for strategy formulation. Much of the research about and many of the practices involved in interpersonal communication are applicable to group communication situations. Paying attention to group formation and group processes can help ensure that groups are productive. Special attention may need to be paid to decision-making processes and conflict resolution to ensure that the potential benefits of groups are achieved.

A good team leader needs to be flexible and have a broad repertoire of actions or skills to meet the team's diverse needs. The leader's role is to function in a manner that will help the group achieve effectiveness. The leader's goal is to solve team problems by analyzing the internal and external situation and selecting and implementing the appropriate behaviors to ensure team effectiveness. The model of team leadership begins with the decisions that a leader must make; the next step is to take action and, hopefully, these actions will result in team effectiveness.

As with other communication contexts, the success of virtual teams largely depends on adequate planning and preparation. An effective virtual team must align its mission, clarify each member's role, understand members' differing communication and work styles, decide how the team will make decisions in its virtual workspace, and document and agree on team norms.

Key Terms

group **258**

team **258**

comparison level (CL) **230**

comparison level for alternatives (CL_{alt}) **260**

intermember relations **263**

ground rules **266**

groupthink **267**

informational influence **268**

normative influence **268**

interpersonal influence **268**

process losses **269**

social loafing **270**

free-riding **270**

oversampling **273**

competitors **276**

cooperators **276**

individualists **276**

fundamental attribution error **277**

creativity **280**

stinking thinking **280**

brainstorming **281**

nominal-group technique **282**

silent brainstorming **282**

Delphi technique **283**

distributed leadership **284**

Discussion Questions

1. What are group norms, and how do they structure interactions within a group?
2. What are group roles and which roles occur most frequently in groups? Which roles are productive and why? Which roles are destructive and why?
3. What are the sources of conflict in groups? How can conflict be managed effectively?
4. Describe Hill's team leadership model. What communication skills are required to enhance team effectiveness in task accomplishment? Effectiveness of team relationships? Team effectiveness in terms of its relationship with its environment?
5. What is the critical aspect in the success of virtual teams? How might this aspect be ensured?

Applications

1. Observe a group meeting. Attempt to identify the stage of group formation for the team. Identify the roles that the respective members of the group play. If conflict occurs, what type is it? What types of conflict resolution behaviors are used to deal with the conflict? After completing your observation, write a report to the team summarizing your findings and providing recommendations for how they might improve their team processes.

2. Write a group contract. One way to ensure that a group has the discussion that is necessary to begin on the path of performing is to create a group contract. Creating a group contract ensures that you have discussed your expectations of one another, assigned task responsibilities, created deadlines, and talked about group member roles. In addition, a group contract details the procedure for dealing with the failure to meet these agreed-upon expectations. To complete a group contract, review the following steps:

   a. You and your group members should discuss and identify your expectations of one another regarding the completion of a team project. These expectations generally include concerns about participation, the meeting of deadlines, attendance at in-class group meetings and at other group meetings, and the revision of individual sections of your presentation or paper to meet group standards. Group standards regarding the quality of work expected or the grade desired are also often useful. In addition, you may want to agree upon deadlines for the various components of the project as well as assign group roles and responsibilities.

   b. You and your group members should discuss and identify the consequences for not fulfilling these expectations. Specifying consequences is important for two reasons: (1) It provides an opportunity to empower group members; and (2) it mitigates against the enabling of free-riding and social loafing. An example of a consequence includes reducing the percentage of an individual's group grade if deadlines are not met or if revisions are not made to individual assignments as expected by the team. Another example of a consequence might be the termination of an individual's membership in the group if a certain number of contract transgressions occur.

   c. Each group should write a contract that specifies its expectations of individual members as well as the consequences for not fulfilling these expectations. You should be as specific as possible. For example, you should specify what constitutes poor attendance, inadequate participation, and low-quality work. Consequences for not fulfilling expectations should be as specific as your group's expectations. As discussed previously, your contract might also include a schedule as well as the assignment of group members' responsibilities.

3. Team member evaluations. Use the following template to generate an internal team review. Please rank team members according to their value to the team. Additionally, provide each team member with a short paragraph outlining this individual's strengths, and an additional paragraph outlining an area where this individual needs to improve. To begin this process, record each team member's name and score his or her performance on a scale of 1 to 5 (1 being lowest and 5 being highest) for each of the team-related activities, using the following template.

Team Member:	
Establishing decision-making policies	
Setting meeting agendas	
Setting timelines and meeting deadlines	
Identifying team needs	
Defining project goals	
Planning strategies to meet group goals	
Facilitating problem solving	
Developing conflict resolution rules	
Organizing collaborative sessions	
Assigning task responsibility	
Remaining flexible and accommodating the group	
Recommending action	

4. Conduct research and develop a plan to improve teamwork at your workplace. Write an informal proposal to your manager outlining your plan and explaining its benefits.

5. Conduct research on the benefits of virtual teams. Prepare a proposal for your manager, outlining the benefits and proposing a shift to virtual teams at your workplace.

Endnotes

1. Eisenberg, E. M., & Goodall, H. L., Jr. (1993). *Organizational Communication: Balancing Creativity and Constraint.* New York: St. Martin's Press, p. 286.

2. Eisenberg & Goodall, 1993, p. 187.

3. Festinger, L. (1954). A theory of social comparison processes. *Human Relations,* 7, 117–140.

4. Insko, C. A., & Schopler, J. (1972). *Experimental Social Psychology.* New York: Academic Press.

5. Arkin, R. M., & Burger, J. M. (1980). Effects of unit relation tendencies on interpersonal attraction. *Social Psychology Quarterly,* 43, 380–391.

6. Festinger, L. (1957). *A Theory of Cognitive Dissonance.* Stanford, CA: Stanford University Press; Heider, F. (1958). *The Psychology of Interpersonal Relations.* New York: Wiley.

7. Kerckhoff, A. C., & Davis, K. E. (1962). Value consensus and need complementarity in mate selection. *American Sociological Review,* 27, 295–303; Levinger, G., Senn, D. J., & Jorgensen, B. W. (1970). Progress toward permanence in courtship: A test of the Kerckhoff-Davis hypothesis. *Sociometry,* 33, 427–433; Meyer, J. P., & Pepper, S. (1977). Need compatibility and marital adjustment in young married couples. *Journal of Personality and Social Psychology,* 35, 331–342.

8. Kelley, H. H., & Thibaut, J. W. (1978). *Interpersonal Relations: A Theory of Interdependence.* New York: Wiley; Moreland, R. L., & Levine, J. M. (1982). Socialization in small groups: Temporal changes in individual-group relations. *Advances in Experimental Social Psychology,* 15, 137–192; Thibaut, J. W., & Kelley, H. H. (1959). *The Social Psychology of Groups.* New York: Wiley.

9. Bonney, M. E. (1947). Popular and unpopular children: A sociometric study. *Sociometry Monographs,* No. 99, A80; Thibaut & Kelley, 1959.

10. Gilchrist, J. C. (1952). The formation of social groups under conditions of success and failure. *Journal of Abnormal and Social Psychology,* 47, 174–187; Iverson, M. A. (1964). Personality impressions of punitive stimulus persons of differential status. *Journal of Abnormal and Social Psychology,* 68, 617–626.

11. Thibaut and Kelley, 1959.

12. Maassen, G. H., Akkermans, W., & Van der Linden, J. L. (1996). Two-dimensional sociometric status determination with rating scales. *Small Group Research,* 27, 56–78.

13. Coie, J. D., Dodge, K. A., & Kupersmidt, J. B. (1990). Peer group behavior and social status. In S. R. Asher & J. D. Coie (Eds.), *Peer rejection in childhood* (pp. 17–59). New York: Cambridge University Press; Newcomb, A. E., Bukowski, W. M., & Pattee, L. (1993). Children's peer relations: A meta-analytic review of popular, rejected, neglected, controversial, and average sociometric status. *Psychological Bulletin,* 113, 99–128.

14. Shaw, M. E. (1964). Communication networks. *Advances in Experimental Social Psychology,* 1, 111–147.

15. Leavitt, H. (1951). Some effects of certain communication patterns on group performance. *Journal of Abnormal and Social Psychology,* 51, 38–50.

16. Engleberg & Wynn.

17. Tuckman, B. W. (1965). Developmental sequences in small groups. *Psychological Bulletin,* 63, 384–399; and Tuckman, B. W.,

& Jensen, M. A. C. (1977). Stages of small group development revisited. *Group and Organizational Studies,* 2, 419–427.

18. Myers, A. E. (1962). Team competition, success, and the adjustment of group members. *Journal of Abnormal and Social Psychology,* 65, 325–332; Shaw, M. E., & Shaw, L. M. (1962). Some effects of sociometric grouping upon learning in a second grade classroom. *Journal of Social Psychology,* 57, 453–458.

19. Reitan, H. T. & Shaw, M. E. (1964). Group membership, sex-composition of the group, and conformity behavior. *Journal of Social Psychology* 64, 45–51.

20. Gibson, J., & Hodgetts, R. (1986). *Organizational Communication: A Managerial Approach.* New York: Academic Press.

21. Schachter, S. (1951). Deviation, rejection, and communication. *Journal of Abnormal and Social Psychology,* 46, 190–207.

22. French, J. R. P., Jr. (1941). The disruption and cohesion of groups. *Journal of Abnormal and Social Psychology,* 36, 361–377; Pepitone, A., & Reichling, G. (1955). Group cohesiveness and the expression of hostility. *Human Relations,* 8, 327–337.

23. Gibson, J., & Hodgetts, R. (1986). *Organizational Communication: A Managerial Approach.* New York: Academic Press.

24. Mullen, B., & Copper, C. (1994). The relation between group cohesiveness and performance: An integration. *British Journal of Social Psychology,* 27, 333–356.

25. Gully, S. M., Devine, D. J., & Whitney, D. J. (1995). A meta-analysis of cohesion and performance: Effects of levels of analysis and task interdependence. *Small Group Research,* 26, 497–520.

26. Gerard, H. B., & Orive, R. (1987). The dynamics of opinion formation. *Advances in Experimental Social Psychology,* 20, 171–202; Orive, R. (1988a). Group consensus, action immediacy, and opinion confidence. *Personality and Social Psychology Bulletin,* 14, 573–577; and Orive, R. (1988b). Social projection and social comparison of opinions. *Journal of Personality and Social Psychology,* 54, 943–964.

27. Schachter, 1951.

28. Bornstein, R. F. (1992). The dependent personality: Developmental, social, and clinical perspectives. *Psychological Bulletin,* 112, 3–23.

29. Schachter, 1951.

30. Tziner, A., & Eden, D. (1985). Effects of crew composition on crew performance: Does the whole equal the sum of its parts? *Journal of Applied Psychology,* 70, 85–93.

31. Shaw, M. E. (1981). *Group Dynamics: The Psychology of Small Group Behavior* (3rd ed.). New York: McGraw-Hill.

32. Bond, M. H., & Shiu, W. Y. (1997). The relationship between a group's personality resources and the two dimensions of its group process. *Small Group Research,* 28, 194–217.

33. Williams, K. D., Harkins, S., & Latane, B. (1981). Identifiability as a deterrent to social loafing: Two cheering experiments. *Journal of Personality and Social Psychology,* 40, 303–311.

34. Harkins, S. G., & Jackson, J. M. (1985). The role of evaluation in eliminating social loafing. *Personality and Social Psychology Bulletin,* 11, 457–465; Harkins, S. G., & Szymanski, K. (1987).

Social loafing and facilitation: New wine in old bottles. *Review of Personality and Social Psychology*, 9, 167–188; Harkins, S. G., & Szymanski, K. (1988). Social loafing and self-evaluation with an objective standard. *Journal of Experimental Social Psychology*, 24, 354–365; Jackson, J. M., & Latane, B. (1981). All alone in front of all those people: Stage fright as a function of number and type of co-performances and audience. *Journal of Personality and Social Psychology*, 40, 73–85; Szymanski, K., & Harkins, S. G. (1987). Social loafing and self-evaluation with a social standard. *Journal of Personality and Social Psychology*, 53, 891–897; Williams, Harkins, & Latane, 1981.

35. Polzer, J. T., Kramer, R. M., & Neale, M. A. (1997). Positive illusions about oneself and one's group. *Small Group Research*, 28, 243–266.

36. Brickner, M. A., Harkins, S. G., & Ostrom, T. M. (1986). Effects of personal involvement: Thought-provoking implications for social loafing. *Journal of Personality and Social Psychology*, 51, 763–770.

37. Weldon, E., & Weingart, L. R. (1993). Group goals and group performance. *British Journal of Social Psychology*, 32, 307–334.

38. Hinsz, V. B. (1995). Goal setting by groups performing an additive task: A comparison with individual goal setting. *Journal of Applied Social Psychology*, 25, 965–990.

39. Rothwell, J. D. (1998). *In Mixed Company: Small Group Communication* (3rd ed.). Fort Worth, TX: Harcourt Brace College Publishers, pp. 84–85.

40. Gouran, D., & Hirokawa, R. (1996). Functional theory and communication in decision making and problem solving groups: An expanded view. In R. Hirokawa & M. Poole (Eds.), Communication and group decision making, 2nd ed. (pp. 55–80). Thousand Oaks, CA: Sage, 69.

41. Rettinger, D. A., & Hastie, R. (2001, July). Content effects on decision making. *Organizational Behavior and Human Decision Processes 85*, 336–59.

42. Chernyshenko, S., Miner, A. G., Baumann, M. R. , & Sniezek, J. A. (2003). The impact of information distribuc weighting model. *Organizational Behavior and Human Decision Processes 91*, 12–25.

43. Dennis, A. R. (1996). Information exchange and use in small group decision making. *Small Group Research 27*, 532–50; see also Wittenbaum, G. M. (1998). Information sampling in decision making groups: The impact of members' task-relevant status. *Small Group Research 29*, 57–84; Propp, K. M. (1997). Information utilization in small group decision making: A study of the evaluation interaction model. *Small Group Research 28*, 424–53; Gonzalez, C. (2005). Decision support for real-time, dynamic decision-making tasks. *Organizational Behavior and Human Decision Processes 96*, 142–54.

44. Oetzel, J. G. (1998). Explaining individual communication processes in homogeneous and heterogeneous groups through individual-collectivism and self-construal. *Human Communication Research 25*, 202–24.

45. Price, K. H., Lavelle, J. J., Henley, A. B., Cocchiara, F. B., & Buchanan, F. R. (2006). Judging the fairness of voice-based participation across multiple and interrelated stages of decision making. *Organizational Behavior and Human Decision Processes 99*, 212–26.

46. Hirokawa, R. W., & Scheerhorn, D. R. (1986). Communication in faulty group decision making," in R. Y. Hirokawa and M. S. Poole, (eds.) *Communication and Group Decision Making*, p. 67. Beverly Hills, CA: Sage.

47. Stasser, G. (1992). Pooling of unshared information during group discussions. In S. Worchel, W. Wood, & J. A. Simpson (Eds.) *Group Process and Productivity* (pp. 48–67). Newbury Park, CA: Sage; Stasser, G., Taylor, L. A., & Hanna, C. (1989). Information sampling in structured and unstructured discussions of three- and six-person groups. *Journal of Personality and Social Psychology*, 57, 67–78; and Wittenbaum, G. M., & Stasser, G. (1996). Management of information in small groups. In J. L. Nye & A. M. Brower (Eds.), *What's Social About Social Cognition? Research on Socially Shared Cognitions in Small Groups* (pp. 3–28). Thousand Oaks, CA: Sage.

48. Di Salvo, V. S., Nikkel, E., & Monroe, C. (1989). Theory and practice: A field investigation and identification of group members' perceptions of problems facing natural work groups. *Small Group Behavior*, 20, 551–567.

49. Myers, D. G., & Lamm, H. (1976). The group polarization phenomenon. *Psychological Bulletin*, 83, 602–627.

50. Clark, K. B. (1971). The pathos of power. *American Psychologist*, 26, 1047–57; Myers, D. G., & Lamm, H. (1975). The polarizing effect of group discussion. *American Scientist*, 63, 297–303; Myers & Lamm, 1976; Goethals, G. R., & Zanna, M. P. (1979). The role of social comparison in choice shifts. *Journal of Personality and Social Psychology*, 37, 1469–76; Myers, D. G. (1978). The polarizing effects of social comparison. *Journal of Experimental Social Psychology*, 14, 554–63; and Sanders, G. S., & Baron, R. S. (1977). Is social comparison irrelevant for producing choice shifts? *Journal of Experimental Social Psychology*, 13, 303–14.

51. Davis, J. H., Kameda, T., & Stasson, M. (1992). Group risk taking: Selected topics. In J. F. Yates (Ed.), *Risk-taking behavior* (pp. 63–199). Chichester: Wiley; Laughlin, P. R., & Earley, P. C. (1982). Social combination models, persuasive arguments theory, social comparison theory, and choice shift. *Journal of Personality and Social Psychology*, 42, 273–80; and Zuber, J. A., Crott, J. W., & Werner, J. (1992). Choice shift and group polarization: An analysis of the status of arguments and social decision schemes. *Journal of Personality and Social Psychology*, 62, 50–61.

52. Chaney, L. H., & Martin, J. S. (2011). *Intercultural Business Communication* (5th ed.). Boston: Prentice Hall.

53. Eisenberg & Goodall, 1993.

54. Hirokawa, R., & Rost, K. (1992). Effective group decision making in organizations. *Management Communication Quarterly*, 5, 267–388.

55. Ohbuchi, K., Chiba, S., & Fukushima, O. (1996). Mitigation of interpersonal conflicts: Politeness and time pressure. *Personality and Social Psychology Bulletin*, 22, 1035–42.

56. Rosenbaum, M. E. (1986). The repulsion hypothesis: On the nondevelopment of relationships. *Personality and Social Psychology*, 51, 1156–66.

57. Haythorn, W., Couch, A. S., Haefner, D., Langham, P., & Carter, L. F. (1956). The effects of varying combinations of authoritarian and equalitarian leaders and followers. *Journal of Abnormal and Social Psychology*, 53, 210–19; Shaw, 1981.

58. Moreland, R. L., Levine, J. M., & Wingert, M. L. (1996). Creating the ideal group: Composition effects at work. In E. Witte & J. Davis (Eds.), *Understanding group behavior: Small group*

processes and interpersonal relations (vol. 2, pp. 11–35). Mahwah, NJ: Erlbaum.

59. McGrath, J. E. (1984). Small group research, that once and future field: An interpretation of the past with an eye to the future. *Group Dynamics: Theory, Research, and Practice*, 1, 7–27.

60. Houle, C. O. (1989). *Governing Boards: Their Nature and Nurture*. San Francisco: Jossey-Bass.

61. Franken, R. E., & Brown, D. J. (1995). Why do people like competition? The motivation for winning, putting forth effort, improving one's performance, performing well, being instrumental, and expressing forceful/aggressive behavior. *Personality and Individual Differences*, 19, 175–84; Franken, R. E., & Prpich, W. (1996). Dislike of competition and the need to win: Self-image concerns, performance concerns, and the distraction of attention. *Journal of Social Behavior and Personality*, 11, 695–712; Steers, R. M., & Porter, L. W. (1991). *Motivation and Work Behavior* (4th ed.). New York: McGraw-Hill; and Tjosvold, D. (1995). Cooperation theory, constructive controversy, and effectiveness: Learning from crisis. In R. A. Guzzo, E. Salas, & Associates, *Team effectiveness and decision making in organizations* (pp. 79–112). San Francisco: Jossey-Bass.

62. Tjosvold, 1995.

63. Kelley, H. H. (1997). Expanding the analysis of social orientations by reference to the sequential-temporal structures of situations. *European Journal of Social Psychology*, 27, 373–404; McClintock, C. G., Messick, D. M., Kuhlman, D. M., & Campos, F. T. (1973). Motivational bases of choice in three-choice decomposed games. *Journal of Experimental Psychology*, 9, 572–90; Swap, W. C., & Rubin, J. Z. (1983). Measurement of interpersonal orientation. *Journal of Personality and Social Psychology*, 44, 208–19.

64. Bonta, B. D. (1997). Cooperation and competition in peaceful societies. *Pyschological Bulletin*, 121, 299–320; Fry, D. P., & Bjorkqvist, K. (Eds.). (1997). *Cultural Variations in Conflict Resolution: Alternatives to Violence*. Mahwah, NJ: Erlbaum; Van Lange, P. A. M., De Bruin, E. M. N., Otten, W., & Joireman, J. A. (1997). Development of prosocial, individualistic, and competitive orientations: Theory and preliminary evidence. *Journal of Personality and Social Psychology*, 37, 858–64.

65. Hofstede, G., & Hofstede, G. J. (2005). *Cultures and Organizations* (2nd ed.). New York: McGraw-Hill.

66. McCord, L. B., & Richardson, J. (2001), Are workplace bullies sabotaging your ability to compete? Retrieved September 4, 2005, from *http://gbr.pepperdine.edu/2010/08/are-workplace-bullies-sabotaging-your-ability-to-compete/#10#10*.

67. McCord & Richardson, 2001.

68. Ibid.

69. Ibid.

70. Lencioni, P. M. (2002). *The Five Dysfunctions of a Team*. San Francisco: Jossey-Bass.

71. Blake, R., & Mouton, J. (1964). *The Managerial Grid*. Houston: Gulf Publishing; Kilmann, R., & Thomas, K. (1977). Developing a force-choice measure of conflict-handling behavior: The "MODE" instrument. *Educational and Psychological Measurement*, 37, 309–25.

72. Morrill, C. (1995). *The Executive Way*. Chicago: University of Chicago Press.

73. Wall, V. D., Jr., & Nolan, L. L. (1987). Small group conflict: A look at equity, satisfaction, and styles of conflict management. *Small Group Behavior*, 18, 188–211.

74. Ting-Toomey, S. (1985). Toward a theory of conflict and culture. In W. Gudykunst, L. Stewart, and S. Ting-Toomey, eds., *Communication, Culture, and Organizational Processes*. Beverly Hills, CA: Sage.

75. Ting-Toomey, S. (1988). A face negotiation theory. In Y. Kim and W. Gudykunst, eds., *Theories in Intercultural Communication*. Newbury Park, CA: Sage.

76. Ting-Toomey, "Toward a Theory of Conflict and Culture."

77. See also an excellent review of conflict and culture research in Gudykunst, W. B. (1994). *Bridging Difference: Effective Intergroup Communication*. Newbury Park, CA.

78. Ting-Toomey, "A Face Negotiation Theory."

79. See Olsen, J. M. (1978). *The Process of Social Organization*. New York: Holt, Rinehart and Winston; Ivy. D. K., & Backlund, P. (2008). *Genderspeak: Personal Effectiveness in Gender Communication*. Pearson/Allyn & Bacon, 257–61.

80. For an excellent review of conflict and gender, see Argyle, M. (1994). *The Psychology of Interpersonal Behavior*. London: Penguin Books.

81. See Michalko, M. (2006). *Thinkertoys: A Book of Creative-Thinking Techniques*. Berkeley, CA: Ten Speed Press, 5.

82. Nemiro, J. E. (2002). The creative processes in virtual teams. *Creativity Research Journal 14* (1), 69–83.

83. Gilson, L. L., Mathieu, J. E., Shalley, C. E., & Ruddy, T. M. (2005). Creativity and standardization: Complementary or conflicting driver of team effectiveness? *Academy of Management Journal 48*, 521–31.

84. Kramer, T. J., Fleming, G. P., & Mannis, S. M. (2001). Improving face-to-face brainstorming through modeling and facilitation. *Small Group Research 32*, 533–57.

85. Osborn, A. F. (1962). *Applied Imagination*. New York: Scribner's.

86. Rietzschel, E. F., Nijstad, B. A., & Stroebe, W. (2006). Productivity is not enough: A comparison of interactive and nominal brainstorming groups on idea generation and selection. *Journal of Experimental Social Psychology 42*, 244–51; also see Paulus, P. B., & Dzindolet, M. T. (1993). Social influence processes in group brainstorming. *Journal of Personality and Social Psychology 64*, 575–86; Paulus, P. B., Dugosh, K. L., Dzindolet, M. T., Coskun, H., & Putman, V. K. (2002). Social and cognitive influences in group brainstorming: Predicting production gains and losses. *European Review of Social Psychology 12*, 299–326.

87. McGlynn, R. P., McGurk, D., Effland, V. S., Johll, N. L., & Harding, D. J. (2004). Brainstorming and task performance in groups constrained by evidence. *Organizational Behavior and Human Decision Processes 93*, 75–87.

88. Nijstad, B. A., van Vianen, A. E. M., Stroebe, W., & Lodewijkx, H. F. M. (2004). Persistence in brainstorming: Exploring stop rules in same-sex groups. *Group Processes & Intergroup Relations 7*, 195–206.

89. Nijstad, van Vianen, Stroebe, & Lodewijkx, "Persistence in Brainstorming."

90. Nakui, T., Paulus, P. B., & van der Zee, K. I. (2011). The role of attitudes in reactions towards diversity in workgroups. *Journal of Applied Social Psychology 41* (10), 2327–51; also see Giambatista,

R. C., & Bhappu, A. D. (2010). Diversity's harvest: Interactions of diversity sources and communication technology on creativity group performance. *Organizational Behavior and Human Decision Processes* 111, 116–126.

91. Delbecq, A. L., Van de Ven, A. H., & Gustafson, D. H. (1975). *Group Techniques for Program Planning: A Guide to Nominal-Group and Delphi Processes.* Glenview, IL: Scott, Foresman, 7–16.

92. Paulus, P. B., Levine, D. S., Brown, V., Minai, A. A., & Doboli, S. (2010). Modeling ideational creativity in groups: Connecting Cognitive, neural, and computational approaches. *Small Group Research 41* (6), 688–724; also see Hess, T. M., Queen, T. L., & Patterson, T. R. (2012). To deliberate or not to deliberate: Interactions between age, task characteristics, and cognitive activity on decision making. *Journal of Behavioral Decision Making 25*, 29–40.

93. Smith, B. L. (1993). Interpersonal behaviors that damage the productivity of creative problem-solving groups. *The Journal of Creative Behavior 27* (3),171–87.

94. Stewart, D. D., Stewart, C. B., & Walden, J. (2007). Self-Reference effect and the group-reference effect in the recall of shared and unshared information in nominal groups and interacting groups. *Group Processes and Intergroup Relations 10*, 323–39.

95. Philipsen, G., Mulac, A., & Dietrich, D. (1979, June). The effects of social interaction on group generation of ideas. *Communication Monographs 46*, 119–25; Jablin, F. M. (1981, Spring). Cultivating imagination: Factors that enhance and inhibit creativity in brainstorming groups. *Human Communication Research 7* (3), 245–58; Jarboe, S. (1988, June). A comparison of input-output, process-output, and input-process-output models of small group problem-solving effectiveness. *Communication Monographs 55*, 121–42.

96. Sosik, J. J., Avolio, B. J., & Kahai, S. S. (1998). Inspiring group creativity: Comparing anonymous and identified electronic brainstorming. *Small Group Research* 29, 3–31.

97. Barki, H. (2001). Small group brainstorming and idea quality: Is electronic brainstorming the most effective approach? *Small Group Research 32*, 158–205.

98. Engleberg & Wynn.

99. Roy, M. C., Gauvin, S., & Limayem, M. (1996). Electronic group brainstorming: The role of feedback on productivity. *Small Group Research 27*, 215–47.

100. Sosik, Avolio, & Kahai; Cooper, W. H., Gallupe, R. B., Pollard, S., & Cadsby, J. (1998). Some liberating effects of anonymous electronic brainstorming. *Small Group Research 29*, 147–77.

101. Zaccaro, S. J., Rittman, A. L., & Marks, M. A. (2001). Team leadership. *Leadership Quarterly*, 12, 451–483.

102. Stewart, G. L., & Manz, C. C. (1995). Leadership for self-managing work teams: A typology and integrative model. *Human Relations*, 48 (7), 747–70.

103. Fleishman, E. A., Mumford, M. D., Zaccaro, S. J., Levin, K. Y., Korotkin, A. L., & Hein, M. B. (1991). Taxonomic efforts in the description of leader behavior: A synthesis and functional interpretation. *Leadership Quarterly*, 2 (4), 245–87.

104. Nadler, D. A. (1998). Executive team effectiveness: Teamwork at the top. In D. A. Nadler & J. L. Spencer (Eds.), *Executive teams* (pp. 21–39). San Francisco, CA: Jossey-Bass, p. 24.

105. Hackman, J. R., & Walton, R. E. (1986). Leading groups in organizations. In P. S. Goodman & Associates (Eds.), *Designing Effective Work Groups* (pp. 72–119). San Francisco, CA: Jossey-Bass.

106. Hackman, J. R., & Walton, R. E., 1986; LaFasto, F. M. J., & Larson, C. E. (2001). *When Teams Work Best: 6000 Team Members and Leaders Tell What It Takes to Succeed.* Thousand Oaks, CA: Sage; and Larson, C. E., & LaFasto, F. M. J. (1989). *Teamwork: What Must Go Right/What Can Go Wrong.* Newbury Park, CA: Sage.

107. The Challenges of Working in Virtual Teams. (2010). *The challenges of working in virtual teams: Virtual teams survey report 2010.* New York: RW3 Culture Wizard. Retrieved February 4, 2013, from *http://www.communicationcache.com/uploads/1/0/8/8/10887248/the_challenges_of_working_in_virtual_teams.pdf.*

108. The Challenges of Working in Virtual Teams, 2010.

109. Ibid.

110. Peters, L., & Karren, R J. (2009). An examination of the roles of trust and functional diversity on virtual team performance ratings. *Group and Organizational Management 34*, 479–504.

111. Hill, N. S., Bartol, K. M., Tesluk, P. E., & Langa, G. A. (2009). Organizational context and face-to-face interaction: Influences on the development of trust and collaborative behaviors in computer-mediated groups. *Organizational Behavior and Human Decision Processes 108*, 187–201.

112. Sivunen, A. (2006). Strengthening identification with the team in virtual teams: The leaders' perspective. *Group Decision and Negotiation 15*, 345–66.

113. Dorado, M. A., Medina, F. J., Munduate, L., Cisneros, I. F. J., & Euwema, M. (2002). Computer-mediated negotiation of an escalated conflict. *Small Group Research 33*, 509–24.

114. Walther, J. B. (2009, August). In point of practice, computer-mediated communication and virtual groups: Applications to interethnic conflict. *Journal Applied Communication Research 37* (3), 225–238.

115. Zornoza, A., Ripoll, P., & Peiro, J. M. (2002). Conflict management in groups that work in two different communication contexts: Face-to-face and computer-mediated communication. *Small Group Research 33*, 481–508.

116. Walsh, J. P., & Maloney, N.G. (2007). Collaboration structure, communication media, and problems in scientific work teams. *Journal of Computer-Mediated Communication 12*, 712–32. Also see Bosch-Sijtsema, P. (2007). The impact of individual expectations and expectation conflicts on virtual teams, *Group Organization Management 32*, 358–88.

117. Montoya-Weiss, M., Massey, A. P., & Song, M. (2001, December). Getting it together: Temporal coordination and conflict management in global virtual teams. *Academy of Management Journal 44*, 1251–62.

118. Messaging. (2010). *Decision Sciences 41* (4), 845–886.

119. Engleberg & Wynn.

120. Dorsett, L. (2001, January) A week in a digital collaboration space: Fast electronic work groups. *Training & Development*.

121. Pauleen, D. J. (2004). An inductively derived model of leader-initiated relationship building with virtual team members. *Journal of Management Information Systems*, 20 (3), 227–256, p. 229.

122. Dorsett, 2001.

Nokia, OYJ: *A Case Study about the Impact of Communication on Innovation*

Introduction

In 2006, Fappe Berglund* loved going to work. He was proud to tell people he developed software for Nokia and often received celebrity-like treatment throughout Finland. Wherever he went, people were using phones running Symbian, the mobile operating system he helped to create. Little did Fappe know how soon his stardom would disintegrate. On June 29, 2007, Apple released the first iPhone, which rapidly transformed the entire phone industry and challenged Nokia's market dominance.

Despite the iPhone's growing popularity, Nokia continued to focus on creating the highest quality hardware, leaving software as an afterthought. Fappe, however, knew that Nokia needed to incorporate new, innovative features to remain competitive. He pleaded with management, "Let my team show you software is important. Give us a year to build an application store and build a wall between us and the competition." The approval committee, which operated bureaucratically, would retort, "Nokia does not pursue insignificant, novel software features. Next time, please submit an opportunity with a large, immediate payout for consideration."

Remaining steadfast in its ways, Nokia watched its market share plummet at an alarming rate. In a panic, Nokia issued a notice to employees: "Over the coming weeks, resources and funding will be shifted towards teams that enjoy the most immediate success. Good luck!"

Fappe, now fearful of losing his job, pushed management even harder to allow his team to develop riskier features but with immediate payout. Several months later, management finally granted his request. By this point, however, the first-mover advantage was gone. Nonetheless, Fappe's team rushed to put together the new features that Fappe had envisioned before they were rendered obsolete. They quickly sent the completed update to the hardware team, at which point things began to go terribly wrong.

The hardware team had complete freedom to change any feature of the phone before it went in to final production. They decided to reduce the memory for the software to 25 percent of the specified allocation, unaware that the operating system would suffer as a result. Then, when software errors delayed the phone's release and third-party developers refused to release apps for Symbian (an open-source platform used predominantly by Nokia), the blame was put on Fappe, further reducing his team's available resources.

At this point, Fappe's frustration peaked. He was flown to Mainz, Germany, where he and 100 other senior engineers spent several days strategizing and proving why their teams should continue to be funded. At one point Fappe spoke out, "Look everyone, we're spending more time fighting politics than doing design. If Nokia will ever be as great as it once was, we need to actually produce a phone and it had better be a phone that's smart."

Soon thereafter the company's recently appointed Canada-born CEO, Stephen Elop, issued a company-wide memo nicknamed "The Burning Platform," in which he foretold the end of Symbian, among other Nokia platforms.

Layoffs at Nokia then began by the thousands. Fappe started to feel more like a politician than a software engineer. He spent most of his time ensuring his team continued to receive its allocation of the company's budget. To add to that, he was now looked down upon as a significant reason for the company's decline. Fappe had had enough and exclaimed, "How can this company's slogan possibly be 'connecting people'? I can barely keep my own team together let alone get any work done." And with that he retired early. As many talented employees were laid off or left, Nokia began the struggle of reasserting its market dominance.

This Case was originally written by Adrienne Argenbright, Shivangi Bhatnagar, Maggie Chen, Mengya Feng, Ian Malave, Melissa Barba, Zoe Jablow, Nadhira Raffai, David Soroudi, and Michael Chung for a course taught by Dr. Robyn Walker and Dr. RS Hubbard at the USC Marshall School of Business. Written spring, 2014, used by permission of the USC Marshall School Case Study Initiative.

* Fictional name used to personify the situation and illustrate the type of issues some in this position would experience.

Company Background

By the late 1900s, Nokia, OYJ (the Finnish equivalent of INC) had been well established in electronics and mobile telephones. It had become involved in many different markets through a number of acquisitions and its innovative history. Some notable creations were:

- First electronic device in 1962, which was used in nuclear power plants
- Development on radio telephones in 1963 for army and emergency services
- First car phone in 1982, called the Mobira Senator
- First handheld mobile phone in 1987 called the Mobira Cityman
- Global System for Mobile Communications, which could carry data as well as regular voice movement
- Nokia 1011 mobile phone, which blazed the path to newer phones because it could send and receive SMS messages and could hold as many as 99 phone numbers in its memory

In the late 1990s and early 2000s, Nokia was the world's number 1 mobile maker. Nokia phones were so common that "Nokia" was almost synonymous with "mobile phone." The company had established itself as a world leader in mobile sales. Between 1996 and 2001, its turnover (annual sales) increased from €6.5 billion to €31 billion. For several years, it had struggled with failed product launches, financial problems, and some organizational changes internally. However, Nokia has endeavored so far and has continued to try new products, though it is hindered by internal politics and reorganizations. For example, in 2003 the company launched its Nokia 1100 handset, which was the best-selling mobile phone of all time and the world's top-selling consumer electronics product.

Some major changes in the recent history of Nokia include:

- In 2006, Nokia and Siemens AG announced a partnership, creating Nokia Siemens Networks. This merger was to combine the mobile and fixed-line phone network equipment businesses.
- From 2006 to 2012, Nokia acquired companies like Twango, Enpocket, Navteq, Cellity, Meta Carta, and Smarterphone. These companies are of various market segments, such as software, mobile web browsing, and a developer of an operating system for feature phones.
- In 2011, Nokia's CEO Stephen Elop announced an alliance with Microsoft. This effort would lead towards development of smartphone technology.

With its innovative past, Nokia was the world's leader in mobile phones for 14 years. It sold its billionth phone in 2005 just as other mobile device companies were on the rise. A turning point came when Apple released its first generation iPhone in 2007, changing the landscape in the smartphone segment.

However, the company was facing threats due to the inability to produce competitive devices for the smartphone market. In 2009, Nokia faced its first quarterly loss in more than a decade. By 2010, Nokia's first quarter loss rose to €929 million, and mobile device sales were down 24%. Losses are directly correlated to the rise of new operating systems like Google's Android and Apple's iOS. In the years following these struggles, Stephen Elop, a former Microsoft executive and Nokia's first non-Finnish CEO, was hired to turn profits around.

Elop's job was to streamline operations at Nokia by cutting costs to create products that are more competitive. Another task for Elop is to reform Nokia's strategy. The new alliance with Microsoft to use an operating system made by another company marks a turning point for Nokia. It has plans to release the new Lumia 920, a smartphone that runs the Windows Phone 8 operating system.

Analysts and the media have stated that the decline in Nokia's performance results from transitioning to the smartphone strategy "too late." Recounts from insiders in the company show that there were several organizational problems hindering the company from moving forward.

Discussion of the Problem

Nokia has seen enormous amounts of success in the basic mobile phones industry during the 1990s and early 2000s. Durable, affordable mobile phones were manufactured and shipped for sale like large-scale commodities. Nokia's engineers were experts at value engineering, using affordable materials and designing hardware to achieve cost efficiency. In essence, Nokia's expertise lies in the design and manufacture of mobile phone hardware, which had seen great success before the arrival of smartphones. Over time, Nokia has remained focused on basic mobile phones as it has been the bread and butter of its business and was slow to adapt to the smartphone market.

Ideas never left the company's boardroom

The lack of successful cell phone products from Nokia caused the market to question the company's creativity. In fact, in 1999, more than 7 years before the launch of the first iPhone, Nokia had created a mobile phone with colored touch screen and a single button. In addition, Nokia's engineers had also developed a tablet computer with touch screen and wireless function—features seen in today's leading tablet devices. However, neither product was released to the market because of the company's hesitation to enter the smartphone market. CEO Stephen Elop stated that if the inventions had landed in products, "Nokia would have been in a different place." On average, Nokia spends 6-9 months assessing new opportunities in the market before designing products. In 2011 Nokia spent €5 billion on R&D, 30% of industry total.

An Engineering-Dominant Organization

Nokia is a highly engineering-centric organization. "At Nokia, engineering has been allowed to displace what is properly the company's *design* prerogative almost entirely," said former head of design for user-interface and services Adam Greenfield. In fact, even though consumers are being drawn away from Nokia by Apple's user-friendlier operating system, Nokia's engineers continued to focus on making the best hardware. Greenfield also recalls that the dominance of engineers in the decision making of what products get released meant that design and user-experience were not key priorities in product development at Nokia.

The scale of profits they can generate measures the viability of projects. In other words, projects are selected based on how much ROI on absolute terms it can create. Smaller initiatives are often set aside. One example is the Nokia Sports Tracker—a fitness activity-monitoring app that Greenfield thought would lend the brand "an aura of futurity, build consumer enthusiasm and loyalty." The project was not given enough funding and eventually dropped by the company. According to Greenfield, senior management often ignores homegrown projects and inventions that are small in scale.

Competition Overload and Inability to Reach Consensus

By 2008, Nokia executives realized the need to develop a more appealing software operating system, but despite spending more than four times in internal research and development than its competitors, Nokia had trouble generating workable innovations from meetings. Internal competition was intense between two groups with different beliefs of what would be best for the company. One team advocated for continuation of the old operating system Symbian, while another team supported building a brand new system—MeeGo.

The teams competed with each other for top executives' attention. Nokia's chief designer Alastair Curtis said, "[the teams] were spending more time fighting politics than doing design." Decision making and ideas generation at Nokia involved more than 100 engineers from all over the world packed in a hotel conference room, with representatives from Symbian and MeeGo fighting to make their voices heard and to keep their jobs.

Nokia's Corporate Structure

Nokia is a large company with many departments and layers of management. Products are put into two core product segments: Mobile Phones (traditional, basic cell phones) and Smart Devices (smartphones and tablets). The Markets unit runs sales, marketing, and global supply chain functions. Cross-product functions such as Services and Developer Experience, Design and CTO Office (the firm's technology unit) are separated into their own departments (see below for Nokia's structure).

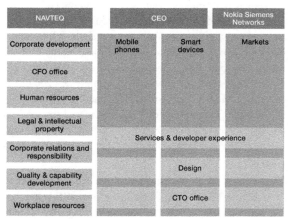

Nokia's Organization Structure

Although the matrix structure of Nokia's organization should drive knowledge sharing and more communication between departments and product units, chief designer Curtis still sees the organization structure as convoluted. He stated, "It was hard for the team to drive through a coherent, consistent, beautiful experience."

CEO Stephen Elop's Response

After his appointment as CEO in 2010, Stephen Elop vowed to craft a clear strategy for the company after years of indecisiveness. In an attempt to rally the troops, CEO Stephen Elop issued a controversial memo to Nokia employees through the company's internal network. In the memo Elop suggests that the company is standing on a "burning platform" and "must change its behavior." The memo was called "brutally honest" by the media. Here is an excerpt:

We poured gasoline on our own burning platform. I believe we have lacked accountability and leadership to align and direct the company through these disruptive times. We had a series of misses. We haven't been delivering innovation fast enough. We're not collaborating internally. Nokia, our platform is burning.

Furthermore, the memo went on to describe the ineffectiveness of all of Nokia's software platforms, both the Symbian and the MeeGo. He stated, "…Symbian is proving to be an increasingly difficult environment in which to develop and meet the continuously expanding consumer requirements…" Sales of Symbian devices declined 30% in the next three months following the release of the memo. Moreover, employees perceived the memo poorly, believed that Elop was working as a mole from Microsoft, and thought the goal of the memo was to stir up a need for change to facilitate an acquisition deal with Microsoft. An anonymous employee claimed that the memo did not work, describing that car parks were empty and there was an unwillingness to work.

Discussion Question

1. What are the most pertinent questions that should be asked in order to address the critical issues, main decisions and possible solutions to this case?

Sources

Arghire, Ionut. "Nokia Is Preparing "Beautiful Phones," CEO Says." *Softpedia*. N.p., 22 Mar. 2013. Web. 01 Apr. 2013.

Global Market Share Held by Nokia Smartphones Q1 2007-Q4 2012. *Statista*. IDC, Jan. 2013. Web. 01 Apr. 2013.

Gruber, John. "What's Next For Nokia?" *Daring Fireball*. N.p., 15 Sept. 2010. Web. 25 Mar. 2013.

Heidi. "Finnish Companies Are Preparing to Move Windows Phone." *Nokia Ääni*. N.p., 30 Mar. 2012. Web. 26 Mar. 2013.

"iPhone Premieres This Friday Night at Apple Retail Stores." *Apple*. N.p., 28 June 2007. Web. 25 Mar. 2013.

Johnson, Bobbie. "Nokia Crisis Highlights Internal Struggle." *BBC News*. BBC, 02 Oct. 2011. Web. 01 Apr. 2013

Lomas, Natasha. "Innovate Or Die: Nokia's Long-Drawn-Out Decline." *TechCrunch.com*. Tech Crunch, 31 Dec. 2012. Web. 25 Mar. 2013.

"Nokia: A Business Culture Problem?" *Nokia: A Business Culture Problem?* N.p., n.d. Web. 01 Apr. 2013.

Nokia Corporation (NOK). *Yahoo Finance*. Web. 26 Mar. 2013.

"Nokia: Elop on Culture, Technology and the Economy." *Nokia: Elop on Culture, Technology and the Economy*. N.p., n.d. Web. 01 Apr. 2013.

Reisinger, Don. "Nokia Quietly Kills Linux-based Meltemi, Report Says." *Cnet.com*. C|net, 26 July 2012. Web. 25 Mar. 2013.

Ricker, Thomas, "Visuallized: Nokia R&D spending, almost 3 times it's peers." *Engadget*. 3 Feb 2011. Web. Retrieved 27 March 2013.

Rodriguez, Salvador. "At Nokia: Hefty Layoffs, Facilities to Close, Changes in Leadership." Los Angeles Times. *Los Angeles Times*, 14 June 2012. Web. 25 Mar. 2013.

Schonfield, Erick. Jack Dorsey's Advice to Nokia: " You make too many products. Focus on 3." 26 October 2011. Web. 27 March 2013.

Smith, David. *Is Nokia doing too much?* 26 October 2011. Web. 26 March 2013.

Smith, Jake. Phil Schiller reveals Apple's Marketing Budget for 2009 and 2010. 3 August 2012. Web. 27 March 2013.

Troianovski, Anton, and Sven Grundberg. "Nokia's Bad Call on Smartphones." *WSJ.com*. The Wall Street Journal, 18 July 2012. Web. 25 Mar. 2013.

Ziegler, Chris. "Nokia CEO Stephen Elop Rallies Troops in Brutally Honest 'Burning Platform' Memo?" *Engadget*. N.p., 8 Feb. 2011. Web. 26 Mar. 2013.

Chapter 11

Strategic Organizational Communication

© Bigedhar / bigstockphoto.com

The Case of the Exploding Muffler

"Did you see the news this morning?" Dolores Kaiser asked. She slapped the newspaper she was carrying down on the desk in front of her.

"Now what?" was the reply from Kevin LaPlace, North American president of Kerckhoff Motors, as he picked it up to review the front page.

"Another exploding muffler," Kaiser replied. "Fortunately, this time, though, the car didn't catch fire."

"Well, that's a relief—no one was injured or killed, I assume," said LaPlace.

"No, but we need to do something to stop this insanity. Our reputation is taking a huge hit here in the States. Is there any evidence that Germany is going to budge on our request for a recall?" Kaiser asked.

"I guess I'm going to have to fly to Frankfurt to make a case for how serious this is in terms of the effects on sales," LaPlace remarked. "You'd think the numbers I've been sending would be enough to persuade the management team over there that a recall is in order."

"I still can't believe that you as the North American president don't have the power to make these kinds of decisions," Kaiser said as she turned to the door. "Do you want me to ask Mark to bring you some coffee on my way out?"

"How about a double-shot espresso?" LaPlace said with a weak laugh. "This is going to be one of those days."

After reading this chapter, you will be able to

- *Identify the three basic models for strategic organizational communication.*

- *Understand the value of creating a strategic communication plan for your organization.*

- *Conduct a communication audit to assess the current state of internal communication and identify areas for improvement.*

- *Develop an internal communication plan and assess its effectiveness.*

- *Understand the components of an external relations program.*

- *Understand the key functions of many external relations programs, which include public relations and image building, investor relations, issues management, risk and crisis communication.*

- *Deal successfully with the media, including performing interviews and handling crisis situations.*

Case Questions

1. How important is the role of managing an organization's reputation in its goal to remain a profitable institution?

2. How important is it for organizations to have effective internal communication plans to manage routine information flow and to support timely decision making across departmental and international office boundaries?

3. How should an organization proactively plan for dealing with crisis situations to effectively manage public perception and to maintain the company's image and reputation?

This chapter looks at communication from the organizational perspective. Sadly, this may be the only exposure you receive to organizational communication, particularly from a strategic perspective, if you are a student in a business school. That is because communication largely goes unrecognized as a discipline within business schools because of the political power struggles that characterize these institutions. Existing disciplines in business schools do not want to lose any of their power to a new, "upstart" discipline and thus often fight to keep communication all but invisible in curricula. This is a startling disservice to students who are thus likely never exposed to the need for and complexity of designing effective communication plans, structures, and processes for their workgroups, departments, and organizations.

One way that other disciplines within business schools marginalize communication is by gendering it as a "soft skill." This reflects the largely unreflective, masculinist cultures of many business schools. Technical skills, such as finance, marketing, and logistics, are valorized as "hard" skills without any recognition that all of these occur through and within a larger field of communication practice. Ignoring this larger field is analogous to assuming that life can take place without oxygen with the resulting illness and eventual death of the organism. This situation also applies to organizations whose administrators may be ignorant of the importance and complexity of communication and thus lack the knowledge and skills needed to design successful, productive communication processes and systems.

Because communication is often vigorously marginalized as a remedial, soft skill by business schools and their research regimes, its processes as a strategic activity are underdeveloped. As a result a strategic approach to organizational communication is still very much in its infancy, particularly in a business school setting. No one definition for it exists. Argenti, Howell, and Beck (2005) define strategic communication as "aligned with the company's overall strategy, to enhance strategic positioning", while Hallahan, Holtzhausen, van Ruler, Vercic, and Sriramesh (2007) define it as "the purposeful use of communication by an organization to fulfill its mission."

A special journal issue on strategic communication edited by Gail Fann Thomas and Kimberlie Stephens (2015) provides a useful schema for beginning to think about strategic organizational communication. The first theme that they propose is the central role that stakeholders play in strategic communication. One study in the special issue, for instance, examines the role of public citizens, activist groups, and governmental agencies in shaping an organization's strategic agenda. Stakeholders both inside and outside the organization should be considered in its strategic planning. Even without this effort, these stakeholders will affect the organization's success. As some of the case studies published in this text show, an organization can ignore such stakeholders in their planning, but this doesn't stop the effects of doing so upon the organization. Therefore, it is useful to recognize the fluidity of organizational boundaries and how stakeholders can shape an organization's strategy from either inside or outside the organization. What this means is that communication strategy needs to take into account the needs of both internal and external stakeholders if it is to be effective.

A second theme proposed by the authors of this special issue is that of the need for alignment of an organization's strategic position. This alignment must be achieved in a multitude of directions. Internal and external strategies, for example, need to be aligned and draw upon the same values, those that are core to the organization's vision and mission. Misalignment of stakeholders' perception of an event can dramatically influence the meaning of communication surrounding it and can alter an organization's strategic approach.

A third theme, but one that is not distinct from the other two, is the need for strategic communication at all levels. In order for firms to reap the benefits of effective communication practices and objectives, these need to be practiced at all levels of the organization, from top managers to the front-line employees. This need underscores the importance of alignment of both internal and external messaging.

This chapter thus provides a quick overview of the basic models of strategic communication and then looks at methods to plan both internal and external communication. The themes of strategic communication both internally and externally indicate that this planning needs to be aligned with the broader goals and values of the organization and with each other. Planning starts with the organization's goals and values but should also take into account its stakeholders when developing that vision. This chapter serves as a basic introduction to organizational communication, a topic deserving its own course or series of courses because of its importance and complexity. For now, though, it might be helpful to recognize the parallels between the steps of strategic message formulation and how they apply to both individuals and organizations.

Models of Strategic Organizational Communication

Chaffee identified the three basic models of strategic communication at the organizational level as

- Linear
- Adaptive
- Interpretive[1]

In the **linear model,** "strategy consists of integrated decisions, actions or plans that will set and achieve viable organizational goals."[2] Using this model, managers identify goals, generate alternatives for achieving those goals, weigh the likelihood of success for each alternative, and then decide which to implement. This model is concerned with presenting managerial plans to stakeholders and with stakeholders' acceptance of those plans.

The **adaptive model** shifts the focus of strategy from sequential planning and implementation to continuous adjustment of the relationship between the organization and its environment. In the adaptive model, the organization is an open system in a dynamic environment where the "goal" is represented by co-alignment of the organization with its environment. **Co-alignment** refers to matching up opportunities and risks in the environment with the capabilities and resources of the organization. This model is less centralized than the linear model, but it still places strategy in the domain of management. It involves more than just messages aimed at informing and influencing stakeholders; it includes all of the communication processes involved in adapting to the organizational environment. These include information exchange and feedback processes within the organization and between the organization and its environment. (The adaptive model is based on systems theory.)

The **interpretive model** is concerned with the social construction of reality, which was discussed in Chapter 1. This model is based on a social contract view that "portrays the organization as a collection of cooperative agreements entered into by individuals with free will."[3] In this model, strategy is concerned with the management of meaning and with symbol construction aimed at legitimizing the organization by providing "orienting metaphors and frames of reference that allow the organization and its environment to be understood by organizational stakeholders."[4] Strategic communication is about negotiating and shaping stakeholders' understandings of what the organization is and what it does.

Even though these three models appear to be distinct, Chaffee argued that they are interrelated and interdependent and that more than one may be operating at the same time within an organization.

The relevant audiences for strategic communication at the organizational level are organizational stakeholders.[5] Organizational stakeholders include shareholders or owners, employees, customers or clients, or any important constituency that can be affected or can affect the organization.[6] These might include the government, media, activist groups, special interest coalitions, and communities.

linear model
Strategy consists of integrated decisions, actions or plans that will set and achieve viable organizational goals.

adaptive model
Strategy is focused on the continuous adjustment of the relationship between the organization and its environment.

co-alignment
Matching up opportunities and risks in the environment with the capabilities and resources of the organization.

interpretive model
Strategy is concerned with the management of meaning and with symbol construction aimed at legitimizing the organization by providing orienting metaphors and frames of reference that allow the organization and its environment to be understood by organizational stakeholders.

Messages intended for strategic communication in organizations often are originated and produced by organizational subsystems composed of many individuals. Strategic communication can be a complex process in which a number of organizational units and individuals contribute to the design and dissemination of messages.

Strategic Internal Communication

internal strategic communication

Management's efforts to provide information to and exert influence with the organizational membership.

Internal strategic communication or employee communication is management's efforts to provide information to and exert influence with the organizational membership. Internal communication should be an important feature of any management written plan and considered a key contributor to organizational effectiveness and productivity.

Research by Gallup and others shows that engaged employees are more productive. They are more profitable, more customer-focused, safer, and more likely to withstand temptations to leave. The best-performing companies know that an employee engagement improvement strategy linked to the achievement of corporate goals will help them win in the marketplace.

However, there is evidence that many companies "do not apply the same analytical rigor to employee communications" as they do to financial and operational components of management strategy.[7] This is apparent if one recognizes the predominance of chief financial officer positions found at most large organizations without the analogous title of chief communication officer. In fact, organizations that recognize the value of communication may have a Corporate Communications department or officer but this function is generally focused narrowly on external communication duties. This oversight can be measured in terms of the effect on productivity. According to Gallup's research, in average organizations, the ratio of engaged to actively disengaged employees is 1.5:1. Actively disengaged employees erode an organization's bottom line while breaking the spirits of colleagues in the process. Within the U.S. workforce, Gallup estimates this cost to be more than $300 billion in lost productivity alone. Specifically, the costs to an organization from poor employee communication include

- Increased employee turnover
- Increased absenteeism
- Dissatisfied customers from poor customer service
- Higher product defect rates
- Lack of focus on business objectives
- Stifled innovation

Some of the common reasons for a lack of an internal communication program include the following attitudes of management:

1. **If I know it, then everyone must know it.** Management often assumes that because its members are aware of some piece of information, then everyone else is, too. Typically, employees aren't aware unless management makes a deliberate attempt to carefully convey information.

2. **Communication just happens.** Another frequent problem is that management does not really value communications or assumes that it just happens.

3. **We hate bureaucracy—we're "lean and mean."** When organizations are just getting started, their leaders can often pride themselves on not being burdened with what seems like bureaucratic overhead, such as extensive written policies and procedures. As the organization grows, it needs more communication and feedback to remain healthy, but the organization doesn't adjust to the growth and provide the appropriate communication plan. As a result, increasing confusion ensues—unless management matures and realizes the need for increased communication.

Responsible Communication

The Gallup Organization created a feedback system for employers that would identify and measure elements of worker engagement most tied to the bottom line. After hundreds of focus groups and thousands of interviews with employees in a variety of industries, Gallup came up with the Q12, a twelve-question survey that identifies strong feelings of employee engagement. Results from the survey show a strong correlation between high scores and superior job performance. Here are those twelve questions:

■ Do you know what is expected of you at work?

■ Do you have the materials and equipment you need to do your work right?

■ At work, do you have the opportunity to do what you do best every day?

■ In the last seven days, have you received recognition or praise for doing good work?

■ Does your supervisor, or someone at work, seem to care about you as a person?

■ Is there someone at work who encourages your development?

■ At work, do your opinions seem to count?

■ Does the mission/purpose of your company make you feel your job is important?

■ Are your associates (fellow employees) committed to doing quality work?

■ Do you have a best friend at work?

■ In the last six months, has someone at work talked to you about your progress?

■ In the last year, have you had opportunities at work to learn and grow?

Questions for Discussion

1. What are the benefits to an organization of assessing employee engagement?

2. What are concrete steps that an organization might take to ensure high levels of employee engagement?

3. As a leader, what steps might you take to better ensure employee engagement?

Source: The Gallup Organization (Princeton, NJ, 2008).

4. **Did you hear what I meant for you to hear?** As discussed earlier in this text, with today's increasingly diverse workforce, it's easy to believe you've conveyed information, but you may not be aware that they interpreted it differently than you intended.

5. **We need a solution now!** Particularly when personnel are tired or under stress, it's easy to do what's urgent rather than what's important.

6. **So what's to talk about?** Communications problems can arise when inexperienced management interprets its job to be solving problems and assumes that if there aren't any problems/crises, then there's nothing that needs to be communicated.

7. **If I need your opinion, I'll tell it to you.** Communications problems can arise when management simply sees no value whatsoever in communicating with subordinates, believing subordinates should shut up and do their jobs.[8]

As should be clear after reading the contents of this text, these ideas arise from a lack of knowledge about communication and its complexity, or ignorance of simple perceptual challenges. To combat this mindset, it is important that management comprehends and fully supports the premise that organizations must have high degrees of communication. Too often, management learns the need for communication by having to respond to the lack of it, as many of the case studies in this text, which are based on real situations, attest.

One way to think about an organization's internal activities is to group them by functional area. Four common functional areas are orientation and indoctrination of employees, morale and satisfaction, compensation and benefits, and organizational change and development.[9]

■ **Orientation and indoctrination.** Many organizations provide formal training sessions for new employees to orient them to the organization and their new position. Many organizations also have programs to socialize organizational members by reinforcing corporate values, beliefs, and practices.

■ **Morale and satisfaction.** Special events, newsletters, and company magazines are instances of media that are often intended to improve employee's self-concepts, interpersonal relationships, and attitudes toward the organization.

- **Compensation and benefits.** The Employee Retirement Income Security Act (ERISA) requires organizations to make full and understandable disclosure of employee benefit programs.
- **Organizational change and development.** Change is a stressful process and as such, organizations should attempt to help employees deal with change. Employees may need a great deal of new information to understand the purposes and effects of major change and to cope with it. Common types of change in an organizational setting include mergers, new ventures, restructuring, and downsizing.

Most of these functions are housed in the human resources department; however, responsibility for newsletters, company magazines, special events, and activities of this nature are generally handled by corporate communication departments. It is thus important that activities managed by different departments be well coordinated. One way to manage this process is to create an internal communication plan grounded in organizational values and mission.

? Critical Thinking

Does your organization have an internal or employee communication plan? If so, what are its elements? What works and what might be improved? If not, what kind of communication policies need to be developed and why?

Creating an Internal Communication Plan

Employees need to know the direction of the organization—how they can engage and participate—and provide feedback. To ensure that employees receive this information in an effective manner, an internal communication plan should be developed.

Five aspects of successful internal communication programs are:

- Management is supportive. Top and middle managers are involved in and responsible for communication.
- Professional communication staff is close to the issues and included in strategic planning. Communication is part of the business plan.
- Communication reinforces strategic objectives to all employees. Messages must be consistent yet adapted to their audience.
- Communication uses all appropriate media, but face-to-face is best.
- The communication program is formally and frequently assessed for effectiveness.

Before starting to develop any form of strategy for improvement, it is important to know where the organization currently stands in terms of the quality of communication with employees. The use of organizational diagnostics in the form of an audit is a suitable place to start. This audit should be company-wide and differentiate divisions and job levels, since identifying barriers to communication for everyone is important. The audit should help answer a number of important questions, including

- Are employees receiving accurate information?
- How are employees receiving regular information?
- Are messages consistent across the company?
- Do employees understand both the goals and the results of communications?[10]

Table 11-1 identifies sixteen essential strategic communications practices within organizations. They are grouped into three categories: (1) strategy, (2) implementation, and (3) support and alignment.

- **Strategy.** Includes the core tasks of communications planning and strategy development.
- **Implementation.** Includes practices most common to an organization with an *active* communications function.
- **Support and alignment.** Includes noncommunications-specific practices within the organization that help to ensure the communications function is successful.[11]

The table also offers quality standards or criteria for each practice. They describe in brief what the practices should look like. This list can be of value in the audit process. It can be used as a checklist to help determine if an organization is performing each strategic communications practice. But more importantly, the audit process can reveal if quality criteria are being met, and if not, where improvements can be made in how the practice is performed.

Table 11-1 Strategic Communications Practices

	Strategic Communications Practices	Quality Criteria/Standards
Strategy	■ Identify the vision	The communications vision is aligned with, but distinct from, the organization's overall mission.
	■ Choose goals and outcomes	Goals and outcomes are well defined, measurable, and help guide a defined plan of action.
	■ Select target audiences	Audiences are specific and include key decision makers or individuals with influence on the issue.
	■ Develop messages	Messages are specific, clear, persuasive, reflect audience values, and include a solution or course of action.
	■ Identify credible messengers	Messengers are seen as credible by the target audiences and can be recruited and available to the cause.
	■ Choose communications channels and media	Channels and media are chosen for their access and availability to target audiences.
	■ Scan the context and competition	Risks and contextual variables that can affect communications success are identified and factored into planning when possible.
Implementation	■ Develop effective materials	Materials are developed in attractive, accessible, and varied formats for maximum exposure and visibility.
	■ Build valuable partnerships	Linkages exist with internal and external stakeholders who can help align with and carry the message.
	■ Train messengers	Internal messengers are trained in key messages and are consistent in their delivery.
	■ Conduct steady outreach	Outreach and dissemination to audiences through multiple outlets is regular and sustained.
	■ Monitor and evaluate	Activities and outcomes are regularly monitored and evaluated for purposes of accountability and continuous improvement.
Support and integration	■ Support communications at the leadership level	Management understands and supports communications as an integral part of organizational viability and success.
	■ Earmark sufficient resources	Fundraising regularly includes dedicated resources for communications practice.
	■ Integrate communications throughout the organization	Communications is seen as an integral part of every organizational project or strategy.
	■ Involve staff at all levels	Communications is not seen as an isolated function; most if not all staff members have some knowledge and/or participation in communications efforts.

Source: Adapted from Coffman, J. (2004). *Strategic Communications Audits*. Working paper prepared for Communications Consortium Media Center. Retrieved November 1, 2009, from *http://www.mediaevaluationproject.org/WorkingPaper1.pdf*.

Conducting a Communication Audit

A communication audit collects data about current communication practices and uses that data to make assessments about organizational performance and capacity.

When planning to conduct a communication audit, it is important to first determine if assessments about organizational practices will be made internally or by outside experts. The advantages of doing it internally are that direct costs are likely to be lower and the process may become an engaging organizational exercise that builds communications capacity in and of itself. The advantages to using outside experts are their objectivity, time and availability, the knowledge they bring from other organizations for comparison purposes, and the credibility that may accompany their credentials and expertise.

Regardless of whether the audit is done internally or externally, a common set of methods can be used to gather data needed to make assessments about practices. Common methods for gathering data include:

- **Participant observation.** The individual conducting the audit participates in organizational activities involving communications in order to see how and when practices are performed.

- **Document review.** Communications documents (e.g., publications, campaign materials, press releases, etc.) are reviewed to assess the development and targeting of materials as a communications practice.

- **Focus groups.** Groups of five to fifteen people meet together in a moderated discussion and respond to open-ended questions about communications practices and organizational capacity. Their main advantage is the group interaction that takes place as participants react to and build on one another's responses.

- **Interviews.** Probably the most common audit method, interviews allow the person conducting the audit to better understand communications-related work processes. Interviews allow respondents to provide a rich qualitative sense of how practices are performed and how the organization treats communications. Interviews can also be conducted with the organization's external stakeholders or target audiences.

- **Surveys.** Surveys or questionnaires are the second most common audit method. They can be administered cheaply to all organizational staff within a short time frame, and they allow for standardization and comparison of responses.

- **Critical incident analysis.** Staff is asked to describe, through an interview or questionnaire, specific effective and ineffective experiences with communications. The purpose is to collect examples of experiences that staff find memorable in order to "see" how communications practices are performed within situational contexts.

- **Analysis of digital communication platforms and networks.** As more and more communication takes place electronically within organizations, software tools can be developed to analyze those communications, particularly in terms of numbers of users, frequency, purposes, etc.

Table 11-2 compares these methods on the basis of time, cost, and information yielded. While the use of one or more of these methods is recommended, it is also possible to conduct the strategic communications audit informally by, for example, asking each staff member to give his or her own independent and subjective assessments based on existing knowledge and experience, or convening staff to make collective assessments.

Once the assessments are completed, the next step is to identify areas in which the organization can improve. The assessment of where the organization should be must be based on an accounting of the organization's realistic capabilities with respect to communications.

Table 11-2 Comparison of Audit Methods

Method	Time	Cost	Information Yield
Interviews	30–60 minutes each	Moderately expensive (time to conduct, analyze)	Qualitative, in-depth data
Surveys	20–30 minutes each	Moderately expensive	Standardized data
Critical incident analysis	20–30 minutes each	Inexpensive	Specific examples of practice/process flow
Network analysis	20–30 minutes each	Expensive (analysis, software)	Process flow/interaction and integration
Participant observation	Variable	Expensive (time)	Process flow
Document review	20–60 minutes each	Expensive (time)	Material, message evaluation
Focus groups	1–2 hours	Moderately expensive (depends on number)	Qualitative in-depth data; specific

Source: Coffman, J. (2004). *Strategic Communications Audits*. Working paper prepared for Communications Consortium Media Center. Retrieved November 1, 2009, from *http://www.mediaevaluationproject.org/WorkingPaper1.pdf*.

The strategic communications audit should result in more than just an identification of areas or practices that need to be improved. To maximize the chances that audit findings will be used and actual practice improved as a result, the audit should:

■ Demonstrate through data how communications problems are causing problems *in the present* (as opposed to speculating about their future impact). At the same time, the audit should reinforce practices that are current organizational strengths.

■ Generate specific recommendations for *how* actual communication practice can be enhanced. Data need to be linked to concrete actions.

■ Make transparent the organizational benefits of adopting those actions in addition to the weaknesses they are designed to address.

■ Prioritize recommendations so organizations are not immobilized by the prospect of implementing them.[12]

Formal communications audits should be conducted about every five years. Informal audits on which organizations internally revisit their strategic communication capacity and performance levels may be done more frequently. Audits should also be considered after an organization experiences a critical incident that might affect communications, such as when the organization changes mission, changes leadership, or experiences a crisis.

? Critical Thinking

Of data-gathering techniques discussed for conducting a communication audit, which would collect the best information and why? Which techniques might present problems and how might these be overcome or compensated for?

Developing the Internal Communication Plan

Once the organization has assessed its current communication practices and identified areas for improvement, an internal strategic communication plan can be developed. An effective approach in the development of the communications strategy is to answer the following:

■ What are the organization's goals, ambitions, and strategic aspirations for the future?

■ What do the people in the organization need to think, feel, and do in order to make those goals a reality?

- Where are employees now and what needs to change in their current perceptions, attitudes, or access to basic information?
- What is the role of the internal communication function in helping close the gap of what management wants for the future and what exists today?
- What are the roles and responsibilities of leaders, managers, employees, and communication professionals?
- What are the communication activities the organization is going to need—and who will be responsible for those activities?
- What are the resource levels needed?[13]

Twelve essential elements of a successful internal communications strategy are:

1. **Effective employee-directed communications must be led from the top.** Effective communications require the active commitment and endorsement of senior managers. It is not enough simply to develop a vision statement or formulate in general terms the values by which the company lives. Behavior is what counts. Managers must be seen to behave in a manner that is consistent with the ethos they are promoting.

2. **The essence of good communications is consistency.** If management tries to improve communications and fails because messages are inconsistent or are "good news only," the organization probably will settle back into the way they used to be.

3. **Successful employee communications owe as much to consistency, careful planning, and attention to detail as they do to charisma or natural gifts.** We might not all be another Zig Ziglar, Tony Robbins, or Bill Clinton, but with planning and attention to detail, successful communication plans can be implemented.

4. **Communication via the line manager is most effective.** Line manager-to-employee communication is an opportunity for people to ask questions and check that they have understood the issues correctly. However, be aware that business urgency and reality may dictate the need, on many occasions, to inform employees directly rather than relying entirely on communication down through the organizational hierarchy.

5. **Employee communications are not optional; they are part of business as usual and should be planned and budgeted for as such.** An employee communications plan—key themes, targets, objectives, and resources—provides a context in which to deliver initiatives that arise at short notice.

6. **There must be integration between internal and external communications.** There must be a fit between what management is telling people and what is being told to customers, shareholders, and the public. (By the same token, there must be a fit between what management is telling people, and what the external media is telling them.)

7. **Timing is critical.** However clearly expressed and well-presented your message may be, if it arrives at the wrong time you might as well not have bothered. Old news is often worse than no news. Consequently, it is important to ensure that the channels you use can really deliver at the time you need them to.

8. **Tone is important.** Expressing overly gushing enthusiasm about a technical change of little real significance to employees or the public at large may detract from your credibility as well as the messages.

9. **State your message from your audience's point of view.** Never lose sight of the "what's in it for your audience?" factor. People are more likely to listen if it is clear how the message affects them.

10. **Communication is a two-way process.** Employee communications are NOT a one-way information dump. Capturing feedback is of critical importance, and if management is not

perceived as listening and acting on what it has been told, it risks no longer being able to solicit information.

11. **A single key theme or a couple of key themes is a means of giving coherence to a range of diverse employee communication initiatives.** In recent years, the overriding theme of many corporate employee communications has been the impact on the business of competition, regulation, and economic forces. Many messages and initiatives can therefore be evaluated according to the light they shed on one or more of these key themes.

12. **Set standards and stick to them.** Determine which channels of communication and media should be mandatory and which should be optional; establish quality standards for all channels and media and review these at least annually.[14]

The following sections provide two approaches to internal communication plans; one is an example of a plan developed by communication medium while the second focuses on upward and downward communication flow. (Upward and downward flow of communication was discussed in Chapter 5.)

An Internal Communication Plan Focused on Medium

Examples of employee communication media include the Intranet, websites, social media platforms, newsletters, memos, notice boards, the press, company magazines, blogs, and employee forums. Table 11-3, based on an actual example, illustrates how an organization might manage its internal communications with a focus on communication medium. The table also identifies the purpose for each media, its intended result, the communication department's role, and the frequency of the message.

More and more organizations are experimenting with collaborative software platforms and internal social media as ways of enhancing communication among employees. These platforms have been adopted with expectation of producing more open, transparent, and collaborative communication across all levels of an organization. Some organizations have experienced dramatic success through this implementation while others have shown little or no improvement in collaboration and communication. According to Cardon (2016), this lack of improvement may be the result of seeing such implementations as technological solutions rather than providing tools for enhanced communication. Recent research seems to indicate that successful use of these platforms is linked to positive organizational culture and communication[15] (Please review discussion of organizational culture in Chapter 5). What this means is that the use of such tools to empower employees, for example, can support the development of a more participative, egalitarian organizational culture.[16] Proper implementation of social platforms can also enhance a sense of community among employees.[17] These findings support the earlier assertion of the importance of alignment when develop strategic communication plans, alignment of organizational goals, values, and the creation of the type of culture needed to attain those goals and values.

An Internal Communication Plan Focused on Flow

As was discussed in Chapter 5, communication flows typically in three directions in an organization: upward, downward, and horizontally. One way to think about an effective internal communication program is to consider the flow of communication between management and employees—upward and downward—and create a plan to ensure that this flow is optimal. The following steps may be followed to create an internal communication plan designed around the flow of communication.[18]

Downward Communication To ensure the effective downward flow of communication, an internal communication plan should:

- Ensure every employee receives a copy of the strategic plan, which includes the organization's mission, vision, values statement, strategic goals, and strategies about how those goals will be reached.

Table 11-3 Example of an Internal Communication Plan Organized by Medium

Medium	Purpose	Intended Result	Communications Department Role	Frequency
E-mails				
Information bulletins Director messages Other organizational information	Inform, engage	Employees understand our purpose, progress, and how they connect	Consult, develop, publish	Weekly and as necessary
Activity reports	Inform	Employees understand what the rest of the organization is doing	Collect and publish	Monthly
Meetings				
Coffee with director	Inform, clarify, exchange	Employees connected with organization	Attend, notes if required	Twice a month
Brown bag lunch/info sessions	Inform, clarify, exchange	Employees connected with organization	Plan, announce	Varies
Leadership team staff meeting (open to employees)	Model open organization, inform	Establish public record	Take notes	Weekly
All-manager meetings	Inform, clarify	Employees connected with organization	Note taking	Monthly
All-employee meetings	Inform, clarify	Employees connected with organization	Planning, logistics	Twice a year
Wednesday stand-up	Public forum to surface issues	Leadership visibility over problems, employee questions answered	Facilitate, record, track status	Weekly
Staff meetings	Inform, clarify		None	Various
Team meetings	Daily work		None	Various
Hallway conversations	Various		None	Various
Café conversations	Understanding		Facilitate	Various
Web pages				
Monthly news e-zine	Connect people to colleagues, to organization, to job	Employees connected and informed	Develop, publish	Monthly
Director staff meeting notes	Connect people to organization, document organization history	Employees connected and informed	Develop, publish	Weekly
Organization calendar	Provide visibility over organization activities		Maintain	As necessary
Stand-up meeting actions	Provide organization accountability	Employees connected and informed	Develop, publish	Weekly
Decision log	Document organizational decisions	Organization has record of decisions	Develop, publish	As necessary
Field guide to organization	Connections to organization	Employees understand how organization fits together	Develop, publish	As necessary

Source: Adapted from Coyote Enterprises. (2002). Retrieved October 31, 2009, from *http://www.coyotecom.biz/commun/intcomplan.htm*.

- Ensure every employee receives an employee handbook that contains all up-to-date personnel policies.
- Develop a basic set of procedures for how routine tasks are conducted and include them in a standard operating manual.
- Ensure every employee has a copy of their job description and the organization chart.

- Regularly hold management meetings (at least every two weeks), even if there's nothing pressing to report. If meetings are held only when there's something to report, then communications will occur only when management has something to say. The result is that communication will be one-way and the organization will suffer. Have meetings anyway, if only to establish that nothing significant has changed and there are no immediate problems.

- Hold full staff meetings every month to report how the organization is doing, major accomplishments, concerns, announcements about staff, and so on.

- Leaders and managers should have face-to-face contact with employees at least once a week. Even if the organization has more than twenty employees, management should stroll by once in a while.

- Regularly hold meetings to celebrate major accomplishments. This helps employees perceive what's important, gives them a sense of direction and fulfillment, and lets them know that leadership is on top of things.

- Ensure all employees receive yearly performance reviews, including their goals for the year, updated job descriptions, accomplishments, needs for improvement, and plans to help the employee accomplish the improvements.

Upward Communication To ensure the effective upward flow of communication, an internal communication plan should:

- Ensure all employees give regular status reports to their supervisors. Include a section for what they did last week, will do next week, and any actions/issues to address.

- Ensure all supervisors meet one-on-one at least once a month with their employees to discuss how they are doing and hear about any current concerns. Even if the meeting is chitchat, it cultivates an important relationship between supervisor and employee.

- Use management and staff meetings to solicit feedback. Ask how it's going. Do a round table approach to hear from each person.

- Act on feedback from others. Write it down. Get back to it—if only to say you can't do anything about the reported problem or suggestion.

- Respect the "grapevine." It's probably one of the most prevalent and reliable forms of communications. Major "movements" in the organization usually first appear when employees feel it safe to share their feelings or opinions with peers.

Effective internal communication is a means to an end, not an end in itself. For employees to be fully engaged in their work and the organization, it needs to be demonstrated how an effective communication plan is linked to the solution of business problems.

Strategic External Communication

As a form of public or external communication, strategic organizational communication can require a substantial commitment of resources, including the purchase of advertising space in print and electronic media; time, space, and materials for special events; production facilities for websites, newsletters, company magazines, and video programs; and salaries and benefits for those who write, edit, and create the messages. **Public communication** is described as the process of one communicating with many.[19] This definition, however, oversimplifies the idea of a "source" for strategic communication activities and fails to recognize the transactional and dialogic nature of communication.

public communication
The process of one communicating with many.

External strategic communication includes public relations and issues management efforts designed to influence consumers, communities, special-interest groups, voters, regulators, legislators, and others outside the organization.

External communication occurs in at least three major forms: (1) advertising and promoting products and services, (2) creating and maintaining a desirable public image and reputation for the organization, and (3) shaping public opinion on issues important to the organization. Traditionally, communication concerned with image building has been the responsibility of public relations practitioners. This area has expanded to include investor relations programs to market the company's stock to individuals and institutional investors and programs to manage and communicate about risk and crises situations.

In addition, many organizations have expanded external communication to include a new function—identifying and tracking public issues that concern the organization. An organization might try to change to respond to public criticism or try to influence public opinion on important issues by advocating its own position in the public arena.[20]

As this discussion indicates, external communication involves numerous stakeholders with differing interests. An organization that understands the value of communication will coordinate external messaging among departments and ideally, provide spokespersons with a carefully drawn external communication plan that helps to deliver information in line with its core values and objectives.

External Communication Issues

This section discusses the topics of external communication—public relations, issues management, and investor, risk and crisis communication. From an individual communication perspective, it also explains how to handle the news media, a discussion that is particularly useful for dealing with crisis situations.

Public Relations, Reputation Management, and Image Building

Many large corporations have public relations departments that are focused on creating an image and reputation of the organization for public consumption. Public relations departments were initially focused on enhancing relations with the media but have broadened to include attempts to shape public perception of the organization. **Reputation management** is the practice of attempting to shape public perception of a person or organization by influencing information about that entity.[21]

What necessitates this shaping of perceptions is the role of consumers in any organization and recognition of how ignoring these perceptions may harm a company's performance.[22] For businesses, reputation management usually involves an attempt to bridge the gap between how a company perceives itself and how others view it, not unlike impression management at the individual level.[23] Not only do reputation management practices reinforce and aid a corporation's branding objectives, which play a paramount role in helping it to meet its marketing and business communication goals, it helps to determine how well a company can increase profits and market share. Good reputation management practices are also important in helping any entity manage staff confidence. If a negative reputation is allowed to develop, staff morale may also be negatively affected, in turn negatively affecting company performance.[24]

With the explosive growth of the Internet and electronic communication, reputation management has evolved to include the monitoring of the reputation of an organization or a brand on the Internet, addressing content which is potentially damaging to it, and using customer feedback to try to solve problems before they damage the organization's or brand's reputation.[25]

One example of a reputation management campaign involves the controversy that arose when the Taco Bell restaurant chain was accused of using only 35 percent beef in their "seasoned beef" product. A class action lawsuit was subsequently filed against the organization. The suit was voluntarily withdrawn, with no verdict reached, settlement made, or money exchanged, but with the law firm that represented the class action saying, "From the inception of this case, we stated that if Taco Bell would make certain changes regarding disclosure and marketing of its 'seasoned beef' product, the case could be dismissed."[26] Taco Bell responded to the case being withdrawn by launching a reputation management campaign titled "Would it kill you to say you're sorry?" that ran advertisements in various news outlets in print and online with the intent of drawing attention to the voluntary withdrawal of the case.[27]

Some businesses have adopted unethical means to falsely improve their reputations. For instance, a study by the University of California Berkeley found that some sellers on eBay were undertaking to enhance their reputation by selling products at a discount in exchange for positive feedback to "game" the system.[28] Online reputation management can also involve suppressing negative search results, while highlighting positive ones.[29]

However, companies can manage their reputation ethically as well as effectively if they use a strategy that is "built in" rather than "bolted on," according to professors Grahame Dowling and Peter Moran. "Built in" reputation management programs are based on either the normative, economic, or competitive logic of the organization. Because these fundamental characteristics of an organization drive core operations and deliver value to stakeholders, a reputation emerging from them becomes both an honest and reliable signal of future behavior. Built-in reputations stand in contrast to those based on tactical initiatives such as ad hoc "checkbook" philanthropy and non-core corporate social responsibility (CSR) programs. These are considered "bolted on" approaches to reputation management. Because many of these programs do not reflect the fundamental objectives of the organization, they send conflicting signals about its reason for being. In addition, because they are easily copied by competitors, they are unlikely to confer long-term advantage, according to Dowling and Moran.

As part of their reputation management endeavors, many companies also devote significant resources to image building. **Image building** is defined as the process of creating the identity an organization wants its relevant publics to perceive.[30] **Identity** is the visual manifestation of the image of the organization as conveyed through its logo, products, services, buildings, stationery, uniforms, and other tangible items created by the organization to communicate with a variety of constituencies.[31]

Image building has typically been associated with the field of public relations. Public relations may involve other activities, such as media relations, marketing publicity, and internal relations. **Public relations** is "the management function which evaluates public attitudes, identifies the policies and procedures of an individual or an organization with the public interest, and executes a program of action to earn public understanding and acceptance."[32]

Managing the Organization's Identity

One common process for managing an organization's identity is detailed below.

1. **Conduct an identity audit.** Similar in function to an internal communications audit, an external audit is intended to discover how the public currently views the organization, what its symbols represent to different constituencies, and whether the identity is up to date. It may involve interviews with top managers and other relevant constituencies, and a review of company literature, advertising, products, services, and facilities.

2. **Set identity objectives.** These goals should be set by top management and should explain how each constituency should react to specific identity proposals.

3. **Develop designs and names.** Once the audit is complete and objectives are in place, new designs for the company logo or product labeling and names of the company or products are developed to communicate these objectives.

image building

The process of creating the identity an organization wants its relevant public to perceive.

identity

The visual manifestation of the image of the organization as conveyed through its logo, products, services, buildings, stationery, uniforms, and other tangible items created by the organization to communicate with a variety of constituencies.

public relations

The management function that evaluates public attitudes, identifies the policies and procedures of an individual or an organization with the public interest, and executes a program of action to earn public understanding and acceptance.

4. **Develop prototypes.** Once the final designs are approved, prototypes are developed to identify reactions from the relevant publics.

5. **Launch and communicate.** This step typically involves public relations and advertising campaigns.

6. **Implement the program.** This step might take some time but usually is best approached by developing identity standards to ensure consistency across all uses of the new identity materials.

? Critical Thinking

Can you identify an organization that has managed its identity successfully? What were the elements of that program? Can you identify an organization that has not been so successful at identity management? How might it improve its image?

Creating a Web Presence and Social Media Strategy

The Internet is a key component for corporate communication because of its speed, international access, and affordability. Creating a company website enables organizations to accomplish a number of activities, including:

- Updating employees and customers about organizational changes.
- Selling products and services.
- Advertising employment opportunities.
- Creating a first point of contact for customers through order entry, customer service systems, and online call centers.

When you're building an online presence, the most important aspect is the company website. It's the hub for communication and provides a first impression of the company for visitors. It should include the right elements to maximize its effectiveness.

However, an effective web presence may extend beyond the creation of an effective web page. It will likely also include maintaining a blog that can help the website stand out and help consumers better understand the business. For one, it shows that you know what you're talking about. It helps you identify yourself as an expert or unique. Secondly, a blog is constantly updated. It gives readers a reason to come back to your site. The more contact you have with your consumers, the more likely they are to buy from you.

A third element of an effective web presence is to develop an electronic newsletter that automatically updates customers on company, product, and services developments and offers them specials. E-mail marketing is one of the most effective ways to generate sales. Getting consumers to sign up for the e-mail list means organizations no longer have to wait for them to come to it.

Organizations also need to recognize the value of using social media to generate leads and capture interest in their products and services. Doing so well requires a significant investment of time and money to produce a successful social media strategy and to implement it. Jay Baer, an executive at the consulting firm Convince & Convert, says that with all the new tools and platforms constantly emerging, it's very easy to fall into the trap of thinking about social media through a tactical prism instead of a strategic one. What he means by this is that "Companies should focus more on how to BE social, and less on how to DO social media."[33]

The steps he puts forth to build a social media strategy are condensed and paraphrased below. Many can be mapped to the steps in the strategic process for message formulation discussed in Part 1 of this text.

Create a cross-functional team to create the strategy. Baer says nobody should "own" social media strategy in your organization. Social impacts all corners of the company, and should be more like air (everywhere) than like water (you have to go get it).

Listen to customers and competitors. The reality is that your customers (and competitors) will give you a good guide to where and how you should be active in social media, if you broaden your social listening beyond your brand name.

Select a narrow objective. You can use social media to help accomplish several business objectives. But the best social media strategies are those that focus (at least initially) on a more narrow rationale for social. What do you primarily want to use social for? Awareness? Sales? Loyalty and retention? Pick one. Jayson DeMers suggests four social media goals.

- If you're looking to **generate traffic**, your metric should be to identify the number of new visitors to the social websites where you have run your social media campaigns.

- If you're looking to **create a following**, your metric should be to identify the number of new subscribers or followers on your social channels (Facebook, Twitter, etc.).

- If you're looking to **generate interaction**, your metric should be the quantity and type of commentary you receive (Facebook comments, Twitter replies/mentions).

- If you're looking to **generate revenue**, your metric should be the precise dollar value of every lead a social post generates.[34]

Identify success metrics. Your team needs to identify how you are going to determine whether the message is actually making a difference in your business. What key measures will you use to evaluate social media strategy effectiveness? How will you transcend likes and engagement? Will you measure return on investment, for example?

Analyze your audiences. Your team needs to determine with whom you will be interacting using social media. What are the demographic and psychographic characteristics of your current or prospective customers? How does that impact what you can and should attempt to accomplish using social media?

Determine your key theme. Product features and benefits aren't enough to create a passion-worthy interest in your audience. Your team needs to identify how your organization will appeal to the heart of your audience, rather than its head. Disney isn't about movies, it's about magic. Apple isn't about technology, it's about innovation. What are you about?

Create a channel plan. Only after you know why you're active in the social media realm and how you will measure your social media strategy success should you turn your attention to how you will use the various social media channels: Facebook, Twitter, Tumblr and the rest. This channel plan should be distinct, in that you have a specific, defensible reason for participating in each.[35]

A good deal of information can be found creating social media content online. It is important to recognize that using social media well involves a serious commitment of time and resources. For example, Leo Widrich suggests that an organization be prepared to post 5-10 times a day on Twitter and 1-4 times a day on Facebook for optimal outcome. Research suggests that the best times to tweet and post to Facebook are 8 a.m. till 8 p.m., well beyond the normal work day.[36] Both of these tactical steps require a significant investment in social media by any organization.

? Critical Thinking

What makes a website useful and memorable in your opinion? Based upon your own website use, what should organizations avoid when designing web pages?

Gaining Publicity

A major purpose of many public relations programs is to provide information to the media in the hope that it will be published or broadcast. The resulting coverage is called *publicity*. To be an effective publicist, one must be familiar with journalistic news values and know how to identify a news angle that will be interesting to journalists and the public.

Table 11-4 lists ways to create news for an organization. In general, aspects of news include the following:

- **Timeliness.** One way to makes news timely is to announce something when it happens. Another way is to offer information linked to events or holidays already of interest to the public. A third approach is to link announcements to current issues that are already in the news.

- **Prominence.** Prominence relates to the importance of the person or company involved in the announcement. Celebrities are more likely to get news attention, just as are influential business leaders and organizations.

- **Proximity.** News that has a local angle is more likely to get published or broadcast, so it is important to "localize" information to the media outlets being targeted.

- **Significance.** Any event that affects a large number of people is more likely to get publicized by the media.

- **Unusualness.** Events or announcements that are out of the ordinary make them more attractive to the media.

- **Human interest.** Stories about other people are more interesting to the public, so it can be helpful to "humanize" announcements by connecting them to real people and telling the story through their eyes.

- **Conflict.** Controversial issues are more likely to get coverage in the news media.

- **Newness.** Information about new products or services is more likely to get publicized.

Table 11-4 Ways to Create News for Your Organization

■ Tie in with news events of the day.	■ Make a trip.
■ Cooperate with another organization on a joint project.	■ Make an award.
■ Conduct a poll or a survey.	■ Hold a contest.
■ Tie in with a newspaper or broadcast station on a mutual project.	■ Pass a resolution.
■ Issue a report.	■ Appear before public bodies.
■ Arrange an interview with a celebrity.	■ Stage a special event.
■ Take part in a controversy.	■ Write a letter.
■ Arrange for a testimonial.	■ Release a letter you received (with permission).
■ Make an analysis or a prediction.	■ Adapt national reports and surveys for local use.
■ Form and announce names for a committee.	■ Stage a debate.
■ Hold an election.	■ Tie in to a well-known week or day.
■ Announce an appointment.	■ Honor an institution.
■ Celebrate an anniversary.	■ Organize a tour.
■ Issue a summary of facts.	■ Inspect a project.
■ Tie in with a holiday.	■ Issue a commendation.
	■ Issue a protest.

Source: Wilcox, D. L., Ault, P. H., & Agee, W. K. (1995). *Public Relations Strategies and Tactics*, 4th ed. (New York: HarperCollins).

Responsible Communication

Corporate social responsibility (CSR) is a concept whereby companies integrate social and environmental concerns into their business operations and in their interaction with their stakeholders (employees, customers, shareholders, investors, local communities, government) on a voluntary basis.

CSR is closely linked with the principles of sustainability, which argues that enterprises should make decisions based not only on financial factors, such as profits or dividends, but also based on the immediate and long-term social and environmental consequences of their activities.

CSR has become prominent in the language and strategy of business and by the growth of dedicated CSR organizations globally. Governments and international governmental organizations are increasingly encouraging CSR and forming CSR partnerships.

CSR is rapidly becoming a major part of all business management courses and a key global issue.

CSR provides a number of potential benefits to both the community and business, including:

- Reduced costs
- Increased business leads
- Increased reputation
- Increased staff morale and skills development
- Improved relationships with the local community, partners, and clients
- Innovation in processes, products, and services
- Managing the risks a company faces

There are critics of CSR, however, who argue that it distracts from the fundamental economic role of businesses, while others say it may be used cynically and superficially as a public relations campaign in an attempt to preempt the role of governments as a watchdog over multinational corporations.

Questions for Discussion

1. What are some examples of CSR efforts that you have seen or with which you have been involved? Were these true attempts at more responsible business practices or more superficial in the sense that they were being used to simply affect an organization's image?

2. How were these CSR efforts communicated to the public and other stakeholders? Were these messages effective in terms of the medium chosen to communicate the message and the content of the message? Were they appropriately targeted to their intended audience or audiences?

Investor Relations

Over the past forty years, investor relations has become an important part of corporate communication's function. Broadly speaking, those involved in investor relations are responsible for marketing the stock of public companies to investors either directly or through securities analysts. They provide information that analysts need to recommend the company's stock and that investors need to buy it.

Investor relations manages relations with both individual shareholders and institutional investors, such as pension and mutual funds, banks, and insurance companies. Individuals hold about 55 percent of all equities in the United States while institutional investors hold the remaining 45 percent. The financial community is typically targeted through "buy-side" and "sell-side" analysts. The buy-side represents individuals, fund and portfolio managers, and institutional analysts, while the sell-side represents individual and institutional brokers as well as investment banks.

Those working in investor relations reach institutions often through face-to-face meetings and the telephone. In addition, CEOs may address industry conferences or analyst or broker societies. Companies also host meetings in major financial centers and invite investors who own or may want to buy company stock.

To reach individuals, investor relations professionals may use direct mail to contact current shareholders, customers, or suppliers or try to generate visibility in the media.

Companies reach both types of investors through annual and quarterly reports, proxy statements, press releases, and annual meetings.

In order to develop a formal investor relations program, companies must answer four critical questions:

- **What is the current perception of the company in the investment community?** This question is best answered by surveying the financial community to determine what it needs from the company and how the company is viewed.

- **Where does investor relations fit within the company?** Investor relations is in a sensitive position both legally and ethically in terms of what can and cannot be shared with the public, investors, and the media. The person or persons given the job must be able to use judgment as well as to maintain good relations with those inside and outside the company.

- **What are the objectives of the investor relations program?** An effective investor relations program must provide a proactive marketing function that ensures the company's stock price is appropriate for the earnings outlook and the economy, limits stock price volatility, and understands the shareholder base as well as what is common in the industry. With this knowledge, the program should build the shareholder base and provide feedback to management regarding investor concerns.

- **What activities are necessary to achieve these objectives?** In order to achieve these objectives, the company must develop a message that includes management's philosophy, current conditions in the industry, and earnings potential.[37]

This and other information needs to be communicated to analysts and institutional investors in a timely manner. That is the role of investor relations.

Issues Management

issues management

The organized activity of identifying emerging trends, concerns, or issues likely to affect an organization in the next few years, and developing a wider and more positive range of organizational responses.

In the past few decades, large organizations have moved beyond traditional image-building functions of public relations to deal more effectively with social and political issues that affect organizations and their relationships with various publics.[38] **Issues management** is "the organized activity of identifying emerging trends, concerns, or issues likely to affect an organization in the next few years and developing a wider and more positive range of organizational responses."[39] Issues management is related to risk and crisis management, two additional concepts related to organizational strategic communication that will be discussed later in this chapter.

Many of these attempts to influence the development of public policy decisions arise from conflicts among industries, which often involve legal regulation. Traditionally, many heavily regulated industries have relied upon lobbyists to influence the regulatory process. But many public issues do not become objects of legislative action until the issue has become highly politicized, and many organizations have used lobbying in ways that are almost exclusively self-serving. These approaches can be criticized as reactive as well as insensitive to the importance of public interest and response to such issues.

Issues management has become a concern because executives and managers tend to avoid dealing with public issues. "The most significant explanation of the failure of business to gain respect for its positions on public issues is that corporate leadership either does not recognize or ignores, the discernible trends which always precede issues."[40]

One model developed to explain how such failures occur characterizes organizational responses by two factors (1) the organization's stake in maintaining the status quo and (2) the perceived legitimacy of the public's complaints against the status quo.[41] According to the model, organizations will avoid a public issue if the stakes and perceived legitimacy are low. If the stakes are high and perceived legitimacy is low, organizations will tend to "stonewall" with cover-ups, distortions, and other methods. When stakes are low and perceived legitimacy is high, the organization attempts to accommodate critics through some sort of change. If both the stakes and the perceived legitimacy are high, the organization attempts to collaborate with critics.

The problem that this model identifies is that executive's perceptions of legitimacy may have little to do with the actual impact that a public issue may have on an organization. Because of this problem, organizations should develop some means of tracking and monitoring issues as they develop. Several techniques that organizations can use to track and predict the development of such issues include

- **Trend extrapolation.** A factor or variable is measured over time and statistical forecasting techniques are used to project a trend from these measurements.
- **Trend impact analysis.** After a trend is extrapolated, future events are identified that would affect the extrapolation and the trend is modified in light of these possible events.
- **Scanning.** Issues that might affect an organization are identified and monitored by use of volunteers who regularly scan print and electronic media for information.
- **Monitoring.** Monitoring tracks issues that have been identified through scanning using a systematic analysis of data. Monitoring may include public opinion polling, focus groups, and other forms of social science research.
- **Scenario writing.** Some organizations hire writers to develop and write scenarios that address the question, "What would happen if X came to pass?"[42]

These tools help organizations gather information about emerging public issues. But issues management doesn't stop here. The information that has been gathered can be used to affect decision making. This action typically takes one of two forms: organizational change or issue advocacy.

? Critical Thinking

What public issues are you aware of that might have a negative effect on organizations? What industries would potentially be most affected by certain outcomes of these public concerns? What could organizations do to affect these outcomes?

Organizational Change and Issues Management

Issues management may be used to address potential regulatory challenges, but some managers use the information to create social responsibility programs. Such efforts are grounded in Chaffee's adaptive model of strategy that assumes an interdependency between the organization and its environment.

Starbucks Corp. is one example of a company that has created a social responsibility program. One aspect of Starbucks's program is its commitment to ethically sourcing and roasting its coffee. In fiscal 2007, 65 percent of Starbucks's coffee was purchased from C.A.F.E. (Coffee and Farmer Equity) Practices, which are approved suppliers who have integrated the company's standards for sustainability throughout the coffee supply chain. C.A.F.E. Practices suppliers—and other entities within Starbucks's supply network—must have certain practices in place that ensure safe, fair, and humane working conditions; the protection of workers' rights; and adequate living conditions. The minimum wage requirements and addressing child labor/forced labor/discrimination indicators are mandatory. In addition, in the growing and/or processing of coffee, measures must be in place to manage waste, protect water quality, conserve water and energy use, preserve biodiversity, and reduce agrochemical use. Starbucks set a goal of ensuring that 100 percent of its coffee was ethically sourced by 2015. Starbucks uses such programs to differentiate itself as a leader in the coffee industry.

Issues Advocacy

Another form of action is advocacy of the organization's position on the issues. Public communication programs based on issues advocacy are different from typical image-building activities.

Traditional image building is "usually rather general in scope and bland in character," whereas issues advocacy "addresses itself to specific controversial issues, presenting facts and arguments that project the sponsor's viewpoint … to try to influence political decisions by molding public opinion."[43]

ExxonMobil, for example, engages in issues advocacy on a range of issues, including climate change, energy policy, and energy pricing. A recent ExxonMobil advocacy campaign on global warming acknowledged that it exists but tries to undermine the belief that it was caused by human activity. ExxonMobil's issues advocacy is carefully crafted to serve its strategic goals.

Risk Communication and Crisis Communication

risk

The chance of loss (or gain).

Risk and crisis communication are closely related but separate activities. **Risk** is "the chance of loss (or gain)."[44] In contrast, a crisis is more urgent and immediate and is commonly associated with a potential negative outcome. Crisis is thus an event or episode that is caused by risk.

Risk Communication

Risk management is concerned with identifying an organization's exposure to potential losses, preventing or reducing the likelihood of their occurrence, and mitigating potential loss. Risk management may include risk of theft, fraud, and workplace accidents, to larger catastrophic events, such as terrorist attacks and natural disasters. **Risk communication** is "the process of communicating responsibly and effectively about the risk factors associated with industrial technologies, natural hazards, and human activities."[45]

risk communication

The process of communicating responsibly and effectively about the risk factors associated with industrial technologies, natural hazards, and human activities.

The basic responsibility of risk communication practitioners is promotion of "reasoned dialogue among stakeholders on the nature of the relevant risk factors and on acceptable risk management strategies."[46] Practitioners thus must understand how risks are perceived by relevant publics, be able to present expert risk assessments in ways non-experts can understand, and help interested parties reach a shared understanding of risk.

Risk communication as an area of practice and scholarly attention has experienced rapid growth. A number of university centers exist to study risk communication, consulting firms offer risk communication services, degree programs in risk communication have been started, and hundreds of scholarly articles have been published on the subject in the past twenty years.

Crisis Communication

Crisis communication is an often overlooked aspect of an organization's management strategy. A 2004 study found that only between 5 and 25 percent of the Fortune 500 companies were prepared to manage an unfamiliar crisis.[47]

Crisis communication requires management in situations that affect an organization's relationships with its stakeholders, particularly those that draw media attention. Much of the crisis communication literature is concerned with this issue. For example, Benoit's theory of image restoration is concerned with crisis situations in which relevant audiences believe an organization is responsible for an offensive act. For Benoit, the important point is not whether the organization is actually responsible, but whether the public believes it is responsible. According to Benoit's theory, organizations can respond to crisis situations in five ways: They can deny responsibility, evade responsibility, reduce offensiveness of the act, take corrective action, or apologize.[48]

Discussions of crisis management typically focus on three issues: (1) planning and preparing for crisis events, (2) behavior of the organization during a crisis, and (3) communicating with important publics during the crisis.[49] Although this model separates communicating about the crisis from the planning and behavior stages, both of these latter issues are relevant to what is communicated and how.

Five steps in the planning process are to:

1. Identify the potential crises.
2. Evaluate the impact of a crisis, not only in terms of the actual event but the public response to it.
3. Assign responsibility for execution of the crisis management program.
4. Put the plan in writing.
5. Rehearse the actions outlined in the plan.[50]

The types of disasters that an organization might face have been categorized as natural disasters, normal accidents, and abnormal or intentional accidents. Natural disasters include fires, earthquakes, or hurricanes.[51] Normal accidents is a term coined to describe industrial disasters such as those that occurred at Three Mile Island, Chernobyl, Bhopal, and Alaska due to the Exxon Valdez spill. Abnormal accidents occur because of deliberate action, such as bombings, kidnappings, cyberattacks, and other types of sabotage.[52]

One tool for accomplishing the first two steps in the planning process is to apply the "worst case scenario" technique.[53] The third step should be accomplished by limiting the number of people involved. "If you manage crisis by committee, you are doomed to failure.... There needs to be a chain of command and agreement on who's going to do the speaking."[54]

The communication objective in any crisis management strategy should depend upon the stage of the crisis.[55] In cases when communication programs can begin before a crisis occurs, messages should provide internalizing information to build a positive public opinion toward the organization. When it appears a crisis is imminent, the strategy should shift from internalizing messages to instructing messages that tell the public how to respond to the crisis. During the breakout stage of the crisis, instructing communication should intensify so that the affected publics know what to do. As the crisis subsides, communication may shift to adjusting messages intended to help people cope with the effects of the crisis. When the crisis is over, the organization can shift back to an internalizing message strategy.

Any crisis communication plan should provide training for dealing with the media regarding crisis management; identify communication lines with local communities and intervening agencies, such as the police; and provide a strategy for communicating with employees.

During a crisis, an organization should follow the steps outlined below:

1. **Get control of the situation.** This involves defining the problem and setting measurable communication objectives. In addition, it is important to communicate to employees how and where to get information.
2. **Gather information about the situation.** It is important that an organization has a means to stay up to date with the situation as it is happening so that it can respond quickly and appropriately. One way to accomplish this task is to create a crisis center that creates crisis response plans, monitors potential crises, and develops crisis response capabilities.
3. **Communicate early and often.** It will benefit the organization's credibility to be prepared and to explain what is happening and what the company is doing about it, and to provide information about resources available to affected parties to deal with the situation.
4. **Communicate directly with affected parties.** It is important to be prepared to communicate with the media and to do so promptly; it is also important to communicate directly with others who are affected, such as employees, customers, shareholders, and communities.

Handling the News Media

An organization should not wait for a crisis to develop relationships with members of the media if it wants to take advantage of the media's image-building capabilities. It is important that someone in the organization takes time to cultivate these relationships. Building relationships with the media is generally considered a better method than sending out mass-produced public releases, which may average a response rate of only 2 percent.[56]

An alternative is for corporate communication professionals to target their audience by doing research on the publications and writers who cover their industry or company. Ideally, someone in the company would keep a record of all articles published on the firm to make this job easier. Not only is it important to know who is covering the organization but also the angle the writer often takes.

In addition to identifying writers who cover your industry and targeting stories to them specifically, it is important that communication professionals within the organization are responsive to calls from the media. This means that those taking the calls need to be informed about the writer and need to gather information about the specifics of the call so that they can best identify the proper person within the company to address the issue. All of this needs to be done in a timely manner because of the constant deadline that most news organizations are under.

Preparing for a News Interview

Once an interview is scheduled, it is important for the person who is being interviewed to properly prepare. As with most other communication situations, preparation is the key to success in handling interviews with the media.

1. **Develop a strategy.** As with other messages, you should identify the purposes that you hope to achieve during the interview. You should also have a clear idea of who the intended audience is. Knowledge about these two issues should help you to determine the general content of your message and whether visuals or photos would be appropriate and, if so, what kind.

   Additional questions to consider involve those that your audience, the media, will be concerned about. These include what makes your story different from others or what makes it newsworthy.

2. **Refine and rehearse the message.** As with presentations and employment interviews, you should be clear about your central theme or message and develop examples, illustrations, and anecdotes that support the message. Your message should also be phrased in terms of the public's interests, not the company's.

3. **Confirm the details and ground rules.** Confirm the time, day, date, and location of the interview. If the interview is not at your office, make sure that you know how to get to the location and the time it will take to get there. For telephone or face-to-face interviews, find out whether the interview is being recorded and consider whether it is necessary for you to record the conversation as well. You must notify the party if you are recording a conversation.

4. **Make sure that you are up on the news.** You don't want to be taken by surprise, so it is important to be abreast of what is happening in the news that might affect your company or your industry.

5. **Prepare a note card with important details.** If you have trouble remembering numbers, put these on a small note card that you can refer to discreetly. Be judicious in your use of the card, since reading from it can detract from your ability to maintain a confident, credible image.

Performing the News Interview

Make sure that you arrive on time for the interview and that you look professional. It might be helpful to take a page from presidential candidates and consider whether loosening your tie or taking off your jacket will help you to better establish common ground with an audience who doesn't wear a suit to work. During the interview, practice the following points:

- **Lead with your main point.** Since you have a limited amount of time, make sure that you get your key message in early. Don't wait for the reporter to ask you a question that allows you to communicate your main message—he or she may not.

- **Express your key points from the public's point of view.** Telling the audience how the company's actions will contribute to better health or preserve jobs in the community may help it to better appreciate your points.

- **Use plain language.** Avoid language with which only those in your industry, company, or professional specialization are familiar.

- **Maintain control.** Focus on your goals for the interview and offer responses aimed at achieving those goals.

- **Be honest.** Tell the truth. If there is a problem, then focus the bulk of your discussion on the steps you are taking to avoid the problem in the future. Don't guess at the answer. If you don't know something, say so.

- **Take responsibility.** Again, unless the corporate attorney has advised otherwise, take responsibility for problems rather than blaming others.

- **Remain calm and avoid arguments.** Becoming emotional can undermine your credibility and make you look as if you have lost control and composure.

- **Rephrase the question.** You don't need to accept a reporter's premise. If a reporter uses words you wouldn't, don't repeat them. Correct them, if necessary.

- **Try to be friendly, helpful, and patient.** Shake hands with reporters and call them by name. Be enthusiastic about your company and your job, if appropriate for the occasion. Avoid becoming impatient with reporters or acting as if they or their questions are stupid.

The important thing is that you maintain your composure and appear to be likeable. Be honest, humble, and use humor when appropriate.

? Critical Thinking

As you reflect upon interviews with organizational representatives that you have seen or heard in the media, what are the characteristics or abilities of an effective interviewee? What sort of statements should company representatives avoid during interview situations? What kinds of difficult questions might you anticipate in an interview with a media representative, and how might these questions be effectively answered?

Communicating During a Crisis

Many of the steps discussed above for handling the news media apply to communicating with the press during a crisis situation. Additional guidelines for dealing with the media during a crisis include:

- Anticipate questions and determine who will answer them. Ideally, question-and-answer sheets should be prepared for management personnel who may be asked questions by the news media. Anticipate which questions might be asked during a briefing and who should best respond.

- Prepare and deliver a brief statement. After introducing yourself and others representing your company, deliver a brief statement (less than two minutes in length) that focuses only on the facts that can be confirmed at that time.

- Outline your organization's current response effort and action plan.
- Limit the question-and-answer session to no more than ten minutes.
- Don't speculate or make predictions.
- Don't make any remarks "off the record." Such comments might lead reporters to believe there is more to the story that they can pursue.

As with many other types of professional communication situations, adequate preparation is often the key to a successful crisis briefing.

Summary

The three basic models of strategic communication at the organizational level are linear, adaptive, and interpretive. In the linear model, managers identify goals, generate alternatives for achieving those goals, weigh the likelihood of success for each alternative, and then decide which to implement. The adaptive model shifts the focus of strategy from sequential planning and implementation to continuous adjustment of the relationship between the organization and its environment. The interpretive model is concerned with the social construction of reality. In this model, strategic communication is about negotiating and shaping stakeholders' understandings of what the organization is and what it does. Even though these three models appear to be distinct, they are interrelated and interdependent and more than one may be operating at the same time within an organization.

The relevant audiences for strategic communication at the organizational level are organizational stakeholders. Organizational stakeholders include shareholders or owners, employees, customers or clients, or any important constituency that can be affected or can affect the organization. These might include the government, media, activist groups, special interest coalitions, and communities.

The first step in creating an internal communication plan is to assess the current communication situation. This is commonly done by performing a communication audit, which not only assesses the current state of internal communication but also identifies areas for improvement. Once the assessment is complete, an internal communication plan can be developed. It is important to periodically assess the plan for its effectiveness and make changes as needed to ensure effective communication throughout the organization.

As a form of public communication, strategic external communication can require a substantial commitment of resources, including the purchase of advertising space in print and electronic media; time, space, and materials for special events; production facilities for websites, newsletters, company magazines, and video programs; and salaries and benefits for those who write, edit, and create the messages. Strategic external communication can be a complex process in which a number of organizational units and individuals contribute to the design and dissemination of messages. External strategic communication includes public relations and issues management efforts designed to influence consumers, communities, special-interest groups, voters, regulators, legislators, and others outside the organization. It may also include investor relations, which is intended to manage relationships with the investment community.

Other external strategic communication issues are risk and crisis communication, which are closely related but separate activities. Risk management is concerned with identifying an organization's exposure to potential losses, preventing or reducing the likelihood of their occurrence, and mitigating potential loss. Risk communication is the process of communicating responsibly and effectively about the risk factors associated with industrial technologies, natural hazards, and human activities. Crisis communication requires management in situations that affect an organization's relationships with its stakeholders, particularly those that draw media attention.

Key Terms

linear model **304**

adaptive model **304**

co-alignment **304**

interpretive model **304**

internal strategic communication **305**

public communication **314**

external strategic communication **315**

reputation management **315**

image building **316**

identity **316**

public relations **316**

issues management **321**

risk **323**

risk communication **323**

Discussion Questions

1. What are the three models of organizational strategy proposed by Chaffee? What are the characteristics of each?
2. What are some of the costs to an organization of poor employee communication? What are some of the common reasons that are cited for a lack of an employee communication plan?
3. What are the elements of a successful employee communication program?
4. What are some of the barriers to effective interdepartmental communication? What are some of the steps that can be taken to improve interdepartmental communication?
5. What are the steps involved in developing a strategic external relations program? What challenges might you anticipate in developing such a program and how might they be addressed?

Applications

1. Use participant observation to conduct a "mini" communication audit of an organization of which you are a part. Participant observation involves participating in organizational activities involving communication and assessing how and when communication is performed. Summarize the results of your observations in an informal report you address to the leader of the group.
2. Collect a variety of documents created by an organization. These might include publications, campaign materials, press releases, a website, and so on. Review the documents to assess their effectiveness in terms of strategic communication issues. That is, identify the audiences for the message, their purposes, and the channel and media used, and assess how well the documents meet these strategic goals. Write an informal report to the leader of the organization that summarizes your findings.
3. Select an organization to which you have access. Prepare a list of open-ended questions intended to elicit responses from employees or members of the organization about its communication practices. Conduct interviews with five persons who are members of the organization. Write an informal report to the leader of the organization that summarizes your findings.
4. Select an organization that has a web presence. Then prepare an informal report in which you identify and analyze the effectiveness of the organization's logo, slogans, letterhead, product designs, and promotional materials in terms of how well you think they reinforce the themes identified in the company mission statement. In performing your analysis, take into consideration how they might be perceived by the major audiences or stakeholders for the materials.
5. Identify a recent crisis that an organization has faced. Conduct research on that crisis and write an informal report in which you (a) summarize the facts of the crisis situation, (b) prepare a two-minute statement that could be delivered to the press, and (c) identify potential questions you might receive from the press and provide your responses to them.

Endnotes

1. Chaffee, E. E. (1985). Three models of strategy. *The Academy of Management Review* 10 (1), 89–98,
2. Chaffee, 1985, p. 90.
3. Ibid., 1985, p. 93.
4. Ibid., 1985, p. 93.
5. Ibid., 1985.
6. Lim, G., Ahn, H., & Lee, H. (2005). Formulating strategy for stakeholder management: A case-based reasoning approach. *Expert Systems with Applications*, 28, 831–40.
7. Barrett, D. J. (2002). Change communication: Using strategic employee communication to facilitate major change. *Corporate Communication: An International Journal*, 7 (4), 219–231, p. 219.
8. McNamara, C. (2008). Basics in internal organizational communications. Adapted from the *Field Guide to Leadership and Supervision*. Retrieved October 31, 2009 from *http://managementhelp.org/mrktng/org_cmm.htm.*
9. Papa, M. J., Daniels, D. D., & Spiker, B. K. (2008). *Organizational Communication: Perspectives and Trends.* Los Angeles, CA: Sage Publications.
10. Morrison, M. (2008). How to write an internal communications plan and strategy. *http://rapidbi.com/created/howtowriteaninternalcommunicationsplanandstrategy.html*
11. Barrett, D. J. (2002). Change communication: Using strategic employee communication to facilitate major change. *Corporate Communication: An International Journal*, 7 (4), 219–231.

12. Coffman, J. (2004). Strategic communications audits. Prepared for the Communications Consortium Media Center. Retrieved October 12, 2005, from *http://www.mediaevaluationproject.org/WorkingPaper1.pdf.*

13. Morrison, M. (2008). How to write an internal communications plan and strategy. *http://rapidbi.com/created/howtowriteaninternalcommunicationsplanandstrategy.html*

14. Hopkins, L. (2009). Internal Communication: 12 Essential Elements. Retrieved October 31, 2009 from *http://ezinearticles.com/?Internal-Communication:-12-Essential-Elements&id=12286.*

15. Cardon, P.W. (2016). Community, culture, and affordances in social collaboration and communication. *International Journal of Business Communication 53*(2), 141-147.

16. Ibid.

17. Ibid.

18. Morrison, 2008.

19. Wiseman, G., and Barker, L. (1967). *Speech—Interpersonal Communication.* Chicago, IL.: Chandler.

20. Sethi, S. P. (1982). *Up Against the Corporate Wall: Modern Corporations and Social Issues of the Eighties* (4th ed.). Englewood Cliffs, NJ: Prentice Hall.

21. What is reputation management? (n.d.) Definition from *WhatIs.com.* Retrieved December 1, 2015 from *WhatIs.com.*

22. Kamvar, S. D., Schlosser, M. T., Garcia-Molina, H. (2003). The EigenTrust algorithm for reputation management in P2P networks. WWW '03 Proceedings of the 12th international conference on World Wide Web. doi:10.1145/775152.775242.

23. *Management Today* Masterclass – Reputation management. (2007, May 1). *Management Today.*

24. Cravens, K. S., & Oliver, E. G. (2006, July 1). Employees: The key link to corporate reputation management. *Business Horizons 49* (4): 293–302. doi:10.1016/j.bushor.2005.10.006 – via ScienceDirect.

25. Moryt, M. (2013, May 17). Great businesses lean forward, respond fast. *Silicon Valley Business Journal.*

26. Alabama's Beasley Allen law firm drops suit against Taco Bell over 'seasoned beef' claims. (n.d.) Retrieved June 13, 2016 from *AL.com* and With lawsuit over, Taco Bell's mystery meat is a mystery no longer. (n.d.) Retrieved June 13, 2016 from *NPR.org.*

27. Macedo, D. (2011, April 26). Taco Bell still has beef with firm that dropped lawsuit. Fox News. Retrieved June 13, 2016 from *foxnews.com.*

28. Mills, E. (2007, January 11). Study: eBay sellers gaming the reputation system? CNET. Retrieved July 14, 2012 from *cnet.com.*

29. Lieb, R. (2012, July 10). How your content strategy is critical for reputation management. *MarketingLand.* Retrieved June 12, 2012 from *marketingland.com.*

30. Goldhaber, G. M. (1993). *Organizational Communication* (6th ed.). Dubuque, IA: Brown & Benchmark.

31. Argenti, P. (1998). *Corporate Communication* (2nd ed.). Boston, MA.: Irwin/McGraw-Hill.

32. Cutlip, S. M., & Center, A. H. (1964). *Effective Public Relations* (3rd ed.). Englewood Cliffs, NJ: Prentice Hall, p. 4.

33. Baer, J. (n.d.) Social media strategy in 8 steps. Retrieved August 29, 2017 from *http://www.convinceandconvert.com/social-media-strategy/social-media-strategy-in-8-steps/.*

34. Hemley, D. (2013). 26 tips to create a strong social media content strategy. Retrieved August 28, 2017 from *http://www.socialmediaexaminer.com/26-tips-to-create-a-strong-social-media-content-strategy/.*

35. Baer.

36. Hemley.

37. Argenti, P. (1998). *Corporate Communication* (2nd ed.). Boston, MA: Irwin/McGraw-Hill.

38. Gaunt, P., & Ollenburger, J. (1995). Issues management revisited: A tool that deserves another look. *Public Relations Review,* 21 (3), 199–210.

39. Coates, J., Coates, V., Jarratt, J., & Heinz, L. (1986). *Issues Management: How You Can Plan, Organize, and Manage for the Future.* Mt. Airy, MD: Lomond, p. ix.

40. Jones, B. L., & Chase, W. H. (1979). Managing public policy issues. *Public Relations Review,* 5, 3–23, p. 3.

41. Post, J. E. (1978). Corporate response models and public affairs management. *Public Relations Quarterly,* 24, 27–32.

42. Ewing, R. P. (1979, Winter). The uses of futurist techniques in issues management. *Public Relations Quarterly,* 15–18.

43. Sethi, 1982, p. 162.

44. Leiss, W. (2004). Effective risk communication practice. *Toxicology Letters,* 149, 399–404, p. 399.

45. Leiss, 2004, p. 401.

46. Ibid., 2004, p. 402.

47. Mitroff, I. I., & Alpasian, M. C. (2004, Spring). A toolkit for managing crises and preparing for the unthinkable. *The Mitroff Report,* 1, 81–88.

48. Benoit, W. L., (1997). Image repair discourse and crisis communication. *Public Relations Review,* 23 (2), 177–186 and Benoit, W. L. (1995). *Apologies, Excuses, and Accounts: A Theory of Image Restoration Strategies.* Albany, NY: State University of New York Press.

49. Sturges, D. L. (1994). Communicating through crisis: A strategy for organizational survival. *Management Communication Quarterly,* 7, 297–316.

50. Englehart, B. (1995). Crisis communication: Communicating under fire. *The Journal of Management Advocacy Communication,* 1, 23–28, p. 28.

51. Mitroff. & Alpasian, 2004, Spring.

52. Perrow, C. (1984). *Normal Accidents: Living with High-Risk Technologies.* New York: Basic Books.

53. Barton, L. (1993). *Crisis in Organizations: Managing and Communicating in the Heat of Crisis.* Cincinnati, OH: SouthWestern.

54. Englehart, 1995, p. 28.

55. Sturges, 1994.

56. Argenti, 1998.

Amazon.com, Inc.: *Big Ideas in a Bruising Workplace*

A small startup company may regard operational efficiency as its top priority, to yield profits. A bigger company, however, will often face a much larger set of stakeholders with various concerns, forcing it to strike a balance between economic gains and basic social needs.

Big companies sometimes resemble a government or an empire unto themselves. If the corporate culture that has effectively served the company in the growth stage lags behind rapid growth, serious problems may occur as some interest groups feel neglected or ignored and begin to push back, asking for attention, or even major reforms.

The Upheaval

August 15, 2015 was a tough day for Amazon. *The New York Times* published an investigative article entitled, "Inside Amazon: Wrestling Big Ideas in a Bruising Workplace."[1] The headline was accompanied by a subhead, "The company is conducting an experiment in how far it can push white-collar workers to get them to achieve its ever-expanding ambitions." The article offered up sharp criticism of Amazon, the biggest e-commerce and cloud computing company in the United States today.

Sampling more than 100 current and former Amazon employees' personal experiences, reporters from *The Times* depicted a dark side to the corporate behemoth that often boasts about its 14 leadership principles.[2]

The company's radical departure from current management norms had long been tolerated as a necessary tradeoff for its survival and prosperity. But now its distinctive corporate culture, as illustrated by personal accounts, was beginning to make readers think twice.

Workplace Conflicts for the Best Idea Generation

At Amazon, the conflicts among team members, between work and personal life, and between hourly employees and salaried management have been viewed positively as the right recipe for creativity. In its fourth leadership principle "Are Right, A Lot," Amazon states, "[leaders] seek diverse perspectives and work to disconfirm their beliefs."[3] A confrontational approach has been adopted to fend off the bureaucracy of a typical large company, keeping every team member on their toes.

However, this much desired work efficiency may have been achieved at the sacrifice of harmony and cohesion as experienced by people interviewed for the *Times* article. Straightforward challenges during meetings made mature employees cry. Longer working hours and prompt e-mail reply, even at midnight, are a widely accepted norm. Secret commentary software was introduced for employees to report on managers' performance. The pressure to keep performing better was perceived as an implicit exploitation, a natural consequence from Amazon's single-minded obsession with its ever-expanding success.[4]

Worse still, those who were interviewed spoke of the rampant use of "hostile language" that frightened some employees, forcing them to remain silent and ultimately quit. Productivity was hurt in unseen ways.[5]

This case was prepared by research assistants Seokbong Choi and Cynthia (Huijuan) Li under the direction of James S. O'Rourke, IV, Teaching Professor of Management, as the basis for class discussion rather than to illustrate either effective or ineffective handling of an administrative situation. Information was gathered from corporate as well as public sources. Editorial assistance: Judy Bradford.

1. Kantor, Jodi and Streitfeld, David, "Inside Amazon: Wrestling Big Ideas in a Bruising Workplace," *The New York Times*, August 15, 2015. *<http://www.nytimes.com/2015/08/16/technology/inside-amazon-wrestling-big-ideas-in-a-bruising-workplace.html?_r=0>*

2. Amazon Leadership Principles. *<http://www.amazon.jobs/principles>*

3. Ibid.

4. Kantor, Jodi and Streitfeld, David, "Inside Amazon: Wrestling Big Ideas in a Bruising Workplace," *The New York Times*, August 15, 2015 *<http://www.nytimes.com/2015/08/16/technology/inside-amazon-wrestling-big-ideas-in-a-bruising-workplace.html?_r=0>*

5. Ibid.

Purposeful Darwinism for the Optimal Resource Utilization

The internal competition at Amazon does not stop with the daily operation and generation of ideas, according to *The Times* article. Staffing decisions are made with the lowest-performer-out principle. Managers were forced to identify the so-called "least performers" even if there were none during cut-throat sessions at performance evaluations.[6]

In some extreme instances, workers who suffered from cancer, experienced miscarriage or other personal crises were said to be forced out to make room for other workers to move up. Secret reporting to management was sometimes abused as a tool for telling on other workers.[7]

Amazon could attempt to justify all these internal struggles by pointing to its ninth leadership principle: Frugality. Accomplish more with less. "Constraints breed resourcefulness, self-sufficiency and invention. There are no extra points for growing headcount, budget size or fixed expense."[8]

Tight budget control seems to explain the inhumane treatment at Amazon. No replacement could be found when an employee had to cut back on overtime work due to personal reasons, such as tending to a seriously ill relative or a newborn.[9] A corporate culture that seemed to view personal life as the diametrical opposite of work performance compelled mature workers to leave in disagreement, or simply after being marginalized.

Getting and Keeping the Best, The Elitism Cult

Elitism is apparently preferred, as is stated in the fifth Amazon Principle: "Hire and Develop The Best."[10] The best had long been defined as people who work "long, hard and smart" by Bezos in his letter to shareholders in 1997:

"It's not easy to work here (when I interview, people I tell them, "You can work long, hard, or smart, but at Amazon.com you can't choose two out of three"), but we are working to build something important, something that matters to our customers, something that we can all tell our grandchildren about. Such things aren't meant to be easy. We are incredibly fortunate to have this group of dedicated employees whose sacrifices and passion build Amazon.com." [11]

One of the manifestations of this elite culture is Amazon's "Just Do It" award which recognizes employees who have tried and failed, as well as those who have tried and succeeded—the message being that taking risks is better than being frozen with fear.[12]

Aspiring young engineers, in Bezos's view, want to be pushed. The Just Do It award brings a sense of accomplishment and the joy of self-actualization. Just as Bezos described in the shareholder letter above, Amazon has been seen as a great place to work for young and ambitious adventurers who want to be part of something big and powerful and who have few interests outside of work.

But the fundamental business question for Amazon may be: Does the best always mean young and with few personal commitments?

Once again, such a seemingly healthy incentive mechanism may turn out to be less effective and sustainable than expected. Some of those interviewed for the *Times* article said they had observed co-workers on drugs for depression, drinking too much, and experiencing severe sleeping problems. "I didn't even realize how disgustingly abusive it was until I left," a former, anonymous employee said in a follow-up report by *The Times*.[13]

6. Ibid

7. Ibid.

8. Amazon Leadership Principles. <http://www.amazon.jobs/principles>

9. Kantor, Jodi and Streitfeld, David, "Inside Amazon: Wrestling Big Ideas in a Bruising Workplace," *The New York Times*, August 15, 2015 <http://www.nytimes.com/2015/08/16/technology/inside-amazon-wrestling-big-ideas-in-a-bruising-workplace.html?_r=0>

10. Amazon Leadership Principles. <http://www.amazon.jobs/principles>

11. Amazon Letter to Shareholders 1997. <http://media.corporate-ir.net/media_files/irol/97/97664/reports/Shareholderletter97.pdf>

12. Klein, Sebastian. "7 Habits You Can Learn From Jeff Bezos and Amazon.com," Lifehack. Work. <http://www.lifehack.org/articles/work/7-habits-you-can-learn-from-jeff-bezos-and-amazon-com.html>

13. "Depiction of Amazon Stirs a Debate about Work Culture," *The New York Times*, August 18, 2015 <http://www.nytimes.com/2015/08/19/technology/amazon-workplace-reactions-comments.html?_r=0>

Amazon: The Dream of Being the Biggest

A highly competitive work environment, strict control of internal resources, and a clear preference for the strongest have been the secrets of success for this pioneering online retail company.

Founded by Jeff Bezos, a computer science major from Princeton University and former Vice President at a Wall Street firm in 1994, Amazon was initially an online bookstore.

Bezos originally wanted the name "Cadabra," but soon changed it to "Amazon" after "cadabra" was misheard as "cadaver."[14] He selected the name "Amazon" because it refers to a place "exotic and different" and the "biggest" river in the world, which coincides with his idea of making the company the "biggest" store in the world. The name starts with "A", which would also put it at the top of any alphabetically ordered list.[15]

Following such an ambition is Amazon's number one leadership principle: "Customer Obsession":

Leaders start with the customer and work backwards. They work vigorously to earn and keep customer trust. Although leaders pay attention to competitors, they obsess over customers.[16]

The single-minded focus on customers has made Amazon's business goals very consistent ever since its Initial Public Offering in 1997. In a letter to shareholders that same year, Bezos wrote:

We are still in the early stages of learning how to bring new value to our customers through Internet commerce and merchandising. Our goal remains to continue to solidify and extend our brand and customer base. This requires sustained investment in systems and infrastructure to support outstanding customer convenience, selection, and service while we grow.[17]

In the general statement about its business in Amazon's 2014 annual report, the company still proclaims its unwavering goals in the most clear-cut way: "We seek to be Earth's most customer-centric company."[18] Primary customers were defined as consumers (at Amazon retail websites), sellers (at Amazon retail websites), enterprises (Amazon Web Services), and content creators (at Kindle Direct Publishing).[19]

Following the customer-focus approach is the eighth Amazon Leadership Principle: "Bias for Action":

Speed matters in business. Many decisions and actions are reversible and do not need extensive study. We value calculated risk taking.[20]

Amazon has been known for its aggressive investment in fulfillment centers and servers and has made its name synonymous with online shopping in the United States, successfully distancing itself from brick-and-mortar retailers, as well as dominant online search engines. The company prides itself on Amazon Prime, the free two-day shipping, and now free two-hour delivery in some cities. It even expanded one-hour Prime Now deliveries to London in October 2015.[21]

In July of 2015, the company's market value, at US$250 billion, surpassed Walmart's market value of US$230 billion after Amazon's stock price increased by more than 14 percent a share. Walmart's annual sales of US$486 billion in 2014, however, still dwarfed Amazon's annual sales of US$89 billion in mid-year, 2015.[22]

---

14. Elliott, Amy-Mae. "Amazon.com Facts: 10 Things You Didn't Know About the Web's Biggest Retailer," Mashable, July 22, 2011 <http://mashable.com/2011/07/22/facts-amazon-com/#nhxpdkvj7iqa>

15 Byers, Ann (2006), Jeff Bezos: the founder of *Amazon.com*, The Rosen Publishing Group, pp. 46–47

16 Amazon Leadership Principle. <http://www.amazon.jobs/principles>

17 Amazon Letter to Shareholders 1997. <http://media.corporate-ir.net/media_files/irol/97/97664/reports/Shareholderletter97.pdf>

18 Amazon 2014 Annual Report. United States Securities and Exchange Commission, Form 10-K. <https://www.sec.gov/Archives/edgar/data/1018724/000101872415000006/amzn-20141231x10k.htm>

19 Ibid. Pages 3 and 4.

20 Amazon Leadership Principle. <http://www.amazon.jobs/principles>

21 Brian, Matt. "Amazon Expands One-hour Prime Now Deliveries in London," *Engadget*, Oct. 6, 2015 <http://www.engadget.com/2015/10/06/amazon-expands-prime-now-london/>

22. Prigg, Mark, "Amazon overtakes Walmart as firm reveals record profits causing its market value to rocket to over $250 billion (and makes Jeff Bezos $7 bn in 45 minutes), *DailyMail.com*. <http://www.dailymail.co.uk/sciencetech/article-3172655/Amazon-overtakes-Walmart-firm-reveals-record-profits-c ausing-worth-rocket-250-billion.html>

Gross margin has steadily increased from 24.8% ($15,122 million) in 2012 to 29.5% ($26,236 million) in 2014. Fulfillment costs 12% of its net sales; technology and content came in second (10.4%) and general and administrative cost remained the lowest (1.7%) after marketing (4.9%). But general and administrative expenses have grown at a relatively higher rate (36% in 2012, 26% in 2013, and 37% in 2014) due to increases in payroll and related expenses, along with professional service fees.[23]

The Company is still bent on maximizing its growth potential, which has been accomplished in several ways: increase fulfillment center productivity, expand customer base and sales channels, and obtain technologies for product development. Amazon is frequently involved in cash acquisitions, sometimes resulting in a net loss, despite its huge earning capacity. In 2013, its net income was US$180 million, and in 2014, it incurred a net loss of US$287million.[24]

As of January 2015, Amazon had 2,744 common stock shareholders. Over 67% are institutional shareholders. While its stock price stood at US$541.94 on October 7, 2015, Amazon never declared a dividend payout (which is also true for Google and many other high tech companies). Instead, Amazon increased stock-based compensation awards to existing and new employees with the total amount of US$833 million in 2012, US$1.1 billion in 2013 and US$1.5 billion in 2014.[25]

With higher revenue, lower expenses, and robust cloud services, Amazon reported a profit of US$0.19 per share in July 2015 when Wall Street was expecting a loss of US$0.14 per share.[26] Amazon shares stood at US$534 on September 24, 2015, while Google closed at $626. The market is wondering which one will cross the $1,000 per share line first.[27]

High Turnover Rate, Legal Risks and The Hidden Problem of Long Term Growth

Amazon's rapid expansion has been accompanied by a sharp increase in the number of employees. As of December 31, 2014, Amazon employed 154,100 full-time and part-time employees, as well as independent contractors and temporary personnel for peak seasons. As compared to itself in 1997, Amazon's workforce has increased by more than 250 times.[28]

Amazon number of employees (full time and part time)

Source: Amazon Annual Reports

Despite the generous stock compensation program, there is a common understanding among those interviewed in *The Times* article that working there is unsustainable. Amazon is increasingly viewed as a worthy starting point – a place where "brief stints helped their careers take off." Even the company describes its standards as "unreasonably high."[29]

PayScale, an online salary, benefit and compensation information company, looked into loyalty levels of employees at Fortune 500 companies. Amazon, though with an impressive median pay of US$93,000, was ranked 464th out of 466, with 466 being the least loyal. Amazon's median employee age is 32 and the median tenure is one year.[30] The turnover rate is among the highest in the retail and information technology sector.

23. Amazon 2014 Annual Report. United States Securities and Exchange Commission, Form 10-K.
    <*https://www.sec.gov/Archives/edgar/data/1018724/000101872415000006/amzn-20141231x10k.htm*>

24. Ibid.

25. Ibid.

26. Hoium, Travis. "The Race to $1,000 Per Share: Will Google or Amazon Cross the Finish Line First?," The Motley Fool, Sept. 27, 2015. <*http://www.fool.com/investing/general/2015/09/27/the-race-to-1000-will-google-or-amazon-cross-the-f.aspx*>

27. Ibid.

28. Amazon 2014 Annual Report. United States Securities and Exchange Commission, Form 10-K.
    <*https://www.sec.gov/Archives/edgar/data/1018724/000101872415000006/amzn-20141231x10k.htm*>

29. Kantor, Jodi and Streitfeld, David, "Inside Amazon: Wrestling Big Ideas in a Bruising Workplace," *The New York Times*, August 15, 2015 <*http://www.nytimes.com/2015/08/16/technology/inside-amazon-wrestling-big-ideas-in-a-bruising-workplace.html?_r=0*>

30. PayScale: Full List of Most and Least Loyal Employees. <*http://www.payscale.com/data-packages/employee-loyalty/full-list*>

This loss of talent benefits other high tech companies, while the outflow at Amazon is immediately compensated by the influx of fresh talent attracted by high pay and the brand itself.

The jury is still out as to whether the Amazon brand is in jeopardy due to *The Times* article. But there is plenty of speculation.

"Now, why should it matter if employees in the contact center are happy?" wrote Paul Segre for *The CX Report*, "Because they're directly engaging with customers all day long. Sentiment is easily transmitted from one person to another, and there are few bigger turnoffs for customers than having to resolve an issue with a disengaged, irritated, or clearly miserable customer service agent."[31]

In the same *CX Report* article, Segre, who is the CEO for Genesys, which sells call center software to mid-sized and large businesses, wrote: "The fact is, customers will speak with their wallets if they perceive too much injustice in the way a company conducts its business."[32]

When white-collar Amazon employees made phone calls to law firms in the Seattle area to complain about the unfair treatment, lawyers told them there was no basis for lawsuits without evidence of discrimination.[33]

Spelling it out in more certain terms was Jim Shrimp, a Pennsylvania attorney who specializes in discrimination cases and defending businesses in wage and hour disputes:

"Employees may think it's unfair, but there is nothing *per se* unlawful about requiring employees to work long hours and to judge those who don't harshly," Shrimp wrote in an August 25, 2015 blog. "Employees may think it's unfair, but there is nothing *per se* unlawful about requiring employees to log-in during vacation. Employees may think it's unfair,

but there is nothing *per se* unlawful about asking employees to report poor performance by co-workers (although in my opinion this is terrible for morale). Employees may think it's unfair, but there is nothing *per se* unlawful about memorizing 14 leadership principles and punishing those who don't. As long as Amazon is complying with wage and hour and discrimination statutes, the employee must decide whether to stay at Amazon or leave."[34]

In all U.S. states except Montana, employment relationships are predominantly based on the "at-will" principle in favor of freedom of contract and employer deference, yet at the cost of job security.[35]

An employer can terminate employment at any time for any reason or no reason at all, except for illegal reasons such as written promises, implied promises, discrimination or violation of public policy, all of which are extremely difficult for a low-level employee to prove.[36] So employee discontent usually stays at the level of business ethics with the rectification of corporate culture as the only possible remedy.

Amazon has come under fire for its treatment of blue-collar warehouse workers. In 2011, its warehouse in Breinigsville, Pennsylvania was the focus of an in-depth story by *The Morning Call,* of Allentown. The newspaper's exposé revealed that Amazon employees were forced to work in brutal heat in the summer, so much so that ambulances were called in to wait outside to treat those suffering from the stress.[37] Amazon later spent US$52 million to install cooling systems.[38]

Lawsuits in five states also targeted warehouse labor-abuse allegations in 2013. Workers said they were not paid for waiting up to 20 minutes in security-check lines daily

---

31. Segre, Paul. "Connecting Amazon's Employee Experience to Its Customer Experience," *The CX Report*, Sept. 16, 2015.
   <http://thecxreport.genesys.com/2015/09/16/connecting-amazons-employee-experience-to-customer-experience/>

32. Ibid.

33. Kantor, Jodi and Streitfeld, David, "Inside Amazon: Wrestling Big Ideas in a Bruising Workplace," *The New York Times*, August 15, 2015 *<http://www.nytimes.com/2015/08/16/technology/inside-amazon-wrestling-big-ideas-in-a-bruising-workplace.html?_r=0>*

34. Shrimp, James B. "Working at Amazon: A Demanding Workplace or Just Normal?" High Swartz blog, Aug. 25, 2015.
   <http://www.highswartz.com/blog/employment-law/working-at-amazon-a-demanding-workplace-or-just-normal/>

35. "The At-will Presumption and Exceptions to the Rule," National Conference of State Legislatures.
   <http://www.ncsl.org/research/labor-and-employment/at-will-employment-overview.aspx>

36. Ibid.

37. Soper, Spencer, "Inside Amazon's Warehouse," *The Morning Call*, August 17, 2015
   <http://www.mcall.com/news/local/amazon/mc-allentown-amazon-complaints-20110917-story.html>

38 Young, Angelo. "Amazon.com's Workers Are Low-Paid, Overworked And Unhappy; Is This The New Employee Model for The Internet Age?*" International Business Times*, Dec. 19, 2013
   <http://www.ibtimes.com/amazoncoms-workers-are-low-paid-overworked-unhappy-new-employee-model-internet-a ge-1514780>

to exit the warehouse. Nor were they paid for time spent walking daily to and from lunch from one end of the warehouse to the other. (The walking time was counted as part of their unpaid, 30-minute lunch break.)[39]

Tim Gimbel, the CEO and founder of the LaSalle Network, a professional staffing a recruiting service, wrote for *Fortune* that the Amazon workplace culture fosters growth overall:

"People shouldn't stay at a job they don't enjoy," Gimbel wrote. "My guess is people stay at Amazon because they're pushed. They're expected to grow professionally and produce results."[40]

"There is no one-size fits-all definition of how a workplace should be run," he added. And I'm not sure why people would want every environment to be the same. Amazon's environment isn't for everyone. But just because the people quoted in the article didn't like it, doesn't mean others won't. Plenty of people do, and that's why Amazon continues to grow."[41]

The Gathering Momentum of Discontent

Positioning itself as a new-age company that "strives to do really big, innovative, groundbreaking things,"[42] Amazon seems to readily accept the downside of a peculiar work culture and reasons that the nature of the work is really challenging. So for some people, it doesn't work.

The question is: When and where should stakeholders draw the line between uniqueness and outright inappropriateness? Even before *The Times* article was published, challenges to Amazon's work culture surfaced periodically.

For example, self-employed workers at Mechanical Turk, a crowdsourcing Internet marketplace under Amazon Web Services (AWS), initiated a letter-writing campaign to Jeff Bezos[43] during the 2014 Christmas season.

Mechanical Turk began in 2005, allowing companies to hire freelancers to do digital tasks such as transcribing, writing and tagging images. Amazon has used them without setting minimum rates for their work. The company also takes a 10 percent commission with every transaction.

At the Mechanical Turk website, task requesters do not have to file for payroll taxes. But there is no minimum wage, and average hourly pay is as low as one dollar. The voluntary workers are especially vulnerable as their submissions can be turned down by the requesters without cause.

In the letter-writing campaign, these Turkers protested to Jeff Bezos, asking Amazon to stop selling them as cheap labor and give them more power at the bargaining table with the online task requesters.[44]

As there is still an apparent legal vacuum regarding online freelance work, Amazon has become a *de facto* authority that the general public looks up to. Whether Amazon admits it or not, its role has changed from a simple online book retailer to a powerful influence on fair employment and social welfare.

The Epilogue: A Positive Reaction or A Subtle Denial

"I strongly believe that anyone working in a company that really is like the one described in the NYT would be crazy to stay. I know I would leave such a company,"[45] Jeff

---

39. Ibid.

40. Gimbel, Tom. "Why some of Amazon's 'problems' aren't really problems," Fortune.com, Sept. 2, 2015. Commentary. <*http://fortune.com/2015/09/02/amazon-workplace-problems/*>

41. Ibid.

42. Quote by Susan Harker, Amazon recruiter interviewed in "Inside Amazon: Wrestling Big Ideas in a Bruising Workplace." *The New York Times*. http://www.nytimes.com/2015/08/16/technology/inside-amazon-wrestling-big-ideas-in-a-bruising-workplace.html?_r=0

43. Harris, Mark. "Amazon's Mechanical Turk workers protest: 'I am a human being, not an algorithm'," *The Guardian*, December 3, 2014. <*http://www.theguardian.com/technology/2014/dec/03/amazon-mechanical-turk-workers-protest-jeff-bezos*>

44. Ibid.

45. Cook, John. "Full memo: Jeff Bezos responds to brutal NYT story, says it doesn't represent the Amazon he leads," GeekWire, Aug. 16, 2015. <*http://www.geekwire.com/2015/full-memo-jeff-bezos-responds-to-cutting-nyt-expose-says-tolerance-for-lack-of-empathy-needs-to-be-zero/*>

Bezos wrote in an internal e-mail to Amazon employees on August 16, 2015. The CEO said Amazon will not tolerate the "shockingly callous management practices" described in the article. He urged any employees who knew of "stories like those reported" to contact him directly.[46]

On the other hand, Jeff Bezos had previously been quoted: "If push comes to shove, we'll settle for intense,"[47] regarding the choice for the company's culture.

Does the evolution of a company's size call for a corresponding evolution of its corporate mechanism and corporate culture? And ultimately, how can a successful small firm adapt its culture to its bigger self without looking bad in the eyes of its employees and the public?

Discussion Questions

1. Has this newspaper article seriously undermined the brand reputation of Amazon.com?
2. Should Jeff Bezos change the firm's leadership principle? Or, should he stick with his view of leadership at Amazon?
3. What should the balance be between encouraging fair competition and fostering a spirit of cooperation?
4. Was the internal memo written to employees after publication of the *Times* article the best way for Jeff to communicate and alleviate employee concerns? Has he chosen the right message and proper channel for that message?

---

46. Ibid
47. Kantor, Jodi and Streitfeld, David, "Jeff Bezos and Amazon Employees Join Debate Over Its Culture," *The New York Times*. August 17, 2015. <*http://www.nytimes.com/2015/08/18/technology/amazon-bezos-workplace-management-practices.html*>

Exhibit 1: Amazon Leadership Principles

1. **Customer Obsession.** Leaders start with the customer and work backwards. They work vigorously to earn and keep customer trust. Although leaders pay attention to competitors, they obsess over customers.

2. **Ownership.** Leaders are owners. They think long term and don't sacrifice long-term value for short-term results. They act on behalf of the entire company, beyond just their own team. They never say "that's not my job".|

3. **Invent and Simplify.** Leaders expect and require innovation and invention from their teams and always find ways to simplify. They are externally aware, look for new ideas from everywhere, and are not limited by "not invented here". As we do new things, we accept that we may be misunderstood for long periods of time.

4. **Are Right, A Lot.** Leaders are right a lot. They have strong business judgment and good instincts. They seek diverse perspectives and work to disconfirm their belief.

5. **Hire and Develop The Best.** Leaders raise the performance bar with every hire and promotion. They recognize exceptional talent and willingly move them throughout the organization. Leaders develop leaders and take seriously their role in coaching others. We work on behalf of our people to invent mechanisms for development like Career Choice.

6. **Insist on the Highest Standards.** Leaders have relentlessly high standards – many people may think these standards are unreasonably high. Leaders are continually raising the bar and driving their teams to deliver high quality products, services and processes. Leaders ensure that defects do not get sent down the line and that problems are fixed so they stay fixed.

7. **Think Big.** Thinking small is a self-fulfilling prophecy. Leaders create and communicate a bold direction that inspires results. They think differently and look around corners for ways to serve customers.

8. **Bias for Action.** Speed matters in business. Many decisions and actions are reversible and do not need extensive study. We value calculated risk taking.

9. **Frugality.** Accomplish more with less. Constraints breed resourcefulness, self-sufficiency and invention. There are no extra points for growing headcount, budget size or fixed expense.

10. **Learn and Be Curious.** Leaders are never done learning and always seek to improve themselves. They are curious about new possibilities and act to explore them.

11. **Earn Trust.** Leaders listen attentively, speak candidly, and treat others respectfully. They are vocally self-critical, even when doing so is awkward or embarrassing. Leaders do not believe their or their team's body odor smells of perfume. They benchmark themselves and their teams against the best.

12. **Dive Deep.** Leaders operate at all levels, stay connected to the details, audit frequently, and are skeptical when metrics and anecdote differ. No task is beneath them.

13. **Have Backbone; Disagree and Commit.** Leaders are obligated to respectfully challenge decisions when they disagree, even when doing so is uncomfortable or exhausting. Leaders have conviction and are tenacious. They do not compromise for the sake of social cohesion. Once a decision is determined, they commit wholly.

14. **Deliver Results.** Leaders focus on the key inputs for their business and deliver them with the right quality and in a timely fashion. Despite setbacks, they rise to the occasion and never settle.

Source: Amazon Leadership Principles. *<http://www.amazon.jobs/principles>*

Exhibit 2: Jeff Bezos's letter to employees after publication of the *New York Times* article

Dear Amazonians,

If you haven't already, I encourage you to give this (very long) New York Times article a careful read:

http://www.nytimes.com/2015/08/16/technology/inside-amazon-wrestling-big-ideas-in-a-bruising-workplace.html

I also encourage you to read this very different take by a current Amazonian:

https://www.linkedin.com/pulse/amazonians-response-inside-amazon-wrestling-big-ideas-nick-ciubotariu

Here's why I'm writing you. The NYT article prominently features anecdotes describing shockingly callous management practices, including people being treated without empathy while enduring family tragedies and serious health problems. The article doesn't describe the Amazon I know or the caring Amazonians I work with every day. But if you know of any stories like those reported, I want you to escalate to HR. You can also e-mail me directly at jeff@amazon.com. Even if it's rare or isolated, our tolerance for any such lack of empathy needs to be zero.

The article goes further than reporting isolated anecdotes. It claims that our intentional approach is to create a soulless, dystopian workplace where no fun is had and no laughter heard. Again, I don't recognize this Amazon and I very much hope you don't, either. More broadly, I don't think any company adopting the approach portrayed could survive, much less thrive, in today's highly competitive tech hiring market. The people we hire here are the best of the best. You are recruited every day by other world-class companies, and you can work anywhere you want.

I strongly believe that anyone working in a company that really is like the one described in the NYT would be crazy to stay. I know I would leave such a company.

But hopefully, you don't recognize the company described. Hopefully, you're having fun working with a bunch of brilliant teammates, helping invent the future, and laughing along the way.

Thank you, Jeff

Source: Geek Wire <*http://www.geekwire.com/2015/full-memo-jeff-bezos-responds-to-cutting-nyt-expose-says-tolerance-for-lack-of-empathy-needs-to-be-zero/*>

Exhibit 3: Amazon Results of Operations 2014

	Year Ended December 31,		
	2014	2013	2012
Net Sales:			
North America	$ 55,469	$ 44,517	$ 34,813
International	33,519	29,935	26,280
Total consolidated	$ 88,988	$ 74,452	$ 61,093
Year-over-year Percentage Growth:			
North America	25%	28%	30%
International	12	14	23
Total consolidated	20	22	27
Year-over-year Percentage Growth, excluding effect of foreign exchange rates:			
North America	25%	28%	30%
International	14	19	27
Total consolidated	20	24	29
Net Sales Mix:			
North America	62%	60%	57%
International	38	40	43
Total consolidated	100%	100%	100%

Source: Amazon 2014 Annual Report. United States Securities and Exchange Commission, Form 10-K. Page 3.
<*https://www.sec.gov/Archives/edgar/data/1018724/000101872415000006/amzn-20141231x10k.htm*>

Exhibit 4: Amazon Sales Division Performances 2014

		Year Ended December 31,				
		2014		**2013**		**2012**
Net Sales:						
North America						
Media	$	11,567	$	10,809	$	9,189
Electronics and other general merchandise		38,517		29,985		23,273
Other (1)		5,385		3,723		2,351
Total North America	$	55,469	$	44,517	$	34,813
International						
Media	$	10,938	$	10,907	$	10,753
Electronics and other general merchandise		22,369		18,817		15,355
Other (1)		212		211		172
Total International	$	33,519	$	29,935	$	26,280
Consolidated						
Media	$	22,505	$	21,716	$	19,942
Electronics and other general merchandise		60,886		48,802		38,628
Other (1)		5,597		3,934		2,523
Total consolidated	$	88,988	$	74,452	$	61,093
Year-over-year Percentage Growth:						
North America						
Media		7%		18%		15%
Electronics and other general merchandise		28		29		34
Other		45		58		64
Total North America		25		28		30
International						
Media		—%		1%		9%
Electronics and other general merchandise		19		23		35
Other		1		22		11
Total International		12		14		23
Consolidated						
Media		4%		9%		12%
Electronics and other general merchandise		25		26		35
Other		42		56		59
Total consolidated		20		22		27
Year-over-year Percentage Growth, excluding effect of foreign exchange rates:						
International						
Media		2%		7%		12%
Electronics and other general merchandise		21		27		40
Other		1		26		15
Total International		14		19		27
Consolidated						
Media		5%		12%		14%
Electronics and other general merchandise		26		28		36
Other		42		56		59
Total consolidated		20		24		29
Consolidated Net Sales Mix:						
Media		25%		29%		33%
Electronics and other general merchandise		68		66		63
Other		7		5		4
Total consolidated		100%		100%		100%

(1) Includes sales from non-retail activities, such as AWS sales, which are included in the North America segment, and advertising services and our co-branded credit card agreements, which are included in both segments.

Source: Amazon 2014 Annual Report. United States Securities and Exchange Commission, Form 10-K. Page 3.
<https://www.sec.gov/Archives/edgar/data/1018724/000101872415000006/amzn-20141231x10k.htm>

Exhibit 5: Amazon Operating Expenses 2014

Operating Expenses

Information about operating expenses with and without stock-based compensation is as follows (in millions):

	Year Ended December 31, 2014			Year Ended December 31, 2013			Year Ended December 31, 2012		
	As Reported	Stock-Based Compensation	Net	As Reported	Stock-Based Compensation	Net	As Reported	Stock-Based Compensation	Net
Operating Expenses:									
Cost of sales	$ 62,752	$ —	$ 62,752	$ 54,181	$ —	$ 54,181	$ 45,971	$ —	$ 45,971
Fulfillment	10,766	(375)	10,391	8,585	(294)	8,291	6,419	(212)	6,207
Marketing	4,332	(125)	4,207	3,133	(88)	3,045	2,408	(61)	2,347
Technology and content	9,275	(804)	8,471	6,565	(603)	5,962	4,564	(434)	4,130
General and administrative	1,552	(193)	1,359	1,129	(149)	980	896	(126)	770
Other operating expense (income), net	133	—	133	114	—	114	159	—	159
Total operating expenses	$ 88,810	$ (1,497)	$ 87,313	$ 73,707	$ (1,134)	$ 72,573	$ 60,417	$ (833)	$ 59,584
Year-over-year Percentage Growth:									
Fulfillment	25%		25%	34%		34%	40%		40%
Marketing	38		38	30		30	48		47
Technology and content	41		42	44		44	57		58
General and administrative	37		39	26		27	36		36
Percent of Net Sales:									
Fulfillment	12.1%		11.7%	11.5%		11.1%	10.5%		10.2%
Marketing	4.9		4.7	4.2		4.1	3.9		3.8
Technology and content	10.4		9.5	8.8		8.0	7.5		6.8
General and administrative	1.7		1.5	1.5		1.3	1.5		1.3

Source: Amazon 2014 Annual Report. United States Securities and Exchange Commission, Form 10-K. Page 3.
<https://www.sec.gov/Archives/edgar/data/1018724/000101872415000006/amzn-20141231x10k.htm>

Exhibit 6: Amazon Income Statement 2014

AMAZON.COM, INC.

CONSOLIDATED STATEMENTS OF OPERATIONS
(in millions, except per share data)

	Year Ended December 31,		
	2014	2013	2012
Net product sales	$ 70,080	$ 60,903	$ 51,733
Net service sales	18,908	13,549	9,360
Total net sales	88,988	74,452	61,093
Operating expenses (1):			
Cost of sales	62,752	54,181	45,971
Fulfillment	10,766	8,585	6,419
Marketing	4,332	3,133	2,408
Technology and content	9,275	6,565	4,564
General and administrative	1,552	1,129	896
Other operating expense (income), net	133	114	159
Total operating expenses	88,810	73,707	60,417
Income from operations	178	745	676
Interest income	39	38	40
Interest expense	(210)	(141)	(92)
Other income (expense), net	(118)	(136)	(80)
Total non-operating income (expense)	(289)	(239)	(132)
Income (loss) before income taxes	(111)	506	544
Provision for income taxes	(167)	(161)	(428)
Equity-method investment activity, net of tax	37	(71)	(155)
Net income (loss)	$ (241)	$ 274	$ (39)
Basic earnings per share	$ (0.52)	$ 0.60	$ (0.09)
Diluted earnings per share	$ (0.52)	$ 0.59	$ (0.09)
Weighted average shares used in computation of earnings per share:			
Basic	462	457	453
Diluted	462	465	453
(1) Includes stock-based compensation as follows:			
Fulfillment	$ 375	$ 294	$ 212
Marketing	125	88	61
Technology and content	804	603	434
General and administrative	193	149	126

See accompanying notes to consolidated financial statements.

Exhibit 7: Amazon Balance Sheet 2014

AMAZON.COM, INC.

CONSOLIDATED BALANCE SHEETS
(in millions, except per share data)

	December 31,	
	2014	2013
ASSETS		
Current assets:		
Cash and cash equivalents	$ 14,557	$ 8,658
Marketable securities	2,859	3,789
Inventories	8,299	7,411
Accounts receivable, net and other	5,612	4,767
Total current assets	31,327	24,625
Property and equipment, net	16,967	10,949
Goodwill	3,319	2,655
Other assets	2,892	1,930
Total assets	$ 54,505	$ 40,159
LIABILITIES AND STOCKHOLDERS' EQUITY		
Current liabilities:		
Accounts payable	$ 16,459	$ 15,133
Accrued expenses and other	9,807	6,688
Unearned revenue	1,823	1,159
Total current liabilities	28,089	22,980
Long-term debt	8,265	3,191
Other long-term liabilities	7,410	4,242
Commitments and contingencies (Note 8)		
Stockholders' equity:		
Preferred stock, $0.01 par value:		
Authorized shares — 500		
Issued and outstanding shares — none	—	—
Common stock, $0.01 par value:		
Authorized shares — 5,000		
Issued shares — 488 and 483		
Outstanding shares — 465 and 459	5	5
Treasury stock, at cost	(1,837)	(1,837)
Additional paid-in capital	11,135	9,573
Accumulated other comprehensive loss	(511)	(185)
Retained earnings	1,949	2,190
Total stockholders' equity	10,741	9,746
Total liabilities and stockholders' equity	$ 54,505	$ 40,159

See accompanying notes to consolidated financial statements.

Source: Amazon 2014 Annual Report. United States Securities and Exchange Commission, Form 10-K. Page 3.
<https://www.sec.gov/Archives/edgar/data/1018724/000101872415000006/amzn-20141231x10k.htm>

Model Documents

This appendix opens with a discussion of some key elements of message formatting and design and then provides examples of a variety of business message formats, including memos, e-mails, letters, employment messages, short reports and proposals, and press releases. In addition to formatting examples, you will also find examples of messages intended for different purposes: routine claims, bad news, direct requests, and persuasive messages.

Design Elements

There are several aspects of visual impression to consider when designing a written message. These include the following:

- Format
- Use of space
- Font selection.

Format

The *format* of the document should use the conventions of business writing. Most business audiences know what a memo should look like, just as they know the conventional format for a letter. Reports also have conventional formats with which most business audiences are familiar. If you do not follow these formats, you indicate to your reader that you are not familiar with those conventions and thus are undereducated in this regard or are not a professional, since you aren't aware of professional expectations and practices. This perception, of course, can affect your credibility.

The proper format to use depends upon your audience and purpose. If you are writing a hard-copy message to an audience that is *internal* to your organization, you should use a memo format. If you are writing a hard-copy message to an audience that is *external* to your organization, you should use a letter format. E-mail messages to both internal and external audiences use a combination of features from both letters and memos. Similarly, reports and proposals can be prepared for both internal and external audiences. These formats are typically used to deliver longer, more complex messages than those conveyed in a memo, letter, or e-mail message. Another common business format is that of the résumé. Examples of each of these common business formats can be found later in this appendix.

Use of Space

Use of *space* on the page involves decisions about various design elements, including the width of the margins, the space between paragraphs, and the use of lists, headings, and graphics. Using space appropriately can make a document more pleasing and inviting to read. Use of space can have subtle effects upon the reader and can also send messages about you as the writer.

Typically, the margin width of business documents is one inch at the top, sides, and bottom of the page. Margins should not be too wide, since that sends the message that you are attempting to make your document look longer or more complete. They should not be too narrow, since that sends the message that you need to edit your document to make it fit the space provided, and that you may have failed to do so.

The conventional spacing of business documents, regardless of the format, is single spacing within paragraphs and double spacing between paragraphs. Because of this visual cue—a blank space between paragraphs—indenting the beginning of each paragraph is not necessary. Use of too much space between paragraphs can also make your document look as if it is not substantial in content or that you are stretching your information to make it look more substantial than it is.

Paragraphs in business documents should be seven to eight lines in length. Creating paragraphs that are shorter in length is called *chunking*. Chunking has a psychological effect on the reader that makes a document look easier to skim; provides more white space, which makes it more pleasing in appearance; and makes a document look easier to read overall. Readers may be discouraged from reading a document that contains one large paragraph or a few large paragraphs, because the document looks too difficult to skim or too time-consuming to read.

Font Choice

Font choice can affect the readability of a document as well as subtly set a tone for the document. There are two types of font: serif and sans serif. Examples of serif type include Times New Roman, Courier, and Bookman. Examples of sans serif type are Arial, Univers, and Verdana. Serif is typically used for large blocks of text, because it provides more information for the eye and is thus considered easier to read. However, serif type also gives a document a more conservative visual impression. It can therefore be used as a design element to create a particular image for your company.

Sans serif type, because of its cleaner appearance, gives a document a more modern look. If you wish your documents to look more modern, yet still be highly readable for your audiences, you might use sans serif type for headings and other design elements and serif for large blocks of text.

Another consideration when selecting a font is its size. Typically, a 12-point font size for written messages is considered large enough to be easily read by most audiences.

Message Formats

This section provides examples of a variety of messages, including memos, e-mails, letters, employment messages, reports and proposals, and press releases.

Memo Format

Much of the difficulty of properly formatting business messages has been eliminated by word processing and other types of software that provide document templates. An example of a memo format is provided in Figure A-1.

A memorandum is an internal message that is characterized by its header, as shown in the example above. An important feature of the header is the Subject line. The Subject line should contain a specific, informative phrase intended to capture your audience's attention.

Like most business messages, memos are typically single-spaced, with double spaces between paragraphs. Typically, memos are not signed by the sender. However, if you wish to personalize a memo, signing your initials by your name is a common practice.

Letter Formats

As stated earlier, letters rather than memos are used to communicate more formally with audiences external to an organization. You may choose from several types of letter formats. The two most common are the block and the modified block format. An example of a block format for a letter is provided in Figure A-2.

Figure A-1 Example of a Memo Format

Memorandum

To: All employees
From: Jane Doe, HR supervisor
Date: May 14, 2018
From: Memorial Day holiday observance

As you may know, the Memorial Day holiday falls on Monday, May 28, this year. That means that we will be closing our offices on Monday, May 28, to honor the holiday. Our offices will reopen on Tuesday, May 29.

We in the Human Resources department wish you all a happy and safe Memorial Day holiday.

Figure A-2 Example of a Block Format Letter

Salestek, Inc.
128 Main Street
Middletown, IA 73220

December 2, 2018

Melanie Smith
ABC Products Co.
346 Center Avenue
Berg, PA 23009

Dear Ms. Smith:

Your order of November 19, 2018 has been received and processed by our company. You should be receiving the shipment in five to seven business days.

Your business is appreciated, so please let us know how we might continue to provide you the best service possible. If you have any questions about the products you receive, please call me toll free at 1-800-644-9900.

Sincerely,

Todd Jones

Todd Jones
Shipping Manager

As shown in Figure A-2, all text in a block format letter is left justified, or lined up with the left margin. This format is probably the most commonly used because the left justification makes it easier and faster to create.

An example of the second common type of letter format, modified block, is provided in Figure A-3.

In the modified block format letter, you will notice that the address of the sender, the date, and the signature block are aligned on the right side of the page.

E-mail Format

Formatting e-mail messages is fairly simple, since the computer program you are using prompts you for the elements of the header. These elements are similar to those used in a memo: To, From, and Subject. Typically, the program you are using will automatically insert the information for the sender (yourself), while you need to type in the receiver's e-mail address and the subject line. As in a memo, you should insert a specific, informative phrase intended to capture your audience's attention.

An e-mail message also incorporates elements from a letter format. Both letters and e-mail messages, for example, typically include a salutation at the beginning and a signature at the end. Most e-mail programs enable you to create a signature file that will automatically be added to the

Figure A-3 Example of a Modified Block Format Letter

Salestek, Inc.
128 Main Street
Middletown, IA 73220

December 2, 2018

Melanie Smith
ABC Products Co.
346 Center Avenue
Berg, PA 23009

Dear Ms. Smith:

Your order of November 19, 2018 has been received and processed by our company. You should be receiving the shipment in five to seven business days.

Your business is appreciated, so please let us know how we might continue to provide you the best service possible. If you have any questions about the products you receive, please call me toll free at 1-800-644-9900.

Sincerely,

Todd Jones

Todd Jones
Shipping Manager

end of each message when it is sent. A signature file includes the name, title, organization, and contact information of the sender.

Finally, it is important for an e-mail message to be as grammatically correct as any other type of written message and to use correct punctuation and spelling, since errors can negatively affect the clarity of the message as well as the credibility of the sender. You should avoid using all capital letters when writing e-mail messages, because it can appear as if you are shouting at the receiver. The use of all capital letters in an e-mail can thus negatively affect the tone of the message.

Attention to tone is particularly important in e-mail messages, since they can be written so quickly and sent. You should never write an e-mail message when you are experiencing negative emotions, such as frustration, impatience, or anger, since the emotions will undoubtedly come through in your message and may negatively affect your credibility and relationship with your audience. An example of an e-mail message is provided in Figure A-4.

Figure A-4 Example of an E-mail Message

To:	Linda Roberts, Loan Officer
From:	Juan Alvarez, Director of Loan Compliance
Subject:	New Policies Affect Loans to Real-Estate Investors

Linda,

Please be aware of the new policies regarding mortgages to real-estate investors.

Loans can no longer be made to mortgage applicants who already have four or more outstanding mortgages. Because of the problems caused by the sub-prime lending situation, we are required to limit our exposure to mortgage debt. Applicants who have four or more active mortgages are now considered too risky because of a potential lack of liquidity in their current asset portfolio.

You will find this latest policy change attached to this message. Please come by my office if you have additional questions after reading the attached policy statement.

Regards,
Juan

Résumé Formats

Another conventional format used in business situations is the résumé. The contents of a résumé should be narrowly targeted to show that you are well qualified for a particular position. Information is typically provided in three areas: work experience, education, and leadership or organization membership. Under each of these categories, information is typically provided in the form of bullet lists. Using complete sentences and paragraphs should be avoided in a résumé, since they require your reader to spend more time retrieving the information he or she is looking for.

Several formats for résumés exist, but the most common and often most favored is the chronological résumé, in which you present your qualifications chronologically. In other words, your most recent experiences should appear at the top of each category, followed in descending order by those that are your least recent in time. An example of a chronological résumé is provided in Figure A-5.

An element that you might consider adding to a chronological résumé is an "objective" statement at its beginning. Experts disagree about the inclusion of an objective statement. Some say it is a necessary element, while others say that the objective statement often adds little to a résumé. All agree that excellent objective statements are difficult to write. An excellent objective statement should identify the unique contributions that you can make to a particular employer. Reading the job description carefully can give you some idea of the specific skills, abilities, and personal characteristics that a particular employer is looking for.

Increasingly, résumés are being submitted electronically to Web job banks. Résumés submitted to job banks are reviewed by a search engine that is programmed to search for keywords that correspond to the qualifications for which the employer is looking. For this reason, it is important to list the qualifications for the job in a keywords section of the résumé. Of course, it is important that you do in fact have these qualifications, since eventually a human being will read your résumé carefully and discover whether you are indeed qualified for the job.

Figure A-5 Example of a Chronological Résumé

Joan Donne
348 Elm Street
Middletown, MO 73301
203-667-3211

Work Experience

May 2014 to present

Staff Accountant, EST International
Jonestown, MO

- Prepared accounting reports for wholesale importer ($1 million annual sales)
- Handled budgeting, billing, and credit-processing functions
- Audited financial transactions with suppliers in three Asian countries

August 2012 – May 2014

Accounting Intern, Outerwear Sports
St. Louis, MO

- Assisted in billing and credit-processing functions of retail business ($500,000 annual sales)
- Assisted in launching an online computer system to automate all accounting functions

Education

Bachelor's degree, Accounting, University of Missouri, 2009–2012
Dean's List 2010, 2011, 2012

Volunteer and Professional Experience

- Volunteer for Habitat for Humanity
- Secretary of Accounting Association of America

As you may note, electronic résumés often do not contain some of the design elements of paper résumés because these may not appear as they do in a word processing program. An example of an electronic résumé is provided in Figure A-6.

Figure A-6 Example of an Electronic Résumé

JOSEPH PRIESTLEY
89 Lincoln Street
Santa Fe, NM 78285-9063
512-555-9823
jpriestley@hotmail.com

Professional Profile
- Technical proficiency in ERP systems, ACL, database, and spreadsheet software.
- Hands-on experience in accounting gained through internship with well-regarded local firm.
- Excellent interpersonal communication and teamwork skills developed through course projects and active involvement in student organizations.
- Ability to manage time effectively, excellent work ethic, and dedication to high-quality work as demonstrated by 3.87 GPA and part-time work to finance my education.

Keywords
Bachelor's degree in accounting. Entry-level accounting experience. Knowledge of basic accounting principles and practices. Excellent communication skills. Personal characteristics, including good work ethic, ability to manage time efficiently, and dedicated to producing quality work.

Education
B.B.A., Accounting, University of New Mexico, May 2018, GPA 3.87
- Dean's List, 2016, 2017, 2018
- Deanna D. Darling Academic Scholarship

Technical Skills
Proficient in Microsoft Office Suite, database and spreadsheet software, ERP systems, and ACL.

Related Employment
Intern, Gerald and Associates, CPAs, Santa Fe, NM, June–August 2016
- Shadowed auditor and helped to write numerous auditing reports for corporate clients.
- Created and maintained spreadsheets and databases containing client audit information.
- Worked with audit teams to hone communication skills and developed phone skills necessary to effectively interact with professional clientele.

Other Employment
- Server, Bubba's BBQ, Santa Fe, NM, 2014–2017
- Stockperson, University of New Mexico Bookstore, Santa Fe, NM, 2014–2015

Leadership Activities
Beta Alpha Psi, honorary accounting society, 2014–2017, chapter president, 2016–2017, chess team, 2014–2017, president, 2015–2016

An attractive and fully formatted hard copy version of this document is available upon request.

Additional Employment Messages

Additional types of employment messages include application letters, follow-up or thank-you letters, job refusal and job acceptance letters, and resignation letters.

An application letter is often sent as a cover message for a résumé, while a follow-up letter is sent to thank the interviewer for an interview. A well-written application letter would focus on the audience's or employer's needs and concerns and show how the applicant will meet these needs and benefit the employer. Furthermore, a well-written application letter would provide concrete evidence to illustrate that the potential employee has the skills and abilities for which the employer is looking. It should be noted that an application letter differs from a résumé in that the information in a résumé is more general: it could be sent to any company or organization with a similar job opening. A letter, on the other hand, should be more specific to the needs of a particular organization.

Figure A-7 provides an example of an application letter that is audience-centered and that provides the information for which an employer is looking. The letter is in response to the following job advertisement:

Example of a Job Advertisement

Entry-Level Accounting Position

XYZ Accounting Consultants is an international company that provides accounting services to large corporate clients. XYZ Accounting Consultants is currently looking for applicants for its entry-level accounting position. The qualified applicant should have the following:

- A bachelor's degree in accounting.
- Entry-level accounting experience.
- Knowledge of basic accounting principles and practices.
- Excellent communication skills.
- Such personal characteristics as being hardworking, able to manage time efficiently, and dedicated to producing quality work.

Please send letters of application and résumés to the manager of our Los Angeles office, 345 Figueroa Street, Los Angeles, CA 90001.

A job advertisement is often the best source for identifying what an employer is looking for in an applicant. A well-written application letter will use the same language as the advertisement to refer to the applicant's skills. Using the same language makes it easier for the employer to read the message, since he or she is looking for that information; it also shows that the applicant is knowledgeable about those qualifications and addresses them specifically.

It is often acceptable nowadays to send application letters via e-mail. Figure A-8 provides a sample message to accompany an electronic submission of employment materials.

Another type of employment message is the follow-up letter or thank-you note. These messages should be sent after an interview to thank the interviewer for taking the time to speak with you and to emphasize your key selling points. The message also might be used to provide information that may be relevant to the position but which was not covered during the interview. A follow-up letter can be helpful in establishing goodwill and distinguishing you from other candidates who do not attend to the importance of goodwill in business relationships. An example of a follow-up letter is provided in Figure A-9.

Once you have been offered a job, it may be a good idea to formally accept the offer by sending a job acceptance message. An example of a job acceptance message sent via e-mail is provided in Figure A-10.

Figure A-7 Example of an Audience-Focused Application

JoAnn Dunn
123 Sepulveda Street
Los Angeles, CA 90001
(213) 741-4567
jdunn@midtown.edu

February 1, 2018

Maria Munoz, Manager
XYZ Accounting Consultants
345 Figueroa Street
Los Angeles, CA 90001

Dear Ms. Munoz:

I am responding to your ad for an entry-level accountant that was posted on JOBSTAR. I have all the attributes your company is looking for in a new employee. I am knowledgeable of accounting principles and practices, I have recent accounting experience, and I am a hard worker with excellent time management skills.

As a student at Midtown University, I have taken many accounting courses to help me prepare for a career in accounting. These course include Financial Accounting, Tax Accounting, and Accounting and the Law. I did very well in these courses, earning an 'A' grade for my work in each. This knowledge prepares me well to begin contributing to your company's goals immediately as an entry-level accountant.

I have had the additional opportunity to put this knowledge into practice during my internship last summer at Deloitte and Touche. I assisted an account executive to audit and prepare reports for three Fortune 500 companies. This experience also enabled me to practice and improve my writing and speaking skills, which will benefit you by enabling me to represent your company as a well-spoken and credible professional.

I also work hard and have excellent time management skills. Not only was I able to attend college full-time and maintain a 3.5 GPA, but I also worked full-time as a sales associate at Office Max to fund my education. These characteristics will enable me to be an efficient employee who doesn't stop until I get the job done while still maintaining quality work.

I would like to schedule an interview with you to discuss my qualifications further. I will call you next week to set up an appointment at your earliest convenience.

Sincerely,

JoAnn Dunn

JoAnn Dunn

Figure A-8 Example of a Job Application Message Sent Electronically

To:	mthomas@axumpharma.com
From:	mmarvel@unj.edu
Subject:	Career Fair Follow-up: Résumé for Mary Anne Marvel

October 24, 2018

Monte Thomas
Human Resources Manager
Azum Pharmaceuticals, Inc.
1208 West 34th Street
New York, NY 23140-1000

Dear Mr. Thomas:

It was a pleasure meeting you at the career fair this morning. The opportunities offered in pharmaceutical sales identify your company as a leader in today's global marketplace.

My education and related work experience in sales enable me to be a valuable asset to your company.

- A degree in communication with a minor in marketing from the University of New Jersey.
- Knowledge of the medical field gained as an administrative assistant at Dr. Joan Petti's internal medicine practice.
- Customer service skills gained as a sales associate at North Street Drug and Pharmacy.
- Excellent communication skills gained through numerous group projects in an academic setting and through three years' experience working with colleagues and customers in fast-paced retail and healthcare environments.

Please review the attached résumé that you requested for additional information about my education and work experience. Please contact me so we can discuss my joining Axum Pharmaceuticals.

Sincerely,
MaryAnne Marvel

Figure A-9 Example of a Follow-up Letter

Alma Rosario
42 Doe Court
Miramar, CA 92145

September 18, 2018

William Wagner
Human Resources Director
Carson Fine Foods
301 Torrey Pines Road
La Jolla, CA 92037

Dear Mr. Wagner:

Thank you for taking the time to meet with me today to discuss the position of Financial Planning Analyst with Carson Fine Foods. During our discussion, you stated that you're looking for an organized and outgoing candidate to join your team. Through my previous work and life experience, I gained organizational and customer development skills and learned how to meet goals through teamwork. In my position with Biotech Inc., I communicated with internal and external customers and assisted in efficiency and customer relations for the Fraud Detection program. I am confident that my skills and background will make me as asset as a Financial Planning Analyst with Carson Fine Foods.

I am eager to discuss this opportunity with you further. Please let me know what additional information I can provide you and your colleagues in order to secure this position and begin working for your organization.

Sincerely,

Alma Rosario
Alma Rosario

Figure A-10 Example of a Job Acceptance Message

To:	llouis@kmart.com
From:	tturner@pmi.edu
Subject:	Job Offer Follow-Up: I Accept

Leonard,

I accept your employment offer as a management trainee. Thank you for responding so quickly after our discussion on Tuesday.

As you requested, I have signed the agreement outlining the specific details of my employment. You should receive the signed agreement today. I have kept a copy for my records.

If you should need to speak with me before I report to work on June 15, please call me at 999-4321.

Best regards,
Tony

You may receive job offers that you choose not to accept. In this case, you may wish to send a job refusal message. An example of a job refusal message sent via e-mail is provided in Figure A-11.

Figure A-11 Example of a Job Refusal Message

To:	tmilburn@sunfashions.com
From:	rosborne@smu.edu
Subject:	Job Offer Decision

Tony,

I appreciate your spending time with me discussing the sales associate position.

Your feedback regarding my fit for your organization and the opportunities available to me were particularly valuable. Having received offers in both sales and marketing, I feel that a career in the latter field better suits my personality and long-term career goals. Today, I am accepting an entry-level marketing position with Fashion Trends Inc.

Thank you for your confidence demonstrated by the offer. When I hear about Sun Fashion's continued success, I will think of the dedicated people who work for the company

Sincerely,
Renee

On the other end of the career spectrum, there may come a time when you want to quit a job to take another or to take a break from employment. Figure A-12 provides an example of a message sent to resign from an employment situation using e-mail.

Figure A-12 Example of a Resignation Message

To:	bromans@firstnational.com
From:	mromirez@firsnational.com
Subject:	Pleasure of Serving First National Bank

Betsy,

My job as a customer service associate at First National Bank the past year has been a rewarding experience. It has taught me a great deal about the banking industry and providing excellent customer service.

Learning about the business of banking has been particularly exciting. From the time I declared a major in finance, I have wanted to work with investment products. Before I accepted my current position, that goal was discussed. Now, that goal is becoming a reality, as I have accepted a job as a sales trainee in the investment division of WideWorld beginning one month from today. If satisfactory with you, I would like June 1 to be may last day here.

Thank you for the confidence you placed in me, you support of customer service associates, and your feedback to help me continue growing as a value employee. As I continue my career in investment banking, I will take with me many pleasant memories of my time with First National.

Best regards,
Maria

Components of Reports and Proposals

Reports and proposals can be either informal or formal in design, style, and content. Informal reports and proposals typically use memo formats. The components that are often included in a formal report are listed below:

- Title page
- Table of contents
- Executive summary
- Introduction
- Background
- Discussion of the problem
- Conclusions
- Recommendations
- Appendixes, if appropriate.

Figure A-13 provides a sample of an informal report delivered to an external audience using a letter format.

Figure A-13 Example of an Informal Report Using a Letter Format

April 3, 2018

Linda Ruiz
President, Massive Corp.
600 Western Avenue
Atlanta, GA 30360-1660

Dear Ms. Ruiz:

RECOMMENDATIONS FOR IMPLEMENTING INTERNAL COMMUNICATION PLAN AT MASSIVE

Thank you for allowing us to assist you in the recent communication audit of your organization. Studies have shown that improved communication practices can minimize costly mistakes, improve morale, and improve customer relations, all of which can add to the corporate bottom line.

Procedures

In preparing this report, data was gathered using a variety of methods. Interviews were conducted with all management personnel regarding the flow and channels of communication used in the organization as well as their perceptions of communication effectiveness. Focus groups composed of employees from each of the company's departments were also used to gather similar information and perceptions from the rank and file. To double-check the validity of these methods and response that we received to our questions, an online survey was disseminated to all employees. The responses from these methods of data gathering along with our proven knowledge of corporate communication policies and practices led to the recommendations in this report.

Findings

Research revealed useful information concerning Massive's current communication processes and practices.

<u>Results of Interviews with Management Personnel</u>

Across the board, management stated that it did not see any problems with the communication flow and channels currently used at Massive. However, when specific questions were asked about productivity, efficiency, morale, and losses from mistakes and misunderstadings, a different picture emerged. Eighty percent of management personnel answered affirmatively to the following questions:

- Have you witnessed or heard about mistakes being made by employees because the information or instructions provided to them was interpreted incorrectly?
- Have you ever had an employee express frustration to you because he or she believed that management did not know what was occurring in his or her department or at lower levels of the organization?
- Do you think that the current communication process used by your organization could be streamlined to help make task completion by employees faster?

1

Figure A-13 Example of an Informal Report Using a Letter Format *(continued)*

Internal Communication Plan, Page 2

From our interviews with management personnel, two pictures emerged; on the surface, they believe communication practices and processes at Massive are sufficient, but when pressed about particular issues, the majority believed improvements could be made.

Results of Focus Groups with Employees

Nine focus groups were conducted with employees from each of Massive's departments. Focus group size ranged from eight to twelve persons. Unlike the responses we initially received from management, employees generally believed there were numerous areas for improvement in Massive's communication practices.

All participants said that management did not listen to employees at lower levels and did not solicit suggestions from them. The results, according to employees, were that management did not value employees, did not have the information it needed to make good decisions, and was reactive when dealing with problems rather than proactive.

Furthermore, employees said that they did not feel that management clearly communicated organizational goals, activities, and events. The result was that employees often felt disconnected and devalued because they were not seen as a source for solutions. Employees said that Massive did not have a team culture. In the words of one employee, Massive is "a collection of individuals, all going their own separate way."

Results of Company-Wide Questionnaire

Of the 405 questionnaires sent out via e-mail, we received responses from 349 employees. The responses to the questionnaire closely followed the responses we received from employee focus groups. The results from the survey are summarized below. The questionnaire can be found in the Appendix.

Question	Always	Sometimes	Never
1	5 percent	34 percent	61 percent
2	10 percent	50 percent	40 percent
3			
4	16 percent	60 percent	24 percent
5	6 percent	42 percent	51 percent
6	20 percent	62 percent	15 percent
7	11 percent	34 percent	55 percent
8	19 percent	48 percent	31 percent

Figure A-13 Example of an Informal Report Using a Letter Format *(continued)*

Internal Communication Plan, Page 3

Recommendations

The primary recommendations for Massive are:

1. Improve the upward flow of communication from employees to management. Not only does this recommendation require changes in the company's communication practices but also its organizational culture. Management needs to become more open to others' ideas and more informal with its interactions with employees. It also needs to become much more active in, and present at, daily operations throughout the company. More formally, departments need to have regular meetings to gather ideas from employees and this information needs to be spread throughout the organization. Management should encourage employees to send them suggestions through all channels of communication.
2. Improved downward flow of communication from employees to management. Management needs to actively share corporate goals, strategies, activities, and events that affect the company and its employees. This can be done through a variety of channels, including regular e-mail messages, weekly or monthly company meetings, and a monthly company newsletter posted on the company website.
3. Improved horizontal flow of communication. This issue has been addressed in Step 1. Regular meetings among all department heads that share departmental activities and concerns as well as those of employees can lead to better decision making through better coordination of solutions.

Advantages of Implementing Recommendations

Organizational studies have shown that implementing such a communication plan may result in a number of advantages:

- **Improved attitudes.** People who feel valued for their ideas and appreciated by management and colleagues generally have higher morale.
- **Increased productivity.** Enhanced, systematic communication plans can lead to higher-quality work, greater professional commitment, and increased company loyalty.
- **Better decision making.** Communication practices that enable companies to gather more information from knowledgeable parties often lead to better, more effective solutions.
- **Greater profitability.** Higher morale, increased productivity, and more effective solutions lead to greater profitability.

Thank you for the opportunity to audit Massive's internal communication practices and to provide our results and recommendations for improvement. Please let us know how we can assist you further with the implementation of our proposed plan and the monitoring of its effectiveness.

Sincerely,

Hasan Hassoud

Hasan Hassoud, Consultant

ksm

Enclosure: Appendix

Proposals are sales documents that are intended to recommend changes or purchases within a company, or to show how your organization can meet the needs of another, if intended for an external audience. A formal proposal may include the following components:

- Proposed idea and purpose, or what is often called the "project description"
- Scope, or what you propose to do
- Methods or procedures to be used
- Materials and equipment needed
- Qualifications of personnel who will be working on the project
- Follow-up and/or evaluation of the project
- Budget or costs of the project
- Summary of proposal
- Appendices, if appropriate.

An example of a short proposal is provided in Figure A-14.

Press Releases

An example of a press release is provided in Figure A-15.

Messages for Differing Purposes

This section provides examples of messages for a variety of purposes: routine claims (Figure A-16), confirming order receipt (Figure A-17), extending credit (Figure A-18), bad news (claim denial) (Figure A-19), and a sales message for promoting a service (Figure A-20).

Figure A-14 Example of a Short Proposal

PROPOSAL FOR IMPLEMENTATION OF
INTERNAL COMMUNICATION PLAN

for Massive Corp.

by Hasan Hassoud, Communications Consultant

May 1, 2018

Purpose

After careful study, the management of Massive Corp. has decided to implement the internal communication plan that was recommended last month. The internal communication plan is designed to improve communication at every level of Massive Corp.

Proposed Plan Implementation

The implementation of the internal communication plan will be directed by myself, Hasan Hassoud. Three additional consultants, Jana Lowry, Teresa Warner, and Ted Mitchell, will complete the team involved with plan implementation.

Implementation Process

The implementation process will begin with a two-day retreat for all management personnel. This retreat will provide a number of sessions, including "Bringing about Corporate Culture Change," "Creating and Sharing Corporate Visions," "Leading Effective Meetings," and "Managing by Walking Around." The retreat will conclude with the creation of a schedule for regular meetings to be held at all levels of the organization. These meetings are intended to impart the new cultural values to employees and to provide for the transmission of information from employees to management and vice versa.

The next step in the process will take place at the scheduled meetings. Our consultants will attend the first of each of these departmental meetings. Consultants will then meet with each manager to provide feedback and coaching (if necessary) to support him or her in effective transmission of the corporate message as well as the gathering of information from employees.

After the initial visit to each department meeting as well as those at the management and company-wide level, our consultants will visit a second meeting to observe how well managers are implementing their new skills and provide any needed feedback. If certain managers need additional support, this can be arranged. Subsequent meeting visits will be provided monthly for a period of six months.

1

Figure A-14 Example of a Short Proposal *(continued)*

Plan Assessment

At the end of the six-month period, our consultants will assess how well the plan has been implemented and whether employees believe it has been successful. This assessment will be performed using two methods: two focus groups composed of a random selection of employees and a second online questionnaire disseminated to all employees. The findings from this assessment will be communicated to Massive's corporate team.

Length of Plan Implementation

As outlined above, implementation of the plan will be performed over a six-month period, beginning with a two-day retreat and consisting of seven additional visits to all departmental, management, and company-wide meetings. If desired, an assessment of the plan implementation will be conducted at the end of six months. This assessment will consist of two one-hour focus groups and the dissemination of an online questionnaire to all employees.

Number of Participants

The plan will serve all Massive employees, which is reportedly 405.

Cost

Exact cost figures are as follows:

Professional fees for retreat workshop	$ 2,400.00
Rental of retreat site and meals for 20 persons	3,500.00
Professional fees for meeting visits and coaching	10,000.00
Plan assessment	2,000.00
Total	$17,900.00

Figure A-15 Example of a Press Release

Marine Industrial Corporation Acquires Renowned
Process Improvement TechKron Inc.

Date: October 11, 2018

CONTACT INFORMATION:
Belinda Morales
Director OEM Sales
Tel: 502-210-1652
Email: bmorales@marineindustrial.com

TECHKRON INC. JOINS MARINE INDUSTRIAL CORPORATION
(EMAILWIRE.COM, October 11, 2018) San Diego, CA — Marine Industrial Corporation (QIS) acquires TechKron Inc. Known as an industry leader in quality assurance, Marine Industrial brings in TechKron, an ISO/IEC 17025:2005 accredited company with engineering capabilities, Advanced Product Quality Planning, Six Sigma, and Coordinate Measuring Machine Services to take its business to new heights in the automotive manufacturing processes.

The acquisition will improve Marine Industrial's Quality Engineering Department, add 100 employees to its workforce, and increase its market share and geographic footprint to Saginaw, MI, Baltimore, MD, Indianapolis, IN, and Spartanburg, SC.

Belinda Morales, director of Business Development, said, "The addition of TechKron's specialty services and expanded geographic footprint will allow Marine Industrial to provide a broader range of capabilities to our customers. In today's competitive manufacturing market, many organizations are faced with the never-ending challenge of continual cost reductions. Outsourcing of noncritical production services is becoming a more prevalent approach to such savings. Marine Industrial can facilitate this need by now offering even more cost-effective solutions with a greater diversity of services."

Leo Cragmoor, COO of TechKron, states, "The acquisition of TechKron by Marine Industrial will provide a major benefit to our existing and future customers. They bring a level of expertise and experience that will compliment and enhance our core services. I am confident that the acquisition will allow us to further improve our quality of service and dramatically expand our market share."

Marine Industrial Corporation is an ISO-certified Quality Assurance Service provider that specializes in a diverse line of services targeted at reducing automotive manufacturing costs while increasing quality, productivity, and efficiency.

Marine Industrials' core competencies include Engineering, Inspection, Sorting, Containment, Rework, Light Assembly, CMM, Training, Kitting, and Packaging. Marine Industrial is one of the largest such suppliers in the nation with 23 U.S. locations, six Mexico locations, and one Canadian location. Marine Industrial is an approved vendor for most major OEMs and has more than 2,500 active customers to date. By providing skilled and trained employees to our customers, Marine Industrial has become an integral part of the supply chain in every aspect of automotive production.

Figure A-16 Example of a Routine Claim

To:	Tom Bowls <tbowls@computersolutions.com>
From:	Jennifer Reagan <jreagan@lauder.com>
Subject:	Laptop Repair or Replacement Needed

Mr. Bowls,

Please repair or send us a replacement for the laptop computer listed on the attached sales agreement. It has a faulty cooling fan. You should receive the computer tomorrow via overnight freight.

The computer was purchased six months ago under our agreement with your company to provide our salespeople with laptops. The computers are covered by a twelve-month warranty for faulty parts replacement. I spoke with your sales manager, Tom Wilkins, this morning and he instructed me to contact you for extradited service.

Our salesperson Maria Rodriguez eagerly awaits the return of her laptop. Our salespeople are highly dependent on their computers because they spend so much time on the road.

Thanks,
Jennifer Reagan

Purchasing Manager

Figure A-17 Example of an Online Order Confirmation

To:	Dillon McCrea <dmcrea@pmail.com>
From:	Maggie Fielding <mfielding@firstline.com>
Subject:	Firstline welcomes Dillon as valued customer

Dillon,

Welcome to Firstline Insurance! I'm excited to see that you have enrolled as a new customer.

You will be contacted soon by your personal customer service representative, Lucille Burns. Lucille has been with the company for ten years and is well versed in our product line and receives top rankings in customer service.

Lucille will make sure that you have the right financial products to suit you and your family's needs. She will keep in touch regarding your family's changing needs and will inform you about beneficial changes to your financial planning.

I have complete confidence in the care you will receive from Lucille, but if for any reason you aren't completely satisfied or have other concerns, please let me know right away.

You can reach me at 213-561-8300, extension 201, or you can e-mail me at mfielding@firstline.com.

Thank you for trusting in us for your insurance needs.

Best regards,

Maggie Fielding
Customer Service Manager
Firstline Insurance Corp.

P.S. Be sure to watch your mailbox for our Welcome to Firstline package sent to new customers. You will receive coupons for discounts at several retail and restaurant outlets in your area as sign of our appreciation for your business.

Figure A-18 Example of Letter Extending Credit

January 23, 2018

Frances Ford
Purchasing Department
Pots and Pantries, Inc.
123 Colville Avenue
Spokane, WA 89001

Dear Ms. Ford:

Welcome to the most unique designs in glassware available in the U.S. Our expert buyers tour every region of the world to find the most innovative creations in kitchen and dining glassware.

Because of your current favorable credit rating, we are please to provide you with a $15,000 credit line subject to our standard 2/10, n/30 terms. By paying your invoice within ten days, you can save 2 percent on your glassware purchases.

You can use our convenient online ordering system to search our extensive line of glassware products and to place your orders. If you need additional assistance, please call our 24-hour service line, where you will be assisted by our number one-rated customer service personnel.

The most innovative glassware designs are now available to you and your customers, so please take some time to familiarize yourself with our extensive line.

Sincerely,

Luther Crosby

Luther Crosby
Credit Manager

Figure A-19 Example of a Claim Denial

June 14, 2018

Snowcap Limited
Attention: Lindsey Tucker
1905 Southhaven Street
Santa Fe, NM 87501-7313

Ladies and Gentlemen:

Restocking of Returned Merchandise

The HighFly skis you stocked this past season are skillfully crafted and made from the most innovative materials available. Maintaining a wide selection of quality skiing products is an excellent strategy for developing customer loyalty and maximizing your sales.

Our refund policies provide you the opportunity to keep a fully-stocked inventory at the lowest possible cost. You receive full refunds for merchandise returned within 10 days of receipt. For unsold merchandise returned after the primary selling season, a modest 15 percent restocking fee is charged to cover our costs of holding this merchandise until next season. The credit applied to your account for $2,069.75 covers merchandise you returned at the end of February.

While relaxing from another great skiing season, take a look at our new HighFly skis and other items available in the enclosed catalog for the 2019 season. You can save 10 percent by ordering premium ski products before March 10.

Sincerely,

Galen Fondren
Credit Manager

Enclosure: Catalog

Figure A-20 Example of a Sales Message Promoting a Service

April 1, 2018

Louisa Fox, Marketing Manager
Learner Consumer Products Group
2304 Pike Market Street
Seattle, WA 90322

Dear Ms. Fox:

Are you looking for help developing your organization's social media platform? ... improving your retail marketing? ... planning your external communication program? ... enhancing your mass advertising strategy? Then you need the services of the full-service brand engagement firm Souther and Associates to develop an integrated media plan that ensures your company's continued success.

With Souther and Associates' full-service capabilities, you will receive support in all of the following areas:

- Social media. Leverage the millions of conversations taking place through the use of social media by taking advantage of our four-step approach, which tracks conversations and dialogue; extracts insights from consumer conversations; interacts with key influences, brand advocates, and detractors; and measures consumer sentiment, advocacy, and engagement.

- Retail marketing. Engage consumers away from the noise and competing advertising, and reach them on an intimate, meaningful, and locally relevant level that will help you to drive trial, traffic, and sales.

- Communication planning. Build preference for your brand by translating emotional insights into high-impact brand strategy and innovation. Our experts bypass consumers' rational thinking with tools and techniques that are reactive and observational. Then, we integrate these emotional insights with your brand's functional benefits to create the foundation for lasting behavior change.

- Influence marketing. Mass advertising still plays an important role in branding, but these days, credibility is especially important, and who is more credible than a trusted professional? We identify professionals to give your products that powerful endorsement.

Visit www.souther.com today and check out the list of consulting services we provide and read real-life stories from past clients about how we increased brand awareness for them. If you contact us before May 15, you will also receive a free assessment of your current marketing program from our proprietary MarketLab analysis tool. Our team is ready to assist you in improving the impact of your marketing programs today. Please call me at 509-788-1302 to make an appointment with a consultant.

Sincerely,

Frank Forester

Frank Forester
Engagement Director

Enclosure

Punctuation, Sentence Structure, and Usage

This appendix contains the rules for common problems that occur in writing regarding punctuation, sentence structure, and grammar usage.

Punctuation

This section contains the rules for punctuation. These include the use of apostrophes, colons, commas, dashes, ellipses, hyphens, and semicolons.

Apostrophes

An apostrophe indicates possession. In addition, it is used to prevent misreading of confusing words.

1. Use an apostrophe to show possession.

   a. To form the possessive case of most singular nouns, add an apostrophe and an **-s**, such as "the **child's** backpack."

   b. When singular nouns end in **-s** or **-es**, add an apostrophe and an **-s** to the end of the word, such as "the **boss's** office."

   c. Add an apostrophe and an **-s** to show the possessive case of plural nouns that do not end in -s or -es, such as "the **children's** party."

   d. To show the possessive case of plural nouns ending in **-s** or **-es**, add only an apostrophe, such as "the **boys'** clubhouse."

   e. Add an apostrophe to show the possessive form of amounts, time, and the word "sake," such as in "one week's pay" or "for Pete's sake."

2. Use an apostrophe to replace missing letters or numbers, such as in can't (cannot) or class of '09 (class of 2009). In measurement, an apostrophe is used as a symbol for feet, such as in 3' × 11".

3. Use an apostrophe in words, letters, or abbreviations if it is confusing without the use of an apostrophe, such as in "crossing the i's and dotting the t's" or "polka-dotted pj's."

Colons

A colon (:) is primarily a mark of introduction of something that follows in a sentence. Use a colon only after a complete sentence.

1. Use a colon to introduce a series or list after a complete sentence:

   I needed to get several things at the grocery store: breakfast cereal, milk, bread, cheese, and fruit.

2. Use a colon to introduce an element that explains the previous sentence:

    The instructor concluded with an important thought: The early bird gets the worm.

3. Use a colon to form an appositive (a word that further explains a noun or pronoun):

    We will learn presentation skills from the best of the best: Tony Robbins.

4. Use a colon in special situations:

    a. A salutation in a business letter—Dear Ms. Hershell:

    b. Figures giving time—11:30 p.m. or 6:00 a.m.

    c. Subtitles of books or magazines—*Eating like a King: Three Weeks in France's Wine Country.*

    d. Biblical references to clarify between the chapter and verse—Luke 17:21.

Commas

A comma is used to define the relationships of various elements of a sentence and to clarify meaning for the reader.

1. Use a comma before a coordinating conjunction (*and, but, so, yet, for, nor*) between two main clauses:

    Interest rates are low, but people still aren't buying houses.

2. Use a comma to set off nonessential elements from the rest of the sentence:

    The company, which is headquartered in St. Louis, is planning to close ten regional offices.

3. Use a comma between items in a series of three or more:

    We had fried chicken, cole slaw, and apple cobbler at Uncle Bob's birthday party.

4. Use a comma to set off introductory elements at the beginning of a sentence:

    When her children went off to college, Carol started her own business.

5. Use a comma between two or more adjectives that equally modify the same word (these are called coordinate adjectives because each adjective describes the noun independently):

    The winding, gravel road led up to Martin's fishing cabin.

6. Use a comma to separate adjectives following a noun:

    Rudolpho, tanned and rested, returned to work ready for anything.

7. Use a comma in dates with at least three parts: day, month, year (place comma after the day):

    Jennifer's birthday is March 4, 1993.

8. Use a comma to separate the city from the state and the state from the rest of the sentence:

    Tucson, Arizona, is the best place to be in the winter.

9. Use a comma in numbers larger than three digits:

    The number of migrating birds returning this winter is estimated to be more than 240,000.

10. Use a comma to set off an appositive (a word that further explains a noun or pronoun).

    Theda, George's first wife, lives across town.

11. Use a comma after the name of a person being addressed in the beginning of a sentence:

    Leo, please drop off the mail on your way to school.

12. Use a comma before *such as, including,* and *especially* when the information that follows is not essential to the meaning of the sentence:

    We use a variety of communication media in the office, including e-mail, telephone, and fax.

13. Use a comma to separate transitional words from the rest of the sentence:

    Cecilia, however, will not be joining us for dinner.

14. Use a comma after a conjunctive adverb (*however, consequently, furthermore, therefore, otherwise*) that separates two complete sentences. (A semicolon must also be used before the conjunctive adverb.)

    I should go to bed early tonight; otherwise, I will be very tired for tomorrow's exam.

15. Use a comma inside quotation marks:

    "Man the lifeboats," the captain yelled.

Dashes

Dashes (—) are used to provide emphasis or clarity. Create a dash with two hyphens, and do not space before or after the dash.

1. Use a dash to create emphasis:

   The team leader—if you can call her that—missed our last meeting.

2. Use a dash to create greater clarity when other punctuation is used in a sentence:

   Some of the things needed to remodel the living room—paint, a ladder, and drop cloths—still need to be purchased.

3. Use a dash to separate elements in the sentence that abruptly interrupt the meaning:

   The children need 10,000 points—more or less—to qualify for the prize.

4. Use a dash to introduce items in a series when you want to create greater emphasis than a colon:

   We ate everything on the buffet—roast beef, barbecued chicken, poached salmon, grilled pork chops, and three kinds of dessert.

Ellipsis Points

Ellipsis points consist of three dots with spaces in between each dot (. . .). Ellipsis points are used to indicate missing words in a direct quotation. Ellipsis points can also be used at the end of a sentence when it seems to fade out before completing the thought.

1. Use ellipsis points to indicate missing words in a direct quotation:

   The minister said, "We must learn to love our neighbor … as we love ourselves."

2. Use ellipsis points to indicate the sentence fades out before completing the thought:

   Lisa yawned and said, "I'm just SO tired … When are we going to get there?"

Hyphens

A hyphen is used to connect two or more words in a sentence. Hyphenated words can act as modifiers or as compound words that can stand alone.

1. Use a hyphen with a compound modifier (two words used together to modify another word) when it comes before a noun:

   There is nothing like an old-fashioned root-beer float in the summer.

2. Use a hyphen with numbers between twenty-one and ninety-nine that are written out:

   Twenty-four children attended the birthday party.

3. Use a hyphen with some prefixes and suffixes (the prefixes *pre, post, self, pro,* and *ex* always require a hyphen, and the suffix *elect* always requires a hyphen):

   The leader of the group was a self-proclaimed minister.

4. Use a hyphen with short fractions:

   One-half of the men had graduated from college.

5. Use a hyphen with some computer terms that contain *e*:

   She downloaded a new book on her e-reader.

6. Use a hyphen between numbers to indicate a sequence of numbers:

   Seats are still available in rows 5–10.

Semicolons

A semicolon is stronger than a comma but weaker than a period because it does not indicate the end of a complete thought. Use a semicolon only when two sentences are closely related. Use a semicolon to separate the following elements:

1. Two complete sentences that are closely related when no conjunction (*and, but, or, nor, for, yet, so*) is between them:

   It rained for eight hours straight; the main roads were flooded.

2. Items in a series when one or more of the main elements already contains commas:

   The concert is scheduled for Chicago, Illinois; Boston, Massachusetts; and St. Louis, Missouri.

3. Two complete sentences joined by a transitional expression that functions as a conjunctive adverb (*however, moreover, consequently,* etc.):

   We had three weeks' vacation; however, we were unable to leave home because our car had broken down.

4. Elements in a sentence that would become confusing with the addition of another comma:

   When you sell the house, leave the stove; but take the refrigerator.

Sentence Structure

This section discusses common problems related to correct sentence structure. The topics are subject–verb agreement, pronoun–antecedent agreement, fragments, run-on sentences, comma splices, and clauses.

Subject–Verb Agreement

In grammatically correct sentences, the subject should agree with the verb. To determine if the subject and verb agree in a sentence, first locate the subject. Second, decide whether the subject is singular or plural. Finally, write the appropriate form of the verb. Using the following rules will help you to write sentences free from subject–verb agreement errors.

1. Use a singular verb with a singular subject and a plural verb with a plural subject:

   Singular: Bill [singular subject] drives [singular verb] to work on Tuesdays and Thursdays.

   Plural: The girls [plural subject] fly [plural verb] whenever they get the opportunity.

2. Use a plural verb with two or more subjects joined by *and*. This is known as a compound subject:

   A policeman [subject 1] and a fireman [subject 2] were [plural verb] injured in the explosion.

3. Use a singular verb with two or more singular subjects joined by *or* or *nor*:

   Lisa [subject 1] or Connie [subject 2] is going [singular verb] to work the night shift.

4. Use a verb that agrees with the closer subject when a singular subject and a plural subject are joined by *or* or *nor*:

   Todd [singular subject] or the children [plural subject] walk [plural verb] the dog to the park every day.

5. Use a singular verb with a collective noun that names a group of people acting as a single unit:

   The staff [collective noun] has had [singular verb] a pay freeze for the past year.

6. Use a plural verb with a collective noun that names a group of people acting independently of one another (club, family, class, team, platoon, faculty, jury, staff, board, audience, committee, etc.):

   The team [collective noun] are beginning [plural verb indicates the collective noun was acting independently] their own projects to ensure that the company's financial goals are met.

7. Use a singular verb with a title even though the title might be plural:

   The Little Foxes [plural title] is [singular verb] a popular play.

8. Use a singular verb with the name of one company even though it might contain a compound noun:

   Dewie, Jones, and Cheatham [company] is [singular verb] the best accounting firm in the city.

9. Use a singular verb with an amount (money, distance, time) when it is expressed as a single unit:

   Fifteen hundred dollars [amount expressed as a single unit] is [singular verb] the advertised price of the mountain bike.

10. Use a verb that agrees with the antecedent of the pronoun with *who*, *which*, and *that*:

    John wants the dogs [antecedent of who] who run [plural verb] the neighborhood secured.

11. Use the appropriate singular or plural verb form with an indefinite pronoun, depending on whether the indefinite pronoun is singular or plural:

    Singular: Each [singular indefinite pronoun] of the teams has [singular verb] an equal chance of winning.

    Plural: Both [plural indefinite pronoun] of the teams have [plural verb] an equal chance of winning.

Pronoun–Antecedent Agreement

The function of pronouns—*I, me, you, he, him, she, her, it, we, us, they, them*—is to replace nouns or other pronouns in a sentence. The antecedent is the word to which the pronoun refers. Be certain that a pronoun agrees with its antecedent.

1. The basic idea behind pronoun–antecedent agreement is for the singular or plural construction to remain parallel.

   Singular: The *boy* sent a present to *his* sick friend, Joshua.

   Plural: The *boys* sent a present to *their* sick friend, Joshua.

2. When using pronouns to refer to collective nouns, remember such nouns are always considered singular because they are taken as a single entity.

Incorrect: Goldman Sachs sent quarterly reports to their shareholders.

Correct: Goldman Sachs sent quarterly reports to its shareholders.

3. Pronouns should clearly reference a particular word. Avoid using vague pronouns alone. Common vague pronouns include *it, that, these, they, this, those, which.*

Vague: *They* are always handing in their assignments late. (To whom does the word *they* refer?)

Fragments

A sentence fragment is a group of words that does not express a complete thought. Sentence fragments can be turned into complete sentences by adding words that will complete the thought. Remember—a sentence must contain a subject (noun) and a verb. The following are reasons that fragments occur:

1. The fragment contains no subject.

Fragment: Splashing water on his face and wiping it with a towel.

Sentence with subject: Splashing water on his face and wiping it with a towel, Luther tried to clear his head.

2. The fragment contains no verb.

Fragment: Fuchsias, daisies, hollyhocks, roses, and marigolds.

Sentence with verb: Fuchsias, daisies, hollyhocks, roses, and marigolds ringed the restored Victorian home.

3. The fragment results from using a dependent clause.

Dependent clause: Although Terry said he would return it to the store.

Complete sentence: Although Terry said he would return it to the store, the defective toaster still sat on the kitchen counter.

Run-on Sentences

A run-on sentence is two complete sentences (main clauses) that are run together without correct punctuation. The following rules are for correcting run-on sentences:

1. Place an end punctuation mark (period, question mark, exclamation mark) between the two sentences:

Lisa wanted a cup of coffee. She hoped it would help wake her up.

2. Use a comma and a coordinating conjunction (*and, but, or, nor, for, so, yet*) to link the two sentences:

Lisa wanted a cup of coffee, but she wasn't sure it would help wake her up.

3. Use a semicolon to separate and connect the two closely related ideas:

Lisa wanted a cup of coffee; she hoped it would help wake her up.

4. Form a simple sentence by adding a word to subordinate one sentence to the other:

Lisa wanted a cup of coffee because she hoped it would help wake her up.

Comma Splices

A comma splice occurs when two main clauses are separated by a comma without a coordinating conjunction (*and, but, or, nor, for, so, yet*). The following rules are ways to correct a comma splice.

1. Place an end mark (period, question mark, exclamation mark) between the two clauses to form two sentences.

    Comma splice: The house was enormous, it was four stories tall.

    Correction with end mark: The house was enormous. It was four stories tall.

2. Leave the comma and add a coordinating conjunction (*and, but, or, nor, for, so, yet*) to link the sentences.

    Comma splice: The house was enormous, it was four stories tall.

    Correction with coordinating conjunction: The house was enormous, and it was four stories tall.

3. Use a semicolon to separate and connect the two closely related ideas.

    Comma splice: The house was enormous, it was four stories tall.

    Correction with semicolon: The house was enormous; it was four stories tall.

Clauses

A clause contains a subject, verb, and modifiers—but is not necessarily a complete sentence. The following are some types of clauses that should help you ensure that you write clear, concise sentences:

1. **Independent clause:** An independent clause is a group of words that can stand alone as a complete sentence. While independent and dependent clauses can have a subject and a verb, only an independent clause can stand alone. Another name for an independent clause is main clause.

    The cat [subject] is [verb] waiting at the door.

2. **Compound sentence:** Two independent clauses can be joined together to make a compound sentence by either adding a comma and a coordinating conjunction or a semicolon between the two clauses.

    The cat is waiting at the door [independent clause 1], and the dog is lying on the couch [independent clause 2].

3. **Dependent clause:** A dependent clause is a group of words containing a subject and a verb that cannot stand alone. Dependent clauses are introduced by subordinating conjunctions and followed by a comma. The following example could be added to the independent clause example to form a complex sentence; however, the phrase is not a complete sentence on its own.

    But [subordinating conjunction] it [subject] is [verb] wet from the rain [modifier].

4. **Relative clause:** A relative clause is the clause introduced by a relative pronoun. Relative pronouns are *who, whom, which,* and *that.*

    The cat that is waiting at the door [that is waiting at the door = relative clause] is wet from the rain.

5. **Nonrestrictive clause:** A nonrestrictive clause adds information about the antecedent but does not limit the antecedent. Remember, an antecedent is the word being referred to.

    The cat [antecedent], which is wet from the rain, [which is wet from the rain = nonrestrictive clause] is waiting at the door.

6. **Restrictive clause:** A restrictive clause limits the antecedent and is necessary to the meaning of the sentence.

Everyone [antecedent] who has seasonal flu [who has seasonal flu = restrictive clause] is required to stay home during the fever stage. (The clause, "who has seasonal flu," restricts the antecedent, "everyone," because it further defines who "everyone" is in the sentence.)

Usage

This section discusses common problems involving the use of adjectives and adverbs, capitalization, and *who* and *whom*.

Adjectives and Adverbs

Adjectives and adverbs are modifiers or words that further explain or restrict another word in a sentence.

Adjectives

An adjective modifies a noun or pronoun by describing what it is. Adjectives are placed before a noun or pronoun.

Correct: The red [adjective = describes the color of the apple] apple [noun] sat on the teacher's desk.

Incorrect: The apple [noun] red [adjective] sat on the teacher's desk.

Adverbs

An adverb modifies a verb to describe how something is done or an adjective to further describe a noun or pronoun's state of being.

1. Adverbs are often formed by adding –ly to an adjective, and an adverb can go after *or before* the verb.

   Correct: He paints [verb] beautifully [adverb = describes how he paints].

   Correct: She quickly [adverb = describes how she moved] threw [verb] the hot pan in the sink.

2. An adverb can describe an adjective. When using an adverb to describe an adjective, place the adverb before the adjective.

   Correct: Tim's extremely [adverb = describes how fast Tim's motorcycle is] fast [adjective = describes Tim's motorcycle] motorcycle is going to be ridden in this weekend's race.

   Incorrect: Tim's fast [adjective] extremely [adverb] motorcycle is going to be ridden in this weekend's race.

3. An adverb that describes frequency (*always, never, sometimes, often,* etc.) usually comes before the main verb or phrase it is describing.

   Correct: Melinda is often [adverb that describes how late Melinda is for work] late for work [adjective clause that describes the subject *Melinda*].

   Incorrect: Melinda is late for work [adjective] often [adverb].

Capitalization

Capitalization is used to begin a sentence and indicate proper nouns in a sentence to make reading easier.

1. Capitalize the first word to begin a sentence, direct quotation, each line in a list, or the first word after a colon when a complete sentence follows the colon:

   - Katie crossed the street.
   - The teacher will discuss
     - Writing e-mail messages
     - Preparing for the mid-term exam
     - Completing the team assignments.
   - This is my favorite saying: A bird in hand is worth two in the bush.

2. Capitalize a proper noun (a name that specifies a specific person, place, or thing):

   - *Someone's name:* Lisa Rogers was elected class president.
   - *Geographical names:* The group visited China during spring break.
   - *Nouns followed by numbers or letters:* Our airplane is Flight 1203 to Los Angeles.
   - *Titles before a person's name:* Chief Running Bull spoke to the crowd.
   - *Titles of high distinction:* The President will appear on television tonight.
   - *Course titles:* All students are required to take Business Communication 105.
   - *A specific degree:* Lisa is studying to earn a master's degree in Political Science.
   - *Organizations and departments within organizations:* The Boys and Girls Clubs of America organized its annual fund-raiser.
   - *Brand names and trademarks:* John ordered a Pepsi with his hamburger.
   - *Government groups and laws:* Congress passed a bill to support the First Amendment.
   - *Historical events and time periods:* We are studying the Middle Ages now, but I am really looking forward to reading about the Renaissance later in the term.
   - *Days of the week, months, and holidays:* My favorite holiday is Christmas.
   - *Religious references:* The Methodist minister will read from the Bible on Sunday.
   - *Races, languages, and nationalities:* While many Americans are Caucasian or of African descent, a growing proportion are Hispanic.
   - *Computer terminology:* The teacher instructed us to use the Internet for our research.
   - *Celestial bodies:* The Earth revolves around the Sun.

3. Capitalize the pronoun *I.*

Who versus Whom

Who and *whom* are pronouns. The following charts identify (1) the correct pronoun case for *who* and *whom* and (2) how to use *who* and *whom*, depending upon their case in a sentence.

	Subjective Case	Objective Case	Possessive Case
Singular	Who	Whom	Whose
	Whoever	Whomever	Whosever
Plural	Who	Whom	Whose
	Whoever	Whomever	Whosever

Using Who and Whom

Case	Pronoun	Use in a Sentence
Subjective	Who	Subject of a verb or a complement
	Whoever	
Objective	Whom	Direct object, indirect object,
	Whomever	object of a preposition
Possessive	Whose	Indicates ownership
	Whosever	

Who or Whoever

1. Use *who* or *whoever* when the pronoun is the subject of a verb:

   Who wants to eat at Wendy's?

2. Use *who* or *whoever* when the pronoun is a subject complement:

   The man who was hospitalized was who?

3. Use *who* or *whoever* when the pronoun is the subject of a subordinate clause:

   I wonder who threw the rock through the store window?

Whom or Whomever

1. Use *whom* or *whomever* when the pronoun is the direct object of a verb:

   Whom did he finally ask to take him home?

2. Use *whom* or *whomever* when the pronoun is the object of a preposition:

   With whom were you planning to spend the weekend?

3. Use *whom* or *whomever* when the pronoun is the object of a verb in a subordinate clause:

   I wonder whom the teacher will select to play the Tin Man in the school play.

active listening "Listening with a purpose" which involves paraphrasing, asking questions for clarification, and providing feedback.

adaptive capacity The ability to change one's style and approach to fit the culture, context, or condition of an organization.

adaptive model Strategy is focused on the continuous adjustment of the relationship between the organization and its environment.

aggressiveness Asserting one's rights and needs at the expense of others through hurtful expression, self-promotion, attempts to control others, and argumentativeness.

AIDA approach A popular model for organizing persuasive messages; AIDA is the acronym for *attention, interest, desire,* and *action.*

anticipatory socialization The process we use to develop a set of expectations and beliefs about how people communicate in various formal and informal work settings.

appropriate feedback Feedback that is honest, reflects the communicator's true understanding and judgment, and is appropriate for the subject, audience, and occasion or context.

articulate To pronounce all words clearly and fluently.

assertiveness Self-enhancing, expressive communication that takes into account one's own needs as well as those of others.

attribution The assignment of meaning to other people's behavior.

audience-centered communication Communication that considers the needs, concerns, and expectations of the audience.

avoidance A conscious attempt to avoid engaging with people in the dominant group.

boundary spanners Connect an informal network with another information network.

brainstorming A creative technique designed to help a group generate several solutions to a problem.

call to action A conclusion to a persuasive message that is intended to convince the reader to fully consider the writer's or speaker's proposal and, ideally, commit to a decision or take the next step.

central connectors Link most people in an informal network with one another.

chronemics Values related to time, refers to the way that people organize and use time and the messages that are created because of our organization and use of time.

claim Often a general or abstract idea presented as fact.

co-alignment Matching up opportunities and risks in the environment with the capabilities and resources of the organization.

coherence The logical flow of ideas throughout a paragraph.

collectivist culture A culture in which cooperation rather than competition is encouraged and in which individual goals are sacrificed for the good of the group.

common ground The interests, goals, and commonalities of belief that the communicator shares with the audience.

comparison level (CL) The standard by which individuals evaluate the desirability of group membership; CL is strongly influenced by previous relationships.

comparison level for alternatives (CL$_{alt}$) The lowest level of outcomes a member will accept in light of available alternative opportunities.

competitors People who view group disagreements as win–lose situations and find satisfaction in forcing their views on others.

compliance-gaining Attempts made by a communicator to influence another person to do something that the person otherwise might not do.

compliance-resisting The refusal to comply with another person's attempts at influence.

confirmation bias A tendency to distort information that contradicts the beliefs and attitudes we currently hold.

context The situation or setting in which communication occurs.

contextual intelligence The awareness of and ability to adapt to the context.

cooperators Individuals who value accommodative interpersonal strategies in groups.

correlation A consistent relationship between two or more variables.

creativity The generation, application, combination, and extension of new ideas.

critical listening Listening used to evaluate the accuracy, meaningfulness, and usefulness of a message.

critical thinking The intellectually disciplined process of actively and skillfully conceptualizing, applying, analyzing, synthesizing, and/or evaluating information gathered from, or generated by, observation, experience, reflection, reasoning, or communication as a guide to belief and action.

culture The learned beliefs, values, rules, norms, symbols, and traditions that are common to a group of people.

defensive communication climate An organizational climate in which individuals feel threatened.

Delphi technique Method, named after the ancient oracle at Delphi, has been called "absentee brainstorming" because individuals share ideas in writing or via e-mail, without meeting face-to-face.

demographics The statistical data about a particular population, including its age, income, education level, and so on.

diagram A two-dimensional drawing that shows the important parts of objects.

dialogic model of communication This model of communication takes other people's points of view into account, acknowledging that the speaker and the listener may have different perspectives.

dialogue A conversation among two or more persons. From the dialogic perspective, that dialogue would be characterized by such attributes as trust, lack of pretense, sincerity, humility, respect, directness, open-mindedness, honesty, concern for others, empathy, nonmanipulative intent, equality, and acceptance of others as individuals with intrinsic worth, regardless of differences of opinion or belief.

distributed leadership A situation in which team members share team leadership.

drive The state of an individual associated with a need, such as hunger or thirst.

egocentric Concerned with the self rather than others or society.

emotional intelligence The assortment of non-cognitive skills that influence our ability to cope with the pressures and demands of the environment.

empathic listening A form of active listening with the goal of understanding the other person.

ethnocentrism The belief that your own cultural background—including its ways of analyzing problems, values, beliefs, language, and verbal and nonverbal communication—is correct and that other cultures are somehow inferior.

ethos An ethical appeal that refers to information that provides credibility to ourselves or our position.

evidence More specific statement of fact that supports a statement.

extemporaneous speaking Public speaking that is delivered spontaneously rather than being read or memorized in advance.

external strategic communication Management's public relations and issues management efforts designed to influence consumers, communities, special-interest groups, voters, regulators, legislators, and others outside the organization.

faces The public image of individuals, or groups, that their society sees and evaluates based on cultural norms and values.

false dichotomy A dichotomy that is not jointly exhaustive (i.e., there are other alternatives) or that is not mutually exclusive (i.e., the alternatives overlap). A false dichotomy may be the product of either–or thinking.

feedback The listener's verbal and nonverbal responses to the speaker and his or her message.

forecasting Elements of a text or oral presentation that tell the audience what the reader or speaker will cover next.

free-riding When group members do not work as hard when they believe others will compensate for this lack of effort.

fundamental attribution error Conflict that is exacerbated by members' tendencies to misperceive others and to assume that the other party's behavior is caused by personal rather than situational factors.

goal The outcome that the person perceives will eliminate the need.

goodwill In the business communication context, the ability to create and maintain positive, productive relationships with others.

graph A visual element used to compare the values of several items; sometimes called *charts*.

ground rules Explicit, agreed-on prescriptions for acceptable and appropriate behavior.

group A collection of people who share a common purpose, feel a sense of belonging to the group, and who exert influence on one another.

groupthink Conformity-seeking behavior of cohesive groups that interferes with effective decision making.

haptics Communicating through the use of bodily contact or touch.

high self-monitors People who are highly aware of their impression-management behavior and efforts.

identity The visual manifestation of the image of the organization as conveyed through its logo, products, services, buildings, stationery, uniforms, and other tangible items created by the organization to communicate with a variety of constituencies.

image building The process of creating the identity an organization wants its relevant public to perceive.

impression formation The process of integrating a variety of observations about a person into a coherent impression of that person.

impression management The attempt to control the impression of ourselves that we present to others in any communication situation.

individualistic culture A culture with an "I" focus in which competition, not cooperation, is encouraged and individual initiative and achievement are highly valued.

individualists Individuals who are concerned only with their own outcomes in group situations.

inference A conclusion about the unknown based upon the known.

influence The power to affect the thoughts or actions of others.

information brokers Keep the different subgroups in an informal network together.

informational influence When the group provides members with information that they can use to make decisions and form opinions.

intercultural communication The exchange of information among people of different cultural backgrounds.

intermember relations The relations of the group members to one another, which are determined by patterns of status, attraction, and communication.

internal strategic communication Management's efforts to provide information to and exert influence with the organizational membership.

Internet conferencing Sometimes known as *webcasting*, allows one a group to conduct a presentation in real time over the Internet simultaneously with VOIP or a conference telephone call.

interpersonal communication Communication involving mutual influence, usually for the purpose of managing relationships.

interpersonal dominance The relational, behavioral, and interactional state that reflects the actual achievement—by means of communication—of influence or control over another person.

interpersonal influence When the group uses verbal and nonverbal influence tactics to induce change.

interpersonal intelligence The ability to understand others.

interpretive model Strategy is concerned with the management of meaning and with symbol construction aimed at legitimizing the organization by providing orienting metaphors and frames of reference that allow the organization and its environment to be understood by organizational stakeholders.

intimate distance This distance is used to communicate affection, give comfort, and to protect. It is used more in private than in public and extends to about 18 inches.

intrapersonal communication One's communication with oneself, including memories, experiences, feelings, ideas, and attitudes.

intrapersonal intelligence The ability to form an accurate model of oneself and to use this model effectively.

issues management The organized activity of identifying emerging trends, concerns, or issues likely to affect an organization in the next few years, and developing a wider and more positive range of organizational responses.

kinesics The study of posture, movement, gestures, and facial expression as channels of communication.

leadership Influence of people within an organizational setting through the orchestration of relationships.

linear model Strategy consists of integrated decisions, actions or plans that will set and achieve viable organizational goals.

logos Consists of information such as facts or statistics; also known as *logical appeal*.

low self-monitors People who have little awareness about how others perceive them and little knowledge about how to interact appropriately with others.

management The coordination and organization of activities within an organization.

mindfulness The psychological process of bringing one's attention to the internal and external experiences occurring in the present moment.

monochronic time (M-time) A cultural orientation to time in which people do one thing at a time and are more task oriented than relationship-oriented.

monologue Talking to oneself. From a dialogic perspective, a monologue is characterized by such qualities as deception, superiority, exploitation, dogmatism, domination, insincerity, pretense, personal self-display, self-aggrandizement, judgmentalism that stifles free expression, coercion, possessiveness, condescension, self-defensiveness, and viewing others as objects to be manipulated.

motive The learned state that affects behavior by moving an individual toward a perceived goal.

need A lack or imbalance that creates dissatisfaction in an individual.

networking Establishing and maintaining relationships with others.

nominal-group technique A procedure that uses some of the principles and methods of active brainstorming but has members write their ideas while being quiet and thinking before sharing them with the group.

nonverbal communication The "attributes or actions of humans, other than the use of words themselves, which have socially shared meaning, are intentionally sent or interpreted as intentional, are consciously sent or consciously received, and have the potential for feedback from the receiver."

normative influence When group members tailor their actions to fit the group's standards and conventions.

organizational culture The system of shared meanings and practices within an organization that distinguish it from other organizations.

outgroup homogeneity effect The tendency to think members of other groups are all the same.

oversampling The tendency for groups to spend too much of their discussion time examining shared information—details that two or more of the group members know in common—rather than unshared information.

pathos An emotional appeal; an attempt to win over the audience by appealing to its emotions, often by telling a story or evoking a picture with which the audience can empathize.

pauses Temporary breaks in speech used to emphasize important points and enhance the meanings of words and phrases.

perception Awareness of the elements of the environment made possible through our senses.

perceptual mindsets Our cognitive and psychological predispositions to see the world in a certain way.

performance appraisal A structured formal interaction between a subordinate and supervisor that usually takes the form of a periodic interview in which the work performance of the subordinate is examined and discussed, with a view to identifying weaknesses and strengths as well as opportunities for improvement and skills development.

peripheral specialists Those in informal networks that others rely on for specialized expertise.

personal distance The distance ranging from 18 inches to 4 feet used by those in the United States for conversation and non-intimate exchanges.

personal space The physical distance between you and others with which you feel comfortable.

pitch The sound quality of the speaker's voice, ranging from low and deep to high and squeaky.

plain language Communication your audience can understand the first time they read or hear it.

plurality The recognition that there are multiple different interpretations of any situation and that no one communicator can control all these interpretations.

polychronic time (P-time) A cultural orientation to time in which people are well adapted to working on several activities simultaneously.

power bases The differing sources or bases of power within an organization.

process losses Reductions in performance effectiveness or efficiency caused by faulty group processes, including motivational and coordination problems.

projected cognitive similarity The tendency to assume others have the same norms and values as your own cultural group.

proxemics The study of human space that revolves around two concepts: territoriality and personal space.

public communication The process of one communicating with many.

public distance The distance exceeds 12 feet and is used most often for public speaking.

public relations The management function that evaluates public attitudes, identifies the policies and procedures of an individual or an organization with the public interest, and executes a program of action to earn public understanding and acceptance.

rate of delivery The speed at which one speaks.

rational explanation Explanation that includes some sort of formal presentation, analysis, or proposal and usually involves the presentation of evidence.

reasoned skepticism The process of actively searching for meaning, analyzing and synthesizing information, and judging the worth of that information.

reflexivity The capacity for reflection.

reputation management The practice of attempting to shape public perception of a person or organization by influencing information about that entity.

risk The chance of loss (or gain).

risk communication The process of communicating responsibly and effectively about the risk factors associated with industrial technologies, natural hazards, and human activities.

self-awareness An understanding of the self, including one's attitudes, values, beliefs, strengths, and weaknesses.

self-centered communication Communication that fails to consider the needs, concerns, or interests of its audience.

self-concept How we think about ourselves and describe ourselves to others.

self-esteem How we like and value ourselves and how we feel about ourselves.

self-fulfilling prophecy The idea that we see ourselves in ways that are consistent with how others see us.

self-reflexive Having an accurate image or reflection of one's self.

silent brainstorming Overcome some of the disadvantages in oral brainstorming by encouraging apprehensive team members to participate by first writing their ideas.

social construction or social construct Any phenomenon "invented" or "constructed" by participants in a particular culture or society and existing because people agree to behave as if it exists or to follow certain conventional rules.

social distance The distance ranges from 4 to 8 feet and is used for professional communication.

social loafing The reduction of effort by individuals working in groups.

somatotype Body type comprised of a combination of height, weight, and muscularity.

stereotyping A standardized mental picture that is held in common by members of a group and that represents an oversimplified opinion, prejudiced attitude, or uncritical judgment.

stinking thinking Consists of thoughts that limit the possibilities of an individual, group, or organization.

strategic alignment The degree in which your oral messages match your nonverbal ones.

strategy Plan for obtaining a specific goal or result that involves big-picture analysis.

style The level of formality in written communications.

supportive communication climate An organizational climate in which individuals do not feel threatened.

table A visual element used to present data in words, numbers, or both, in columns and rows.

tactics Concrete actions taken to implement a strategy.

team A coordinated group of individuals organized to work together to achieve a specific, common goal.

territoriality Our need to establish and maintain certain spaces as your own.

tone The implied attitude of the communicator toward his or her audience.

transitions Elements that assist the audience in moving from one topic to another through words and phrases that link the ideas being developed by the writer or speaker.

trust The confidence that others' intentions are good.

vocal distractions or disfluencies Speaking "errors" such as stammers, stutters, double starts, and excessive use of filler words such as *um* and *uh*.

vocal variety The varying use of the vocal aspects of volume, rate, and pitch.

volume The relative sound level of speech; it must be loud enough to be heard, but not so loud as to be overwhelming.

Index

Page numbers with an *f* refer to a figure; *b* indicates a box.

A

abstractions, vivid images vs., 33
abuses of power, 58–59
Academically Adrift (Arum), 30
accent errors, 151
accident communication, 187, 324
accommodation, in conflict resolution, 278, *278f*
active listening, 229, 235–236, *237t*
adaptive capacity, 95
adaptive model, 304, 328
adjectives, 376
adjourning phase, 265
advantages-disadvantages format, 139
adverbs, 376
advertising, word of mouth, 46
advocacy, 60
African American cultures, as collectivist, 77
aggressive-defensive culture, 97, 99–100
aggressiveness, 48, 228, *278f*
AIDA approach, 136, *136f*
Airbnb, 191–200
Amazon, 331–343
ambiguity, 104–105
American Red Cross, 117–121
analogies, faulty, 135
anger, 54, 150
Anglo cluster, 74–75, *75t*
Ansoff, Igor, 3
anticipatory socialization, 56
anxiety, 176, 179
apostrophes, 369
appeals, types of, 133–134
appearance
    body type/attractiveness, 231
    clothing/artifacts, 233
    professional image, 54–55
Apple technology problem (hypothetical),
        90–92
application letters, employment
    overview, 207–208, 221, 351
    as audience-centered communication,
        85–87
    electronic, *353f*
    samples of, *86–87f, 208f, 352f*
appropriate feedback, 54
Argenti, Paul A., 303
argumentation, 133
Aristotle
    on communication purposes, 45

evidence, types of, 133
    Rhetoric, 3, 46–47
articulation, 175
Arum, Richard
    Academically Adrift, 30
assertiveness
    characteristics of, 48, 228
    as cultural characteristic, 74–75, *75t*
attention, interest, desire, action.
        See AIDA approach
attention getters, 166–167, *167f*
attitudes, of audience, 81
attraction relations, 263
attribution, 25, 34
audience analysis
    overview
        about, 71–72
        audience-centered communication,
            84–87
        business audiences, 82–84, 88
        demographics, 72–77
        gender, 77–80
        knowledge/interests/attitudes/concerns,
            81–82
        language, 80
        Speedy Travel Inc, 70
    in communicating change, *247f*
    culturally diversity in, 181–183
    in job hunting, 203–204
    messaging from, 21
    for online presence, 318
audience-centered communication,
        84–87
audits
    overview, 307, 328
    data gathering for, 309
    methods, comparison of, *310t*
    self-auditing, 219
authority
    as earned/inherited, 77
    influence as replacement for, 5
    leadership vs. management in, 6, 59
averages, misleading, *146b*
averaging rankings/ratings, 272, *273t*
Avery, Christopher M.
    Teamwork Is an Individual Skill,
        258
avoidance
    overview, 48, 228
    in conflict resolution, 278, *278f*

B

baby boomers, 73
bad news messages
    delivery of, 248
    example of, *129f*
    indirect approach for, 127, 128
Baer, Jay, 317–318
bar graphs, 144–145, *144f, 172f*
Barnaby Consulting Corp., 44
Barnlund, Dean C.
    on ethics, 21
    on intent, 22
    on self-concept, 26
Barton, Clara, 118
Beck, Karen A., 303
beginning, in oral presentations, 166–167
behavioral interviewing, *211f*, 216
Bennis, Warren
    Geeks & Geezers, 95
Benoit, W. L., 323
Berger, Peter L.
    The Social Construction of Reality, 9
bias, in CNN reporting, 64–69
biased samples, *146b*
blame, avoiding, 150
Blecharczyk, Nathan, 192
Blitzer, Wolf, 64
block format letters, *346f*
blogs, 111–112, 317
Bloom's Taxonomy, 30, *31f*
body
    in application letters, 208
    in informative messages, 128
    in oral presentations, 167–168
    in PowerPoint presentations, 171–173,
        171–173f
    in reports/proposals, 139, 140
body movement, in oral presentations, 175
body type (somatotype), 231
"border" persons, 71
boundary spanners, 245
brainstorming
    overview, 281–282
    advantages/disadvantages of, *284t*
    in virtual teamwork, 290–291
bridging presentation segments, 184
Brooks Brothers brand, 39–43
bullet lists, 143, 206–207
bullying, *277b*
Burgoon, J. K., 59

business audiences, 82–84
business communication
    overview, 1
    strategic elements of, 2–121
    tactics of, 122–343
    See also communication
business etiquette, 182–183
business literacy, 18
business travel, videoconferencing vs., 185
business writing
    overview, 124, 153
    Cerner Corporation e-mail, 156–158
    genre of, 124–126
    informative messages
        overview, 153
        e-mail, 126
        parts of, 127–130
        steps in, *126f*
    persuasive messages
        overview, 153
        appeals, 133–134
        components of, 133, *168f*
        evidence for, 135
        organizing, 135–136
        resistance to, 137
        strategy questions, 130–132
    reports/proposals
        overview, 153
        about, 137
        format of, 139–140
        preparations for, 138
        type/organization of, 138–139
    steps in, *125f*
    tactless, 123
    visual impression in
        about, 140
        graphics, 143–147
        headings, 141–143
        lists, 143
        proofreading, 150–151
        revision, 147–150
        submission, 151–152
        white space, 141

C
Cable News Network (CNN), 64–69
Cafferty, Jack, 64, 66, 68
California Design, Inc., 17
call to action, 130, 169
candidate screening, 202, 214–216
capital letters, in e-mail, 348
capitalization, 377
Case, Thomas, 59–60
case study analysis
    overview, 10–11
    reality construction rules, *11f*
    steps in, 11–12
cause-and-effect organization, 139, 164–165, *164f*
central connectors, 245, *245f*
Cerner Corporation, e-mail memo of, 156–158
Chaffee, E. E., 304, 322
Chandler, Alfred D., 3

change, as leadership function, 7, *7t*
channel plans, 318
channels/media
    Airbnb, 193
    selection considerations, 103–108, *103f*
    types of, 103
charts, 144–145
Chesky, Brian, 191–192
chronemics (time), 232–233
chronological context, 95
chronological organization, 138, 164–165, *164f*
chronological résumés, 206, *349f*
chunking information, 141, 345
CL (comparison level), 260
claims (damages/repairs), *364f*
claims (denial), *367f*
claims (in persuasive messages), 133, *168f*
CL$_{alt}$ (comparison level for alternatives), 260
clauses, 375–376
close, in business writing, 128–130, 139
closed systems, 25, 31
CNN (Cable News Network), 64–69
co-alignment, 304, 328
coalition building, 60
codes, nonverbal, 104–105
coercion, 6, 58–59
coherence, 148
cohesion, 266–268
collaboration
    in conflict resolution, 278, *278f*
    stonewalling vs., 321
    trust as basis for, 277
collective endeavors, groups as, 259
collectivism
    conflict resolution and, 279
    individualism vs., 76, *76t*, 77, *261t*
colons, 369–370
comma splices, 375
commas, 370–371
common ground, in persuasion, 57
communication
    adaptation of, 10
    audience-centered, 84–87
    context
        overview, 114
        definition/dimensions of, 94–96
        organizational culture. *See* organizational culture
        virtual teams, 93
    delivery of, 248–249
    employment. *See* employees
    foundations of
        about, 18, 36
        California Design, Inc., 17
        ethics of, 30–35
        models of, 18–23
        perception, 23–26
        self-awareness, 26–30
    marginalization of, 303
    media. *See* media
    networks for
        analysis map, *245f*
        centralized/decentralized, 263–264

formal/informal, 102–103
    types of, 244–246, *264f*
nonverbal, 175–177
purposes of
    about, 45, *45f*, 61
    Barnaby Consulting Corp., 44
    credibility, 48–56
    goodwill, 46–48
    information, 46
    responsible, 53–54
    strategic. *See* strategic communication
    strategic organizational. *See* strategic organizational communication
    written. *See* business writing; written communication
compare-contrast organization, 139, 164–165, *164f*
comparison level (CL), 260
comparison level for alternatives (CL$_{alt}$), 260
competence, 49–50
competition, conflict and, 276, 278, *278f*
competitive edge, in persuasive messages, 132
complementary principle, 260
compliance-gaining/resisting behaviors, 58–59
compromise in conflict resolution, 278, *278f*
concerns, of audience, 82
conclusions
    in application letters, 209
    in oral presentations, 168–169
    in PowerPoint presentations, 173–174
    in reports/proposals, 140
conducting meetings, 240–241
conference telephone calls, 185
confidence, nonverbal signals, 176–177
confirmation bias, 32
conflict
    assertiveness as response to, 228
    during meetings, 241
    in performance appraisals, 219–220
    in virtual teamwork, 289–290
conformity, 266–268
Confucian Asia regional cluster, 75, *75t*
Conger, J., 46, 57–58
consensus, decisions by, 272, *273t*
consistency, as management function, 7, *7t*
constructive criticism, 219
constructive culture, 97–98
context
    analysis of, *247f*
    in virtual teamwork, *289t*
contextual intelligence, 95
contingency theory, in leadership, 30
Cooke, Robert A., 97
cooperation, in conflict resolution, *278f*
cooperators, 276
corporate social responsibility (CSR), 320, 322
correlation, 33
cost, of communication, 106
Coute, Joe, 214
creativity, 280–284, *284t*
credibility
    overview, 48–56

credibility (*cont.*)
    anger as counterproductive to, 150
    building, 134
    during crisis briefings, 187
    establishing, 6
    factors in, *49f*
    maintaining/enhancing, 8
    in performance appraisals, 219
    in persuasion, 57
credit approvals, *366f*
crisis communication
    overview, 187–188
    Airbnb approach to, 197–199
    steps in, 323–324, 326–327
    written communication for, 107
critical listening, 236
critical thinking
    overview, 34–35
    skills for, 30
    strategy as, 4
CSR (corporate social responsibility), 320,
        322
cues, verbal/nonverbal, 76, 104–105
cultural context, 96
cultural diversity
    in brainstorming, 281
    in communication, 7, 104–105
    conflict from, 275
    in conflict resolution, 279
    in decision making, 274, *275t*
    in paralanguage/body language, 230
    in personal space, 232
    in seating arrangements, 232
    and social values, 276
    in virtual teamwork, 288
cultural intelligence, 28–30
cultural literacy, 18
culturally diverse audiences, 181–183
culture
    overview, 74–77
    of Amazon, 331–337
    change adaptation, 249
    creating, 9
    vocal delivery as reflection of, 174

D
dashes, 371
Davis, Lauren D., 290
Day, Julian, 223–224
DDOS (distributed denial of service), 68
debate, dialogic style vs., *228f*
decision by consensus, 272, *273t*
decision making
    overview
        challenges of, 273–274, *274t*
        methods of, 272–273, *273t*
        stages of, 271–272
    indecision, losses from, 298–301
    in leadership, 284–285, *285f*
defensive communication climate, 101–102,
        101t
defensiveness, 150, 220
delivery
    overview, 174–181

for crisis communication, 187–189
    for culturally diverse audiences, 181–183
    for distance presentations, 184–186
    for group presentations, 183–184
    in oral presentations, 174–181
Delphi technique, 283, *284t*
demographics, 72–77
devil's advocate role, 275
diagrams
    overview, 145
    organizational chart as, *145f*
    in PowerPoint presentations, 173, *173f*
dialogic process
    characteristics/disadvantages of, *22f*, 36
    communication as, 21–23
dialogic style, debate vs., *228f*
dialogue, monologue vs., 21–22
dichotomies, 32
direct approach, in business writing, 127–128
direct eye contact, 176, 182, 230, 238
direct requests, 130
discarding data, *146b*
discussions, 239
disfluencies, 175
distance presentations, 184–186
distributed denial of service (DDOS), 68
diversity. *See* cultural diversity
dominance, 59
Dowling, Grahame, 316
downward flow communication, 102,
        312–314
drawings
    overview, 145
    misleading, *146b*
    in PowerPoint presentations, 173
dress/appearance
    from culturally diverse audiences, 182
    for job interviews, 213
    for oral presentations, 177
Drexel Burnham Lambert, 100
drives, 243
Drucker, Peter, 3
DuFrene, Debbie, 51

E
Eastern Europe regional cluster, 75, *75t*
economic loss, from change, 246
Edelman Trust Barometer, 67
EEOC (Equal Employment Opportunity
        Commission), 216
effective listening
    overview, 250
    importance of, 48, 229
    questionnaire for, *235t*
    styles of, 234–235
    tactics for, 236–238
    types of, 235–236
egocentrism, monologues as, 22
Eisenberg, E. M., 51
Eisenberg, Eric, 60
electronic brainstorming, 283–284, *284t*
electronic meetings, 243
electronic résumés, *350f*
ellipsis points, 371

Elop, Stephen, 298–301
e-mail
    overview, 109–111
    application letters sent by, 351
    brainstorming by, 282
    characteristics of, *110t*
    formats
        about, 344, 347–348
        example of, *348f*
    spell checking with, 150
    subject line, 140–141
    termination by, 225
emotional connection, 58
emotional control, 54
emotional intelligence, 27–28
emotions, as obstacle, 35
empathic listening, 236
empathy, 71
employees
    communicating change to, 246–249, *247f*
    communication with
        overview, 227
        Bezos memo to, 336–337
        nonverbal, 229–233, 250
        style of, 228–229
    effective listening. *See* effective listening
    meeting management. *See* meeting
        management
    motivating, 243–246
employment
    overview, 202, 221
    application process, 202–209
    Gen-Y workforce, 201
    job interviews
        overview, 221
        applicants, 209–215
        employers, 215–217
    performance appraisals, 217–220
    social media use in, 209
    terminations, 223–225
employment messages, 85–87
end (conclusions). *See* conclusions
English for Specific Purposes (ESP), 125–126
entitlement, 28
entry points, 125
environmental actions, *285f*, 286
Equal Employment Opportunity
        Commission (EEOC), 216
ESP (English for Specific Purposes), 125–126
ethical sourcing, 322
ethics
    overview, 30–35
    in communication, 22, *53t*
    in critical thinking, 34–35
    mindfulness in, 4
    reputation management and, 316
    trust and, 50–54, *52t*
ethos (ethical appeal), 134, *168f*
evaluation apprehension, 270
Evered, R., 27
Everson, Mark W., 118, 120
evidence
    for claims, 133
    gathering, 138

in persuasion, 57, *168f*
quality of, 135
executive summary, 139
expert audiences, 83
expert decisions, 272, *273t*
expertise, 49–50
extemporaneous speaking, 178
external communications, risks from, 112–113
external plans
overview, 314–315
crisis communication. *See* crisis communication
investor relations, 320–321
issues, 315–319, 321–323
news media, 324–327
risk communication, 323
external strategic communication, 315
ExxonMobil issues crafting, 323
eye contact
cultural differences in, 230
direct, 176, 182, 230, 238

F
face negotiation theory, 77
Facebook
in business, 109, 111
optimal use of, 318
face-to-face communication
ambiguity of, 105
components of, 229–233
as richest channel, 104
facial expressions, 177
facilitators, 240–241
false causality, *146b*
false dichotomies, 32
FedEx Express, 254–256
feedback
about, 19
appropriate, 54
from culturally diverse audiences, 182
Gallup system for, *306b*
Internet conferencing polls for, 185
in performance appraisals, 218–220
positive/negative, 235
speed of, 105–106
femininity, masculinity vs., 76, *289t*
filtering information, 34
The Five Dysfunctions of a Team (Lencioni), 258–259
flattening of organizational hierarchies, 227
fluency, in oral presentations, 175
follow-up letters, 351, *354f*
font choices, 142, 345
forecasting, 148, 167
formal authority, influence vs., 59
formats
for business writing, 138–139, 344–345
for résumés, 205–206, *205f*
forming stage, 265
fragments, 374
free-riding, 270–271
French, J. R. P., *6t*

functional résumés, 206
fundamental attribution error, 277
future orientation, 74–75, *75t*

G
Gallup Organization feedback system, *306b*
Gardner, H., 27, 28
gaze/eye contact, 230
Gebbia, Joe, 191–192
Geeks & Geezers (Bennis & Thomas), 95
gender
in brainstorming, 281
in conflict resolution, 279
egalitarianism, 74–75, *75t*
leadership attributes by, 79–80, *79f*
gendered communication, 77–78, *78t*
general norms, 267
general to specific organization, 164–165, *164f*
generation Xers (nexters), 73
generational differences, 73
Gen-Y workforce, 201
Germanic Europe regional cluster, 75, *75t*
gestures, 230
Gibson, Stacey, 157
global communication competence, *29f*
Global Leadership and Organizational Behavior Effectiveness. *See* GLOBE studies
Global Literacy Competence (GLC) Model, 28–30, *29f*
globalization
business writing for, 125–126
challenges of, 5
cultural diversity and, 15
differing social realities, 9
ethical practices and, 51
message distortion and, 8
opportunities/challenges of, 2
GLOBE studies, 74–75
goals, 243
Goffman, Erving, 55
Goodall, H. L, Jr., 51
goodwill
in conclusions, 129
conveying, 46–48
in persuasion, 58
Google+, 111
Gould, Stephen Jay, 33
"grapevine," 103
graphics
in business writing, 143–147, *146b*
in PowerPoint, 171–173
in videoconferencing, 186
graphs
in PowerPoint presentations, *172f*
truncation of, *146b*
types of, 144–145
gratification delay, 28
Gross, Ronald, 94
ground rules, 266
group presentations, 183–184
group productivity, illusion of, 270–271
group-oriented cultures, 276, 279

groups
overview, 292
challenges of, 258–259
cohesion/conformity, 266–268
conflict in
resolution of, 277–280
sources of, 274–277
creativity enhancement, 280–284, *284t*
decision making. *See* decision making
definition of, 258
development of, 265–266
forming, 259–261
influence within, 268–269
member relations, 263–264
performance of, 269–271
power and, 264–265
roles of, 261–262
status effects on, *263t*
groupthink, 267–268, 275

H
Hall, Challis A., 254
Hall, Edward T., 76, 232
haptics (touching), 233
hard skills, soft skills vs., 8
headings, 141–143, *142f*
Herzberg, F., 244
Heskett, J. L., 100
hierarchical ordering of information, 141–142
high self-monitors, 56
high-context cultures
conflict resolution in, 279
low-context cultures vs., 76–77, *77t*
as polychronic, 233
higher-order thinking skills, 30
hiring costs, 216
Hofstede, Geert, cultural dimensions of, 75–76, 288, *289t*
Holtzhausen, Derina, 303
horizontal flow communication, 102
hostile questions, 180–181
Howell, Robert A., 303
Huckin, Tom, 82
human space, 231–232
humane orientation, 74–75, *75t*
hygiene factors, 244
hyphens, 371–372

I
IBM virtual teamwork, 291
identity, 316–317
illustrations list, 139
image building
definition of, 316
issues advocacy vs., 323
media relationships and, 324–325
image restoration theory, 323
implementation, in organizational communication, 308, *308t*
impression formation/management, 25, 55
improvement focus, 150
In Their Time (Mayo), 95

indecision, losses, 298–301
indirect approach, in business writing, 127, 128, 137
individualism
    collectivism vs., 7, 76, *76t*, 77, *261t*, *289t*
    as counterproductive, 30
    ethics vs., 51
individualistic roles, 261, *262t*
individualists, 276
individual-oriented cultures, 276, 279
industrial disasters, communication after, 187, 324
industry analysis, 203–204
inferences/inferential errors, 32–33
influence, in persuasion, 58–59
informal network analysis map, *245f*
information
    amount conveyed, 106–107
    chunking, 141
    as communication purpose, 46
    distortion, 8, 19
    hierarchical ordering of, 141–142
    in résumés, 205–206
information brokers, 245
information overload, 30
information transfer
    characteristics/disadvantages of, *22f*
    communication as, 19, *19f*
informational influence, 268–269
informative meetings, 239
in-group collectivism, 74–75, *75t*
institutional collectivism, 74–75, *75t*
institutional stock investors, 320–321
integrity, trust and, 50–54, *52t*
intercultural communication, 23
interdependency, in organizational communication, 20
interest, creating, 163
interests, of audience, 81
intermember relations, 263
internal communications, risks from, 112
internal plans
    audits, 309–310, *310t*
    developing
        elements of, 310–312
        flow downward/upward, 312
        medium for, 312, *313t*
    practices/criteria for, 307–308, *308t*
internal strategic communication, 305
international audiences, 83–84
Internet conferencing, 185–186
interpersonal attraction, 259–261
interpersonal communication
    overview, 227
    in relationships, 6
    richness of, 104
    styles, 48
interpersonal dominance, 59
interpersonal influence, 268–269
interpersonal intelligence, 27
interpersonal style, 228–229, 250
interpretation, 104–105
interpretive model, 304

intimate distance, 232
intrapersonal communication, 27
intrapersonal intelligence, 27
introduction
    in application letters, 208
    in informative messages, 127–128
    in oral presentations, 166–167
    in PowerPoint presentations, 171, *171f*
    in reports/proposals, 139
investor relations, 320–321
issues advocacy, 322–323
issues management, 321–322

J
jargon use, 80, *80f*
Jemison, D.B., 3
job acceptance messages, 351, *355f*
job advertisements, 351, *351f*
job climate analysis, 203–204
job descriptions, 204, *204f*
job hunting. *See* employment
job refusal messages, *355f*
job satisfaction, motivators in, 244
Jobs, Steve, 162
Johnson, Belinda, 199
Johnson, James Wood, 118
Johnson, Robert Wood, 118
Johnson & Johnson, 117–121
Jordan, Ray, 117, 119, 120
Jourard, Sidney, 233
Jude-York, Deborah, 290

K
Ketchum Leadership Communication Monitor, 79
Keynote software, 169
Keys, Bernard, 59–60
keywords, in résumés, 207
kinesics, 230
knowledge, of audience, 81
knowledge/expertise, leadership through, 6
Kotter, J. P.
    on management/leadership functions, 7, 243
    on organizational effectiveness, 100
Krechevsky, M., 27
Krein, T. J., 219

L
language
    clarity of, 80
    sexist, *78b*
large-power-distance culture, 77
Latin America regional cluster, 75, *75t*
Latin Europe regional cluster, 75, *75t*
leadership
    in communicating change, 226, 247–248, *248f*
    construction of, 10
    functions of, 7, *7t*
    gratification delay in, 28
    influence through, 6, 15
    management vs., 5–6

meaning management, 10
    relationship orchestration as, 59
    in teamwork
        overview, 292
        decisions, 284–285, *285f*
        internal/external, *285f*, 286
    traits for, 55
lean media, 104
learning organizations, 31
Leavitt, H., 264
Lecky, Prescott, 280
Lehman, Carol, 51
Lencioni, Patrick M.
    The Five Dysfunctions of a Team, 258–259
Lerner, Michael, 51
letters
    formats
        about, 344, 345, 347
        examples of, *346–347f*
    use of, 140
level-one listeners, 234
linear model, 304, 328
LinkedIn, 111
listening skills. *See* effective listening
Lister, Joseph, 118
lists, 143
logos (logical appeal), 133–134, *168f*
long-term orientation, short-term orientation vs., 76
low self-monitors, 56
low-context cultures
    conflict resolution in, 279
    high-context cultures vs., 76–77, *77t*
Luckmann, Thomas
    The Social Construction of Reality, 9

M
majority rule, 272, *273t*
management
    functions of, 7, *7t*
    leadership vs., 5–6
management strategy, 3
managerial audiences, 82–83
margin width, 344–345
Marriott, Airbnb vs., 194
Martin, Carrie, 120
masculinity, femininity vs., 76, *289t*
Mayo, Tony
    In Their Time, 95
McGregor, Douglas, 99
meaning making, 9
mechanical correctness, 150–151, *151b*
media
    overview, 114
    new media, 108–113
    relationships with, 187
    types of, *108t*
meeting management
    overview, 238–239, 250
    agendas, *240f*, 241–242
    minutes, 242
    steps in, 239–242
    types of, 239, 243

Mehrabian, Albert, 231
memos
    formats
        about, 344, 345
        example of, *346f*
    reports/proposals formatted as, 138–139
    use of, 140
messages
    alignment of, 5
    audience-centered, 10, 84–87
    control over, 107
    distortion of, 8
    multiple entry points, 125
    targeting, 249
    unethical, *53t*
metrics, of online presence, 318
microblogs, 112
middle (body), in oral presentations, 167–168
Middle East regional cluster, 75, *75t*
Milken, Mike, 100
millennials (or generation Y), 73
mindfulness, 4, 30
minimax principle, 260
Mintzberg, Henry, 82
Mitchell, Terence, 51
mixed audiences, 84
mobile conferencing, 243
model documents
    design elements, 344–345
    for differing purposes, 360–368
    message formats, 345–360
modified block format letters, *347f*
money, as social construct, 9
monochronic time (M-time), 232–233
monologue, dialogue vs., 21–22
Moore, Gary, 210
moral exclusion, *23b*
Moran, Peter, 316
motivation, 243–246
motivator-hygiene theory, 244
motives, definition of, 243
movement in presentation area, 177
M-time (monochronic time), 232–233
multicultural audiences, 83–84

N
National Communication Association Credo
        for Communication Ethics, *53t*
National Council for Excellence in Critical
        Thinking, 34
natural disasters, communication after, 187,
        324
natural gestures, 176
natural world, social reality vs., *10f*
needs, 243
negative focus, 34
negative reciprocity, 260
Nemiro, J. E., 280
networking, 46
neutral buffer, 128
neutral tone, 150–151
news interviews, 325–326
news media, 324–326

newsletters, electronic, 317
Nokia, 298–301
nominal-group technique, 282–283, *284t*
nonexpert audiences, 83
nonverbal communication
    components of, 104–105, 250
    cultural differences in, 182
    in effective listening, 237–238
    with employees, 229–233
    significance of, 8
    in videoconferencing, 186
nonverbal signals, 176–177
Nordic Europe regional cluster, 75, *75t*
norm of reciprocity, 276
normal accidents, communication after, 324
normative influence, 268–269
norming stage, 265
norms, 267, 269
note cards, 178
Nulty, Christopher, 195
number lists, 143

O
objectives, of online presence, 318
Oetzel, John, 271
old information before new, 164–165, *164f*
Olsen, Leslie, 82
online order confirmations, *365f*
online presence
    overview, 317–318
    advertising, 193
    social media. *See* social media
open-ended questions, 219
operationalized norms, 267
Opotow, Susan, *23b*
oral communication, 107
oral presentations
    overview, 161, 189
    appropriate uses of, 161–162
    delivery in. *See* delivery
    developing, 165–169
    novice, 160
    organization of, 164–165
    persuasive elements in, *168f*
    planning, 162–164
    steps in, 161
    visual aids, 169–174
order, as management function, 7, *7t*
order confirmations, *365f*
organizational change, issues management
        and, 322
organizational chart, *145f*
organizational culture
    characteristics of, 96–97, *97t*
    climate of, 101–102
    communication in, 2, 8, 20
    communication role in, 4
    networks for, 102–103
    types of, 97–102
Organizational Culture Inventory, 97–102,
        101t
Osborn, Alex, 281
outgroup homogeneity effect, 25, 71

oversampling, 273
oversimplification, 33
ownership of problems, 220

P
Papas, Nick, 198–199
paragraph coherence, 148
paragraph spacing, 345
paralanguage, 230
parallel structure, lists, 143
passive-defensive culture, 97, 98–99
pathos (emotional appeal), 134, *168f*
Patterson, Neal L., 156–157
pauses, in oral presentations, 175
perception, 23–26, 36
perceptual mindsets, 36, '36
perceptual process steps, *24f*
performance appraisals, 217–221
performance goals, 219
performance meetings, 239
performance orientation, 74–75, *75t*
performing stage, 265
peripheral specialists, 245, *245f*
personal conflict, 274–275
personal distance, 232
personal literacy, 18
personal power, 6
personal space, 231–232
persuasion
    overview, 56–58
    in business writing. *See* business writing
    in oral presentations. *See* oral presentations
    as a process, 247
physical context, 95
pie graphs, *144f, 172f*
Pisani, Elisabeth, 162–163
pitch, in oral presentations, 175
plain language, 80
plan articulation/execution, 247–248
planning
    of group presentations, 183
    meetings, 239–240
    oral presentations, 177
Playfair, William, 169
plurality, 7, 22–23
polarization, in decision making, 273–274
politics, in organizational communication, 20
polychronic time (P-time), 232–233
position power, 6
positional authority, 5
positive focus, 150–151
posture, 176
power, differences in, *289t*
power, groups and, 264–265
power bases, 6, *6t*
power distance, 74–76, *75t*
PowerPoint presentations
    designing, 170
    organizing, 171–174
    in videoconferencing, 185
press releases, example of, *363f*
Prezi software, 169
problem-solution format, 138

problem-solution organization, 164–165, *164f*
problem-solving orientation, 150
procedural conflict, 276
process losses, 269–270
professional image, 54–56
project teams, 258
projected cognitive similarity, 25, 71
pronoun–antecedent agreement, 373–374
proofreading, 150–151
proposals
    components of, 140, 360
    example of, *361–362f*
    See also business writing; reports/proposals
proxemics, 231–232
proximity, in group formation, 259
P-time (polychronic time), 232–233
public communication, 314
public distance, 232
public issues tracking, 315, 321–322
public policy, influence on, 321
public relations, 315, 316
publicity, creating, 319, *319t*
punctuation, 369–372

Q

qualification language, 32
question choices, *146b*
question-and-answer (Q&A) sessions
    during crisis briefings, 187
    in job interviews, 210–213, *211f, 213t*
    in oral presentations, 179–181, 189
questions, audience, 82

R

RadioShack, 223–225
rate of delivery, 174–175
rational explanation, 60
Raven, B., *6t*
readability, in videoconferencing, 186
reality construction rules, *11f*
Reardon, Kathleen, 20
reasoned skepticism, 54
recency effect, 128
reciprocity principle, 260
recommendations, in reports/proposals, 140
Red Cross trademark, 117–121
red flags, in social media, 209
Redding, W. Charles, 52, *53t*
reflexivity, 27
regional cultures, 77
regulation, influence on, 321
rehearsals
    for group presentations, 183–184
    for job interviews, 211
Reitan, Harold, 267
relational actions/behaviors, 6, *285f*, 286
relationship building, as business precedent, 76
relationships
    in business, 227
    disruption of, 246
    mapping, 245
    orchestration of, 6, 59

repetition
    in business writing, 130, 149
    in oral presentations, 167–168
reports/proposals
    about, 356
    formats, 344, *357f*
    See also business writing
representative samples, 33
reputation management, 315–316
request for proposal (RFP), 140
research
    credibility from, 177
    for job interviews, 210
    primary/secondary, 138
resignation messages, *356f*
resistance, overcoming, 132, 134, 137
resources, 277, 328
responsible communication, 53–54
résumés
    overview, 204–207, 221
    as audience-centered communication, 85
    formats
        about, 344, 348–350
        examples of, *349–350f*
    lies on, *214b*
    sample of, *205f*
revision, 147–150
RFP (request for proposal), 140
Rhetoric (Aristotle), 3, 46–47
rich/lean communication, 104
Riley, Patricia, 60
risk, definition of, 323
risk communication, 323, 328
risk management, 323, 328
roles, threats to, 246
rote learning, 30
Rothwell, J. D., 32
Ruler, Betteke va, 303
run-on sentences, 374

S

sales
    conclusions, 130, 169
    messages, *368f*
samples, biased, *146b*
sans serif fonts, 345
Savas, Stephen D., 157
Scott, William, 51
seating arrangements, 232
self-auditing, 219
self-awareness, 26–30
self-centered writing, 84–85
self-concept, 26–27, 56
self-confirmation, 32
self-esteem, 27–28
self-fulfilling prophecy, 26–27
self-inventory, 203
self-monitoring, 56
self-presentation, 55
self-reflexiveness, 26
self-serving bias, 34
Selznick, Philip, 3
semicolons, 372

Senge, Peter, 31
sentence structure, 372–376
sequential organization, 138
serif fonts, 345
setting of presentation, 178–179
sexist language, *78b*
shared meaning, 7, 19
sharing economy, 191, 193–194
Shaw, Marvin, 267
short-term orientation, long-term orientation vs., 76
short-term rentals, 191–200
signature file, 348
silent brainstorming, 282
similarity principle, 259–260
simplicity, of oral presentations, 162–163
skimmability, 141
slide presentation software, 169–174
small-power-distance culture, 77
Smircich, L., 3
Smith, Frederick W., 254–255
social comparison theory, 268–269
social construction of reality, 9–10, 304
The Social Construction of Reality (Berger & Luckmann), 9
social context, 95
social dilemmas, 277
social distance, 232
social literacy, 18
social loafing, 269–271
social media
    overview, 111–113
    employer review of, 209
    FedEx snafus exposed by, 254–256
    strategy for, 317–318
social network analysis, 245–246
social networking, 108–109, 111
social realities
    communication in, 2
    constructing, 6
    natural world vs., *10f*
social relationships. *See* relationships
social responsibility programs, 322
social status, 9, 263
socioemotional (social maintenance) roles, 261, *262t*
soft skills, 8, 303
somatotype (body type), 231
Souther, James, 83
Southern Asia regional cluster, 75, *75t*
space, in document layout, 344
spatial organization, 138–139, 164–165, *164f*
speed, in communication, 105
Speedy Travel Inc, 70
spelling/grammar checkers, 150–151
spontaneity of presentation, 178
Sriramesh, Krishnamurthy, 303
stakeholders
    communication role of, 4
    messaging for, 20–21
    organizational, 304, 328
Starbucks social responsibility programs, 322
statistics, erroneous/misused, *146b*

status hierarchies, 263
    See also social status
Stephens, Kimberlie, 303
stereotyping, 24–25
stinking thinking, 280
stock markets
    Cerner Corporation performance, 156–158
    communication with, 320–321
stonewalling, collaboration vs., 321
stories, in oral presentations, 163
storming (conflict) stage, 265
strategic alignment, 229
strategic communication
    overview, 3–5
    case study analysis, 10–12
    context of, 94–95
    globalization challenges in, 2
    importance of, 5–9
    practices/criteria for, 308, *308t*
    social construction of reality, 9–10
strategic communicators, 18
strategic control, 20–21, *22f*
strategic design, *247f*
strategic management, 3
strategic organizational communication
    overview, 303–304
    models of, 304–307, 328
    plans for
        external. *See* external plans
        internal. *See* internal plans
strategy
    overview, 3
    military as origin of, 15
    practices/criteria for, 308
Stubbart, C., 3
style, 148–149
subject–verb agreement, 372–373
Sub-Saharan Africa regional cluster, 75, *75t*
substantive conflict, 275
summary conclusions, 129–130, 169
support/integration, in organizational
    communication, 308, *308t*
supportive communication climate, 101–102,
    101t
sustainability, 320
symbols, in communication, 9

T
table of contents, 139
tables
    overview, 145
    example of, *145f*
    in PowerPoint presentations, 172–173, *173f*
Taco Bell legal issues, 315–316
tactical analysis, *247f*
tactics, 3
Tannebaum, R., 27
task actions, *285f*, 286
task roles, 261, *262t*
teams, definition of, 258

teamwork
    overview, 227
    decision making. *See* decision making
    dysfunctions of, 258–259
    effectiveness of, 286–287
    features of, 248
    leadership in, 284–286, *285f*, 292
    virtual, 258, 287–292
Teamwork Is an Individual Skill (Avery), 258
technology advances, 7–8
teleconferencing, 243
telephone interviews, 213–214, 216
templates
    for résumés, 205
    in word processors, 140, 150–151
territoriality, 231–232
testimonies, bias in, 135
thank-you messages/e-mails, 214–215, 351
Theory X assumptions, 99
thinking styles, 34–35
Thomas, Gail Fann, 303
Thomas, Robert
    Geeks & Geezers, 95
360-degree feedback, 218
tick-tock technique, 280
time (chronemics), 232–233
time-consuming formalities, 182
Ting-Toomey, Stella, 77, 279
title page, 139
Tobin, Glenn, 157
tone, 149–150, 348
topic sentences, 147
topical organization, 139
touching (haptics), 233
trademark dispute, 117–121
traditionalists, 73
trained mindlessness, 4, 95
training
    in crisis communication, 187
    FedEx, 255
    mindfulness, 4
    online, 106, 109
    for virtual teamwork, 291
trait theory, 55
transactional process
    characteristics/disadvantages of, *22f*
    communication as, 19–20, *20f*
transitions, 148, 167–168
transmittal document/cover letter, 139
trust
    overview, 47–48
    components of, *47f*
    in conflict resolution, 277
    in television news, 67
    in virtual teamwork, 288
    in workplace communication, 227
Twitter
    in business, 109, 112
    optimal use of, 318

U
uncertainty avoidance, 74–75, *75t*, 76, *289t*
United States
    emblem/insignia legal protection, 118
    as "low-context" culture, 105
    Patent and Trademark Office, 119
    regional cultures, 77
upward flow communication, 102, 314
usage, 376–378

V
Veil, Shari, 4
verbal/nonverbal cues, 76
Vercic, Dejan, 303
videoconferencing
    overview, 184–186
    considerations for, 243
    job interviews by, 213
Virtual Teaming, 290
virtual teams, 258, 287–292
vivid images, abstractions vs., 33
vividness, in oral presentations, 163
vocal delivery, 174–175
vocal distractions, 175
vocal variety, 175
voice communication, 104
VOIP (voice over internet protocol), 185
volume, 174

W
Warren, Nigel, 197
Web conferencing, 243
Web load time, 186
Web messages, 141
webcasting, 185–186
websites, 317
Weiss, Brent, 214
Weldon, William C., 118
white space, 141
whom/whomever, 378
who/whoever, 378
who/whom, 378
Widrich, Leo, 318
Wikipedia, 111
wikis, 111
women, in double bind situations, 32, 78
word-of-mouth advertising, 46, 193
work teams, 258
workplace changes, 5–8
workplace harassment, 113
written communication
    business writing. *See* business writing
    as least ambiguous channel, 105
    for lengthy communication, 106
    for permanent records, 107

Z
Zappos, 96

CPSIA information can be obtained
at www.ICGtesting.com
Printed in the USA
LVHW061520171219
640804LV00004B/30/P

9 780999 486122